What's on the CD?

The CD included with the *MCSE: NT Server 4 Study Guide* contains several valuable tools to help you prepare for your MCSE exams. The contents of the folders you'll find on the CD, and the steps for installing the various programs are described below. Please consult the README file located in the root directory of the CD for further product information.

The Edge Tests: Windows NT Server 4 Exam Preparation Software

This Edge Test demo provides sample test questions similar to those you'll encounter when you take the MCSE NT Server 4.0 exam. Two versions of the test are provided, one for Windows 3.1 & 3.11 systems, and one for Windows 95 and NT systems. To install the *Windows NT Server 4* exam prep software for Windows 3.1 or 95, run the SETUP.EXE file located in the folder that coincides with your operating system (EDGETEST\WIN3_1 or EDGETEST\WIN95_NT). For Windows NT 4.0, you must first copy the contents of the Win95_NT folder into a subdirectory on your hard drive and run the DELIVERY.EXE file from there.

Microsoft Train_Cert Offline Web Site and Internet Explorer 3.0

Look to Microsoft's *Train_Cert Offline* Web site, a quarterly snap-shot of Microsoft's Education and Certification Web site, for all of the information you need to plot your course for MCSE certification. You'll need to run *Internet Explorer* 3.0 to access all of the features of the *Train_Cert Offline* Web site, so we've included a free copy on the CD. To install *Internet Explorer 3.0*, run the SETUP.EXE file located in the MICROSFT\IE3\CD folder. To install the *Train_Cert Offline* Web site to your system, run the SETUP file located in the MICROSFT\OFFLINE folder.

Transcender Corporation's NT-ServerCert 4.0 Demo & Certification Sampler

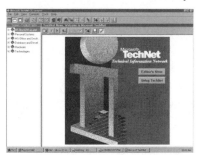

Transcender's *NT-ServerCert 4.0* exam prep software provides you with a selection of sample test questions similar to those you'll encounter in the MCSE NT Server 4.0 exam. To install the demo, run the SETUP.EXE file located in the TRANSCND\NT4EXAM folder. The Transcender *Certification Sampler* lets you preview samples of all of Transcender's Microsoft exam simulations. To install the Transcender demos, simply run the SETUP.EXE file located in the TRANSCND\SAMPLER folder.

Microsoft TechNet Technical Information Network

This evaluation copy of Microsoft's *TechNet Technical Information Network* gives you access to a vast database of information related to Microsoft products and technologies. It includes more than 100,000 pages of articles, technical notes, service packs, and Knowledge Bases. To install the *TechNet Technical Information Network* program to your computer, run the SETUP.EXE file located in the TECHNET folder. For further installation instructions or to review the user license for this product, please read the MANSETUP text file located in the TECHNET folder.

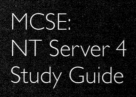

MCSE:
NT Server 4
Study Guide

October 9, 1996

Dear SYBEX Inc. Customer:

Microsoft is pleased to inform you SYBEX Inc. is a participant in the Microsoft®
Independent Courseware Vendor (ICV) program. Microsoft ICVs design,
develop, and market self-paced courseware, books, and other products that
support Microsoft software and the Microsoft Certified Professional (MCP)
program.

To be accepted into the Microsoft ICV program, an ICV must meet set criteria. In
addition, Microsoft reviews and approves each ICV training product before
permission is granted to use the Microsoft Certified Professional Approved Study
Guide logo on that product. This logo assures the consumer that the product has
passed the following Microsoft standards:

- The course contains accurate product information.
- The course includes labs and activities during which the student can
  apply knowledge and skills learned from the course.
- The course teaches skills that help prepare the student to take
  corresponding MCP exams.

Microsoft ICVs continually develop and release new MCP Approved Study
Guides. To prepare for a particular Microsoft certification exam, a student may
choose one or more single, self-paced training courses or a series of training
courses.

You will be pleased with the quality and effectiveness of the MCP Approved
Study Guides available from SYBEX Inc..

Sincerely,

Holly Heath
ICV/OCV Account Manager
Microsoft Channel Programs, Education & Certification

MICROSOFT INDEPENDENT COURSEWARE VENDOR PROGRAM

MCSE:
NT® Server 4
Study Guide

Matthew Strebe
Charles Perkins
with **James Chellis**

NETWORK PRESS ®
SYBEX

San Francisco ■ Paris ■ Düsseldorf ■ Soest

Associate Publisher: Guy Hart-Davis
Acquisitions Manager: Kristine Plachy
Acquisitions and Developmental Editor: Neil Edde
Editor: June Waldman
Project Editor: Kimberley Askew-Qasem
Technical Editor: Heather Osterloh
Book Design Director: Catalin Dulfu
Book Designer: Seventeenth Street Studio
Graphic Illustrator: Patrick Dintino
Electronic Publishing Specialist: Bill Gibson
Production Coordinator: Robin Kibby
Indexer: Matthew Spence
Cover Designer: Archer Design

Screen reproductions produced with Collage Complete.
Collage Complete is a trademark of Inner Media Inc.

SYBEX is a registered trademark of SYBEX Inc.
Network Press and the Network Press logo are trademarks of SYBEX Inc.

TRADEMARKS: SYBEX has attempted throughout this book to distinguish proprietary trademarks from descriptive terms by following the capitalization style used by the manufacturer.

The authors and publisher have used their best efforts to prepare this book and the content is based upon final release software whenever possible. Portions of the manuscript may be based upon pre-release versions supplied by software manufacturer(s). The authors and the publisher make no representation or warranties of any kind with regard to the completeness or accuracy of the contents herein and accept no liability of any kind including but not limited to performance, merchantability, fitness for any particular purpose, or any losses or damages of any kind caused or alleged to be caused directly or indirectly from this book.

©1996 Microsoft Corporation. All rights reserved. Microsoft, the Microsoft Internet Explorer logo, Windows, Windows NT, and the Windows logo are either registered trademarks or trademarks of Microsoft Corporation in the United States and/or other countries.

SYBEX is an independent entity from Microsoft Corporation, and not affiliated with Microsoft Corporation in any manner. This publication may be used in assisting students to prepare for a Microsoft Certified Professional Exam. Neither Microsoft Corporation, its designated review company, nor SYBEX warrants that use of this publication will ensure passing the relevant Exam. Microsoft is either a registered trademark or trademark of Microsoft Corporation in the United States and/or other countries.

Library of Congress Card Number: 96-72286
ISBN: 0-7821-1972-7

Manufactured in the United States of America

10 9 8 7 6

Matthew Strebe: To Christy

Charles Perkins: To Kathy

Acknowledgments

Matthew Strebe: No one has enough time to write without stealing it from loved ones, so I'd like to thank my wife for her continued support and understanding. I'd also like to thank Charles Perkins, James Chellis, and Mike Moncur who are to blame for dragging me into writing; Sybex and all the good people there (Neil, Kim, and June); Dan McMurtrey for buying me my first computer book and getting me started down this path; Dad, Mom, Roy, Duane, Gretchen, Susan, Victor, Chris, Jacquie, daan, Rachel, and Ruth; and Shron & Kendo.

Charles Perkins: I want to thank my family (of course!) with special appreciation to my grandparents. Grandpa, stick around to read this. Grandma, keep moving his bucket. Joe, graduate and you can be as cool as I am.

Contents at a Glance

Table of Contents

Table of Exercises

Introduction

WHETHER YOU ARE just getting started or are ready to move ahead in the computer industry, the knowledge and skills you have are your most valuable assets. Microsoft, recognizing this, has developed its Microsoft Certified Professional (MCP) program to give you credentials that verify your ability to work with Microsoft products effectively and professionally.

The premier MCP certification for individuals who work with Microsoft networks is the Microsoft Certified Systems Engineer (MCSE.) This certification designates that you have the ability to work professionally with Windows NT and related products.

Central to the MCSE program is Windows NT Server. This book covers the Microsoft Windows NT Server operating system. Here you will find the information you need to acquire a solid foundation in Windows NT, to prepare for the Windows NT Server exam, and to take a big step toward MCSE certification.

Is This Book for You?

If you want to learn how Windows NT Server works, this book is for you. You'll find clear explanations of the fundamental concepts you need to grasp.

If your goal is to become certified as an MCSE, this book is also for you. The MCSE is *the* hot ticket in the field of professional computer networking. Microsoft is putting its weight behind the program, so now is the time to act. This book will help you get started.

What Does This Book Cover?

Today personal computers are more powerful than even mainframes and supercomputers were a few years ago. Personal computer users often have gigabytes of hard disk space, megabytes of memory, and even hundreds of megahertz of processing power at their disposal. Personal computers are being used for much more than their original purposes of editing text and calculating spreadsheet values. The incredible computing capacity of today's computers is being harnessed to combine audio, video, and textual information in multimedia software; to edit and present three-dimensional graphics and animation; and to communicate with other computers around the world via the Internet—just to name a few of the tasks.

Windows NT is the operating system that Microsoft developed to support today's computing requirements. (The *NT* stands for "New Technology.") Windows NT is actually two products: NT Server and NT Workstation. You can think of this book as your guide to Windows NT Server. It begins by covering the basic Server concepts, for example:

- What is it?

- How do you install it?

Next you will learn how to perform important tasks, for example:

- Administering users and groups

- Configuring file systems and security

- Configuring local and network printing

- Creating a coherent server environment

You will also learn how to configure aspects of the operating system, tune your server's performance, work with applications, and troubleshoot your system.

How Do You Become an MCSE?

Attaining MCSE status is a serious challenge. The exams cover a wide range of topics and require dedicated study and expertise. Many who have achieved other computer industry credentials have had troubles with the MCSE, which is why the MCSE certificate is so valuable. If achieving MCSE status were easy, MCSEs would quickly flood the market and the certification would become meaningless. Microsoft, keenly aware of this fact, has taken steps to ensure that the certification means its holder is truly knowledgeable and skilled.

To become an MCSE, you must pass four core requirements and two electives. Most people select the following exam combination for the MCSE core requirements for the 4.0 track (the most current track):

WINDOWS NT SERVER 4.0 REQUIREMENT

70-67: Implementing and Supporting Windows NT Server 4.0

CLIENT REQUIREMENT

70-73: Implementing and Supporting Windows NT Workstation 4.0

NETWORKING REQUIREMENT

70-58: Networking Essentials

WINDOWS NT SERVER 4.0 IN THE ENTERPRISE REQUIREMENT

70-68: Implementing and Supporting Windows NT Server 4.0 in the Enterprise

For the electives, you have about ten choices. The two most popular electives at present are

70-53: Internetworking Microsoft TCP/IP on Microsoft Windows NT 3.51 (4.0 will be available soon.)

70-75: Implementing and Supporting Microsoft Exchange Server 4.0

For a complete description of all the MCSE options, see the Microsoft Roadmap to Education and Certification on the CD that comes with this book.

This book is part of a series of MCSE study guides, published by Network Press (Sybex), that covers four core requirements and two electives—the entire MCSE track.

Where Do You Take the Exams?

You may take the exams at any of more than 800 Authorized Prometric Testing Centers (APTCs) around the world. For the location of an APTC near you, call (800) 755-EXAM (755-3926). Outside the United States and Canada, contact your local Sylvan Prometric Registration Center.

To register for a Microsoft Certified Professional exam:

1. Determine the number of the exam you want to take.

2. Register with the Sylvan Prometric Registration Center that is nearest to you. At this point you will be asked for advance payment for the exam. At this writing, the exams are $100 each. Exams must be taken within one year of payment. You can schedule exams up to six weeks in advance or as late as one working day prior to the date of the exam. You can cancel or reschedule your exam if you contact Sylvan Prometric at least two working days prior to the exam. Same-day registration is available in some locations, although this option is subject to space availability. Where same-day registration is available, you must register a minimum of two hours before test time.

3. After you receive a registration and payment confirmation letter from Sylvan Prometric, call a nearby Authorized Prometric Testing Center (APTC) to schedule your exam.

When you schedule the exam, you will receive instructions regarding appointment and cancellation procedures, ID requirements, and information about the testing center location.

What the Windows NT Server Exam Measures

The Windows NT Server exam covers concepts and skills required for the support of Windows NT Server computers. It emphasizes the following areas of Server support:

- Standards and terminology

- Planning

- Implementation

- Troubleshooting

This exam can be quite specific regarding Windows NT requirements and operational settings, and it can be very particular about how administrative tasks are performed within the operating system. It also focuses on fundamental concepts relating to Windows NT Server's operation. Careful study of this book, along with hands-on experience with the operating system itself, will be especially helpful in preparing for the exam.

Tips for Taking the Windows NT Server Exam

Here are some general tips for taking the exam successfully:

- Arrive early at the exam center so you can relax and take one last review of your study materials, particularly tables and lists of exam-related information.

- Read the questions carefully. Don't be tempted to jump to an early conclusion. Make sure you know *exactly* what the question is asking.

- Don't leave any unanswered questions. They count against you.

- When answering multiple-choice questions you're not sure about, use a process of elimination to get rid of the obviously incorrect questions first. This method will improve your odds if you need to make an educated guess.

- Because the hard questions will eat up the most time, save them for last. You can move forward and back through the exam.

How to Use This Book

This book can provide a solid foundation for the serious effort of preparing for the Windows NT Server 4.0 exam. To best benefit from this book, you might want to use the following study method:

1. Study a chapter carefully, making sure you fully understand the information.

2. Complete all hands-on exercises in the chapter, referring to the chapter so that you understand each step you take.

3. Answer the exercise questions related to that chapter. (You will find the answers to these questions in Appendix A.)

4. Note which questions you did not understand and study those sections of the book again.

5. Study each chapter in the same manner.

6. Try the practice exams included on the CD that comes with this book. They will give you a good idea of what you can expect to see on the real thing.

If you prefer to use this book in conjunction with other types of training, you have many options. Both classroom and online training are widely available. Cyberstate University, for example, offers an online MCSE training program that centers around this book, and the other books in this series. You can reach Cyberstate at (888) 438-3382. Many companies offer local classroom training. Free network training referral services, such as EdgeTek, at (800) 800-1638, can help you locate available resources.

To learn all the material covered in this book, you will need to study regularly and with discipline. Try to set aside the same time every day to study and select a comfortable and quiet place in which to do it. If you work hard, you will be surprised at how quickly you can learn this material. Good luck.

What's on the CD?

The CD contains several valuable tools to help you study for your MCSE exams:

- The Edge Test for NT Server 4.0 demo provides an excellent supplement for reviewing the materials in this book.

- Transcender Corporation's NT-ServerCert 4.0 demo also provides an excellent supplement for reviewing the materials in this book.

- An evaluation copy of Microsoft's TechNet Database is a wealth of useful articles on Microsoft products and technologies, valuable network utilities, and service packs.

- Microsoft's Train_Cert Offline provides information about Microsoft Education, as well as the MCSE program.

- Microsoft's Internet Explorer 3.0 is a popular Web browser that you can use to view Train_Cert Offline and to surf the Internet.

Introduction to Windows NT Server

YOU ARE READING this book to learn more about the Windows NT Server operating system. Perhaps you will be administering an NT network. Perhaps you are already familiar with Windows 95 and are wondering what Windows NT can do for you. Perhaps you are preparing for the Windows NT Server exam in the MCSE series of tests. Whatever the case, this book will lead you through the Windows NT Server operating system and environment, illustrate important concepts, show you how NT works, point out pitfalls and offer hints and tips, quiz your knowledge, and provide opportunities for you to practice the skills you will need to work professionally with Windows NT.

In the first chapter we explain what Windows NT Server is, where it came from, and where it is going. You will find out where Windows NT Server belongs in your network and what kind of computer you need to run it effectively.

What Is Windows NT Server?

TWO IDENTICAL BEIGE computers are on a counter in front of you. They are both running Microsoft operating systems, and at first glance they look exactly the same. They both have a Taskbar with a clock in one corner and a start button in the other. Windows on the screen contain running programs, and buttons on the Taskbar switch between them. You notice the first difference when you press the start button—one computer displays the text Windows 95 alongside the buttons, the other displays Windows NT Server (see Figure 1.1).

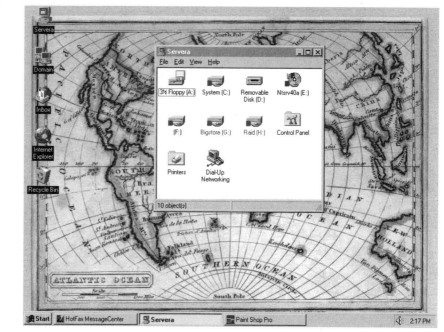

What are the differences between Windows NT Server and Windows 95? Where does each belong in your network? What are the capabilities and hardware requirements of Windows NT Server, and what are the alternatives? The following sections will help you answer these questions.

How Does Windows NT Differ from Windows 95?

Windows NT Server, as its name implies, is a server operating system. It is optimized to provide network services to client computers. Although Windows NT Server could be used as a client operating system, Windows NT Workstation is more suited to that task because it costs less. Windows NT Server is at home at the center of your network providing file and print services, routing mail and other network traffic, and supporting back-end software such as database servers and Internet host packages.

You should use client operating systems such as Windows 95 or Windows NT Workstation to run word processing and spreadsheet applications, and you should use a server operating system such as Windows NT Server to store files on the network.

Windows NT Server may look like Windows 95, but in actuality it is completely different internally. Although Windows 95 can trace its genealogy all the way back to the first versions of Windows, Microsoft wrote the Windows NT operating system from scratch in the late 1980s. This fresh beginning allowed the developers of Windows NT to take advantage of such developments in operating systems and computer hardware as preemptive multitasking, multiprocessing, multiplatform support, secure file systems, and fault tolerance.

Windows NT Server and Windows NT Workstation are essentially the same operating system with different features enabled.

Users do have to pay a small price for this new technology. Because Windows NT is a completely new operating system, many programs that depend on the peculiarities of the original Windows or DOS operating systems will not operate from within Windows NT. However, the price is more than returned in the advanced features that Windows NT provides.

Windows 95 is actually much more complicated than Windows NT because Windows 95 must be able to run all programs written for previous versions of Windows and DOS. And meeting that requirement is not easy. Windows NT, on the other hand, has to run only programs written for Windows NT and those programs for Windows and DOS that do not interfere with Windows NT security mechanisms.

Windows NT maintains a degree of compatibility with older software running under MS-DOS, Windows 3.11, and OS/2 1.3 through the use of environment subsystems. *Environment subsystems* are services of Windows NT that provide a complete shell in which programs written for the above operating systems run. Inside this environment subsystem shell, the computer appears to be operating under DOS, Windows, or OS/2. The subsystem then translates commands from the applications running inside it to their Windows NT equivalents and passes them on to the appropriate Windows NT service.

Where Did Windows NT Server Come From?

In the late 1980s software developers created Windows as a graphical environment for programs running on Microsoft DOS. Microsoft and IBM collaborated on a replacement for DOS on Intel computers. Their new operating system had many advanced features and was called OS/2. At the same time Microsoft recognized the need for another more advanced operating system that would have not only all the features of OS/2 (and more) but also the ability to run on other microprocessors, especially reduced instruction set computers (RISC) microprocessors, which were much faster than Intel microprocessors. This visionary operating system would have to be written in a high-level language such as C that could be ported to other microprocessors, instead of in Intel assembly language, which was not portable.

Microsoft recruited operating system architects and programmers who had experience with advanced operating systems on minicomputers and mainframes. Microsoft hired Dave Cutler, who had led several operating system development project for Digital Equipment Corporation, to lead the development program for the new operating system. The operating system at that time was called OS/2 NT. (*NT* stood for "new technology.")

Windows NT was originally going to be named OS/2 NT!

In 1990 Microsoft released version 3.0 of its Windows operating system, which became very popular. Shortly thereafter, Microsoft and IBM disagreed on how their two operating systems—OS/2 and Windows—should be marketed. IBM wanted Windows to be viewed as a stepping stone to the more advanced OS/2, whereas Microsoft wanted to expand the capabilities and features of Windows to compete with OS/2. When cooperation broke down, IBM retained the OS/2 operating system, and Microsoft changed the name of the OS/2 NT project to Windows NT.

The first version of Windows NT released to the public (in 1993 as Windows NT Advanced Server version 3.1) had the same user interface as the regular version of Windows. It was a true 32-bit operating system, and it provided a 32-bit environment for Windows programs to run in. This capability made the job of writing large, powerful programs easier because programmers did not have to work around memory boundaries and unprotected memory areas that plagued MS-DOS and Windows 3.0 software. Windows NT Advanced Server version 3.1 also provided a 16-bit environment in which programs written for earlier versions of Windows could run. In addition, it could run DOS and OS/2 version 1.3 programs (a legacy of its earlier incarnation as OS/2 NT). The Windows NT development team also made it possible for developers to compile POSIX programs to run on Windows NT, thereby making it more attractive to government organizations and more suited to UNIX environments. POSIX, which stands for Portable Open Systems Interface, is a government standard that promotes the standards for client/server software by providing an application environment similar to UNIX.

You can run programs written for OS/2 version1.3 under Windows NT.

Windows NT has since influenced the development of Microsoft's Windows client operating systems. In 1994 Microsoft released the Win32s software package, which allowed Windows 3.11 and earlier Windows computers to run a subset of 32-bit Windows NT software. In late 1995 Microsoft released Windows 95, which includes most of the 32-bit software interfaces, including those supported by Win32s.

Windows 95, however, gave users a new interface that was much more flexible and easy to use than the interface in Windows 3.*x*. Users of Windows NT had to wait until the release of version 4.0 in 1996 to experience the new interface. Version 4.0 also debuted services for support of the World Wide Web and the Internet.

Where Does Windows NT Server Belong in Your Network?

As a server operating system, Windows NT belongs at the heart of your network, providing services to client computers. You could use Windows NT Server for other less demanding tasks, such as running word processor and spreadsheet applications, but other operating systems are more appropriate for that purpose.

The most common use for Windows NT Server is as a file server. In this capacity it provides a place for storing files for all the client computers on the network, and it enforces security on the network by ensuring that only individuals holding the proper permissions can access the files. One Windows NT server in a domain will also maintain a database of usernames and passwords; that server and other Windows NT servers on the network use the database to log people on to the network. The server that maintains the database is called the primary domain controller (PDC).

Windows NT Server is a software product. A Windows NT server is a machine running that product.

Computers running Windows NT Server can also perform other server functions such as hosting and controlling access to databases; routing e-mail, fax, and network traffic in and out of a local area network (LAN); and hosting Internet or intranet information. Figure 1.2 illustrates some server roles.

FIGURE 1.2

Windows NT Server can perform many roles in a local area network.

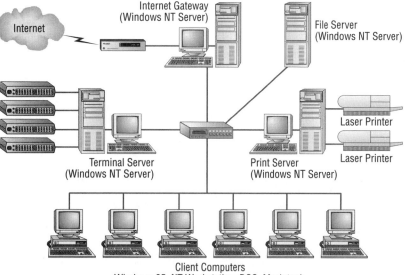

Where Is Windows NT Server Going?

Windows NT is Microsoft's path to the future of network computing. Microsoft is committed to extending Windows NT technology into every aspect of computing, from handheld computers (the latest handheld computer specification from Microsoft provides a 32-bit application programming interface—or software environment—much like that first introduced by Windows NT) to large multiple-processor enterprise servers at the center of corporate networks. Windows NT currently supports multiple processors in the fastest RISC microcomputers available.

You can expect Microsoft to make Windows NT Server computers even easier to manage in a large corporate network environment. You can also expect Microsoft to fine-tune the user interface, increase operating system performance, and integrate features of Windows 95, such as Plug and Play and power management support, into Windows NT Server.

As new microprocessor technologies become available and widely accepted, Windows NT Server will probably be ported to run on those microprocessors. Another feature that will most likely appear in the near future is support for 64-bit computing under Windows NT; several of today's microprocessors already support 64-bit computing, and many more will in the future.

Windows NT Features and Capabilities

ALTHOUGH WINDOWS NT Server is a full-featured operating system capable of functioning as a client, supporting spreadsheets, word processing programs, World Wide Web browsers, database access programs, and any other type of application that you might find running under Windows NT Workstation or Windows 95, running client applications is not its primary purpose. Windows NT Server is intended to provide network services to other computers on a network, and for that reason it has features and capabilities that client operating systems seldom have.

The Windows NT Server is a large and complex operating system with many modular components. However, three major constituents—the operating system kernel, the file system, and the networking services—interact to provide Windows NT Server's characteristic features and capabilities as a network server. Figure 1.3 illustrates the components of Windows NT Server.

FIGURE 1.3

The operating system's kernel, file system, and networking services provide the characteristic features of Windows NT Server as a server on the network.

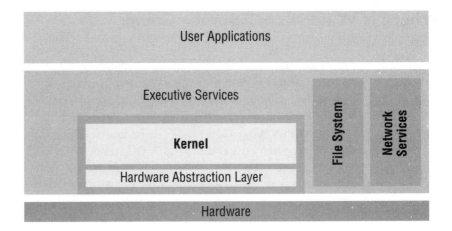

Operating System Kernel Features

The kernel, as its name implies, lies at the heart of the operating system. The kernel provides services to the programs running on the computer. Several features of the Windows NT kernel make it an excellent choice for a network server.

Pervasive Security Mechanisms

Security is an integral part of the Windows NT kernel. The system administrator establishes certain security privileges for every user of the operating system, and the kernel prevents users from performing any actions that would violate the security of the operating system. Normal users, for instance, are not allowed to install device drivers or to change the server's networking protocols, even if they are logged on directly to the server. These functions are reserved for users with system administrator's privileges.

Fault Tolerance

The Windows NT kernel provides a fault-tolerant environment for the execution of programs and services by giving every program its own area in which to execute. No program may violate another program's access space or the access space of the server unless it has permission from the kernel to do so. This partitioning system keeps errant or malicious programs from causing damage to other executing programs or perhaps even to the kernel itself.

Preemptive Multitasking

Windows NT has a preemptive multitasking kernel; that is, the kernel provides the illusion of many programs executing at once on the computer by dividing processor time among the programs and ensuring that no program can monopolize the time of the processor.

Symmetric Multiprocessing

The kernel also supports the use of up to 32 microprocessors in the computer. With this feature, as many programs as there are microprocessors in the computer can actually be executing at the same time. The kernel preemptively multitasks each microprocessor so that every program gets its proper share of executing time. Multiprocessing is *symmetric* in Windows NT because Windows NT does not associate particular types of programs with any particular microprocessor in the computer; instead any task can execute on any microprocessor.

Platform Independence

Windows NT was designed not only for Intel-based computers but also for computers using RISC microprocessors such as PowerPC, MIPS, and Digital Alpha. RISC microprocessors often deliver more processing power than do

Intel-based microprocessors, but they do so at a price—computers using RISC chips cannot directly run programs or operating systems that have been written for Intel-based computers. Because Windows NT was designed to be independent of any particular microprocessor platform, it can run on the most powerful microcomputers available.

File System and Disk Subsystem Features

The Windows NT File System (NTFS) provides reliable and secure storage for files in a Windows NT Server computer. Although Windows NT supports the FAT file system used in MS-DOS and Windows, NTFS was designed specifically to meet the needs of storing information in a shared network environment.

File System Reliability

NTFS provides features for greater reliability than most other file systems do. NTFS can do so because it doesn't store files on the hard disk in the same manner that the FAT file system (used in MS-DOS and Microsoft Windows) does. NTFS does not use a file allocation table (which is what gives the FAT system its name); instead, NTFS records changes to the stored data in a log on the hard disk. If a write operation is interrupted, NTFS (unlike FAT) can use the log to roll back any changes made to the data stored on the hard disk so that the data is not left in an inconsistent state. The FAT system does not have a log, and therefore operating systems that use a FAT may not be able to tell that an operation has been interrupted and the data corrupted.

Files stored in an NTFS drive from within Windows NT will not be accessible from any other operating system because only Windows NT supports NTFS.

Windows NT Server supports one feature that is often used in conjunction with NTFS. That feature (although it is a feature of the Windows NT disk subsystem rather than of NTFS itself) is RAID, which stands for Redundant Array of Inexpensive Disks. RAID allows Windows NT to continue operating even if the physical hard disk drive fails. RAID can also speed up Windows NT's disk access.

Redundant Arrays of Inexpensive Disks are also referred to as Redundant Arrays of Independent Disks or disk arrays. All three terms are appropriate. In any event, RAID can speed up disk access as well as provide fault tolerance because Windows NT can request data from several drives simultaneously.

The file system fault tolerance and RAID subsystem features of Windows NT Server are covered in greater detail in Chapter 4.

File System Security

A file system that provides file storage for many users on a network must have features that are not required for a stand-alone computer or a client operating system. Primary among these features is support for security. NTFS complements the security in the Windows NT kernel, maintaining ownership information and providing file-and-directory level access control and auditing. This security system allows the network administrator to specify which users and groups have access to which files and directories, and it also allows the administrator to log successful or unsuccessful attempts to access those files or directories.

Chapter 7 covers NTFS security features and shows you how to establish a secure networking environment on your server.

Networking Services Features

The third essential aspect of network server operating systems is network services. Most network server operating systems work best with one protocol or set of protocols, are designed to serve a certain kind of client, and expect to operate in a particular network environment. Windows NT, however, arrived on the networking scene after many of the other network operating systems were already well established and therefore had to adapt to those other networking environments rather than create its own. Therefore, the networking services on Windows NT are among the most flexible of any network operating system.

Chapter 4, Chapter 7, and Chapters 9 through 14 guide you through the various networking protocols and services of Windows NT networking.

Flexible Protocol Support

When you install Windows NT, by default you are given the choice of three protocols (IPX, NetBEUI, and TCP/IP) to use for networking; you can configure Windows NT Server to provide network services over any one or all three. These protocols are not the only ones that Windows NT supports, however. You can also configure Windows NT to use AppleTalk or DLC, for example.

Windows NT is flexible about the type of protocol it uses because it makes few assumptions about the protocol used to transport data over the network. For networking, Windows NT can use any transport protocol that is written to the Transport Driver Interface (TDI), which means that future protocols such as ATM will surely be supported.

Because Windows NT is flexible about the protocols it uses, you can expect to find it in many different types of networks—Windows NT is just as at home in a primarily Novell NetWare network as it is in a network of UNIX workstations using TCP/IP or a Microsoft Windows/ NetBEUI environment.

Chapter 6 describes each of the Windows NT networking protocols.

Support for Multiple Client Operating Systems

Windows NT is meant to be a server operating system and therefore comes with software to support most client operating systems such as DOS, Windows, Windows NT Workstation, OS/2, and the Apple Macintosh. Windows NT can also provide network file services for UNIX computers, which are not often classified as clients.

Integration with Windows Clients and Other Windows Servers

Microsoft has paid special attention to providing network services for Windows client operating systems such as Windows 95. Windows NT Server contains many features intended to make managing a large network of Windows computers easier and to make Windows NT and Windows 95 interoperate seamlessly. Windows NT Server also works well with other Windows NT servers, and it is easy to manage the servers remotely using the graphical tools provided with the operating system.

Windows NT servers can be organized into domains, which greatly simplifies administration of a Windows NT network. One Windows NT Server becomes the primary domain controller, which maintains the security database and controls various aspects of the network's operation. In a domain-based network, the network users do not log on to each of the servers in the domain; rather they log on once to the domain as a whole, and the information stored in the security database in the primary domain controller determines which elements on the various servers the user can access. This method is much easier than maintaining account information and logging on to each server individually. Domains may contain backup domain controllers that can take over logon authentication in the event that the primary domain controller is busy or unreachable.

Chapter 14 focuses on the support of network clients.

Enhanced Scalability

A network based on Windows NT servers can easily grow into an enterprise network with many domains distributed throughout a building, across a campus, or even wider across wide area network (WAN) links. With Windows NT you can establish trust relationships between domains so that users on one network can access resources on another network or so that one network can allow users defined in another network to log on locally. You can use the pass-through nature of trust in a Windows NT network to develop sophisticated network environments that reduce the administrative burden and maximize the flexibility of your network.

Chapter 2 and Chapters 10 through 12 show you how Windows NT networks can easily grow to encompass thousands of users, and another book in this series, MCSE: NT Server 4 in the Enterprise Study Guide, *shows you how to implement these large networks with Windows NT servers.*

Other Servers Compared to Windows NT

Windows NT IS one of many available server operating systems. Alternative server operating systems include

- Novell NetWare
- Banyan Vines
- UNIX
- Macintosh

Each operating system has its advantages and disadvantages, and no operating system is the best system for every environment.

Novell NetWare

Novell NetWare is the most widely installed network operating system. Novell was one of the earliest companies to provide a complete network operating system and network environment for IBM-compatible computers, and Novell NetWare file servers have always been among the fastest available. Two variants of NetWare are in widespread use today: NetWare 3.12 and NetWare 4.*x*.

NetWare 3.12

This operating system is the product of years of evolution of the operating system and networking environment that Novell developed more than a decade ago. It is a fast and stable operating system optimized to serve files on a local area network. It is very conservative in its hardware requirements—NetWare 3.12 will run comfortably on many computers that would strain to support Windows NT Server.

Drawbacks to NetWare 3.12 arise from its simplicity and age. Primary among them is that each NetWare 3.12 server must be logged in to separately—you cannot log in to the network as a whole. In contrast, in Windows NT domains, you log on to the domain once, and the resources of all of the servers in that domain become available to you. Logging in to a NetWare 3.12 network can become cumbersome in a network with many servers. A related drawback is that NetWare 3.12 does not have built-in facilities to manage a number of servers as a group (Windows NT does). NetWare 3.12 servers act as independent entities.

The NetWare 3.12 operating system is so specialized for serving files that you cannot execute programs on the server that were not specifically designed for NetWare. On the other hand, Windows NT Server can run any programs that Windows NT Workstation can run as well as most programs that Windows 95 and earlier operating systems can run. A further limitation to NetWare 3.12 is that programs developed for this system are multitasked cooperatively within NetWare. Consequently, any one program can crash the operating system, which makes for a significantly less stable operating system when the programs are not well tested.

Because NetWare runs programs written only for NetWare, you cannot use programs written for a more widely adopted operating system (such as DOS, Windows, or Windows 95) to provide network services on the file server. This restriction obviously limits the range of software available to be run on the file server.

A minor irritant with NetWare 3.12 is that the file server console is text based rather than graphical.

NetWare 4.x

NetWare 4.x represents the culmination of Novell's years of experience designing and implementing network operating systems. It addresses several of the shortcomings of Novell's earlier operating systems, introduces new features, and provides innovative mechanisms for constructing very large networks.

With NetWare 4.x, as with Windows NT, you can provide one network username and password and be allowed to access resources on many servers. In addition, NetWare 4.x provides sophisticated directory services and true multiple-server support. Windows NT Server version 4.0 provides limited support for NetWare Directory Services and will provide more support in the future.

Nevertheless, this new NetWare version is still limited to running only Net-Ware programs (although NetWare 4.x can run programs in a separate memory space, thereby protecting the operating system from program errors). Another drawback is that even though NetWare 4.x provides many more graphical tools for administering the network than does NetWare 3.12, the server console is still a command-line interface.

Banyan Vines

Banyan Vines is a network environment that runs on top of a host operating system such as SCO UNIX. The host operating system performs the functions of controlling the hard disk drives, memory, and the network interface; Banyan Vines implements the protocol by which client computers are granted access to the file storage provided by the host operating system.

Windows NT, in contrast, is a complete operating system that provides both the basic file and compute services as well as the networking services required by a network file server.

Banyan Vines was the first PC-based network operating environment to provide sophisticated directory services with true multiple-server support.

Banyan Vines, however, is not implemented widely beyond very large PC LAN networks, such as those used by the government. A StreetTalk directory services component (implementing directory services and support for multiple servers) has been implemented for Windows NT, and this feature facilitates the migration of networks from Banyan Vines to Windows NT.

UNIX

UNIX is not a single operating system, but rather a name for a family of related operating systems from various companies that have a common heritage and functionality. Like Windows NT, the various versions of UNIX are complete operating systems; they can run applications as well as network services. UNIX does not differentiate between clients and servers. If a computer is used as a client, it is a client; if it is used as a server, it is a server. UNIX computers can also be servers to other client operating systems such as Windows 95, DOS, the Macintosh operating system, or even Windows NT.

Most versions of UNIX, like NetWare, present a command-line interface for configuration and control of the operating system. However, with the X-Windows windowing system, which is similar to the Microsoft Windows graphical user interface, you can have as many command-line interfaces as you want.

Macintosh

The Apple Macintosh operating system with AppleShare Server naturally provides file services for Macintosh computers over a network and is very easy to use and administer. Macintosh computers seldom provide file services for non-Macintosh computers. Windows NT provides all the file and print services that AppleShare Server provides, and it does so on a wider set of hardware platforms, including inexpensive Intel-based computers.

NT Hardware Requirements

SPECIFYING HARDWARE REQUIREMENTS for operating systems is difficult because computer hardware improves at a rapid pace and the performance expectations of users grow with what hardware can produce. Table 1.1 shows the Microsoft published minimum standards to run Windows NT Server on Intel and RISC-based computers; however, the hardware listed here will not provide a very useful machine. Another set of requirements represents the minimum hardware for acceptable performance of Windows NT as a server operating system.

TABLE 1.1	COMPONENT	INTEL	RISC
Minimum Hardware Requirements for Windows NT Server	Microprocessor	80486/25 or higher; any Pentium will provide acceptable performance.	MIPS, PowerPC, or Digital Alpha will provide acceptable performance.
	Disk storage	120MB	150MB
	Memory	12MB (16MB is recommended; 24 will reduce virtual memory usage and provide acceptable performance; 48 will increase performance.)	16MB (24MB is recommended; 32 will reduce virtual memory usage and provide acceptable performance; 64 will increase performance.)
	Display	VGA or higher resolution video display adapter.	VGA or higher resolution video display adapter.
	Required additional drive	CD-ROM or access to files from a networked CD-ROM.	SCSI CD-ROM drive or access to files from a networked CD-ROM.

Windows NT Server requirements for microprocessors, memory, disk space, and peripheral devices are explained in more detail in the following sections.

Microprocessor

Windows NT Server will run on most microprocessors used in microcomputers today. Most Windows NT Servers are run on Intel-based computers because most microcomputers sold today are Intel-based computers. The minimum capacity Intel-based microprocessor specified for use with Windows NT is an 80486SX running at 25MHz. This microprocessor will run the Windows NT Server operating system, but it would be painfully slow for any real use. A more realistic minimum to meet today's networking requirements for a small network is a Pentium-class microprocessor running at 60MHz.

Windows NT Server also supports RISC microprocessors such as the MIPS, Digital Alpha, and PowerPC. All versions of these microprocessors provide sufficient computing power to comfortably run Windows NT Server.

Memory

Windows NT Server requires more memory to run than most other client operating systems. Whereas 16MB might be plenty for Windows 95, it is barely enough for Windows NT. In order for Windows NT Server to perform any useful function in that small amount of memory, it can swap memory out to disk to create more room and then bring that memory back when it's needed again.

On an Intel-based computer, Windows NT Server needs 24MB to provide an "acceptable" level of performance, and in 48MB it will run well.

On a RISC-based computer, Windows NT Server needs 32MB to provide an acceptable level of performance, and in 64MB it will run well. RISC-based computers require more memory than Intel-based computers require because the programs that run on them are larger (and an operating system is a computer program). The designers of RISC microprocessors chose to allow program instructions to take more space so that they would execute more quickly—this is one of the reasons that RISC-based computers are often faster than Intel-based ones.

Disk Space

The disk files for Windows NT Server occupy 120MB to 150MB of disk space, and the amount of disk space required does not vary much. A RISC-based computer requires a little more space than an Intel-based computer requires. You can select not to install parts of the operating system for modest savings in required disk space, but the amount of space saved would most likely not be worth the effort.

The primary consideration for configuring disk space in a computer for Windows NT Server is the amount of program and user data that will be stored, rather than the space required for operating system files. The amount of space required for programs and data vastly exceeds the storage requirements of Windows NT.

Peripherals

A final consideration is the various computer peripherals that you will be inserting in or attaching to your Windows NT Server computer. Devices you attach to your computer must have drivers for Windows NT. Some devices are supported by Windows NT itself (the keyboard and mouse, for instance); others come with driver software that you can install from within Windows NT.

The computer hardware market is characterized by an almost unlimited array of computers and hardware devices (network adapters, video cards, etc.). Windows NT supports most computers and hardware devices for sale today. However, Windows NT does not support every computer and every hardware device ever manufactured. Some hardware devices may appear to work with Windows NT initially, but eventually they conflict with other hardware devices or cause Windows NT to become unstable.

The Windows NT *Hardware Compatibility List* (HCL) lists the computers certified by Microsoft to run Windows NT. Using a computer from the *Hardware Compatibility List* will considerably reduce incompatibility problems and will assist the Microsoft help line staff in resolving any difficulties you may have. You can use the NT Hardware Qualifier (NTHQ) to test any machine for Windows NT compatibility before trying to install the operating system.

The Hardware Compatibility List *is a book that ships as part of the Windows NT documentation package. Microsoft also maintains an electronic version of the HCL at its site on the World Wide Web.*

The HCL covers various types of hardware:

- Storage devices, including SCSI and RAID I/O subsystems

- Monitors, modems, network adapters, CD-ROMs, UPS systems, keyboards, and pointing devices

- CPUs

The Windows NT distribution CD-ROM contains many device drivers for Windows NT. You are much more likely to find a device driver on the CD-ROM for your device if your device is on the HCL than if it isn't.

If your hardware is not on the HCL, you may have, or be able to obtain, drivers from the hardware manufacturer. When buying new hardware, make sure that, if the hardware is not on the HCL, the manufacturer includes a Windows NT device driver with the hardware.

Summary

W INDOWS NT SERVER is a server operating system with the powerful architecture of earlier versions of Windows NT and the ease of use of Windows 95. Although it can run application programs (spreadsheets, word processors, etc.) like Windows 95 can, the primary function of Windows NT Server is to provide network services such as file storage, mail routing, network routing, database hosting, and Internet hosting.

Windows NT is a completely different operating system internally from Windows 95. Unlike Windows 95, which is a direct descendent of earlier versions of Windows, Windows NT is not an updated version of any other operating system. Because Windows NT was never tied to implementation decisions of prior operating systems, Microsoft was free to implement powerful, new features, such as fault tolerance, security, preemptive multitasking, symmetrical multiprocessing, platform independence, RAID, and log file system support.

Windows NT Server requires at least an 80486 microprocessor with 12MB of memory; however, you need a Pentium computer with 48MB of memory to attain optimal performance. A RISC-based computer requires more memory.

Review Questions

1. You would most likely use Windows NT Server to run application programs such as spreadsheets and word processors.

    A. True

    B. False

2. Windows 95 is not a descendent of Windows NT.

    A. True

    B. False

3. Windows NT will run every program that other versions of Windows and DOS will run.

  A. True

  B. False

4. Windows NT can run some OS/2 programs.

  A. True

  B. False

5. Windows NT 4 uses the Windows 95 interface.

  A. True

  B. False

6. Normal users are allowed to install alternative device drivers in the kernel.

  A. True

  B. False

7. The Windows NT kernel provides a fault-tolerant environment for the execution of programs and services

  A. True

  B. False

8. Windows 95 is platform dependent because it runs on Intel-based computers only.

  A. True

  B. False

9. Windows NT Server can provide network services for DOS, Windows, Windows NT Workstation, OS/2, and the Apple Macintosh.

  A. True

  B. False

10. Windows NT Server is a _____ operating system.

11. Windows NT Server as a _____ server provides a place for storing files for all of the client computers on the network

12. The _____ lies at the heart of the operating system and provides services to the programs running on the computer.

13. A _____ _____ kernel provides the illusion of many programs executing at once on the computer by dividing processor time between each program and ensuring that no program can monopolize the time of the processor.

14. A _____ kernel supports the use of more than one microprocessor in the computer.

15. NTFS does not use a _____ _____ _____ (FAT).

16. RAID stands for _____ _____ _____ _____.

17. TDI stands for _____ _____ _____.

18. One Windows NT Server becomes the _____ _____ _____ (PDC), which maintains the security database and controls various aspects of the network's operation.

19. Windows NT Server also supports RISC microprocessors such as _____, _____ _____, and _____.

20. Microsoft maintains a list of computers and peripheral equipment that has been tested to work with Windows NT; the list is called the _____ _____ _____, or HCL.

Planning Your
Network

AT THE RISK of stating the obvious, planning your Windows NT network is by far the most important part of setting up your network. Nevertheless, the vast majority of networks are never planned at all—they are simply installed to meet current needs and evolve ad hoc to keep a minimum of service available to users. Networks installed in this manner tend to outgrow resources such as server capacities quickly; it soon becomes very difficult to tell why these networks run slowly and figure out how to improve their performance.

Planning your network correctly from the start will prevent this chaos from happening to you. If your organization is growing at a steady and predictable pace (most established businesses follow this pattern), you should have no problem defining your network. If your organization is new or is growing rapidly, you can apply the same planning principles by designing the network for its maximum size in three to five years and then implementing the network plan as your organization grows into it. This approach will keep you from being overwhelmed by rapid growth or from investing in technologies that will not be sustainable as your organization grows.

The first section of this chapter walks you through designing a medium-sized network from the ground up. You will be able to apply the design principles used for this type of network to any smaller network. After designing the physical, data link, and network layers of your network, you will be ready to concentrate on network operating system issues. The second section of this chapter discusses the security models that Windows NT supports. The third section focuses on the different roles your Windows NT server may play to support your chosen security model. The fourth section covers other special functions you may need your servers to perform. The fifth and final section introduces the different types of software licensing Windows NT supports and shows you how to choose the type appropriate for your network.

Planning the Network Foundation

NETWORKS, LIKE BUILDINGS, are built in many layers. Buildings rely upon a solid foundation to support their framework, which gives shape and structure to the building. Buildings are subdivided into floors to make efficient use of the available space. Floors are then further subdivided into rooms to create privacy and security and to prevent people from constantly interfering with one another. Imagine how unproductive a large organization would be if all its employees worked in one undivided space.

In the same way, networks rely upon sound cabling to transmit data among computers and networked devices. Data link equipment requires properly designed cabling to communicate. Data link equipment transmits information in units called *frames*, which address data to specific recipients and ensure the integrity of data transmissions.

Transport protocols allow data to move between different types of data link equipment and guarantee the delivery of all data between any two nodes on the same internetwork. Transport protocols work by providing additional addressing embedded in units called *packets*, which are carried inside frames and tell routers and gateways how to switch the packet onto other data link networks to which the gateway is attached. Network file systems and interprocess communication protocols rely upon transport protocols to provide seamless data streams by simulating the operation of local hard disks and message-passing systems. They hide the packet-based transmission of transport protocols so that software need not deal with or require any specific transport protocol.

Network operating systems rely upon network file systems and interprocess communication protocols to transfer data between servers and clients, to manage the logon and security processes, and to allow communications between clients and servers in client/server applications. Applications rely upon clients seamlessly connected to resource servers to perform their tasks. Finally, users rely upon networked applications to perform their work.

Each network layer requires thought and planning to ensure the proper operation of the entire network. But rather than starting at the foundation, the physical cable plant, you will start your planning at the top—with the needs of the end user. As you clarify the requirements for each level from the top down, your choices for the next lower level become clear.

The steps in creating a well-designed network are as follows:

- Conduct a survey of existing conditions

- Plan network requirements

- Plan the network operating system

- Plan the network

- Plan the physical plant

The following sections explain each step in detail, and the exercises show you how to perform each step in your organization.

Conduct a Survey of Existing Conditions

The first step in planning a network is to record what you know about your organization's computing needs. Survey your organization to determine the following information:

- **How many computers are in use?** This answer will determine the size of your network, the number of servers you will need, and the quantity and type of data link equipment you will require.

- **What types of computers are being used?** This answer will define the network operating system you should use, the transport protocols you can use, and some of the services you will need.

- **What special pieces of computing equipment, such as printers, are in use?** This step will identify additional special equipment, such as print servers, that might be required.

- **What services, such as Internet or private wide area network services, are in use?** This step will further isolate which network operating system you should use, as well as help you identify any third-party software that might be required.

- **What software is currently being used?** Some network-ready software will operate only under certain network operating systems. If your network is using this type of software, your choice of network operating systems may be limited.

- **Will you be integrating existing local area subnetworks into the new network?** These existing networks will have to be compatible with the network you install, or you will have to migrate them to other technologies.

Once you've surveyed your existing network, you can come up with a list of requirements for the network you are planning.

Plan Your Network Requirements

The next step in network planning is to define what you want to be able to do with your network. Common requirements include

- **Supporting collaboration through groupware and e-mail.** How collaborative is your company? Some companies do not require teamwork because the tasks are individual in nature, while other companies may depend on hundreds of carefully coordinated individuals to create a product.

- **Providing resource sharing for file storage and printing.** Nearly every network in existence must meet this requirement.

- **Providing easy access to the Internet or to private wide area networks.** This requirement is becoming more commonplace every day—but it is full of pitfalls and security risks.

- **Establishing a central point of network security and control.** For some organizations, the security of data is more important than networking. For others, security is of no concern at all. Find out what your security requirements are.

- **Centralizing administration and reducing training burden.** Networks do not have to grow into unmanageable beasts, and users can learn to assist with network administration. Putting together a set of procedures for common tasks such as adding new users, assigning passwords, and providing common training will help to keep your network running smoothly.

- **Supporting all existing computer hardware.** Few organizations can afford to throw away their existing computer and network equipment, so supporting legacy systems is an important priority when migrating to new technologies.

- **Implementing data archiving and disaster recovery.** This requirement is easy to implement in server-based networks because they provide central points of data storage.

- **Providing for the distribution of shared databases.** Servers support the replication of shared data among different servers to guarantee that a common set of information is available to everyone in the organization. Replication can keep the databases in different offices synchronized.

- **Increasing the speed at which information can be shared throughout the organization.** Years ago—before overnight delivery services and networks—sharing a document with colleagues in another city meant spending a week waiting for the mail. Even faxing did not really facilitate the sharing of complex information. But e-mail and groupware can transmit everything from blueprints to video presentations quickly and painlessly anywhere in the world.

Your organization will have its own requirements. Use the list above to start thinking about the purpose of your network. Combine this list with the information generated from the existing-conditions survey of your organization's computing environment. These two sets of requirements constitute your networking goal and serve as your checklist for evaluating technologies and systems.

Plan the Network Operating System

After surveying your network, create a list of network operating systems you are considering using. This step comes before all others because it determines what sort of server hardware you can use, and it may determine which transport protocols you will support. These choices in turn can force your hand when you select data link layer equipment, which in turn will determine what sort of cabling you will use. Notice that this sequence of decisions reinforces the top-down design structure.

Although you have many network operating systems from which to choose, Windows NT is the most modern network operating system available. Its support for advanced features such as symmetric multiprocessing, deeply embedded security, preemptive multitasking, and software fault tolerance systems (including disk mirroring and striping with parity) make Windows NT the most secure and reliable network operating system on the market. Outstanding security and reliability, coupled with strong support for TCP/IP and intra/Internet services and lower cost than most other network operating systems, make Windows NT the obvious choice for new network installations.

Check each network operating system candidate to ensure that it can serve your existing conditions and your planned network requirements. Then select the operating system that comes closest to fulfilling your requirements.

Once you've selected a network operating system, make sure that it will not introduce any problems of its own. For instance, many older network operating systems require users to log in to each server separately. Although this process is of little consequence in small networks, it can become very intrusive in larger multiple-server networks.

You will also want to consider the administrative burden that network operating systems create. Some network operating systems are very easy to administer, whereas others can be so difficult as to become a work hindrance to users in larger networks. If you intend to implement automated administration tools such as Simple Network Management Protocol (SNMP) or Dynamic Host Configuration Protocol (DHCP), you will have to plan these now so you can ensure that the hardware and software you purchase will support them.

Windows NT fills all these needs and is an excellent choice for both general network requirements, such as file and print sharing, and for special purpose applications, such as application serving, Internet serving, and for use as a gateway or firewall.

Windows NT supports all common network protocols, such as TCP/IP (used in UNIX networks and the global Internet), IPX (used in Novell NetWare networks), NetBEUI (used by Microsoft and IBM networks), and AppleTalk (used by Apple Macintosh networks). Nearly every computer in existence supports these protocols, which makes Windows NT Server an easy choice. Before you decide on a network operating system, answer the question at the end of Exercise 2.1. Then create your own list of requirements and make sure the network operating system you choose can satisfy them.

Plan the Logical Network

Planning the logical network involves selecting a transport protocol, selecting data link technologies, and dividing the network into subnetworks and security domains.

EXERCISE 2.1

Choosing a Network Operating System

You have a client who wants to integrate many small networks into a single organizational network. Current equipment includes

- A Novell NetWare network used in accounting

- Apple Macintoshes networked in a peer environment in the marketing area

- OS/2 and Windows NT Workstations for research and development

- UNIX computers in the software development department

Which network operating system(s) can support these existing conditions without loading new software on the client computers?

Networking Terminology

Network terminology is characterized by confusion and inconsistency. This brief glossary defines network terms as we use them in this book.

- **Subnetwork** refers to a single shared media network such as an Ethernet collision domain or a Token Ring.

- **Network** refers to a group of similar subnetworks that are bridged or switched together.

- **Internetwork** refers to networks that are connected via routers.

- **Internet** refers to the global internetwork of TCP/IP hosts to which most major governments and businesses are now attached.

- **Intranet** refers to TCP/IP internetworks that exist entirely inside an organization but use the software and methods made standard by the global Internet.

- **Domain** refers to a shared security domain wherein a user can log on to a one authentication server that will then introduce the user to all other secure shared resources. This type of domain is not the same as an *Internet domain*, which is a logical grouping of TCP/IP hosts, or an *Ethernet collision domain*, which is a single Ethernet subnetwork.

Planning the logical network is often the most difficult portion of network planning, because you won't have any obvious or easy ways to measure or determine network requirements or usage. Fortunately, we can spare you some trouble by passing on the experience of many network technicians.

If you were going to build a warehouse to store engines, you could simply measure the size of each engine, determine how high you can stack them, add floor space for access, and build a warehouse of the exact size you need. Most architects also add room for expansion and growth. Another method is to simply buy more space than you will ever need, but this approach obviously requires deep pockets.

Both techniques are used in networking, and unfortunately, the second is more common. Many organizations waste a tremendous amount of money on hardware to guarantee that they will not have a capacity problem. In very small networks buying more hardware than you need can actually make financial sense because network architects may charge more than the extra equipment will cost to design a network of the proper size. We will assume, however, that you intend to spend as little as you can to create a well-designed network. The steps in designing the logical network are as follows:

- Estimate the client load

- Determine which data link technologies will support that load

- Determine which types of cable support that data link layer technology

- Decide whether you will centralize or distribute servers on the network

- Lay out a network map

Estimating Client Load

To estimate load capacities of networks, you need a metric with which you can compare very different network technologies and relate them to client computer requirements, often without the benefit of knowing exactly how those client computers will be used. Seasoned network integrators base their estimates on what they've done and seen work in the past.

Although no simple method will replace an experienced network integrator, experience can be distilled into methods that are useful for planning and estimating. A good working methodology will serve a number of roles:

- It will be useful for comparing data link technologies.

- It will be useful for planning the network's physical layout.

- It will be able to predict the amount and type of hardware necessary to implement the network.

We have developed a simple method that will help you plan your network based upon the client load limit of various current data link technologies. For instance, a single 10Mb/s Ethernet network can support a maximum of about 50 DOS clients. The same Ethernet network can reliably serve 20 or so Windows NT Workstations.

Of course, these estimations are not absolute—the way the client is used will affect its load on the network greatly, and as technology changes so will the load estimates for various clients. The law of averages comes to our aid here by smoothing the usage characteristics of a single computer over the number of computers attached to the network. This method doesn't always work well, however. Consider the case of a diskless DOS workstation that must boot its operating system from a network server. This client will typically demand more from a network than a typical client because even its memory page file is being sent over the network.

You can use the method presented here if your operations conform to the common uses of computers. If you are doing something you know will require more bandwidth, consider revising the load values for clients upwards. We have presented worst-case capacities in this method, so resist the temptation to revise them downward.

LOAD REQUIREMENTS OF TYPICAL NETWORK CLIENTS We determined the client load requirements shown in Table 2.1 by dividing 100 by the maximum useful number of clients of that type that could operate on a single Ethernet segment.

Make a map of all the computers in your organization based on their rough location in your facility, matching them to one of the types in Table 2.1. Sum the values to determine your organization's total client load.

TABLE 2.1 Load Requirements of Network Clients	**CLIENT**	**METRIC**	**EXPLANATION**
	Macintosh	1	Macintoshes typically require very little from a network, so we used a typical Macintosh client as the basis for our network metric.
	DOS	2	MS-DOS machines tend to run simpler application software that does not demand much from a network.
	Diskless DOS Client	6	Diskless MS-DOS clients, however, are much more demanding. These computers must use the network for every I/O command that would normally go to a local hard disk drive.

	CLIENT	METRIC	EXPLANATION
TABLE 2.1 Load Requirements of Network Clients (continued)	Windows	3	Windows is a more complex platform than MS-DOS is, and applications built to run on Windows are more complex and network aware.
	Power Macintosh	3	Macintosh computers based on the PowerPC microprocessor are very fast. Although Macintoshes demand less from a network than most PC file-sharing schemes demand, these computers can hit the network hard because of their speed.
	Diskless Windows	9	Diskless Windows clients are extremely demanding of network bandwidth—more so than any other type of computer.
	Windows 95	4	Windows 95 is a powerful multitasking operating system that typically runs on fast client computers.
	OS/2	4	OS/2 is very similar to Windows 95 in most respects. It runs on similar hardware and runs similar applications.
	Windows NT Workstation	5	Windows NT Workstation is the most powerful operating system available for PCs. Its ability to multitask multiple network applications smoothly requires much from a network.
	UNIX workstation	5	UNIX workstations are usually used by bandwidth-intensive users like programmers, graphic artists, and CAD operators.
	UNIX X-terminal	3	X-terminals are diskless, but they operate as simple displays. Screen updates are sent from a server that actually performs the work requested by the user.
	TCP/IP print server	10	Although print servers technically do not generate load of their own, printed documents do. Every document you print to a print server moves across the network twice—when it is sent from your computer to the Windows NT Server that processes it and again when it is sent to the print server attached to the printer. Because printed documents can also be quite large, they can create quite a load on your network.

LOAD CAPACITIES OF DATA LINK TECHNOLOGIES Data link technologies use various methods to arbitrate the sharing of media, which makes a comparison difficult. For example, although Token Ring uses a faster bit rate than Ethernet uses, a client must wait for the token before transmitting, which can make Ethernet seem more responsive. Adding clients to a Token Ring will slow the network in a simple deterministic manner, whereas overloading an Ethernet can cause it to suddenly cease operating all together. These differences mean that comparisons based on simple bit rate are meaningless.

We chose to use the worst-case number of clients we felt could be usefully attached to a single shared media network rather than to use a comparison of raw throughput. We then applied this metric to the capacities of other types of networks that are not shared media, such as asynchronous transfer mode (ATM), to show how these networks can be aggregated into large internetworks.

When creating internetworks, the capacity number used for a subnetwork becomes its load. For instance, a Fiber Distributed Data Interface (FDDI) ring with a capacity rating of 1,000 can handle up to ten Ethernet networks, each with a capacity rating of 100. Table 2.2 shows the load capacities of various network data link technologies.

TABLE 2.2 Load Capacities of Network Technologies	**NETWORK**	**CAPACITY**	**EXPLANATION**
	Ethernet	100	Ethernet was used as the basis for comparison because it is the most common network data link technology. You can expect to attach 50 DOS clients to a single Ethernet subnetwork before it bogs down.
	Token Ring	200	A single Token Ring can support roughly twice as many computers as a single Ethernet subnetwork. Because Token Ring degrades gracefully, you can continue to load a Token Ring past this point, but your network will slow considerably.
	Fast Ethernet	500	Although the bit rate for fast Ethernet is ten times the rate of Ethernet, it cannot handle ten times the traffic because of the delay involved in resolving collisions.

TABLE 2.2 Load Capacities of Network Technologies (continued)	NETWORK	CAPACITY	EXPLANATION
	Fiber Distributed Data Interface	1,000	You can reasonably connect ten Ethernet networks on a single FDDI ring. This arrangement depends greatly upon where you've chosen to place your servers—centralized servers demand more from the backbone.
	FiberChannel (1GB/s)	10,000	Gigabit Ethernet will operate over FiberChannel at one gigabit per second. Although gigabit Ethernet retains the Ethernet name, it is full duplex point to point and does not have collisions. It is a perfect backbone technology in campus environments.
	ATM-155 OC-3	1000	ATM is a switched network technology. It is not shared. For this reason, you can count on being able to use about 80 percent of the bit rate for useable traffic so long as you maintain constant connections between servers.
	ATM OC-12	4000	ATM bandwidth increases linearly with speed. At 622 Mb/s, ATM OC-12 is sufficient for the most demanding backbone applications.
	ATM OC-48	16,000	ATM at OC-48 (2.2 Gb/s) is typically used for metropolitan area networks. This capacity is appropriate for metropolitan area high-speed links.
	AMT OC-192	48,000	ATM at OC-192 (8.8Gb/s) is used for major trunks between metropolitan areas by the telephone companies. It is included here for completeness.

When calculating load versus capacity, remember that these numbers are maximum capacity estimates. Erring on the side of excess capacity is preferable to being tied to a slow network. You should try to avoid coming within 25 percent of the maximum values presented here if you want your network to run smoothly.

Make a rough map of the computers in your organization based on location. Select a network technology and group clients into networks based upon location. Then sum the client load values of each group to make sure you are well within the load capacity for the network type you've selected.

Backbones are high-speed links connecting shared media subnetworks. Backbones may be shared media networks themselves, point-to-point links, or switched networks.

A NETWORK DESIGN EXAMPLE Figure 2.1 shows an organization's physical layout; the computers in use are represented as client loads. Using this map, the network administrator was able to segregate the network into Ethernet subnetworks as shown in Figure 2.2. This network will operate properly under normal load conditions because the administrator stayed well below the worst-case capacity of Ethernet during the design. Exercise 2.2 will give you some practice in designing networks.

FIGURE 2.1

Typical client loads for an organization.

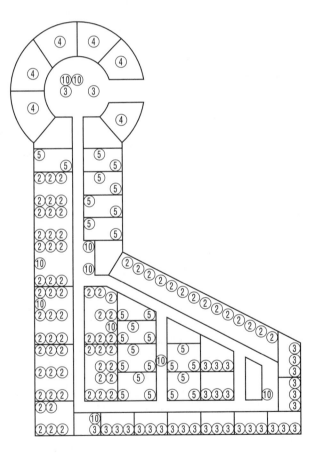

FIGURE 2.2

Creating subnetworks based upon estimated client load.

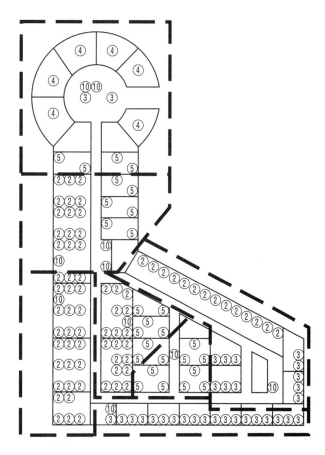

EXERCISE 2.2

Designing a Network

Given the following information and using the method described above, determine how many Ethernet subnetworks you need to comfortably support these clients, allowing for 25 percent growth:

- 15 Windows NT computers

- 250 MS-DOS clients

- 95 Macintosh computers

- 99 Power Macintosh computers

- 35 OS/2 workstations

- 155 Windows clients

Locating Servers

Once you have laid out your network, you can determine the best place to install servers. Many organizations opt to collect all the servers into a central computer room, which reduces the administrative burden. Centralizing servers also makes access to different servers equally fast for organizations where users will attach to many different application servers. Unfortunately, centralizing servers requires the use of a very fast network backbone because this arrangement guarantees that all network traffic will pass through the backbone to the central server farm. Figure 2.3 shows a network with centralized servers.

FIGURE 2.3

Centralized servers.

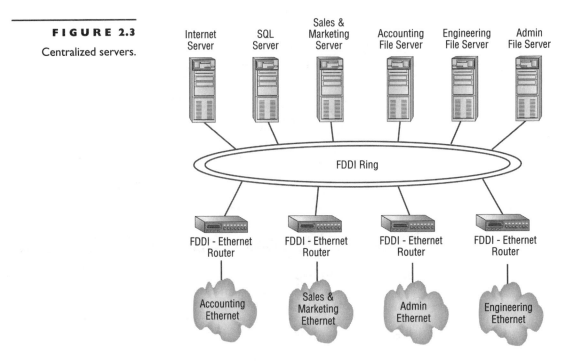

Other organizations distribute servers to the individual subnetworks and rely upon a slower backbone to connect users to resources outside their subnetwork. The backbone does not need to be high speed because (we hope) about 80 percent of all client traffic will be to the local server, which is on the subnetwork with the clients. Distributing servers physically throughout the organization reduces the cost of the network, but it tends to increase the administrative burden. Distributed serving can be very slow if users frequently need to access other servers on the network; if this situation exists in your organization, centralized servers (or a combination of centralized and local servers) may be more appropriate. Figure 2.4 shows a network with local servers.

FIGURE 2.4

Local servers.

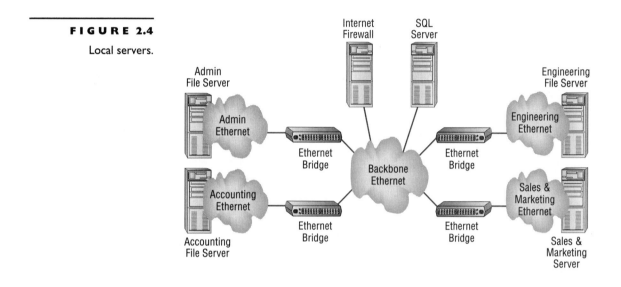

Plan the Network Technology

Each type of shared media data link technology can support only a limited number of clients. The actual number varies between networks depending upon the load, but even the fastest shared media networks don't get very large. To create larger networks than those supported by a single shared media network, you must use internetworking devices.

Once you've installed your physical plant, you will need to connect the various subnetworks. You create connections between subnetworks with devices called bridges, routers, and switches. *Bridges* connect two similar subnetworks. *Routers* connect subnetworks of different technologies. *Switches*, depending upon the type, can connect many subnetworks of similar or different technologies.

Choosing Network Technologies

Once you've determined what your client load will be, you can determine which network technologies are most appropriate to handle that load. Current popular network technologies include

- Ethernet

- Token Ring

- ATM-25

- Fast Ethernet

- FDDI

- ATM-155

Although technically you have many choices, the inexpensive, easy-to-use data link technology called Ethernet outdistances most network data link technologies.

Now available in two flavors, 10 and 100M/bit, Ethernet is fast enough to handle even the most demanding client loads. Another variant (due out soon) called gigabit Ethernet promises to eliminate the need for high-speed, high-cost technologies to connect even the largest campus networks. The dominance of Ethernet in the data link technology market makes this choice very easy.

Ethernet supports all popular cable plant technologies. You can run Ethernet over coaxial cable, twisted pair telephone cabling, and optical fiber. Most new installations will opt for twisted pair wiring, as it solves many of the problems associated with coaxial wiring and is less expensive than optical fiber. Optical fiber is usually used for internetwork connectivity in large buildings and campuses.

Choosing Backbone Technologies

Choosing a backbone technology is somewhat more complex than choosing a shared media network technology. Unlike subnetworks for which your choice should be obvious, no single backbone technology surpasses others in price, performance, or ease of use.

Most high-speed backbones in operation today run on 100Mb/s FDDI, which is a ring technology that can support very large and distant networks. FDDI is expensive, however, and despite (and partly because of) its redundancy features, it can be difficult to work with. FDDI is also nearly obsolete as a backbone technology at a mere 100Mb/s.

Many network integrators are using ATM as a backbone technology. ATM uses high-speed circuit switches to connect the various parts of a network in star hierarchies. ATM was designed primarily as a telephony, voice, and video service, however, and has some problems encapsulating the large packets typically used by transport protocols such as TCP/IP. Because ATM is new and because many vendors are building devices that do not interoperate properly, ATM can be a risky choice. However, ATM will probably be installed worldwide as the telephony transport over the next 20 years, which will make it a more obvious choice as time goes by and incompatibilities are ironed out.

Gigabit Ethernet over FiberChannel may represent a simple and (relatively) inexpensive alternative to the two heavy-duty backbone technologies presented earlier. However, this new technology will carry a high price tag.

Full-duplex Fast Ethernet over fiber optic cable is the least expensive high-speed backbone technology currently available, but it suffers from distance limitations that make it difficult to use in larger campuses or metropolitan area networks.

Plan the Physical Plant

Just as Ethernet is the easy choice for data link technology, star-wired, category 5, unshielded twisted pair (UTP) cable plants are the easy choice for physical plants. The combination of star wiring and UTP makes troubleshooting easy, since no cable fault affects more than one computer. There are no rules for termination, transceiver counts, or any of the myriad of problems that can occur with coaxial-based plants. UTP cabling operates at up to 100MHz, providing bit rates up to 155Mb/s. If you anticipate a greater need, you will need to install optical fiber throughout your network.

All modern networks operate over one of two types of cable: category 5 unshielded twisted pair (UTP) or optical fiber. The distance limitations of UTP wiring restrict its use to connecting clients in a relatively small area (within 100 meters of a wiring closet) in a star architecture. Optical fiber connects these wiring closets to form the backbone of the network.

Although many other network cabling styles exist, they are all obsolete except in special circumstances. The advantages of the star-wired–UTP/optical fiber network far outweigh the minor cost advantages of coaxial wiring in all but the smallest peer-to-peer networks. If a network spans beyond a single room, it should use the architecture presented here. Figure 2.5 shows a typical star-wired network with optical fiber backbone.

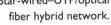

FIGURE 2.5

Star-wired–UTP/optical fiber hybrid network.

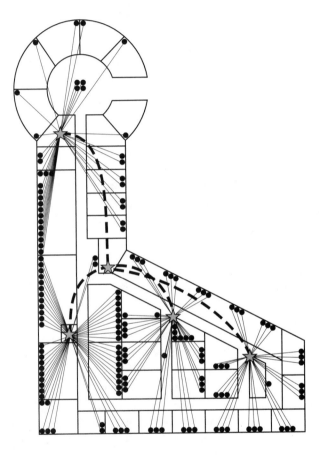

The advantages of star-wired networks are many:

- They can emulate all other wiring topologies (ring or bus).

- They are inexpensive.

- You can add more stations simply by pulling a new cable.

- Cable faults typically affect only one computer and are easy to isolate.

Star-wired networks have only one disadvantage—they require more cable. But when you consider that UTP is typically one-tenth the cost of the coaxial cable required for bus networks, the difference in cost is inconsequential.

To plan your physical plant, simply lay out where you want UTP station locations, also called *drops*, on blueprints of your facility. You don't have to lay out cable paths, as you can count on the contractor who installs your network to make the shortest path to a wiring closet to save work.

Note that your physical plant should map somewhat to your subnetwork layout created in the client load section, but it does not have to match exactly. You can create more than one subnetwork in a single wiring closet, but it might be difficult (and unnecessary) for one subnetwork to span more than one wiring closet.

Each network device and computer attached to the network will require a drop. Note where you have space for wiring closets, also known as *intermediate distribution frames* (IDFs), which are generally required for the central point of each star. The *main distribution frame* (MDF) closet is where the backbone runs for each IDF end. If you have more than one floor, the MDF on each floor will terminate in the computer room.

Windows NT Network Security Models

YOU NEED TO be aware of two security models when you network with Windows NT Server: workgroup and domain. The first model, *workgroup*, governs the interactions of Windows and Windows NT computers in a peer network; the second model, *domain*, governs the interactions of clients and Windows NT servers in a server-based network with a Windows NT server (designated the primary domain controller) coordinating the security of the network. The two models fulfill different security requirements.

The Workgroup Security Model

Windows NT local area networks that are small and that do not need centralized network control or centralized data storage can be organized into workgroups. Workgroups are essentially peer-to-peer networks, which means that the users of each workstation select and manage the resources on that workstation that are made available to other users on the network. The user accounts and resources on the workstation are administered from that workstation, not from a network server.

A workgroup is a good choice for your networking model if your organization is small (ten users or less), the workstation users have the ability to administer their own workstations, and central file storage and central control of network security are not important.

The workgroup security model does not support user accounts in the same way that logging on to a domain does. Workgroup resources are simply protected by a password (or in the case of Windows NT, by an account name and password). Anyone knowing the password to a shared resource on a workgroup has access to that resource—without passing an account name.

Windows NT allows servers to participate in workgroups as stand-alone servers. *Stand-alone servers* are servers that run Windows NT Server but do not participate in any domain security. Stand-alone servers are discussed later in this chapter.

A workgroup is not a good choice for your networking model if you have many users, if you need to centralize user account management and network security, or if you cannot rely on the users of your network to administer their own workstations.

The Domain Security Model

Domains provide much more coherent security and network administration than the workgroup security model provides. In domains, accounts are managed on a single computer, called the primary domain controller, which permits or denies access to all the shared resources in the domain. (Backup domain controllers keep a copy of the security accounts database and can log on users if the primary domain controller is busy or unavailable.) Because accounts are managed centrally, users have to log on only once to gain access to all servers in the domain. The domain controller that logged them on will "introduce" the user to other servers in the domain by forwarding their account information in the form of a security access token.

The domain model of networking is a good choice if you have strict security requirements, multiple servers, or if you cannot rely on your users to administrate their own computers.

Because this information is centrally controlled, the task of managing a large network is easier for the network administrator than it would be if the information had to be maintained individually on each computer in the network. Centralizing this information also means that users do not have to perform their own administration tasks for their workstations.

In a domain one or more servers store the shared network files for all workstations in the domain. The primary domain controller controls workstation access to the files stored on the servers, using account and security information it stores in a central database. Storing the network files in servers helps the network administrator control access to information. A central location also helps to streamline the task of data backup.

Structuring Domains

A large network may have more than one domain. An organization that is divided into functional units, for instance a business that is split into marketing, finance, manufacturing, and research departments, may divide its domain-based network along those same functional lines. Organizations that have offices in different parts of the country would probably choose to have a domain in each office.

This book focuses on single-domain networks. The companion book in this series, MCSE: NT Server 4 in the Enterprise Study Guide *by Lisa Donald, covers multiple-domain networks in detail.*

Workgroup User Accounts and Domain User Accounts

The User Manager program that comes with Windows NT Workstation cannot administer the domain user and administrator accounts. Instead, these accounts are administered by the User Manager for Domains program on the Windows NT Server or computers with remote server management software.

Local user and group accounts for individual workgroup resources are not added to the domain database. Local users and groups are still administered with the User Manager program. When you log on from the workstation that is part of a domain, you are given the choice of logging on to the domain (using an account in the domain user account database) or of logging on to the workstation computer (using an account in the workstation's local user account database). If you log on using a user account that is local to the workstation, you may not have access to resources on the domain.

Trust Relationships

Trust relationships extend the domain logon process beyond the bound of a single domain. You can establish trust relationships between Windows NT domain controllers so that they can "introduce" clients from their domains to the domain controllers in the foreign trusted domain, thus allowing access to information in the foreign trusted domain without requiring another logon to that domain. The trust relationship then determines what access the foreign client is given.

Trust relationships are outside the scope of this book, but are covered in the companion book, MCSE: NT Server 4 in the Enterprise Study Guide *by Lisa Donald.*

Choosing a Security Model

Your choice of security models depends primarily upon two things: the level of security you require and the level of control you wish to exercise over your network.

Generally, you will choose the domain security model over the workgroup model.

The advantages of the domain model are numerous, and the disadvantages few. For most server-based networks, the workgroup model has no advantage, since you must normally log on to a server anyway. The domain model supports a single logon to all shared resources in the domain, whereas the workgroup model requires a separate logon for each workstation shared resource. The domain model also supports centralized account management and user control.

The workgroup model is typically used only in networks where the users are computer experts and wish to retain a high level of control over resources that they share from their computers, as in peer-to-peer networks. Adding a server to an existing peer-to-peer network might be slightly easier if you choose the workgroup model.

You can have both domain and workgroup security in the same network at the same time, allowing users to share their computing resources while retaining central control over server-based resources.

The domain and workgroup models are not mutually exclusive—they can be used at the same time in the same network. In fact, most Windows NT–based networks have a server-based centralized domain security structure for important data and a workgroup for sharing less security-sensitive resources such as CD-ROM readers. Use Exercise 2.3 to practice selecting security models for different network requirements.

EXERCISE 2.3

Selecting a Security Model

You've just installed a ten-user Ethernet network for a group of real estate agents who intend to share e-mail, scheduling information, and a laser printer. Which security model is appropriate?

You've just installed a 400-user, six-server Fast Ethernet network for a consumer credit bureau. Which security model is appropriate in this case?

Windows NT Server Roles

WINDOWS NT DEFINES the role of a Windows NT server by its participation in the domain security model. You must choose from the four defined roles for a Windows NT server during the initial installation of Windows NT.

- **Primary domain controllers** must be the first server operating in the domain because all other computers to this server to get permission to participate in the domain.

- **Backup domain controllers** assist the primary domain controller in authenticating logons.

- **Member servers** are servers in the domain, that do not participate as domain controllers.

- **Stand-alone servers** are not members of a domain, so they must provide their own local logon and security.

Primary Domain Controller

In a security domain one computer acts as the primary domain controller. This computer authenticates logons for clients by validating the supplied username and password in the accounts database and returning a security token to the requesting client. The security token introduces that client to all other domain security participants on the network whenever the user requests a resource shared by that participant. The security token scheme gives transparent access to the user and provides for a single logon to the domain without sacrificing security.

The first Windows NT server in your network must be the primary domain controller if you intend to use the domain security model. You indicate this decision during the installation of Windows NT Server. This first server will be responsible for storing the security accounts database. It also names the domain. If you don't want the first server you install to remain the primary domain controller, you can always promote a backup domain controller later.

Backup Domain Controllers

Backup domain controllers keep a copy of the entire security accounts database and can log on clients if the primary domain controller is busy or cannot be reached.

Backup domain controllers keep copies of the security accounts database, and they cannot change their copies. You can use the Server Manager for Domains utility to promote any backup domain controller to primary domain controller. (The current primary then becomes a backup.)

Server

Servers not configured as either primary domain controller or backup domain controller cannot create a security access token, so they cannot log clients on to the domain. Two types of servers are not domain controllers: member servers and stand-alone servers. Neither of these types of servers can be promoted to domain controller status. You must reinstall Windows NT Server if you want to use these computers as domain controllers.

Member Servers

Member servers participate in domain security, but they cannot authenticate logons. Therefore, they cannot function alone. Users must log on to a primary domain controller in order to gain access to member server resources.

Stand-Alone Servers

Stand-alone servers do not participate in domain security at all—they require their own specific logon. These servers are used in the workgroup security model.

Special Purpose Servers

S PECIAL PURPOSE SERVERS are computers configured to provide a network service other than file and print services. These servers are usually special cases of the basic application server. Your organization may have no special purpose servers, or you may have many, depending upon your needs and your business model.

Application Servers

Application servers run powerful programs designed to serve the server portion of a client/server application. The server portion of a client/server application is often referred to as the "back end," and the client portion is often referred to as the "front end." Consequently, application servers are called back-end servers. All the Microsoft BackOffice applications are designed to be run on application servers. Figure 2.6 shows an application server in a local area network.

Application servers are optimized for software execution speed. Typically, they have very fast processors, are likely to use symmetric multiprocessing, and generally have more RAM than any other type of server. Hard disk space for these servers varies widely depending upon the type of application being served.

FIGURE 2.6

Local area network with
an application server.

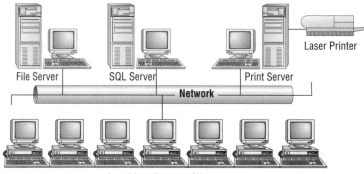

Local Area Network Clients

Application servers are most commonly implemented as back-end database servers using the Structured Query Language (SQL) protocol. SQL servers perform the computer-intensive task of tracking down data relations and returning a complete set of data based upon a user's request. Microsoft SQL server is an example of an SQL back end. Microsoft Access would typically be used as a front end to an SQL server.

Internet Servers

Internet servers are special application servers that answer (most commonly) Hypertext Transfer Protocol (HTTP—the protocol of the World Wide Web), File Transfer Protocol (FTP), and Gopher requests from the Internet. Internet servers allow organizations to publish Web pages on the Internet, as well as post information files and programs. Uniform resource locator (URL) addresses are the addresses to Internet servers.

The Internet Information Server (IIS) package that comes with Windows NT Server 4 provides all the functionality necessary to use a Windows NT Server as an Internet server. It provides secure storage and publication of HTTP, FTP, and Gopher information from a Windows NT Server and keeps Internet traffic securely separated from other information on your server. However, IIS cannot keep hackers from penetrating other computers on your network, so you will still want to place a firewall between your Internet server and your in-house network. This requirement means that, for the most part, you will not be storing secure data on your Internet server.

Firewalls

The explosion of the Internet has forced companies to protect their computing resources from intrusion by unauthorized parties. The Internet protocols were not designed with security in mind—they were optimized for ease of connectivity instead. Special security servers called *firewalls* patch the holes in Internet security.

Firewalls act as gatekeepers to the network and attempt to prevent unauthorized intrusion into the network through a number of complex security measures. Typically, firewalls can be configured to allow only computers from certain IP addresses to attach to your network. Firewalls also prevent external computers on the Internet from "seeing" IP addresses inside the network, thus preventing intruders from exploiting shared resources on interior servers. The only computer that can be seen is the firewall itself. Figure 2.7 shows an Internet server being isolated by a firewall in a local area network.

FIGURE 2.7

A firewall isolating an Internet server from a local area network.

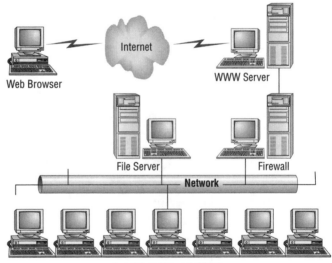

Messaging Servers

Messaging servers aggregate the many different types of messaging services that an organization requires. They typically run a LAN groupware package, such as Microsoft Exchange or Lotus Notes, and are usually configured as

Internet e-mail gateways. Messaging servers may also be configured with modems to dial into paging services to contact personnel or forward high priority messages to alphanumeric pagers. Message servers can also sort through Internet or private news services for articles that may be of interest to anyone on the network and forwarding them as e-mail. Figure 2.8 shows how a message gateway attaches to the various components of a network.

FIGURE 2.8

A message gateway connecting network resources.

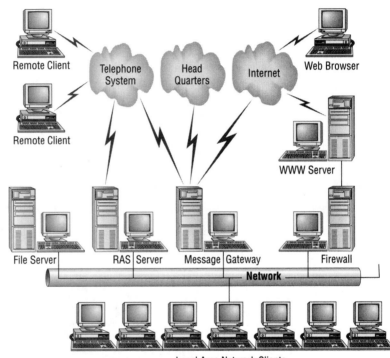

Gateways

Gateways are servers configured to provide a link between two distinct networks, protocols, or services. Gateways may provide any sort of translation necessary to extend one network's service to another network. The Gateway Service for NetWare (GSNW) is built into Windows NT Server. GSNW allows Microsoft network clients to attach to resources on a NetWare network. This configuration is a perfect example of a gateway.

Routers are a type of gateway optimized for connecting networks of dissimilar data link technology that run the same transport protocol. Gateways might also be configured to translate an older mainframe interface to a local area network protocol or to periodically poll a private news, e-mail, or database server to allow clients not configured to attach to the service directly to access the information. Remote access servers can be considered a serial-to-network gateway. Figure 2.9 shows a Windows NT server acting as a GSNW provider.

FIGURE 2.9

Windows NT can act as a gateway to NetWare servers.

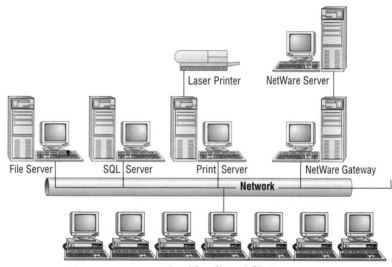

Remote Access Servers

Remote access servers answer incoming connections from remote clients. Typically, modems, ISDN interfaces, or Point-to-Point Tunneling Protocol (PPTP) connections from the Internet perform this function.

These servers have special security requirements because they are gateways to your network from public locations. For this reason, they may restrict access to confidential or sensitive information.

Because Remote Access Service (RAS) connections are very slow compared to LAN connections, RAS servers do not need to be located on high-bandwidth backbones. In Figure 2.8 a RAS server provides service to remote clients.

Licensing

THE FINAL STEP in planning your network is satisfying the legal aspects of client licensing. Client licensing is the purchase of a license to attach to a network operating system, thus providing a way to scale the price of a network operating system by the number of people who will be using it, rather than simply charging all organizations, large or small, the same price.

Per Server Licensing

Most network operating systems, including Windows NT and Novell NetWare, have stringent licensing requirements. Novell NetWare, for instance, limits the number of users who can attach to a NetWare server simultaneously and will not allow additional users to attach. This arrangement is called "per server licensing" because licenses are issued per server operating system sold.

Per Seat Licensing

Windows NT allows per server licensing but gives you the choice of using per seat licensing if that arrangement fits your needs better. *Per seat licensing* means purchasing a separate client access license (CAL) for each computer on your network, which gives that computer license to attach to any number of Windows NT Servers. It is called per seat licensing because you purchase a license for every computer in your organization, thus freeing you from per server license limits.

How Purchase Licenses Are Applied

If you choose to use per server licensing, client access licenses are applied to the server. For instance, purchasing 50 client access licenses means you can have 50 users simultaneously logged on to a specific server.

If you choose to use per seat licensing, client access licenses are applied individually to computers in your organization. For instance, if you buy 50 client access licenses, you can allow 50 computers to log into any number of Windows NT Servers simultaneously.

Selecting a Licensing Method

Microsoft recommends choosing per server licensing for small, single-server organizations. Microsoft allows a one-time conversion of per server licenses into per seat licenses if your organization grows beyond one server. Choosing per server licensing will allow you to save on access costs if your computers are generally not all attached to the server at the same time. Microsoft recommends choosing per seat licensing for all networks larger than a single server.

We recommend using per seat licensing in all cases. The amount of money you may save using per server licensing is small, and the restrictions are simply not worth the savings. By adding the cost of a per seat license to every workstation purchase, you will have the administrative freedom to add servers as you please and will never have to worry about licensing issues. Practice choosing a licensing method with Exercise 2.4.

EXERCISE 2.4

Choosing a Licensing Method

You have installed a network with four Windows NT Servers in an organization that will be using two of them as departmental servers and the other two as application servers. Which licensing method is appropriate?

Summary

PLANNING A NETWORK is not particularly difficult if you follow the proper steps and familiarize yourself with the available technologies. Planning a network involves determining your existing computing conditions, deciding what you want your network to do for you, selecting a network operating system that will satisfy those requirements, selecting data link technologies that can provide the capacity you need for your clients, and installing a cable plant that can support that data link technology.

After installing the physical plant and logical link devices, you will select domain or workgroup security in a Windows NT environment and determine the specific roles of all the servers on your network. Different types of servers fulfill different networked computing requirements.

Once your network is installed and your servers are up, you will have to purchase client access licenses on a per server or per seat basis for your network. Per seat licensing is the method to use for networks that have more than a single server or whenever you don't want to deal with licensing issues on a continuing basis.

Review Questions

1. You do not have to worry about supporting legacy systems, because the network will usually replace them.

   A. True

   B. False

2. Many older network operating systems require a separate login to each server.

   A. True

   B. False

3. Computers configured for domain security cannot participate in workgroups.

   A. True

   B. False

4. Organizational requirements are the same for all organizations.

   A. True

   B. False

5. Collecting servers in a central location reduces the administrative burden.

   A. True

   B. False

6. Collecting servers in a central location reduces traffic on the backbone.

    A. True

    B. False

7. It is always better to distribute servers rather than to centralize them.

    A. True

    B. False

8. Generally, you will choose the _____ security model.

9. The _____ security model governs the interactions of Windows and Windows NT computers in a peer network.

10. What is the most important part of setting up a network?

    A. Designing the physical plant

    B. Determining the client load

    C. Planning

    D. Calculating the number of licenses you will require

11. _____ are high-speed links that connect shared media networks.

    A. Routers

    B. FDDI

    C. Backbones

    D. Bridges

12. _____ is the most popular data link technology.

    A. Token Ring

    B. FDDI

    C. ATM

    D. Ethernet

    E. FiberChannel

13. _____ wired physical plant architectures can simulate all other wiring architectures.

   A. Bus

   B. Star

   C. Ring

   D. Full-duplex

14. The _____ is responsible for security in the domain security model.

   A. application server

   B. security server

   C. domain security controller

   D. primary domain controller

   E. primary domain server

Server Hardware

3

S ERVERS ARE JUST computers. They operate the same way that client stations do, and in most cases they use the same hardware architecture. So what is the difference between a server and a standard computer? Network operating system software and high-performance hardware components give servers their distinct capabilities. The hardware in each type of server is optimized to perform that server's primary role.

We outlined the minimum hardware requirements for running Windows NT Server in Chapter 1. However, those minimums do not represent a realistic hardware configuration, and a computer built to those minimums could not provide service as a Windows NT server.

In this chapter we describe the hardware you should be using to get the performance you expect out of a server. We also point out the configuration differences between different types of servers and explain how to configure the devices you install in a server.

Server Hardware

F IGURE 3.1 SHOWS the basic components of any computer. A functional server requires all of these components. We use the following terms throughout this discussion:

- **Microprocessors** are the brains of the computer. They perform lists of instructions called programs.

Since the dawn of time (which in computing terms is about 1960), CPU has stood for central processing unit, including everything that was required for computation but not those components of a computer system responsible for data storage or input and output. The closest analogy in your computer today is the entire box that is your computer minus anything attached to it (such as the monitor, keyboard, and any external disk drives). Because there is no longer any direct analogy (your "CPU" has disk drives in it), the term CPU has come to mean the microprocessor chip itself. In this book we prefer to use the more precise term, microprocessor.

- A **motherboard** is the nervous system of a computer. It connects all the components of a computer into one functional device.

- **Random access memory** (RAM) is the short-term memory of a computer. Programs are stored in RAM, as is the data upon which programs operate. RAM is erased every time a computer is shut off.

- **Video adapters** create images from image maps stored in RAM and created by the microprocessor. You must have a video adapter to interact with a computer, and most machines will not operate without one.

- **Hard disk drives** are the long-term storage areas of a computer. Programs can be stored permanently on hard disk drives and loaded into RAM when they are needed. Data files can be stored permanently on hard disk drives.

- **Hard disk drive controllers** are high-speed peripherals that connect computers to hard disk drives. Simple hard disk controllers are usually built into motherboards, but servers usually require the installation of more complex disk controllers.

- **Network adapters** attach individual computers to a network of computers. They manage communications with other computers.

- **Input/output (I/O) devices** provide low-speed connections to simple peripherals such as keyboards, printers, modems, and uninterruptible power supplies. These devices do not need complex high-speed network or disk interfaces.

FIGURE 3.1

Basic computer hardware
components.

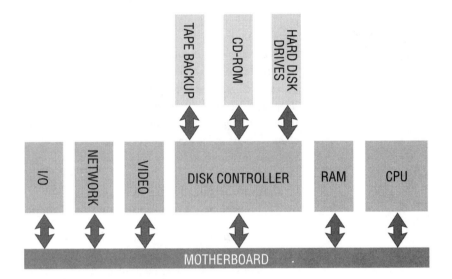

Selecting Server Hardware by Role

SERVERS USE VASTLY different hardware depending upon the services
they provide. For example, a typical file server will have copious
amounts of hard disk space, whereas an application server may have
two to four times as much RAM as a file server. Internet or Remote Access
Services servers(RAS) may be attached to banks of modems, while an entire
print server may be no larger than a deck of cards. Some specialized servers
include

- File and print servers

- Application servers

- Internet/intranet servers

- Messaging servers

- Remote Access Services servers

- Firewalls

The following discussion assumes that the server performs only the role in question, although this type of utilization is normally not the case in most installations. For instance, almost all Windows NT servers operate as file servers, regardless of their primary role. Many servers perform double duty as RAS servers, application servers, or Internet servers. Small organizations may rely upon a single server to provide all of the functions that follow.

We are describing the roles separately to highlight the exact hardware that is necessary to perform that role. You can then mix the hardware requirements for the different roles to create servers capable of performing multiple roles.

File and Print Servers

Most Windows NT servers provide both file and print services because file storage and printing are the two most commonly centralized services on a network. Consequently, the term *file and print server* is almost as common as *file server*. We begin our discussion with the file server aspect of file and print servers.

File servers emphasize hard disk space and speed to quickly serve client requests. They must also have adequate network capacity to serve many simultaneous requests. File server response time (which is what network users perceive to be the "speed" of the file server) does not depend as much on the microprocessor speed as it does on network connection speed, available memory, and hard disk drive speed. Consequently, the file server on your network may use a "slower" microprocessor than your workstation uses to run your applications. Table 3.1 shows a typical configuration for a file server that supports approximately 50 users. Use the estimation tables shown in Chapter 2 to determine how much disk space your servers will require.

Because the primary bottlenecks (or performance-limiting components) of file servers are the network interface and the hard disk drive speeds, adding a faster microprocessor, additional microprocessors, or memory beyond a certain point will not significantly increase the performance of your file server. Using a faster network interface or increasing hard drive speed by using faster drives or using more drives in a RAID array will help. RAID technology is explained later in this chapter and again in Chapter 5.

Another way to increase file server speed when your file server is at capacity is to add another file server to your network. You can then split the network load between the file servers, increasing overall network performance.

Many file servers also have print devices attached to them and allow network users to print documents to the printers (the print server part of file and print servers). A print server is actually any device that accepts print jobs from the network and sends them to a print device. Some organizations use dedicated print servers; however, most client computers can also accept print jobs from the network for printing on print devices

Microsoft terminology reserves the term printer for the software component in a server or client computer that accepts print requests and feeds it to an actual print device. The print device accepts the print request and makes marks on blank pieces of paper. This print device is the device that everyone but Microsoft calls printer. This book uses the term print device to describe the mechanism that produces marks on paper and other similar devices, such as fax modems, that can accept print requests.

Other specialty devices called network print servers operate as network interfaces to printers. These devices typically have one network port; one, two, or three printer (print device) ports; and an operating system burned into ROM. A print server is accessed directly by its network port address.

TABLE 3.1	COMPONENT	QUANTITY	PURPOSE
Typical File Server Hardware	Processor	Pentium—150MHz	File servers are rarely CPU bound. Striping creates additional load, however.
	RAM	48MB	Provides large disk cache for fast response.
	Disk space	8GB	Four 2GB disks striped with parity to provide 6GB of storage; plenty for 50 average users.
	Tape backup	DAT 4GB native	Capacity sufficient to back up entire server with 2:1 compression.
	Network adapter	Fast Ethernet	Bandwidth to file server should be at least four times the speed of normal clients. Provide multiple Ethernet adapters if you don't want to use Fast Ethernet.
	CD-ROM	Two 4x CD-ROMs	File servers are often used as CD-ROM jukeboxes.
	Special hardware	None	Avoid unnecessary hardware such as sound cards or video accelerators.

You can configure Windows NT to spool print jobs to these network print servers by adding the appropriate TCP/IP address as a port in the printer configuration control panel. Print services take very little CPU or disk space, and any Windows NT computer—regardless of its primary function—can perform them.

Application Servers

Most application servers don't require as much hard disk space as file servers do, but they do need a lot of RAM to cache database requests and a fast connection to the network to respond quickly to numerous interprocess communication requests. Application servers typically make use of multiprocessing, which allows the use of more than one microprocessor at the same time.

Many organizations rely on application servers for their primary business functions, and the speed of an application server can become a bottleneck that limits the total number of transactions that can be performed. If you've ever talked to an order entry clerk who had to "wait for the system" to complete your transaction, you know exactly what we mean. For this reason, many organizations make a bigger investment in an application server than they do in a file server.

Many businesses require near-line storage of all transactions for a number of years so that they can quickly resolve accounting, legal, and customer service issues. Therefore, many application servers use optical write-once/read-many (WORM) drives to permanently record each transaction. These drives are read from when "archived" data is required. These systems may have jukebox style carriages that mount old disks in seconds without human intervention.

Table 3.2 shows a typical database application server configuration.

TABLE 3.2 Typical Application Server Hardware	COMPONENT	QUANTITY	PURPOSE
	Processor	Dual Pentium Pro—200MHz; or a 433MHz Alpha	Application servers need fast CPUs for responsiveness.
	RAM	128MB	Provides large disk cache for fast response.
	Disk space	5GB	Hardware RAID 5 across five 1GB SCSI disks provides fastest access to database records.
	Backup	Near-line optical disk WORM jukebox	Writes each database record out for permanent archiving.
	Network adapter	Fast Ethernet; separate adapter for each subnetwork	Bandwidth to application server should be as fast as you can afford.
	CD-ROM	One 2x CD-ROM	For software installation only.
	Special hardware	None	Avoid unnecessary hardware.

Internet/Intranet Servers

Internet/intranet servers are unique among servers in that they do not require high speed from any of their components. Because the Internet protocols are optimized for low-bandwidth modem connections, a server can easily keep up with requests. With the addition of an interface to the wide area network (WAN), a light-duty file server can also act as an Internet server that handles moderate to heavy traffic. Internet servers often do double duty as Internet routers because they are easy to attach to both the WAN and the local area network (LAN) and because they are faster than even the fastest current WAN links.

An intranet server is similar to an Internet server. The primary difference between these two types of servers is in their orientation. An Internet server provides data using Internet protocols such as FTP and HTTP that can be accessed from the Internet and World Wide Web, whereas an intranet server provides data using Internet protocols such as FTP and HTTP that can be accessed from within the organization's own network, but not necessarily from outside the organization. Internets and intranets are explained in more detail in Chapter 12.

You should locate Internet servers and routers outside the company firewall to allow maximum access to Web services while protecting internal company resources. Table 3.3 shows the hardware you would use in an Internet server.

TABLE 3.3 Typical Internet/Intranet Server Hardware	COMPONENT	QUANTITY	PURPOSE
	Processor	Pentium—100MHz	Internet servers are almost never CPU bound. Routing to low-bandwidth connections is also not very taxing.
	RAM	32MB	No need for large caches when your maximum connected bandwidth is so slow.
	Disk space	2GB	Web sites are rarely this large, and they are almost never subject to rampant growth.
	Tape backup	QIC 2.0GB native	Sufficient to back up hard disks.
	Network adapter	Ethernet	Usually adequate for Internet servers. Intranet servers may use Fast Ethernet.

	COMPONENT	QUANTITY	PURPOSE
TABLE 3.3 Typical Internet/Intranet Server Hardware (continued)	CD-ROM	One 4x CD-ROM	For loading software.
	Special hardware	T-1 interface to Internet	Web servers must use leased-line constant connections to the Internet, usually at the T-1 rate.

Messaging Servers

Messaging servers are really a special case of the application server, but because messaging does not usually occur in real time, a messaging server doesn't require the same level of responsiveness as an application server does. Quite often, messaging servers are configured similarly to Internet servers, but they are located inside the company firewall to protect user names and identities from outside scrutiny. Table 3.4 shows the hardware of a typical messaging server.

Message servers sometimes run rather complex messaging applications that perform database replication among multiple sites. These servers may require significantly more hardware than the configuration shown in Table 3.4. Whenever you install a server to support a specific application, use the manufacturer's recommended hardware configuration.

	COMPONENT	QUANTITY	PURPOSE
TABLE 3.4 Typical Message Server Hardware	Processor	Pentium—100MHz	Message servers have no real-time requirements, nor do users attach directly to them.
	RAM	32MB	No need for large caches when you aren't serving files or database records.
	Disk space	2GB	Sufficient for nearly any messaging server.
	Tape backup	QIC 2.0GB native	Sufficient to backup hard disks.
	Network adapter	Ethernet	Sufficient for messaging servers.
	CD-ROM	One 4x CD-ROM	For loading software
	Special hardware	Two high-speed modems	For dialing into Internet or online message service providers, alphanumeric paging, and faxing.

Remote Access Services Servers

RAS servers require very little hard disk space or processing power compared to other file servers. They do require a tremendous amount of additional communications equipment, however. RAS servers are normally configured with multiple-port serial cards; they can be attached to external modems that answer incoming phone lines. RAS servers may also be configured with wide area network lines to support inbound Point-to-Point Tunneling Protocol (PPTP) links from the Internet.

Light-duty RAS servers (those supporting four or fewer simultaneous connections) are generally implemented on file servers because they generate very little load to the system. Table 3.5 shows the special hardware required for RAS servers.

TABLE 3.5 Typical Remote Access Server Hardware	**COMPONENT**	**QUANTITY**	**PURPOSE**
	Processor	Pentium—100MHz	RAS servers are almost never CPU bound.
	RAM	32MB	No need for large caches for RAS hosts.
	Disk space	1GB	More than enough for RAS hosting.
	Tape backup	None	No user files are stored here, so you can restore from CD-ROM.
	Network adapter	Ethernet	You won't need more than this for RAS servers because the inbound bandwidth is so low.
	CD-ROM	One 2x CD-ROM	For loading software.
	Special hardware	16-port serial board with modems	Answers inbound dial-up RAS connections. May be as few as one or as many as 256.

Firewalls

Firewalls are security gateways that protect networks connected to the Internet from intrusion (called "attack" in security circles) by unauthorized parties. A firewall is the only computer on the internal secure network that is attached to the external nonsecure network (the Internet). The firewall then acts as a proxy for each client on the internal network, hiding its identity and exposing only a single IP address to the Internet. The firewall performs many other security services such as checking IP addresses for permission to access the internal network and denying access to unlisted addresses. Figure 3.2 shows how firewall partitions secure resources from nonsecure networks.

FIGURE 3.2

Local area network protected by a firewall.

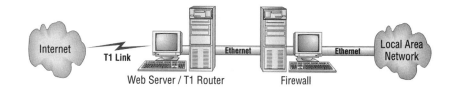

Web Server / T1 Router   Firewall

You should never run services other than the firewall services on a computer acting as a firewall. The reason is that hackers may be able to exploit bugs in your software to bypass the security functions of firewalls. In fact, most firewall server software for Windows NT will shut down all services not directly related to the firewall service. Installing firewall software on a computer you use for other purposes is a surefire way to trash your Windows NT installation.

The only exception to that rule is the role of Internet routing. Firewalls must have two (and only two) network connections: one connection to the secure LAN and one connection to the Internet. Your LAN connection will be Ethernet or Token Ring, but your Internet connection will usually be an X.25 PAD (the interface commonly used for dedicated circuit connections to the Internet such as T1) or a high-speed modem. The firewall will automatically perform the service of Internet routing in this configuration.

Because they can't be used to perform other services, firewalls need only be faster than the fastest network connections attached to them and have enough disk space to store the firewall software. In fact, you would be able to use Windows NT Workstation 4 as the operating system platform for your firewall were it not limited to ten simultaneous IP connections. Windows NT Workstation 3.51 (the version prior to version 4), which is not encumbered by this limitation, is perfect for use as a firewall platform. Table 3.6 shows the hardware requirements for a typical firewall.

TABLE 3.6	COMPONENT	QUANTITY	PURPOSE
Typical Firewall Hardware	Processor	Pentium—150MHz	Firewalls are usually attached to slower bandwidth connections, so speed is not a big issue.
	RAM	32MB	No need for large caches on firewall hosts.
	Disk space	1GB	More than enough for the operating system and firewall.
	Tape backup	None	No user files are stored here, so you can restore from CD-ROM.
	Network adapter	Dual Ethernet	You need a network connection for the internal and the external network. You can use a firewall as a router if you don't have any servers outside your firewall.
	CD-ROM	One 2x CD-ROM	For loading software.
	Special hardware	None	Do not install unnecessary hardware in a firewall.

The Care and Feeding of Microprocessors

ONE OF THE major design requirements for Windows NT was support for multiple microprocessors. This criterion was mandated both to allow the customer to choose the microprocessor best suited to the task and to emancipate Microsoft from Intel. Currently, Windows NT supports four popular microprocessors:

- Intel's *x*86 family (80386, i486, Pentium, and Pentium Pro)
- Digital Equipment Corporation's Alpha
- The MIPS family of RISC microprocessors
- The IBM and Motorola PowerPC series

Windows NT looks and works exactly the same on all these microprocessors. The hardware abstraction layer, which is essentially a device driver for the motherboard and microprocessor, makes the hardware of these different computers look the same to higher-level services. It does not, however, translate the machine code of one processor to another. Machine code is the "native language" of a microprocessor. The Windows NT Server CD-ROM contains a native version of Windows NT for each of the supported microprocessors. Third-party application software that runs under Windows NT must be recompiled to work on each different microprocessor.

Applications compiled for Intel processors will not run on Windows NT machines using other processors unless the CPU manufacturer provides an emulator.

Hardware abstraction is similar to having an automobile operator's manual in four languages. Drivers who speak those languages can read the manual and operate the car in exactly the same way, even though they probably can't communicate directly with each other. The hardware abstraction layer is an operator's manual for the different microprocessors.

Selecting a Microprocessor

Windows NT was designed to take advantage of the latest advances in microprocessor design and implementation. For that reason, it is available for many reduced instruction set computer (RISC) processors that represent the cutting edge of processor speed. The only complex instruction set computer (CISC) processor supported by Windows NT is the Intel $x86$ family used in IBM PC–compatible computers.

RISC machine languages are simpler than CISC machine languages. RISC microprocessors lack many of the features that are implemented in CISC microprocessors, such as hardware floating-point mathematics circuitry. RISC machine languages usually implement only instructions that can be executed in a single machine cycle, whereas CISC microprocessors have instructions that may take many hundreds of machine cycles. However, because the simpler circuitry of RISC can be clocked faster than the complex circuitry of CISC, RISC machines can execute equivalent software routines faster than a CISC microprocessor can perform the same operation in hardware.

Consequently, you cannot compare the speed of microprocessors based on their speed rating in MHz. This comparison would be analogous to comparing car speeds based on their engine RPM ratings. (A smaller engine running at a higher RPM may produce the same amount of power as a larger engine running at a lower RPM.) Unless you know how much work the processor can do in how many cycles, you have no basis for comparison.

CPU benchmarks compare the relative speeds of microprocessors. CPU benchmarks are like the 0-60 speed rating of an automobile—they take the engineering of the entire car into account and provide a useful metric for comparing speed regardless of engineering differences. Table 3.7 shows a comparison of manufacturers' claimed ratings for microprocessors supported by Windows NT, normalized to the speed of a Pentium at 100MHz. Column one shows the relative amount of work done per clock cycle (relative efficiency); column two shows the power of the CPU at its top, current-shipping speed relative to an Intel Pentium processor at 100MHz (actual performance); column three shows the clock speed of the processor.

We compiled these benchmarks from SPECint95s claimed by the manufacturers on similarly configured workstations and mathematically normalized to a Pentium at 100MHz. These numbers are for general comparison only and cannot be used to estimate the actual performance of a real machine.

TABLE 3.7 Specmark95 for Windows NT Microprocessors	PROCESSOR	RELATIVE EFFICIENCY	ACTUAL PERFORMANCE	CLOCK SPEED
	Intel 486	52%	62%	120
	Pentium	100%	170%	200
	Pentium Pro	137%	276%	200
	Alpha 21064	43%	144%	333
	Alpha 21164	97%	420%	433
	Alpha 21264	189%	949%	500
	PowerPC 603e	69%	165%	240
	PowerPC 604	109%	262%	240
	MIPS R5000	86%	215%	250
	MIPS R10000	138%	379%	275

As you can see, most RISC processors do less work per cycle than a Pentium 100 does. However, because many RISC processors use simpler circuitry, they can run much faster, yielding overall system performance many times faster than a typical Intel CISC processor. The three RISC processors that clock faster than the Pentium use newer semiconductor technology. Since RISC chips are simple, they can quickly incorporate advancements in semiconductor design, often outpacing their CISC cousins after only a few years in development. This flexibility is another fundamental advantage of RISC technology.

Table 3.7 also shows the decreasing returns of faster clock speeds. The Pentium 200 shows a speed increase of only 70 percent compared to the Pentium 100. If speed scaled linearly, we would see a 100 percent increase. The difference is associated with the speed of memory. Typical dynamic random access memory (DRAM) can respond to a read request in 60 nanoseconds. A RISC processor running at 100MHz could require memory response in as little as 10 nanoseconds. The processor in this case may have to "idle" for six cycles waiting for slow DRAM requests. Caches alleviate most of this problem, but unless all your RAM is made from expensive fast cache memory, your computer will suffer from the decreasing returns problem. Fast microprocessors like the Alpha 21264 typically use four times the cache memory as Intel processors to minimize this effect.

Next we take a closer look at the Intel, Alpha, MIPS, and PowerPC microprocessor families.

Intel

Intel microprocessors include the i486, Pentium, Pentium Pro, and clone microprocessors such as the Cyrix 6x86 family and the AMD k5 series. The Intel microprocessors are the only CISC microprocessors that Windows NT supports.

The initial production release of Windows NT 4 checks for Cyrix processors and disables the on-chip, write-back cache of certain Cyrix chip versions to reduce stability problems. This procedure reduces the speed of the affected Cyrix processors by a factor of about 30 percent. Earlier versions of Windows NT do not perform this check and may have stability problems on certain Cyrix chips. Later versions of Cyrix chips do not have the stability problem and will execute under Windows NT 4 at their full rated speed.

Intel microprocessors are capable of running all software written for MS-DOS, Windows, and Windows 95 under Windows NT. Consequently, Intel is the most popular brand of microprocessor for use with Windows NT despite the fact that Intel chips are slower than their RISC cousins.

Intel processors will have the fewest software compatibility problems of all these microprocessors. To minimize incompatibility issues, you should use Intel processors unless you are running an application server that requires more power than Intel processors can deliver.

Intel Pentium and Pentium Pro computers have on-chip support for multiprocessing, whereas the i486 and the Cyrix and AMD brand processors do not. The Intel microprocessors are ideal for low-cost multiprocessing servers.

Alpha

Digital Equipment Corporation created the Alpha series of RISC microprocessors to power its line of midrange servers. Digital expressed early interest in the development of Windows NT because of its architectural similarity to VMS, Digital's minicomputer operating system that the Alpha was designed to run. These processors provide clock speeds in excess of 500MHz.

Digital provides an i486 emulator that allows the use of most Windows and MS-DOS programs on the Alpha series of microprocessors.

To encourage the use of its microprocessor, Digital has created an Intel microprocessor emulator that can run applications designed for the Intel family of microprocessors under Windows NT. Some very clever optimizations enable this software to run applications at up to 70 percent of the native speed of the Alpha processor. This software ships with DEC Alpha systems that are preloaded with Windows NT.

MIPS

The first MIPS microprocessors, commercial implementation of the RISC ideas studied at Stanford and other universities, were among the earliest true RISC microprocessor made. Windows NT was originally developed on computers using MIPS microprocessors—at the time, MIPS-based computers were seen as the future for high-performance personal computing. Current MIPS microprocessors incorporate the technological advancements of other RISC microprocessors, including multiple dispatch, out-of-order execution, long pipelines, and high clock speeds. MIPS microprocessors are not tied to the fortunes of a single manufacturer because MIPS technology is widely licensed and produced.

The MIPS family of processors will only run software compiled for MIPS. They will not run all Windows software. Check with your software provider to ensure that MIPS versions of third-party software you want to use is available before choosing this microprocessor. Most Microsoft BackOffice software supports the MIPS family of microprocessors.

PowerPC

IBM developed the PowerPC line of RISC microprocessors to compete against Intel in the workstation market. This line of microprocessors is "second sourced" by many companies, including Motorola. The PowerPC microprocessor is available in a line of workstations from IBM and in the Power Macintosh series of workstations from Apple Computer. Although current Power Macintosh computers cannot run Windows NT, the next generation will be based on a new industrial standard for PowerPC-based computers from IBM, Apple, and other companies called the PowerPC Platform (PPCP), also known as the Common Hardware Reference Platform (CHRP), which will allow computers produced by Apple, Motorola, IBM, and other PowerPC computer manufacturers to run a number of operating systems written for the PowerPC, including the MacOS and Windows NT.

Only software compiled for the PowerPC will run on the PowerPC family of processors. These processors will not run all Windows software. Check with your software provider to ensure that PowerPC versions of third-party software you want to use are available before choosing this microprocessor. Most Microsoft BackOffice software supports the PowerPC.

The PowerPC microprocessor is the newest line of microprocessors that Windows NT supports. These processors are fast and very inexpensive compared to their more esoteric cousins. Versions of these chips are currently sampling at speeds in excess of 500MHz, making them serious contenders with the Alpha 21264 for the title of Windows NT heavyweight champion.

Multiprocessing

Using more than one microprocessor in a computer is called *multiprocessing*. Windows NT can distribute processes among microprocessors if your computer is capable of operating with more than one microprocessor. Multiprocessing multiplies your computing power by the number of processors in use, similar to the way that adding more hard disks multiplies storage capacity.

However, multiprocessing suffers from decreasing returns. Because of the overhead involved in determining which processor should handle interrupts and other system events, you won't see a linear increase in processing power as you add processors. Under Windows NT, you can expect to add about 50 percent of the computer's speed with one processor for each processor you add.

Applications can take advantage of multiprocessing by breaking the computational workload into more than one thread of execution. Windows NT itself is *multithreaded*, so you will see a speed advantage in any case, but your application may not run any faster in a machine with four processors than it does in a machine with two processors unless the application itself is multithreaded.

Windows NT implements *symmetrical multiprocessing*, which means that the system will attempt to balance the computational load across the number of processors in your system rather than simply assign processes to certain processors regardless of the load they generate. Symmetrical multiprocessing requires additional overhead, but it scales very well as the number of processors increases (in contrast to the other method called *asymmetrical multiprocessing*).

Selecting the Right Motherboard

MANY FACTORS OTHER than the raw performance capability of a microprocessor affect overall system speed. Although we do not recommend building your Windows NT server from scratch, you should know how the components in your machine work and which factors affect performance. Each of the following factors has a major effect on the overall speed of the system:

- Amount of cache memory

- Peripheral bus type, speed, and width

- Memory interface width and speed

- Compatibility of integrated components

- Plug-and-Play and power-management BIOS options

Complete system providers that make their own motherboards, such as Dell and Compaq, are especially likely to include integrated components.

Cache

Don't even consider using a motherboard with less than 128K of cache; 256K is typical for workstations, and 512K is better for servers. RISC microprocessors should have two to four times that amount because their higher clock speeds and larger program sizes.

Peripheral Bus

Peripheral bus type and speed vary greatly among motherboards. The ISA bus is only 16 bits wide, meaning that a 64-bit microprocessor wastes 75 percent of its bandwidth accessing these peripherals. EISA, VESA local bus, and microchannel are all limited to 32 bits in width, wasting 50 percent of memory bandwidth for 64-bit reads.

The PCI bus, on the other hand, can scale with the microprocessor to 32, 64, or 128 bits of width. Thus PCI is the obvious choice for peripheral buses, and it is supported by each of the microprocessor types supported by Windows NT. You should consider only motherboards that implement the PCI bus.

Memory Interface

The memory interface of a motherboard is also important. Although you can't tell by looking at it, the motherboard may be using a 32-bit path, 64-bit path, or 128-bit path to memory. The wider the path, the faster your memory accesses will occur.

Integrated Peripherals

Integrated components, such as onboard IDE interfaces, floppy disk drive interfaces, and I/O ports are common. These standards are fixed and do not vary by manufacturer, so Windows NT will support them fully no matter who makes your motherboard.

Some motherboards include support for other peripherals, such as SCSI controllers, sound cards, and video. Although these are convenient and can save you money, the downside is that Windows NT may not support the peripheral correctly.

Even when using a "name brand" chip set, the motherboard manufacturer may not implement the chip set the same way the peripheral manufacturer did, causing slight incompatibilities. Manufacturers of peripherals will usually not support embedded peripherals in motherboards they did not manufacture, so you may be left out in the cold if you need customer support.

Embedded peripherals may become obsolete before the rest of the motherboard does, causing you to disable the device and replace it with a peripheral card anyway. For these reasons, we recommend avoiding embedded peripherals beyond the standard set.

BIOS

Motherboard BIOS options control how the motherboard and peripherals interact. Most of these settings will be factory configured for optimal performance and should not be modified.

Two settings that are common on machines that did not ship with Windows NT that do need to be disabled are Plug and Play support and power management. Windows NT version 4 does not support Plug and Play, so it cannot configure Plug-and-Play peripherals correctly. Make sure the BIOS of your motherboard supports disabling Plug and Play so you can manually configure your peripherals using a Plug-and-Play configuration manager.

Power management can wreak havoc with a Windows NT server. File servers are usually under moderate load, so power management features usually won't kick in, but many strange problems can occur when they do. Network errors, hard disk errors, and freezing on return from a "sleep" state can all occur, depending upon how the peripherals you use support power management. Make sure you can disable power-management features on your motherboard to prevent these problems.

Mass Storage Devices

Mass storage devices store files on a permanent basis. Although many ways to store data exist, only a few types of mass storage are really practical enough to actually warrant serious consideration for computers. These are

- Hard disk drives

- Magnetic tape drives

- CD-ROM drives

- Removable cartridge hard disk drives

- Magneto-optical drives

- Write-once/read-many and CD-recordable drives

Most computers use only the first three items. The others are for more esoteric purposes such as near-line massive storage, software distribution, or rapid archiving.

Mass storage devices are the only components in a computer that are not solid state (aside from cooling fans). Their use of moving parts makes them the components most likely to fail. Every server should have some method of fault tolerance to minimize the effects of this eventuality.

Hard Disk Drives

Hard disk drives store everything that is important on a server or computer. They are the only part whose failure is truly catastrophic—you can replace all other components in less than ten minutes of down time if you have spares available. Without fault tolerance measures such as disk mirroring or striping with parity, a hard disk failure will require you to completely restore all the files on the disk from backup tape. If the drive containing your boot partitions fails, you will probably have to reinstall the operating system just to run the tape restoration.

Because they are the only components of a server that can cause data loss, choosing the right hard disks and the right fault tolerance scheme is critical. Chapter 5 covers fault tolerance schemes in detail. If you don't already know which fault tolerance schemes you plan to implement, you should read Chapter 5 *before* ordering your server so you know how many drives you will need.

Choosing Hard Disks

Manufacturers often rate and advertise their hard disks by their seek time, that is, the amount of time it takes on average for the drive head to seek to a specific element of data. Seek time is rarely important in file servers because they have large caches and implement a variety of automatic defragmentation schemes to reduce disk seeking.

Overall throughput is far more important. The amount of data that a hard disk can transfer in a given time period determines how fast a server can respond to a user's request for data if that data isn't cached. Choosing fast hard disks, or a fault tolerance scheme that improves disk-read speed, will do more to make your server responsive to users than nearly any other optimization.

Multiple Physical Disks

Consider using multiple physical disks for your servers, rather than a single large disk, for two reasons: speed and redundancy. Windows NT can read from more than one disk simultaneously. Having multiple physical disks allows you to implement striping and mirroring, both of which reduce read time.

Having more than one disk and implementing a fault tolerance scheme (e.g., mirroring or striping with parity) allow one hard disk to fail in your system without taking the system down. Using multiple physical disks appropriately can save you quite a bit of trouble because tape restorations are never easy or painless. With disk fault tolerance, you can simply wait for a time when the server is idle, bring it down, replace the disk, and reboot. You won't lose any data, and you won't have to spend hours restoring a file server. Some disks and controllers will even let you replace a disk while the server is operational.

Small Computer System Interface (SCSI)

The small computer system interface (SCSI) was derived in the early 1980s from the earlier SASI standard to address the need for a standard in hard disk drive and mass storage interfaces. SCSI-II clarified and amended the standard to allow higher-speed synchronous transfer rates. A new, wide version doubles the number of available peripherals and further improves performance.

The SCSI specification handles up to eight devices on a single SCSI bus. Because one of those devices must be the controller, room for seven mass storage devices remains. SCSI devices must have built-in SCSI controllers that can translate data from the physical geometry of the device into contiguous blocks. The SCSI controller simply assumes that SCSI devices have linearly addressed blocks in which they can store data. The device itself must translate the request into a head movement, tape seek, or whatever positioning is necessary in order to fulfill the request. Because SCSI devices require sophisticated electronics, they are more expensive than comparable peripherals that do not incorporate control electronics.

The original SCSI specification was limited to 6MB/sec and was slightly vague in its treatment of some commands, giving rise to a few incompatibilities between SCSI components. SCSI-II improved performance to 10MB/sec, added some commands, and clarified the specification to eliminate compatibility problems. All SCSI devices made in the last few years meet the SCSI-II standard.

Because of its versatility, SCSI can interface a number of nonstorage peripherals, such as scanners and some printers. SCSI network adapters and video monitors have even appeared for some computers that had no other high-bandwidth interfaces.

SCSI is the fastest standard bus for the interconnection of mass storage devices in typical servers. As such, it is the obvious choice for most servers. Unless responsiveness is not an issue, you should use SCSI controllers and peripherals for your speed-critical mass storage devices.

You do not need to use SCSI for your tape or CD-ROM if your computer comes with an IDE controller on the motherboard (and most do). You can use the slower IDE bus for peripherals such as tape or CD-ROM drives, leaving the SCSI bus for the exclusive use of your hard disk drives. Typically, you would include at least one hard disk drive, your tape backup device, and your CD-ROM on the SCSI bus. High-speed servers may elect to put the boot/system hard disk on the same SCSI bus as the CD-ROM and tape and have a separate SCSI controller for an array of striped disks. Many servers even boot a mirrored IDE disk because the boot partition cannot be part of a stripe set. Boot speed rarely affects performance once the server is up and running. Thus the entire SCSI bus is available for use as a stripe set.

SCSI adapters are not all the same, and they do not all perform equally well under Windows NT. Some are not capable of addressing more than one device at a time, so they lose much of the advantage of disk striping. Some do not adhere to industry format standards and require you to reformat any hard disk drive you use with them. Check the Microsoft Hardware Compatibility List and the Microsoft Knowledge Base for a listing of SCSI controller compatibility issues before selecting a specific model.

IDE

Integrated device electronics (IDE) hard disks evolved from the original "dumb" modified frequency modulation (MFM) and run-length limited (RLL) drives used by IBM PCs in the early 1980s. MFM and RLL devices had no inherent control logic—the computer directly controlled their hard disk mechanisms. Although this design reduced cost, it required the computer to know exactly how to control the disk. If the computer was not set up to work with the drive correctly, the drive could be permanently damaged. To alleviate this problem, 286-class computers and their successors came with BIOS setup pages that allowed you to select which hard disk drive you wanted to use by number. But BIOS setup made it easier to select the wrong setting, and if support for your hard disk wasn't built into the BIOS, you couldn't use it. Consequently, new hard disk technology had to coincide with BIOS updates.

IDE disks eliminate the need to constantly change the BIOS settings of new computers to match currently available hard disks. By including a more complex control circuit with the hard disk that knew how to translate disk requests from the computer to the geometry of the hard disk, IDE disks could simulate MFM or RLL disks of a similar size.

IDE disks are mass market hard drives that go into nearly every PC made today. Their control circuits are relatively simple, and they don't emphasize speed; their cost is about half that of SCSI devices of the same size. IDE disks transfer data at about half the speed of SCSI devices, and you can connect only two drives to a single controller. Most computers come with two built-in controllers, allowing up to four drives to be attached.

CD-ROM drives and tape drives are also now being built to interface as IDE peripherals, which reduces cost and increases compatibility. These devices are not nearly as fast as the IDE bus, so they are a perfect fit.

Although you should select SCSI peripherals for any application in which performance is important, IDE peripherals can complement a server nicely as described earlier.

RAID Controllers

Redundant array of inexpensive disk (RAID) controllers are SCSI controllers that make an array of same-sized disks look like a single massive storage device to the computer. They control the drives in parallel, splitting the read and write load among all disks equally and thereby multiplying throughput by the number of disks attached. RAID controllers also shoulder the burden of calculating the parity stripe, thus reducing the load on the CPU.

RAID systems are the fastest mass storage controllers available and are typically used in database application servers that need extreme speed. However, because the data transfer speed of the network limits the speed of file server access in most networks, RAID is used in file servers to provide fault tolerance rather than to increase the speed of file access. This functionality is especially appropriate if the network uses regular 10MB Ethernet, which is not capable of exceeding typical disk throughput anyway.

Tape Backup

The primary consideration when selecting a tape backup device is capacity. You should have enough capacity to archive all the hard disk drives on your machine on a single tape. If you have a total of 8GB of hard disk space, your tape drive and media should match that capacity.

Consider selecting a tape device that has drivers on the NT CD-ROM. Having a driver on the CD-ROM guarantees that you won't have compatibility problems or have to wait for drivers from the manufacturer.

Most tape drives are sold showing both their native and compressed capacities. (The compressed capacity is about double the native capacity.) However, you shouldn't rely on compressed capacity ratings when selecting a tape for three reasons:

- Your data may not have much redundancy, so you may not achieve the compression ratio stated. For instance, if have 4GB to archive using a tape drive with 4GB compressed capacity but you achieve only a 1.5:1 compression ratio, you will run out of tape before your archive is finished.

- The Windows NT backup program does not perform compression. Unless your tape device performs hardware compression (many do not, as compression circuitry adds to the cost), then NT backup will archive only up to the native capacity of the tape.

- Many NTFS partitions use compressed files, which already have much of their redundancy removed. Since recompressing data does not remove any more redundancy, you must have 4GB of native capacity to store 4GB of already-compressed data.

These potential pitfalls don't mean that you shouldn't use tape compression. They just mean that you shouldn't rely upon it. It's perfectly acceptable to use compression as a buffer zone for archive devices that are slightly smaller than the total capacity you need or to store multiple archive sets on a single tape.

The three most popular ways to interface tape backup units to computers are to use SCSI devices, IDE devices, and floppy drive controllers. SCSI is the most popular and is used with most 8mm and 4mm digital audio tape (DAT) drives. These drives are high capacity and very fast. SCSI tape drives usually implement compression in hardware, so you can use them with NT backup to provide compression. You should seriously consider these drives for servers.

IDE tape backup units are becoming very popular. These tape devices are built to similar specifications as their SCSI cousins, but they usually cost a little less because their control circuitry is less complex. These units usually do not implement hardware compression. They are sufficient for light file servers or other types of servers that do not have heavy-duty archiving requirements.

Floppy tape backup units interface through the floppy disk drive controller. These units are slower than the hard disk interfaced tape units and don't have nearly the capacity of the SCSI and IDE tapes, topping out at 2GB native capacity. You may hear these devices referred to as quarter-inch cartridge (QIC) or Travan tape drives. Although these tape drives work well, their low capacity and slower speeds make them suitable only for small servers. These tape drives are intended for use in workstations.

CD-ROM

Selecting a CD-ROM is easy. If you are going to serve CD-ROMs to a network, you should get the fastest variety you can find. Currently, 12x CD-ROMs are available, and 8x CD-ROMs are not very expensive. If you do not plan on serving CD-ROMs, speed doesn't matter that much because you will only be using the device to install software. Any 2x or faster CD-ROM will do.

Compared to hard disk drives, CD-ROMs are not high-performance devices, so don't pay more for a SCSI version if an IDE version will do. Avoid proprietary controller CD-ROMs, as they require their own drivers and additional interrupt and port resources.

You may want to use servers dedicated to serving CD-ROMs, called *CD-ROM jukeboxes*. These servers will need only enough hard disk space to run Windows NT and will not require particularly fast microprocessors. Since you can put seven CD-ROM devices on a SCSI bus, you may wish to go that route. Jukeboxes also have room for four IDE devices, which you should use to add inexpensive IDE CD-ROMs. If your CD-ROMS will not be in use all the time, you may want to consider using CD-ROM changers, which can mount multiple CD-ROMs in a single mechanism and swap them as necessary. Avoid this arrangement if different CD-ROMs might be in use at the same time, as the changer will have to constantly switch between them.

CD jukeboxes are usually not under tremendous load, so you should consider using them as print servers, RAS servers, domain controllers, or other low-load service providers if you have the need.

Removable Cartridge Hard Disks

Removable cartridge hard disk drives are becoming more popular as file and application sizes have ballooned beyond the capacity of floppy disk drives. These drives use either magnetic or magneto-optical platters stored in rugged plastic cases that can be mounted and removed from their drives. Most drives are compatible only with media made specifically for their mechanism, so if you purchase one of these devices, be sure to standardize all your purchases on a popular model if you intend to move cartridges between computers.

Removable cartridge hard disks are usually not appropriate for servers because the sharing of information requires it to be accessible at all times. Windows NT will not let you make a removable cartridge hard drive part of a stripe, mirror, or volume set. These devices normally store files for workstations that generate large files, which are of no use to others on the network, or for applications that are rarely used.

Some network administrators prefer to use removable cartridge hard disk drives for backup purposes because they are fast. However, their high cost per gigabyte of storage compared to tape usually makes this use prohibitively expensive.

WORM and CD-R Drives

WORM and CD-R drives are popular in server applications that permanently retain data. These devices use lasers to etch the digital image of stored data on to optical platters. Since the disks cannot be erased and last for decades, these disks are useful for taking snapshots of current configurations or for any other data that should be permanently recorded, such as medical, legal, or financial information.

CD-R has become a very popular form of WORM because the platters it creates can be read by any normal CD-ROM reader. This technology provides a very inexpensive method of distributing a large amount of data physically or through the mail.

Because the media cost for CD-R is relatively low compared to removable cartridge hard disks, CD-Rs are appropriate for archival purposes when backup sets must be retained indefinitely.

Interfaces and Adapters

S ERVERS TYPICALLY HAVE network and video adapters installed, and they usually have modems attached to support light RAS or fax sharing. The rest of this chapter explains which criteria are important when you select interfaces and adapters for your server.

Network Adapters

Network adapters have become much easier to work with than they were in the early days of networking. Almost all network adapters are software configurable, and most brands come with Windows NT drivers that work correctly.

However, you should be aware of some differences among adapters. Most manufacturers make two lines of cards for each network technology: a line for workstations and a line for servers. Although both models will work in a server, adapters made specifically for servers create less load on the CPU and have larger caches; these features reduce the overall burden on the server and increase responsiveness. You should use network adapters made specifically for servers in file and application servers. Other lower-load servers will not be limited by their network speed, so this distinction is not as critical.

Choose a network controller that operates in the highest speed bus in your server, especially if the controller operates faster than 25Mb/sec. The ISA bus is physically limited to about 25Mb/sec, so you will waste any bandwidth above that your network adapter provides. Regular Ethernet adapters are slow enough that this distinction does not matter.

Many servers have multiple network adapters. Make sure you choose an adapter that supports as many different interrupt and port settings as you need.

Modems

The criterion for selecting a modem is simple: compatibility. Your modem should be compatible with any modem you connect to and with all the software you use. The modem should also support the standard Hayes command set. Most modern modems meet these requirements.

You should use the fastest modems you can afford. The new 56Kb/ps modems operate at the theoretical limit for analog telephone lines, so you should purchase these when an industry standard emerges. Modems will not get any faster than 56Kb/ps because the digital transports that move modem data between telephone central offices operate at this speed (in the United States).

The only practical difference between an internal and external modem is that you can power off an external modem to reset it without shutting down your computer. If you are considering putting many modems in a computer, you should use a multiport serial board attached to external modems to conserve bus slots inside your machine. Make sure the multiport serial board comes with Windows NT drivers before you purchase it.

Video

Video performance and speed are of no concern to a file server. Many servers go months without being attached to a monitor. Select the least expensive video adapter you can find that works with Windows NT. Don't be afraid to use an ISA bus video adapter if you have any reason to conserve PCI slots in your server—it won't make much difference.

The only reason to want high-performance video is if you are using your file server for some purpose other than network services. This arrangement is acceptable, and even common practice in small networks, as long as the tasks being performed on the server don't take much compute time away from the primary function of the server. Many small networks use a file server as a light-duty workstation, perhaps for reception or network administration. If your file server is being used for these purposes, use the same video adapter you use in your other workstation computers.

Summary

THE ROLE A server fills in your network determines its hardware. File servers require abundant hard disk space, whereas application servers emphasize RAM capacity and microprocessor speed. Most other roles do not require much of either; instead, they require specialized hardware such as modems or wide area network adapters to fulfill their requirements. Most file servers fill multiple roles, so they will be configured to meet multiple needs.

The microprocessor you select is important because, although Windows NT runs on many different processors, applications must be compiled for the specific processor you are using. The speed of esoteric RISC microprocessors is tempered by their inability to run many applications, thereby limiting the pool of third-party software you can use. Most software is written for Intel microprocessors.

Multiprocessing is an effective way to increase compute power without sacrificing compatibility. Motherboards also have a major impact on performance. They differ widely in the bus standards they implement, the amount of cache RAM they provide, and their integrated peripherals.

Mass storage devices are the only components in a computer that are not solid state; they are the devices most likely to fail, which necessitates the use of fault tolerance or fault recovery systems. Hard disk drives are one of the two primary bottlenecks in file servers—the speed of a file server is directly proportional to the speed of its hard disk drives. You should use the fastest hard disk drive controllers you can afford in a file server. In addition, the native capacity of your tape device should equal the sum of the capacities of all the hard disk drives in your system. Consider using WORM or CD-R drives if you must permanently archive data.

The network adapter is the other primary bottleneck in file server performance. Use a network adapter specialized for servers when you are specifying file or application servers; also make sure any high-speed network interfaces are installed in the highest-speed bus available in your computer. You can use a single internal modem, but if you require multiple modems, installing external modems conserves bus slots. Video is required, but video performance is not important for servers.

Review Questions

1. Servers use completely different architectures than typical PC computers use.

    A. True

    B. False

2. The minimum requirements published by Microsoft to run Windows NT are sufficient for small servers.

    A. True

    B. False

3. You can use any Windows NT application on any microprocessor supported by Windows NT.

  A. True

  B. False

4. Servers use vastly different hardware depending on the services they provide.

  A. True

  B. False

5. Almost all servers perform more than one service role.

  A. True

  B. False

6. Almost all servers provide file services.

  A. True

  B. False

7. Almost all servers provide application services.

  A. True

  B. False

8. File servers are rarely CPU bound.

  A. True

  B. False

9. Application servers need more RAM than any other type of server.

  A. True

  B. False

10. Because the Internet protocols are optimized for low speed, Internet servers do not need to be fast.

   A. True

   B. False

11. Firewalls should be the only computer attached to both the secure and nonsecure networks.

   A. True

   B. False

12. Your firewall can safely do double duty as an Internet server.

   A. True

   B. False

13. Your firewall can safely do double duty as an Internet router.

   A. True

   B. False

14. RISC microprocessors are always faster than CISC microprocessors.

   A. True

   B. False

15. A Pentium running at 200MHz delivers twice the computing power of a Pentium running at 100MHz.

   A. True

   B. False

16. Two processors deliver twice the performance of a single processor.

   A. True

   B. False

17. An application server will not benefit from multiprocessing unless the application is written to support multiprocessing.

   A. True

   B. False

18. Fault tolerance schemes such as mirroring and striping with parity allow your hard disk controller to fail without bringing the system down.

A. True

B. False

19. If you have a SCSI controller, you should not use IDE peripherals.

A. True

B. False

20. SCSI controllers should be embedded on the motherboard for maximum performance.

A. True

B. False

21. Hard drives wear out from normal use.

A. True

B. False

22. Windows NT supports _____ families of microprocessors.

23. _____ microprocessors are the fastest microprocessors supported by Windows NT.

24. _____ microprocessors have the most applications available for use with Windows NT.

25. Windows NT uses the _____ method of multiprocessing.

26. The only component whose failure is catastrophic in a server is _____.

A. the microprocessor

B. RAM

C. a hard disk drive

D. the video adapter

27. _____ is the fastest standard bus for the interconnection of mass storage devices in typical servers.

    A. PCI

    B. SCSI

    C. IDE

    D. ISA

    E. WORM

28. The _____ is the brain of a computer.

    A. microprocessor

    B. motherboard

    C. RAM

    D. video adapter

    E. hard disk

Installing Windows NT Server

THE PURPOSE OF this chapter is to show you how to install the Windows NT Server operating system software on a computer. The process we describe here installs a minimally configured operating system that does not include services such as TCP/IP, Internet Information Services, and Remote Access Services.

We have deliberately chosen a relatively simple installation process for this chapter; later chapters build on this information.

You will learn to install and configure those services, as well as to configure the operating system to use network adapter cards, in detail in later chapters. The later chapters, however, require you to have an installed Windows NT Server operating system and to be familiar with the operating system (OS) installation process.

Topics covered here include

- Installation media (from boot floppies, from CD-ROM, from a network server)

- Installation roles (primary domain controller, backup domain controller, member server, and stand-alone server)

- Installing Windows NT Server

- Uninstalling Windows NT Server

Installing Windows NT Server

INSTALLING WINDOWS NT Server involves many decisions, quite a few tedious steps, and several rebootings of the server computer. The individual decisions are easy, and the steps are not difficult, but each one element must be correct to perform a successful install.

The complexity of the installation process arises from the various installation media and server roles for Windows NT Server. Before starting the actual installation process, we describe how to prepare the computer hardware for installation and explain the effect of each installation medium and installation role. The following topics are covered in the preliminary discussion:

- Hardware preparation

- Booting multiple operating system

- Installation media

- Installation roles

- Installing versus upgrading

- Domain names

Hardware Preparation

This chapter assumes that your computer is qualified to run Windows NT Server. Refer to Chapter 1 to make sure that your computer satisfies the operating system's hardware requirements. In addition, make sure that the components you intend to use appear on the Hardware Compatibility List or (if the components have not yet been evaluated by Microsoft) that the manufacturer *guarantees* that the components will work with Windows NT. Items that you should be particularly careful about include the CD-ROM, the SCSI controller card (for server computers with SCSI hard disk drives and peripherals), and the network adapter card or cards.

Before you install Windows NT Server, you must be certain that none of the hardware components in the computer conflict. For example, if you have both a SCSI adapter and an Ethernet adapter in the computer, the Ethernet adapter cannot be configured to use the same interrupts as the SCSI adapter. You should be able to boot DOS from a floppy disk, ensuring that your computer hardware will at least boot, but the ability to boot DOS does not prove the absence of device conflicts. (DOS will run even when some of the devices in the computer are in conflict.) You should use the utilities that come with the devices to configure those devices to avoid memory and interrupt conflicts.

Being able to boot DOS is not proof that a computer can run Windows NT Server. However, if Windows 95 can run, reports no errors in configuration, and can use each of the devices, then you usually can be sure that the computer has no configuration problems.

When you use Windows NT Server to host files on a network, you should make one or two partitions for the exclusive use of Windows NT Server and format them for use with NTFS. (Windows NT is the only operating system that can read and write NTFS.) You should format the first partition, which does not have to be very large, with the FAT file system for booting and for DOS and Windows.

You should make at least one partition for NTFS because Windows NT uses the security features of NTFS to provide file-level security for data shared over the network. You might make two partitions for NTFS because you can then dedicate one partition to the Windows NT Server system and administrative files and dedicate the other to user files. When you place user files and system files on separate partitions, you protect the file server from running out of disk space for system services when users fill all available user storage space.

The rest of the book assumes that you have partitioned your hard disk space into two or more partitions. The first partition is formatted with the FAT file system and contains the Windows NT startup files (and perhaps DOS and Windows operating system files); the second partition is dedicated to Windows NT and will be formatted during the installation process with the NTFS file system.

You should keep one small partition formatted with the FAT file system for MS-DOS or a slightly larger one formatted with the FAT file system for DOS and Windows. This arrangement allows you to set up the server to multiboot DOS, Windows (if you leave enough space), and Windows NT Server. You might wish to configure your server in this manner because many computer peripherals, such as some network adapters, SCSI adapters, and sound cards, come with DOS configuration programs. In many cases these DOS programs will not perform correctly under Windows NT Server because they violate the Windows NT security mechanisms by writing directly to the hardware devices, which is how the utilities configure the devices. Therefore, you may wish to keep these utilities in the FAT file system partition and boot to DOS or Windows when you need to configure them.

Booting Multiple Operating Systems

Windows NT Server will coexist happily with other operating systems on your computer. Windows NT Server can be installed in its own NTFS volume (the best choice as described in the previous section), or it can be installed alongside another operating system in a FAT volume. The Windows NT boot loader allows you to choose from the operating systems installed in your computer.

When you install Windows NT Server, the Windows NT boot loader is installed in the boot partition of your computer. Initially, the boot loader's boot menu contains two entries for your Windows NT Server operating system, as well as one for DOS or Windows if either operating system was installed on your computer before you installed Windows NT. Each successive installation of Windows NT adds to the boot loader menu, so you can, for example, install Windows NT Server and Windows NT Workstation along with Windows 95 on the same computer, each with its own boot menu option.

Installation Media

You can install Windows NT Server from a number of different sources. This diversity reflects the many environments in which Windows NT Server will be installed. In many cases it will be installed on a computer using the boot floppies and a CD-ROM directly attached to the computer. In some cases you may not wish to use the floppy disks, or perhaps Windows NT does not support the CD-ROM; then you can use the install method that requires neither a floppy nor a CD-ROM. In some larger networks the installation files may be stored on a central server, and you will use a network share to install the operating system; you may use the Network Client Administrator to make installation disks for the new server.

Most installation methods use the Winnt or the Winnt32 program. Their function is to adopt the Windows NT installation process to the installation environment of your computer. These programs create floppy disks, copy installation files to your hard disk, or both so that the Windows NT Setup program can place Windows NT on your computer.

The Winnt and Winnt32 Programs

The Winnt and the Winnt32 programs perform the same function and take the same command-line switches, but the Winnt32 program runs in the 32-bit Windows NT environment. The command-line switches are as follows:

```
winnt  /S:sourcepath /T:tempdrive
       /I:inffile /OX /X  /F /C /B
       /U:scriptfile /R:directory/E: command
```

/B   Install without installation boot floppies.

/C   Skip free space check on installation boot floppies. Not available in WINNT32.

/E   Specifies command to be executed at the end of GUI setup.

/F   Copy files from the boot floppies without verifying the copies. Not available in WINNT32.

/I   Specifies the filename (but not the path) of the setup information file. The default is dosnet.inf.

/OX   Create boot floppies for floppy-based installation from CD-ROM.

/R   Specifies optimal directory to be installed.

/RX   Specifies optimal directory to be copied. Not available in WINNT32.

/S   Specifies the source location of Windows NT setup files. The source path must be fully qualified, that is, of the form <driveletter>:\[<path>] or \\<servername>\<share>[\<path.]. The default is the current directory.

/T   Specifies the drive to contain the temporary setup files

/U   Specifies unattended operation and optional script file.

/X   Do not create the setup boot floppies.

If you are running from within Windows NT, use WINNT32 *rather than* WINNT.

In the sections that follow, you will learn how to use these programs to install Windows NT Server in various situations.

Installing with a Boot Floppy from the CD-ROM

The simplest method of installing the server software is to use the boot floppies to boot with the Windows NT CD-ROM in a supported CD-ROM drive. You can use the boot floppies that come with the installation CD-ROM, or you can create new copies of the boot floppies using the Winnt or Winnt32 program on the CD-ROM. Later in this chapter, the section titled "Creating the Installation Boot Floppies from the CD-ROM" shows you how to re-create the boot floppies.

This method of installation does not require the hard disks in the computer to have any partitions or formatted file systems on them, not even DOS FAT. After booting from these installation disks, you have the option of creating partitions and formatting file systems on your server computer from within the installation program.

If your SCSI controller or BIOS supports booting from CD-ROM, you can skip creating boot floppies and simply boot the Windows NT Server CD-ROM.

Installing without a Floppy Disk from an Unsupported CD-ROM Drive or from the Network

This method of installation copies the installation files from the CD-ROM before continuing with the installation, but it also copies the files that would otherwise be copied to the boot disks to the hard disk so that the boot disks are not necessary. The drive must have enough free space to hold the installation temporary files.

- **If you use this method to install from a CD-ROM drive,** you must have DOS or Windows installed with drivers for using that CD-ROM drive.

- **If you use this method to install from the network,** you must have DOS or Windows installed with drivers that allow you to connect to the network share that holds the Windows NT installation files. The /b option of Winnt and Winnt32 tells the installation program to perform an installation without a floppy disk.

Installing with a Floppy Disk from the Network

If you wish to install from the network and you do not have an operating system installed on the computer that can connect to the network share that holds the installation files, then you can use the Windows NT Client Administrator to transform a bootable DOS floppy disk into a network boot disk. You can then use this network boot disk to connect to the network share and begin the installation.

If you use this method to install Windows NT Server, you must have a partition on the hard disk of the computer large enough to contain installation files that will be stored temporarily during the installation. To facilitate this type of installation, you should make DOS tools such as FDISK and FORMAT available from a network share on the file server.

Exercise 4.1 shows you how to create a network boot floppy with the Client Administrator that will log on to a Windows NT Server and allow you to use the Winnt program and installation files stored in a share on the server.

EXERCISE 4.1

Creating a Network Boot Disk Using the Windows NT Client Administrator

1. Log on to your Windows NT Server as the administrator.

2. Select Start ➤ Programs ➤ Administrative Tools ➤ Network Client Administrator.

3. Select the Make Network Installation Startup Disk radio button and then click Continue.

4. Select the Share Files radio button, accept the default share name of Clients, and accept the default path of `<CD-ROM Drive Letter>\Clients` for the source of the client configuration files.

5. Click the OK button. The Network Client Administrator will inform you that it is making the client configuration files available on the network share.

6. Select the type of floppy drive you have in your server. Select Network Client version 3.0 for MS-DOS and Windows. From the Network Adapter Card list, select the type of network adapter card that you have in the computer and on which you will install Windows NT Server. Click OK.

7. Enter a name for the computer on which you will install Windows NT Server. This name does not have to be the name that the server will use after it is installed; this designation is a temporary name for use during the installation process.

8. Note that the Username field is filled with the account name of the account from which you ran the Network Client Administrator (in this case the administrator account). The computer for which you are making the floppy disk will use this account when it connects to the server.

9. Note that the domain name recorded in the next field is the same as the name of the server from which you are running Network Client Administrator. The computer will attach to this server when you boot the floppy disk.

10. Select a network protocol for the computer to use to attach to the server. The simplest network protocol is NetBEUI. If you choose TCP/IP, you may have to enter more information (the TCP/IP address, network mask, etc.) in the next set of fields. You must select a network protocol that your server supports. Click OK.

11. Insert a floppy disk formatted with DOS system files (format /s from a DOS, Windows, or Windows 95 command prompt) and then click OK.

12. Click OK when the Network Client Administrator tells you that files have been successfully copied to the floppy disk.

13. Click the Exit button in the Network Client Administrator. The program will inform you that certain defaults were used in creating the floppy disk and that you may have to modify some software settings. Click OK. Leave the floppy disk in the disk drive.

14. Open the floppy drive icon from the desktop. (Double-click the My Computer icon and then double-click the 3 1/2-inch floppy icon.)

15. Right-click the `Autoexec.bat` icon and then select Edit menu. This step launches the Notepad program and allows you to edit the `autoexec.bat` file.

16. Edit the line that includes the Net Use command to refer to the network share on your server that will hold the Windows NT Server installation files instead of the share holding the client files. If you follow the exercise in the "Network Preparation for Network Installation" section below and you are installing to an Intel-based computer, the share name will be `I386`.

17. Delete the last two lines of the file (the line that says Echo running setup... and the line that runs the Setup program).

18. Select File ➢ Save from within Notepad and then select File ➢ Exit.

19. You may need to modify the network adapter settings in the `Protocol.ini` file in the net subdirectory of the floppy disk. You will most likely need to do so if the interrupt, memory, or DMA settings are other than the default settings that Windows NT expects.

Creating the Installation Boot Floppies from the CD-ROM

The Windows NT Server software package contains three floppy disks and the Windows NT installation CD-ROM. You do not need to have a previously installed operating system on your computer's hard disk drive if you install Windows NT using these floppy disks. The Winnt and the Winnt32 programs on the installation CD-ROM can re-create these floppy disks if they become damaged or lost. Figure 4.1 shows the MS-DOS Winnt program informing you about the floppy disk requirements.

F I G U R E 4.1

Creating NT boot disks.

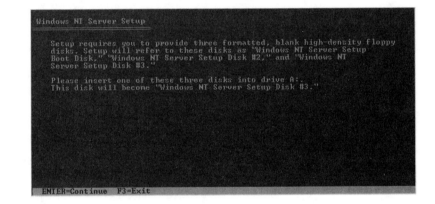

To re-create the floppy disks from your installation CD-ROM, perform the steps described in Exercise 4.2.

EXERCISE 4.2

Re-creating Windows NT Boot Floppies

1. Go to the command prompt. (In Windows NT and Windows 95, select Start ➢ Programs ➢ MS-DOS Prompt; in earlier versions of Windows, exit Windows.)

2. Change drives to the CD-ROM drive. (At the command prompt, type the letter of the drive. For instance, if your CD-ROM is drive F:, type **F** and then press Enter.)

3. Type **CD \I386** (or the directory corresponding to your processor) to change to the I386 directory.

4. Do one of the following, depending on your current operating system:

- If you are at a Windows 95 or a Windows NT command prompt, type **Winnt32 /OX** and then press Enter.

- If you are at an earlier version of Windows or a DOS command prompt, type **Winnt /OX** and then press Enter.

5. Label a blank, formatted floppy disk as Windows NT Server 4 Setup Disk 3 and place it in the disk drive. Press Enter. The program will transfer files to the floppy disk and then ask for the second disk.

6. Label another disk as Windows NT Server 4 Setup Disk 2 and place it in the disk drive. Press Enter. The program will copy files to this second disk and then ask for the final disk.

7. Label a third disk as Windows NT Server 4 Boot Disk, insert it in the disk drive, and then press Enter.

8. Remove the boot disk from the drive after the program has finished transferring information to the boot disk.

Preparing the Network for a Network Installation

If you will be installing Windows NT Server to many computers throughout a network, you may wish to put the Windows NT Server installation files on a central file server and perform a network install of the operating system at each of the computers on the network. If many of your computers are configured exactly the same, you can automate the process by using several of the installation program's software switches.

Another advantage of installing from the network is that when you reconfigure your Windows NT Server (by adding an adapter card such as a new modem or video card, for instance), the operating system provides the network location as the default path for the operating system files it needs, instead of requiring you to insert the installation CD-ROM again.

Before you can install the Windows NT Server operating system to your computer from the network, you must create a network share that contains the Windows NT installation files. If you have many computers on your network, the best way to create the network share is to copy the installation files to a subdirectory on the central file server's hard disk and then share that directory.

On the installation CD-ROM, the basic installation files for a particular computer architecture reside in the subdirectory with the name of that architecture. The Intel files, for example, are in the I386 directory, and the PowerPC files are in the PPC directory. Additional files that are not a basic part of the operating system (new device driver software, demo programs, etc.) reside in other directories off the root directory of the CD-ROM.

If all the computers on your network use the same type of microprocessor (MIPS or Intel, for example), you may create shared network directories only for the installation files for those microprocessors. (In this case you would copy only the files in the MIPS or the I386 subdirectories, respectively.)

Exercise 4.3 shows you how to create a shared installation subdirectory on your central Windows NT 4 file server.

EXERCISE 4.3

Creating a Network Share of the Windows NT Server 4 Installation Files on a Central Windows NT 4 File Server

1. Log on as an administrator.

2. Place the Windows NT Server 4 installation CD into the CD-ROM drive.

3. Click on the Browse This CD button in the Windows NT CD-ROM window that will automatically start up when you insert the CD.

4. Open the My Computer icon on the desktop

5. Open the drive icon that will contain the directory for the installation files.

6. Drag the subdirectory that contains the installation files from the CD-ROM window to the drive window. For example, to copy the Intel installation files to your C drive, drag the I386 directory to the C window. The files will be copied to the hard disk drive from the CD-ROM. This process may take a while. When the file copies are done, a new subdirectory will be present on the disk drive. It will be selected (highlighted).

7. Select File ➢ Sharing in the drive window. Select Shared As in the Directory Properties window.

8. Click the Permissions button at the bottom of the screen. Change the Type of Access from *Everyone* to *Read* in the Access Through Share Permissions window. Click OK.

9. Click the OK button at the bottom of the Directory Properties window.

10. Close the CD-ROM window, close the drive window, and close the My Computer window.

Unattended Installation

You can configure the Windows NT Server installation so that you do not have to respond to any prompts from the installation and Setup programs while NT is being installed. This installation method is called an *unattended install*. It takes a little more preparation to begin with, but if you have to install or upgrade a large number of machines, the unattended install option can save you a lot of time and effort.

To perform the unattended install, you must customize unattended script files and answer files for your particular installation. These script and answer files must contain the information that you otherwise would type into prompts and dialog boxes during the installation process. The unattended install is useful because if you have many computers that are all configured mostly the same, you have to type the information only once—into the unattended install files.

The Windows NT Server 4 CD-ROM includes a file called UNATTEND.TXT that (once you customize it) allows you to install Windows NT in a simple configuration or to upgrade Windows NT versions 3.51 and earlier to Windows NT Server 4. This UNATTEND.TXT file is simple because a basic installation requires very little information, and a Windows NT upgrade from an earlier version of Windows NT will use most of the earlier Windows NT operating system's configuration information.

If you wish to make unattended installation files for a more complex installation of Windows NT, you need to use the Computer Profile Setup utility or the Setup Manager utility. The Setup Manager is briefly described in the next section, but to use the utility most effectively you should refer to the Microsoft Windows NT Resource Kit documentation. The Computer Profile Setup utility comes with the Microsoft Windows NT Resource Kit, and you will need to refer to the documentation in the Resource Kit for instructions.

Using an Unattended Answer File

You can use the SETUPMGR.EXE program included on the Windows NT Server installation CD-ROM to create unattended answer files. The Setup Manager program allows you to specify, before you install the operating system, the answers to questions that you would otherwise have to enter during the installation process. Figure 4.2 shows the Setup Manager.

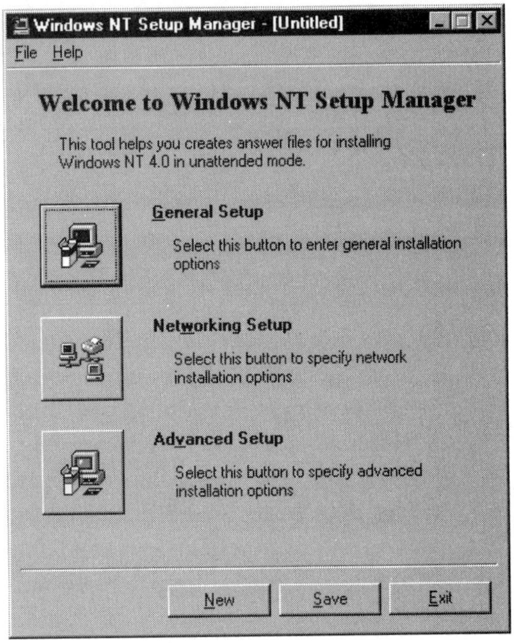

FIGURE 4.2

Setup Manager helps you create answer files.

If you are using an Intel-based computer, you can find the Setup Manager program in the \Support\Deptools\I386 subdirectory of the Windows NT Server installation CD-ROM. Executing the SETUPMGR.EXE program allows you to configure the General Setup, Networking Setup, and Advanced Setup portions of the unattended installation text file. You access each portion (General, Networking, and Advanced) through its own button. Buttons for selecting a new unattended installation file, saving the file, and exiting the program appear at the bottom of the window.

GENERAL

- **User Information:** You enter the user's name, the organization name, the name for the computer, and the product ID.

- **General:** The Setup program can confirm the hardware settings, run a program during setup, and select the type of upgrade you are performing if you are upgrading rather than installing Windows NT.

- **Computer Role:** You can determine which NT operating system you are installing (Workstation or Server), the network architecture (workgroup or domain), and if the operating system is Windows NT Server, if it will be a primary or backup domain controller. You will enter additional information here also, such as the domain or workgroup name and an (optional) computer account name.

- **Install Directory:** You can tell the installation program to install to the default directory, ask the user for a directory, or install to a specified directory.

- **Display Settings:** Sets the display configuration.

- **Time Zone:** Lists time zone settings for the computer's time clock.

- **License Mode:** You can configure a Windows NT Server computer to have a certain number of per seat or per server network connection licenses (applies only to Server installations).

NETWORKING

- **General:** You can specify that networking will be configured during the installation process or that you will configure networking from the Setup Manager program. If you select Unattended Network Installation (which requires you to configure networking from the Setup Manager), you can specify that the Setup program will detect and install a network card using defaults, that the Setup program will detect the card from a list you provide, or that the Setup program will install the network driver for the card you specify.

- **Adapters:** You can select adapter cards to be installed or detected and specify their communications parameters.

- **Protocols:** You can specify the protocols to be installed and set their parameters.

- **Services:** You can specify the services to be installed and set their parameters.

- **Internet:** For Server computers, you can set which of the Internet services will be installed and specify where the Internet services will store their information.

■ **Modem:** If RAS is installed and configured to use one or more ports, you can use this tab to configure what type of modem is connected to your computer and set the modem configuration.

ADVANCED

The advanced options have a number of settings that you will not want to change unless you have a good understanding of the install process and a need to perform an unorthodox installation.

One setting that you may wish to change, however, is the Convert to NTFS option found under the File System tab. This option will convert the Windows NT installation partition to NTFS. You will want to check this option if you wish to use the advanced features that NTFS provides.

After you specify how you want to install Windows NT within the Setup Manager program, select Save from the Setup Manager main screen. At the prompt select a directory and filename for the unattended installation file. If you have created a network share containing the Windows NT setup files, you should save the unattended installation file there.

Exercise 4.4 shows you how to create an unattended installation answer file. This exercise assumes that you are installing a computer to be part of a domain called DOMAIN and that the computer name will be MY_SERVER. The user name is Isaac Newton, and the organizational name is Gravatic Technologies. The exercise assumes that you have an NE2000-compatible Ethernet driver and that you are using an Intel-compatible computer.

The settings in this exercise will most likely not match those required for your computer and your network.

USING THE UNATTENDED ANSWER FILE WITH WINNT AND WINNT32

The /u option in Winnt and Winnt32 allows you to specify an unattended answer file for a Windows NT installation. The /u option requires the /s option to also be selected, specifying the source directory for Windows NT installation files (including the unattended installation file). Type the file name of the unattended installation file after the /u option.

EXERCISE 4.4

Creating an Unattended Installation Answer File

1. Insert the Windows NT Server 4 installation CD-ROM into the CD-ROM drive.

2. Double-click the My Computer icon.

3. Open the CD-ROM icon in the My Computer window. Select Browse This CD-ROM from the Autorun window that appears.

4. Select Support ➤ Deptools ➤ I386.

5. Open the Setupmgr program.

6. Click the New button at the bottom of the screen.

7. Click the General Setup button.

8. Click the User Information tab; type **Isaac Newton** into the User Name field, **Gravatic Technologies** into the Organization field, and **MY_SERVER** into the Computer Name field. Enter the product ID number for your server CD into the Product ID field.

9. Click the Computer Role tab. In the *Select the role of the computer* field, select primary domain controller. Type **DOMAIN** into the Domain Name field.

10. Click the other tabs to observe the settings of each tab. You don't have to change any of them for this exercise.

11. Click the OK button at the bottom of the screen.

12. Click the Networking Setup button.

13. Click the General tab and select Unattended Network Installation. Then select Specify adapters to be installed.

14. Click on the Adapters tab. Click on the Add button. In the Adding Adapters window, select Novell NE2000 Adapter. Click OK.

15. Click the Parameters button. Type **5** for the interrupt number and **320** for the I/O Base Address. Click OK.

16. Click the Protocols tab. Click on the Add button. Select NETBEUI in the Adding Protocols window. Click the OK button. You do not have to set the parameters for NETBEUI.

17. Click OK at the bottom of the Networking Options window.

18. Click the Advanced Setup button. Click the File System tab. Select the Convert to NTFS option. Click OK at the bottom of the Advanced Options window.

19. Click the Save button at the bottom of the Windows NT Setup Manager window. Type `C:\temp\test.txt` in the Name field. Click the Save button. This step saves the unattended installation file as `test.txt` in the temp directory of your C drive.

20. Click the Exit button.

Using a Text Editor to Create the Uniqueness Database File

If you have to install Windows NT workstation to a large number of similarly configured computers, you can use the unattended installation file (which you create just once; it contains the configuration information common to all the computers on which you will install Windows NT) in conjunction with a uniqueness database file that identifies differences among installations, such as the computer name and the user name for that installation. You can then use the /UDF option of Winnt and Winnt32 to specify a uniqueness database file (UDF) file that customizes the installation for a particular computer. An example of a UDF file for three computers follows.

EXAMPLE UDF FILE

```
; UDF file to customize the installation for three
  computers
;
[UniqueIds]
u1 = UserData
u2 = UserData
u3 = UserData
[u1:UserData]
FullName = "Charles Perkins"
OrgName = "Charles Perkins Elucidation"
```

```
ComputerName = YOYO
[u2:UserData]
FullName = "Matthew Strebe"
OrgName = "Netropolis"
ComputerName = BOOMERANG
[u3:UserData]
FullName = "Henry J Tillman"
OrgName = "Tillman World Enterprises Inc."
ComputerName = POGO
```

UDF ORGANIZATION

Each computer in the preceding example has a different FullName, organization name, and computer name. The installation program merges the settings of the unattended text file and the uniqueness database file at the graphics portion of the installation process. An unattended installation answer file will supply all other settings.

When you select the UDF option for Winnt or Winnt32, you can also specify the uniqueness ID for that installation. The sample UDF has three uniqueness IDs listed: u1, u2, and u3. When specifying u1 with the above UDF file, Winnt causes the Setup program to use the first set of sample information.

The format of the UDF file is simple, and it is very similar to the format of the unattended installation answer file. The [u1:UserData] section heading, for example, specifies that the data following it will add to or replace, for the u1 installation, information found in the [UserData] section of the unattended installation file. The FullName setting of Charles Perkins will replace, for the u1 installation, the FullName information stored in the unattended installation file.

The UDF file is different from the unattended answer file in that it has a [UniqueIDs] section containing identifiers for unique installation; the unique ID prefixes each section of the answer file that contains information just for the unique ID.

CREATING AND USING THE UDF

You can create UDF files using a text editor such as Notepad. If you intend to use a UDF file to customize the installation process for several computers, you will need to provide unique settings for at least the computer name for each installation. Use the format outlined above to create UDF entries for each computer.

You use the UDF by specifying the UDF file and the uniqueness identifier for the installation on the Winnt or Winnt32 command line. The UDF file is used with the unattended answer file option (explained in the preceding section, "Using an Unattended Answer File"). You specify that setup will use a UDF file with the /UDF option shown here:

```
/UDF:ID[,database_filename]
```

The next example assumes the following:

- You have created an unattended answer file called `unat1.txt` using Setup Manager.

- You have created a UDF file called `udf1.txt`, which contains a unique ID of id1, with your text editor.

- The installation files (including the answer file and the UDF file) reside on a network share mapped to drive F.

Under these conditions, you can type this command from the DOS prompt:

```
winnt /s:f:\ /u:unat1.txt /UDF:id1,udf1.txt
```

Using the Sysdiff Utility

If you further wish to customize the installation of Windows NT to one or more computers over a network, you can use the Sysdiff utility. This utility records the difference between a normal Windows NT installation and an installation to which you have added other software such as a standard application suite of files. The Sysdiff utility can perform in any of the following modes:

- **Snap:** In this mode Sysdiff takes a snapshot of the state of the Windows NT operating system Registry and the state of the file system files and directories. The information it records is written out to a snapshot file.

- **Diff:** This mode of operation records the differences between the state of a previous snapshot of a Windows NT installation and the state of the installation at the time Sysdiff is run again. Sysdiff /Diff creates a difference file.

- **Apply:** Executing Sysdiff with the apply option can apply the data in the difference file to a Windows NT installation.

- **Inf:** This mode creates an INF file containing information about your installation preferences and installation data from the difference file. You can apply this option to a server-based share of the Windows NT installation files so that the differences captured with the Diff command are automatically applied to installations of Windows NT made from that server-based share.

- **Dump:** This command produces a file that lists the contents of the difference file.

```
sysdiff /snap [/log:log_file] snapshot_file

sysdiff /diff [/log:log_file] snapshot_file
  difference_file

sysdiff /apply [/log:log_file ] difference_file

sysdiff /inf [/u] sysdiff_file oem_root

sysdiff /dump difference_file dump_file
```

The command-line parameters are defined as follows:

- **snapshot_file:** The file containing the state of the original installation

- **difference_file:** The file containing the differences between the original installation and your custom installation

- **log_file:** The file describing the operation of the Sysdiff utility

- **oem_root:** The directory containing the additional directories and files for your custom installation

- **dump_file:** The file containing a description of the data in the difference file

The simplest way to use the Sysdiff utility is illustrated in Exercise 4.5.

The Sysdiff utility is a powerful tool that can automate the distribution of both operating system and application software to a large number of computers. However, you must be very familiar with the installation process and the operation of the Windows NT operating system and applications before you can use the Sysdiff utility to its fullest extent.

EXERCISE 4.5

Using the Sysdiff Utility to Customize an Installation

1. Perform an installation of the Windows NT software to a typical computer.

2. Create a shapshot file with the Sysdiff /snap option.

3. Install to the typical computer the software that you wish to be distributed to each installation.

4. Create a difference file with the /diff option.

5. Install Windows NT to each of the destination computers.

6. Run the Sysdiff utility with the /apply option after each installation is complete.

Installation Roles

Your Windows NT Server can play several different roles in your network:

- It can be configured to be a primary domain controller (PDC), of which there can be only one in a Windows NT domain.

- It can be one of several backup domain controllers (BDC) in which case it will satisfy logon requests for the domain and take over if the PDC fails.

- It can be a member server in which case it will perform neither PDC nor BDC functions but will defer to the PDC and BDCs for domain security and logon.

- It can be set up as a stand-alone server if the server is not part of a domain at all.

If you install a server without making it a domain controller (PDC or BDC), you cannot make it a PDC or a BDC later. You will have to reinstall the operating system software if you wish to change the role of the server.

Primary Domain Controller

The primary domain controller is the central point of control for the network. When your network is organized into a Windows NT domain, you have to log on to the network only once—all workstations and servers defer to the primary domain controller to validate the usernames and passwords. (The PDC may delegate authentication to the backup domain controllers, but the PDC always maintains the master list of acceptable usernames and passwords for the domain.)

Every domain has exactly one primary domain controller. The PDC must be the first server brought up on the network in the domain because it must maintain the database of user accounts and computer domain membership accounts as other computers are brought into the domain.

If you are creating a new domain, you should designate the first server you install as the primary domain controller. If the first computer you bring online is not the computer you want to be the primary domain controller, install it as the primary domain controller anyway. When you install Windows NT Server on the computer you want to be the primary domain controller, intall it as a backup domain controller and then promote it to primary domain controller.

Backup Domain Controller

Backup domain controllers exist for several reasons. First, if the primary domain controller fails and no other domain controllers are available on a network, then network authentications would cease and resources would become unavailable. In addition, the primary domain controller on a large network can become a bottleneck because a domain controller must make all domain authentications. BDCs alleviate the load on the PDC by performing authentications for the PDC. Because you can increase the number of BDCs on the network as the network grows, you can keep the load on the PDC small and maintain optimum network performance.

Backup domain controllers maintain a copy of the primary domain controller's database, and any backup domain controller can become the primary domain controller when the PDC fails.

You should configure the second server on your domain to be the backup domain controller. If you plan to have a large number of servers in your domain, you should select several more servers to be BDCs.

Member Server

Not every server in your network must be a PDC or a BDC. The tasks that the PDC and BDCs perform exact a performance penalty from the server, and you may wish to dedicate some servers in your domain to a single purpose, such as serving files or hosting a database.

If you already have a PDC and BDC and you require the best performance from a server computer, you may wish to designate it a member server in your domain.

Stand-Alone Server

In some cases you will install a server that is not a part of a domain. In this case you can make the computer a stand-alone server and configure it to use the workgroup networking model instead of the domain networking model.

If the server will not be a part of a domain, you should designate it as a stand-alone server.

Installing versus Upgrading

If you have an earlier version of Windows NT Server loaded on the computer, you will have the option of upgrading the earlier version of the operating system to version 4.

You should upgrade your server rather than perform a fresh installation when your computer is already running an earlier version of the software and you do not require a change in the server's role.

Upgrading the current installation is a much easier process than installing a new version of the operating system because when the installation program upgrades from an earlier version it can transfer many of the operating system settings to the new version.

You should be aware, however, that even if you upgrade a member server or stand-alone server, it will still be a member server or stand-alone server. If you wish to make a server that previously was not a PDC or BDC into a PDC or BDC, then you need to reinstall the operating system software.

Server and Domain Names

Before you begin installing servers and naming computers, you should devise a coherent plan to keep track of networked resources. Networks are often brought online chaotically, and servers are named as if they were pets. Although this free-form system is fun for the network administrator, it's not fun for new users who are trying to figure out where certain files reside.

The primary responsibility of a network administrator is to make network resources as easily available as possible. Part of this responsibility is to create a coherent naming scheme for all network resources.

To make a naming scheme, think about what is important in your organization. Are resources divided by department? by use? Should you use an obvious name?

For instance, if you dedicate a server to the accounting department, ACCOUNTING might be a good name for it. On the other hand, if the server stores x-ray files exclusively, XRAYS might be appropriate. Likewise, a printer loaded with invoices should probably be called INVOICE PRINTER.

The rule for naming conventions is consistency and uniqueness. If you name one server by department or location, name them all by department or location. If you find you can't follow through, then department or location naming probably isn't the right scheme for your situation.

You can also devise schemes based on major resource types. For example, you could name servers by department, such as MARKETING, and name printers by function, such as INVOICES or CHECKS, because most printers are used exclusively within departments, whereas servers are accessed throughout the organization. Names must be unique within domains—and should be unique throughout your organization. If you have a CHECKS printer in the accounting domain and a CHECKS printer in finance domain, someone is certain to access one or both of them incorrectly. (Examples of how to resolve this kind of problem follow.)

Create a set of rules for naming shared resources. Give each department, location, purpose, and function a unique mnemonic and combine them to create unique names. For example, ACCSRV would be the accounting server, whereas MKTLPR would be the marketing laser printer, and ACCIPR would be the accounting invoices printer. When users are familiar with your naming scheme, they will know exactly what your named resources refer to when they see them in lists.

Small organizations should create naming schemes with an eye towards the future. Naming your server SERVER because it's the only one you have leaves you out in the cold when you add a second server. PRIMARY might be a bit better, but a name like your organization location or even HEADQUARTERS could easily support the addition of more servers down the line without changing your naming scheme.

If you have several domains in your network, you should choose a similar naming scheme for the each domain. You should at least select a domain name for your domain that will allow easy interoperation with other domains, for instance one based on your physical location, like SANDIEGO. Leaving the domain name set to the default name of DOMAIN is not the best option. You can change your domain name later, but you'll have to go around to every computer in your facility to make the change.

Installation Process

Once you have decided which role the server will play on the network and have determined what media you will use to install the software, you can go on with the installation. The installation process requires four general steps:

1. Gathering information

2. Booting the floppies, starting Winnt, or starting Winnt32

3. Using the text-based Setup program

4. Negotiating the graphical configuration program

The following sections move through these steps one at a time.

Gathering Information

The first step is to gather all of information you will need during the installation process. The information you need includes the computer's name, the domain name, and the interrupt and memory settings of various components. (These settings are particularly hard to determine in the middle of an installation without aborting the installation and starting over.)

You should note at least the following information before you continue with an installation:

- **Computer name:** This name will identify your server on the network. Computer names can be up to 15 characters long and must be unique.

- **Domain name:** (if a member of a domain)

- **Workgroup name:** (if a member of a workgroup)

- **Device settings:** For each device in your computer with an interrupt, DMA, or memory setting, record the model and manufacturer of the device (this information is particularly important for network cards) and record each of the settings for the device.

- **Hard drive partitions:** Record the purpose and format for each of the partitions in your computer. Specify which partition will contain the Windows NT Server system files.

- **Windows NT directory:** Record the directory that will contain the Windows NT Server System files. (The default is \WINNT.)

- **Protocol selection:** Record which protocols you will configure this server to support. (Usual choices include TCP/IP, IPX/SPX, and NetBEUI.)

- **TCP/IP information:** If you will be installing the TCP/IP protocol, you need to record the TCP/IP address, subnet mask, gateway address, DNS address, WINS address, and TCP/IP domain name (which is not the same as the Windows NT networking domain name listed above).

- **IPX information:** If you will be installing the IPX/SPX protocol, you should list the IPX network number for your network.

- **Ethernet information:** If you are installing an Ethernet card in your server (most NT servers have them), you should record the Ethernet frame type that you will be using on your network. You should also record which media type you will use if your card supports several media types (such as twisted pair, fiber optic, or Thinnet).

- **Licensing information:** Record the individual and organization name that this software is licensed to. You should also record the CD key that is printed on a label on the back of the CD-ROM case. Also record whether you will use per seat or per server licensing and the user limit.

- **Administrator password:** Record the administrator password. If at a later point you cannot recall the password, you may have to reinstall the software.

Because this list contains sensitive information such as the administrator password, you should keep the list in a safe place after you have installed the server software. You should not discard the list; however, it may be useful later when you need to reinstall, upgrade, or otherwise maintain the system.

Booting the Floppies, Starting Winnt, or Starting Winnt32

Just starting the installation process can be the most complicated part of installing Windows NT Server, or it can be the easiest. If you use the installation boot floppies that come with the Windows NT Server CD-ROM and you install from a CD-ROM drive that is compatible with Windows NT, then this part of the installation process is very simple—you just insert the CD-ROM in the CD-ROM drive, insert the first floppy disk in the floppy drive, and boot the computer. Figure 4.3 shows the MS-DOS based WINNT.EXE program copying installation files to the hard disk.

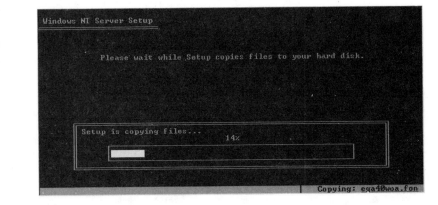

The process becomes more complicated if you don't have the floppy disks or if you are booting from an unsupported CD-ROM drive. In these cases you will use either the Winnt or Winnt32 program to make the floppy disks or start the installation without using the floppies.

- If you need to create floppy disks, refer to "Creating the Installation Boot Floppies from the CD-ROM" earlier in this chapter for instructions.

- If you will be installing from a network share and the installation files have not yet been made available over the network, refer to "Preparing the Network for a Network Installation" earlier in this chapter for instructions.

- If you will be installing from a network share and the computer does not have an operating system already installed that can connect to a network share, refer to "Installing with a Floppy Disk from the Network" for instructions on how to make a network boot disk.

The following exercises will get you started with the boot process. Follow Exercise 4.6a to use the installation boot floppies, Exercise 4.6b to perform a CD-ROM install without a floppy disk, and Exercise 4.6c to perform a network installation from a shared directory on a server.

EXERCISE 4.6a

Starting the Installation Process with Boot Floppies

1. Insert the Windows NT Server installation boot disk.

2. Boot your computer.

3. Insert the Windows NT Server disk 2 when prompted.

4. Press Enter.

5. Proceed to Exercise 4.7.

EXERCISE 4.6b

Starting a CD-ROM Installation Process without Floppy Disks

1. Turn the computer on and boot to MS-DOS or Windows 95. Your current operating system must support your CD-ROM drive. You may boot from an MS-DOS floppy disk if you wish.

2. Go to the command prompt. (If you have booted DOS, then you are already at the command prompt. From Windows for Workgroups and earlier versions of Windows, double click the MS-DOS icon in the Main program group. From Windows 95 select Start ➤ Programs ➤ MS-DOS prompt or Start ➤ Shut Down ➤ Restart in MS-DOS mode.)

3. Change drives to the CD-ROM drive (for instance, type **F:** if your CD-ROM is drive F).

4. Type **CD \I386** to change directories into the I386 subdirectory (for an installation on Intel-based computers).

5. Type **LOCK** at the command prompt to allow direct access to the hard drive if you are performing the installation from MS-DOS 7 or Windows 95.

6. Type **Winnt /b**.

EXERCISE 4.6b (CONTINUED FROM PREVIOUS PAGE)

7. Enter the location of the installation files. The default location will be the I386 directory of the CD-ROM or network share. You can simply accept the default location and press Enter to continue.

8. The Setup program will copy installation files to the hard disk drive of your computer. When the file transfer is complete, remove all floppy disks from the disk drives and then press Enter to reboot your computer. The computer will reboot and welcome you to Windows NT Server Setup. Go to the next section.

EXERCISE 4.6c

Starting a Network Share Installation Process

1. If you are booting from a network boot floppy, insert the boot disk into the floppy disk drive. If you are performing an installation without floppy disks, leave the floppy disk drive empty.

2. Turn on the computer.

3. Go to the command prompt. (If you have booted a network boot disk, then you are already at the command prompt. From Windows for Workgroups and earlier versions of Windows, double-click the MS-DOS icon in the Main program group. From Windows 95 select Start ➤ Programs ➤ MS-DOS prompt.

4. Type **net use z: \\boomerang\I386** to map a drive to the network share that contains the Windows NT Server installation files.

5. Type **Z:** to change drives to the network share.

6. Type **lock** if you are at a DOS 7 (Windows 95) or later command prompt to enable direct disk access for the Windows NT setup program.

7. Type **Winnt /b**.

8. Enter the location of the installation files as **Z:\I386**. The default location will be the I386 directory of the CD-ROM or network share. You can simply accept the default location and press Enter to continue.

9. The Setup program will copy installation files to the hard disk drive of your computer. When the file transfer is complete, remove all floppy disks from disk drives and then press Enter to reboot your computer. If you are in Windows 95, you may have to exit the command prompt and shut down the computer manually. The computer will reboot and welcome you to Windows NT Server Setup. Go to the next section.

Using the Text-Based Setup Program

Once you have performed one of the beginning installation exercises (Exercises 2.4 through 2.8), the Windows NT Setup program executes. The process from here is the same regardless of the method of installation (network, CD-ROM, without a floppy, or with the installation boot disks).

In this portion of the installation process, you must respond to a sequence of text screens that examine your computer's hardware and allow you to select a partition to use with Windows NT, the file system to use on the NT partition, and the directory for the Windows NT files. Then the Setup program copies essential files (but not all the files) to their final location on your hard disk.

Exercise 4.7 shows you how to use the Windows NT Setup program. Each step is explained in the text that follows the exercise.

EXERCISE 4.7

Using the Windows NT Setup Program

1. Press Enter at the initial setup screen.

2. Insert the third floppy disk if necessary. At the hardware identification screen, press S if you need to specify additional adapters.

3. Press Enter to continue.

4. Scroll down through the Windows NT Licensing Agreement until you can press F8 to agree to the license. Press F8 to continue.

5. Select *The above list matches my computer* and then press Enter. If Setup detects a previous version of Windows NT, it will prompt for a fresh installation or an Upgrade.

6. Select the primary partition on your hard drive. If you wish to install NT on another partition, create that partition now.

7. Press C to convert the partition to NTFS. Warning: The partition will no longer be available to MS-DOS or Windows 95. If you need to use these operating systems with this partition, skip this step.

8. Accept the default directory location of \WINNT.

9. Press Enter for an exhaustive examination of the hard disk.

10. Remove any floppy disks or CD-ROM disks from your computer and press Enter to reboot.

THE INITIAL SETUP SCREEN

The initial setup screen displays four options:

- To learn more about Windows NT Setup before continuing, press F1.

- To setup Windows NT now, press Enter.

- To repair a damaged Windows NT version 4 installation, press R.

- To quit Setup without installing Windows NT, press F3.

Press Enter to continue.

THE LICENSE AGREEMENT

You must view and agree to the license agreement before you can continue with the installation of Windows NT Server. Press the Page Down key until you can press the F8 key to agree to the license.

HARDWARE IDENTIFICATION

The Setup program automatically detects many types of hard disk and CD-ROM controllers, but it cannot detect every type of controller. This screen allows you to select additional adapter drivers and if necessary to provide additional adapter drivers on floppy disk. This step is necessary because the Setup program must be able to access a hard disk drive before it can install Windows NT, and you may have an unusual drive that NT does not automatically detect.

If you are installing from the installation boot floppies, you should insert the third floppy disk now.

At this point you can press S to specify additional SCSI adapters, CD-ROM adapters, or special disk controllers. You can choose from the Setup program's list of supported devices or specify a manufacturer's floppy disk as the source for the adapter driver.

If NT is already installed on your computer, Setup skips to the "NT system directory location" step. Otherwise, the next screen shows the computer, display, keyboard, layout, and pointing device (mouse). You can select and change each item, or select *The above list matches my computer* to continue.

In most cases the Setup program provides a correct list.

FILE SYSTEMS AND PARTITIONS

The next screen displays a list of existing partitions and unpartitioned space. You can install Windows NT on an existing partition or on the unpartitioned space. You can also create and delete partitions.

If the partition you choose is unformatted or is of type FAT, the installation program gives you the choice of converting the file system to NTFS or of leaving the file system as FAT. You can make the partition NTFS even if it is the system partition of the hard drive. However, if you do so, the partition will be unavailable to other operating systems. If you are following the recommended procedure and have created a second (large) partition for Windows NT, you should choose the option to convert the file system to NTFS.

The differences between FAT and NTFS, and the best uses for each, are discussed in Chapter 5. At this point, if you have created a partition for use with NT, you should choose NTFS as the format for the partition.

You will be asked to confirm that you wish to convert the partition to NTFS and warned that this step will make the partition unavailable to other operating system such as DOS, Windows, and OS/2.

Press C to convert the partition, which will occur just before the graphical portion of the installation process when you reboot to the actual NT operating system.

WINDOWS NT SYSTEM DIRECTORY LOCATION

If a Windows NT operating system is already installed on the partition, you must now decide whether you are going to upgrade the current operating system or install a new operating system.

If you have another version of Windows installed on the computer, Windows NT will recognize it and ask if you want to install a new version of Windows or upgrade the current version. If you choose to install a new version and give the same file directory name as a version of Windows that is already installed, NT warns you that this installation will destroy the existing version of Windows.

Specify where you want to install the Windows NT system files. The default location is \WINNT. You should keep this default unless you have a good reason to choose a different location. (One good reason is that you do not want to overwrite another version of Windows.)

Accept the default directory location of \WINNT.

HARD DISK EXAMINATION AND EXHAUSTIVE SECONDARY EXAMINATION

The final screen of the second (text-based) part of the installation process allows you to select whether Setup will perform a cursory hard disk examination or an exhaustive examination before your computer reboots and the graphical portion of the installation begins.

The simple examination may take a few seconds if you had a freshly formatted or unformatted drive before you began the installation process, or it may take several minutes if you have many files stored on your hard drive. The exhaustive examination will test every location on your hard drive to find any bad locations and may take several minutes.

Press Enter to perform the exhaustive secondary examination (don't press yet) or press Esc to skip the exhaustive examination. Now press Enter.

Once the examination is complete, the Setup program continues, copying more files to your hard disk drive. When it is done copying files, you are prompted to remove any floppy disks or CD-ROMs from your computer and then press Enter to reboot. After the computer reboots, the graphical portion of the installation continues.

Negotiating the Graphical Configuration Program

The third portion of the installation process is mostly graphical, and your computer is running Windows NT while performing this part of the installation.

The first thing the computer will do after it reboots is to check the file systems on each of the hard disks. Windows NT requires each file system to be in a consistent state (i.e., the directory structure of the file system must be error free). At this time Windows NT converts the file system to NTFS if you selected the Convert option earlier in the installation process. After checking the file systems, Windows NT reboots. This portion of the install process is still text based, but the computer is now running NT instead of running the Windows NT Setup program.

After converting the file system and then rebooting, you continue the installation in a graphical environment. Exercise 4.8 takes you through the graphical portion of the installation process.

EXERCISE 4.8

The Graphical Portion of the Windows NT Installation Process

1. Click Next to begin the graphical portion of the installation.

2. Enter your name in the Name field.

3. Enter the name of your organization in the organization field.

4. Click Next.

5. Enter the CD key into the CD key field.

6. Click Next.

7. Select Per Seat Licensing mode.

8. Click Next.

9. Enter a computer name in the Name field and then click Next.

10. Select the server type (PDC) and then click Next.

11. Enter the Administrator account password twice and then click Next.

12. Select Yes to create an emergency repair disk and then click Next.

13. Accept the components listed and click Next.

14. Click Next to continue past the first Configure Network screen.

15. Check the Wired to the network checkbox.

16. Make sure that the Remote access to the network checkbox is not checked.

17. Click Next.

18. Clear the Install Microsoft Internet Information Services checkbox and then click Next.

19. Select from List and then select the MS Loopback Adapter from the list of adapters. Click OK and then click Next.

20. Select the NetBEUI protocol and make sure that the other protocols are not selected. Click Next.

21. Accept the services listed by clicking Next to continue.

22. Click Next to install the components selected.

23. Respond to any requests for information required to configure the networking components. The only information required for the MS Loopback Adapter is the frame type—choose 802.3 and click Continue.

24. Click Next to continue past the screen that allows you to disable network bindings.

25. Click Next to start the network at the prompt.

26. Supply a domain name. (Type **MCSE_TEST** for the purposes of this exercise.)

27. Click Next.

28. Click Finish.

29. Select the correct time zone in the Time Zone tab of the Date/Time properties window. Click the Close button.

30. Click OK when the Detected Display window shows you what kind of display adapter it has detected.

31. Click the Test button in the Display Properties window and click OK in the Testing mode window. Click Yes when the Testing mode window returns and asks if you saw the test screen properly.

32. Click OK in the Display Settings window and then click OK in the Display Properties window.

33. Insert a blank diskette on which to create the emergency repair disk and click OK.

34. Remove any floppy disks from drives in the computer and click the Restart Computer button at the prompt.

OPTIONS

Windows NT Server has several more setup options than Windows NT Workstation has, but one option you won't see in Windows NT Server is the option of a Typical, Portable, Compact, or Custom setup. Previous versions of Windows NT Server allowed you to select between Express and Custom setups, but that option is not available in Windows NT Server 4. Instead, the Setup program automatically selects all those features that it needs to provide network services and then lets you choose the other components you need.

THE REGISTRATION INFORMATION AND KEY

You will then be asked to provide the name and an organization that this copy of Windows NT is licensed to. You must provide this information or the installation process will not continue.

1. Enter your name in the Name field.

2. Enter the name of your organization in the organization field and then click Next.

3. Enter the CD key in the next screen. The key is recorded on a sticker on the back of the Windows NT Server Installation CD-ROM jewel case. You should also record this key in the installation information you gathered earlier in this chapter.

The next screen allows you to select the licensing mode for this Windows NT Server installation. Refer to Chapter 2 for information on how licensing modes impact the design of your network. For the purposes of this exercise, you should select Per Seat.

4. Select Per Seat and then click Next.

THE COMPUTER NAME, SERVER TYPE, AND ADMINISTRATOR PASSWORD

The computer name you select can be up to 15 characters long. You should make it simple and easy to type. Enter a name in the Name field and then click Next. Select PDC when prompted to select the role of your server in the domain and then click Next.

Next you need to enter an Administrator account password. Although you can install Windows NT without an Administrator account password by leaving both fields blank, some Windows NT functions expect this password and will not operate correctly without it. Specifically, if the password is blank, you won't be able to join domains from the installation screens of other Windows NT machines.

You should choose a password that is difficult to guess but that you will not forget. You should not write it down in a place that is easy for others to get to (such as on a yellow sticky note stuck to the computer's monitor), but if you are configuring this workstation for use in an organization, you should make sure that at least one other (trusted) individual in the organization has the password or can get the password in case you are not available to administer the computer. (You could lock your sticky note in a safe.)

Enter the Administrator account password twice and then click Next to continue.

EMERGENCY REPAIR DISK

The next screen asks if you wish to create an emergency repair disk. The emergency repair disk can rescue your Windows NT installation from system corruption that can happen when the power goes out unexpectedly or when a program or other operating system has disturbed the operating system's boot or system files.

Select Yes and then click Next to continue.

COMMON COMPONENTS

You will then be asked which components you wish to install. Common components have already been selected for you, but you may wish to install some that are not installed by default (such as games or additional communications programs).

Accept the default selection of components and click Next to continue.

NETWORK CONFIGURATION

Next you will need to configure your network. Read the information screen and click Next.

Your first choice is to declare how you want the computer to participate in a network. Your choices are

- Wired to the network

- Remote access to the network

Check the first box (Wired to the network) but not the second (Remote access). Click Next.

Then choose whether to install the Internet Information Services. Since you will be shown how to install and use IIS later in the book, you should skip installing it now.

Clear the Install Microsoft Internet Information Server checkbox and then click Next.

Before you can configure the network adapter for your Windows NT workstation, Windows NT must know what type of adapter is installed in the computer. You can instruct Windows NT to search for the adapter, or you can select the adapter from a list.

If Windows NT finds an adapter, it will display the adapter and you can click Next to continue. If it does not find the adapter, you must select it from a list or provide drivers for the adapter from a floppy disk.

Even if you do not have a network adapter installed in your computer, you can still install the networking portions of the operating system. In that case you will need to select the MS Loopback Adapter from the Windows NT list of adapters. The MS Loopback Adapter is a software driver that pretends to be an adapter but doesn't really control a hardware device. You will not, of course, be able to connect to a network using the MS Loopback Adapter.

Click Select from List and then choose the MS Loopback Adapter. Click OK and then click Next.

PROTOCOLS

The next screen displays checkboxes for the three default networking protocols for Windows NT networking. A checked protocol will be installed and configured during the installation process; an unchecked protocol may be installed later. The default protocols to choose from are

- TCP/IP protocol

- NWLink IPX/SPX compatible transport

- NetBEUI protocol

You can select from the additional protocols list to add other protocols (such as AppleTalk) to the list of protocols to install at this time.

NetBEUI is the simplest protocol and requires the least configuration during the installation process.

For this install, select NetBEUI and make sure that the other protocols are not selected. Then click Next.

The next screen displays networking services that will be installed in your Windows NT server. Accept the default configuration and click Next.

The next screen tells you that you will be configuring the protocols and components you selected earlier. Click Next.

At this point you have to go through a configuration sequence for each of the networking components that you have just selected. For example, if you had selected TCP/IP or IPX/SPX at the protocol screen, you would now be required to enter TCP/IP and IPX/SPX information. (We will show you how to configure these protocols in later chapters.)

We have selected the simplest configurations, but if you have selected anything other than the MS Loopback Adapter, you might have to enter IRQ and DMA numbers and the base memory address of your network adapter card. Each card is different, and some require more information than others. Enter the information that you gathered about your hardware settings when you configured your hardware before installing Windows NT. For the MS Loop-Back Adapter, just enter the frame type (select 802.3) and click Continue.

The next screen allows you to disable network bindings. You should leave the bindings as they are and click Next.

Click Next to start the network and go to the next configuration step.

WORKGROUPS AND DOMAINS

After the network components of Windows NT have been started, you must enter the domain name of the domain your server will participate in. For the exercise in this section, type **MCSE_TEST** as the domain name. Click Next and then Finish.

MISCELLANEOUS SETTINGS

After setting up the network, you still need to configure some miscellaneous components. First you need to configure the date and time and your time zone. The real-time clock on your computer will most likely have the correct date and time.

In the Time Zone tab of the Date/Time Properties window, select the correct time zone. Click the Close button.

The next part of the installation allows you to configure your video adapter and monitor settings. The default configuration is standard VGA with 16 colors. You can change the settings later, but at this point you should accept the default display settings.

The next screen shows you what kind of display adapter Windows NT has detected. Click OK.

You must test the display before you go on, or Windows NT will display a warning box. The display settings you are testing are the current settings, but you should test them anyway.

In the Display Properties window, click the Test button. Click OK in the Testing mode window and watch the test screen. Wait until the Testing mode window returns; if you saw the test screen properly, click Yes. Click OK to save the settings. Click OK in the Display Properties window.

Finishing the Installation

Finally, Windows NT copies a few accessories, applications, and DLLs to the Windows NT partition. It sets up the Start menu and shortcuts and then removes temporary installation files. If you have installed to an NTFS partition, it also sets security on system files.

Windows NT saves the configuration of the operating system and then it creates the emergency repair diskette. The last step is to remove any floppy disks and click the Restart Computer button.

Your computer restarts to an installed version of Windows NT Server 4. Once you log on as an administrator, you can create a user account and configure your printers.

Removing Windows NT Server

W INDOWS NT SERVER doesn't have a "uninstall" routine. If you decide to return to a previous operating system, you install that operating system over Windows NT. However, you need to know a few tricks to make this process work, so follow these three steps:

- Remove the NTFS volume if necessary

- Change the bootstrap routine

- Delete the Windows NT directory

Removing an NTFS Volume

If you have used the NTFS file system for your Windows NT installation, you should remove the NTFS partition before installing another operating system. If you have data files that you want to keep on the NTFS partition, you must copy them onto another mass storage device or back them up to a tape that can be read into the new operating system. Copying these files to a FAT volume is an effective and fast way to make them available to the operating system you move to.

After moving or archiving any data you wish to keep, you are ready to delete the NTFS partition. Removing an NTFS volume can be difficult because some versions of the MS-DOS FDISK program cannot delete an NTFS volume. No version of the MS-DOS FDISK program can remove an NTFS logical drive in an extended MS-DOS partition.

Perhaps the easiest way to remove an NTFS partition is with the Windows NT Setup program used to create them, as shown in Exercise 4.9.

Do not perform Exercise 4.9 unless you actually intend to remove an NTFS partition. This exercise can destroy information on your hard disk.

Removing the NTFS partition in which Windows NT is installed automatically removes the Windows NT files.

EXERCISE 4.9

Deleting an NTFS Partition

1. Insert the Windows NT Setup disk 1 and restart your computer.

2. Insert Setup disk 2 when prompted.

3. Press Enter at the Welcome to Setup screen.

4. Press Enter to automatically detect your mass storage devices or press S if you need to specify them manually.

5. Insert Setup disk 3 when prompted.

6. Press Enter when you have specified all necessary device drivers.

7. Press Page Down until you reach the end of the license agreement on the license page and then press F8.

8. Change your computer settings as necessary and press Enter.

9. Select the NTFS partition you wish to delete and press D.

10. Press L to confirm deletion. Note that the partition now shows up as free space in the partitions list.

11. Press F3 twice to exit NT Setup.

12. Press Enter to restart your computer.

Changing the Boot Operating System

Changing the boot operating system involves simply replacing the boot record of the primary hard disk with the boot loader for the operating system you will be using. In MS-DOS, the SYS utility performs this task. Other operating systems use various methods. Exercise 4.10 shows you how to change the boot loader to MS-DOS in an existing FAT partition, and Exercise 4.11 shows how to create an MS-DOS boot partition.

EXERCISE 4.10

Changing the Boot Loader to MS-DOS in an Existing FAT Partition

1. Boot an MS-DOS floppy disk containing the SYS utility or MS-DOS Setup disk 1.

2. Exit to the command prompt if necessary.

3. Type **SYS C:** at the A: prompt.

4. Restart the computer.

EXERCISE 4.11

Creating an MS-DOS Boot Partition

1. Boot an MS-DOS floppy disk containing the FDISK and format utilities or boot MS-DOS Setup disk 1.

2. Exit to the command prompt if necessary.

3. Type **FDISK** at the A: prompt.

4. Select option 1—Create MS-DOS Primary Partition.

5. Select Y when asked if you wish to use the entire space available and make the partition active.

6. Press Esc to exit FDISK and reboot the computer.

7. Exit to the command prompt if necessary after the computer reboots the system floppy.

8. Type **FORMAT C:/S** at the A: prompt.

9. Remove the floppy disk and reboot the computer when the format finishes.

This command replaces the bootstrap routing on the boot hard disk with the system files for MS-DOS. If you boot MS-DOS Setup disk 1 to install MS-DOS, this step will be performed for you.

Do not perform this exercise unless you intend to create an MS-DOS boot partition.

The exact steps shown in this exercise will not apply if you have other existing partitions on your disk.

Use caution when partitioning a disk containing other partitions.

Other operating systems use other methods too numerous to cover. You usually have an option to replace your current boot strap routine during the operating system installation. If you are installing another operating system, such as OS/2 or a version of UNIX, select the boot option that will replace the Windows NT boot loader.

Removing NT from a FAT Partition

If you have installed Windows NT in a FAT partition, removing it is simple. You need only delete the contents of two directories and a few boot files. Exercise 4.12 shows how to remove a Windows NT installation from a FAT volume in MS-DOS.

EXERCISE 4.12

Removing NT from a FAT Partition

1. Boot MS-DOS from a system disk containing the DELTREE utility.

2. Type **DELTREE WINNT** (or the name of your Windows NT directory) at the C: prompt.

3. Type **CD PROGRA~1**.

4. Type **DELTREE WINDOW~1**.

5. Type **DEL NTLDR**.

6. Type **DEL NTDETECT.COM**.

7. Type **DEL BOOT.INI**.

8. Type **DEL PAGEFILE.SYS**.

9. Type **DEL BOOTSEC.DOS**.

Summary

I NSTALLING WINDOWS NT Server 4 requires careful planning. Although NT runs on almost any Intel-based computer and many RISC-based computers, Windows NT does not support every hardware adapter and computer configuration. Therefore, you should consult the Hardware Compatibility List before making any decisions about which hardware to use.

Before you install Windows NT, you must make sure that your computer is configured properly. One good indication that your computer will work correctly with Windows NT is that it works with another operating system such as Windows 95.

You should carefully plan your Windows NT installation. Before you begin, you should know the name for the computer, the name of the workgroup or domain it will reside on, the network adapter card settings, and so on.

You can install Windows NT Server 4 in various ways: with or without boot disks, over a network, or from a CD-ROM. If you do not use the installation boot disks to boot, you will use either the Winnt program (from DOS or versions of Windows prior to Windows 95) or you will use the Winnt32 program (from Windows 95 and Windows NT).

The first stage of the installation process loads the Setup program and (optionally) stores the setup files on your computer's hard disk. The text-based Setup program detects your computer's hardware and prepares the hard disk and file system for Windows NT installation. The third (graphical) stage installs the various Windows NT components and configures the Windows NT operating system. Finally, once Windows NT is installed, you can log on and create user accounts and configure printers and other devices.

Review Questions

I. Any computer that can run DOS or Windows can run Windows NT Server.

A. True

B. False

2. You can read files on an NTFS partition from within the DOS and Windows operating systems.

    A. True

    B. False

3. You can configure your computer so that Windows NT Server will coexist with other operating systems such as Windows 95 and DOS.

    A. True

    B. False

4. You must have the floppy disks that came with the CD-ROM because that is the only way to install Windows NT Server.

    A. True

    B. False

5. If you perform an installation without a floppy disk, you must have a FAT file system on your computer's hard disk drive with sufficient free space to hold the Windows NT Server installation files.

    A. True

    B. False

6. You should have several primary domain controllers in your domain in case any one PDC fails.

    A. True

    B. False

7. The primary domain controller must be the first computer set up on the domain because it creates the domain.

    A. True

    B. False

8. Backup domain controllers can authenticate logon requests.

    A. True

    B. False

9. You can install a Windows NT Server as a member server or as a stand-alone server and later upgrade it to PDC or BDC status.

    A. True

    B. False

10. Upgrading an earlier version of Windows NT is quicker and easier than installing from scratch.

    A. True

    B. False

11. THE_SERVER is a good name for the server on your network.

    A. True

    B. False

12. You should leave the domain name for your domain to its default, which is DOMAIN.

    A. True

    B. False

13. Any version of DOS FDISK can remove NTFS partitions from your hard disk drive.

    A. True

    B. False

14. You will use the _____ program with the /b option to perform an installation without a floppy disk of Windows NT Server from DOS or Windows.

15. You will use the _____ program with the /ox option to re-create the boot floppies from the CD-ROM from within Windows NT Workstation or Server.

16. You can use the _____ _____ _____ program to create a network boot floppy that will attach to your file server so that you can install Windows NT Server from the network.

17. If you have a large number of similarly configured computers to which you must install Windows NT Server, you can use an _____ answer file to automate the process.

18. The _____ program helps you create files that automate the installation process.

19. A ____ _____ _____ or UDF contains unique information for each computer in automated installations of the Windows NT Server operating system.

20. The _____ utility records the difference between a normal Windows NT installation and an installation to which you have added files.

21. PDC stands for _____ _____ _____.

22. BDC stands for _____ _____ _____.

23. Windows NT Server computers that are members of a domain and are not domain controllers are called _____.

24. Windows NT Servers that are not members of a domain are called _____ _____ _____.

Storage

OST NETWORKS ARE installed to offer safe, reliable sharing and storage of information. Client/server networks use powerful computers called file servers to store data files centrally for access by all authorized users. Networked organizations store most, if not all, of their important information on file servers, so security and safety are critical issues. Most network operating systems, including Windows NT Server, offer many services to protect network data files. Refer to Chapter 10 for a complete discussion of file and network security.

Modern network operating systems also provide many options for file storage that can increase the speed, fault tolerance, and convenience of data mass storage. Windows NT supports disk striping, which allows the use of parallel hard disk drive transfers to improve performance, striping with fault tolerance to decrease the probability of down time, and volume sets, which allow you to easily create or extend large volumes across multiple physical hard disks.

This chapter covers the range of mass storage options available for your file server. The major topics are

- Storage strategies and options

- Fault tolerance and recovery strategies

- File compression and data replication

- Backup procedures

Planning Storage Strategies

LANNING STORAGE ON a regular desktop computer is as simple as installing a single large hard disk and formatting it. With operating systems such as MS-DOS or Windows, you have very little else to worry about. Network file servers, on the other hand, require quite a bit more planning because file storage is central to their purpose.

The three most important services a file server can provide are security, capacity, and speed. Security is a big topic and covers many aspects of server management, including fault tolerance, fault recovery, network security, and file system security. The overall performance and reliability of a file server is directly related to the performance and reliability of the disk subsystem, which is both the slowest and most likely to fail component in a file server. File servers are often "disk bound," or speed limited by their hard disk drives because the servers spend so much time accessing files and servicing multiple file requests from users simultaneously.

Speed is the third most important service a file server can provide, after security and capacity. You can use any of the following strategies to improve file service speed in Windows NT Server:

- Large RAM caches

- Disk striping

- Hardware redundant arrays of inexpensive disks (RAID) systems

Disk striping and mirroring are software implementations of RAID technology. For the sake of brevity, however, when we refer to RAID, we are referring to RAID implemented in hardware as a hard disk controller.

Before you purchase a file server, you should consider what is most important to you in storage options. Is speed critical? For application and database servers, it often is. How much fault tolerance do you need? Some organizations require fully replicated servers so that one can take over immediately if the other fails, while other organizations need only a daily backup to tape. Your answers to these questions will direct you to the appropriate options.

You can use the storage planning matrix in Table 5.1 to determine which technologies are best suited to your needs. Note that cost increases dramatically with both speed and fault tolerance because RAID adapters are expensive and because replication requires two file servers configured similarly. Also note that all forms of fault tolerance reduce speed somewhat. The table assumes you are performing a tape backup on a daily basis—otherwise the title of the One Day Data Lost column would be Data Lost Since Last Backup! Each technology in the matrix is discussed in detail in this chapter.

TABLE 5.1 Storage Planning Matrix		ONE DAY DATA LOST	NO DATA LOSS	NO DOWN TIME
	NORMAL SPEED	Tape Backup	RAID Level 1	Replication + RAID 1
	FAST	Stripe Set	Stripe Set with Parity	Replication + Stripe Set with Parity
	VERY FAST	RAID Level 0	RAID Level 5	Replication + RAID 5

Although you can implement a non-real-time form of replication with the Windows NT directory replication service, the limitations of this service make it far less reliable than the real-time forms of replication available from third-party vendors such as Vinca Corporation and Octopus. If you wish to rely on replication, contact these vendors to evaluate their products.

How Much Disk Space Is Enough?

Determining how much disk space is appropriate for a file server based on the number and types of users is a ritual shrouded in secrecy by the priesthood of network integrators. Their mantra goes something like this: Buy as much as you can afford to stuff in a single server.

We recommend, however, that you use the metric presented in Chapter 2 (for determining network load based upon the type of client used) to determine how much disk space you will need on a file server. Although no estimation can be precise in the absence of information about how users will store files and the policies you will implement, we are confident that this metric is a good, safe planning tool.

Each user on your network will have a file server to which he or she primarily attaches. This file server will store that user's home directory and most of the files the person uses. Organizations with fewer than 50 people usually have only one file server. Larger organizations may have tens or even hundreds of file servers, but they will usually be apportioned along departmental boundaries.

Refer to Table 2.1 for a list of metrics based on client type. To determine how much hard disk space you will need:

1. Sum the values of all clients who will attach to a single server.

2. Multiply that number by 50MB.

3. Add 300MB for the operating system.

4. Round this number to the nearest gigabyte.

If you implement mirroring, duplexing, or RAID level 1, you will need twice as much disk space. If you implement striping with parity or RAID level 5, you will need one additional hard disk to compensate for space taken by parity information.

As an example, if your network has 15 Power Macintoshes, 12 Windows clients, and six Windows NT Workstations, you will need

```
15 x 3 + 12 x 3 + 6 x 5 = 111 * 50 = 5550 + 300 = 5850MB = 6GB
```

of hard disk space.

Exercise 5.1 gives you some practice in estimating storage space. Remember that this metric in no way determines how much space you will use in practice—that value can only be determined empirically. Rather, use this tool for planning and estimating.

EXERCISE 5.1

Estimating Mass Storage Requirements

1. Calculate storage requirements for the following single-file-server network:

- 20 Windows 95 computers

- 10 Windows NT workstations

- 6 UNIX workstations

2. Calculate storage requirements for the following single-file–server network:

- 200 MS-DOS clients

Storage Options

WINDOWS NT HAS a dizzying array of storage options that you can mix and match to create the perfect file-service environment for your network. These options affect the speed, security, and fault tolerance of your network file server.

Choosing a File System

Windows NT currently supports two file systems: New Technology file system (NTFS) and file allocation tables (FAT). NTFS was created for Windows NT, whereas FAT supports smaller volumes like floppy disks and provides backward compatibility.

Windows NT prior to version 4.0 shipped with support for the HPFS file system used by OS/2. Although the operating system no longer ships with the file system driver for OS/2, you can retain support for OS/2 by installing Windows NT 4 as an upgrade to Windows NT 3.5.

You might want to use the FAT file system on a Windows NT Server, especially if you are dual booting another operating system like Windows 95 that requires access to your files and is not compatible with NTFS.

However, you should never use the FAT file system for disk partitions that you will share on a Windows NT Server, unless the volume is too small to support NTFS. Compared to NTFS, FAT is unsafe, unreliable, and likely to cause additional administrative hassle if not outright data loss. FAT does not support features like striping, which increases reliability and access times, or volume sets, which allow you to add storage space as necessary without affecting your users. You should use the FAT file system only on volumes that will be local to the server and not shared, such as a small one containing DOS configuration utilities.

If you are installing a server, use the NTFS file system. There is no good reason to use a FAT file system for shared volumes.

On a single hard disk drive, the FAT file system may be faster than NTFS in certain circumstances because of the overhead (data structures used to keep track of information in the system) associated with providing the security service. This slight performance difference does not compensate for the lack of security or reliability. Table 5.2 compares the features of NTFS and FAT.

TABLE 5.2 NTFS and FAT Compared		

FEATURE	NTFS	FAT
File-level security	Yes	No
POSIX support	Yes	No
Volume set extension	Yes	No

TABLE 5.2 NTFS and FAT Compared (continued)	**FEATURE**	**NTFS**	**FAT**
	Long file names	Yes	Yes*
	Supports multiple file forks for Macintosh files	Yes	No
	Log structured for fault tolerance	Yes	No
	Huge partitions	Yes	No
	Hot fixing	Yes	No
	File-level compression	Yes	No

* Long file names were added to the FAT file system with the release of Windows 95. MS-DOS does not support long file names.

Dual Booting

Dual boot is the feature of the Windows NT loader that allows you to specify alternative operating systems during the boot process. If another Microsoft operating system such as MS-DOS or Windows 95 already occupies the boot sector when you install Windows NT, Windows NT will include it in the operating system selection list. Therefore, if you would want to dual boot between Windows NT and another operating system, install the alternative operating system first.

WARNING

Allowing another operating to boot on a server is a potential security loophole, especially if you are using the FAT file system for file storage.

Many Plug-and-Play or hardware configuration utilities do not run under Windows NT because Windows NT does not allow user applications to access hardware directly. Installing a small (10MB) partition containing MS-DOS and MS-DOS drivers and configuration utilities for the computer is a good idea and is the only reason you would dual boot a computer configured as a server.

If you do have a small MS-DOS partition for drivers and software configuration tools, be sure to use the NTFS file system on your secure directories because it cannot be read from MS-DOS.

NTFS

NTFS represents the culmination of file system development at Microsoft. It is the preferred file system for use with Windows NT for the following reasons:

- NTFS was created specifically for Windows NT.

- NTFS implements many protective features to ensure the reliable storage and retrieval of data.

The following sections highlight the special features of NTFS and explain how to convert your file systems to NTFS.

Windows NT is the only operating system that supports NTFS. If you need to share files with another operating system on the same computer, you will need to choose a file system that is compatible with both operating systems.

NTFS has numerous features that make it more appropriate than FAT for Windows NT. You will need to understand the following NTFS features:

- Fault tolerance

- Security

- File and partition sizes

- File compression

- POSIX support

- Performance

Windows NT servers should without exception use NTFS as the primary file system. You may want to retain a FAT partition for MS-DOS–based drivers and configuration utilities, but it should not be your primary file system. The many virtues of NTFS are extolled in the sections that follow.

FAULT TOLERANCE NTFS logs all changes to the file system, which means that it can redo or undo every file or directory update to correct discrepancies arising from system failures or power losses. This process prevents the inconsistencies that occur in file systems like HPFS and FAT and that eventually lead to data loss if left uncorrected.

NTFS also uses a method called *hot fixing* to repair hard disk failures on the fly; hot fixing does not return an error message to the calling application.

After every write to a hard disk, the sector is reread to verify its integrity. If the data is different, the sector is flagged bad and the write is performed again to a different place.

SECURITY Windows NT objects maintain the permissions and auditing features implemented by the Windows NT security model. Consequently, permission to use (or even see) a file or directory can be maintained for each file by each user if you need that sort of detail. In practice, security is normally implemented on directories, usually by group. Files inherit the security attributes of the directories that contain them when they are created, and users inherit permissions based upon their group memberships.

Files created or copied into a directory inherit the security permissions of the directory. Files moved into a directory retain their original permissions and attributes unless they are moved between volumes.

Here's an easy way to remember how inheritance works: Files inherit directory permissions when they are created. Copying a file actually creates it in a new location, so the file inherits directory permissions. When you move a file within the same volume, Windows NT merely changes the file's directory entry to reflect its new location. (That's why moves are so fast.) Since the file is not being created, its permissions don't change. However, when you move a file between volumes, Windows NT can't simply change a directory entry because different volumes have different directory tables. Therefore, Windows NT copies the file (*creating* it in the new volume; hence the directory inheritance) and then deletes it from the previous location.

NTFS supports security on files and directories, but you need to use third-party utilities to implement data encryption.

FILE AND PARTITION SIZES NTFS can store files up to 16 exabytes in length. An exabyte is $2^{64\text{th}}$ power, or 4GB x 4GB. Windows NT extends considerably the maximum file and partition sizes when compared to FAT and HPFS.

The recommended minimum partition size for NTFS is 50MB. If you have a smaller partition, you should consider using the FAT file system for that partition because of the overhead required for NTFS features (e.g., security) and the more complex directory structure. Figure 5.1 shows the difference in overhead for a small 5MB partition formatted as both FAT and NTFS. Notice that NTFS takes nearly 25 percent of the partition's total space for directory overhead, whereas FAT takes almost none.

FIGURE 5.1

Comparing NFTS to FAT on small volumes.

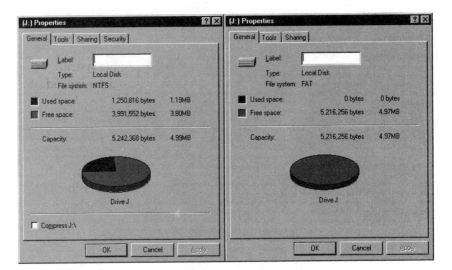

Even though NTFS takes up quite a bit of room on small partitions, you can reclaim that space by setting compression on the entire volume, which isn't available under the FAT file system.

You cannot "undelete," or restore, a deleted file under NTFS. Note that when you drag a file to the Recycle Bin, it is not actually deleted. Dragging files to the Recycle Bin merely copies them to a hidden area on the disk. They are not actually deleted until the size of your Recycle Bin exceeds the threshold programmed for automatic deletion or until you specifically empty it.

Using the Recycle Bin feature of the Explorer to "delete" unwanted files is the only way to restore them.

FILE COMPRESSION In addition to supporting very large file and partition sizes, NTFS provides real-time file compression. File compression removes redundancy from files, thereby decreasing their physical size.

NTFS compresses files on a file-by-file basis, which means that if anything goes wrong physically with a portion of data on the disk, it will affect only one file. This compression scheme differs from that used by MS-DOS, which can lose an entire volume of data if a sector goes bad.

Because NTFS is far more fault tolerant than earlier operating systems and because compression is implemented on a file-by-file basis, you need not be cautious about file compression. A good practice is to compress directories that contain information or programs not often used.

NTFS compression is a native part of the file system, so it is supported throughout Windows NT. In contrast, FAT compression schemes use a number of clever techniques to emulate the FAT file under what amounts to an entirely different compressed file system.

NTFS can compress or decompress individual files or all files in any directory. A compressed attribute bit is set when a file or the content a directory is compressed. This bit tells the system whether to decompress the file when it is read.

Because compression requires a small amount of overhead, compressing files that contain little or no redundancy could possibly make them larger. Although NTFS will leave the compression bit set, it will not actually compress files that would not benefit from compression.

NTFS favors speed over size when compressing and decompressing files. The average compression ratio for Windows NT is about 2 to 1, which means you should be able to store about twice as much data on a disk if you enable file compression. The file compression ratio depends on the amount of redundancy in a file and will vary greatly for files of different types.

When compressed files are moved or copied, the compression bit is maintained in the same manner as all permission information. When files are copied, the compression bit is set to match the target directory. When files are moved within the same partition, the compression bit remains the same regardless of the target directory's compression setting. When files are moved across partition boundaries, the compression bit is inherited from the target directory because a move across partitions actually copies a new file and deletes the old.

POSIX SUPPORT Windows NT supports POSIX standard network naming conventions such as case sensitivity, last access time stamping, and hard links.

Under POSIX applications, the files README.TXT, Readme.TXT, and readme.txt are three different files. You will not be able to test this feature with Windows NT applications, such as Explorer, because they treat file names as case insensitive.

Although Windows NT and NTFS support case-sensitive file names, Windows NT applications including Explorer, File Manager, and DOS command prompts, treat file names as case insensitive. Using Windows NT utilities to manage files created by POSIX applications can result in ambiguities that can cause data loss.

Hard links are directory entries that point to the same file on the disk. *Shortcuts*, on the other hand, are actually small files that contain information Windows NT uses to locate the original file.

Shortcuts actually have an .LNK extension that doesn't show up even when you have Explorer set to show files with their extensions.

To fully support POSIX, NTFS file names can include any characters except the following: ? " /\ <> * | and : .

PERFORMANCE To decrease fragmentation, Windows NT always attempts to save files in contiguous blocks.

Windows NT implements a B-tree directory structure similar to that used by HPFS, rather than the linked list directory structure used by the FAT file system. The B-tree directory speeds file finding considerably and reduces the possibility of a missing link resulting in data loss.

CONVERTING Most computers come with MS-DOS, Windows 95, or OS/2 (which uses the HPFS file system) factory installed, but few currently ship with Windows NT installed. Most users will want to convert their existing FAT or HPFS file systems to NTFS after they become comfortable using Windows NT as their primary operating system.

Converting a file system to NTFS is a one-way process. You cannot convert a file system back to FAT or HPFS if you change your mind.

Windows NT includes a conversion utility called, appropriately, CONVERT.EXE, that can convert FAT and HPFS volumes into NTFS volumes without erasing them or deleting any files. The conversion utility uses command-line syntax. You can launch it either from an MS-DOS box or from the run option in the Start menu.

Because NTFS requires more overhead than FAT and HPFS, you may not have enough free room on a partition to perform the conversion, especially on partitions smaller than 50MB. The conversion utility will let you know if a partition is too small (without changing the contents of your partition).

If you need to retain security attributes of an HPFS386 volume used by LAN Manager or OS/2 Warp Server, get the ACLCONV.EXE *utility from Microsoft and read the associated readme file.*

Exercise 5.2 shows you how to run the conversion utility.

EXERCISE 5.2

Converting FAT or HPFS Volumes to NTFS

1. Open the Start Menu.

2. Select Programs ➤ Command Prompt.

3. Type **CONVERT D:/FS:NTFS** at the command prompt and press Enter.

Notice the progression of the conversion utility.

FAT

The FAT file system was introduced with MS-DOS in 1981. Because of its tenure, it is supported in some sense by almost all computer operating systems, including Windows NT, Windows 95, MacOS, and most UNIX operating systems. Its near-universal support makes FAT appropriate for use on volumes that are used by more than one operating system, although this type of utilization is rare on a computer configured for use as a server.

The FAT file system keeps track of files in a partition using a file allocation table (hence the acronym) stored on the first few clusters of the partition. Each cluster on the disk has an entry in the FAT that indicates whether the cluster is in use or free. A root directory is stored on the disk immediately after the file allocation table containing the file and directory entries that point to the remaining files on the disk.

In the FAT file system, a directory is a list of file entries consisting of a file name—limited to 11 characters—and a period, a date and time stamp, and some attribute bits that show the status of the file, such as read only, deleted, and locked. If the attribute bit *directory* is set, the file is interpreted as another directory containing its own list of file entries. Because the root directory contains pointers to other directories and those directories can contain pointers to other directories, the FAT system is referred to as a *linked list file system*.

The FAT file system is a simple file system that does not store consistency information to ensure that files do not get corrupted in abnormal shutdowns, such as a power failure. Over time, FAT volumes can become increasingly corrupt. MS-DOS, Windows 95, and Windows NT all come with a utility to scan for and correct discrepancies in the FAT file system, but not all discrepancies can be detected or corrected in a FAT file system.

The FAT file system was designed to be used with DOS, which is a single-user operating system. FAT therefore does not record security information such as the owner or access permissions of a file or directory.

The simple structure of FAT does give it some advantages over more complex file systems like NTFS—primarily for volumes under 200MB. FAT has less overhead than do HPFS and NTFS for small volumes.

FAT VERSUS VFAT FAT currently exists in two versions: the original version, used in versions of DOS and Windows up to version 6.22 of MS-DOS and version 3.11 of Windows, and VFAT, which is used in MS-DOS version 7, Windows 95, and Windows NT version 4.0. The main difference between the versions is their file naming conventions.

VFAT is an extension to FAT that supports long file names for newer programs and operating systems while still allowing older programs to use the shorter file names that they expect. The differences between FAT and VFAT are detailed in the companion volume to this book, *MSCE: Windows NT Workstation Study Guide*.

FAT FILE SYSTEM CONSIDERATIONS Despite the FAT file system's security and corruptibility drawbacks, you might decide to use it to complement the NTFS partitions on a file server. For instance, Windows NT running on microprocessors other than the Intel 386 family can boot Windows NT only in a FAT partition.

The FAT file system is the only file system that Windows NT supports for use on floppy disks. It's also a good choice for removable cartridge hard disk drive with a capacity of 50MB or less.

Many Plug-and-Play configuration utilities for network adapters, modems, video adapters, and other hardware devices will not run under Windows NT, which does not allow hardware-level access to User mode programs. These programs will have to reside in a FAT partition to be accessed from MS-DOS. Therefore, you should keep an MS-DOS boot partition large enough to contain hardware configuration utilities and free space for a reinstallation should you ever need it.

SUMMARY OF FAT FEATURES

- FAT supports files and partitions as large as 4GB.

- FAT is accessible by many operating systems, including MS-DOS, Windows NT, Windows 95, OS/2, MacOS, and many variants of the UNIX family of operating systems. FAT is a nearly universal file system.

- FAT has the least file system overhead of any modern file system, which makes it suitable for small partitions (less than 50MB).

- FAT is the only widely supported PC-compatible file system that is used on floppy disks.

FAT SECURITY CONSIDERATIONS   Unfortunately, the FAT file system has no real provisions for security. Windows NT can keep files secure over the network, but if you implement a FAT file system on your file server, nothing prevents a user from walking up to your file server, booting an MS-DOS floppy, and walking away with your data. NTFS embeds security information for each file and is not accessible from MS-DOS, effectively closing this sort of security loophole.

If security is any concern at all in your organization, do not use the FAT file system to store important data on a file server.

Partitions and Volumes

Hard disks, like file cabinets, are not simply vast places to put data. They have a well-defined structure of partitions and volumes that allows the various file systems to coexist peacefully on the same disk. You will encounter partitions and volumes again when you learn how to use the Disk Administrator (later in this chapter). The following sections explain how hard disks are arranged.

Partitions

Hard disks are subdivided into partitions. Each partition contains one volume maintained by any file system. Note that each partition may be created and maintained by any operating system, not just by Windows NT. Volumes are partitions with file systems in them. When you format a partition, you are creating a volume.

Partitions allow one hard disk to appear as many hard disks. This scheme allows you to divide your hard disk according to function or to support foreign file systems on your physical hard disk. (*Foreign file systems* are file systems that are not recognized by Windows NT, such as UNIX file systems.)

Changing the partitions of a disk destroys all the data in the partitions being changed. Consequently, you must partition a disk correctly the first time! Unless you have a reason to do otherwise, create one partition as large as your disk will support.

Windows NT also supports three special types of partitions: stripe sets, stripe sets with parity, and volume sets. These partitions can span multiple hard disk drives a provide a way to implement faster, more fault tolerant, or larger volumes than can be created with a single partition.

When installing the operating system, Windows NT may warn you that your disk has more than 1,024 cylinders. In this case, you should enable sector translation (SCSI disks) or large block allocation (IDE disks) in the BIOS of your disk controller to give Windows NT access to the entire disk without partitioning it.

MASTER BOOT RECORD The master boot record is the first portion of data on a hard disk. It is reserved for the BIOS bootstrap routine, which contains low-level code that redirects the loading of the operating system to the partition marked as active. This indirect method allows up to four bootable partitions to exist on the same disk and, therefore, multiple operating systems.

THE PARTITION TABLE The partition table is the index of partitions used by the bootstrap routine to identify distinct portions of the disk. File systems can create volumes only within partitions. Partition entries in the partition table contain a simple starting position on the disk and the length (or number of clusters) of the partition.

Volumes

A volume is the structure imposed upon a partition to allow files to be indexed. A volume contains the table of contents of the disk, called the *root directory*. The volume also maintains allocation tables that show what space in the volume is occupied, thus ensuring that no file overwrites another by being stored in the same location. File systems operate with volume information to determine where to store files and how to retrieve them.

Standard volumes are simply regular formatted partitions. They are the same as volumes from any other operating system. Windows NT allows two formats for standard volumes: FAT and NTFS.

Some file systems, such as Windows NT, can create logical partitions containing volumes that extend across more than one physical partition. Volume sets and stripe sets are both examples of logical partitions that extend across multiple physical partitions.

DRIVE LETTERS Drive letters are assigned to volumes for easy identification when referring to the exact location of a file. MS-DOS assigned drive letters as it found devices when booting, starting with C for hard disks. Windows NT allows the administrator to assign drive letters as necessary. This system allows drives migrated from DOS to Windows NT to retain their old drive letter even if a new disk is installed.

VOLUME SETS Up to 32 partitions can be combined into one volume known as a *volume set*. That volume set receives a single drive letter and can be treated as a single partition for the purposes of formatting and file system use by the operating system. The partitions combined into a volume set do not have to be the same size or on the same drive or the same type of drive (SCSI, ESDI, or IDE). For example, a 340MB partition on one drive can be combined with a 500MB partition on another drive to make a single 840MB partition. Drive E in Figure 5.2 is a volume set.

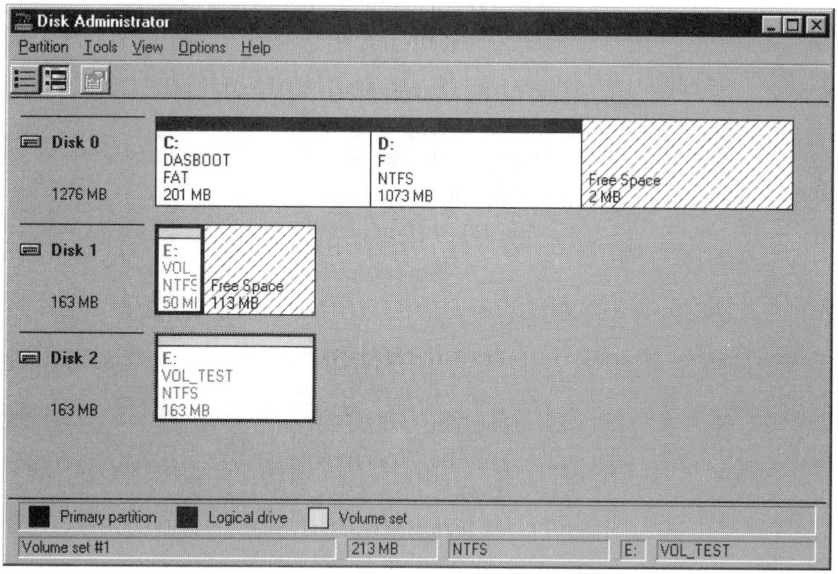

FIGURE 5.2

Drive E in the Disk Administrator window is an example of a volume set.

When data is stored to a volume set, the data is stored to the partitions one partition at a time. When one partition is full, the next partition is used.

The system and boot partitions cannot be a part of a volume or stripe set.

You might wish to create a volume set if you have several small partitions on hard disks or if you have several smaller hard disks that you want to treat as one large hard disk.

Volume sets do not provide fault tolerance to your file storage; they do not implement fault or error recovery information beyond that already provided by the file system. In fact, if a fault occurs with any one partition (or, therefore, hard disk) in a volume set, the whole volume set may be unusable.

STRIPE SETS A stripe set is like a volume set except that all the stripe set's partitions must be on different drives and should be the same size. The space from each of the drives is combined into one large volume like in a volume set, but in a stripe set the data is stored evenly across all of the partitions of the stripe set instead of to one partition at a time. Figure 5.3 shows a stripe set of two drives.

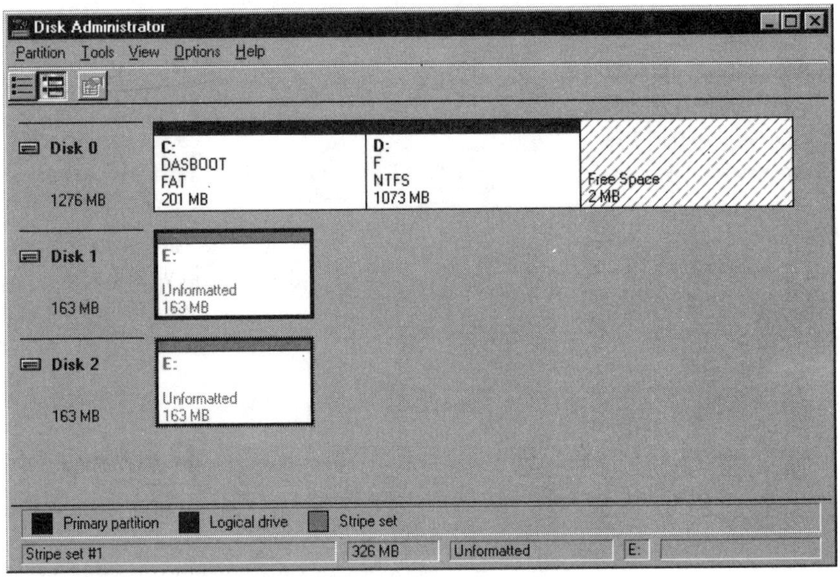

FIGURE 5.3

Drive E is a stripe set that has not yet been formatted with NTFS.

Because of the way data is stored to a stripe set, stripe sets can be much faster than volume sets or even single partitions. A stripe set with multiple disk drive controllers (or a sophisticated disk drive controller that can communicate with several drives at a time) can transfer more information than a single drive controller connected to a single drive can transfer. Figure 5.4 shows how stripe blocks are set up on different disks.

STRIPE SETS WITH PARITY Stripe sets with parity add an extra twist to stripe sets that make them much more fault tolerant than normal volumes. A stripe set with parity reserves an amount of space equal to the size of one hard disk drive for parity information. The parity information is used to re-create information in the event that one of the hard disks in the stripe set fails. The data in the parity blocks stored on the other hard disks will be equal to the data on the failed drive when run through the mathematical operation that created the parity information.

FIGURE 5.4

A stripe volume across
three disks.

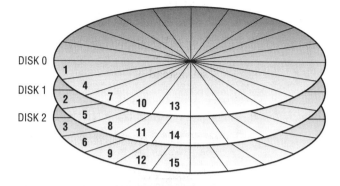

In effect, when a single drive fails, the other drives can pick up the slack until the first drive is replaced. Because drives tend to fail one at a time, in theory your server need never go down to hard disk failure; the administrator will be able to replace disks as they go bad without affecting the data on the disk set. Of course, this strategy only works if the disks fail one at a time.

Fault Tolerance and Fault Recovery

THE NEXT MAJOR topics in this chapter are the critical issues of fault tolerance and fault recovery. *Fault tolerance* encompasses all measures taken to protect data and preserve accessibility in the presence of a hardware failure. Fault tolerance comes in many different degrees and is implemented for many different reasons. Tape backup is actually not fault tolerance, but fault recovery. The difference between the two is that fault tolerance preserves accessibility to data online, while *fault recovery* makes the recovery of data possible but does not preserve accessibility. We discuss the following levels of fault tolerance for servers, starting with the minimum level:

- Tape backup
- Mirroring
- Duplexing
- Striping with parity
- RAID
- Replication

Tape Backup

Tape backup (also called *archiving*) is the minimum level of fault tolerance that should exist for all servers. Tape backup preserves a copy of all the data on a file server on tape in case the server's hard disk drives fail. Data can be restored from the backup tape after a file server has been repaired.

If tape backup is the only fault tolerance system in use, the worst-case scenario for data loss is the amount of information created or changed from the time of the last backup until the server failed. Tape backup systems are most effective when backups occur nightly. This schedule makes the worst-case data loss equal to one work day, which is acceptable for most organizations. When this degree of loss is not acceptable, other fault tolerance systems should be used because the load created by a tape backup operation can be excessive during working hours.

Tape Backup Systems

Tape backup systems can be implemented either locally or over the network.

- **Local tape backup** refers to placing a tape drive in every file server and copying files from that server's hard disk drive to its tape drive.

- **Networked tape backup** refers to copying files from every server on the network to a single tape server that copies all the files to tape in a central location.

The features, benefits, and drawbacks of both methods are discussed below.

LOCAL TAPE BACKUP Local tape backup is the form normally used in single-server networks. The tape software is run on the server and generally set up to automatically backup the network on a daily basis. Windows NT ships with all the software necessary to automate the backup process.

BENEFITS OF LOCAL TAPE BACKUP

- Data is not transmitted over the network.

- Backups can occur during periods of use without causing network load.

- Data closely matches the structure of the hard disk drives.

- Easy access to the Registry.

- Restoration possible without a functioning network.

- Works with Windows NT tape backup software.

DRAWBACKS OF LOCAL TAPE BACKUP

- Additional administrative burden for larger networks.

- Additional hardware cost.

NETWORKED TAPE BACKUP Networked tape backup is generally used in larger multiserver networks, especially when servers are distributed physically throughout the organization. Simply changing daily backup tapes in many servers that are distributed throughout an organization could be a full-time job without networked archiving. Tape servers do not have to be dedicated to archiving. They can be normal file servers, attached to a very large capacity tape device, that act as a file servers during operating hours and as tape servers during periods of inactivity. Another common arrangement is for network administrators to use their own administration workstation as a tape server.

BENEFITS OF NETWORKED TAPE BACKUP

- One tape server can back up multiple servers.

- Less administrative work for larger networks.

DRAWBACKS OF NETWORKED TAPE BACKUP

- Massive archive operations can take longer than overnight, thus causing a network load during operating hours.

- All files are transmitted over the network, creating a possible security loophole for extremely sensitive information.

- Single point of archive failure—if the tape server fails, no archiving occurs.

- Network failure preempts backup operation.

- Additional software costs.

The type of backup system you install depends upon your needs. However, because of the additional software costs and the reduced fault tolerance of networked tape backups, we recommend using local backups unless it is administratively prohibitive.

Backup Styles

Just as you have a choice of backup system types, you also have a choice of ways to perform backups. The two most common methods are full system backups and incremental backups.

FULL SYSTEM BACKUPS Full system backups copy all the server hard disk drives on a daily basis. This method is simple to set up and easy to restore from, since every tape contains every file on the server. You don't have to keep track of tape catalogs or backup databases. You can also perform full system backups in a "copy only" mode that does not disturb the archive bit.

Unfortunately, full system backups require tape drives that are larger than all the data stored on your server and fast enough to transfer all that data during idle periods. If your organization works in two shifts from 6:00 a.m. to 10:00 p.m., your idle time is eight hours. If your tape backup system can back up and verify 10MB per minute, you are limited to backing up 4,800MB—less than the maximum capacity of many networks.

Full system backups also require the use of tape drives and tapes that are larger than the entire capacity of the network. These devices are very expensive, as are the tapes they use.

INCREMENTAL BACKUPS Incremental backups are an alternative to using large expensive tapes and tape drives. An incremental backup uses a file attribute bit called the *archive bit* to mark files as having been backed up.

When the file system modifies or creates a file, the archive bit is set, indicating that the file needs to be backed up. Tape backup programs clear the archive bit when the file is backed up to indicate that it no longer needs to be archived. Incremental backups simply copy those files on the file server that have the archive bit set—those that have not already been backed up.

Generally, a full system backup is performed when free time is available on the network, like weekends, and someone is on hand to change tapes if the tape device capacity is smaller than the capacity of the server. Then daily incremental backups are performed over night.

Incremental backups are more administrative hassle than full system backups. The location of a single file is usually impossible to find unless the tape backup software keeps a database of files and the tape volumes they've been written to. Therefore, restoring a system completely requires restoring the contents of a number of tapes.

TAPE ROTATION Tape rotation refers to the reuse of tape media. It doesn't make much sense to keep a copy of every day of a network's existence in a big tape library if the only purpose for your archiving is to restore the network in the event of a failure. You can reuse tapes on a rotating basis when the tapes are so far out-of-date that you no longer care about the data.

For some organizations, that date might be yesterday, and they may rotate between only two tape sets. Other organizations will keep backup tapes for up to a month. Most organizations rarely need to go longer than a week with incremental backup tapes, which is the rotation recommended by most archive specialists and tape backup companies.

To implement a fail-safe network, you must keep a recent full system copy off-site. All the fault tolerance in the world won't restore your network if your facility is destroyed by an act of Godzilla. If your facility is destroyed (an almost-common event in southern California), your on-site tape backup sets will be destroyed with it. According to a study performed by a major archiving company, almost 80 percent of businesses that suffered a total data loss and did not have an off-site backup went out of business within two years.

Figure 5.5 shows three common tape rotations:

- Every other day, which is implemented simply to keep a backup copy off-site

- Weekly full backups with daily incremental

- Monthly, with four full backups and daily incremental backups

The monthly scheme ensures that files can be restored for up to a month in the event that they have been accidentally erased. There is no fault tolerance reason for keeping more than two full system backups.

FIGURE 5.5

Tape rotation policies.

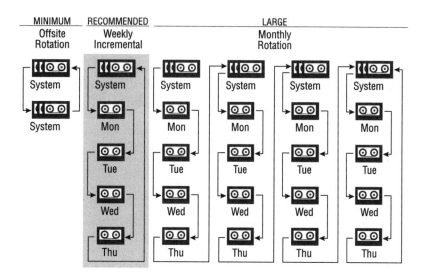

The backup policy of many organizations also stipulates permanently keeping a complete archive on a periodic basis—generally weekly. This policy guarantees that any file of importance can be retrieved even if it was deleted years ago (assuming, of course, that you still have equipment that can read the archived tape!). The policy also guarantees that you will have to purchase backup media on a continuing basis.

Remember that your tape rotation policy does not affect the number of backups you perform—that will always remain constant at one per day. It affects only the way you use your media and how many tapes you must purchase.

Mirroring

Disk mirroring is the process of performing every write operation in a file server to two identical disks. Then, in the event that the primary disk fails, the secondary disk is ready to take over instantly as an exact copy. This technique allows the server to keep the volume online, even though the primary hard disk has failed.

Disk mirroring and duplexing is RAID level 1. Microsoft uses the terms mirroring *and* duplexing *to refer to RAID level 1 as performed by Windows NT.*

Disk mirroring is the most basic form of fault tolerance. It preserves accessibility in the event of a hard disk failure. Windows NT Server supports disk mirroring by marking a partition as a mirror to another partition. Windows NT will keep the two partitions synchronized and will inform you when the primary or secondary disk has failed. Disk mirroring preserves accessibility only in the event of hard disk failure.

Duplexing

Disk duplexing is related to disk mirroring but adds another level of fault tolerance: the hard disk controller. Disk duplexing stipulates that two hard disk controllers are used, with two disks attached, to perform the mirroring function. If one of the hard disk controllers fails, the system will fall over to the other controller, preserving accessibility. Disk mirroring is not tolerant of hard disk controller failure.

Hard disk drive controller failure is far less common than it used to be, so disk duplexing is not as important as it once was. Windows NT Server makes no differentiation between disk mirroring and disk duplexing. To duplex two disks on different controllers, simply install the necessary hardware and mirror the partitions as you would for disk mirroring.

Striping with Parity

Striping with parity is a fault tolerance measure added to shore up disk striping, which alone actually reduces the fault tolerance of a disk subsystem by multiplying the probability of disk subsystem failure by the number of disks in the stripe set. Adding a parity stripe to a stripe set allows any one disk in the stripe set to fail without denying access to the disk set because the data on the failed drive can be calculated from the parity stripe, which exists across the remaining drives. Striping with parity is the Windows NT term for its software implementation of RAID level 5.

Because the failure of more than one disk at a time is very unusual (except when external factors cause the failure), striping with parity affords the same level of fault tolerance as disk mirroring or duplexing, depending upon how many drive controllers are involved.

Setting up a stripe volume with parity is discussed in the "Working with the Disk Administrator" section.

Hardware RAID

RAID refers to the simultaneous use of multiple hard disk drives to increase the fault tolerance and/or speed of a disk subsystem. Windows NT implements the following RAID levels:

- RAID level 0 (striping)

- RAID level 1 (mirroring)

- RAID level 5 (striping with parity) in software

Hardware RAID controllers are, in effect, special hard disk controllers that control all the hard disk drives independently on the same bus and calculate or derive the stripe data. RAID controllers can improve performance significantly because they are not distracted by the other processing chores the CPU must perform and because they relieve the processor of a burdensome task. Think of RAID controllers as disk coprocessors. Although the term *RAID* also applies to software-only systems like those implemented by Windows NT, people usually mean hardware RAID controllers when they use the term.

Level 0

RAID level 0 is not implemented for fault tolerance, as it actually decreases the fault tolerance of the disk subsystem. Rather, RAID level 0 is the ultimate in disk performance: parallel drives without the performance penalty of deriving a parity stripe. RAID level 0 should not be implemented without another fault tolerance or fault recovery system in place.

Level 1

RAID level 1 is disk mirroring. Many less expensive disk controllers offer RAID level 1 as an option, which frees Windows NT from dealing with the overhead of providing the mirrored disk function. Unfortunately, RAID level 1 hardware controllers cannot implement disk duplexing, which requires more than one controller and, therefore, must be controlled by Windows NT.

Level 5

RAID level 5 is the most commonly implemented form of hardware RAID: parallel drives with parity stripe. This level offers a good mix of speed and safety.

RAID controllers are both very fast and fault tolerant for the following reasons:

- Their only purpose is to split data transferred to and from the computer into the optimal size for transfer to the disks attached.

- They usually have robust caches.

- They use a dedicated microprocessor to calculate and derive the stripe set.

Unfortunately, they are also very expensive. The price of a RAID controller can account for one-third of the total cost of a server.

Server Replication

Replication is the ultimate form of fault tolerance. Replication provides a backup in the event of any hardware failure on the primary server by copying data between the primary and the backup server continually. In the event that the primary server is unavailable for any reason, network traffic can be redirected to the backup server.

Any component failure is protected by replication, not just disk or disk controller failures as protected by the fault tolerance systems discussed thus far. Consequently, replication can be the only fault tolerance system you implement, replacing disk mirroring, duplexing, or RAID. And because both servers can be operational servers under Windows NT, replication can be performed very inexpensively if you already have two servers.

Windows NT comes with a limited replication service that can copy data between two computers. One computer must be set up as the export computer (which can only be a Windows NT Server), and the other is set up as the import computer (which can be any Windows NT machine). Data is transferred from the export computer to the import computer as soon as it is closed and has not changed for two minutes.

The directory replicator service replicates files only after they are closed. As a result, files that are constantly open, such as databases, will not be replicated until every user has closed them, which may not occur in the case of database files.

A serious limitation of Microsoft's implementation of directory replication is that it does not copy open files. Therefore, you should consider using a true real-time replication package from a third party (Vinca and Octopus both provide very robust replication software) if you intend to rely on server replication for fault tolerance. Microsoft's implementation is best suited for distributing user profiles, logon scripts, and other administrative files.

Working with the Disk Administrator

THE INFORMATION PRESENTED next builds on what you learned about hard disks and file systems earlier in the chapter. This section shows you how to use the Windows NT Disk Administrator to do the following:

- Create partitions and volume sets

- Format volumes

- Create, extend, delete, stripe, and make active volume sets.

To reach the Disk Administrator:

1. Go to the Start menu.

2. Select Programs ➤ Administrative Tools.

The Disk Administrator shows you a graphical view of the hard disks and partitions that exist in your Windows NT server. The graphical display shows the drives, their capacities, the volumes with their volume names, volume characteristics (stripe set, mirror set, volume set), file system types, volume size, and drive letters. See Figure 5.6 for a view of the main Disk Administrator window.

The Disk Administrator program performs all the functions of the MS-DOS FDISK and Microsoft LAN Manager fault tolerance character-based applications, and more.

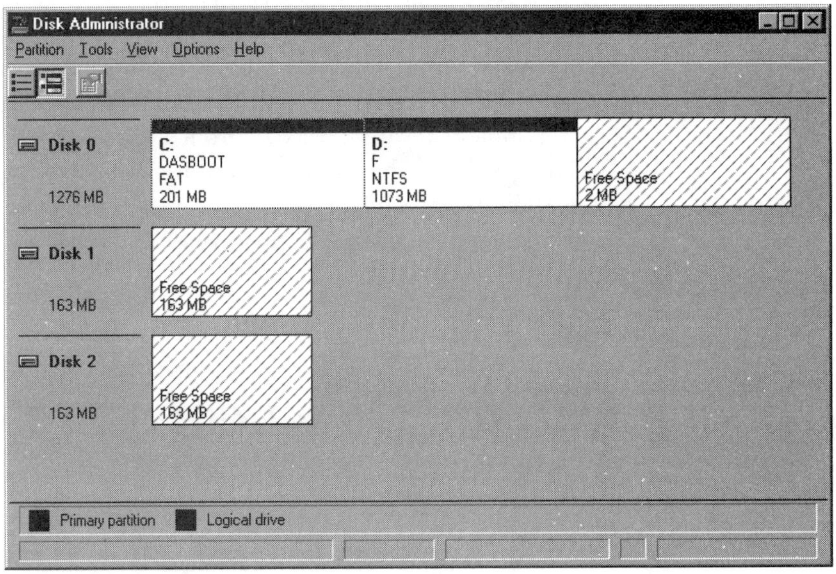

FIGURE 5.6

You use the Disk Administrator to manage volumes and partitions on a Windows NT Server.

Creating and Deleting Partitions

A disk must be partitioned before it is formatted with a file system. Some hard disks come partitioned and formatted (usually with the FAT file system), but many do not. You may need to partition a new hard drive after installing it.

All hard disks sold today come with a low-level, or hardware-level, format applied by hard disk controllers from the factory. Some SCSI hard disk controllers may require you to perform a low-level format with that controller for hard disks. Check the device's documentation to determine if this format is necessary and, if so, how to do it.

A disk with no partitions set up contains only free space. You can create a partition on a hard disk only when free space is available on that hard disk, and the partition will be taken from that free space. Deleting a partition returns the space occupied by that partition to the free space for that drive. If you have two DOS partitions on a drive, for example, and you wish to make one large NTFS partition, you will first have to delete the two DOS partitions so that you can create the NTFS partition.

You may create a partition as large as the available free space or any size (in megabytes) smaller. Any area not used by the new partition will be returned to the free space, which you can use to make more partitions. Exercise 5.3 shows you how to create a partition. Figure 5.7 shows the Create Primary Partition window.

FIGURE 5.7

Select the size of the new partition in the Create Primary Partition window.

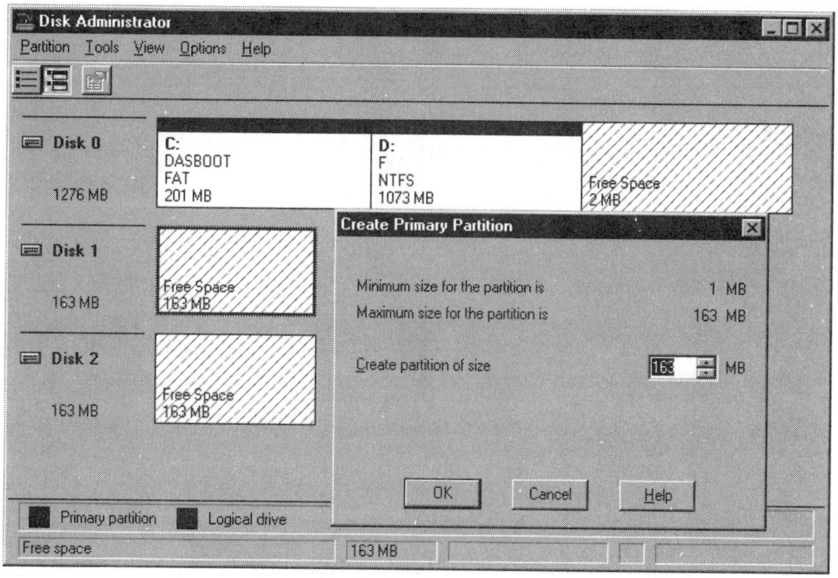

EXERCISE 5.3

Creating a Partition

1. Select Start ➤ Programs ➤ Administrative Tools ➤ Disk Administrator.

2. Select the free space on the drive that will contain the new partition. Refer to Figure 5.7.

3. Select Partition ➤ Create. You will be prompted for the size of the partition. The default is the amount of free space left on the drive.

4. Click OK.

5. Select Partition ➤ Commit Changes Now...

6. Select Yes in the confirmation window.

7. Click OK in the window that announces that Disk Administrator has performed the operation successfully.

Deleting a partition destroys any information stored in a file system on that partition, so be very careful when you delete partitions. The Disk Administrator will warn you when you are attempting to delete a partition that has a file system installed on it. See Exercise 5.4 for an example of deleting a partition.

If you perform Exercise 5.4 on any partition except the one created in Exercise 5.3, you will lose data!

Windows NT assigns a drive letter to each partition as you create it. Windows NT may rearrange the drive letters when it does so, and this change may confuse programs or users that expect files to be on certain drives.

You do not have to leave the partitions with the drive letters that the Disk Administrator has assigned. You can use the Disk Administrator to assign drive letters to partitions. As you install and remove hard drives in your computer, you should make sure that the drive letters for partitions that hold programs remain the same; otherwise, some programs may fail to work.

EXERCISE 5.4

Deleting a Partition

1. Select Start ➤ Programs ➤ Administrative Tools ➤ Disk Administrator.

2. Select the partition you wish to delete.

3. Select Partition ➤ Delete. The Disk Administrator will announce that all data on the partition will be lost and ask if you wish to proceed.

4. Click the Yes button.

5. Select Partition ➤ Commit Changes Now.

6. Select Yes in the confirmation window.

7. Click OK in the window that announces that Disk Administrator has performed the operation successfully.

Primary and Extended Partitions

When you create a partition it can either be a primary partition or an extended partition. The Create... menu item in the Partition menu creates a primary partition in the free space of the hard drive. To create an extended partition, use the Create Extended... menu selection instead.

The maximum number of primary partitions on a hard disk is four. This limitation is an artifact from the way that early IBM PC–compatible computers organized information on hard disks. Early DOS computers using the FAT file system could not use a disk partition larger than 32MB. As hard disks grew to sizes much larger than 128MB, the industry soon determined that four partitions would not be adequate to use the entire space of large drives. To overcome the four-partition limitation, any one (but only one) of the four partitions can be designated an *extended* partition. You can create many logical drives within the extended partition.

MS-DOS 5.0 and earlier versions of DOS could see only one primary partition. These versions of DOS do not see any other primary partitions even if the partitions have been formatted with a DOS file system. Versions of DOS earlier than 3.3 will not be able to use a partition larger than 32MB.

Extended partitions are not really necessary since the advent of operating systems that can handle large partitions. The only good reasons to partition a disk below its maximum size are

- To have more than one bootable operating system on a disk

- To have more than one file system on a disk

- To partition operating system files from user files so user files can't run the operating system out of space

- To use excess space on a stripe volume when smaller drives are part of the stripe set

You are more likely to be combining the space of multiple physical disks rather than splitting the space of a single disk into multiple partitions. For the vast majority of applications, four partitions per disk are more than enough.

After deleting partitions on a hard disk, you may see your free space divided into two portions. This happens because an extended partition exists on the drive. Right-clicking the free space portion that is the extended partition will invoke a pop-up menu that contains a delete option. Use the delete option to remove the unwanted free space portion.

Active Partitions

The partition that your computer boots on startup is the active partition. To mark a partition active, select Partition ➤ Mark Active in the Disk Administrator. Only one primary partition may be marked active at a time.

In IBM compatibles only a primary partition can be a boot partition. However, Windows NT does not have to reside in a primary partition—in fact, Windows NT can reside in any sufficiently large partition on any of the hard disks in your computer. But the Windows NT boot loader must reside in the primary partition that has been marked as the booting partition. The boot loader in the Windows NT boot partition will then load the Windows NT operating system from wherever it has been installed.

Terminology: For Windows NT, Microsoft uses the term system partition to refer to the partition that contains the boot files such as NTLDR and the term boot partition to refer to the volume containing the Windows NT operating system files. This terminology conflicts with prior Microsoft usage for other operating systems, general industry usage, and common sense. The MSCE exams use the Microsoft definitions.

In order for the Windows NT boot loader to run on Intel computers, the active partition must contain the Windows NT startup files, which include NTLDR, BOOT.INI, and NTDETECT.COM. In Windows NT terminology, the partition that contains the startup files is called the *system partition*. The partition with the Windows NT operating system files (the partition that has the System32\ directory) is called the *boot partition*. The boot partition can be the same as the system partition, or it can be in another volume or on another hard disk drive.

Committing Changes

When creating and deleting partitions with the Disk Administrator utility, the changes you make are not committed (saved) to the hard disk until you either exit the program and confirm the changes or until you select Partition ➤ Commit Changes Now.

Unlike some other operating systems, Windows NT Server allows an administrator to delete, create, format, and use a partition without rebooting the computer.

Volumes and Volume Sets

Creating a volume set simply involves selecting the partitions you want to participate in the volume set. Because more than one hard disk is usually part of a volume set, its reliability is reduced to that of the least reliable drive in the set. This makes volume sets less fault tolerant than simply leaving the disks as separate drives, because any single drive failure will cause the data on all drives to be inaccessible. The convenience of volume sets often outweighs their reduced fault tolerance if other fault-tolerant systems are in place. Exercise 5.5 shows the process of creating a volume set. Since Windows NT implements volume and stripe sets in software, NT must be running in order to recognize them. Naturally then, the boot and system partitions cannot be part of a volume or stripe set.

Other operating systems cannot recognize data contained in volume or stripe sets even if they are FAT formatted.

Windows NT may have difficulty repairing a volume set if your drive configuration information is lost. Always use offline backup for volume sets.

EXERCISE 5.5

Creating a Volume Set

1. Select Start ➤ Programs ➤ Administrative Tools ➤ Disk Administrator.

2. Select the free space from which you will make the first part of the volume set.

3. Hold down the Control key and select the additional free space that will contain the extension to the volume set. Repeat this step for as many additional free space areas as will be part of the volume set.

4. Select Create Volume Set from the Partition menu. You will be prompted for the size of the volume set. The default is the current size plus the amount of free space left on the drive.

5. Click OK.

6. Select Partition ➤ Commit Changes Now.

7. Select Yes in the confirmation window.

8. Click OK in the window that announces that Disk Administrator has performed the operation successfully.

You may be prompted to reboot your computer for the changes to take effect.

Extending Volume Sets

If you have formatted a volume set with NTFS, you can also extend the volume set. You may wish to extend a volume set if the file system on the volume set is full or almost full.

Extending a volume set is a great way to add more space to a nearly full NTFS volume. Simply add another hard disk to your computer and add that disk to the volume set with the Disk Administrator utility.

You can create and extend volume sets, but you cannot shrink a volume set. Instead you must delete it, returning the space it occupied to free space (and discarding all information that was stored in the volume set). You can then create a new volume or volume set that is smaller than the original. Follow the steps outlined in Exercise 5.6 to extend a volume set.

EXERCISE 5.6

Extending a Volume Set

1. Select Start ➤ Programs ➤ Administrative Tools ➤ Disk Administrator.

2. Select the NTFS volume set that you will extend.

3. Hold down the Control key and select the free space on the drive that will contain the extension to the volume set. Repeat this step for as many additional partitions as will be part of the volume set.

4. Select Partition ➤ Extend Volume Set. You will be prompted for the new size of the volume set. The default is the current size plus the amount of free space left on the drive.

5. Click OK.

6. Select Partition ➤ Commit Changes Now.

7. Select Yes in the confirmation window.

8. Click OK in the window that announces that Disk Administrator has performed the operation successfully.

You may be prompted to reboot your computer for the changes to take effect.

Creating Stripe Sets

In a stripe set, data is stored evenly across all the disks in the set, one row at a time, in 64K blocks. This arrangement allows the operating system to divide the commands among the drives and issue concurrent commands to each drive; then each drive can perform the operations simultaneously. You must have at least two physical disks to create a stripe set—you can't use two free space areas on the same disk. Using stripe sets can enhance read and write performance in the file system, especially if you have several hard drive controllers or the hard drive controller is sophisticated and can issue multiple commands to multiple drives. Exercise 5.7 explains how to create a stripe set.

EXERCISE 5.7

Creating a Stripe Set

1. Select Start ➢ Programs ➢ Administrative Tools ➢ Disk Administrator.

2. Select the free space on the first drive that will be a part of the stripe set.

3. Hold down the Control key and select the free space on the drive that will contain the next partition of the stripe set. Repeat this step for as many additional drives as will be part of the stripe set.

4. Select Partition ➢ Create Stripe Set. You will be prompted for the size of the stripe set. The default is the smallest free space among the drives multiplied by the number of drives selected.

5. Click OK.

6. Select Partition ➢ Commit Changes Now.

7. Select Yes in the confirmation window.

8. Click OK in the window that announces that Disk Administrator has performed the operation successfully.

You may be prompted to reboot your computer for the changes to take effect.

The system and boot partitions cannot be a part of a stripe set.

Creating Stripe Sets with Parity

In a stripe set with parity, the data is stored evenly across all the disks in the set, one row at a time, in 64K blocks. For each row, a special parity block is calculated and stored on one of the hard disks. The hard disk that stores the parity block changes with each block. This arrangement allows the operating system to divide the commands among the drives and issue concurrent commands to each drive; then each drive can perform the operations simultaneously. The system can derive the data stored on any one failed disk from the parity stripe blocks on the remaining disks.

Striping with parity generally takes longer than a typical volume during writes because of the compute overhead of calculating a stripe block, but it is faster during reads if the stripe set is healthy. You must have at least three physical disks in a stripe set to gain any advantage over disk mirroring, so Windows NT will not allow you to create a stripe set with less than three. See Exercise 5.8 for an example of creating a stripe set.

EXERCISE 5.8

Creating a Stripe Set with Parity

1. Select Start ➤ Programs ➤ Administrative Tools ➤ Disk Administrator.

2. Select the free space on the first drive that will be a part of the stripe set with parity.

3. Hold down the Control key and select the free space on the drive that will contain the next partition of the stripe set. Repeat this step for as many additional partitions as will be part of the stripe set.

4. Select Fault Tolerance ➤ Create Stripe Set with Parity. You will be prompted for the size of the stripe set. The default is the smallest free space among the drives multiplied by the number of drives selected.

5. Click OK.

6. Select Partition ➤ Commit Changes Now.

7. Select Yes in the confirmation window.

8. Click OK in the window that announces that Disk Administrator has performed the operation successfully.

You may be prompted to reboot your computer for the changes to take effect.

The system and boot partitions cannot be a part of a stripe set with parity.

Creating Mirror Sets

Creating a mirror set with the Disk Administrator allows you to provide an automatic fault tolerance fallover in the event that your primary hard disk partition fails to operate. The hard disk mirror will activate and take over the duties of your primary hard disk partition until you can restore it. Exercise 5.9 shows the procedure for creating a mirror set.

If your boot drive fails, a hard disk mirror will not be able to boot unless it is set as the active partition. You should create a fault-tolerant boot floppy disk in case you need to boot the mirror.

EXERCISE 5.9

Creating a Mirror Set

1. Select Start ➢ Programs ➢ Administrative Tools ➢ Disk Administrator.

2. Select the formatted partition you wish to mirror.

3. Hold down the Control key and select a free space area on another physical disk equal to or larger than the partition you wish to mirror.

4. Select Fault Tolerance ➢ Establish Mirror. If you selected you boot drive, click OK to acknowledge the boot floppy notice. The partition bar colors have changed to indicate a mirror set.

5. Select Partition ➢ Commit Changes Now.

6. Click OK.

Windows NT will begin mirroring your hard disk drive. You should notice some hard disk activity, and the Disk Administrator will note that the mirror set is initializing.

Drive Letters

Windows NT assigns drive letters in the same order as MS-DOS does. However, unlike MS-DOS, Windows NT allows you to change the order of their assignment any way you want. This process is called *static drive-letter assignment*.

The MS-DOS drive-letter-assignment order follows these rules:

- Hard disk drive letter assignments start with C.

- Hard disk drive letter assignment always proceeds in physical drive number order.

- The first primary partitions of each drive are assigned drive letters.

- The logical drives of each drive are assigned drive letters.

- The remaining partitions of each drive are assigned drive letters.

Exercise 5.10 shows the static assignment of drive letters. Keep in mind that you can assign only "free" drive letters, that is, drive letters that are not already in use. If you want to free up a drive letter that is currently in use for assignment to another drive, simply assign a new drive letter to the first drive and commit your changes. This step will free up the letter you wish to assign.

EXERCISE 5.10

Assigning a Drive Letter

1. Select Start ➤ Programs ➤ Administrative Tools ➤ Disk Administrator.

2. Select the volume to receive an assigned drive letter.

3. Select Tools ➤ Assign Drive Letter.

4. Pick the drive letter for the volume from the list in the Assign Drive Letter window. Click OK.

5. Select Partition ➤ Commit Changes Now.

6. Select Yes in the confirmation window.

7. Click OK in the window that announces that Disk Administrator has performed the operation successfully.

You may be prompted to reboot your computer for the changes to take effect.

Formatting a Volume

Once you have created a partition, whether it be a single partition, volume set, or stripe set, you must format the partition to make it usable by Windows NT.

Formatting a volume will destroy any data stored on that volume.

To format a partition, you must first select the partition to be formatted. (Click once on the partition in the Disk Administrator window.) The partition must have already been created and committed; you cannot format the free space on a hard disk. Select Tools ➤ Format and then choose the file system you want to put on that volume. Exercise 5.11 explains how to format a volume.

EXERCISE 5.11

Formatting a Volume

1. Select Start ➤ Programs ➤ Administrative Tools ➤ Disk Administrator.

2. Select the volume to format.

3. Select Tools ➤ Format.

4. Enter a label for the drive.

5. Select the file system type for the volume. Your choices are FAT or NTFS. Click OK.

6. Click Yes to confirm that you know that formatting the drive will destroy any data saved on the drive.

7. Click OK when the format is complete.

Recovering Disk Configuration Information

When you install Windows NT, you are asked if you wish to create an emergency repair disk. One piece of information stored on this repair disk is disk configuration information. After you make changes to the configuration of your hard drives, the Disk Administrator allows you to save the configuration.

You should save the information to a floppy disk because an emergency that would require you to recover the disk configuration information most likely would also make it difficult to access information on the hard disk drives.

You can use the RDISK.EXE utility to create the emergency repair disk so you can restore the hard disk configuration to the state it was in the last time you saved the configuration.

Chapter 17 describes various troubleshooting procedures and explains how to use RDISK.EXE.

Recovering from Faults

Windows NT makes working with fault-tolerant volumes very easy, as NT automatically recovers from mirror set asynchrony and regenerates stripe sets from parity information.

Mirror Sets

To repair a failed mirrored drive, you must break the mirror set using the Break Mirror Set command from the Fault Tolerance menu, replace the faulty disk, and create a new mirror set that includes the mirrored drive. Exercise 5.12 explains how to repair a damaged mirror set.

EXERCISE 5.12

Repairing a Damaged Mirror Set

1. Shut down the Windows NT computer.

2. Remove the failed drive. If your primary boot drive failed, make sure you have a fault-tolerant boot floppy to boot from.

3. Install a new drive to replace the failed drive.

4. Reboot.

5. Select Start ➢ Programs ➢ Administrative Tools ➢ Disk Administrator.

6. Click OK to acknowledge the new drive.

7. Delete any partitions installed on the new drive.

8. Select the remaining half of the mirror set.

9. Select Fault Tolerance ➢ Break Mirror Set.

10. Click Yes to break the mirror set.

EXERCISE 5.12 (CONTINUED FROM PREVIOUS PAGE)

11. Select the remaining half of the mirror set.

12. Hold down the Control key and select the free space on the new disk.

13. Select Fault Tolerance ➤ Establish Mirror.

Windows NT will now restore the mirror set in the background.

Stripe with Parity

Windows NT will automatically detect and "orphan" failed members of a stripe set with parity. You will see the following message: *A disk that is part of a fault-tolerant volume can no longer be accessed.* Exercise 5.13 shows the process of repairing a stripe set with parity.

Windows NT will fill the system event log with messages about bad sectors when a disk fails. You may get a warning that the system log is full.

EXERCISE 5.13

Repairing a Damaged Stripe Set with Parity

1. Shut down the Windows NT computer.

2. Remove the failed drive.

3. Install a new drive to replace the failed drive.

4. Reboot.

5. Select Start ➤ Programs ➤ Administrative Tools ➤ Disk Administrator.

6. Click OK to acknowledge the new drive.

7. Delete any partition that is installed on the new drive.

8. Select the stripe set.

9. Hold down the control key and select the free space on the new disk.

10. Select Fault Tolerance ➤ Regenerate.

Windows NT will now restore the stripe set in the background.

Working with Backup

W INDOWS NT PROVIDES a simple tape backup program called backup that allows you to perform routine backup operations for a Windows NT computer. The backup program that comes with Windows NT does not support sophisticated functions such as software compression or file-by-file tape databases. The software also does not come with an unattended tape backup scheduler, but you can use the Windows NT AT command to perform this function. Figure 5.8 shows the Windows NT Backup tool.

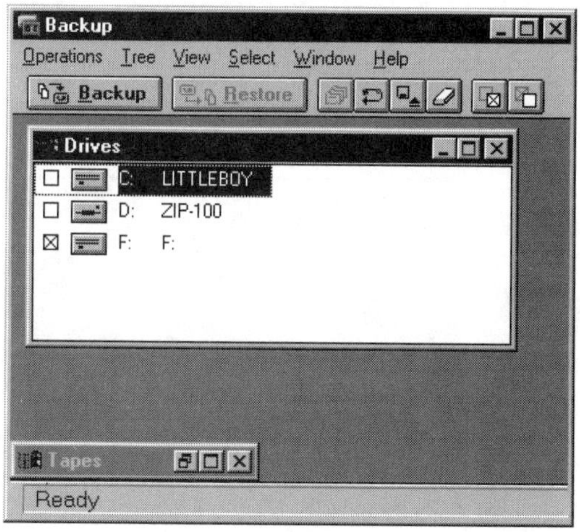

FIGURE 5.8

The Windows NT
Backup tool.

Before you can use the Backup tool to archive your files, you must make your tape device known to Windows NT by installing a driver for it. Exercise 5.14 shows how to install a driver for the tape devices automatically supported by Windows NT. If your tape device came with a driver for Windows NT, install it according to the manufacturer's instructions.

Adding a Tape Device

1. Select Start ➤ Settings ➤ Control Panels.

2. Double-click Tape Devices.

3. Click Detect to automatically detect your installed tape device. If Detect automatically detects the correct tape device, skip to step 7.

4. Select the Drivers tab.

5. Click Add.

6. Select your tape device from the list of manufacturers and products.

7. Click OK.

8. Click Yes to restart your computer.

Backing Up a Volume

Backing up a volume is a simple matter with the Backup tool—you simply select the data to backup, choose the options you want, and start the operation. The options you can choose are simple and mostly self-explanatory, as shown in Exercise 5.15.

The Windows NT Backup tool will not copy files that are in use. You should use the AT command to schedule backups during a time when users are not logged on to the server to ensure that normally open files like databases are archived properly. Some third-party backup utilities can open archive files.

If you need to perform a backup operation without affecting the status of the archive bit, you should choose the Copy operation. This operation copies files without resetting the archive bit. However, because a copy backup does not change the archive bit, you cannot subsequently perform an incremental backup that is incremental to the copy backup. Figure 5.9 shows the Backup Information window.

FIGURE 5.9

The Backup Information
window.

FIGURE 5.9

The Backup Information window.

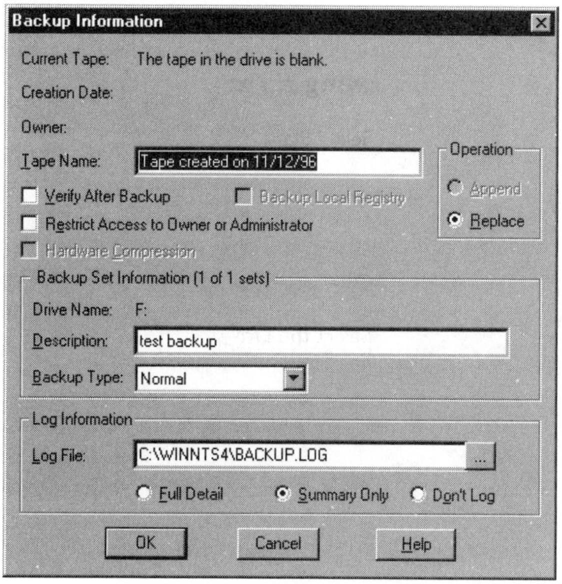

EXERCISE 5.15

Backing Up a Volume

1. Select Start ➢ Administrative Tools ➢ Backup.

2. Check the volumes you wish to back up in the Drives window. You can double-click on the drives to see a directory tree if you wish to back up only certain directories in the volume.

3. Click Backup.

4. Check Verify After Backup.

5. Type a description of this volume in the description edit line.

6. Click OK.

7. Notice the progression of the tape backup.

The backup operation may take anywhere from a few minutes to many hours depending upon the speed of your device and the size of the volume you selected for backup.

Restoring from Backup

We hope that you'll never have to restore a backup tape, but if you do, the procedure is outlined in Exercise 5.16. This procedure restores an entire volume. If you need to restore individual files, you can use the help procedures included in the Backup tool to work through the process.

EXERCISE 5.16

Restoring a Backed Up Volume

1. Select Start ➤ Administrative Tools ➤ Backup.

2. Double-click the tape containing the volume you wish to restore in the Tapes window. You may have to wait a few minutes for the tape device to retrieve the tape catalog. If no catalog sets are on the tape, simply check the tape you wish to restore from.

3. Check the Verify After Restore option.

4. Check the Restore File Permissions option if you backed up an NTFS volume.

5. Click OK. You can watch the status of the restoration in the Status window.

Scheduling Jobs with AT

Windows NT includes a simple command similar to the UNIX chron command, called AT. The AT command simply performs a command or batch file at a specified time. You can use the AT command to automate the Windows NT Backup tool—a feature it sorely needs but lacks.

Before you can use the AT command, you must start the schedule service through the Services control panel, as shown in Exercise 5.17.

EXERCISE 5.17

Starting the Schedule Service

1. Select Start ➤ Settings ➤ Control Panels.

2. Double-click the Services control panel.

3. Select Schedule in the Service pick box.

4. Click Startup.

5. Choose Automatic as the Startup Type.

6. Click OK.

7. Click Start. The service will take a few moments to start.

8. Click Close.

Once you've started the Schedule service, you are ready to schedule a backup job. Since the AT command is a console command, you will need to open a command-prompt window. The Windows NT 4.0 Resource Kit from Microsoft includes a graphical front-end utility for AT that makes it much easier to use. Exercise 5.18 shows the process for adding a backup at a scheduled time.

EXERCISE 5.18

Scheduling a Backup Job

1. Select Start ➤ Programs ➤ Command Prompt.

2. Type the following command:

```
AT 01:00'C:\winnt\system32\ntbackup backup c:/v
```

3. Type **AT** at the command prompt and press Enter. Verify that the job you entered in step 2 is shown in the list of scheduled jobs.

At 1:00 a.m., the Backup tool will be launched and will back up your primary disk partition.

You will have to experiment with the AT command and the Backup tool to find the right set of parameters to implement your tape backup policy. Table 5.3 shows the AT parameters. You can view these at any time by issuing the AT command with the /? help switch.

TABLE 5.3	PARAMETER	EFFECT
Parameters of the AT Command	\\computername	Specifies a remote computer. Local computer is default.
	Id	Specifies a scheduled task id for the delete command.
	/delete	Deletes the scheduled task identified by id, or all jobs if no id present.
	/yes	Skips delete confirmation.
	Time	Sets the schedule time for the operation to occur.
	/interactive	Allows the job to interact with the desktop of the user who is logged on at the time the job runs.
	/every:date,[date,...]	Specifies week days or dates to run the command.
	/next:date,[date,...]	Runs the command on the next occurrence of date.
	"command"	Windows NT command to schedule. Can be an executable or a batch file.

Command line syntax:
AT [\\computername] id /delete [/yes]
AT [\\computername] time [/interactive] [/every:date...] [/next:date ...] "command"

The Windows NT Tape Backup tool has a command-line name of ntbackup.exe, *not* backup.exe. Backup.exe *is another useful program for copying files between directories.*

Using the Backup tool from the command line limits you to backing up directories only. You cannot back up individual files, and you cannot use wildcards to specify files. Table 5.4 shows the Backup tool parameters.

	PARAMETER	EFFECT
TABLE 5.4 Parameters of the NTBACKUP Command	/nopoll	Erase tape. Cannot be used with other parameters.
	/missingtape	Specifies that tapes from a backup set may be missing and makes each tape an individual set, rather than a member of a set.
	operation	Backup or Eject.
	Path	Specifies one or more paths to be backed up.
	/a	Specifies append rather than replace.
	/v	Specifies verify.
	/r	Restricts access.
	/d "text"	Specifies a description for the backup contents.
	/b	Backs up local Registry.
	/hc:on or off	Selects hardware compression if it is supported by the tape device.
	/t option	Specifies the backup type where option is normal, copy, incremental, differential, or daily.
	/l "filename"	Specifies a filename for the log file.
	/e	Write only exceptions to the log file.
	/t:n	Specifies the tape device number from 0 to 9 indicating the tape drive to use.

Ntbackup command syntax:
ntbackup [/nopoll] [/missingtape]
ntbackup operation path [/a] [/v] [/r] [/d "text"] [/b] [/hc:on|off] [/t option] [/l "filename"] [/e] [/tape:n]

Summary

WINDOWS NT PROVIDES a number of sophisticated mass storage options to enhance the fault tolerance and recovery of your network file server. Everything from tape backup to RAID levels 0, 1, and 5 are addressed in software by Windows NT Server. You need to be familiar with the storage options provided by Windows NT so you can implement effective storage and fault tolerance strategies for your organization.

The first step in planning for mass storage is determining how much storage space a file server needs. Knowing that, you can determine the capacity of the requisite tape backup device as well as the capacity for the additional space required by fault tolerance mechanisms such as striping with parity or mirroring.

Your choice of file systems will greatly affect the security and safety of your mass storage systems. With Windows NT Server, you should always choose the NTFS file system for shared volumes because of its enhanced security and inherent fault tolerance features.

Review Questions

1. The FAT file system does not record security information such as the owner or file-sharing access permissions of a file or directory.

   A. True

   B. False

2. The FAT file system has more overhead than NTFS has for small volumes.

   A. True

   B. False

3. Under VFAT, names are not case sensitive, but they do preserve case.

A. True

B. False

4. You must be careful when creating a partition because you might create a partition in the space occupied by an existing partition.

A. True

B. False

5. Windows NT assigns a drive letter to each partition as you create it.

A. True

B. False

6. The partitions combined into a volume set must be the same size and on the same drive.

A. True

B. False

7. The system and boot partitions cannot be a part of a volume set.

A. True

B. False

8. Volume sets provide fault tolerance to your file storage.

A. True

B. False

9. Because of the way data is stored to a stripe set, stripe sets can be much faster than volume sets.

A. True

B. False

10. RAID level 0 increases the fault tolerance of your server.

A. True

B. False

11. The system and boot partitions cannot be a part of a stripe set.

   A. True

   B. False

12. You must use third-party tape backup software if you want to schedule unattended backups under Windows NT.

   A. True

   B. False

13. Formatting a volume will destroy any data stored on that volume.

   A. True

   B. False

14. Under NTFS, files created or copied into a directory retain their original permissions and attributes. Files moved into a directory inherit the security permissions of the directory.

   A. True

   B. False

15. The memory in your computer is _____, which means that it goes away when the power is turned off.

16. Hard disks and floppy disks (and to an increasing extent, CD-ROMs) are the most popular form of nonvolatile or _____ storage in personal computers.

17. The two file systems for hard disks that Windows NT supports are _____ and _____.

18. Hard disks are subdivided into _____.

19. The _____ _____ _____ is the first portion of data on a hard disk and is reserved for the BIOS bootstrap routine.

20. Windows NT supports converting _____ to NTFS for the purpose of easing the migration of a computer from OS/2 to Windows NT.

21. File names under NTFS are limited to _____ characters.

22. _____ is the preferred file system for use with Windows NT Server.

23. The maximum number of primary partitions on a hard disk is _____.

24. The partition that your computer boots when it is turned on is the _____ partition.

25. To recover a mirror set, you must _____ the existing mirror set to remove the failed drive.

26. A _____ is one or more partitions treated as a single unit and given a single drive letter.

27. In a stripe set, the data is stored evenly across all of the disks, one row at a time in _____ K blocks.

28. Once you have created a partition, whether it be a single partition, volume set, or stripe set, you must _____ the partition to make it usable by Windows NT.

29. The recommended minimum partition size for NTFS is _____ MB.

30. File _____ removes redundancy from files, thereby decreasing their physical size.

31. RAID level _____ describes mirroring.

    A. 0

    B. 1

    C. 2

    D. 3

    E. 4

    F. 5

32. Disk _____ creates fault tolerance by keeping an exact copy of the same volumes on two disks controlled by separate controllers.

   A. duplexing

   B. mirroring

   C. striping

   D. RAID

Networking and Network Protocols

WINDOWS NT SERVER was designed to operate at the heart of your network. The server is the focal point of file storage and logon requests. In networks that are used for more than just file storage, the server is also the focal point for such things as printing, e-mail, faxing, and database support. Windows NT Server must be efficient and flexible in how it communicates with client computers because of the large number of computers it must communicate with and the many services (printing, e-mail, etc.) it must provide. The Windows NT Server network protocols provide the framework for all other network activity.

In the first part of this chapter, we describe both networking in general and the operation of a Windows NT network. We then identify and compare the networking protocols most commonly used in Windows NT networks and conclude the chapter by showing you how to install and configure the protocols.

Network Architecture

THE TERM *NETWORK ARCHITECTURE* refers to the way that networks are designed. You can compare the architecture of networks to the architecture of buildings—different parts of networks (and buildings) can be identified by the different tasks they perform.

The foundation of a building, for example, provides the structure on which the rest of the building is constructed. The foundation of one building may be laid out entirely differently from that of another building (an office building is not laid out the same way as your home), and it may be made of entirely different materials (such as steel and concrete for the office building and wood and brick for your home); nevertheless, you would never confuse a building's foundation with its roof or windows.

Similarly, the physical layer of a network, which may be made of twisted strands of copper wire in one network and of glass in another, is easy to identify by the function it performs: conveying the communications signals of the network from one network device to another.

You can identify the parts of a network by what they do, even if the method of accomplishing the function differs from one network to another. The physical layer, for example, physically links computers with a cable, using cable made of light carrying glass in some cases and cable made of coaxial copper wire in others. The network layer sends packets of information over the physical layer, using Token Ring frame types in some cases and Ethernet frame types in others.

The purpose of this section is to

- Introduce several important networking concepts

- Describe the OSI and IEEE networking models, which provide a framework to compare with most networking architectures

- Explain how Windows NT networking components cooperate to implement the networking layers outlined in the IEEE model

Networking Concepts

In order to administer and configure a Windows NT Server, you should have a basic understanding of the fundamental concepts of networking. The diagram in Figure 6.1 shows some of the visible components of local area networks, and the following mini-glossary defines the most important concepts.

- **Local area network:** A local area network (LAN) links personal computers in one general location such as an office building or school. The personal computers use the LAN to communicate. Network components can communicate over copper wire, fiber-optic cable (glass), and radio waves, as well as through the air via infrared light. Other types of networks link other kinds of devices (a video network links closed-circuit television and video cameras, for instance), but only a network linking computers together in one location is called a LAN.

FIGURE 6.1

A local area network requires at least two computers communicating via network interface adapters over a networking medium such as a twisted-pair cable. In addition, a LAN may contain servers, hubs, clients, and peers.

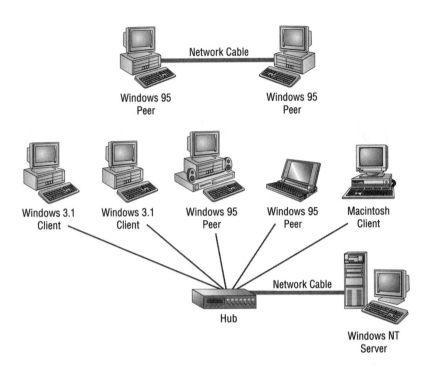

- **Personal computer:** A personal computer is a computer that is designed to be used by one person and can run programs, store information, and display information. A LAN with personal computers and a file server may be connected with wires the same way a mainframe or minicomputer is connected to its terminals, but the LAN is much more flexible because the individual personal computers can execute programs independently of the file server.

- **Network cable:** Most LANs use some form of network cable to connect the computers. You can install many types of cable in a network, including twisted-pair copper cable, Thinnet or Thicknet coaxial cable, and fiber-optic cable. The cable is the medium that conveys the signals exchanged by communicating computers.

- **Network interface adapter:** The network interface adapter or card (often abbreviated NIC) connects the computer to the cable and translates the data from the computer into a form that can be transmitted over the cable medium. For example, an Ethernet NIC accepts data from the computer in chunks called packets and transforms those packets into sequences of electrical pulses to be applied to the copper wires (or sequences of light pulses if the medium is fiber-optic cable). The receiving NIC detects these electrical voltages (or light pulses) and translates them into packets of data, which it transfers to the receiving computer.

- **Networking protocol:** In order for two computers to communicate over the network, they must assign the same meaning to the same sequence of signals. When one computer sends information, the other must be prepared to receive it. Protocols define the meanings assigned to signals, which data is sent and in what order, and how the computers negotiate the sending and the receiving of data. For example, just as Morse code (a protocol for people communicating over radio and the telegraph) assigns letters of the alphabet to sequences of long and short signals, Ethernet (a protocol used by network adapters over network cable) assigns numerical values to sequences of electrical pulses. Also, just as the letters in Morse code must combine to form understandable words, the numbers transmitted over Ethernet must combine to form valid Ethernet packets.

- **Hub:** Some networks, notably twisted-pair Ethernet and Token Ring, arrange the network cables so that they all run from the networked computers to a central point. A hub or concentrator connects the cables at the central point. Some hubs merely rebroadcast a signal received on any one cable over all the other cables. Other more sophisticated hubs can determine the destination of a packet and retransmit only the signal on the corresponding cable. These hubs are called "switching hubs," or switches. Other features of sophisticated hubs include fault detection and isolation, traffic monitoring, and remote management.

- **Server:** The hub is the physical central point of most networks, but the server is the central point of network communications. The computers on the network rely on the server to store data and to validate logon requests. The server is connected to the network as any other computer is; it is the server's software that makes the server special. The server is usually more powerful than the other computers on the network.

- **Client:** A client is a computer that relies on the server for logon validation and file storage. A client usually has some storage (hard disk space) of its own to contain program files, but the user's files are typically stored on the file server rather than to the client. Unlike most servers, the client computer executes programs for the user and interacts directly with the user.

- **Peer:** A peer computer is a computer that not only executes programs for the user and interacts directly with the user (like a client) but also can share its hard disk space or printers with other computers on the network (like a server). A peer does not, however, validate logon requests for other computers and is not usually dedicated to storing files for other computers. Instead a peer is usually used like a client computer, and occasionally files that are stored on the peer computer are made available to other computers on the network.

These definitions certainly don't exhaust the information you need to know about networks, but they provide the foundation you need to understand the rest of this chapter (and the rest of this book). Another book in this series, *MCSE: Networking Essentials Study Guide,* explains these and many other networking concepts in much greater detail.

The Open Systems Interconnect (OSI) Model

The first network was born when someone linked two computers with a cable so that they could exchange information. Before 1969 mainframe computers were often connected, but the links between the mainframes were direct and not shared. A mainframe required as many links as it had other mainframes to talk to. Thus larger networks were formed, but not the kind of networks with which we are familiar today.

In 1969 the Advanced Research Projects Agency (ARPA) tested a new concept in networking, called packet switching, between four major universities. *Packet switching* allows communications links to carry many streams of data by breaking each stream of data into many packets and identifying the sender and recipient of each packet. Computers in the network forward the packet until it reaches its destination. The protocols that implement this kind of a network are called *transport protocols.*

Terminology: Be careful not to confuse the Microsoft use of the term transport protocol with the transport layer of the OSI model. In the Microsoft network architecture, a transport protocol is any protocol stack (group of related protocols) that Microsoft operating systems can use to provide network connectivity for services such as printing and file storage. Transport protocols (a stack of related protocols in the OSI model) that come with Windows NT Server include TCP/IP (which uses TCP at the transport layer), NWLink (which uses IPX and SPX at the transport layer), and NetBEUI (which is not routable because it doesn't have a network layer component).

The original protocols for sending, receiving, and forwarding packets eventually became the TCP/IP protocol suite, which is in worldwide use today and is the set of protocols used to form the Internet.

At about the same time that the TCP/IP protocol suite was first being tested and the Internet was born, the first version of the most popular LAN standard in use today appeared in the form of the ALOHA network in Hawaii. The ALOHA network used the concept of a shared media, wherein more than just two computers could share a cable or other medium (such as radio). Any computer could transmit data, and all of the computers on the network would receive it. This type of network also broke data into packets, and a computer on the network would simply discard any packet that was not marked as having that computer as its destination. This network used the Carrier Sense Multiple Access with Collision Detection physical media access protocol, and the familiar Ethernet networks are manifestations of this kind of network.

Other types of packet-based transport protocols, such as SNA, IPX/SPX, NetBEUI, and AppleTalk, soon joined TCP/IP; and other physical media access protocols, such as Token Ring, ARCnet, FDDI, and LocalTalk, were developed. You will most often use a transport protocol, such as IPX/SPX, in combination with a media access protocol, such as Token Ring.

OSI Model

As new media types were developed and new transports grew on top of them, many people saw the need for the different media types and protocols to be able to work with each other. In the early 1980s, the International Standards Organization developed the open systems interconnection (OSI) model to provide a basis upon which different manufacturers could create interoperable network software components.

The OSI model describes seven standard layers to which all network software and hardware components should conform in a modular operating system like Windows NT. The seven OSI layers are

1. Application

2. Presentation

3. Session

4. Transport

5. Network

6. Data link

7. Physical

Each layer provides a service to the layer directly above it by using the services of the layer below it. For instance, TCP, a transport layer service, guarantees a reliable connection to the layer above it using the unreliable service of IP, a network layer service. TCP works by making as many requests for data as necessary (via IP) to its peer TCP layer on the other computer until it gets what it needs to provide a consistent set of data to the layer above it. This process is shown in Figure 6.2.

FIGURE 6.2

How network components interact.

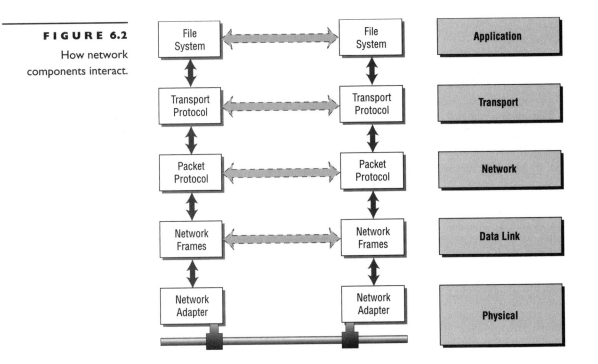

The OSI model represents an abstract ideal that is not always applicable to real-world considerations. For instance, many software components encompass more than one layer of the stack. The OSI model also encompasses some functionality that is not the responsibility of software at all. The physical and data link layers are implemented with electronic equipment and cables. The data link layer encompasses the functionality of the network adapter driver software, which is provided by the network adapter manufacturer, not the operating system manufacturer.

User applications are not prohibited from bypassing higher-level modules and writing directly to lower-level layers if they know how to interface with the lower-level components. The upper layers abstract the differences between interchangeable software modules at lower levels, but user applications are not required to use this abstraction. For example, an application can interact directly with the TCP/IP layer even though NetBIOS is bound above it. The application will break if TCP/IP is replaced by IPX, however. An application that interacts with NetBIOS does not have to worry about which transport layer is installed.

Taking this direct-use scenario to the extreme, a network could be implemented by interfacing directly to the network adapter from the redirector, but the entire network would have to be implemented with exactly the same model network adapter and could never be upgraded to newer technology.

NT's modularity allows layers to be independent of one another, which increases the network's life span and encourages cross-vendor compatibility.

OSI Layers

The following subsections describe the seven OSI layers; after you read this material, you should understand the intent of modular component-based networking. Notice that each layer depends on the services provided by the layer below to implement its functionality.

PHYSICAL LAYER The physical layer and the data link layer (directly above it) are responsible for media access control. The IEEE extensions to the ISO model (see the section "IEEE Enhancements to the OSI Model") are primarily concerned with these two layers. Ethernet and Token Ring are protocols that reside in these two layers.

The physical layer is simply responsible for sending bits (bits are the binary 1s and 0s of digital communication) from one computer to another. The physical layer is not concerned with the meaning of the bits; it deals with the physical connection to the network and with transmission and reception of signals.

This level defines the following kinds of physical and electrical details:

- What will represent a 1 or a 0

- How many pins a network connector will have

- How data will be synchronized

- When the network adapter may or may not transmit the data

Your physical network interface adapter implements this level.

DATA LINK LAYER The data link layer implements the flow of data over a single link from one device to another. It accepts packets from the network layer and packages the information into data units called *frames* to be presented to the physical layer for transmission. The data link layer adds control information, such as frame type, addressing, and error control information, to the data being sent.

This layer ensures the error-free transfer of frames from one computer to another. A cyclic redundancy check (CRC) is added to the data frame to detect damaged frames. If a frame is damaged, the receiving unit ignores it. Higher-level protocols can detect missing frames and request that they be sent again.

The IEEE further subdivides this layer into the logical link control sublayer and the media access control sublayer (see "IEEE Enhancements to the OSI Model"). This layer is also the layer at which Windows NT device drivers operate.

NETWORK LAYER The network layer and the next (the transport layer) contain the Windows NT transport protocols. The network layer defines functions of IP in the TCP/IP stack and many of the functions of IPX in the IPX/SPX protocols.

The network layer is responsible for routing data between networks. It makes routing decisions and forwards packets for devices that are farther away than a single link. (A *link* connects two network devices and is implemented by the data link layer. Two devices connected by a link communicate directly with each other.) Larger networks may have *intermediate systems* between any two *end systems*. The network layer allows the transport layer and layers above it to send packets without being concerned about whether the end system is immediately adjacent or several hops away.

Intermediate devices in the network layer are commonly known as routers. *In UNIX parlance, gateways and routers are the same thing, but Microsoft uses the term* gateway *to refer to devices that act as service gateways for higher-level protocols such as NetBIOS or the Gateway Service for NetWare.*

TRANSPORT LAYER The transport layer defines functions of TCP in the TCP/IP protocol stack and several of the functions of IPX, as well as the functions of SPX in the IPX/SPX protocols.

This layer ensures that packets are delivered error free, in sequence, and with no losses or duplications. The transport layer breaks large messages from the session layer (discussed next) into packets to be sent to the destination computer. On the destination computer, the transport layer reassembles packets into messages to be presented to its session layer. The transport layer typically sends an acknowledgment to the originator for messages received.

SESSION LAYER The session, presentation, and application layers are operating-system specific network services such as printing and file storage.

The session layer includes protocols such as NetBIOS, Named Pipes, Mail Slots (Windows NT logon authentication), Remote Procedure Calls, and some other network file systems.

The session layer allows applications on separate computers to share a connection called a *session*. This layer provides services such as name lookup and security that enable two programs to find each other and establish a communication link. This layer also controls the dialog between two processes, determining who can transmit and who can receive at what point during the communication.

PRESENTATION LAYER The presentation layer translates data between the formats the network requires and the formats the computer expects. The presentation layer performs protocol conversion, data translation, compression and encryption, and character set conversion; it also interprets graphics commands.

Redirectors operate at the presentation and application levels; they make the files on a file server visible to the client computer. Redirectors also make remote printers act as though they are attached to the local computer.

APPLICATION LAYER The Windows NT Workstation and Server networking components operate primarily at the application level, which is the topmost layer of the OSI model. It provides services that directly support user applications, such as database access, e-mail, and file transfers. It also allows applications running on different computers to communicate as though they were on the same computer. When a programmer writes an application program that uses network services, the application program will access this layer.

IEEE Enhancements to the OSI Model

The IEEE further subdivides the second layer of the OSI model, the data link layer. The IEEE enhancements allow several sets of protocols implementing the network and higher layers (such as TCP/IP, NWLink, or NetBEUI) to use the same data link and physical layer (or device driver and network interface adapter). Windows NT uses this capability to run multiple transport protocols over the same network interface adapter. The IEEE subdivision also allows one protocol transport to use several network interface adapters.

The IEEE enhancements are the logical link control sublayer and the media access control sublayer.

LOGICAL LINK CONTROL SUBLAYER The logical link control sublayer acts as an interface between lower-layer protocols (such as Ethernet or Token Ring) and upper-layer network protocols such as TCP/IP or IPX. The IEEE 802.2 standard defines this sublayer.

MEDIA ACCESS CONTROL SUBLAYER The media access control sublayer communicates with the physical device (the physical layer, or layer 1 of the OSI stack). IEEE standards 802.3, 802.4, and 802.5 define implementations of this sublayer for Ethernet, Token Bus, and Token Ring, respectively.

Windows NT Networking Components

MICROSOFT HAS DONE an admirable job mapping its components and boundary layers to layers in the OSI stack (see Figure 6.3). Windows NT has a software component that maps to each OSI stack layer. Figure 6.3 also includes physical disk I/O subsystems to show how the network redirector can make network connections look like local storage.

F I G U R E 6.3

Windows NT and the
OSI model.

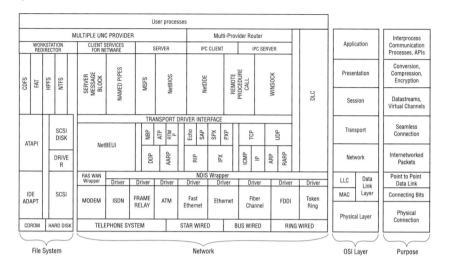

F I G U R E 6.3

Windows NT and the OSI model.

Note that many of the software components appear to cover more than one layer. These components perform services in more than one layer, essentially embodying the function of the layers and interfaces in one package. In the following sections, we introduce each of the components used in Windows NT according to the layers in which they operate.

Do not confuse the application layer of the OSI stack with software applications. The application layer provides services to user applications, which run in the user space above the OSI stack.

Major NT Component Types

Windows NT components work together through interfaces called boundary layers. Each component implements a major network service. Each boundary layer provides a way for components to communicate, but provides no other service. Some boundary layers are implemented as software switches that select the appropriate component to perform a service. Other boundary layers are not really software at all—they are simply rules to which programmers must write components in order for them to work under Windows NT. Components provide a certain service; boundary layers connect components, as shown in Figure 6.4.

FIGURE 6.4

Microsoft component
architecture.

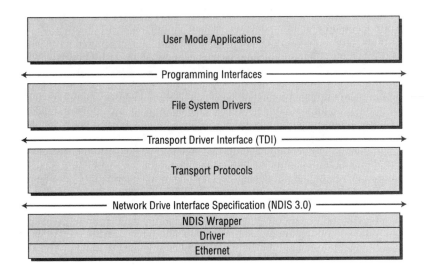

Windows NT divides the network software component layers slightly differently than the OSI model does, so we will use Microsoft terminology for these component layers. You should be familiar with the purposes of the different OSI layers and match them with their Windows NT counterparts as you read this section.

Boundary layers facilitate the task of developing adapter drivers and network components, such as protocols and file systems, because the interfaces to the boundary layers are very well-defined. Boundary layers help realize the goals of the OSI model.

The Windows NT components and boundary layers are

- Programming interfaces (boundary layer)

- File system drivers (component)

- The transport driver interface (boundary layer)

- Transport protocol (component)

- Network driver interface specification (boundary layer)

- Adapter driver (component)

Notice that in the preceding list the boundary layers and components alternate; in fact, each boundary layer provides the interface between the components above and below it. The first boundary layer, programming interfaces, provides the boundary between the user's application and the network itself.

Although the term boundary layer *is used to describe the interface between components, notice that each boundary layer component includes the word* interface *in its name. The terms* interface *and* boundary layer *are synonymous.*

Programming Interfaces

As a boundary layer, programming interfaces provide an established method for user applications to interact with any of a number of file system drivers and network services.

Windows NT supports the following programming interfaces:

- NetBIOS

- Windows Sockets

- Remote Procedure Calls

- Network Dynamic Data Exchange (NetDDE)

These services call on file system drivers as well as transport protocols to perform their functions.

Programming interfaces create the boundary between the application layer and user applications in the OSI model.

File System Drivers

File system drivers are networking components that are treated as Windows NT local storage file systems. Windows NT provides file systems for many of its application and session layer components so that applications do not have to treat local and networked storage differently. By making application and session layer components look like file systems to user applications, you can use applications written to work on your local computer across the network. See Chapter 5 for a detailed discussion of local storage file systems.

These components include the workstation and server services, Named Pipes, and Mailslots. All these components call upon transport protocols to perform their services.

Network file system drivers such as Named Pipes are sometimes called "redirectors" because they redirect I/O that would go to a local disk to go over the network.

Transport Driver Interface

The transport driver interface (TDI) is a boundary layer that makes all the transport protocols look the same to higher-level services such as file systems and redirectors. The transport driver interface is not software—rather, it is a specification to which all Windows NT transport protocols are written. For instance, NWLink, which implements Novell's IPX protocol, looks exactly like TCP/IP for Windows NT to upper-layer file systems and redirectors.

In the OSI model, the TDI is an interface between the transport layer and the session layer.

The transport driver interface is merely a documented specification to which program-mers must write transport protocols if they want them to work correctly with other Windows NT components. It is not a software service or a program running in Win-dows NT. All the interfaces in Windows NT are specifications, not software, including the programming interfaces and the Network Driver Interface Specification (NDIS).

Transport Protocols

Shared media networks are not always available to a computer. Transmission errors occur. Packets are dropped in routers. Collisions happen. Transport protocols convert the unreliable, inconsistent packet bursts delivered by net-work adapter drivers into smooth data transmission streams (albeit with non-deterministic delay characteristics) that can be used for file transmission.

Transport protocols perform such services as packet ordering, guaranteed delivery, and connection maintenance between networks. The transport driver interface enables several protocols to run simultaneously under Windows NT. If a server speaks TCP/IP, IPX, and NetBEUI, it can make reliable connections to clients running any one of those protocols.

Transport protocols make up the network and transport layers of the OSI model. They can be subdivided further; for example, TCP is the transport layer and IP is the network layer in the TCP/IP protocol.

Network Driver Interface

In Windows NT, the network driver interface is implemented by the Network Driver Interface Specification (NDIS 4.0).

NDIS is a specification to which adapter drivers must be written to work with Windows NT. NDIS also includes a small code wrapper that controls the interface between NDIS-compliant drivers and transport protocols. NDIS 4.0 allows multiple network adapter drivers to be bound to an unlimited number of transport protocols.

Adapter Drivers

Adapter drivers are software components that adapter manufacturers design to provide an interface between proprietary hardware and standard software. An adapter driver knows exactly how to make the specific adapter for which it was written perform a certain function, such as transmit a packet.

Each adapter requires an adapter driver written specifically for it. To operate with Windows NT, these drivers must be NDIS 3.0 compliant, which means they must know how to respond to requests from the NDIS wrapper.

Adapter drivers operate at the media access layer of the OSI stack, whereas the adapter itself interfaces the media access layer with the physical layer.

The IEEE 802 model, which was developed in concert with the OSI model, further subdivides the data link layer into the logical link control (LLC) layer and the media access control (MAC) layer. The LLC layer maps directly to the network adapter driver; the MAC layer correlates to the network adapter and other devices that operate using a certain network technology such as Ethernet or Token Ring.

Default Components

A standard Windows NT installation includes a number of default components chosen because they satisfy the requirements of most users.

Windows NT installs a complete set of network components by default to allow most network users to begin using their network as soon as the initial installation completes. This section describes the default components and how they interact. You will also learn how to install, remove, and configure each default component.

Also included with Windows NT, but not installed by default, are standard components that provide additional functionality such as interoperation with NetWare file servers and for networking computers via dial-up telephone lines. These components are covered in detail later in the book.

The following components are installed by default in Windows NT:

- NetBIOS interface

- TCP/IP protocol

- Workstation

- Server

- Computer browser

- Driver for your network interface adapter

- RPC name service provider

Comparing Network Protocols

W HEN YOU INSTALL Windows NT Server you are given a choice of protocols to use on your network. In Chapter 4 you installed NetBEUI because it is the simplest protocol to configure. However, the rest of your network may not be using NetBEUI, so you need to know about the other networking protocols and when to use them. You also need to understand the advantages and disadvantages of each network protocol so that you can make the most appropriate choice when compatibility with currently installed network systems is not an issue. This section describes the following protocols:

- TCP/IP

- NWLink (IPX/SPX)

- NetBEUI

- AppleTalk

TCP/IP

TCP/IP stands for Transmission Control Protocol and Internet Protocol; it is also a suite of related protocols developed by the Defense Department's Advanced Research Projects Agency (ARPA; later DARPA) as part of its project on network interconnection started in 1969. TCP/IP is by far the most widely used protocol for interconnecting computers and is the protocol of the global Internet. ARPA originally created TCP/IP to connect military networks, but provided the protocol standards to government agencies and universities free of charge.

Universities quickly adopted the protocol to interconnect their networks because it worked (and was free). Many academicians collaborated to create higher-level protocols for everything from newsgroups, mail transfer, file transfer, printing, remote booting, and even document browsing.

TCP/IP became the standard for interoperating UNIX computers, especially in military and university environments. With the development of the Hypertext Transfer Protocol (HTTP) for sharing Hypertext Markup Language (HTML) documents freely on the large global network that interconnected universities and government agencies, the World Wide Web (WWW) was born and Internet use exploded into the private sector. TCP/IP rode this wave of expansion to quickly eclipse IPX as the commercial protocol of choice among all network operating systems.

To support NetBIOS over TCP/IP, Microsoft has included NetBT (NetBIOS over TCP/IP) in accordance with Internet Protocol Request for Comments (RFC) 1001 and 1002.

TCP/IP protocol definitions are called Requests for Comments (RFC); they are freely available on the World Wide Web.

Features of TCP/IP

If you have a network that spans more than one metropolitan area, you will probably need to use TCP/IP. TCP/IP is the most flexible transport protocols. It's not fast or easy to use, but it is routable over wide, complex networks and provides more error correction than any other protocol. TCP/IP is supported on every modern computer and operating system. Some other advantages are

- Broad connectivity among all types of computers and servers

- Direct access to the global Internet

- Strong support for routing

- Simple Network Management Protocol (SNMP) support

- Support for Dynamic Host Configuration Protocol (DHCP) to dynamically assign client IP addresses

- Support for the Windows Internet Name Service (WINS) to allow Net-BIOS name resolution among Microsoft clients and servers

- Support for most other Internet protocols such as Post Office Protocol (POP), Hypertext Transfer Protocol (HTTP), and most other protocols with an acronyms ending in *P*

- Centralized TCP/IP domain assignment to allow internetworking between organizations

Don't confuse TCP/IP domains with Windows NT domains. TCP/IP domains are groups related by routing areas, whereas Windows NT domains define authentication and security groups.

Disadvantages of TCP/IP

No protocol is perfect for every situation. TCP/IP is very flexible and can be used in almost any situation requiring a transport protocol, but its flexibility has several drawbacks, including

- Relatively difficult to administer correctly, although new tools like DHCP make it a little easier

- Centralized TCP/IP domain assignment requires registration effort and cost

- Global expansion of the Internet has seriously limited the availability of unique domain numbers

- Difficult to set up

- Relatively high overhead to support seamless connectivity and routing

- Slower than IPX and NetBEUI

NWLink (IPX/SPX)

NWLink is Microsoft's implementation of Novell's IPX/SPX protocol stack used in Novell NetWare. IPX is an outgrowth of the XNS protocol stack that Xerox developed in the late 1970s.

NWLink is IPX for Windows NT. IPX is the protocol; NWLink is the networking component that provides the protocol.

IPX is included with Microsoft Windows NT primarily to support interconnection to Novell NetWare servers. Microsoft clients and servers can then be added to existing network installations gradually, easing the migration between platforms and obviating the need for a complete cut over from one networking standard to another.

NWLink does not by itself allow file and print sharing to and from NetWare clients or servers. Those functions are performed by the Client Services for NetWare (CSNW) redirector that also comes with Windows NT Workstation.

Gateway Services for NetWare (GSNW), which comes with Windows NT Server, can make file and print services on NetWare servers available to Microsoft network clients.

NWLink also includes enhancements to Novell's version of the NetBIOS programming interface. NWLink allows Windows NT to act as either the client or server in Novell IPX/NetBIOS client/server applications.

Features of NWLink

NWLink provides a reasonable middle ground between the simple, unroutable NetBEUI transport protocol and the complex, routable TCP/IP protocol. Like NetBEUI, IPX has many self-tuning characteristics, and it does not require much administrative burden to set up. IPX has the following benefits:

- Easy to set up

- Supports routing between networks

- Faster than the current Windows NT implementation of TCP/IP

- Allows easy connection to installed NetWare servers and clients

Disadvantages of NWLink

On the other hand, truly large networks that connect many distant locations may find it difficult to work over IPX because it does not have an effective central addressing scheme to prevent two networks from using the same address numbers (in contrast to TCP/IP's addressing scheme). IPX does not support the wide range of network management tools available for TCP/IP. In addition:

- The lack of a centralized network numbering scheme stymies interconnection between independent organizations. Although Novell now has a network number registration, it came about after most networks were installed. So few organizations actually use this numbering scheme that it doesn't solve the centralized numbering problem.

- IPX is slower than NetBEUI over slow serial connections.

- IPX doesn't support SNMP.

NetBEUI

NetBEUI stands for NetBIOS extended user interface (and NetBIOS stands for network basic input output system). NetBEUI implements the NetBIOS frame (NBF) transport protocol, which IBM developed in the mid-1980s to support LAN workgroups under OS/2 and LAN Manager.

When IBM developed NetBEUI, it did not target networked PCs for enterprisewide connectivity. Rather, NetBEUI was developed for workgroups of 2 to 200 computers. NetBEUI cannot be routed between networks, so it is constrained to small LANs consisting of Microsoft and IBM clients and servers.

NetBEUI 3.0 is the Microsoft update of IBM's NetBEUI protocol included with early versions Windows NT.

Features of NetBEUI

You can think of NetBEUI as the small, fast sports car of transport protocols. You can't rely on it for long trips (routing), but it's faster than any other TDI-compliant transport protocol for small networks that do not need to take advantage of routing to other networks. NetBEUI has the following advantages:

- Very fast on small networks

- Allows more than 254 sessions (a limitation of earlier versions)

- Better performance over slow serial links than previous versions

- Easy to implement

- Self-tuning

- Good error protection

- Small memory overhead

Disadvantages of NetBEUI

The disadvantages of NetBEUI are similar to the disadvantages of a sports car. It's not suitable for long trips because it can't be routed. Because it's not widely used (outside the realm of Microsoft operating systems), very little software is available to help you analyze NetBEUI problems. Here are some other disadvantages of NetBEUI:

- Cannot be routed between networks

- Few tools, such as protocol analyzers

- Very little cross-platform support

AppleTalk

AppleTalk is the transport protocol developed by Apple for use with Apple Macintosh computers. Every Macintosh computer comes with built-in support for the AppleTalk protocol and is equipped to use the protocol to connect to an AppleShare file server. Although you would probably not use AppleTalk to connect your Windows 95 or Windows NT workstations to your Windows NT server (in fact, this configuration is not possible without third-party software), you can use the AppleTalk protocol that comes with Windows NT to provide file and print services to Apple Macintosh computers on your network.

AppleTalk is an example of a transport protocol that is not TDI compliant. Therefore, you cannot use it to implement the full range of networking features of Windows NT. Microsoft chose to implement AppleTalk as a service that speaks directly to NDIS-compatible network adapters, thus bypassing the NetBIOS features required for clients of Microsoft networks.

Features of AppleTalk

The primary advantage of AppleTalk in a Windows NT network is that Macintosh computers can use AppleTalk and Services for Macintosh to seamlessly access file and print services on a Windows NT server.

Disadvantages of AppleTalk

The most significant disadvantage to AppleTalk is that clients other than Macintosh computers cannot use AppleTalk. Even if you use AppleTalk to connect your Macintosh clients to your Windows NT server, you will have to use another protocol such as NetBEUI alongside AppleTalk to allow other computers to access your server.

Installing and Configuring Network Protocols

YOU ARE NOW ready to learn how to install all three network protocols (TCP/IP, NWLink, and NetBEUI) as well as the AppleTalk protocol.

TCP/IP

TCP/IP can be the most difficult protocol to install in a computer. However, installing TCP/IP can be as easy as installing any other protocol if your network already has Dynamic Host Configuration Protocol (DHCP) services installed to assign IP addresses, subnet masks, and default gateways for you. If your network does not already provide DHCP support, then you will have to manually assign the many TCP/IP configuration options yourself.

When you set up TCP/IP networking on your Windows NT server, you will need certain information about your TCP/IP network:

- The IP address of your server

- The subnet mask for your network or networks if your server has more than one network adapter

- The default gateway

- The domain name server

- DHCP information

- WINS information

Figure 6.5 shows the Microsoft TCP/IP Properties window, which contains these configuration settings.

This section explains the TCP/IP networking settings and walks you through the process of installing TCP/IP on your server.

IP Address

The IP address uniquely identifies your computer on a TCP/IP network. It consists of four numbers separated by dots; each number must be between 0 and 255. For instance, 128.110.121.42 is a valid IP address.

The first one to three numbers (depending on the subnet mask, described below) identify the network that your computer is on. The remaining number(s) identify your computer on that network. The address as a whole should uniquely identify your computer among all computers worldwide.

If the first three numbers identify your network address (indicated by the subnet mask), then your computer is a part of a Class C network, which can handle up to 255 computers. This size is the most common Internet network size. If the first two numbers identify your network address, then you are on a Class B network, which can handle about 65,000 computers. The number of

Class B networks worldwide is much smaller than the number of Class C networks. Most Class B networks are found in very large corporations and universities. If only the first number identifies your network and the remaining three identify the computers on the network, then you are on a Class A network. Class A networks are reserved for other wide area internetworks like major Internet service providers and telephone companies with millions of computers that are linked to the Internet.

If your network is connected to other networks, then you will have received your network ID and perhaps your whole IP address from an outside source such as Internet Network Information Center (InterNIC) or from an Internet provider, which received the numbers from InterNIC.

IP addresses ending in 0 and 255 are special addresses in TCP/IP. Addresses ending in 0 (or equal to zero after the network mask is applied) refer to the network itself. For example, 128.110.121.0 is the network number of the network, not of any computer or component of it. Networks including the number 255 are used to broadcast information. The 255 means this information applies to all the computers in the network.

If you set up your server as a DHCP server, it can automatically assign IP addresses to client computers when they attach to the network during the boot process. The DHCP server frees you from the hassle of assigning IP addresses and resolving IP address conflicts. However, you must manually assign the IP addresses to the DHCP server. Note that your server can have its IP address assigned by another DHCP server on your network. Therefore, you need to manually assign IP addresses to only one computer on a network if DHCP has been installed.

Subnet Mask

The subnet mask, which usually looks like 255.255.0.0 marks which part of the IP address is the network ID and which part is your station ID. A value of 255 means that the number is a part of the network ID. A value of 0 identifies your station ID. For instance, a subnet mask of 255.255.255.0 with an IP address of 198.5.212.40 means that your network is 198.5.212 and you are station 40 on that network.

TCP/IP uses subnet masks because some networks need many station addresses and other networks need few. The subnet scheme provides for a large number of small networks and a small number of large networks, which can be further subdivided into small networks. The subnet mask performs a simple mathematical operation that tells TCP/IP whether the computer you are talking to is local or is accessed through a gateway.

The destination address of each packet is mathematically ANDed with your subnet mask. If the result is not equal to your subnet mask, the computer is not local to your network and the packet is transmitted to the default gateway. The Boolean algebra operator AND works this way: for each bit in a binary number, 0 and 0 = 0; 1 and 0 = 0; 0 and 1 = 0; 1 and 1 = 1.

Sometimes you will see a value other than 0 or 255 in the subnet mask. This additional value divides networks into even smaller subnets. For example, a subnet mask of 255.255.255.128 would give you a network with fewer than 127 available addresses for client stations. Exercise 6.1 shows you how to determine how many IP addresses are available using any valid subnet mask.

EXERCISE 6.1

Viewing a Subnet Mask with the Calculator

1. Select Start ➢ Programs ➢ Accessories ➢ Calculator.

2. Select View ➢ Scientific.

3. Type **224** (which is the last byte of the subnet mask) in the display. The first three bytes are 255.255.255. We know that these equal 11111111, so there's no need to convert them with the calculator.

4. Select the Bin radio button to change the display type from decimal to binary.

5. Notice that the display has changed to 11100000.

This value means that the subnet mask allows five bits for the addressing of computers within the subnet. Because 2 raised to the 5th power is 32, minus the 0 that defines the network and the 31 that addresses all computers in the network, you have 30 unique addresses to assign within this subnet mask. Valid subnet masks can contain only 1s to the left and 0s to the right, but the boundary between 1s and 0s can be anywhere within the 32 bits of the subnet mask.

6. Close the calculator.

Further discussion of dividing subnets is beyond the scope of this book, but you should recognize when a network is being so divided.

The subnet mask identifies a message destination that is beyond your local network. When a destination network ID (identified from your subnet mask) is not the same as your network ID, then the message is sent to a gateway (see below), which will forward the message to the destination computer. This setting can be configured automatically if you have DHCP on your network, or you can configure the subnet mask manually.

Default Gateway

When the destination computer is not on the same network as your computer, the network must forward the message to the destination network. A special device or computer called a *gateway* handles the forwarding request. When your computer recognizes that the destination computer is not on your local network (by combining the subnet mask with the destination IP address), your computer sends the message to the gateway instead.

In TCP/IP parlance, gateways are the same as routers. However, in common usage, gateways are computers, configured as routers, that also provide other network services, whereas routers are dedicated to the task. For instance, a server with more than one network interface adapter is probably routing IP packets between them and therefore acting as a gateway.

Therefore, the gateway must have an address that is on your local network. For instance, you could have a gateway on your network (198.5.212) at address 9. The default gateway IP address would be 198.5.212.9, and any address that did not have 198.5.212 as the first three numbers would not work.

If you do not have a valid gateway IP address, your computer, using TCP/IP, will be limited to communicating with computers on your local network only. This setting can be configured automatically if you have DHCP on your network, or you can configure the subnet mask manually.

Domain Name Server

Computers are very good at keeping track of numbers, but humans are better at dealing with names that mean something. Fortunately, the designers of the Internet provided a means of converting human-friendly names into computer-friendly numbers. The Internet domain name service performs this function, and to use it you need the IP address (numbers) of the closest domain name server (DNS).

When you see an Internet address, such as sybex.com, oeadm.org, or whitehouse.gov, you are seeing a name that the DNS must transform into numbers so that your computer can reach that destination computer.

The DNS address is a string of four numbers separated by dots like any other IP address, and it does not necessarily have to be on your local network. This setting can be configured automatically if you have DHCP on your network, or you can configure the DNS address manually. See Figure 6.6 for a view of the DNS tab of the Microsoft TCP/IP Properties window.

FIGURE 6.6

You can manually enter the location of domain name servers for your network.

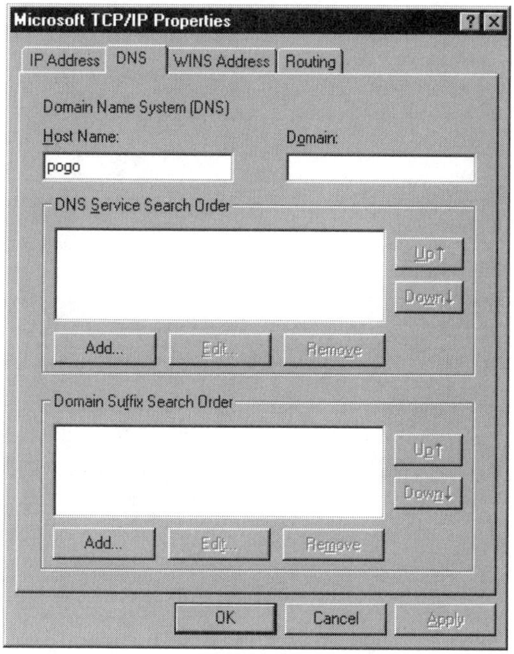

Dynamic Host Configuration Protocol (DHCP)

You can configure your Windows NT server to be automatically configured by a DHCP server elsewhere on your LAN (most likely by another Windows NT server). However, a server that will be the one providing the DHCP service for the rest of the network cannot select this option. (Chapter 15 explains how to configure DHCP.)

Windows Internet Name Service (WINS)

Microsoft developed the WINS protocol to make resolving Internet numeric addresses easier in a local area network. WINS performs the function of mapping Microsoft networking names to the numeric representation (123.123.123.123) of the Internet number. (DNS, on the other hand, looks up the addresses using the hierarchical Internet naming scheme, for example, names such as www.whitehouse.gov.) WINS is designed for keeping track of Microsoft-style computer names in your LAN. You can configure NT Server to use WINS, DNS, or both to translate computer names into Internet addresses. The WINS server will run on a Windows NT server somewhere in your network. See Figure 6.7 for a view of WINS configuration. (Chapter 15 also explains how to configure WINS.)

FIGURE 6.7

WINS translates Microsoft-style network names into numerical Internet addresses.

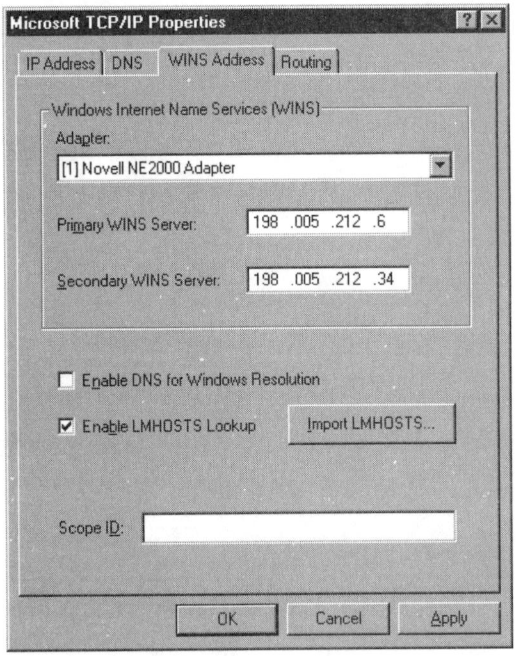

Installing and Configuring TCP/IP

The TCP/IP protocol is one of the protocol options available when you install Windows NT server. If you have already installed this protocol, you won't have to do Exercise 6.2. You will need to work Exercise 6.2 if you need to reconfigure TCP/IP, however.

EXERCISE 6.2

Installing and Configuring TCP/IP

1. Select Start ➤ Settings ➤ Control Panel.

2. Open the Network icon by double-clicking it.

3. Click the Protocols tab in the Networks window.

4. Click the Add button.

5. Select TCP/IP Protocol from the list of protocols. You may be asked to insert the original installation CD-ROM or to specify the location of the installation files.

6. Select Close in the Network window.

7. Select *Obtain an IP address from a DHCP server* if your local area network has a DHCP server. Otherwise, enter the IP address for your computer in the IP address field. Specify the subnet mask and default gateway as well.

8. If you have a DNS server in your LAN or if you have a constant connection to the Internet, click the DNS tab and then enter the DNS address.

9. If you have a WINS server in your network, click the WINS Address tab and then enter the WINS addresses.

10. Press OK to close the TCP/IP Properties dialog box. You will receive a warning if you haven't specified a primary WINS address.

11. Click Close.

12. Restart your computer in order for the changes to take effect. Click Yes to restart your computer.

NWLink (IPX/SPX)

Installing NWLink is very similar to installing other Windows NT transports such as TCP/IP or NetBEUI. NWLink does have some setting information that can be changed after it is installed by double-clicking the NWLink protocol in the Protocols list box, but the default settings will work for most users. Exercise 6.3 takes you through the process of installing NWLink.

EXERCISE 6.3

Installing and Configuring NWLink

1. Right-click the Network Neighborhood icon on the Desktop.

2. Select Properties.

3. Select the Protocols tab.

4. Click the Add button.

5. Select NWLink IPX/SPX Compatible Transport in the Network Protocols list box.

6. Click OK.

7. Enter the path to your Windows NT 4 Server CD-ROM in the Path field of the Windows NT setup dialog box and click continue. If you have RAS installed, you will be asked whether you want to bind NWLink to RAS. Click OK to bind them or cancel to leave them unbound.

8. Click the Close button.

9. Click Yes when asked if you want to restart.

Frame Types

For most users, leaving the default frame type (auto) is the best choice. Unfortunately, some Ethernet adapters can not properly detect frame types automatically and will therefore not work with this setting. For these adapters, you need to set the frame type specifically. The Ethernet 802.2 setting is recommended for new installations. Your setting must match the frame type used by other IPX/SPX-configured computers on the network.

Ethernet frame types control how Ethernet adapters communicate with each other. They include Ethernet source and destination information and a checksum. The different frame types handle this task in slightly different fashions and are therefore incompatible. The differences between them are not important, but the network problems they create are.

Novell NetWare 3.11 and earlier used Ethernet_802.3 as the default frame type. Novell 3.12 and later use the Ethernet_802.2 frame type as the default setting. To avoid reconfiguring clients when new servers are added, many NetWare servers simply load the LAN driver once for each frame type. This method reduces performance a little and takes slightly more memory, but it is a good trade-off to preclude frame incompatibility problems. Exercise 6.4 shows you how to change frame types.

EXERCISE 6.4

Changing the Ethernet Frame Type and IPX Network Number

1. Right-click the Network Neighborhood icon on the Desktop.

2. Select Properties.

3. Select the Protocols tab.

4. Double-click NWLink IPX/SPX Compatible Transport in the Network Protocols list box. If you have more than one adapter in your computer, select the adapter that resides on the same network as other IPX/SPX computers, such as a NetWare file server, in the Adapter drop-down box.

5. Select the Manual Frame Type Detection radio button.

6. Click the Add button.

7. Select the Frame Type you wish to use.

8. Enter the IPX network number to which the adapter is attached in the Network Number field. (If you are using the IPX/SPX protocol to connect to a NetWare file server, you can use the number shown on the NetWare Server's LAN driver information dialog box in the NetWare Monitor NLM.)

9. Click the Add button.

10. Repeat steps 7, 8, and 9 for each additional frame type you wish to use.

11. Click OK.

12. Click the Close button.

13. Click Yes when asked if you want to restart.

You may add as many frame types as you like to the supported frames dialog box. Be aware that many early Ethernet adapters support only certain frame types. If your network adapter is not software configurable (if it uses jumper switches to set the port and interrupt), it probably does not support all four frame types.

Another way to set the network number is through the NWLink setting dialog box. You can use the default setting of 0 to match any network number. If you set a network number, it must match the network number used by other IPX/SPX computers communicating on the LAN to which the adapter is connected.

NetBEUI

NetBEUI is the easiest protocol to install. Follow the steps outlined in Exercise 6.5 to install the NetBEUI protocol. (If you installed Windows NT Server as described in Chapter 4, then NetBEUI is already installed on your operating system.)

EXERCISE 6.5

Installing and Configuring NetBEUI

1. Open the Network Settings control panel.

2. Click the Protocols tab.

3. Click the Add button.

4. Select NetBEUI from the Protocols option list and click OK.

5. Enter the path to your CD-ROM install files and click OK. Normally this would be `D:\I386`.

6. If you have RAS installed, Windows NT will ask if you want to support it using this protocol. Click cancel to leave it unsupported.

7. Click Close to complete the operation.

8. Click Yes to restart your computer.

AppleTalk

The AppleTalk protocol is also very easy to install. You install it by adding Services for Macintosh from the Services tab of the Networks window, rather than from the Protocols tab.

In order to support Macintosh computers, the Windows NT operating system must load other components in addition to the AppleTalk protocol.

You are installing AppleTalk to support Apple Macintosh clients only, and in the process you will also create a network share for use by Apple Macintosh computers. Chapter 15 explains how to install AppleTalk and the related services.

Summary

WINDOWS NT SERVER was designed to be the focal point of your network. It has a flexible network framework that allows it to support many protocols and services.

Network architecture describes the function of networks in the same way that the architecture of buildings describes the function of buildings. Different parts of networks can be identified by their function in the network.

A local area network is composed of personal computers in one geographic location, such as an office building or school, that communicate with each other. Personal computers can execute programs on their own. Network cable links network interface adapters, which allow personal computers to communicate in a network. The networking protocol specifies the meaning of the signals exchanged by computers and the order of the exchange. Many networks have a hub that connects the network cables at the physical center of a network. A server serves files and authenticates logon requests; a client relies on a server for file services and logon authentication; a peer may serve files but does not provide logon authentication for other computers.

The OSI model specifies seven layers of network functionality. The IEEE model further details the operation of the data link layer. The seven layers are

1. Application
2. Presentation
3. Session
4. Transport
5. Network
6. Data link
7. Physical

The IEEE specification subdivides the data link layer into the logical link control and media access control sublayers.

Device drivers and network interface adapters under Windows NT perform services that fall under the data link layer and physical layer of the OSI model. Transport protocols under Windows NT perform services that fall under the network and transport layer of the OSI model. Components of Windows NT networking that fall under the Services tab of the Network control panel usually belong to the top three layers of the OSI model.

The Windows NT networking model specifies components and boundary layers. The components specify software and hardware that perform certain tasks; the boundary layers specify how these components communicate with each other. This combination of components and boundary layers makes components interchangeable and gives Windows NT Server its networking flexibility.

TCP/IP is the most flexible of the networking protocols, and it is the protocol of the Internet (and by extension, of the World Wide Web). It can be the most difficult to configure, however.

NWLink, also known as IPX/SPX, is the transport protocol used in NetWare networks. It is a fast networking protocol and is easy to configure. You should be careful that the frame type matches the frame type used in your network, and if you are connecting to a NetWare server, make sure that the network number matches that of the NetWare server.

NetBEUI is the simplest protocol to install, and it is also a very fast protocol. NetBEUI is a good choice for dial-up network connections if you do not need to transfer Internet information over the same dial-up line. The most significant drawback to NetBEUI is that it is not a routable protocol.

AppleTalk's strength and weakness are its support for Apple Macintosh computers. It is the easiest way to support Macintosh network clients, but you won't use it to support any other kind of computer.

Review Questions

1. Windows NT Server was designed to be the heart of your network.

   A. True

   B. False

2. The OSI model defines 12 layers for network communication.

   A. True

   B. False

3. The physical layer is simply responsible for sending bits from one computer to another.

   A. True

   B. False

4. The IEEE enhancements to the OSI model further subdivide the data link layer into the logical link control sublayer and the media access control sublayer.

   A. True

   B. False

5. The network layer and the transport layer are the layers at which Windows NT transport protocols such as TCP/IP and NWLink operate.

   A. True

   B. False

6. Boundary layers in the Windows NT network architecture isolate components to keep them from communicating with each other.

   A. True

   B. False

7. Boundary layers are the same thing as interfaces.

   A. True

   B. False

8. TCP/IP is the simplest transport protocol you can install.

   A. True

   B. False

9. NWLink supports accessing NetWare file servers.

    A. True

    B. False

10. NetBEUI is routable.

    A. True

    B. False

11. AppleTalk allows you to connect Macintosh computers to your Windows NT Server.

    A. True

    B. False

12. When you install NWLink, any frame type or network number will do.

    A. True

    B. False

13. AppleTalk is installed from the Protocol tab of the Network control panel just like TCP/IP, NWLink, or NetBEUI.

    A. True

    B. False

14. A _____ _____ _____ links personal computers together.

15. A _____ _____ _____ connects the computer to the cable and translates the data from the computer into a form that can be transmitted over the cable medium.

16. _____ define the meanings assigned to signals, which data is sent and in what order, and how the computers negotiate the sending and the receiving of data.

17. A _____ is a computer that relies on the server for logon validation and file storage.

18. A _____ is a computer that not only executes programs for the user and interacts directly with the user (like a client) but also can share its hard disk space with other computers on the network (like a server).

Configuring
Windows NT

THIS CHAPTER FOCUSES on the configuration of Windows NT through the control panel. The control panel contains programs that allow you to control the operation of Windows NT by changing device driver and service settings. Nearly all Windows NT configuration settings are controlled from the control panel.

When Apple developed control panels for the Macintosh OS computers, it called each individual control panel program a control panel and put them all in a folder called the Control Panels folder. When Microsoft borrowed the idea for Windows, it created a monolithic Control Panel application into which individual control panel programs can be installed. Microsoft made this control panel look like a folder, but it's really not—you can't just put anything in it. To avoid confusion, we call the monolithic control panel application the Control Panel and the individual components control panel programs.

You use the various control panel programs to install device drivers and services. Many control panels include a tab that allows you to specify a new device driver for previously installed hardware. Device drivers are installed under the control panel that controls the functionality of the device.

Many of the control panel programs in Windows NT Server are present only for complete compatibility with Windows NT Workstation. They have little or no purpose on a dedicated file server; however, the control panels may be useful for nondedicated servers that are also used as workstations and we mention them (briefly) in this discussion for the sake of completeness.

Other control panels are so fundamental to the operation of a network server that we mention them here and devote one or more chapters to explaining their features.

The Control Panel includes the following control panel programs by default.

- **Accessibility Options** provides user interface extensions for various interface requirements.

- **Add/Remove Programs** installs and removes applications that use the standard Microsoft installer.

- **Console** configures the interface for the command prompt.

- **Date/Time** sets the date and time.

- **Devices** controls the execution of device drivers.

- **Dial-Up Monitor** shows statistics for the Remote Access Service.

- **Display** controls the visual appearance of the Explorer interface.

- **Fonts** adds and removes fonts.

- **Internet** defines a proxy server for TCP/IP.

- **Keyboard** changes keyboard settings and drivers.

- **Licensing** adds licenses for some software packages.

- **Mail** controls your MS-Mail client.

- **Microsoft Mail Postoffice** controls the MS-Mail post office on your messaging server.

- **Modems** controls the modems installed in your computer.

- **Mouse** changes mouse settings and drivers.

- **Multimedia** configures sound cards and related multimedia devices.

- **Network** configures network services and device drivers.

- **ODBC** controls the routing of ODBC database information.

- **PC Card (PCMCIA)** controls the various PC Cards installed in your computer.

- **Ports** controls the configuration of serial and parallel ports.

- **Printers** is a convenient shortcut to the printer settings program.

- **Regional Settings** configures your computer for regional variations.

- **SCSI Adapters** controls any SCSI and IDE adapters installed in your system.

- **Server** controls the server service of a Windows NT Server.

- **Services** controls the execution of the various services installed in your computer.

- **Sounds** assigns various sound files to Windows interface activities.

- **System** controls various systemwide Windows NT configuration settings.

- **Tape Devices** changes tape device drivers.

- **Telephony** controls the TAPI settings for your computer.

- **UPS** changes settings for attached uninterruptible power supplies.

- **MacFile** lets you control how your Windows NT Server acts as an AppleShare server.

- **GSNW** lets you control the gateway and client services for NetWare.

After a short digression to discuss drivers and services, we will explore each control panel application typically installed during the Windows NT installation.

Drivers

DRIVERS ARE SOFTWARE components that act as interfaces between the operating system and a specific hardware component or lower level software service. For instance, a mouse driver watches the input port to which the mouse is attached and converts the numbers it receives from the mouse to positions and movement commands that it provides to Windows NT.

Windows NT must have a driver for each attached hardware device. Windows NT prevents applications from directly accessing hardware device registers; only protected mode software like drivers and the Hardware Abstraction Layer can access hardware directly. Other operating systems, such as MS-DOS and Windows, do not prevent programs from directly accessing memory or hardware registers outside their own space. Therefore, poorly written programs can crash the computer by putting these devices in a state the operating system does not expect. Programs running under Windows NT must access the services of drivers to interact with hardware. Access can be denied to a malfunctioning program without crashing the computer. This protective feature also allows certain security features to be implemented in a way that cannot be circumvented by simply accessing hardware directly. Figure 7.1 shows how drivers interact with hardware devices and the operating system.

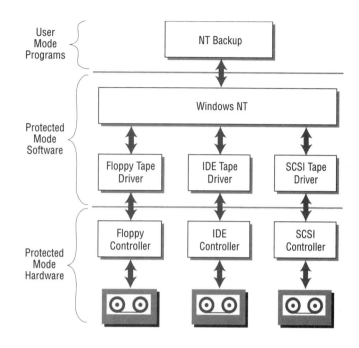

Drivers also allow programs to work with devices from various vendors and with differing functionality without the program having to know anything about the specific device. For example, the NT Backup program can talk to any tape device because all tape device drivers for Windows NT conform to a certain specification that NT Backup and each specific tape device driver understand. The driver translates the commands from NT Backup into the specific commands required to run the physical tape unit. A serendipitous effect of driver abstraction is that programs can use devices invented after the software was released, as long as the devices come with a compatible driver.

Abstraction *means generalizing, so when we say "a driver is abstracted," or when Microsoft refers to the Hardware Abstraction Layer, it means that the hardware has been generalized by the driver so that different hardware devices of the same general type all look the same to the operating system.*

The Windows NT Server and Workstation CD-ROMs contain many device drivers. Most of these drivers were written by the device manufacturers; Microsoft includes them on the CD-ROM as a convenience to you. Some drivers for common peripherals, such as IDE hard disk drives, modems, and

VGA video adapters, were written by Microsoft to provide a basic level of service to Windows NT. Some of the more specialized devices (especially those written after the release of the Windows NT CD-ROM) are available only on floppy disks provided with the device. Select the Have Disk installation option if your device driver is on a floppy disk.

Control Panel Programs

CONTROL PANEL PROGRAMS are your interface to the operation of drivers and services. Most drivers and services are configured to run correctly from the installation without modification, but any time you add or change hardware in your system you will probably need to configure the change through a control panel program. Other control panel programs, such as the Microsoft Mail Postoffice, provide access to the options of an application rather than to a service or device. Figure 7.2 shows the control panel programs included in a typical installation of Windows NT Server. (The control panel programs that appear in your installation may differ from Figure 7.2 depending upon the installation options you select when you install Windows NT.)

FIGURE 7.2

Windows NT Server
Control Panel.

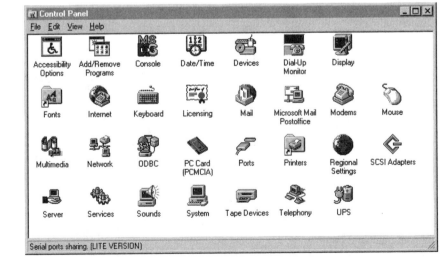

Accessibility Options

The Accessibility Options control panel allows you to adapt the function of the user input devices (keyboard and mouse) to meet the needs or individual preferences of users on that system. For Windows NT Servers, this user is typically the network administrator. This control panel does not appear if you unchecked accessibility options while installing Windows NT Server.

The Mouse Keys feature of the Accessibility Options control panel allows you to control the mouse pointer through the keyboard, affording more precision control over its placement than a mouse can provide.

Accessibility Options has four tabs:

- **Keyboard** controls keyboard settings for StickKeys, FilterKeys, and ToggleKeys.

- **Sound** controls sound settings that show visible indications of system and application sounds.

- **Mouse** controls the MouseKeys feature that allows you to move the mouse pointer with the keyboard.

- **General** controls idle, feature sound, and SerialKey devices that support alternative access to keyboard and mouse features.

Each option changes the standard function of that portion of the user interface.

Add/Remove Programs

Add/Remove Programs allows you invoke the installer or uninstaller for Win32 applications installed on your system and to add or remove components of an operational Windows NT System. This control panel has two tabs:

- Install/Uninstall

- Windows NT Setup

The Add/Remove functionality of this control panel is limited to programs written to use it. Because most programs come with their own install and uninstall programs, you will rarely use the Install/Uninstall tab. However, you may use this panel to add Windows NT system components and some device drivers with the Windows NT Setup tab. You can use the Have Disk feature of this control panel to install any sort of device driver if you can't find a control panel that is more appropriate. Exercise 7.1 shows you how to remove components that may not be necessary for a Windows NT Server.

EXERCISE 7.1

Removing Windows NT Components

1. Select Start ➤ Settings ➤ Control Panel.

2. Double-click the Add/Remove Programs control panel.

3. Select the Windows NT Setup tab.

4. Uncheck the Games option.

5. Click OK. The component will now be removed from your system. You can reinstall the component at any time by reversing this procedure.

Console

The Console control panel allows you to change the configuration of the command prompt. With this control panel you can change cursor and window options, display settings and sizes, and the size of the screen buffer. These settings are more important on systems that run MS-DOS applications, which is rare on a Windows NT Server. This control panel has four tabs:

- **Options** controls the cursor size, command buffer, edit mode, and windows display options.

- **Font** controls the display font. You can choose from monospaced fonts installed in your system.

- **Layout** controls the screen height and width.

- **Colors** controls the display color of the command console.

Date/Time

The name of this control panel says it all. From this control panel you can change the date, time, and time zone of your computer. Because the clock and calendar are useful for everyday purposes, you can also launch this control panel quickly by double-clicking on the time shown in the Taskbar at the bottom of the screen.

Devices

The Devices control panel allows you to control the execution of device drivers. With this control panel you can stop a device driver, thus suspending the service it provides. Stopping a device driver may be necessary if the driver fails to respond to the system or if the operation of a device driver is interfering with the proper operation of the server. Under normal circumstances you will rarely need to use this control panel. Figure 7.3 shows the Devices control panel.

FIGURE 7.3

The Devices control panel.

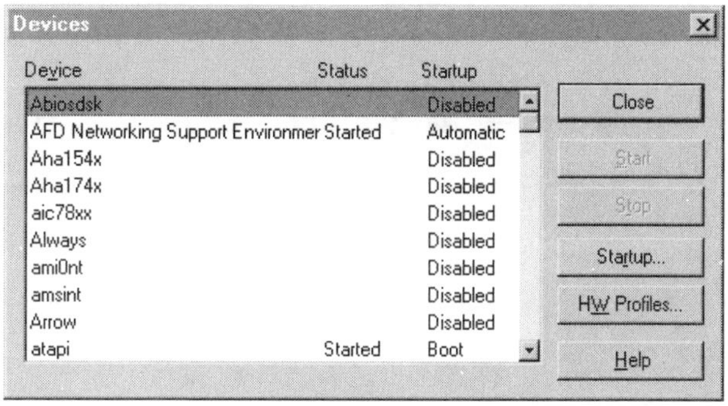

You can also specify how to start a device driver: at boot time, automatically during the later boot process, or manually. You should not change the default settings for devices without a full understanding of the effect the change will have on the system. Many device drivers are required for the system to boot properly—changing their startup options can render your system nonoperational.

If your server has more than one hardware profile (most do not; the hardware profiles feature is included mainly for laptop computers with docking stations), you can use the Devices control panel program to control which devices appear in different hardware profiles. Hardware profiles are covered in more detail in the companion book, *MCSE: NT Workstation Study Guide*.

Dial-Up Monitor

The Dial-Up Monitor shows current statistics for Remote Access Service (RAS) sessions operating in the computer. You can double-click the RAS indicator on the Taskbar to open the dial-up monitor when RAS is active. The Dial-Up control panel program will only be available in the Control

Panel if you have installed the Remote Access Service. The Dial-Up Monitor has three tabs:

- **Status** shows the current throughput and compression statistics for a single RAS connection.

- **Summary** shows summarized connection statistics for all active RAS connections.

- **Preferences** controls RAS features like connection sounds and the display style of the RAS monitor.

Exercise 7.2 shows you how to change the display style of the RAS monitor to emulate the connection status lights of an external modem.

EXERCISE 7.2

Changing RAS Monitor Settings

1. Select Start ➤ Settings ➤ Control Panel.

2. Double-click the Dial-Up Monitor control panel.

3. Select the Preferences tab.

4. Select the *As a window on the desktop* option of the Show status lights control group.

5. Uncheck the *Display the window's title bar* option.

6. Click OK.

7. Move the Monitor window that appears to an inconspicuous location on your desktop and resize it as desired. You can double-click this status window to open the Dial-Up Monitor.

Display

Display settings change the appearance of your Windows NT desktop. Through the Display Settings control panel, you can change the resolution, color depth, color scheme, wallpaper, and many other display-related functions. You can also install video drivers in the Display control panel.

The Display control panel has five tabs:

- **Background** allows you to change the background pattern or wallpaper settings.

- **Screen Saver** allows you to select a screen saver and change its properties.

- **Appearance** allows you to select screen fonts and colors.

- **Plus!** allows you to control miscellaneous features.

- **Settings** allows you to alter the screen resolution, color depth, and refresh frequency; to test display modes; and to change the adapter driver.

Exercise 7.3 shows you how to change a display adapter driver.

Screen savers are a needless waste of compute power on servers that remain logged on to provide some third-party service such as faxing. Setting the screen saver to None will allow energy star–compliant monitors to go to power standby mode without wasting compute power.

EXERCISE 7.3

Changing the Display Adapter

1. Right-click any empty part of the Desktop.

2. Select the Properties menu item. This step is a shortcut to the Display control panel program.

3. Select the Settings tab.

4. Click Display Type.

5. Click Change.

6. Select your adapter from the pick list. If you don't know which adapter you have, click Cancel and use the Detect option. If your adapter is not listed, use the Have Disk option to load a driver from floppy disk.

7. Insert the Windows NT Server CD-ROM and click OK.

8. Follow the on-screen prompts if you are asked to test the adapter.

9. Click OK to acknowledge the reboot message.

10. Click Yes to restart your computer.

Fonts

The Fonts control panel program isn't really a control panel program. It is simply a shortcut to the Fonts folder in your Windows NT Server directory. Double-clicking it opens the Fonts window, allowing you to copy font files to and from the folder or to delete fonts you no longer need.

Internet

The Internet control panel program is used if you have a security server (firewall) on your network that requires it. By checking the Use Proxy Server option and setting the server in the list box, your Internet requests will be filtered by the proxy server rather than passed directly to the Internet. Check the documentation that came with your firewall software to determine if you need to use the Internet control panel program to configure your security services.

Keyboard

The Keyboard control panel program lets you change keyboard settings like the repeat delay, repeat rate, and cursor blink speed. This control panel has three tabs:

- **Speed** allows you to change the keyboard repeat rate, delay, and text cursor blink rate.

- **Input Locale** allow you to assign hotkeys so you can change keyboards on the fly.

- **General** allows you to change keyboard drivers—something most users will never need to do.

Licensing

The Licensing control panel program allows you to add licenses for products that require them and to change the server licensing mode from per server to per seat if you wish. When you buy additional per seat or per server licenses, you can add them to the system through this control panel program.

Mail

The Mail control panel program allows you to add and configure mail services such as Microsoft Mail, Internet Mail, and other third-party mail services (e.g., alphanumeric pager gateway services). This control panel program is installed only if you've installed Microsoft Messaging Services. See Chapter 15 and the companion book *MSCE: TCP/IP Study Guide.*

Microsoft Mail Postoffice

The Microsoft Mail Postoffice control panel program allows you to create and administer Microsoft Mail and Exchange post offices. As with the Mail control panel program, this control panel program is installed only if you've installed the Microsoft Messaging Service. See Chapter 15 and the companion book *MSCE: TCP/IP Study Guide.*

Modems

Modulators/Demodulators (modems) are devices that create analog signals in the audible range from digital data so that the data can be transmitted over regular dial-up telephone lines. These devices are inexpensive and provide a way for any computer in the world to attach to another computer or a network. The only drawback is their bandwidth, which is limited to a theoretical maximum speed of 56Kb/sec (64Kb/sec for European telephone systems). Modem manufacturers have already reached this limit.

Because they are inexpensive and can be used over standard telephone lines, modems are the most popular way of connecting to online services and the Internet. Internet protocols are optimized for low-speed modem connections.

Early dominance in the modem market by a single manufacturer created a de facto standard for establishing protocols and controlling modems. This standard allows Windows NT to treat most modems similarly. Therefore, a single modem driver controls all analog modems. You can accommodate specific differences among modems using the configuration files included in Windows NT and by changing the initialization strings.

When you select which type of modem you are installing in the Modems control panel program, you are not selecting a driver. You are simply telling the unimodem driver which set of initialization strings to use by identifying the type of modem that you have. If you can't find your modem in the list, try using the Hayes Compatible settings.

RAS is designed to provide network connections to low-speed serial devices like modems. To successfully install RAS, you must have at least one serial device in your system. These devices can be modems, ISDN interfaces, or X.25 (leased line) PADs. Figure 7.4 shows the Modems control panel program.

Windows NT will automatically detect the specific modem you have to select the correct initialization string through the Modems control panel program. If the modem you use is not detected, you can choose it manually from a list of modems available on the Windows NT CD-ROM. If your modem is not listed, you will have to choose the closest modem in the Standard Modem Types category. These settings use initialization strings that will work with most modems, but which may not allow you to use some advanced features of your modem. Exercise 7.4 shows the process of adding a modem to Windows NT. This process also activates the universal modem (unimodem) device driver.

EXERCISE 7.4

Adding a Modem to Windows NT

1. Select Start ➤ Settings ➤ Control Panel.

2. Double-click Modems.

3. Click Add if you already have another modem installed.

4. Click Next for Windows NT to automatically detect your modem.

5. Click Next to accept the modem suggested by Windows NT. Click Change to select the modem manually if the modem shown is not correct.

6. Click Finish. The modem will appear in the list of modems in the Modem control panel.

7. Click on the modem you just added in the modem list.

8. Click Properties.

9. Select the maximum bit rate supported by your modem in the Maximum Speed pick box. This rate will be the highest number shown in the pick list.

10. Click Close. If you have RAS installed, click OK to configure RAS for use with this new modem.

Mouse

The Mouse control panel program allows you to change mouse settings to match the way you work. The mouse control panel program has four tabs:

- **Buttons** allows you to change the function of the mouse buttons. Left-handed users can reverse the primary button (although the Microsoft mouse sure feels strange in the left hand!).

- **Pointers** allows you to change the visual style of the pointer.

- **Motion** allows you to change the speed of the mouse.

- **General** allows you to change the mouse driver. Most users will never need to do this.

Many mouse devices come with drivers and control panel programs of their own. Some of these devices add a custom tab to the mouse control panel, whereas others replace the panel with a special configuration program. If your pointing device uses a custom program for configuration, you should use that program instead of the Mouse control panel program.

Multimedia

You control multimedia (or sound and full motion video) functions with the Multimedia control panel program. This program has five tabs:

- **Audio** controls sound card playback volume, preferred playback device (for systems with more than one sound card) and recording level, preferred devices, and record quality.

- **Video** controls the playback size of full motion video files. The two options are windowed at various sizes or full screen.

- **MIDI** controls Musical Instrument Digital Interface output options that let you play MIDI sequences to a synthesizer built into your sound card. You can also add new MIDI synthesized instruments with this tab.

- **CD-Music** allows you to specify the drive letter of your CD-ROM and the headphone output volume.

- **Devices** controls the myriad of device drivers used to add multimedia functions to a computer. You can add, remove, and change the properties of each device driver with this tab.

Dedicated servers have no use for the multimedia functions controlled by this panel. They are included for complete compatibility with Windows NT Workstation. If your server will not be used as a workstation, you should consider removing any installed sound cards and multimedia device drivers.

Network

The Network control panel program (see Figure 7.5) provides access to the network for your server. This control panel program is the most important (and complex) control panel program for a Windows NT Server. It has five tabs:

- **Identification** controls the server name and domain/workgroup membership. Chapter 9 covers domain and workgroup membership as well as network identity.

- **Services** controls the addition, removal, and properties of network-related services. See Chapter 9 for more information about network services.

- **Protocols** controls the network transport protocols used on your server. Windows NT ships with support for the IPX/SPX (using NWLink), TCP/IP, and NetBEUI. The Appletalk transport protocol is controlled through the MacFile control panel. See Chapter 6 for more information on transport protocols.

- **Adapters** controls the properties of installed network adapters. From this tab you can add and remove adapter drivers and control the properties of installed adapters.

- **Bindings** allows you to control precisely which adapters are bound to which transport protocols and which transport protocols are bound to which services. By default, Windows NT enables all possible binding configurations. Bindings are discussed in detail in Chapter 9.

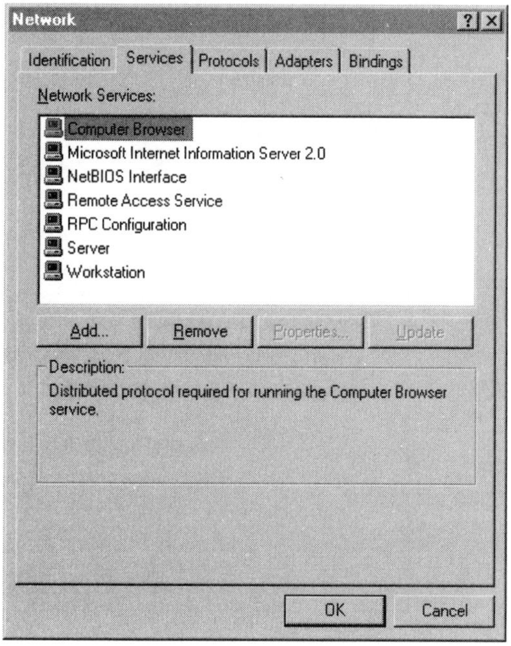

FIGURE 7.5

The Network control panel.

Because this control panel program is central to the functionality of a server, most of its functions are covered elsewhere in this book. Chapter 6 explains how to install transport protocols. Chapter 8 covers installing and configuring network services, changing network identity and domain/workgroup membership, and changing bindings for maximum performance and security.

Exercise 7.5 shows you how to add an adapter driver for an installed network interface adapter. Before performing Exercise 7.5, you must have a network adapter installed. With your computer powered down, install your network adapter. If your adapter is not configured by the BIOS (most PCI cards are) record any IRQ, Port, and DMA settings you configure manually.

EXERCISE 7.5

Adding a Network Adapter Driver

1. Boot the Computer.

2. Right-click the Network Neighborhood icon on the desktop.

3. Select the Properties menu item. This step is a shortcut to the Network control panel program.

4. Select the Adapters tab.

5. Click Add.

6. If your adapter (or a 100% compatible model) is shown in the list, select it. Otherwise, use the Have Disk option to load the driver from a floppy disk.

7. Respond to any adapter-specific dialogs. For many ISA network adapters, you may have to enter the IRQ, Port, or DMA settings. You may also have to enter the IPX frame type used in your network if the NWLink protocol is installed.

8. Click Close. Respond to any binding-related dialogs. You may have to enter a TCP/IP address for the new adapter if you are using the TCP/IP protocol on your network.

9. Click Yes to restart your computer.

Open Database Connectivity (ODBC)

ODBC controls the routing of Open Database Connectivity data sources, allowing you to connect database servers to database clients. This control panel is visible if you have any database software installed in your computer or the Internet Information Server. The functionality provided by this control panel program is of use only to application servers running SQL databases and is beyond the scope of this book.

PC Card (PCMCIA)

The PC Card control panel program allows you to control PC Cards (formerly known as Personal Computer Memory Card Industrial Association cards, or PCMCIA cards) installed in your computer. Because the vast majority of computers having PC Card slots and controllers are laptop computers, which are never used as network servers, this control panel program has no use on most servers. The PC Card control panel program is included mostly for complete compatibility with Windows NT Workstation. Double-clicking the control panel on a computer that has no PC Card controller brings up a dialog noting as much.

Some installations (especially U.S. government classified computers and software developers) have PC Card controllers installed in desktop computers. These controllers support the same PC Cards used in laptop and handheld computers.

If you have a PC Card controller in your server, you will see a control panel program with two tabs:

- **Socket Status** displays a pick list of installed PC Cards. Most PCMCIA controllers have two sockets, so you will usually see two slots listed.

- **Controller** shows the resources used by the PC Card controller. Note that you cannot change the driver for the PC Card controller through this control panel, although you can change drivers for many PC Cards.

Double-clicking an installed PC Card in the Socket Status tab brings up a dialog with three tabs:

- **CardInfo** shows the name of the card, the manufacturer, and a device map if necessary, as well as a device status window.

- **Driver** shows the driver used by the PC Card and the driver's status. Many PC Cards are serial devices, so they will use the `serial.sys` driver.

- **Resources** shows the hardware resources used by the PC Card.

Ports

The Ports control panel allows you to change the default settings for communication (COM) and line printer (LPT) or parallel ports. On Intel computers the NTDETECT portion of the boot process automatically detects COM and LPT ports, but if you have installed devices that use nonstandard IRQ settings, you may have to use the Ports control panel program to change the default resource settings for your computer. This problem frequently occurs with modems using nonstandard IRQ settings to avoid resource conflicts with the built-in COM1 and COM2 serial ports.

When the Ports control panel program launches, it shows the COM ports correctly installed in your system. Most computers have two, or three if a modem is installed. Double-clicking a port in the Ports pick list brings up the settings for that port.

You can click the Advanced button in the settings dialog box to control the COM port number, Base I/O Address, and IRQ level assigned to the port. If these settings do not match the hardware settings of the port, Windows NT will not be able to communicate with the device. Change these settings only if you have determined that Windows NT has improperly detected the resource settings of the port and cannot communicate with it.

Printers

Like the Fonts control panel program, Printers is not really a control panel program. It is a shortcut to the Printers application that controls which printer drivers are installed in your system. The Printers application looks and acts much like a regular Explorer window, but it contains installed printer drivers rather than the names of files or directories. This application is explored in detail in Chapter 14.

Regional Settings

The Regional Settings control panel program allows you to change Windows NT default settings to adapt to conventions in your part of the world. Most versions of Windows NT are localized for the region in which they are sold. You can change the default settings for the version of Windows NT you have to match your specific region. The Regional Settings control panel program has six tabs:

- **Regional Settings** allows you to select regional schemes for number, currency, time, and date symbols from one easy pick list.

- **Number** allows you to change numeric separators for your region. This task is easier to perform in the Regional Settings tab if your region is listed.

- **Currency** allows you to change currency display properties such as the currency symbol, decimal separator, and number of digits after a decimal. Most of these settings should match their equivalents in the Number tab.

- **Time** allows you to change the time separator and clock format.

- **Date** allows you to change the date separator and data format.

- **Input Locales** allows you to choose keyboard settings for your specific region. You can also set up hotkeys and locale indicators on the Taskbar to quickly switch locale settings if you use your computer in more than one locale or language.

SCSI Adapters

SCSI adapters control a wide variety of mass storage and high-bandwidth peripherals, such as hard disk drives, tape drives, removable cartridge hard disk drives, CD-ROM readers and recorders, magneto-optical drives, and scanners. SCSI adapters vary widely in their implementation, so each model requires a driver written specifically for it and for Windows NT. Figure 7.6 shows the SCSI Adapters control panel program.

The Windows NT CD-ROM contains drivers for many popular SCSI controllers, and those controllers can be automatically detected or selected during the Windows NT setup process. The process of adding a SCSI adapter driver to an existing Windows NT installation is similar to the process for adding any device driver and is explained in Exercise 7.6. You must have already installed your SCSI adapter in your computer and attached any hardware peripherals according to the instructions that came with the devices before performing Exercise 7.6.

FIGURE 7.6

The SCSI Adapters
control panel program.

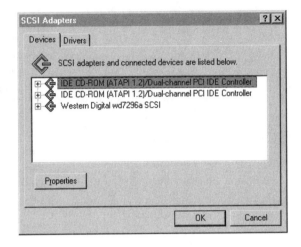

You can install and remove SCSI adapters from the SCSI Adapters control panel, but you cannot configure them here. Configuring your SCSI adapter takes place before the operating system boots. Typically, a message will appear during the BIOS initialization stage of the boot telling you which keystrokes to press to configure the adapter. Each adapter manufacturer uses a different method for BIOS configuration, so you will have to refer to the manual that came with your adapter for specific configuration information.

EXERCISE 7.6

Adding a SCSI Driver

1. Select Start ➢ Settings ➢ Control Panel.

2. Double-click SCSI Adapters.

3. Click the Drivers tab.

4. Click Add.

5. Select your SCSI Adapter manufacturer and model from the list. If your adapter is not shown, click Have Disk to install a driver from floppy disk.

6. Insert the Windows NT Server CD-ROM or other disk as requested and click OK.

7. Click Yes to restart your system.

Server

The Server control panel program(shown in Figure 7.7) shows you summaries of server-related statistics such as sessions in use, files currently locked, number of files open, and number of Named Pipes (explained in the companion book *MCSE: NT Workstation Study Guide*) in use. The Server control panel program has a summary display and five principal command buttons:

- **Users** shows you the connected users by logon and computer name and what resources they are using. From this dialog box you can see how long each user has been connected and how long they've been idle. You can also manually disconnect selected or all users.

- **Shares** shows you the name of each shared resource, the path to each shared resource, and the users connected to each shared resource on the server. You can disconnect users from specific resources with this control panel.

- **In Use** shows the type of resource in use and the permissions granted for that resource.

- **Replication** controls the directory replication setup for this server. You can control import and export replication directories through this dialog box. Replication is covered in greater detail in Chapter 10.

- **Alerts** controls which users or computers receive administrative alerts when they happen.

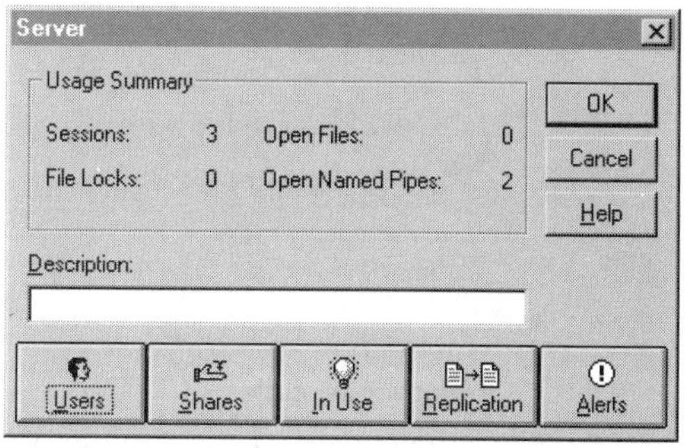

FIGURE 7.7

The Server control panel program.

The Server control panel is a convenient way to monitor how users are using server resources at a specific time. If your server is beginning to run slowly, you can see the number of users logged on to different resources to determine at what thresholds bottlenecks begin to occur.

Services

The Services control panel allows you to control the execution of services in much the same way the Device control panel controls the execution of device drivers. Starting and stopping services is useful if you need to use resources that are locked down by a service. For instance, if your modem is configured to answer incoming RAS calls and you wish to open a terminal session with that modem, you can stop the RAS service in the Services control panel program, access the modem, and restart the RAS service when you finish. Also, print jobs sometimes become "stuck" in the Windows NT print queue if a print device suffers from certain hardware errors. If you've corrected the problem with a print device but the print service doesn't resume, you can stop and then restart the spooler service to resume printing. Exercise 7.7 explains how to start and stop services.

RAS dedicates only modems set to answer incoming calls. You can use modems without stopping the RAS service if the modem is not currently in use and is configured to dial-out only.

EXERCISE 7.7

Stopping and Starting Services

1. Select Start ➤ Settings ➤ Control Panel.

2. Double-click the Services control panel.

3. Select Spooler in the Service pick list.

4. Click Stop. Make sure whatever caused the print device to malfunction has been corrected and that the print device is back online.

5. Click Start. When the Service Manager successfully starts the Spooler service, your printer should print the jammed document successfully.

Sounds

The Sounds control panel program lets you assign different sounds as WAV files to various Windows events, such as errors or acknowledgments. This control panel program is useful only if you have a sound card in your system. It is included with Windows NT primarily to provide complete compatibility with Windows NT Workstation.

Don't waste hardware resources or compute time on multimedia unless someone uses your file server as a workstation and needs to use sound devices.

System

The System control panel (see Figure 7.8) controls various functions and features in Windows NT that are not complex enough to require their own control panel. The System control panel has six tabs:

- **General** displays Windows NT system information such as the version and build of the operating system, the registered user, the type of processor employed, and the amount of physical RAM available.

- **Performance** controls server speed optimization and virtual memory settings.

- **Environment** controls the values of Windows NT environment variables.

- **Startup/Shutdown** controls the NT Boot loader options and crash recovery options.

- **Hardware Profiles** controls the properties and selection of hardware profiles. This feature is of little use in file servers, since their hardware rarely changes.

- **User Profiles** allows you to create roaming profiles for the users of this machine so their preferences will move with them to other machines on the network. User profiles are discussed in detail in Chapter 9, "Managing Users and Groups."

The System control panel program contains miscellaneous operating system features too simple to rate their own control panel program or application. It a good place to look if you are trying to remember where to change a feature that doesn't have its own control panel program.

Perhaps the most important setting controlled from the System control panel program is virtual memory. If you have more than one hard disk drive, you can improve the speed of your computer by creating a virtual memory paging file on each physical disk present. Windows NT can issue read and write commands to different disks simultaneously to speed virtual memory operations. This feature is most important on memory-limited systems. Exercise 7.8 shows you how to split the paging file across multiple physical disks.

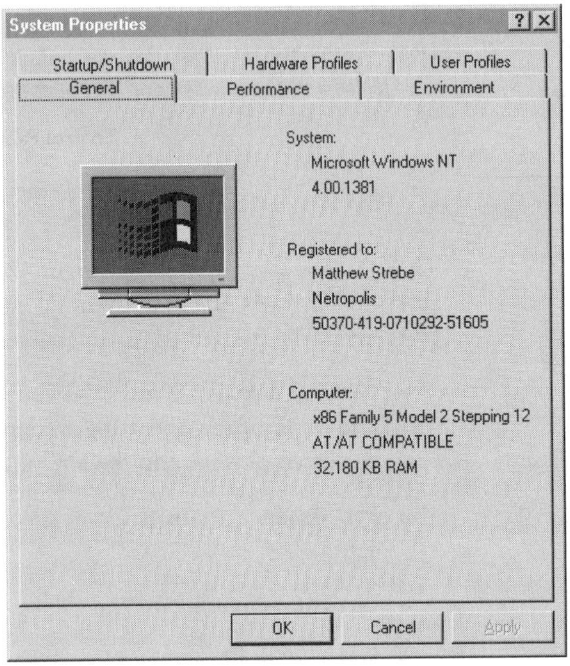

FIGURE 7.8

The System control panel.

Setting the virtual memory paging file size on the boot volume below the amount of physical memory you have plus 1MB disables the recording of debug information to a file if a STOP message is encountered. If you need this feature (most non-beta test installations do not), set the boot volume paging file size to equal at least the amount of physical memory you have plus 1MB or more.

Administrators familiar with Windows 95 will note that the System control panel program in Windows NT does not control device hardware configuration. The reporting functions of the Windows 95 system control panel program are included in the Windows NT Diagnostics utility in the Administrative Tools folder.

Modifying the Environment Path variable to include the windows and windows\system directories of other installations on your computer (such as Windows 95 or NT Workstation) will allow you to run most applications installed under those operating system because Windows NT Server will be able to find the correct dynamic link libraries and settings files.

EXERCISE 7.8

Splitting the Paging File across Multiple Physical Disks

1. Select Start ➤ Settings ➤ Control Panels.

2. Double-click the System control panel.

3. Select the Performance tab.

4. Click the Change button.

5. Divide the recommended value in the Total Paging File Size for All Drives section by the number of physical hard disks in your system, rounding fractions up.

6. Select your boot drive letter in the Drive pick box.

7. Enter the value determined in step 5 as the initial size.

8. Enter the value determined in step 5. Microsoft recommends setting both the initial size and the maximum size to the recommended size for best performance. This setting prevents Windows NT from taking time to increase the paging file size.

9. Repeat steps 6 through 8 for each physical disk in your system.

Tape Devices

You must add tape devices to Windows NT before archive programs such as NT Backup can access them. The Tape Devices control panel has two tabs:

- **Devices** shows the currently installed tape devices.

- **Drivers** shows the currently installed tape device drivers and allows you to add and remove tape device drivers.

You add and remove tape device drivers through the Drivers tab or by pressing the Detect button. You can use the Detect button to automatically detect many tape and backup devices. If Detect doesn't work, or identifies the wrong device, you can add a device manually. Exercise 7.9 shows you how to add a tape device and assumes your tape device has already been physically installed in or attached to your computer.

EXERCISE 7.9

Adding a Tape Device

1. Select Start ➤ Settings ➤ Control Panel.

2. Double-click the Tape Devices control panel program.

3. Select the Drivers tab.

4. Click Add.

5. Select your tape device from the Manufacturers and Tape Devices list box. The Standard tape drivers written by Microsoft can handle many common tape devices.

6. Enter the path to the driver if prompted.

7. Click Yes to restart your computer.

Telephony

The Telephony control panel allows you to create new locations for RAS and modem applications on portable computers. This feature is of little use to file servers, which spend most of their time in a stationary location. The Telephony control panel also allows you to install and remove telephony device drivers. Windows NT automatically installs two device drivers: the Telephony Application Programming Interface (TAPI) kernel-mode service provider and the unimodem service provider. The TAPI device driver provides a common interface to TAPI-enabled telephony applications. The unimodem service provider is a common device driver for modems on COM ports. All modems configured through the Modems control panel use the unimodem device driver for the actual hardware interface to the device. You will probably never need to change settings in the Telephony control panel on a Windows NT server.

UPS

The Uninterruptible Power Supply control panel allows you to configure how your UPS communicates with your server when power events occur. When you install a UPS, you must launch the UPS control panel and configure it to receive commands. Exercise 7.10 explains how to configure an uninterruptible power supply. Figure 7.9 shows the UPS control panel.

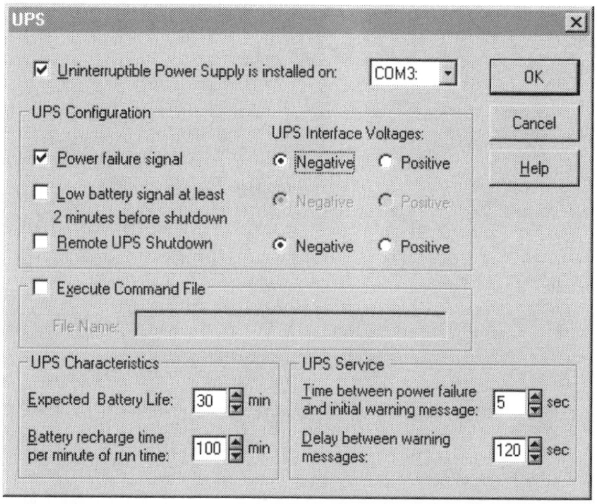

FIGURE 7.9

The UPS control panel.

FIGURE 7.9

The UPS control panel.

EXERCISE 7.10

Configuring an Uninterruptible Power Supply

1. Select Start ➤ Settings ➤ Control Panel.

2. Double-click the UPS control panel.

3. Check the Uninterruptible Power Supply checkbox and select the COM port to which it is attached.

4. Configure the UPS configuration settings to match the signals provided by your UPS; the UPS manual provides the necessary information.

5. Set the UPS Characteristics to match those published in your UPS configuration manual.

6. Change the time periods in UPS Service if you don't want to use the default values. Be sure the server has time to power down within the battery lifetime of the UPS.

7. If you want to execute a command file when a UPS event triggers, specify it in the Execute Command File input box. Do not execute a command file that requires user input.

8. Click OK.

9. Click Yes to start the UPS service.

Other Control Panels

SOME CONTROL PANELS are not installed in a default installation; they are installed only when the service they control is installed. Two services that come with Windows NT have control panels that are installed if you install the related service:

- **MacFile** controls service provision to Macintosh clients. MacFile is covered in Chapter 15.

- **GSNW** controls attachment to NetWare services and the Gateway Service for NetWare. GSNW is covered in Chapter 13.

Many well-written third-party services, such as modem sharing or fax server services, install control panels to configure their various features. Refer to the user manuals that come with these programs for specific information on their configuration and operation.

The Registry

YOU CAN CONFIGURE just about any aspect of Windows NT Server from the Control Panel, and it is both the recommended and the safest place from which to configure your computer. However, the Control Panel is not the only Windows NT configuration tool.

The Control Panel programs you have reviewed in this chapter give you a structured interface for configuring your computer, but they don't actually contain the OS configuration data. Most of that data is stored in the Windows NT Registry. (Some data, such as the default boot option, is stored in other files, but most operating system settings for Windows NT are stored in the Registry.)

The Registry is a very important part of the Windows NT operating system. You should be familiar with its structure and operation in order to use your Windows NT computer to its maximum potential.

Windows NT Server includes two utilities that allow you to modify the data in the Registry directly—REGEDIT.EXE and REGEDT32.EXE. The programs are similar in function, but each has its advantages. REGEDIT, for example, gives you a unified view of the Registry with a My Computer entry at the top, whereas REGEDT32 shows you five top-level keys. REGEDT32 is also a safer program because it allows you to confirm your changes or abandon them at the end of an editing session.

The Registry is a database that contains Windows NT configuration information, such as the following:

- Hardware configuration data

- System software configuration data

- User security data

- Current user data

- Application configuration data

The Registry does for Windows NT what system and configuration files do for other operating systems. You may be familiar with AUTOEXEC.BAT and CONFIG.SYS for MS-DOS, and SYSTEM.INI and WIN.INI for Windows. The Windows NT Registry contains all the information that these other configuration files hold for their respective operating systems—and more. Windows NT maintains versions of these files for compatibility with programs written for older versions of Windows.

In addition, application software can read and store application-specific information in the Registry, read system information, and adapt the application's behavior to match the configuration of your system.

Before you explore the Registry, you may wish to create a Start menu selection for the Registry Editor, REGEDIT.EXE (see Exercise 7.11).

Use REGEDIT.EXE *with caution. You can damage your operating system by entering inappropriate values or removing important Registry information. Therefore, we do not recommend modifying the Registry entries directly if you can use another more conventional way to make changes to your system settings, such as through the Control Panel or through User Manager for Domains.*

EXERCISE 7.11

Creating a Start Menu Selection for the Registry Editor

1. Click the Start button on the desktop.

2. Click Find and then click either Files or Folders.

3. Type **REGEDIT.EXE** in the Named part of the Find:All Files window.

4. Select Local Hard Drives in the Look In drop-down list.

5. Click the Find Now button. REGEDIT.EXE appears in the window when Windows NT finds the file.

6. Drag the REGEDIT.EXE entry to your start button and then let go.

7. Close the Find window.

The REGEDIT.EXE program will appear in your Start menu. You should now be able to run REGEDIT.EXE by clicking the Start button and then selecting the REGEDIT.EXE menu item.

Components of the Registry

The Registry stores a great deal of essential information. The structure of the Registry is hierarchical, much like the file system on your computer's hard drive. Keys and subkeys correspond to directories and subdirectories. Values are much like files in that they have names and types and hold the data in the Registry.

At the top of the Registry, which corresponds to the root of a file system, are five subtrees. The subtrees are like top-level directories. Keys and subkeys within each subtree hold information about your Windows NT computer. Refer to Table 7.1 for an explanation of the Registry elements.

TABLE 7.1 Registry Terms	ITEM	EXPLANATION
	Values	Values contain the information that is stored in the Registry. Each value has three parts: a name, a data type, and a configuration parameter that contains the actual information.
	Keys and Subkeys	Keys and subkeys are containers for subkeys and values.

TABLE 7.1	**ITEM**	**EXPLANATION**
Registry Terms (continued)	Subtree	The subtree (sometimes called subtree key or a predefined key handle) is a top-level key. A Windows NT Registry has five subtrees.
	Hive	A hive is a set of keys, subkeys, and values from the Registry that is stored in its own file in the location \<winnnt_root\SYSTEM32\CONFIG. A hive has its own transaction log to ensure that the data is valid.

The values in the Registry can have one of three types: DWORD value, string value, and binary value. Refer to Table 7.2 for an explanation of the Registry value types.

TABLE 7.2	**VALUES DATA TYPES**	**STRUCTURE AND CONTENTS**
Registry Value Types	DWORD Value	One to eight hexadecimal digits; contains a single value.
	String Value	A string data type of variable length.
	Binary Value	A string of hex digits; each pair of digits forms a byte value.

Editing the Registry

Before you edit the Registry, you must know which keys you wish to change and what you wish to change them to! Many keys in the Registry are not meant to be modified by operating system users, many others are better configured using the programs in the Control Panel. Some settings, however, are safe for you to modify.

It is beyond the scope of this chapter, beyond the capacity of the authors, and perhaps not within the realm of feasibility to list all the Registry settings, what they mean, and what useful values you can set them to. At this point we introduce just one of the Registry settings that you can change. Later in this book you will learn about others. (The next chapter, for example, shows you how to configure the browser status of your server computer by changing some Registry keys.)

Exercise 7.12 shows you how to display a message before people log on to your Windows NT server computer.

EXERCISE 7.12

Editing the Registry

1. Start the Regedit program. Double-click on the My Computer entry.

2. Double-click the HKEY_LOCAL_MACHINE key.

3. Double-click the SOFTWARE key in the above hierarchy.

4. Double-click the Microsoft key in the above hierarchy.

5. Double-click the Windows NT key in the above hierarchy.

6. Double-click the Current Version key in the above hierarchy.

7. Double-click the Winlogon key in the above hierarchy.

8. Double-click the value named LegalNoticeCaption.

9. Type **Authorized Access Warning!** in the Entry field of the Edit String dialog box.

10. Click OK.

11. Double-click the value named LegalNoticeText.

12. Type **Authorized access to this system constitutes an admission that you may be performing useful work. Any useful work performed on behalf of this company will be noted and rewarded. You have been warned!** in the Entry field of the Edit String dialog box.

13. Click OK.

14. Close the Registry Editor.

15. Log out and log on again to check the results. Note that a warning box titled Authorized Access Warning! with the LegalNoticeText now appears, and the user must respond.

Searching the Registry

The information stored in the Registry is exhaustive, and very few individuals know where everything is in it. Select Edit ➤ Find in the Registry Editor to track down things for you.

You can search for keys, values (names), and data. You can find exact matches for the text you type or find all occurrences of the text you type. Once you find a match, you can press [F3] to continue your search or press the Find Next button in the Search window.

When you search for something, the search starts from the currently high-lighted key. It will not branch back. If you wish to search the entire Registry, you must first select the My Computer key at the top of the Registry.

You can find occurrences of the word *Administrator* in the Registry by per-forming the steps outlined in Exercise 7.13.

EXERCISE 7.13

Finding Occurrences of a Word in the Registry

1. Start the Registry Editor.

2. Highlight My Computer by clicking it once.

3. Select Edit ➤ Find from the Registry Editor.

4. Type **Administrator** in the Find What field.

5. Click the Find Next button.

6. Press F3 to find additional occurrences of *Administrator* in the Registry.

Backing Up and Restoring the Registry

Since the Registry contains the information that your operating system needs to run, corruption or damage that occurs in the Registry can render your Win-dows NT Server unusable. Without some way to recover Registry data, you might have to reinstall the operating system from scratch and reconfigure all the system services in your server.

Fortunately, Microsoft has provided a utility that takes a "snapshot" of the state of the Registry and saves that file to a floppy disk so that you can repair your Windows NT installation later. That utility is called the *Repair Disk utility*, and the disk that is created is called the *emergency repair disk*.

The Repair Disk utility (RDISK.EXE) is a simple program whose only func-tions are to update an already existing emergency repair disk or to create a new one. (It also has buttons to exit and to show a minimally informative help window.)

The Repair Disk utility is not a backup utility! It does not save user files to a floppy disk or to tape. The Repair Disk utility merely saves the state of system settings for your Windows NT Server computer. Here is some of the information that is saved:

- The accounts database (including passwords, security settings, groups)

- The configuration of your hard drive

- Hardware Profile information

- Device driver configuration

- Network settings

- Computer identification (name, workgroup, or domain status, etc.)

You should backup your Registry whenever you make a significant change to your computer. You should also back up the files on your hard disk often. Some tape backup programs will store the Registry on the backup tape along with the user files—allowing you to perform both functions in one step!

A Registry stored on backup tape is useful only if your computer is able to run the tape restore program. (The installation boot floppies can only restore a Registry stored on floppy disk, not on tape.) If you back up your Registry to tape, you should also keep an installation boot floppy that can restore your operating system to a state that can at least run the tape backup program!

You should use the Repair Disk utility to update the emergency repair disk for your computer (or create a new one) whenever you make a significant change to your system, such as changing the administrator password, adding a hard drive, upgrading the networking adapter, or adding user accounts. If you do not update your emergency repair disk and have to use an out-of-date emergency repair disk to restore a corrupted Registry, the new information will be lost.

The "Emergency Repair Disk" and the "Restoring Windows NT" sections in Chapter 17 describe how to create and use an emergency repair disk in more detail. Chapter 17 also includes exercises for creating a backup of the Registry on the emergency repair disk and then restoring the Registry from that disk using the installation boot floppies for Windows NT.

Summary

Y OU CAN CONFIGURE most of the features and services of Windows NT Server through the various control panel programs. Control panel programs are small applications that provide an interface through which you can control the specific functions of a service.

You also use the control panel programs to add device drivers to Windows NT. Many control panel programs have tabs, or sections, dedicated to the installation or removal of device drivers. Control panel programs also handle driver configuration.

Many control panels are included for complete compatibility with Windows NT Workstation and have little or no function on a dedicated server. Others are essential and are used often.

Windows NT normally installs the following control panel programs: Accessibility Options (if left checked during the install), Add/Remove Programs, Console, Date/Time, Devices, Dial-Up Monitor (if RAS is installed), Display, Fonts, Internet, Keyboard, Licensing, Mail, Microsoft Mail Postoffice (Mail and MS Mail Postoffice are installed if Microsoft Messaging Service is installed), Modems, Mouse, Multimedia, Network, ODBC (if database software is installed), PC Card, Ports, Printers, Regional Settings, SCSI Adapters, Server, Services, Sounds, System, Tape Devices, Telephony, and UPS.

Other services for Windows NT Server and third-party applications may also install control panels to configure the functions of the services they provide.

Review Questions

1. All hardware devices require a driver in Windows NT.

   A. True

   B. False

2. SCSI controllers are configured with the SCSI Adapters control panel.

   A. True

   B. False

3. All control panels are vital to the functionality of a dedicated Windows NT Server.

   A. True

   B. False

4. Windows NT prevents applications from directly accessing hardware devices.

   A. True

   B. False

5. All the device drivers necessary for any Windows NT Server installation are included on the Windows NT Server CD-ROM.

   A. True

   B. False

6. File servers should always have a sound card so the system administrator can receive audible alerts.

   A. True

   B. False

7. The Add/Remove Programs control panel can be used to install any type of device driver.

   A. True

   B. False

8. The _____ control panel is used to stop and start device drivers.

9. Virtual memory settings are changed through the _____ control panel.

10. If your modem appears in the Modems control panel program and is set to the correct COM port but does not respond to the system, you should check settings in the _____ control panel.

  A. Modems

  B. Devices

  C. Ports

  D. Services

  E. Internet

11. The Accessibility Options control panel controls:

  A. User input and output device alternatives

  B. Access to secure areas of the operating system

  C. Security configuration

  D. Microsoft Access database connectivity

12. User Profiles are managed in which control panel?

  A. Server

  B. System

  C. Licensing

  D. Services

Windows NT
Networking
Services

HAPTER 6 INTRODUCED the basics of networking and explained the protocols that link Windows and Windows NT computers. This chapter describes the services that Windows NT makes available over those protocols. Mastering this information will help you make your network domain a secure and reliable computing environment for your organization.

In the "Services Architecture" section, you will learn about the minimal services required for your server to provide file and print services on the network. These services include the Computer Browser, NetBIOS Interface, RPC Configuration, Server, and Workstation services. You will find out how workgroups and domains are structured, and you will configure your Windows NT Server to join a domain or to be a stand-alone server in a workgroup. In the "Security Architecture" section, you will learn how Windows NT implements security on the network and in the server. You will see how permissions operate and find guidelines for troubleshooting Windows NT security. In the "Troubleshooting Network Connectivity" section, you will learn how to troubleshoot common network connectivity problems.

Services Architecture

EFORE YOU REVIEW the upper-level protocols and services that Windows NT Server supports, you should understand how these upper-level services interoperate. As you learned in Chapter 6, interoperating is a function of the networking architecture.

Chapter 6 started with a survey of the Windows NT networking architecture and then examined the more common transport protocols. The transport protocols rely on device drivers and network interface adapters, which we discussed in Chapter 7. Those transports and the device drivers they use constitute the lower levels of the Windows NT networking architecture. Figure 8.1 shows the services commonly configured in a Windows NT Server computer.

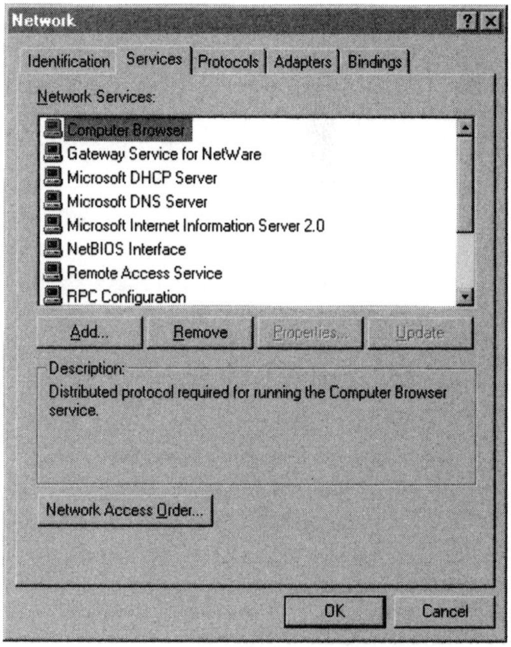

FIGURE 8.1

A number of networking
services are commonly
configured in
Windows NT Server.

Services are the most important aspect of the Windows NT operating system and form the interface between the user and the network server. This chapter explores the services that are the minimal services the server needs to provide file and print services in a Windows NT domain.

- Computer Browser

- NetBIOS Interface

- RPC Configuration

- Server and Workstation

Later chapters show you how to add specific additional services such as Gateway Services for NetWare and Simple TCP/IP Services.

Computer Browser Service

Your server, whether it is a part of a domain or a stand-alone server, must know what network resources are available before it can access those resources. The network browser maintains the list of currently available network resources for the domain. When you open the Network Neighborhood icon on your Windows 95 or Windows NT desktop, you are using the network browser to see what resources are available on the network.

When a computer joins the network at boot time, it announces its presence and provides a list of the resources it makes available on the network. Without a central location in which to store network resource information, every computer would need to keep a list of all the other computers on the network and record all the resources available from those computers. In addition, every computer would need to be notified of every change in network resources. This requirement would produce unnecessary traffic on the network and reduce network performance.

Network browsers reduce the amount of traffic on the network by centrally storing a list of network resources, rather than requiring a broadcast from clients and a response from servers each time a service request is made. Browsers also eliminate the need for every computer on the network to maintain a list of discovered resources. Computers in a network with browsers request the resource list from a browser when they need to find a network resource.

Computers running Microsoft Windows for Workgroups, Windows 95, Windows NT Workstation, and Windows NT Server operating systems can all perform the role of browser in a Windows workgroup or domain.

Browser Roles

Several browser roles exist in a domain or workgroup (see "Browser Roles"), and the browser roles cooperate in the manner described in "Browsing the Network." Figure 8.2 shows network computers configured as master browsers, backup browsers, potential browsers, and non-browsers. If the network has a primary domain controller, it is always the master browser.

If the network does not have a primary domain controller (i.e., the network is a workgroup rather than a domain), any computer running a Microsoft operating system that supports network browsing can perform any of the browsing roles.

MASTER BROWSER The master browser is the computer that maintains the master list of resources available on the network. The list of resources is called the *browse list*. The master browser listens for announcements from computers and adds the computers and their shared resources to the browse list. The master browser distributes this list to the backup browsers and promotes potential browsers to be backup browsers when necessary. If there are no backup browsers, then the master browser also supplies the browse list to computers requesting the list.

Only one master browser can exist in a workgroup or domain, except in the case of TCP/IP internetworks. Because TCP/IP does not route broadcasts, the browsing process will not reveal shared resources through routers. Therefore, a master browser must exist in each TCP/IP network, with the primary domain controller acting as a coordinating or domain master browser.

FIGURE 8.2

If the network has a
primary domain
controller, it is always
the master browser.

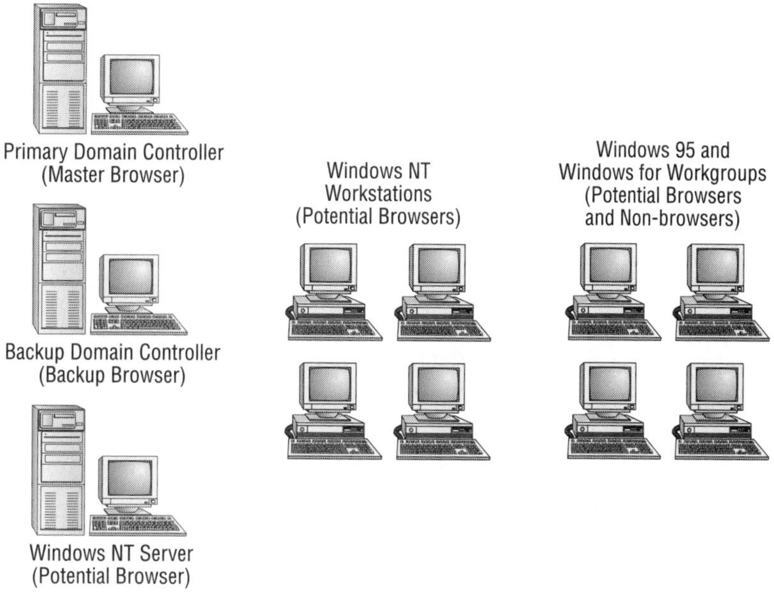

Primary Domain Controller
(Master Browser)

Windows NT
Workstations
(Potential Browsers)

Windows 95 and
Windows for Workgroups
(Potential Browsers
and Non-browsers)

Backup Domain Controller
(Backup Browser)

Windows NT Server
(Potential Browser)

BACKUP BROWSER A backup browser receives a copy of the browse list from the master browser and supplies the browse list to computers requesting the list. The backup browser announces itself periodically to the master browser just as any other computer participating in the workgroup or domain does. It periodically requests the browse list from the master browser, and if it cannot find the master browser, it forces an election on the network. (Elections are described in the section "Configuring Browsers and Browser Elections.")

POTENTIAL BROWSER A potential browser does not receive a copy of the browse list unless it is promoted by a master browser to be a backup browser or unless it becomes the master browser. A potential browser computer, like any other computer participating in a workgroup or domain, will periodically announce its presence and list the services it makes available.

NON-BROWSER A non-browser does not maintain a browse list for other computers or receive a browse list from a master browser for other computers to request. A non-browser computer can still provide network services and request a browse list from network browsers for its own use. A non-browser computer participating in a domain or workgroup will periodically announce its presence and list the services it makes available.

PREFERRED MASTER BROWSER You can designate a computer on the network to be the preferred master browser. When this computer joins the network, it announces itself as the master browser. If the network already has a master browser, it will force an election that reevaluates the roles of computers as browsers in the network. The computer that is designated as the preferred master browser will win the election unless another computer is the primary domain controller or more than one computer is designated as the preferred master browser.

Browsing the Network

Browsers exist to provide networked computers with a list of the resources that are available on the network. The steps that the requesting computer and the network browsers perform before and during a request follow.

1. When each computer starts up and connects to the network, the computer announces its existence to the master browser in the workgroup or domain. If the computer has resources to share, it advertises them to the master browser.

2. When the computer attempts to locate network resources for the first time, the computer contacts the master browser and retrieves a list of backup browsers.

3. The computer contacts a backup browser and requests the network resource list.

4. The backup browser responds with the list of domains and workgroups and the list of servers and client computers participating in the domain or workgroup that the computer is a part of.

5. The computer contacts the server, domain controller, or workstation to request the list of resources shared by that entity.

6. That computer returns a list of resources to the requesting computer. Resources may now be selected by the client and a session established between the client and the share provider.

Configuring Browsers and Browser Elections

Every domain or workgroup must have one and only one master browser (except with TCP/IP as noted above). Microsoft networks hold elections to determine which computer will be the master browser. The factors that determine the outcome of the election are

- The operating system of the computers on the network

- The versions of the operating systems

- The designated role of the computer in network browsing

The computer that is designated the preferred master browser wins the election unless the network has a primary domain controller. If the network has neither a preferred master browser nor a primary domain controller, then other criteria select the master browser.

The following browser roles are presented in the order in which they will be selected as a master browser:

- Preferred master

- Master

- Backup browser

- Potential browser

When computers run different operating systems but have the same browsing role, the operating system decides the election. Here's the order of priority by system:

- Windows NT Server that is the primary domain controller

- Windows NT Server acting as a backup domain controller

- Windows NT Server

- Windows NT Workstation

- Windows 95

- Windows for Workgroups

When Windows NT computers have the same role and the same operating system, the computer first in the list according to operating system version will win.

- 4.0

- 3.51

- 3.5

- 3.1

An election is held whenever the master browser is unavailable, when the master browser forces an election because it is being shut down, or when more than one master browser exists. A client computer, a backup browser, or a preferred master browser can cause an election to occur by broadcasting an *election packet* over the network.

All the browsers receive the election packet and evaluate their precedence in relation to it according to the priorities described above. For example, if a Windows NT workstation receives an election packet sent by a Windows NT Server, it will determine that it has a lower precedence, so it will not respond with another election packet. If any browser determines that it has precedence over the browser that sent the election packet, the contender will broadcast an election packet. For example, if a Windows NT Server 4 receives an election packet from a Windows NT Server 3.51, NT Server 4 determines that it has a higher precedence and broadcasts an election packet containing its election credentials (e.g., that it is a Windows NT Server 4 backup domain controller). This process continues until no one challenges with a new election packet. The result of this election process is that the "highest ranking" computer on the network designates itself the master browser. A network in which election packets are being exchanged is in an *election-in-progress state*.

When browsers stop producing election packets, the last browser to produce an election packet is the new master browser.

You can configure your Windows NT server to never be a browser, always be either the master browser or a backup browser, or be a potential browser. You do so by modifying the following setting in the Windows NT Registry:

```
\HKEY_LOCAL_MACHINE\SYSTEM\CurrentControlSet\
    Services\Browser\Parameters\MaintainServerList
```

This setting has three values:

- **No:** A computer with this setting will not be a network browser.

- **Yes:** A computer with this setting will be either a master browser or a backup browser. This is the default for Windows NT Server primary or backup domain controller computers.

- **Auto:** A Windows NT Workstation or Windows NT member or stand-alone server with this setting will either become the master browser, a backup browser, or a potential browser depending on the number of currently active browsers on the network. Auto is the default for Windows NT workstation computers and Windows NT server computers that are not domain controllers.

You can configure your Windows NT server to be the master browser in the absence of a primary domain controller by changing the following setting in the Windows NT Registry of your server:

```
\HKEY_LOCAL_MACHINE\SYSTEM\CurrentControlSet\
    Services\Browser\Parameters\IsDomainMaster.
```

The default for this setting is No or False, even if the computer is currently the master browser of the network. Changing the value to Yes or True will cause the server to win any election other than one with a primary domain controller.

You can configure your server to never be a browser, always be a browser, or be a potential browser by following the steps in Exercise 8.1. Exercise 8.2 shows you how to change the preferred master browser status of your computer.

EXERCISE 8.1

Configuring the Server's Browser Status

1. Start the Registry editor program (REGEDIT.EXE).

2. Open the HKEY_LOCAL_MACHINE subtree by clicking the plus sign beside HKEY_LOCAL_MACHINE.

3. Open the SYSTEM key.

4. Open the CurrentControlSet key.

5. Open the Services key.

6. Open the Browser key.

7. Open the Parameters key.

8. Select the MaintainServerList value by double-clicking it. The Edit String dialog box appears.

9. Type in **No**, **Yes**, or **Auto**.

10. Click OK.

11. Exit the Registry editor and restart your computer to enforce the changes.

EXERCISE 8.2

Changing the Server's Preferred Master Browser Status

1. Start the Registry editor program (REGEDIT.EXE).

2. Open the HKEY_LOCAL_MACHINE subtree by clicking the plus sign beside HKEY_LOCAL_MACHINE.

3. Open the SYSTEM key.

4. Open the CurrentControlSet key.

5. Open the Services key.

6. Open the Browser key.

7. Open the Parameters key.

8. Select the IsDomainMaster value by double-clicking it. The Edit String dialog box appears.

9. Type **True** to make your computer the preferred master browser; type **False** to leave the default setting.

10. Click OK.

11. Exit the Registry editor and restart your computer to enforce the changes.

Browser Interactions

All the browsers on the network cooperate to provide a browsing service to the users of the domain or workgroup. The browsers and the computers exchange information periodically, and specific timing constraints exist for each interaction.

ALL DOMAIN PARTICIPANTS A computer that provides services in the workgroup or domain (such as a Windows NT Server computer) must inform the master browser that it is available when it starts up and must periodically broadcast its continued existence. Initially the computer must announce itself once a minute, but as the computer continues to run, the announcement interval increases until it reaches 12 minutes. If the master browser does not receive a message from a computer for longer than three announcement periods (perhaps it was shut down), it removes that computer from the browse list.

A 36-minute delay can occur between the time a computer goes down and the computer entry is removed from the browse list. Consequently, the master browser's list may not accurately reflect a given computer's condition.

BACKUP BROWSERS Backup browsers announce themselves on the networks the same way non-browsers do. They also poll the master browser at 15-minute intervals to retrieve the browse list. The backup browser delay in combination with the delay caused when the computer announces itself to the master browser could result in a 51-minute period during which an unavailable resource appears on a backup browser's list.

If the backup browser polls the master browser and the master browser does not respond, the backup browser will force an election on the network.

MASTER BROWSER The master browser periodically broadcasts updated master browser information to all the backup browsers. The maximum size of the browse list that the master browser maintains is 64K. This size limits the number of computers on a single workgroup or domain to about 2,500 computers, depending on how long their names are and other factors.

The master browser can broadcast a *request announcement* packet, which requires all computers participating in the domain or workgroup to respond within 30 seconds. If during the response to a request announcement packet (or at any other time), the master browser receives an announcement from another computer claiming to be a master browser, the master browser forces an election on the network.

NUMBER OF BROWSERS A workgroup or domain always has one master browser. The maximum number of backup browsers in a domain is three, regardless of the size of the domain. The number of potential browsers in a domain or workgroup is unlimited. In a workgroup in which the Maintain-ServerList parameter on the workstations is set to Auto, the master browser will select one potential browser to be a backup browser for every 32 computers that are a part of the workgroup.

Because TCP/IP broadcasts are not routed, each TCP/IP network separated by routers counts as a single network for the purpose of browsing. In this case, the primary domain controller acts as the domain master browser to coordinate the browse lists of all network master browsers.

BROWSING OTHER WORKGROUPS AND DOMAINS In addition to maintaining a list of computers in its own domain or workgroup, the master browser is also responsible for maintaining a list of other domains and workgroups. When a computer becomes the master browser, it broadcasts a "domain announcement" message to each workgroup or domain. It does so every minute for 5 minutes and then every 15 minutes thereafter.

The master browser listens for broadcasts from other master browsers, and if another domain has not sent an announcement message for three times its announcement delay, the master browser removes that domain or workgroup from its list. With a waiting period of three times the default 15-minute delay, a domain or workgroup can be down for as long as 45 minutes before it is removed from the master browse list. This list of other workgroups and domains is given to the backup browsers with the list of computers in the master browser's domain.

The master browser can force other domains to announce themselves in the same manner that it can force all computers in a domain to announce themselves. However, a master browser forces other domains to announce themselves only if it has an empty domain list.

NetBIOS Interface Service

NetBIOS is an essential part of Microsoft workgroups and domains (which are described later in the section titled "Workstation and Server Services"). Many of the basic functions of a Windows NT network, such as browsing network resources, are handled over NetBIOS, and a Microsoft Windows network cannot operate without it.

NetBIOS has been the standard PC client/server interprocess communication (IPC) mechanism since IBM introduced it in the early 1980s, and you can't do much to configure how the NetBIOS service operates on your network. Because of its age, NetBIOS is somewhat primitive compared to other, more flexible interfaces like Named Pipes and Remote Procedure Call, both of which operate on a wider range of operating systems than NetBIOS does.

NetBIOS can communicate over any TDI-compliant transport, including the following:

- NetBIOS over NetBEUI (NBF)

- NetBIOS over NWLink (NWNBLink)

- NetBIOS over TCP/IP (NetBT)

RPC Configuration Service

Remote Procedure Call implements an IPC mechanism for starting programs on foreign computers, feeding them input, and accepting their output. This facility allows computers to spread the processing load among a number of computers.

Windows NT networks use RPC during the logon process. Therefore, the RPC service must be installed in a Windows NT Server.

RPC allows the client and server portion of the application to exist on the same machine by using the Local Procedure Call (LPC) mechanism. Because this mechanism is transparent to the application, you can distribute the processing load as you please among computers, even if that means putting the entire load on a single machine.

RPC has four major components:

- **Remote Procedure Stub** packages remote procedure calls to be sent to the server.

- **RPC Runtime** passes data and parameters between the local and remote computers.

- **Application Stub** accepts RPC requests from RPC Runtime, formats the RPC request for the executing computer, and makes the appropriate call to the remote procedure.

- **Remote Procedure** is the actual procedure called over the network.

Workstation and Server Services

These services provide the network environment that is visible to network users. They also provide network resources to application programs. When you connect to a *network share* (a directory made available from another computer over the network), you are using the Workstation service; and when you make a network share on your machine available to other computers, you are using the Server service.

The Workstation and the Server services use the services already introduced (the Browser, NetBIOS, and RPC services) to provide the networking environment of network shares of files, directories, and printers; of user account connections; and of mapped network drives.

You cannot directly configure the Workstation and Server services, but when you modify other Windows NT networking settings such as the computer name, domain name, or workgroup name, you are indirectly modifying Workstation and Server settings because these services rely on that information to function. The one exception to this rule is that you can change your server's overall service optimization through the server service in the Network control panel program.

- **Minimize Memory Used** controls how much allocated memory the server service uses. You should select this option only if you have ten or fewer clients or because this computer is primarily used as a workstation rather than a server.

- **Balance** configures Windows NT Server for optimum support for up to 64 concurrent clients while supporting networked applications or a local user.

- **Maximize throughput for file sharing** is appropriate if the primary function of this server is file service.

- **Maximize throughput for network applications** is appropriate if you are supporting network applications, such as database servers or other back-end software, that perform computations on the file server.

The Workstation and Server services have two primary modes of operation:

- Participation in a workgroup (in which case your Windows NT server computer will be a stand-alone server)

- Participation in a domain (in which case your computer will be a member server, backup domain controller, or primary domain controller)

Exercise 8.3 shows you how to optimize the server service for the role your computer typically performs.

EXERCISE 8.3

Changing a Server's Overall Service Optimization

1. Right-click the Network Neighborhood icon on the desktop.

2. Select Properties.

3. Click the Services tab.

4. Double-click the Server entry in the Services list box.

5. Select the optimization most important to the function of this server:

- Select Minimize Memory Used if this computer is rarely used as a server.

- Select Balance if this server is typically used as both a server and workstation.

- Select Maximize Throughput for File Sharing if this computer is a dedicated file server.

- Select Maximize Throughput for Network Applications if this computer is an application server, including Internet Information Server or any BackOffice application.

6. Click OK.

7. Click Close.

8. Click Yes to restart your computer.

Workgroups

You can organize Windows NT local area networks that are small and that do not need centralized network control or centralized data storage into workgroups. *Workgroups* are peer-to-peer networks, which means that the users of each workstation select and manage the resources on that workstation that are made available to other computers on the network. The user accounts and resources on the workstation are administered from that workstation, not from a network server. Figure 8.3 shows a typical workgroup.

FIGURE 8.3

A workgroup has a small
number of computers
with no computer
dedicated to serving files
for the other computers.

When you configure your Windows NT server to be a part of a workgroup, you configure it to be a stand-alone server. A Windows NT server set up in this manner will not be a domain controller, nor will it defer to another computer (a primary domain controller or backup domain controller) to control network access or authenticate logon attempts.

A workgroup is a good choice for your networking model under the following conditions:

- Your organization is small (maximum of ten users).

- The users know how to administer their computers.

- Central file storage and central control of network security are not important.

Because the user accounts for one computer are independent of the other computers, a user on one computer that accesses a resource on another computer (other than simple directory sharing, which may not require a password) may need to have an account on that other computer as well. This situation occurs, for example, if you have more than one Windows NT server in the workgroup and you require file-level access to resources on the servers. In the extreme, you might have a workgroup in which each user in the workgroup has a separate account on each computer in the workgroup. The same account name can be used on each computer as well, adding to the confusion, especially when you want to change your password or perform other administrative tasks.

A workgroup is not a good choice for your networking model under the following conditions:

- You have more than ten users.

- You need to centralize user account management and network security.

- You cannot depend on the users of your network to administer their workstations.

- You need to store data centrally on your network.

You can also change your computer's name in the Network Identification control panel.

Exercise 8.4 leads you through the process of joining a workgroup.

EXERCISE 8.4

Configuring Your Stand-Alone Server to Join a Workgroup

1. Log on as Administrator.

2. Open the Network icon in the Control Panel. A Network window will appear.

3. Click the Identification tab if it is not already the active tab.

4. Click the Change button to display the Identification Changes window.

5. Select the Workgroup option and enter the name of the workgroup of which your workstation will be a part. If you want to change your computer's name, enter the new name in the Computer Name field.

6. Click the OK button.

7. Click the OK button in the Network window. You must restart your computer for the changes to take effect.

Domains

Most networks with more than ten workstations are server-based networks. In a *server-based network*, a central computer stores network files, enforces network security, and maintains network data such as user account information and trust relationships between domains. The Windows NT networking model that implements this type of network is the domain model. The controlling computer in a Windows NT domain is called the primary domain controller, and it must be running the Windows NT Server operating system. Figure 8.4 shows a small domain with a primary domain controller, a server, and several client computers.

DOMAIN OVERVIEW In a Windows NT domain, a central server called the primary domain controller controls and can administer the user accounts, group accounts, account policies, and security information. All the domain

FIGURE 8.4

A domain consists of one or more servers, one of which must be a primary domain controller, and client computers that communicate with the server computers.

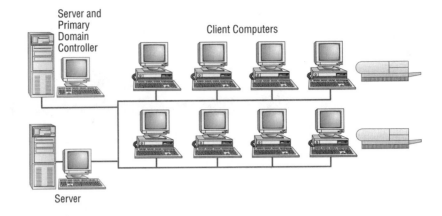

controllers in the domain share the information controlled by the primary domain controller.

Because this information is centrally controlled, the task of managing a large network is easier for the network administrator than it would be if the information had to be maintained individually on each computer in the network. Centralizing this information also means that users do not have to perform administration tasks for their workstations.

One or more servers store the shared network files for all the workstations in the domain. The primary domain controller controls workstation access to the files stored on the servers using account and security information it stores in a central database. Storing the network files in servers helps the network administrator to control who has access to the information. Backing up the data is also easier when the data is centrally located.

STRUCTURING DOMAINS A large network may have more than one domain. An organization that is divided into functional units, for instance, a business that is split into marketing, finance, manufacturing, and research departments, may divide its domain-based network along those functional lines. In this example, four domains could provide resources specific to the needs of the department it serves. Figure 8.5 shows a larger network that has several domains.

Each domain has one or more servers to store the network files for workstations and to provide other network services such as network printing, e-mail routing, and network faxing.

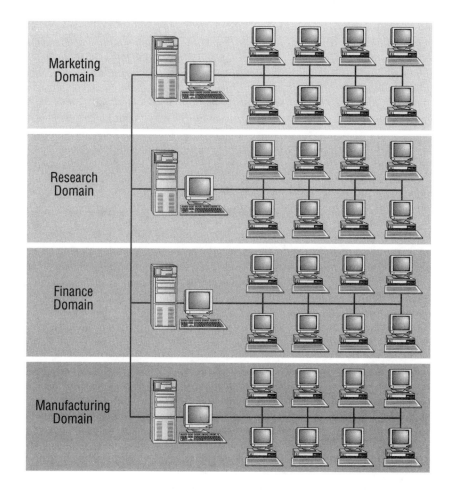

FIGURE 8.5

A large network may consist of several domains.

- **Primary domain controller:** One (and only one) server in the domain must be the primary domain controller for the domain. Only a computer running the Windows NT Server operating system can be a primary domain controller. The primary domain controller maintains a database that contains the user and group account information and the account and security policies.

- **Backup domain controllers:** Other servers (running the Windows NT Server operating system) can be designated backup domain controllers. Backup domain controllers maintain a copy of the primary domain controller's database. They can authenticate and log on domain users, and if the network does not have a primary domain controller, a backup domain controller can be promoted to primary domain controller.

- **Member servers:** You may wish to leave some of your Windows NT Server computers as simple servers. This arrangement will spare these servers the overhead of coordinating with the primary domain controller to maintain a copy of the domain database and authenticate client logons.

You must designate a server as a primary or backup domain controller when you install Windows NT Server on the computer. If you designate a server to be a backup domain controller, you can later promote it to be a primary domain controller. If you do not designate a server as a primary or backup domain controller, you cannot convert it later; instead, you will have to reinstall the operating system.

PROMOTING A BACKUP DOMAIN CONTROLLER TO PRIMARY DOMAIN CONTROLLER A backup domain controller automatically assumes the duties of the primary domain controller if it wins the election resulting from the absence or loss of a primary domain controller on the network. Although it takes over the duties of the primary domain controller, it does not turn itself into the primary domain controller—it will return primary authentication duties to the primary domain controller when it comes back on line and forces an election. However, simply shutting down a primary domain controller is not the most elegant way to transfer control of the domain from one server to another. A much better way to make a new (perhaps faster or equipped with more storage space) computer the primary domain controller is to first install it as a backup domain controller on the network and then promote it to be a primary domain controller.

Removing the old primary domain controller and then installing a new primary domain controller with the same domain name does not re-create the domain that originally existed. This sequence creates a new domain with the same name as the old domain, which can cause havoc when the network clients attempt to attach to the original domain and are denied access because they do not have proper privileges for accessing the new domain.

To promote a backup domain controller to be a primary domain controller, follow the instructions outlined in Exercise 8.5.

JOINING A MEMBER SERVER TO A DOMAIN In order for your server to participate in a domain-based network, it must join the domain. Joining your server to the domain requires making changes in two places on the network:

- The primary domain controller must create an account for the server.

- The server must be configured to join a domain and be told which domain to join.

EXERCISE 8.5

Promoting a Backup Domain Controller to Primary Domain Controller

1. Select Start ➤ Programs ➤ Administrative Tools ➤ Server Manager.

2. Select the backup domain controller you wish to promote in the Computer list box.

3. Select Computer ➤ Promote to Primary Domain Controller.

4. Click OK.

5. Close the Server Manager.

You can create an account for a member server from within the Server Manager program (found in the Programs ➤ Administrative Tools part of the Start menu). You can also create the account by supplying a valid administrator account name and password for the domain when you configure your member server to join the domain.

To configure your Windows NT server to connect to a domain, follow the steps outlined in Exercise 8.6. You can also change your computer's name when you configure your computer to join a domain.

TRUST RELATIONSHIPS Domains are easier to use and administer in medium-size networks than workgroups are because you only have to log on once to the network. You are not required to provide a password for each network share or printer you attach to, and you are not required to log on to each server in the domain. Trust relationships extend the utility of the single username and password logon to networks composed of multiple domains.

When you have more than one domain in your network (controlled by more than one primary domain controller), you can configure your network so that resources in one domain are available in other domains. You make the resources available by establishing trust relationships among the domains. Each domain can specify other domains that they trust to make security decisions about who can log on to and access which resources. For example, if Fred is a member of Domain Finance, which is trusted by Domain Engineering, then Fred can log on to Domain Engineering without a user account in that domain because Engineering trusts users from Finance.

EXERCISE 8.6

Configuring Your Server to Join a Domain

1. Log on as Administrator.

2. Open the Network icon in the Control Panel.

3. Click the Identification tab if it is not already the active tab.

4. Click the Change button to display the Identification Changes window.

5. Select the Domain option and type in the name of the domain of which your server will be a part. If you want to change your computer's name, type in the new name in the Computer Name field.

6. If the primary domain controller does not have an account set up for your computer, check the Create a Computer Account in the Domain box and then enter the username and password for an Administrator account for the domain.

7. Click the OK button.

8. Click the OK button in the Network window. You must restart your computer for the changes to take effect.

Properly establishing trust relationships between several domains in a large network requires an intimate understanding of the Windows NT security architecture and the interactions of user accounts, groups, and network resources such as shares, files, directories, and printers. Creating a trust relationship is simple, but the action has security ramifications beyond the scope of this book. Another book in this series, *MCSE: NT Server 4 in the Enterprise Study Guide,* explores the issues of trust relationships, large networks, and multiple-domain management in great detail.

Security Architecture

WINDOWS NT ALLOWS access to resources based upon user identity and group membership, rather than requiring a password for each resource requested.

Windows NT security is based around trusted access that is confirmed by passwords during the logon process. Once the user has logged on, Windows NT compares the user's identity to access permissions stored in objects to determine whether the user has the authority to access the object as requested.

Chapter 9 describes the logon process and permissions in more detail and explains how the Windows NT security model provides a safe working environment. Chapter 10 shows you how to configure your server to support your organization's style of work and how to troubleshoot network security.

The current section introduces these topics:

- The logon process and user identity

- Objects and security

- Permissions

- Access control lists

The method by which a Windows NT domain deals with security for you is somewhat complex; it starts with the logon process.

Logon Process and User Identity

You have to log on to a domain only once. Subsequently, the computer keeps track of the details of what you can and cannot access; for example, the computer will determine whether you have access to a particular file or directory. You are not required to justify your access privileges with a username and password each time you access a new server resource or network share.

This process is something like opening a safe and taking out a set of keys (*security identifiers*). Once you have your personal key (*account security identifier*) for things only you can access and a key for each of the groups you belong to (*group security identifiers*), you'll be able to open the resources they allow without providing another combination. Windows NT automatically creates a "one use only" key ring called a security identifier containing the necessary codes for all the resources you're allowed access to when you log on. For example, if you are a member of the Finance department, one of the keys you will get when you log on is the key to the finance closet. You don't have to select the key to use or deal with the security process at all. Windows NT simply tries each of your keys and only bothers you when none of them work.

The Ctrl+Alt+Delete logon dialog is the gatekeeper of a Windows NT computer and is presented when no user is logged on to a Windows NT Server. This dialog appears when the computer is booted and when a user has logged off but left the machine running.

When you turn on your Windows NT server, the Win32s subsystem of the operating system software starts the WinLogon process (a *process* is software that is currently running), which generates the logon dialog box. When a username and password are entered into the dialog box, the WinLogon process passes that information to a process called the security accounts manager (SAM).

When you log on to the domain from a network client, the client computer asks for your username and password and (over a network connection) presents them to the security accounts manager.

The security accounts manager is the Windows NT process that is responsible for ensuring that each user (and by extension, each process started by the user) has only those security privileges established by the system administrator or allocated by default by the operating system.

The security accounts manager queries the security accounts database to check the validity of the user name. If the name is valid and the password for that user is correct, the security accounts manager generates an access token (which contains the user and the user's group memberships in encoded form) and passes it back to the WinLogon process or (if you connect via a network client) to the server process maintaining the network client's connection.

All processes have access tokens, even those started by the system or by automatic software.

Objects and Security

The purpose of the Windows NT security system is to control who has access to what. The logon process determines the who; objects in Windows NT are the what. *Objects* comprise attributes, services, and a permissions list organized into an access control list that users and groups can use to access the services of the object. Most of the resources provided by Windows NT are composed of objects.

An object's *attributes* are the data contained in the object. Attributes describe such information as the filename, the data contained in a file, and the access control list of permissions. The actions that an object performs are called services. Some examples of object services are Open, Edit, Delete, or Close. *Permissions* are granted by object and service. For instance, a file contains information to which a user may have access. In other words, the user has Open access, but that user may not have access to the write service of that object. Windows NT represents its resources as objects, and all objects have access control lists (ACLs) so you can set access permissions for any NT resource based on a user's account or group membership. A typical object is shown in Figure 8.6.

FIGURE 8.6

A typical Windows NT object.

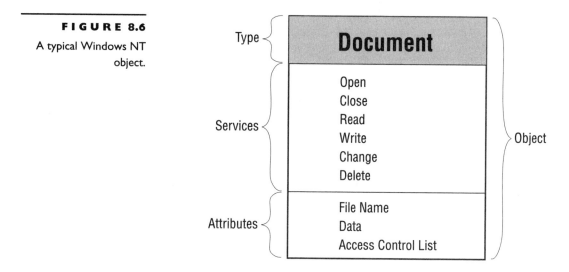

Windows NT contains many types of objects. Here are some examples:

- Directories
- Symbolic links
- Printers
- Processes
- Network shares
- Ports
- Devices
- Windows
- Files
- Threads

Every object has an ACL that Windows NT uses to determine whether a certain user has the authority to access that object.

Permissions

The logon process defines who you are to the operating system, and objects define what you can access. Permissions define the operations you can perform on the objects or, more often, the operations the programs you use can perform on the objects.

Access Control

Windows NT manages access control by assigning an access token (in the key analogy, an access token is the key ring) when you log on. The access token comprises the security identifiers (which are analogous to the keys) for your user account and all the groups to which you belong. When you attempt to access a resource, the security accounts manager on the computer sharing the resource compares your access token to the access control list of the requested object. If one of the security identifiers in your security token matches an access control entry in the access control list, you'll be granted access. Suppose you are accessing a file that only members of the engineering domain and administrators are allowed to access. Because you are a member of the engineering group, you have a key that will open the resource. Think of the administrator's security ID as the master key that will open anything. Figure 8.7 depicts this analogy.

Access Tokens

When you log on, Windows NT assigns you an access token (i.e., a representation of your account and each group to which you belong) that remains valid until you log off. Windows NT compares the individual security identifiers (keys) in this token to entries in an object's access control list (locks) to determine whether you have permission to access the object.

Access tokens are objects. Like any other Windows NT object, they contain attributes and services that describe them to the system and provide their services. Important attributes in the access token include

- **Security ID** representing the logged-on user

- **Security IDs** representing the logged-on user's group memberships

- **Permissions** allowed for the user

SECURITY ID FOR USERS Windows NT creates unique security identifiers for each user and group in the user accounts database. Because security IDs are unique, if an account or group is deleted, any new account or group created will

FIGURE 8.7

A security analogy.

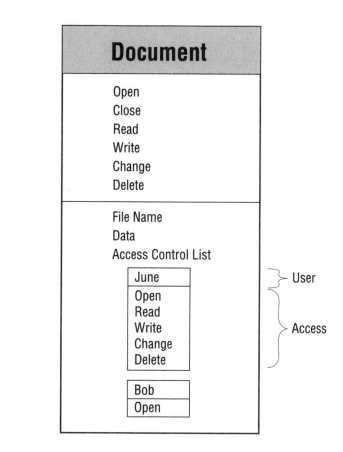

not have the same permissions as its similarly named predecessor. Security IDs can never be repeated, so the system will never mistake one user for another.

SECURITY ID FOR GROUPS Security IDs for groups are like Security IDs for users in that they allow certain permissions. Unlike Security IDs for users, however, security IDs for groups do not represent an individual user. Rather, these Security ID objects contain permissions assigned to groups of users based on some common criteria, such as department or work function. When a user is made a member of a group, the security ID for that group is attached to the user's access token. You will learn more about users and groups and the privileges that can be assigned to both in the next chapter.

When the administrator grants or denies access to an object based on a group, that group's security ID is added to the object's ACL along with the specific permission. Because the access token for a user contains the user's security ID and all the security IDs for groups to which the user belongs, the ACL and the access token will contain a matching ID, telling Windows NT which permissions to allow. ACLs and access control entries are covered in detail in the "Access Control Lists" section later in this chapter.

More than one ID match may occur if a user is a member of more than one group with permissions to the object. Windows NT combines the access permissions; therefore, if you have read access to an object because you are a member of group A and you have write access to the same object because you are a member of group B, you have both read and write access to the object.

PERMISSIONS Permissions are the specific access control entries contained in an object's ACL. An access control entry contains a security ID and the permission to which that security ID is assigned, such as read access, write access, or full control access. Access control entries are covered in the "Access Control Lists" section.

ATTACHING ACCESS TOKENS TO PROCESSES When a process attempts to access an object, the process's access token is checked against the object's ACL. If the ACL allows the specific access requested, the new process is started and the access token from the calling process is attached to it for the duration of its execution.

Because no process can be started without an access token and all processes receive the access token of the process that initiated them, you cannot bypass the security subsystem by starting a process that has a higher security clearance than the process that called it.

Access Control Lists

Each object has an ACL attribute that describes which user or group accounts have access to the object and what type of access they have. If a user does not have an entry in the ACL allowing access to a service of an object, Windows NT will not allow that user to perform the requested action on that object.

For instance, if a user attempts to open a file, the user must have open and read access to that file or be a member of a group that has open and read access to that file. Otherwise, Windows NT will not allow the user to open the file.

Access Control Entries

ACLs for objects contain access control entries, each of which describes a specific permission for a specific service for a user or a group (see Figure 8.8).

FIGURE 8.8

Access control entries in
an ACL.

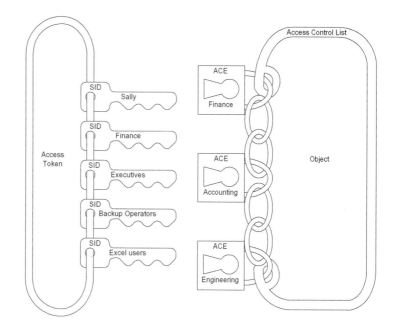

Checking Permissions

When you request access to an object (when you invoke a service of an object), Windows NT compares the security identifiers in the access token of the calling process to each entry in the ACL to see if the access is explicitly denied to you or to any group to which you belong. It then checks to see if the requested access is specifically permitted. Windows NT repeats these steps until it encounters a deny or until it has collected all the necessary permissions to grant the requested access. If the ACL does not specifically allow permission for each requested access, access is denied.

Windows NT optimizes access control by performing all security access checking when the object is first opened. All allowable requested accesses are copied into the object's process table when the object is opened. Any subsequent accesses to the object will succeed if the access appears in the process table and will fail if it does not.

Owing to this optimization, Windows NT has very little computer overhead for security once an object is started. However, any change to a user's or group's permissions will not take effect for any process currently running until that process is shut down and restarted. You may have to reboot because you won't be able to shut down and restart many system services.

Also note that only those permissions requested when the object is opened are copied to the object's process table. Consequently, a file opened only for read/write access, for example, cannot be deleted until it is closed and then reopened with a delete request.

Troubleshooting Network Connectivity

A T THIS POINT in your study of the Windows NT Server operating system, you should be able to install and configure your server to be a part of a workgroup or domain. However the real world of local area networking is not a simple place, and you may have network trouble when your server attempts to connect to other computers on your network or when other computers on the network attempt to connect to your server. Consequently, you must know how to troubleshoot your network.

The trick to troubleshooting is knowing where to start. A good understanding of networking technology and a familiarity with the errors that specific network problems cause will improve your network troubleshooting skills by enabling you to start the process with the most likely suspects.

Because few people have years of experience with specific network hardware and software (networking technology moves too fast), the following list of trouble spots will help you solve problems and maintain your network. Refer to Exercise 8.7 for a concise listing of the steps you should follow to diagnose your network problem.

- Cable connections

- Network interface adapter installation

- Resource conflicts

- Device driver installation

- Protocol configuration

- Domain/workgroup membership

- Network logon

- Share access

Cable Connections

The first thing to check when you lose a network connection is whether you are still physically connected to the network. When a connection has previously existed for a computer, the most common cause of network failure is a disconnected or bad network cable.

If you have a twisted-pair Ethernet network, make sure that the network cable is securely connected to the network interface adapter of your computer. Most network adapters have lights to indicate that the card has an active link to a central (twisted-pair) hub. If the lights indicate that you don't have a connection or that the connection is bad, you should ensure that the cable is good and then reinsert it.

Twisted-pair Ethernet networks and some other networks (such as Token Ring and ARCNET) have hubs at the center of the network. The hub must be operating correctly and in most cases must be supplied with power. Most powered hubs have lights to indicate their status. If the link light is on at the hub and at the network adapter, it's a safe bet that your cable is working correctly. Ensure that the hub is operating correctly and that the cable is securely attached to the hub. You might want to plug your cable into a different hub port to be sure the original hub port hasn't gone bad.

If you have a Thinnet or Thicknet Ethernet network, in addition to ensuring that the cable is securely connected to the network interface adapter, you should also make sure that the Ethernet cable segment is terminated properly at both ends. If other computers on the network are also having problems, you may have a termination problem. Unfortunately, bad transceiver and network adapters can wreak havoc on shared cables, so finding the exact source of the problem can be very difficult. Try turning off all the computers except for the server and the client closest to it. Bring computers up one at a time, moving away from the server, until the problem reappears; then troubleshoot that client. Cabling and termination issues are explored in detail in the companion book *MCSE: Networking Essentials Study Guide*.

A networked computer must have another computer to communicate with, and that computer must be connected to the network by a network cable. Your computer may be functioning correctly while the other computer exhibits the network fault. In this and the other aspects of network troubleshooting (hardware installation, resource conflicts, etc.), you must verify the correct operation of both computers.

Network Interface Adapter Installation

If your computer is physically connected to the network and the network interface adapter reports that the link is good, the next thing to check is whether the adapter is installed correctly and that no resource conflicts exist between the network adapter and other hardware in your computer.

If your network connection was working properly before and you have not added hardware or changed the settings for your adapter, then the adapter is probably not the source of your problem. However, if you have just installed the network interface adapter or if you have just installed other hardware in your computer and you are having a problem, then your adapter resources are probably conflicting with other hardware resources in your computer. Remove the adapter that you suspect may be conflicting with the network adapter (modems and sound cards are especially suspect) until the problem goes away. The only NICs your computer needs to operate are the video board and (perhaps) a hard disk controller card (if your computer doesn't have one built onto the motherboard). You may have to remove all but these essential cards to find the problem if you don't have any software that will report the hardware configuration of the cards in your computer.

Verify that the network interface adapter is installed and working correctly. Most adapters come with configuration software that can diagnose card problems and inform you of its resource settings. Then use the Windows NT Diagnostics utility to verify that the settings for the network adapter are not in conflict with other hardware devices.

Device Driver Installation

Another source of problems the first time you install and configure a network adapter in a computer is the device driver installation and configuration. Every network interface adapter must have a device driver that allows the operating system to use the adapter. This device driver must be the right device driver for the adapter (different adapters from different manufacturers often require different device drivers), and the device driver must be configured with the resource settings (IRQ, DMA, base memory, etc.) used by the adapter.

Most network interface adapters come with floppy disks containing Windows NT device drivers for the adapter. You should make sure that you've installed and configured the driver to use the adapter and that the settings match the settings reported by the configuration software that came with the card.

Protocol Configuration

Protocol misconfiguration is a common problem that arises when you reinstall Windows NT Server or install Windows NT Server for the first time (especially when the computer you are installing the software on has previously connected to the network with no problems). Each protocol has configuration options that must be correctly set to access the network effectively. NetBEUI, NWLink, and TCP/IP are the most commonly used transport protocols and each has its characteristic problems.

- **NetBEUI** is an exception to the rule because it doesn't have any easily modifiable settings. The only concern you may have with NetBEUI is ensuring that the other computers on the network use this protocol. Remember that you can't route NetBEUI, so if you can't see computers on the other side of a router, that's why.

- **NWLink** is only slightly more difficult than NetBEUI is to set up properly. Three things to watch for are the frame type setting (Ethernet 802.2, 802.3, II, or SNAP), the network number, and internal network number. The frame types are associated with network numbers, and must match the network number and frame types being used by other computers on your network.

- **TCP/IP** can be a difficult to configure correctly if your network doesn't have mechanisms such as the dynamic host configuration protocol (DHCP) to do the job for you. Your network address must be the same as the other computers on the TCP/IP subnet, your station address must be unique, your subnet mask must match the class of your network, and if you are using a gateway, its address must be set correctly. This configuration is sufficient for using TCP/IP as a simple transport. If you wish to use TCP/IP for accessing the Internet or an intranet, you must configure other settings such as the domain name server address. Don't confuse the *domain name server* in Internet verbiage with a Windows NT *domain controller*—Internet domains refer to a different concept entirely.

Ensure that the protocols you use are configured correctly for access to your network and make sure that you are using the same protocols as other computers on your network.

Domain/Workgroup Membership

If all the above aspects of Windows NT networking are working properly, then you need to make sure that you are a member of the right domain or workgroup. It does no good to attach to DOMAIN_B, for instance, if every other computer in your network is a member of DOMAIN_A.

Check the settings in the network control panel to make sure that you are connecting to the same domain or workgroup as the computer(s) with which you want to communicate.

Network Logon

You will be denied domain access if you do not supply a valid username and password. The user account must also have privileges to perform network operations. If you can log on using the Administrator account and the problem goes away, then the permissions assigned to the user account may be the source of the problem.

Share Access

Finally, if you wish to connect your computer to a network service, you must make that service available on the network. For example, if you wish to access the directory `test_dir` on `server_a`, then `server_a` must share `test_dir`. Likewise, if you wish to allow others to access the directory `my_dir` on your server computer, then you must share `my_dir`. If the directory is shared and you still cannot make the connection, then you should check the share permissions on that directory. If the share permissions have been changed from the default, then certain users may not be able to access the share. Try accessing the share while logged on as administrator. If the problem goes away, you may have a security problem. If you can access the share, but are unable to open folders or files, check file permissions. Again, if the problem goes away when you log in as administrator, it's probably a security problem.

EXERCISE 8.7

Troubleshooting Network Connectivity

1. Check the network cable. Is it firmly connected to the network interface adapter? Is it a good cable?

2. Check that the adapter is physically installed correctly.

3. Check the network hub for proper operation and link status on the different ports.

4. Check the indicator lights on the network interface adapter and the network hub to ensure a proper link is being made.

5. Repeat steps 1 to 4 for the other computer.

6. Check network termination if the network cabling is Thinnet or Thicknet.

7. Check that the card is configured correctly and passes the diagnostics of the configuration software. Record the resources the adapter uses.

8. Use the Windows NT Diagnostics utility to verify that the settings of the network interface adapter do not conflict with other hardware devices.

9. Make sure that the appropriate device driver is loaded.

10. Make sure that the device driver is configured to communicate with the card using the resource settings you recorded in step 7.

11. Repeat steps 7 through 10 for the other computer.

12. Ensure that both computers are using the same protocols.

13. If you are using NWLink, ensure that the frame type settings match and that the network numbers match.

14. If you are using TCP/IP, make sure that either you are using an automatic configuration service such as DHCP (and that the DHCP service is actually being provided by the network) or that the various TCP/IP settings are configured correctly.

15. Make sure that the computers are a part of the same domain or workgroup.

16. Check to see if you can log on as administrator.

17. Check to see if the problem goes away when you log on as administrator.

Summary

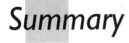

S ERVICES ARE THE most important aspect of the Windows NT operating system and form the interface between the user and the network server. They are the part of the operating system that provides the characteristic attributes of Windows NT networking such as domains, workgroups, mapped drives, network shares, and the logon process. Five default services are Computer Browser, NetBIOS Interface, Remote Procedure Call, Server, and Workstation.

The Browser service retrieves a list of the computers on the network and the services that they make available. The master browser maintains the list, backup browsers keep copies of the list and supply the list to requesting computers, and potential browsers can become backup browsers or master browsers. The primary domain controller of the domain will always be the master browser.

NetBIOS implements the functionality that the Server and Workstation networking components use to provide their services. NetBIOS can run over any TDI-compliant transport. NetBIOS is required for your Windows NT server to function in a domain or workgroup on the network.

Remote Procedure Call (RPC) is a mechanism that allows programs on different computers to call each other as though they were on the same computer. Several Windows NT components, including the logon process, use RPC, and therefore it is a required component for a functioning Windows NT server.

The Workstation and the Server services use the services already introduced (Browser, NetBIOS, and RPC) to provide the networking environment of network shares of files, directories, and printers; of user account connections; and of mapped network drives. These services allow you to participate in either a workgroup or a domain.

If you configure your server to be a part of a workgroup, then it will be a stand-alone server. It will not maintain a security database, will not authenticate log on requests for other computers, and will not look to another computer for logon authentication. Workgroups are most often used in small networks with fewer than ten networked computers.

If you configure your server to be a part of a domain, it can either be a primary domain controller, a backup domain controller, or a member server. The primary domain controller will maintain the security database and can authenticate logon requests. A backup domain controller keeps a copy of the security database and can also authenticate logon requests. A member server does not maintain a copy of the database and does not authenticate logon requests. However, a member server does defer to a primary domain controller or to a backup domain controller for logon authentication and access security.

To maintain a consistent security database when you wish to change primary domain controllers, you should first install the new computer as a backup domain controller and then promote it to primary domain controller status. This procedure avoids the problem of creating a new domain with the same name as the old domain without transferring the old domain's security database, which can cause network problems for computers that are configured to attach to the old domain.

When your network grows beyond a single domain, you can establish trust relationships between domains so that your network users still have to present only one username and password to the network in order to access all appropriate resources on the network. Trust relationships are established by listing trusted domains and trusting domains.

As part of the Windows NT security architecture, when a user logs on, the security manager gives him or her an access token, which identifies which user account is being used and which groups the user is a member of. That access token is associated with all the processes (programs) the user starts. Whenever that user (or a program started by that user) attempts to access a resource object (such as a file or printer), the access token is compared with entries in the object's access control list. If the user has sufficient permissions to access the service of the object, then the user is allowed to perform the action. Otherwise access is denied.

The trick in troubleshooting is knowing where to start. If the computer had been working properly, a change in the computer or network configuration is the most likely source of the problem. Test one thing at a time, eliminating problem areas, until you discover the source of the fault.

Review Questions

1. Network browsers increase the amount of traffic on the network by storing a list of network resources centrally.

   A. True

   B. False

2. Only Windows NT computers can perform the role of browser in a domain.

   A. True

   B. False

3. A preferred master browser will win an election over a primary domain controller.

   A. True

   B. False

4. A Windows 95 computer will be elected master browser over a Windows NT workstation.

   A. True

   B. False

5. Because of the delay between the time when a computer goes down and the computer entry is removed from the browse list, up to 36 minutes can elapse before the master browser's list reflects the computer's condition.

   A. True

   B. False

6. The backup browser delay in combination with the delay for the computer to announce itself to the master browser could result in a resource not being available for as long as 99 minutes while a backup browser list maintains the resource in its browse list.

   A. True

   B. False

7. The maximum number of backup browser in a domain is three, regardless of the size of the domain.

A. True

B. False

8. NetBIOS is not an essential part of Windows NT Server networking services.

A. True

B. False

9. The logon process uses the RPC service.

A. True

B. False

10. Using the Workstation service means you are participating in a workgroup, and using the Server service means you are participating in a domain.

A. True

B. False

11. A workgroup is a good choice for your networking model if you have many users and you need to centralize user account management and network security.

A. True

B. False

12. One and only one server in the domain must be the primary domain controller for the domain.

A. True

B. False

13. A network _____ maintains the list of currently available network resources for the domain.

14. The _____ browser is the computer that maintains the master list of resources available on the network.

15. A _____ browser receives a copy of the browse list from the master browser and supplies the browse list to computers requesting the list.

16. A _____ browser can become a backup browser or a master browser.

17. A _____ will not be promoted to backup browser status nor will it assume master browser status in the absence of a master browser on the network.

18. Microsoft networks hold _____ to determine which computer will be the master browser.

19. When you connect to a network share, you are using the _____ service.

20. When you make a network share on your machine available to other computers, you are using the _____ service.

21. A Windows NT Server in a workgroup is called a _____ _____ _____ .

22. The _____ _____ _____ maintains a database that contains the user and group account information and the account and security policies.

23. The _____ _____ _____ maintain a copy of the primary domain controller's database.

24. A _____ _____ in a domain does not maintain the security database nor does it keep a copy of the security database.

25. _____ _____ extend the utility of the single username and password logon to networks composed of multiple domains.

26. Most of the resources provided by Windows NT are composed of _____ .

27. An object's _____ are the data contained in the object.

28. The actions that an object performs are called _____ .

29. _____ are granted by object and service.

30. All objects have _____ _____ _____ , or ACLs, so you can set access permissions for any NT resource based on a user's account or group membership.

31. An _____ _____ is simply a representation of the user's account that Windows NT compares to entries in an object's access control list to determine if the user is permitted to perform the requested service.

Creating a Secure User Environment

ETWORK OPERATING SYSTEMS such as Windows NT use the concept of User accounts to control security and account-ability for the information contained on network servers. Using a process called logging on, which initiates a connection to the network by providing a username and a password, the network is able to identify which user account to use for each person who accesses the network. Logging on enables the network to

- Present information appropriate for each user

- Customize the network session for each user

- Allow the correct access to information for each user

In this chapter we explain how to create and maintain user accounts, discuss the topics of security and account policies, and describe ways of grouping users to increase security and administrative control and decrease administrative burden.

User Accounts, Groups, and Security

O PROVIDE SPECIFIC resources to specific users and to secure some resources against unauthorized disclosure, a network operating system has to know the identity of each attached user. This introduction is provided by logon authentication. *Logon authentication* restricts access to computers and to the network until a valid account name and the correct password for that account name are entered into a logon dialog. The logon name identifies each unique user and must be distinct for each account in a domain. The password keeps the use of that account private—only individuals who know the password can use that account. In most instances, account privacy extends to a single person. When you use account groups, two or more people have little reason to share a single account even if their access permissions are the same.

For example, suppose June and Ward are engineers who need access to the same CAD and spreadsheet applications. You could reduce your administrative hassles by having them use the same logon account. This procedure was relatively common on some older mainframe computers and in simpler network operating systems that didn't have a strong concept of grouping. By using the same account, June and Ward will have the same security permissions. Unfortunately, Ward won't be able to keep any files private from June (she has access to everything he has access to), and if June changes her password, Ward won't be able to log on until he finds out what the new password is.

So the better option is to create a group—actually more than one group—and make June and Ward members of that group. In this example you should create at least three groups: engineers, who have access to all engineering-specific files; CAD users, who have access to the computer-aided drafting software; and spreadsheet users, who have access to the spreadsheet software.

Why would you bother creating groups for specific applications though, when you could simply secure them with file permissions in such a way that no user could damage the installation? One reason is that you may need to control simultaneous access to these applications for licensing purposes. Let's say you have 50 network users, but only five CAD licenses. You're using the license manager or a similar tool to track concurrent access to your applications and have discovered that no more than five copies are ever in use at one time—perhaps only five engineers work at your company. But suppose that Wally, who is an accountant, launches a copy of the CAD application just to check it out. The license manager tallies up a sixth concurrent user, and your company is out another $5,000 just so Wally could draw some lines and boxes.

After you log on to a domain, the network knows which resources you are allowed to access and will deny you access to resources for which you do not have specific permission.

User accounts can be grouped together for the assignment of permissions that apply to many people. For instance, access to financial information can be assigned to the Finance group, and any member of the Finance group inherits permission from the group to access finance information. From an administrative perspective, groups allow administrators to manage all permissions at the group level. Consequently, they can effectively control security without being overwhelmed by the number of users in a domain.

In a domain User accounts reside on the primary domain controller in the security accounts manager portion of the primary domain controller's Registry. Users who appear as part of the domain are really global users because they can log on to any computer attached to the domain. Local user accounts are set up on individual computers for access only to that specific machine—local user accounts do not provide access to the domain.

Domains enable many servers to share accounts. Global user accounts created on the primary domain controller are available to every computer participating in the domain.

In the same sense, local groups are groups of local user accounts. Global groups are groups of global user accounts that are available to all computers logged on to the network.

Local groups can contain global groups and global (domain user) accounts, but the reverse is not true.

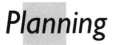

Be careful not create a global group with the same name as a local group. These accounts are not the same—members with the privileges of one will not have the privileges of the other.

Planning

PLANNING YOUR ACCOUNT policies, security structure, naming conventions, and groups provides a foundation from which you can create a coherent and secure network environment. Adding users ad hoc, assigning directory permissions when you realize someone has excessive rights, and creating groups only when they are most obviously necessary eventually produces a disorganized environment that will confuse and frustrate your users and leave many security loopholes.

Creating a coherent network environment requires planning, and a written plan will keep you from forgetting anything between administrative sessions. Your plan should include the following elements:

- **Natural groups in your organization,** such as Accounting, Finance, Managers, Executives, New Employees, and CAD users: List every group you can think of, even if you don't think you'll need it.

- **A standard naming convention**: We recommend using the Internet naming convention, which prefaces the last name with the first initial. Some organizations prefer to use titles, ranks, or grades as account names, especially if these designations are unique.

- **Security permissions** for network shares and directories: Determine which network shares you will create and what permissions should be assigned to those shares. On NTFS volumes, you should usually create a single network share and allow unlimited access to it. Then secure the subdirectories with file-level permissions. With FAT volumes, you will have to explicitly share every directory that needs unique permissions.

- **Default account policies** such as password lengths, account lockout features, and audit policy: Most installations that do not have specific security requirements (e.g., organizations that are not government or defense related) will not need to change account policies from the Windows NT defaults.

- **Resource shares** that need to be accessed by users of your network: Planning your shares up front will keep your networked mass storage (i.e., your file server) from becoming a morass of disorganized files and directories.

The following sections address the details of a complete network environment.

Planning Groups

Planning your groups correctly will make the task of administering the users on your network much easier. Experienced administrators seldom assign access permissions to individual accounts. Instead, they create a group and then make individual accounts a part of that group. For instance, rather than giving individual users the access permissions to back up the system, the administrator creates a Backup group with those permissions and then adds users to that group. That way, when the backup process changes (e.g., you add another server), the administrator has to make changes only to the group account, rather than to each account.

Windows NT Server uses global groups to maintain groups across all computers in a domain. Global groups are different from the local groups you can create using Windows NT Workstation.

Assigning users to groups allows you to keep track of who needs what resource. For example, word processing users might need access to the word processing application, to its data files, and to a shared directory that contains your organization's common documents and templates. You can give all three rights to a group, called Word Processing, and then in one action give the rights to an individual account by adding the account to the group.

You can assign permissions to everyone in a domain by assigning those access rights to the Domain Users group.

When you are creating the network groups for your network, you should determine which network resources the users on your network will need to access. Observe what different users have in common and create groups to give users that access. Ideally, you will assign permissions to groups and allow access to users by making them members of the appropriate groups. You can base groups on the following criteria:

- Organization functional units (marketing)

- Network programs (word processing)

- Network resources (Canon Laser)

- Location (area 51)

- Individual function (backup operator)

You should create global groups before creating shares because you can assign permissions to shares as you create them, as long as the groups already exist.

Naming Conventions

When administering a network, you should develop a consistent and coherent naming convention. A good naming convention has three characteristics:

- It is easy to use and understand. If users don't understand the naming convention, they won't use it.

- Anyone familiar with the naming convention should be able to construct an object name in a few moments. For a user, the name may include his or her full name and function in the company. For a printer, the name might include the model number and configuration details, physical location in the building, and what kind of work the printer is intended for.

- An object name should have an obvious and meaningful relationship with the object it corresponds to. If the object represents a printer, the name should correspond to the printer, for example, the Hewlett-Packard LaserJet III printer on the third floor. If the object is a user account, users should be able to determine that JASMITH corresponds to John A. Smith. Constructing a naming convention that produces meaningful names for objects is fairly easy; constructing a naming convention that translates easily in both directions is more difficult.

Security Planning

Security planning involves securing resources from unauthorized access. You can take two approaches to security:

- Optimistic, wherein users are allowed maximum permission to access information except in those specific cases where information should not be available to them

- Pessimistic, wherein users are allowed to access only the information they need to perform their jobs

Both methods are equally valid approaches to take for security. The nature of your organization and the work it performs will largely determine the method you choose. For instance, many government organizations follow the pessimistic approach because access to the information they store could cause damage to the security of the country.

On the other hand, most medium to small businesses use optimistic security policies because they have not created information that would be useful to someone outside their organization.

Pessimistic security policies take vastly more administrative effort than optimistic policies do, but they are far more secure and do not rely on users to safeguard data on their own. For instance, under a pessimistic policy any time someone needs access to information that is outside his or her need to know, a network administrator has to specifically allow permission for the person to access that information.

Optimistic security policies require very little administrative effort, but they are not very secure—nearly everyone on the network has access to most of the information on it. For that reason, specifically assigning permission to access a resource is usually not necessary.

These two policies are the extremes—most network security policies fall somewhere in the middle. But deciding at the onset which extreme policy is best for your organization will guide you through the rest of the security planning process. Security is presented in detail in Chapter 8.

A quick summary of permissions: Your access token is created when you log on. It contains your user identity and the identity of all groups you belong to. This access token is compared to each secured resource, such as a share, file, or directory, you attempt to access. These resources contain access control lists, which list each security id permitted to use the resource. If any of the identifiers in your access token match identifiers in the resources access control list, you are allowed access as specified by that access control entry in the access control list.

Share Permissions

Share permissions control how access to a shared resource is managed. Table 9.1 shows the effects of share-level permissions.

TABLE 9.1	PERMISSION	EFFECT
Share Permissions	No Access	Prevents access to the shared directory regardless of other allowed permissions.
	Read	Allows viewing of contained files and directories, loading of files, and executing software.
	Change	All read permissions plus creating, deleting, and changing contained directories and files.
	Full Control	All change permissions plus changing file system permissions and taking ownership.

File System Permissions

File system permissions complement the basic share-level permissions. Older file systems (e.g., FAT) do not have a rich enough set of file and directory attributes to implement security on a file or directory basis, so file system permissions are not available for these volumes. Share permissions are implemented by the server service to secure access to file systems that do not implement security.

File system permissions are available for NTFS volumes only.

Modern file systems like NTFS implement finer security control over the sharing of information with file system permissions, which are assigned to individual files and directories using file system attribute bits that are stored in the directory tables of the file system.

Therefore, file system permissions work even on stand-alone computers. For instance, if Jane creates a directory and assigns permissions for only herself, then no one else can access that directory (except administrators) even when other users are logged on to the same machine.

You can also use file system permissions to restrict which files are available to resource shares. Even though a share permission may allow access to a directory, a file system permission can still restrict it. Table 9.2 details the file system permissions available in NTFS volumes.

	PERMISSION	EFFECT
TABLE 9.2	No Access	Prevents any access to the directory and its files even if the user has been granted share or file level full control.
Directory Permissions	List	Viewing, browsing directory, without access to files unless overridden by other file or directory permissions.
	Read	Opening files and executing applications.
	Add	Adding files and subdirectories without read access.
	Change	Add and read permissions, plus delete.
	Full Control	Change plus taking ownership and assigning permissions.

Conflicting Permissions

With the myriad of shares, groups, files, and directories that can be created in a network environment, some resource permission conflicts are bound to occur. When a user is a member of many groups, some of those groups may specifically allow access to a resource while other group memberships deny it. Also, cumulative permissions may occur. For example, a user may have read access to a directory because he's a domain user but also have full control because he's a member of the Engineers group. Windows NT determines access privileges in the following manner:

- Administrators always have full access to all resources.

- A specific denial (No Access permission) always overrides specific access to a resource.

- When resolving conflicts between share permissions and file permissions, Windows NT chooses the most restrictive. For instance, if the share permission allows full control, but the file permissions allow read-only, the file is read-only.

- When a user is a member of multiple groups, the user always has the combined permissions of all group memberships.

Combinations of permissions include the No Access permission. So if membership in the Engineering group allows access to a directory, but membership in the New_Employee group allows No Access, the user will have No Access.

Choosing Permissions

Share permissions and file system permissions are two methods for securing files. Use the following criteria to help you decide which to use:

- If you are sharing from the FAT file system, you cannot use file system security, so you must share each directory that needs unique permissions.

- If you need to secure access to files on a system that users will log on to locally, you must use file system security. Share security applies only to network connections, not to local users.

- Generally, you should create the fewest number of shares possible in your networking environment. For instance, rather than sharing each subdirectory on a server, consider sharing just the higher-level directory and then securing the subdirectories with file-level permissions. Some shares should be reserved for sharing hardware devices such as entire hard disks or CD-ROMs.

- File system security allows a richer set of permissions and can be more finely controlled. Use it whenever possible.

Policy Planning

Policies are general operational characteristics of Windows NT. Changing policies basically means you are changing the default way Windows NT establishes security. Think of policies as the security behavior of Windows NT as it affects all users. The four major categories of policies are

- Account Policies

- User Rights

- Audit Policy

- System Policy

You control the first three, Account Policy, User Rights, and Audit Policy, from the Policy menu of the User Manager for Domains (or the User Manager in Windows NT Workstation) and control the fourth from the System Policy Editor.

Account Policies

Account Policy allows you to control universal security settings for user accounts. You can set the following user account policies:

- Maximum length of time before users are forced to change their password.

- The minimum age if necessary.

- The minimum length of passwords.

- Whether or not passwords must be unique between changes.

- How many passwords a user must rotate among.

- Whether or not account lockouts take place.

- The number of attempts before lockout occurs.

- How long the count remains in effect.

- The length of lockout duration.

- Whether logon hours are strictly enforced.

- Whether users must log on to change their password. In other words, if their logon age expires, can they still change their password or must they contact an administrator.

These policies are self-explanatory and usually don't need to be changed unless you have specific security policy in place or expect a higher level of intrusion attempts (for instance, your server is directly connected to the Internet). Exercise 9.1 shows you how to modify user account policies.

EXERCISE 9.1

Changing Account Policies

1. Select Start ➤ Programs ➤ Administrative Tools ➤ User Manager for Domains.

2. Select Policies ➤ Account.

3. Select Expires In and type **30 days** in the Maximum Password Age control.

4. Select At Least and type **6** in the Minimum Password Length control.

5. Select Account Lockout and type **5** in the Lockout After control.

6. Select Duration and type **60** in the Lockout Duration control.

7. Check *Forcibly disconnect remote users from server when logon hours expire.*

8. Click OK.

9. Close the User Manager for Domains.

User Rights

User Rights policy allows you to control what activity users can engage in on this specific machine. Rights apply to the system as a whole, rather than to specific objects, which are controlled by permissions. Table 9.3 shows the rights that are assigned by default to Windows NT.

TABLE 9.3 Default Rights	RIGHT	GRANTED TO
	Access this computer from network	Administrators, Everyone
	Add workstations to domain	No default group
	Back up files and directories	Administrators, Backup Operators, Server Operators
	Change the system time	Administrators, Server Operators
	Force shutdown from a remote system	Administrators, Server Operators

	RIGHT	GRANTED TO
TABLE 9.3 Default Rights (continued)	Load and unload device drivers	Administrators
	Log on locally	Account Operators, Administrators, Backup Operators, Print Operators, Server Operators
	Manage auditing and security log	Administrators
	Restore files and directories	Administrators, Backup Operators, Server Operators
	Shut down the system	Account Operators, Administrators, Backup Operators, Print Operators, Print Operators, Server Operators
	Take ownership of files or other directories	Administrators

Unlike permissions, rights affect the overall operation of the computer or domain, not a specific resource. Very few users will have a need to change User Rights unless you don't plan on using the groups Windows NT provides for certain functions such as server administration or backing up the system. Exercise 9.2 shows you how to change User Rights.

EXERCISE 9.2

Modifying User Rights

1. Select Start ➢ Programs ➢ Administrative Tools ➢ User Manager for Domains.

2. Select Policies ➢ User Rights.

3. Select Change the System Time in the right pick box.

4. Click Add.

5. Double-click the Everyone group.

6. Click OK.

7. Close the User Manager for Domains.

Audit Policy

Audit Policy tells Windows NT which security events you are interested in tracking. Auditing creates entries in the Security Event log whenever an audited event occurs. You can track events such as failed logons, attempts to change security policies, and other security-critical actions. Specifically, you can audit the success or failure of the following events:

- Logon and logoff

- File and object access

- Use of User Rights controlled functions

- User and group management activities

- Changes to Security Policy

- System restarts and shutdowns

- Processes (such as launching applications)

Some security policies require the tracking of failed logon attempts to identify accounts that are subject to frequent failures or to indicate the level of external attack to the network. You may want to enable auditing if you suspect attempts at hacking your system, even if your security policy does not specifically prescribe it. Exercise 9.3 shows you how to enable auditing.

EXERCISE 9.3

Enabling Auditing

1. Select Start ➢ Programs ➢ Administrative Tools ➢ User Manager for Domains.

2. Select Policies ➢ Audit.

3. Select Audit These Events.

4. Check Logon and Logoff Failure.

5. Click OK.

6. Close the User Manager for Domains.

Auditing frequent events like file and object access can seriously degrade the performance of your server. You should audit these events only as a last resort when attempting to track down a specific intrusion.

System Policies

System policies are slightly different from the other policies in that they are managed through the System Policy Editor, which was introduced in Windows NT 4. The System Policy Editor provides a convenient way to edit system policies that were previously accessible only through the Registry Editor. You can modify a number of system settings through the System Policy Editor. Important settings include

- Programs to run at startup

- Creation of hidden shares

- Print priorities and settings

- RAS security settings

- Availability of logon security features such as banners and shutdown

- File system features

- Local user restrictions

- Disabling Registry editing tools

As you can see, the System Policy Editor presents a very mixed bag of security settings. The System Policy Editor handles any Registry setting Microsoft thought someone might like to control. Feel free to browse through the different policy settings in the Registry—but be certain you understand the implications of changing a setting before you do. System policy changes can lock a computer so securely that even an administrator cannot unlock it. Exercise 9.4 shows you how to modify system policy. Figure 9.1 shows the System Policy Editor.

You can improve file system performance (and thereby the performance of your server) by changing a simple setting in the policy editor. Using the System Policy Editor, select Registry ➢ Local Computer ➢ Windows NT System ➢ File System and check Do not update last access time. This setting disables the NTFS feature that records the last time a file was read (changing a file still updates the time for backup purposes), which eliminates an unnecessary drive seek and directory write each time a read file is closed. If you still need to audit access to certain files, use file auditing—it does a better job anyway.

FIGURE 9.1

The System Policy Editor.

FIGURE 9.1

The System Policy Editor.

EXERCISE 9.4

Modifying System Policy

1. Select Start ➢ Programs ➢ Administrative Tools ➢ System Policy Editor.

2. Select File ➢ Open Registry.

3. Double-click Local Computer.

4. Expand Windows NT System.

5. Expand Logon.

6. Check Logon Banner.

7. Type **Security Notice** in the Caption input box.

8. Type **Unauthorized use of this system may result serious legal penalties.** in the Text input box.

9. Check *Enable shutdown from Authentication dialog box.*

10. Click OK.

11. Close the System Policy Editor.

12. Answer Yes to the Save Changes? prompt.

Share Planning

Creating a coherent shared directory structure is not difficult, but it does require a bit of thinking. What resources do your users need? What natural boundaries or groups might need their own shares? What information needs to remain private?

Creating shares is simple: Select a folder, or a mass storage device if you want to share the entire device, on your server and share it. You can then assign permissions for each group to that share as appropriate. For example, consider the directory structure for a server shown in Figure 9.2. The directories in the root of drive M have the functions and assigned permissions shown in Table 9.4.

FIGURE 9.2

Sample shares structure.

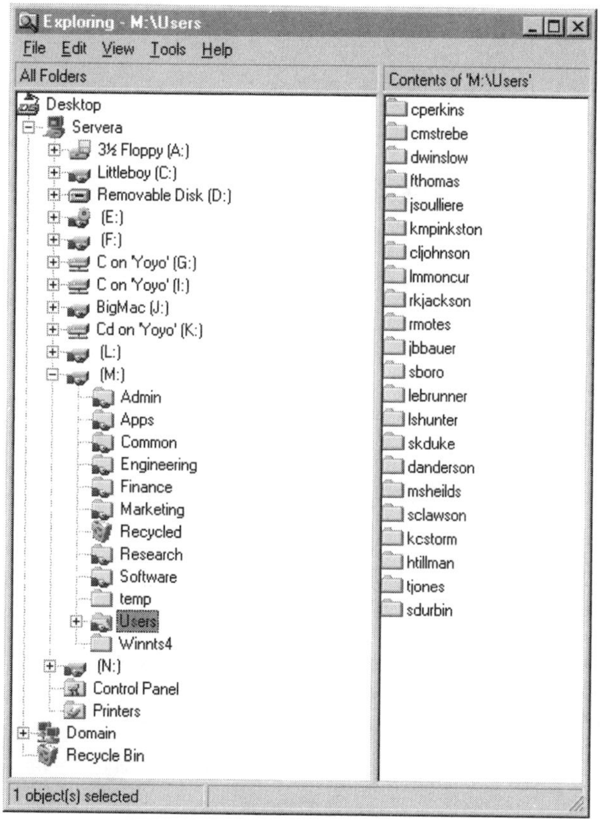

TABLE 9.4	DIRECTORY	FUNCTION	PERMISSIONS
Creating Secure Shares	Admin	Files private to members of the Admin department	Admin:Full Control
	Apps	Installed applications to be run from the server	Domain Users:Read
	Common	Files public to everyone in the domain	Domain Users:Full Control
	Engineering	Files private to the Engineering global group	Engineering:Full Control
	Finance	Files private to the Finance global group	Finance:Full Control
	Marketing	Files private to the Marketing global group	Marketing:Full Control
	Research	Files private to the Research global group	Research:Full Control
	Software	Applications that can be installed off the network onto local computers	Domain Users:Read
	temp	Files used by Windows NT and server resident software	No access is necessary. This directory is not shared.
	Users	Container for subdirectories private to each user	Domain Users:Read
	Winnts4	The system directory containing Windows NT	No explicit access is necessary. This directory is not shared.

Don't confuse the group created for the Admin department above with the built-in Administrators group created for the administration of the domain. Many organizations have an Admin department, so get used to the idea that you will often encounter an Admin group that doesn't have Administrator permissions.

Note that none of the permissions in Table 9.4 contain the Everyone group. Omitting Everyone keeps information private to this domain—users of other domains do not necessarily have access to the shares on this server. Removing Everyone access also keeps guests from accessing information on your server if the Guest account is enabled.

This server is now set up to allow specific users to share specific directories. Marketing users cannot view or use files in the Engineering group. If members of these groups need to exchange files, they can use the common share. Exercise 9.5 shows you how to create a directory, share it, and assign share-level permissions.

EXERCISE 9.5

Creating a Network Share

1. Go to the Desktop and double-click My Computer.

2. Double-click drive C.

3. Select File ➢ New ➢ Folder.

4. Type **Share** to rename the new folder to share.

5. Right-click the Share folder you just created and select Properties.

6. Click the Sharing tab.

7. Click Shared As.

8. Click Permissions.

9. Click Remove to remove the Everyone permission.

10. Click Add.

11. Select Domain Users in the Groups list box.

12. Click Add.

13. Select Full Control in the Type of Access pick box.

14. Click OK.

15. Click OK. The Share directory is now shared in the domain under share name *Share*.

Exercise 9.6 shows you how to set file system permissions on an NTFS volume. Remember that file system permissions are not available to non-NTFS volumes; the Security tab will not be available.

EXERCISE 9.6

Setting File System Permissions

1. Double-click My Computer.

2. Double-click drive C (or an NTFS volume if it is not C).

3. Select File ➢ New ➢ Folder in the window for that drive.

4. Type **Secure** to rename the folder.

5. Right-click the Secure folder you just created and select Properties.

6. Select the Security tab. If the Security tab is not available, you have not selected an NTFS volume.

7. Click Permissions.

8. Select the Everyone ➢ Full Control permission.

9. Select the Finance group you created earlier in the Names list box.

10. Select Full Control from the Type of Access pick box.

11. Click Add.

12. Click OK.

13. Click OK. You have now changed the folder so that only members of the Finance group (and administrators, of course) have access. Try logging on as a nonmember user and accessing this directory.

Managing Groups

SETTING SPECIFIC PERMISSIONS for many users of a network can be an error-prone and time-consuming exercise. Most organizations do not have security requirements that change for every user. Setting permissions is more manageable with the security groups concept, where permissions are assigned to groups rather than to individual users. Users who are members of a group have all the permissions assigned to that group. Group memberships are especially important in large networks and are discussed in further detail in the companion book *MCSE: Networking Essentials Study Guide.*

Groups are useful in many situations. For instance, the finance department in your organization can have permissions set to access all the financial data stored on a computer. You would then create a group called Finance in the User Manager for Domains and make each individual in the finance department a member of this group. Every member of the Finance group will have access to all the financial data.

Groups also make changing permissions easier. Permissions assigned to a group affect every member of the group, so changes can be made across the entire group by changing permissions for the group. For instance, adding a new directory for the finance group requires merely assigning the group permission to the directory to give each member access. This process is much easier than assigning permission to a number of individual accounts.

The two basic types of groups are local groups and global groups. Local groups affect only the Windows NT computer on which they are created. Global groups affect the entire network and are stored on the primary domain controller. We are focusing on global groups in this chapter.

One individual account can belong to many groups. This arrangement facilitates setting up groups for many purposes. You might define groups corresponding to the functional areas in your organization—administration, marketing, finance, manufacturing, etc. You might create another group for supervisors, another for network support staff, and another for new employees.

For example, a member of the Finance group may have permission to access accounting information and financial statements, but a member of the New Users group may have the No Access permission to accounting information. By assigning membership in both groups, you would be allowing access to financial statements without permitting access to accounting information until the new user becomes a trusted employee and is removed from the New Users group.

Windows NT networks have a default group called Domain Users through which you can assign rights and permissions for every user on the domain. When accounts are created, they are automatically assigned membership in the default Domain Users group.

Windows NT networks also have a special Everyone group that contains all members of the domain and any trusted domains. Resources with Everyone access are available to anyone attached to the domain and trusted domain.

Changing permissions assigned to the default Domain Users group will change permissions for everyone who has access to the domain. All users must be members of the Domain Users group—Windows NT Server does not allow you to remove this membership.

Microsoft Exchange uses the Windows NT group information to define its groups. Therefore, all members of a security group will also become members of message groups when you install Microsoft Exchange.

Global versus Local Groups

Windows NT supports two types of groups: global, or network groups, and local groups that apply only to a single computer. Windows NT servers acting as domain controllers create global groups with the User Manager for Domains. Windows NT workstations can only create groups local to that workstation.

Local groups are not especially important on Windows NT servers because users usually don't log in at the server. All the exercises in this chapter concern global groups. See the companion book *MCSE: NT Workstation Study Guide* for a detailed explanation of local groups.

Special Groups and Built-in Groups

Windows NT has many built-in groups that cover a wide array of typical functions and have permissions already assigned to support those functions. The Guests local group is included for complete compatibility with Windows NT Workstation and should remain disabled on dedicated servers. A list of the groups built into Windows NT Server appears in Table 9.5.

Windows NT also includes a special group that does not show up in group lists: Everyone. The Everyone group contains all users attached to the domain in any way, including users on trusted domains and guests, and is used to assign permissions regardless of group membership.

	GROUP	TYPE	FUNCTION
TABLE 9.5 Windows NT Server Built-in Groups	Account Operators	Local	Members can administer domain user and group accounts.
	Administrators	Local	Members can fully administer the server and the domain.
	Backup Operators	Local	Members can bypass file security to archive files.
	Domain Admins	Global	Members can administer domain accounts and computers in the domain.
	Domain Guests	Global	Members have Guest rights to all domain resources.
	Domain Users	Global	All domain users are part of this group.
	Guests	Local	Members have guest access to the domain. This group should remain empty.
	Print Operators	Local	Members can administer domain printers.
	Replicator	Local	A special group for directory replication.
	Server Operators	Local	Members can administer domain servers.
	Users	Local	Server users.

You create, modify, and delete groups with the User Manager for Domains shown in Figure 9.3. Exercise 9.7 shows you how to make a global group. The process for making a local group is similar; you simply select the local group menu item.

EXERCISE 9.7

Creating a Global Group

1. Select Start ➢ Programs ➢ Administrative Tools ➢ User Manager for Domains.

2. Select User ➢ New Global Group.

3. Type **Finance** in the Group Name input box.

4. Type **Members of the Finance and Accounting Departments** in the Description input box.

EXERCISE 9.7 (CONTINUED FROM PREVIOUS PAGE)

5. Click OK. If you want to add members to this group from the existing list of users, you can do so now by double-clicking the Username in the Not a Member of list box. (We will also show you how to add users as you create them.)
6. Close the User Manager for Domains.

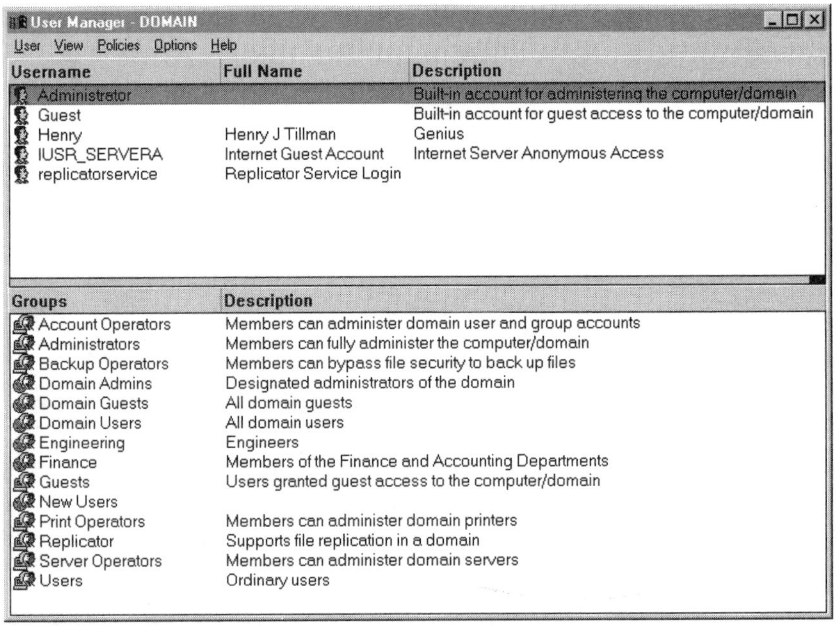

FIGURE 9.3 The User Manager for Domains.

Special Groups

In addition to the many built-in groups, Windows NT has two groups with special functions: Everyone and Guests. You can use these two groups to create special sets of permissions without creating them yourself.

EVERYONE In Windows NT, Everyone is a special group that applies not only to domain users (as does the Domain Users global group) but also to all members of any trusted domains. The Everyone group cannot be deleted or disabled; it is the default permission group granted to any resource when you share it. You must specifically delete the Everyone permission and assign permissions to other groups if you do not want to allow global access to your shared resources.

GUESTS Guests are accounts attached to the domain that could not provide a valid logon because they do not have an account. Windows NT is not like other network operating systems, such as NetWare or UNIX, that treat guests as specific accounts. A Guest is anyone who failed to log on properly to a Windows NT computer or domain.

Guest users are members of the Everyone group. If you allow Everyone access permissions to a share (which is the default) and have Guest Logons enabled, anyone with access to your network will have access to everything on that share. Do not leave guest groups enabled.

Besides these two groups, several internal special groups appear in certain instances. You cannot assign permissions to these groups, so they are of little consequence, but they do reveal how Windows NT manages groups and connections internally. The internal special groups are

- **Interactive:** anyone using the computer locally

- **Network:** all users connected over the network

- **System:** the operating system

- **Creator/Owner:** an alias for the user who created the subdirectory, file, or print job in question

You need not be concerned with the operation or effect of these groups as they are entirely internal to the function of Windows NT.

Managing User Accounts

MANAGING USERS CONSISTS of creating and maintaining user accounts for the people who work on your network. We decided to discuss security and group access before mentioning users because the easiest way to create a user environment is to create your groups first, then create secure shares with permissions assigned by group membership, and finally create users and assign them to groups.

Networked and Local Users

As with groups, Windows NT has two types of users—local and global. *Local users* are users who are allowed to log on to the computer itself. *Global users* are users who are allowed to log on to the network domain. You create local users with the User Manager included with Windows NT Workstation and Windows NT Servers designated as stand-alone servers. You create global users with the User Manager for Domains included with Windows NT Server on servers designated as primary domain controllers, backup domain controllers, or member servers. Global user accounts are created on the primary domain controller. The primary domain controller replicates its account database to all Windows NT servers designated as backup domain controllers in the domain. Backup domain controllers will respond to a logon attempt if the primary domain controller fails to log on the client after a short time; that is, the primary domain controller is busy or temporarily unreachable.

Special Built-in Accounts

Windows NT creates two user accounts by default: the Administrator account and the Guest account.

The Administrator account is always present and should be protected with a strong password. This account manages the overall configuration of the computer and can be used to manage security policies, to create or change users and groups, to set shared directories for networking, and to perform other hardware maintenance tasks. You can rename this account, but you cannot delete it.

You should rename the Administrator account to make guessing its password harder. Hackers know that Windows NT defaults to an Administrator account that cannot be locked out, so they will attempt to hack the password of that account. Changing the Administrator account name defeats this security loophole.

The Guest account enables one-time users or users with low or no security access to use the computer in a limited fashion. The Guest account does not save user preferences or configuration changes, so any changes that a guest user makes are lost when that user logs off. The Guest account is installed with a blank password. If you leave the password blank, remote users can connect to the computer using the Guest account. You can rename and disable the Guest account, but you cannot delete it.

You should leave the Guest account disabled unless you need to allow a specific service to users without passwords. Remember that the special group Everyone includes Guest users and that shares give full control to Everyone by default. If you use the Guest account, be especially careful about share permissions.

Creating User Accounts

You can add user accounts to your NT network in two ways: You can create new user accounts, or you can make copies of existing user accounts. In either case you may make changes in these three areas:

- User account information

- Group membership information

- User account profile information

To add a new user account, you will be working with the New User dialog box, as shown in Figure 9.4.

When you create users with the User Manager for Domains, you are creating global user accounts.

FIGURE 9.4

The New User dialog box.

Figure 9.4 — The New User dialog box, showing fields for Username, Full Name, Description, Password, Confirm Password; checkboxes for User Must Change Password at Next Logon (checked), User Cannot Change Password, Password Never Expires, Account Disabled; Add, Cancel, and Help buttons; and buttons for Groups, Profile, Hours, Logon To, Account, and Dialin.

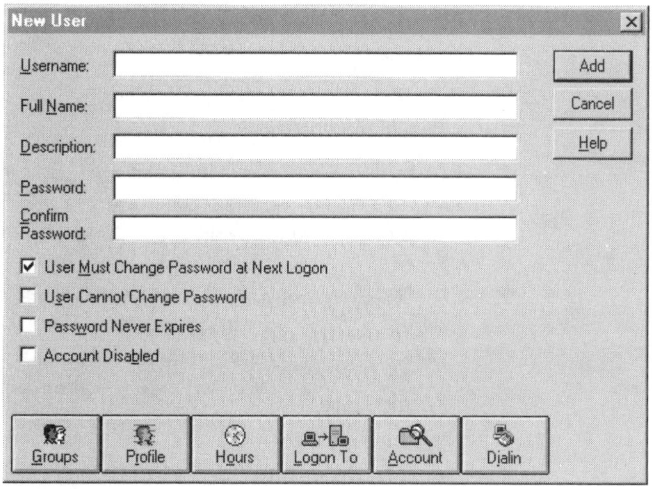

Table 9.6 describes the properties of the user account that are accessible from the New User dialog box.

TABLE 9.6	FIELD	VALUE
User Account Properties	Username	A required text field of up to 20 characters. Uses both uppercase and lowercase letters except " / \ [ ] : ; | = , + * ? < > but is not case sensitive. This name must be unique among workstation users or among network domain members if attached to a network.
	Full Name	An optional text field typically used for the complete name of the user. For instance, a user whose full name is Mae West may have a username of mwest.
	Description	An optional text field used to more fully describe the user and his or her position in the firm, home office, etc. This field is limited to any 48 characters.
	Password	A text field up to 14 characters and case sensitive. This field displays asterisks, rather than the characters typed, to keep your password secure.
	Confirm Password	A text field used to confirm the password field. This method avoids typing errors, which result in unknown passwords. As with the Password field, the Confirm Password field displays asterisks.
	User Must Change Password at Next Logon	A checkbox field used to force a password change at next logon. Note that Windows NT will not allow you to apply changes to a user account if this field and User Cannot Change Password field are both checked.
	User Cannot Change Password	A checkbox field that makes it impossible for users to change their own password. This feature is used for shared accounts (such as the Guest account) where a user changing the account password would prevent other users of the account from logging on. You would not normally check this account for typical users.
	Password Never Expires	A checkbox field that prevents a password from expiring according to the password policy. This setting is normally used for automated software services that must be logged on as a user. Note that setting Password Never Expires overrides User Must Change Password At Next Logon.

	FIELD	VALUE
TABLE 9.6 User Account Properties (continued)	Account Disabled	A checkbox field that when set prevents users from logging on to the network with this account. This field provides an easy way to place an account out of service temporarily.
	Account Locked Out	This option will be checked if the account is currently locked out due to failed logon attempts. You can clear it to restore access to the account, but it cannot be set.
	Groups button	Assigns Group membership.
	Profile button	Activates the user environment profile information.
	Hours button	Sets the hours during which the user may log on. The default is Always.
	Logon To button	Specifies which computers the user can log on to the network from. The default is All Computers.
	Account button	Specifies the account expiration date and the account type. Defaults are never and global account.
	Dialin button	Allows users to dial into this computer using Remote Access Service. See Chapter 12 for more information.

Use the Hours button to disallow network access for all users sometime when your office is closed and set policy to forcibly disconnect logged on users when that time occurs. Schedule your backups to run in this period so you can ensure that no files are open during the backup. The NT tape backup utility can't back up files that are open.

User accounts are administered with the User Manager for Domains administrative tool. Exercise 9.8 shows the process of creating new user accounts. (Subsequent exercises in this chapter assume that you have already opened the User Manager for Domains.)

You should record the Administrator account password, seal it in an envelope, and secure it in a safe or other secure location. Make sure at least one other trusted individual knows where the password is stored in case you get hit by a meteor.

EXERCISE 9.8

Creating a New User Account

1. Log on to the network as an administrator.

2. Click the Start menu and select Programs ➤ Administrative Tools ➤ User Manager for Domains.

3. Select User ➤ New User.

4. Type **mwest** in the Username field.

5. Type **Mae West** in the Full Name field.

6. Type **Movie Star/Pop Culture Icon** in the Description field.

7. Type in any password you want in the Password field. A good password is at least eight characters long and includes at least one punctuation mark. Passwords are case sensitive.

8. Type exactly the same password in the confirm password field.

9. Leave the checkboxes as they are for now.

10. Click OK.

11. Do not record this password anywhere. If you forget it, use the Administrator account to assign a new password to this account.

Copying User Accounts

If you have to create accounts for many users, for instance, in an academic environment where hundreds of students come and go every year, you can create a few basic user account templates and copy them as needed. A user account template is a user account that provides all the features new users will need and has its Account Disabled field enabled. When you need to add a user account, you can copy the template. When you copy a user account, Windows NT automatically copies some of the user account field values from the template; you provide the remaining necessary information.

Windows NT copies these values from the template to the new user account:

- Description

- Group Account Memberships

- Profile Settings

- User Cannot Change Password

- Password Never Expires

- User must Change Password at Next Logon

Windows NT leaves the following fields blank in the New User dialog box:

- Username

- Full Name

- Account Disabled

The Username and Full Name fields are left blank for you to enter the new user information. The User Must Change Password at Next Logon checkbox is checked by default. As a security precaution, leave this setting if you want to force new users to change from your assigned password when they first log on. Exercise 9.9 explains the process of copying a user account.

EXERCISE 9.9

Copying a User Account

1. Select the mwest user account in the User Manager for Domains.

2. Select User ➤ Copy or press F8.

3. Enter the following information into the Copy of mwest dialog box. Leave the checkbox fields in their default states.

4. Type **rvalentino** into the Username field.

5. Type **Rudolf Valentino** into the Full Name field.

6. Notice that the Description field is copied from the original New User dialog box. Although it remains correct in this example, it will usually change it.

7. Type **ruvaruva!** in the Password field.

8. Type **ruvaruva!** in the Confirm Password field.

9. Explore the User Accounts profile and group settings to note that the assignments for mwest have been automatically assigned to rvalentino. To do this inspection, click the Profile and Group buttons and then click OK to return to the Copy of mwest dialog box.

10. Click OK to complete the creation of the rvalentino account.

Notice that we assigned an initial password loosely based on the user's name but mangled according to specific rules. This method is a relatively secure initial password scheme to keep individuals outside your organization from easily guessing new user passwords. However, the only entirely secure method is to assign randomly generated passwords, which are passed to the user through some physical means. Your security needs may require more rigorous precautions to keep initial passwords from creating a hole in your security measures.

Disabling and Deleting User Accounts

When access to the domain is no longer appropriate for a user, you should disable that account. Leaving unused active accounts in the user accounts database permits potential intruders to continue logon attempts after accounts they've already tried lock them out. Disabling an account prevents it from being used, but retains the account information for future use.

This technique is useful for temporarily locking the accounts of employees who are absent or for temporarily denying access to an account that may have been compromised. Deleting an account removes all the user account information from the system. If a user account has been deleted and that user requires access again, you will have to set up a new account with all new permissions. Creating a new user account with the same name will not restore previous account information, as each user account is internally identified by a unique security identifier, not by user name. Exercise 9.10 explains how to disable a user account.

EXERCISE 9.10

Disabling a User Account

1. Double-click user account rvalentino in the User Manager for Domains.

2. Check the Account Disabled field.

3. Click OK to complete the operation.

4. Log off and attempt to log on as rvalentino.

If a user will no longer be using the system, you should delete his or her account, rather than disable it. Deleting an account will destroy all user preferences and permissions, so be certain the user will never again require access before taking this step. Exercise 9.11 explains the process of deleting a user account.

EXERCISE 9.11

Deleting a User Account

1. Log on to the network as an administrator. Go to the Start menu.

2. Select Programs ➤ Administrative Tools ➤ User Manager for Domains.

3. Select user account rvalentino.

4. Select User ➤ Delete (or hit the Del key).

5. Click OK in the Warning dialog.

6. Click Yes to confirm the deletion.

7. Log off and attempt to log on as rvalentino.

Renaming User Accounts

You can rename any user account with the User Manager for Domains, including the Administrator and Guest default accounts. You may need to change an account user name if an account that is associated with a specific job is assigned to another individual or if your organization changes its network naming policy.

Changing the name does not change any other properties of the account. You may want to change the names of the Administrator and Guest accounts so an intruder familiar with Windows NT default user account names cannot gain access to your system simply by guessing a password. Exercise 9.12 will walk you through the steps.

EXERCISE 9.12

Rename a User Account

1. Log on to the network as an administrator and go to the Start menu.

2. Select Programs ➤ Administrative Tools ➤ User Manager for Domains.

3. Select mwest in the User Accounts list.

4. Select User ➤ Rename.

5. Type **wema** in the Change To box.

6. Click OK to complete the operation.

Editing User Environment Profiles

User environment profiles allow you to change some default behavior of Windows NT based on which user is logged on. For instance, the profiles allow you to change the default file location based upon the current user or to map a drive letter to a user's home directory on a server if the person is logging on to a network.

User environment profiles also allow you to run a batch file or executable program that changes as each user logs on. You can use this batch file to set paths, environment variables, and drive mappings, or for any other purpose that will change from user to user.

You should not use user environment profiles simply to start a program when users log on unless the profile somehow depends on the user's name. The Startup folder provides a much easier method for running programs automatically.

Logon Scripts

You can use logon scripts to maintain a consistent set of network connections. In addition, logon scripts provide a way to migrate users from older network operating systems that use logon scripts to Windows NT without changing the user's familiar environment. They are generally not used for individual workstations.

A logon script is usually implemented as a DOS batch file (with a BAT extension), but it can be an executable file under Windows NT 3.5 and later. Certain environment variables enable you to change settings from within a logon script:

- **%PROCESSOR%** changes to the CPU type of the machine.

- **%HOMEDRIVE%** changes to the system hard disk drive.

- **%HOMEPATH%** changes to the user's home path.

- **%HOMESHARE%** changes to the user's home share name.

- **%OS%** changes to the operating system being used.

- **%USERDOMAIN%** changes to the user's home network domain.

- **%USERNAME%** changes to the user's name.

If you are migrating from Novell NetWare, you can take advantage of Windows NT Server's ability to process NetWare login scripts without changing them to Windows NT logon scripts.

If your network uses Windows clients exclusively and few users run MS-DOS programs, you probably don't need to create logon scripts because your drive mappings will persist from session to session automatically. In addition, environment variables aren't as important in this environment as they were in MS-DOS. You can save yourself a lot of hassle by using logon scripts only if you require some functionality that can't be provided any other way.

Maintaining logon scripts is an administrative burden that isn't necessary for most networks anymore.

Home Directories

Home directories give users a place to store their files. By changing the home directory through the user profile, each user can have a private location in which to store files. Windows NT automatically assigns permissions for that user to access his or her home directory if it does not already exist. If it does, you should set permissions on home directories so that only the user specified has access to the data in the directory.

Windows NT makes the home directory the default save location for programs that do not specify one in their Save dialog box. The home directory is also the default directory when launching an MS-DOS prompt. Figure 9.5 shows the user environment profile where you can change these settings. Follow the steps in Exercise 9.13 to create a user directory.

FIGURE 9.5

The User Environment Profile dialog box.

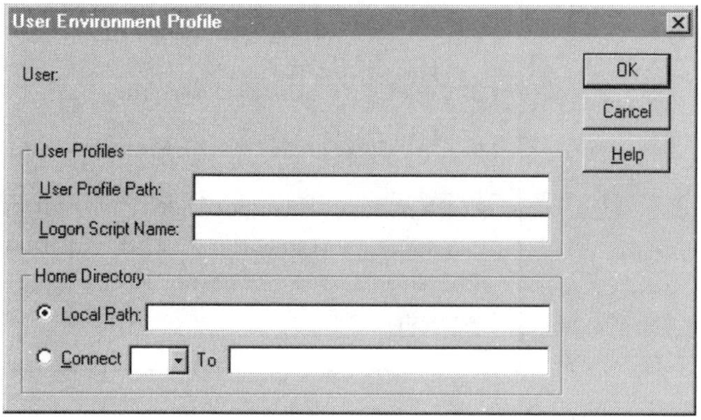

EXERCISE 9.13

Creating User Directories

1. Log on to the network as an administrator.

2. Open the My Computer Icon.

3. Open drive C.

4. Click the right mouse button and select New ➤ Folder.

5. Type **users** as the folder Name.

6. Right-click on the folder.

7. Select Sharing.

8. Select Shared As.

9. Click OK.

10. Select Start ➤ Programs ➤ Administrative Tools ➤ User Manager for Domains.

11. Double-click wema in the User Accounts list.

12. Click the Profile button.

13. Select Z in the Connect To pick box.

14. Type \\{server_name}\users\%username% in the text box. Replace the {server_share} text including the curly brackets with the name of your server.

15. Click OK to close the User Environment Profile dialog box.

16. Click the Profile button again. Windows NT has replaced the environment variable %username% with wema, the name of our user. (Using the %username% variable ensures that the name will be changed when you copy user templates.)

17. Click OK to close the User Environment Profile dialog box.

18. Click OK to close the User dialog box.

19. Click Close in the User Manager for Domains.

When you open the user's folder, you will see that Windows NT has created a directory called wema and that wema has full permissions to the directory—no other users do. Even administrators will not be able to open the directory without first taking ownership of it.

Why did we create a new share for users when we could have simply included the share path for drive C and the user directory, thereby eliminated a step and a share? The reason is that unlike most other shares, your user directories are likely to be moved between volumes during the lifetime of your server. Having an independent share name is convenient for this purpose. This condition is one of the very rare exceptions to the rule that you should create as few shares as possible and use directory permissions to create a secure environment.

Another good idea is to create a volume specifically and only for user files. This technique sets a natural limit to the size user files can take up on your hard disk (since Windows NT doesn't support account-based disk quotas like other network operating systems) and guarantees your system and boot volumes won't run out of space when those downloaded picture files start taking up too much space.

Windows NT cannot create more than one level of directory structure automatically in the User Environment Profile dialog box. If we had entered the path suggested above without having created the user directory first, Windows NT would have set the profile but warned us to create the directory manually. Creating the path for user directories prior to changing the profile information ensures that you will not forget this step or misspell the user name when you create the directory.

Despite its obvious utility, the Connect Drive Letter to UNC Path function works only on Windows NT clients. It does not function on DOS, Windows, or Macintosh clients. You can still use it to create folders with permissions specific to each user, however.

Although creating home directories is simple, it's a little time-consuming. However, you can select multiple users in the user list and use the %username% variable to create many home directories at once.

Profiles

User profiles control Windows NT features such as desktop colors and settings, program groups and start menu settings, and network connections. Because these settings are different for each user, storing them separately allows users to customize and control their Windows NT environment. Bob will always log on to the same environment, even if Susan changes her wallpaper.

Local

Windows NT stores each user's settings in special directories contained in the Profiles directory under your Windows NT System WINNT_ROOT directory. Each user's local profile is stored in a subdirectory named after the user. These directories contain all user-specific settings. A special directory called All Users stores the settings that are global to all users.

Each profile contains many subdirectories. Applications such as Word and Excel store user preferences in the Application Data subdirectory so that shared copies of these applications can maintain different customized features for each user. NetHood contains persistent network connections. Many other directories may exist and contain other settings such as Start menu programs and program groups.

Roaming

Roaming profiles are like the local profiles stored above, except that they are stored on a Windows NT server. Storing one profile on the server, instead of storing a local profile on each of the Windows NT computers that you use, means that changes to your environment will be in effect for all the computers you use, rather than on just the one on which you made the change.

When you specify a roaming profile in the user settings for your user account, the profile is downloaded from the server every time you log on. Changes you make are then sent back to the server so that they will still be in effect the next time you log on and download the profile. Exercise 9.14 shows you how to create a roaming profile.

Windows NT profiles affect only Windows NT. Logging on to a Windows 95 computer will not bring down your Windows NT roaming profile.

You may want each user's home directory to contain the user's profile. You can use the %username% environment variable to automate this process (see Exercise 9.13).

EXERCISE 9.14

Creating a Roaming Profile

1. Select Start ≻ Programs ≻ Administrative Tools ≻ User Manager for Domains.

2. Double-click Administrator.

3. Click Profile.

4. Type **\\\name_of_your_server\winnt\profiles** in the User Profile Path input box. (Replace *name_of_your_server* with the share name of your server and replace *winnt* with the name of your Windows NT directory share name.) If your Windows NT directory is not shared, use the following path: **\\\name_of_your_server\c_drive_share\winnt\profiles**.

5. Click OK to close the User Profiles window.

6. Click OK to close the User window.

7. Close the User Manager for Domains.

8. Log on as administrator on another Windows NT machine in the domain to observe the results.

Summary

JUST AS PROVIDING service to network users is the primary purpose of a network, creating a coherent, secure, and useful user environment is the primary function of network administration. Windows NT Server allows you to create such an environment using group accounts, security permissions, user rights and policies, and network shares.

Effective groups make administering large numbers of users easy. Rather than assigning permissions to individual users, you can assign rights to groups and simply indicate membership in different groups for each user. Windows NT will manage the combinations of rights for users with multiple group memberships.

Security keeps resources from being exposed to unauthorized access. Optimistic security policy allows maximum access to information and secures only specific information. Pessimistic security policy secures all resources and grants access only where necessary. Both approaches are valid, and your choice will depend on your physical security environment. Windows NT supports two types of secured resources: network shares and file system objects. File system objects provide more control over security than shares do. When resolving conflicting file system and share restrictions, Windows NT chooses the most restrictive permission.

Policies are the general security characteristics of Windows NT. Policy changes affect the entire system, not just individual users or groups. Windows NT implements four types of Policy: Account Policies control access to user accounts, User Rights permit or restrict security-related activities, Audit Policy controls the auditing of user activity, and System Policy controls all other security-related system settings.

Setting specific permissions for many users of a network can be an error-prone and time-consuming exercise. Most organizations do not have security requirements that change for every user. Setting permissions is more manageable with the security groups concept in which permissions are assigned to groups rather than to individual users. Users who are members of a group have all the permissions assigned to that group. Windows NT implements two types of groups: those local to the machine and those global to the domain. Global groups are stored on the primary domain controller and replicated to all backup domain controllers.

User accounts allow you to control security on a per person basis. Every person who accesses a Windows NT domain receives a user account through which his or her identity is established to the network and by which permissions to resources are granted. Windows NT also provides two types of user accounts: accounts local to the machine and accounts global to the domain. As with groups, global accounts are stored on the primary domain controller and backed up to the backup domain controllers. User accounts can have logon scripts, home directories, and roaming user preference profiles to allow users to work comfortably at any computer in the network.

Review Questions

1. Share permissions work on a computer even if it's not networked.

   A. True

   B. False

2. Windows NT always favors file permissions over share permissions.

   A. True

   B. False

3. A specific No Access denial always overrides specific access to a resource.

   A. True

   B. False

4. When a user is a member of multiple groups, the user always has the combined permissions of all group memberships.

   A. True

   B. False

5. Share permissions and file system permissions are the same thing.

   A. True

   B. False

6. File system permissions increase control over security beyond that provided by share permissions.

   A. True

   B. False

7. Windows NT makes file system permissions available to all supported file systems.

   A. True

   B. False

8. Windows NT makes share permissions available to all supported file systems.

   A. True

   B. False

9. File system permissions work on a computer even if it's not networked.

   A. True

   B. False

10. Generally, you should create the fewest number of shares possible in your networking environment.

    A. True

    B. False

11. Policy is set on a per group or per user basis.

    A. True

    B. False

12. Shares allowing access to the Everyone group are available to members of trusted domains.

    A. True

    B. False

13. Guests are members of the Everyone group, so they have permission to access any resource that allows Everyone access.

    A. True

    B. False

14. Users who are members of a group have all the permissions assigned to that group.

    A. True

    B. False

15. The Guest account does not save user preferences or configuration changes.

  A. True

  B. False

16. Global groups are stored locally on each machine.

  A. True

  B. False

17. You should always implement pessimistic security policies because you never know what might happen.

  A. True

  B. False

18. Account names must be _____.

19. Permissions control access to _____ based on user account.

20. In a domain, user accounts are kept on the _____ and replicated to _____.

21. A good naming convention should be _____.

22. Security planning involves securing resources from _____.

23. A logon script is usually implemented as a DOS _____ file.

24. Your access token is created when you _____.

  A. log on

  B. launch an application

  C. access a resource

  D. share a resource

Server
Management

ERVER MANAGEMENT EMBODIES a number of different but related topics concerning the security and sharing of resources from Windows NT Server. This chapter touches on the following file-sharing issues:

- Copying and moving files

- Creating shared resources

- Implementing share and file security

- Auditing server file usage

- Installing server tools for remote management from client computers

- Implementing distributed file system shares in multiple-server networks

- Remotely administering servers

- Distributing files with the directory replication service

Most of these topics have little to do with a newly installed server—they are issues that arise over time. Servers reach their storage capacity, requiring the migration of files and directories to other servers. Organizations grow, requiring the seamless addition of file servers. Administrators grow tired of traveling to and from servers to make simple administrative changes.

In this chapter we show you how to maintain an operational network indefinitely and how to manage growth by moving files and redirecting access to network shares without creating additional hassles for your users. We also explain how to implement network security with either share or file security. Finally we discuss implementing distributed file systems and replicated directories that enable you to seamlessly add file servers to your network without changing the way your users interact with it.

File Service

FILE SERVICE IS the primary function of most network servers—hence the common term *file server*. Centralized file storage allows the easy sharing of files among a number of users. It also provides a single point of backup for files and allows users to move between client stations without losing access to their files. While it's quite obvious that shared files should be stored on file servers, it's also important to store private files on the server so they are backed up and available at other workstations if the user who owns them moves to another machine.

Copying and Moving Files

One of the basic tasks network administrators deal with is the copying and moving of files between directories and network shares. You may need to copy files for a myriad of reasons—few users have done anything useful on a computer without copying files. When you copy a file, the original file is referred to as the *source file* and the duplicate is referred to as the *destination file*.

A directory entry is an entry in a file system directory that associates a file name (and attributes) with a specific location in the volume where the actual file data resides. This entry is similar to the table of contents of this book, which contains entries pointing to the actual chapters and sections within.

The difference between copying and moving is that copying creates a duplicate file and makes a directory entry for it in another directory or disk, whereas moving creates a new directory entry for the existing file and removes the old directory entry without actually changing the location of the file data.

The preceding explanation is only half the story. Moving really works only when you move a file on the same volume. If you move a file to another volume, Windows NT simulates a move by copying the file to the new volume and then deleting the old file. This condition occurs because a volume directory entry cannot refer to a file in another volume, so a new file in the destination volume must be created and the original file must be deleted. This difference in behavior explains one of the stranger nuances of Windows NT—permissions on copied and moved files.

When you copy a file, you are actually creating a new destination file from the contents of the source file—two files now exist, even on the same volume. Whenever you create a file on an NTFS volume, the new file inherits the access permissions of the directory in which it is created. Exercise 10.1 shows you how to copy files in Windows NT.

EXERCISE 10.1

Copying Files between Directories

1. Double-click My Computer.

2. Double-click the C drive.

3. Double-click your Windows NT directory folder.

4. Double-click the temp folder in the C drive window. You should now have your Windows NT folder and the temp folder open and visible on the desktop. If you don't have a temp folder, create one by right clicking on a white area in the C drive, selecting New ➤ Folder, and naming the folder temp.

5. Browse through your Windows NT folder until you find the file `BlueMonday.bmp`.

6. Right-drag (drag using the right mouse button rather than the left) this file to the `temp` directory.

7. Select Copy Here in the menu that pops up when you release the drag. The bold option is the default behavior of the drag if you use the left mouse button. The file now exists in both locations.

8. Close all the Windows on your Explorer desktop.

The behavior of permissions when you are moving files is somewhat stranger than it is when you are copying files. Because moving a file within the same volume does not create a file (remember—it just moves the directory entry to a new location, not the file itself), the permissions the file had before the move are retained in the new location regardless of the new directory's access permissions. Consequently, moving a file to a new location on the same volume won't necessarily make it available to people who have access to that directory.

Moving a file to a different volume, however, acts just like a copy—because it is a copy. Windows NT can't update the directory entries because two directories are involved, so it must copy the file to the new volume and delete the original. Because the new file is in fact created on a new volume, the directory permissions for the directory it is created in are inherited. Exercise 10.2 shows you how to move files in Windows NT.

Files in copy and move operations always inherit directory permissions except when a file moves within the same volume.

EXERCISE 10.2

Moving Files between Directories in the Same Volume

1. Double-click My Computer.

2. Double-click the C drive.

3. Double-click your Windows NT directory folder.

4. Double-click the temp folder in your C drive window. You should now have your Windows NT folder and the temp folder open and visible on the desktop.

5. Left-drag the file `BlueMonday.bmp` down one row and release. You have just copied the file to the same directory. Windows NT renames the file `Copy of BlueMonday.bmp` to avoid a file name conflict.

6. Browse through the Windows NT directory until you find the `Copy of BlueMonday.bmp` file.

7. Right-drag this file to the `temp` directory.

8. Select Move Here in the pop-up menu. The file `Copy of BlueMonday.bmp` no longer exists in the Windows NT directory.

9. Close all the windows on your explorer desktop.

Sharing Resources

Sharing resources means making a resource such as a directory or a printer that is available to a Windows NT server also available to clients. Sharing allows you to use another set of permissions, called *share permissions*, to restrict access to the shared resource if necessary. Share permissions work regardless of the file system security measures implemented, so you can use them on both NTFS and FAT shared volumes. If you have directory permissions set up on an NTFS volume, users will be restricted by both sets of permissions.

Windows NT selects the most restrictive permission when combining share permissions and file system permissions.

Creating a share is simple: Select a directory, volume, or printer and right-click to select properties. Selecting the Sharing tab allows you to create and name a new share and set the share permissions, as shown in Exercise 10.3.

MS-DOS users will not be able to access shares with names that violate the MS-DOS eight-plus-three file-naming conventions for length or characters not supported in MS-DOS file names.

EXERCISE 10.3

Creating a Network Share

1. Double-click My Computer.

2. Double-click the C drive in the My Computer window. If your C drive is not formatted with the NTFS file system, select a drive that is. If you don't have one, you can still follow along with the exercises in this chapter, but you will not be able to complete Exercises 10.5 or 10.7.

3. Right-click on a white area (an area without any icons or files).

4. Select New ≻ Folder in the menu that appears.

5. Type **Test Share** as the name of the folder. You must do this entry immediately or the focus will change. If you aren't quick enough and you can't rename the file, right-click on the folder and select the Rename option.

6. Right-click on your newly created **Test Share** folder.

7. Select Sharing.

8. Select Shared As:. The name of the folder automatically appears as the share name. You can change the share name if you wish.

9. Click OK.

10. Click Yes to acknowledge the warning about MS-DOS clients.

Implementing Permissions and Security

Windows NT implements two types of security: share level and file level. Share-level security works with any file system by controlling access to the network share. Users logged on locally are not limited by share-level security, so they will be able to see and manipulate any files not protected by file-level security. File-level security works only with NTFS volumes and limits access on a directory or file basis. Users logged on locally are limited by file-level security.

When you design your share structure, you can use either of two methods:

■ Share each directory independently, using share permissions to control access. This option is your only real choice when using file systems other than NTFS.

■ Share a single directory and then use file-level permissions within that shared volume to control access to individual directories. This vastly superior option is available when using NTFS. File-level security is more comprehensive than share-level security and limits locally logged on users.

Exercise 10.4 shows how to modify share permissions using share security.

In NetWare, all permissions are handled on a file system level, similar to NTFS file-level security. In Windows for Workgroups and Windows 95 peer networks, all permissions are handled on a share level.

EXERCISE 10.4

Implementing Share-Level Security

1. Right-click your newly created **Test Share** folder.

2. Select Sharing.

3. Click Permissions.

4. Select the Everyone/Full Control permission.

5. Click Remove.

6. Click Add.

7. Double-click Domain Users.

8. Select Change in the Type of Access pick box.

EXERCISE 10.4 (CONTINUED FROM PREVIOUS PAGE)

9. Click OK.

10. Click Add.

11. Double-click Domain Guests.

12. Select Read in the Type of Access pick box.

13. Click OK three times.

You can control file-level security to a finer detail than you can control share-level security, and file-level security applies even when users are logged on locally. For these reasons, you should use file security rather than share security whenever possible. For most server installations, you should create only a few shares (one per volume is usually enough) and then use file security to further restrict access to directories or files. Exercise 10.5 shows how to secure individual files and directories.

Currently, Windows NT supports file security only on NTFS volumes. Third-party vendors or Microsoft may release file systems in the future that also work with file-level security.

EXERCISE 10.5

Implementing File-Level Security

1. Right-click your newly created **Test Share** folder.

2. Select Properties.

3. Select the Security tab. The Security tab appears only on NTFS volumes.

4. Click Permissions.

5. Select Everyone/Special Access.

6. Click Remove.

7. Click Add.

8. Click Domain Users

9. Select Change.

10. Click OK two times.

File Auditing

File auditing is an important security technique used primarily to trace access to files when you suspect that intrusion or improper use is occurring. Unless you have external security requirements that require auditing (as some government agencies do), you won't want to leave file auditing enabled because of the severe additional burden that logging file accesses requires. File auditing is available only on NTFS volumes.

Auditing can put a serious load on your server. Be very careful about the number of files you audit and the frequency of their access.

The exception to this rule is when you have a small but extremely sensitive group of files on the disk. If these files are infrequently accessed (say, less than ten times a day), then you can and should enable auditing for these files on a continual basis. But don't audit large directories of frequently accessed files unless you want your server to run like a snail. You might want to turn on file auditing for short periods of time (a few hours, for instance, or overnight) if you suspect unauthorized access is occurring at certain times. This approach will keep your Security log relatively small and shouldn't burden your users excessively.

File auditing makes a record of each audited access to a file. You can audit files for the success or failure (attempt) of the following types of file access:

- **Read** makes a Security log entry every time the file is read.

- **Write** makes a Security log entry every time the file is written to.

- **Execute** makes a Security log entry each time the program is run.

- **Delete** make a Security log entry if the file is deleted.

- **Change Permissions** makes a Security log entry when permissions are changed.

- **Take Ownership** records each attempt to take ownership of a file or directory.

Entries in the Security log differ from object to object. Figure 10.1 shows a typical delete entry in the Security log.

FIGURE 10.1

A delete record in the
Security log.

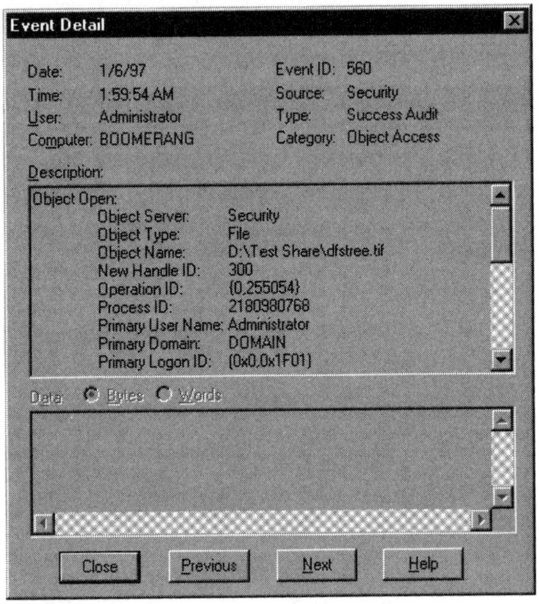

Here's the full text:

```
Object Open:

     Object Server:      Security

     Object Type:        File

     Object Name:        D:\Test Share\SMSROOT

     New Handle ID:      308

     Operation ID:       {0,92981}

  Process ID: 2186148160

  Primary User Name:Administrator

     Primary Domain:     DOMAIN

     Primary Logon ID: (0x0,0x3F36)

     Client User Name:   -

     Client Domain:      -

     Client Logon ID:    -

     Accesses            DELETE
```

```
READ_CONTROL

SYNCHRONIZE

WriteData (or AddFile)

AppendData (or AddSubdirectory or
CreatePipeInstance)

WriteEA

ReadAttributes

WriteAttributes
```

```
Privileges
```

The above example contains four important fields:

- **Object Type** shows that the access applied to a file object.

- **Object Name** shows the specific file and the path to it.

- **Primary User Name** tells you who performed the operation.

- **Accesses** tells you which specific operations occurred.

As you can see, file auditing provides you with a very detailed record of any type of access you care to monitor.

Before you can perform any file auditing, you must enable Audit policy in the User Manager for Domains, as shown in Exercise 10.6.

EXERCISE 10.6

Enabling File Auditing

1. Select Start ➢ Programs ➢ Administrative Tools ➢ User Manager for Domains.

2. Select Policies ➢ Audit.

3. Select Audit These Events.

4. Check File and Object Access Success.

5. Check File and Object Access Failure.

6. Click OK.

7. Close the User Manager for Domains.

Once you've enabled Audit policy, you can select the specific files or directories you wish to audit. Enabling auditing is similar to setting permissions on files and directories, as shown in Exercise 10.7. Remember that file auditing is available only on NTFS volumes, so Exercise 10.7 won't work on FAT volumes.

EXERCISE 10.7

Auditing File Access

1. Right-click your newly created **Test Share** folder.

2. Select Properties.

3. Select the Security tab.

4. Click Auditing.

5. Click Add.

6. Click Everyone

7. Click OK.

8. Click Delete Success

9. Click Delete Failure

10. Click OK. Attempts to delete files in this directory will now be recorded in the Security log.

Enabling auditing and auditing certain directories is only half the picture. You need to see the audit results or the whole process is a waste of time. Exercise 10.8 shows you how to view security events in the Event viewer's Security log. Figure 10.2 shows the Security log after only a single user action—deleting an audited file. Because many different file system events occur for every user action, many audit records are created, which is why enabling Audit policy all the time or for your entire disk doesn't make sense. Even if a security breach did occur, you would have to browse through so many audit records that you might never find it.

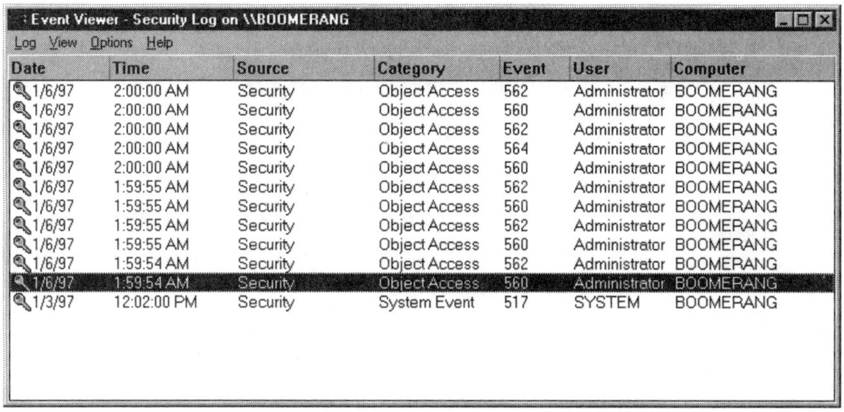

Event Viewer - Security Log on \\BOOMERANG

Log View Options Help

Date	Time	Source	Category	Event	User	Computer
1/6/97	2:00:00 AM	Security	Object Access	562	Administrator	BOOMERANG
1/6/97	2:00:00 AM	Security	Object Access	560	Administrator	BOOMERANG
1/6/97	2:00:00 AM	Security	Object Access	562	Administrator	BOOMERANG
1/6/97	2:00:00 AM	Security	Object Access	564	Administrator	BOOMERANG
1/6/97	2:00:00 AM	Security	Object Access	560	Administrator	BOOMERANG
1/6/97	1:59:55 AM	Security	Object Access	562	Administrator	BOOMERANG
1/6/97	1:59:55 AM	Security	Object Access	560	Administrator	BOOMERANG
1/6/97	1:59:55 AM	Security	Object Access	562	Administrator	BOOMERANG
1/6/97	1:59:55 AM	Security	Object Access	560	Administrator	BOOMERANG
1/6/97	1:59:54 AM	Security	Object Access	562	Administrator	BOOMERANG
1/6/97	1:59:54 AM	Security	Object Access	560	Administrator	BOOMERANG
1/3/97	12:02:00 PM	Security	System Event	517	SYSTEM	BOOMERANG

FIGURE 10.2 The Event viewer's Security log.

EXERCISE 10.8

Viewing Audited File Events

1. Follow the steps in Exercise 10.1 to copy a file into the **Test Share** folder.
2. Drag that newly copied file to the Recycle Bin. This action will cause an audited event to occur.
3. Select Start ➢ Programs ➢ Administrative Tools ➢ Event Viewer.
4. Select Log ➢ Security.
5. Double-click the oldest security event. Notice that Windows NT is reporting the deletion of a file in the **Test Share** folder. The other events in the Security log also relate to this single activity.

Distributed File System

THE DISTRIBUTED FILE system (Dfs—for some reason, Microsoft capitalizes only the first letter of this abbreviation) is an important new tool for Windows NT Server that allows administrators to simulate a single (or, if you prefer, many) coherent server share environment that actually exists across multiple servers. Dfs allows you to create links to other servers that look like subdirectories on a single server.

Distributed file system directory structures are called trees, and they are roughly analogous to the NetWare Directory Service (NDS) provided in NetWare 4.1.

Dfs allows you to graft a share located on any server into the directory hierarchy of any Dfs tree. You can make your share environment appear to be a single hierarchical environment.

One major benefit of the ability of Dfs to provide a single view of all the shares on your network is that by backing up the root share and all its subdirectories, your backup will actually span all the servers with shares grafted into the tree. This mechanism makes backing up an entire network easy and painless.

Dfs does not limit you to a single tree, however. You can provide multiple distributed trees for as many users, groups, or purposes you desire. Multiple trees allow you to provide multiple "views" of your network, customized for unique purposes. For example, the engineering department can use a tree that shows engineering and corporate resources while the finance department uses a different tree that shows financial and corporate resources.

Although only Windows NT Servers can host Dfs trees, shares from Windows NT Workstations and Windows 95 Workstations (with the Dfs client software for Windows 95) can be grafted into Dfs trees.

Another benefit of Dfs is that you can create trees that look exactly the same, but point to different servers, for different departments. This technique allows you to replicate data to other servers and seamlessly split the load among them. This approach works best with read-only information, however, because of the time delays involved with replication service of Windows NT Server.

In the case of Dfs, a picture is worth a thousand words, so take a close look at Figure 10.3. It looks like any regular Network Neighborhood view, right?

Here's what's going on in Figure 10.3:

- Server Boomerang is hosting a Dfs tree called Dfs root.

- The localc subdirectory is local to Boomerang.

- The Space subdirectory is located on another server called Yoyo.

- The sys subdirectory is a NetWare 4.1 server!

FIGURE 10.3

A server hosting a
Dfs tree.

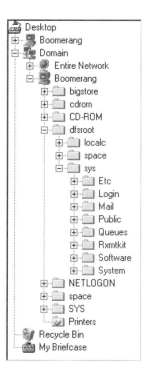

But to a user, all these resources seem to be available on a single server called boomerang. Users don't have to know or care that other file servers are active on the network—Dfs provides the illusion of one large, centralized store.

Dfs currently works only with Windows NT 4 and Windows 95 computers running the Dfs client for Windows 95. If you are using other clients (such as MS-DOS or Macintosh), the leaf shares inside the Dfs tree will appear empty. You can still access the shares on other computers by using their normal share names.

Using Dfs to Manage Growing Networks

Dfs really shines when you are ready to add servers to your network. Many networks start small and grow with the company. For instance, your company may have only 30 clients when you start, with files located on a single server in four different shared directories. Figure 10.4 shows how this server might look.

FIGURE 10.4

The first server in a
growing network.

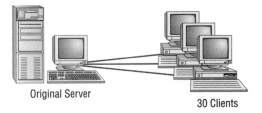

Original Server

30 Clients

By the time your network has grown to 100 users, that server has become quite strained trying to keep up with the load. So you purchase another server and decide to move half the files over to it, as shown in Figure 10.5.

FIGURE 10.5

The second server in a
growing network.

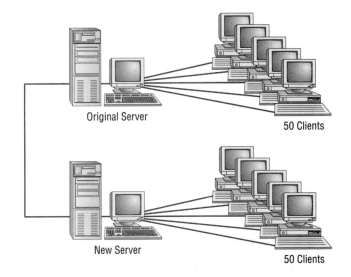

Original Server

50 Clients

New Server

50 Clients

If you don't use Dfs, you will have to go to about 50 different client stations and change all their share mappings to point to the new server. If you do use Dfs, you can simply graft the shares back into the original server's Dfs root. Fortunately, you don't have to start out using Dfs; you can add it at any time. You should start your servers with a single root share that you can later turn into a Dfs root—otherwise, you'll need multiple Dfs roots if you want to simulate multiple root shares.

The next stage, a few years down the road, is when Dfs really shines. For example, suppose our hypothetical company grows to 400 client computers, attached to eight servers, as shown in Figure 10.6.

FIGURE 10.6

A larger hypothetical
company.

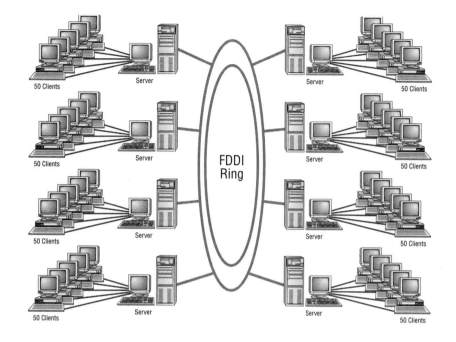

Without Dfs, each additional server would require new share mappings throughout the company for users that need to attach to it. In this situation, servers are usually brought online and given a specific purpose, such as storing financial data. When that data exceeds the capacity of a single server, administrators wind up with servers called FINANCE1 and FINANCE2. This situation continues ad infinitum, with users becoming more and more frustrated as they have dig through multiple servers to find data.

With Dfs, the company still looks like the good old days when everything fit nicely on a single server. Although financial data is spread across four servers, the user sees it as subdirectories of a single finance folder in the original root share—just like it was before. You can use the network monitor and the performance monitor to determine which servers are loaded and which ones have excess capacity, and simply move shares from the loaded servers to those less loaded. All you have to do is update the Dfs tree using the Dfs administrator, and your users won't know anything happened at all. Best of all, you won't be spending weeks updating the share mappings of 2,000 computers.

How Dfs Works

So how does the distributed file system perform its magic? The answer is surprisingly simple. Dfs replaces universal naming convention (UNC) path names (see *MSCE: NT Workstation Study Guide* for an explanation of UNC) that point to grafted subdirectories in the Dfs root with the UNC path name of the actual network share. That's it.

A slightly more technical explanation of this technique follows. The Dfs service on the server containing the Dfs root reports the true UNC path to the share grafted into the Dfs directory structure to the client. The client then initiates a connection to that server in a manner transparent to the user.

UNC path names follow the convention:\\{servername}\{sharename}\ {directory_path}.

For example, in Figure 10.3 the UNC path \\boomerang\dfsroot\sys is actually \\netware\sys. If a user requests files from \\boomerang\ dfsroot\sys\public, the Dfs service running on boomerang redirects the client to \\netware\sys\public, according to the Dfs structure mappings you created with the Dfs Administrator tool.

This process has two important effects:

1. Dfs puts a slight load on the root server. Accordingly, you should make this server's file service load lighter than the loads of other servers on your network. Because most Dfs root servers start out as the only server on the network, it's a good bet that server is also the primary domain controller, a service that also puts a slight load on the server.

2. You can't browse through the Dfs tree on the disk volume hosting the Dfs root because local disk requests go through the multiple provider router, which is not redirected by Dfs, rather than through the multiple UNC router, which is.

When a Dfs server receives a UNC request that resolves to a share located on another computer, the Dfs service tells the multiple UNC router on the client to replace the Dfs root path with the UNC path of the server where the files are actually located.

Because the multiple provider router that resolves local disk requests (like those issued using the My Computer icon) doesn't see these redirection messages, it can't browse through the Dfs tree. In addition, client computers that don't support Dfs see only empty directories—they don't understand the redirection messages sent by the Dfs server.

Therefore, if you map the Dfs share as a local drive, you will be able to browse it because the multiple provider router sends requests for shares mapped as drives to the multiple UNC provider, which is redirected by Dfs.

Dfs can even redirect inbound requests for files and Web pages from the Internet, so your Web site can grow to multiple servers without changing your www root *directory structure if you create a Dfs tree containing your* www root *and graft other server shares into it. However, Dfs cannot currently redirect share names that identify the server using IP addresses, such as* \\128.110.121.13\sharename.

Obtaining Dfs

Dfs was not finished in time for inclusion with the initial release of Windows NT Server 4, so if it is not on your CD-ROM, you will have to download it from the Microsoft Web site. Exercise 10.9 shows exactly how to do this. The Dfs package is small, and the download doesn't take long.

EXERCISE 10.9

Downloading Dfs from the Microsoft Web Site

1. Use Dial-up Networking to connect to the Internet if your computer does not maintain a constant connection.

2. Launch Internet Explorer or your preferred Web browser.

3. Type www.microsoft.com in the location/URL input box of your Web browser.

4. Click the SEARCH link.

5. Type **distributed file system** in the Search input box.

6. Find the link pointing to Microsoft Distributed File System Download Instructions and click it.

7. Read the instructions on the Web page, continuing through each step until you are able to select the link pointing directly to the Dfs file. You will have to agree to a licensing statement, fill in a form asking about you and your network, and select the type of microprocessor you use.

8. Select the `dfs-v40-i386.exe` (differs for other processors) link to begin downloading the Dfs installation package.

9. Respond to the Save as prompt. Browse to the root of your system directory and create a new folder. Name the folder dfs and double-click to browse into the new folder. Save the Dfs package in this folder.

The file should take about five minutes to download. You may also want to download the Dfs client for Windows 95 computers, which will allow you to see Dfs trees from Windows 95 clients and treat Windows 95 shares as part of a Dfs tree.

10. Close your Web browser when the download completes.

11. Double-click My Computer ➤ C drive ➤ DFS ➤ `dfs-v40-i386.exe` (or to wherever you stored the Dfs package).

12. Click Yes to agree to the software license.

13. Click Continue.

14. Click Exit.

15. Read the Release Notes and exit WordPad.

Installing Dfs

Once you've obtained Dfs, installing it is very simple. Exercise 10.10 walks you through the steps necessary to install Dfs assuming you've downloaded it from the Microsoft Web site. If Dfs came on your Windows NT Server 4 CD-ROM, use the instructions on the CD-ROM to install it. It should install like any other network-related service.

Creating Dfs

After installing Dfs on your machine, you are ready to create a Dfs share through the Dfs Administrator tool located in the Administrative tools group. Figure 10.7 shows the Dfs Administrator, and Exercise 10.11 explains the creation process. The Dfs Administrator allows you to assign shared directories on any server to a subdirectory (called a *graft*) that the administrator will create within your Dfs tree.

EXERCISE 10.10

Installing the Distributed File System Service

1. Right-click Network Neighborhood.
2. Select Properties.
3. Click the Services tab
4. Click Add.
5. Click Have Disk. If Distributed File System appears in the Network Service list, do not select it; use Have Disk instead.
6. Type **C:\winnt\system32\dfs** (or wherever your Windows NT boot directory resides).
7. Press Enter.
8. Click OK to select Dfs for installation.
9. Check Host a Dfs on share.
10. Click New Share
11. Type `C:\dfsroot` in the input box.
12. Click Yes to create the `dfsroot` directory.
13. Select Shared As.
14. Click OK
15. Click OK
16. Click Close.
17. Click Yes to restart the computer.

FIGURE 10.7

The Dfs Administrator.

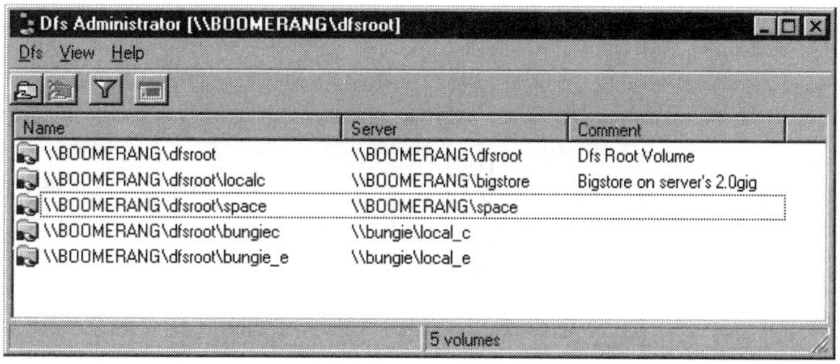
Dfs Administrator [\\BOOMERANG\dfsroot]
Dfs View Help
Name
Server
Comment
\\BOOMERANG\dfsroot
\\BOOMERANG\dfsroot
Dfs Root Volume
\\BOOMERANG\dfsroot\localc
\\BOOMERANG\bigstore
Bigstore on server's 2.0gig
\\BOOMERANG\dfsroot\space
\\BOOMERANG\space
\\BOOMERANG\dfsroot\bungiec
\\bungie\local_c
\\BOOMERANG\dfsroot\bungie_e
\\bungie\local_e
5 volumes

Don't create Dfs shares until you plan a coherent, unified directory tree. You should create only the shares necessary to implement that tree. Then use the network and performance monitors to find out where to move directories to balance your file service load. No matter where resources actually exist on your network, your Dfs tree should remain the same— that's the point of Dfs.

EXERCISE 10.11

Creating and Managing Distributed File Systems

1. Select Start ➤ Programs ➤ Administrative Tools ➤ Dfs Administrator.

2. Select Dfs ➤ Add to Dfs (or click the yellow Shared Folder tool on the toolbar).

3. Type **localc** in the When a user references this path input box.

4. Click the Browse button next to the Send the user to this network path input box.

5. Click your computer to expand it. Notice that you could click on any server, work-station, or Windows 95 computer running the Dfs client for Windows 95 in your domain.

6. Select the share you created in Exercise 10.3 to add to the Dfs volume.

7. Close the Dfs Administrator.

Exploring with Dfs

Now that you have a Dfs share grafted into your Dfs root, let's do a little exploring to see the behavior of Dfs under various circumstances. Follow the steps in Exercise 10.12; then log on to your server from a client on the network and map a drive to the Dfs root share. Browse through that to see how Dfs looks from the client side.

Exercise 10.12 highlights a very important aspect of Dfs. The difference in behavior between the My Computer directory browser and the Network Neighborhood share browser is caused by the services that provide path name resolution to those browsers. The Network Neighborhood browses through the multiple UNC provider service, which is redirected by Dfs, whereas My Computer browses through the multiple provider router service, which is not redirected by Dfs.

EXERCISE 10.12

Exploring with Dfs

1. Double-click My Computer.

2. Double-click the C drive (or the drive containing your Dfs root).

3. Double-click Dfs root.

The folder called localc is a security object created to provide a presence in the file system that matches the Dfs.

4. Double-click localc. Notice that it is empty, although your share may not be.

5. Use the procedure shown in Exercise 10.1 to attempt to copy a file by right dragging and dropping it onto the localc folder.

6. Click OK to acknowledge that access is denied. The localc folder is not a true directory object, so you cannot copy files into it through the Explorer.

7. Close all the windows you have open on the desktop.

8. Double-click Network Neighborhood.

9. Double-click the computer that contains the Dfs root.

10. Double-click Dfs root.

11. Double-click localc.

12. Your Browse window now contains all the files and folders you would expect.

When you double-clicked localc this time, Dfs modified the UNC path to return the true UNC path name of the localc share. This behavior is invisible to the end user, thus providing the invisible redirection of shares anywhere on your network without the interaction of your users or the necessity to reconfigure clients when you move directory shares.

Remote Administration

WINDOWS NT SERVER comes with tools you can install on Windows NT workstations or Windows 95 clients that allow you to administer your file servers without being logged on to the file server. You can install these tools at the client station from which you wish to administer the network. You get two sets of tools: one set for operation from a Windows 95 client and one set for operation from a Windows NT workstation client.

All tools covered in this section are detailed in other areas of the book. Their function from a client station is exactly the same as from the server, so we will not reiterate their use in this section.

Using Server Tools for Windows 95

The server tools for Windows 95 allow you to administer your domain from a Windows 95 client. This technique can be very convenient for administrators who work on a Windows 95 computer and whose servers are located some distance away. You can administer the following tools from a Windows 95 client:

- **Event Viewer** for viewing the server Event log, Security log, and Application log

- **Server Manager** for managing server functions, services, replication, and Macintosh shares

- **User Manager for Domains** for creating and managing domain users and groups

- **Explorer extensions** for managing file system security on NTFS shares

These tools are the most important tools for the day-to-day management of a network. Nevertheless, you will still have to travel to a Windows NT machine if you need to make changes that these tools do not control.

Here are a few things you should be aware of when administering your network from a Windows 95 client:

- Using the Windows 95–based Server Manager, you can create trust relationships between domains, but you cannot verify them.

- You may have to provide your logon account name and password when you connect to new domains or servers.

- You must have administrative privileges on any computer you wish to administer.

- You cannot administer shared printers because the printers shown for the Windows 95 client are local to the Windows 95 client even with server tools installed.

Exercise 10.13 shows you how to install the server tools for Windows 95.

EXERCISE 10.13

Installing Remote Server Tools on a Windows 95 Client

1. Insert the Windows NT Server CD-ROM into the CD-ROM reader at your Windows 95–based client computer.

2. Select Start ➢ Settings ➢ Control Panel.

3. Double-click Add/Remove Programs.

4. Select the Windows Setup tab.

5. Click Have Disk.

6. Type your CD-ROM drive letter followed by `:\clients\srvtools\win95` and press Enter.

7. Check Windows NT Server Tools.

8. Click Install.

9. Click OK.

10. Close the Control Panel windows.

11. Double-click My Computer.

12. Double-click your C drive.

13. Right-click on the `Autoexec.bat` file and select Edit. If you do not have an `Autoexec.bat`, right-click the C window in a blank area, select New ➢ Text Document, and name the new text document `Autoexec.bat`.

14. Find the path statement in the `Autoexec.bat` file. The path statement starts with the command `Path=`. Type `;c:\srvtools` at the end of the path statement. If your `Autoexec.bat` does not contain a path statement, add a line containing `Path=c:\srvtools`.

15. Close all the windows on your desktop and restart your computer.

Once you've installed server tools for Windows 95, you'll be able to administer most of the important functions of your domain servers easily. Exercise 10.14 gives a brief overview of the tools. More detailed information on how to use these tools is provided elsewhere in this chapter and throughout the remainder of the book.

EXERCISE 10.14

Using Server Tools from a Windows 95 Client

1. Select Start ➤ Programs ➤ Windows NT Server Tools ➤ Event Viewer.

2. Type the name of the server you want to view in the Select Computer input box and press Enter. If you are attached via RAS, check the Low Speed Connection checkbox.

3. Browse through the events. Use the Log ➤ Select Computer dialog to view events on other servers.

4. Close the Event Viewer.

5. Select Start ➤ Programs ➤ Windows NT Server Tools ➤ User Manager for Domains.

6. (Optional) If you are dialing in from a RAS connection, select Options ➤ Low Speed Connection.

7. (Optional) If you want to administer a different domain, select User ➤ Select Domain and browse through the domain list. You may have to log on to the new domain before you can administer it.

8. Close the User Manager for Domains.

9. Right-click Network Neighborhood.

10. Select Map Network Drive.

11. Pick a shared NTFS volume from a Windows NT File server in the Path pick box.

12. Click OK.

13. Right-click a directory in the Directory Browser window.

14. Select Properties. Note that the Security tab that does not appear on Windows 95 clients that do not have Server Tools installed.

You can now set permissions, auditing and ownership from a Windows 95 client.

Using Server Tools for Windows NT Workstation

The tools provided for server management from a Windows NT workstation are the same tools used on the server. The only difference is that they are run from a Windows NT workstation. Since these tools don't come with the standard Windows NT Workstation installation, they must be installed from the Windows NT Server 4 CD-ROM. The following tools are provided for administration from a Windows NT workstation:

- DHCP Manager

- System Policy Editor

- Remote Access Server Administrator

- Remote Boot Server Manager

- Server Manager

- User Manager for Domains

- WINS Manager

Exercise 10.15 shows how to install the server administration tools on a Windows NT workstation. Their use is exactly the same as if they were being used from a Windows NT server, as covered throughout the rest of the book.

EXERCISE 10.15

Installing Server Tools for Windows NT Workstation

1. Insert the Windows NT Server 4 disk in your Windows NT workstation.

2. Double-click My Computer.

3. Double-click your CD-ROM drive.

4. Click Browse this CD.

5. Double-click Clients.

6. Double-click Srvtools.

7. Double-click Winnt.

8. Double-click Setup.bat. The proper files for your microprocessor will be installed.

Simple Network Management Protocol (SNMP)

SNMP is an Internet protocol that allows network managers to control network hardware and computers from a central site. Hubs, routers, bridges, switches, gateways, and computers (both clients and servers) support SNMP. With SNMP you can do the following:

- View the operational status of the device

- View various statistics such as throughput and collisions

- Send commands to reconfigure the device

Most network hardware sold today comes in two versions: managed and unmanaged. *Managed hardware* (usually) includes a microprocessor and software that allows it to support SNMP. *Unmanaged hardware* does not include management modules, and it is generally quite a bit cheaper. Some devices allow you to buy management modules later when you decide you need them.

SNMP is generally not worth the cost for small networks contained in a single small site. If you can easily walk around to all of your network devices, managing them manually is easier and more cost effective than installing SNMP hardware and software. However, in a large network SNMP is invaluable because it enables you to monitor the status of every managed device from a single computer.

As with most Internet protocols, SNMP uses a client/server architecture. Every managed device is an SNMP client, and the computer from which you run your SNMP management software is the server. Windows NT comes with an SNMP agent that allows you to support SNMP remote management for the server, but it does not come with the management reporting software. If you intend to use SNMP, you will have to buy SNMP management software separately.

Windows NT does not come with SNMP management software; it has only an SNMP agent to report the status of Windows NT computers.

Directory Replication

WINDOWS NT SERVER provides a directory replication service capable of automatically copying files from one server (called the export server) to another (called the import server) automatically. With this service, you can distribute entire directories between servers to reduce your administrative load and to spread the file access load among a number of servers. Whenever a file in a replicated directory changes, that file is copied to all the import servers set up to receive it.

Directory replication allows a server to publish a directory for replication in the domain. This server is called an export server because it sends data. Other servers can then subscribe to that published directory. These servers are called import servers because they receive data. Only servers running Windows NT Server can export directories, but Windows NT Workstation machines can import them.

When you configure a computer to export or import directories, you do not need to specify which computer you are exporting or importing from—you can simply name the domain. You should avoid exporting to a domain if some of the import computers are located across a slow, wide area network (WAN) link because export traffic will create an unpredictable load on the WAN connection.

The directory replication service that comes with Windows NT Server is crippled by two unfortunate restrictions:

- The directory replication service cannot replicate open files. Because many critical files, such as address books and database files, tend to remain open constantly, they will never be replicated.

- The replication service is unidirectional, meaning files go from one server to another. It is not capable of synchronizing files that have been changed at the same time on different servers.

These two restrictions mean that you can't use directory replication to balance the client access load in your network by maintaining synchronized copies of all your files on different servers and allowing users to attach to any server they wish to access the files.

The directory replication service makes copies of files, not synchronized replicas. Every time replication occurs, imported directories are overwritten. Therefore, you should use directory replication only for read-only files or files that are rarely changed.

You can, however, use directory replication to copy administrative files such as logon scripts and user profiles from the primary domain controller to backup domain controllers and for the distribution of read-only material such as company policies, word processing templates, software master copies, and static Web and FTP sites.

Replication occurs from the export server to the import computer. In other words, the import computer logs on to the export server's REPL$ share and performs the file copy. That's why only the export directory is shared.

Directory replication currently works only between file systems of the same type, for instance, FAT to FAT or NTFS to NTFS.

Configuring Servers for Replication

Before configuring servers for replication, you will need to create a domain user that is a member of both the Backup Operators and the Replicators built-in groups. The directory replicator service on the import computer will use this account to log on to the REPL$ on the export server. Therefore, the account must have some relatively complex permissions set up. Exercise 10.16 shows how to create this account properly.

You may have security problems with the user account you set up if you have changed any of the default permissions of the Windows NT groups or have made policies especially stringent. If directory replication fails, try setting your servers to use the domain adminis-trator account. If that works, you'll know you have a security permissions problem with the replication user.

EXERCISE 10.16

Creating the Replication User

1. Select Start ➤ Programs ➤ Administrative Tools ➤ User Manager for Domains.

2. Select User ➤ New.

3. Type **Replicant** in the Username input box.

4. Type **Logon user for the directory replication service** in the Full Name box.

5. Uncheck Must change password at next logon.

6. Check User cannot change password.

7. Check Password never expires.

8. Click Groups.

9. Click Backup Operators in the Not a member of list box.

10. Click Add.

11. Click Replicator in the Not a member of list box.

12. Click Add.

13. Click OK.

14. Click OK.

15. Close the User Manager for Domains.

Once you set up this account, you are ready to configure your servers for replication. Remember—you can also import to Windows NT Workstation (as well as OS/2 LANManager Servers and OS/2 peer servers), but you can only export from Windows NT Server. You have to configure each computer for directory replication. The procedure is shown in Exercise 10.17. The replication setup dialog box is shown in Figure 10.8.

FIGURE 10.8

The Directory
Replication Setup
dialog box.

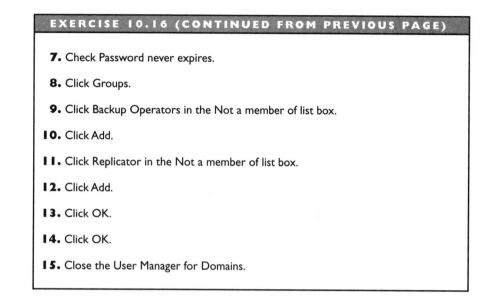

If you have two export servers exporting the same directory names to the same import computer, one of those directories will overwrite the other. Make sure that both export servers use unique export directory names.

EXERCISE 10.17

Configuring the Directory Replicator Service

1. Select Start ➤ Programs ➤ Administrative Tools ➤ Server Manager.

2. Select the first export server (usually the primary domain controller).

3. Select Computer ➤ Services.

4. Double-click Directory Replicator in the Service list box.

5. Select Automatic.

6. Select This Account.

7. Select the Replicant account you created in Exercise 10.16.

8. Enter the password you assigned in the Password and Confirm Password input boxes.

9. Click OK to close the Service Configuration page.

10. Click OK to acknowledge the logon as a service right.

11. Click Start.

12. Click Close to close the Services window.

13. Select Computer ➤ Properties in the Server Manager.

14. Click Replication.

15. Click Add in the Export Directories control group.

16. Select the computer you wish to export to in the domain browser.

17. Click OK.

18. Click Add in the Import Directories control group.

19. Select the computers you wish to import from in the domain browser.

20. Click OK.

21. Click Alerts.

22. Verify that the Administrative account you are logged on as appears in the Send alerts to list box. If not, enter your account name in the New Computer or User-name input box and click Add. Click OK; then stop and restart the Alerter service.

23. Click OK.

24. Click OK.

25. Select the other servers you wish to configure for Directory Replication in the Computer list box of the Server Manager and repeat steps 2 through 8.

26. Close the Server Manager.

Your directory replication should begin after a short wait. You still need to know one more thing about directory replication: Only directories—not files—placed in the `\system32\repl\export` directory will be exported. Files and directories within those directories will be exported, however. You can use Exercise 10.18 to verify the proper operation of the Directory Replication Service.

Verifying Directory Replication

1. Use the procedures shown in Exercise 10.1 to copy some information into the `\Winnt\System32\Repl\Export` directory of your export server.

2. Wait about ten minutes for the replication service to notice the change and copy files.

3. Check the contents of the `\Winnt\System32\Repl\Import` directory on the import server. It should contain the same information as the export directory on your export server.

Microsoft currently acknowledges a number of problems with the Directory Replication Service. Even if you've done everything correctly, under many circumstances directory replication may fail to work for reasons too numerous and arcane to go into here. If you can't get it to work, browse through the Windows NT Server Knowledge Base at www.microsoft.com *using the search key word* replication.

Now that you've copied some files into the export directory of your export server and verified that they've been copied to the import server, let's take a look at the Server Manager tools for viewing the status of directory replication. The Server Manager will report the following conditions in the status column for each directory imported from an export server:

- **OK** indicates that replication is occurring normally.

- **No Master** indicates that the subdirectory is not receiving updates. The export server may not be responding or may no longer be exporting the directory.

- **No Sync** indicates that the subdirectory has received updates but is not currently up-to-date. This status could be due to communications failures, open files, permissions problems, or malfunction of the export server.

- A blank entry indicates that replication has never occurred for that directory. The replication service is either not properly configured or is malfunctioning.

Exercise 10.19 shows you how to view the status of the Directory Replication Service. Figure 10.9 shows the status window of a properly functioning Directory Replication Service.

FIGURE 10.9

Directory replication status.

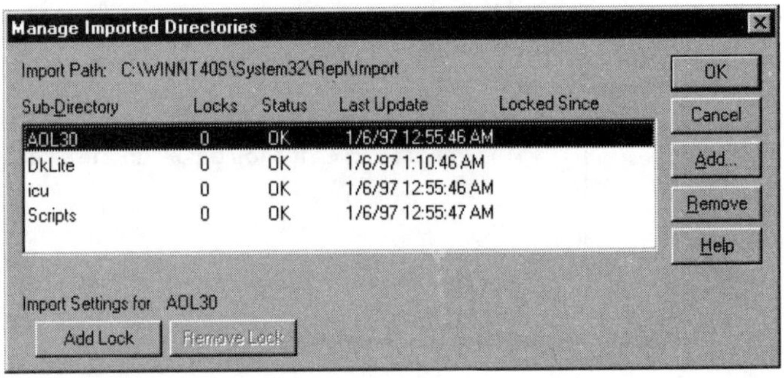

EXERCISE 10.19

Viewing Directory Replication Status

1. Select Start ➤ Programs ➤ Administrative Tools ➤ Server Manager.

2. Double-click the server on the Import side of your test replication performed in Exercise 10.18.

3. Click Replication.

4. Click Manage on the Import side of the replication configuration dialog.

5. Note the status and last replication date. If replication is occurring normally, you will see a status of OK.

6. Click OK three times.

7. Close the Server Manager.

Summary

NSTALLING A SINGLE server is relatively simple. Maintaining a coherent network environment over time as your network grows is considerably more difficult. The best laid plans of network administrators often go awry as unforeseen changes to the network occur and new technologies and methods emerge.

You can use techniques as simple as basic file copying and moving or as complex as distributed file systems to help you manage a growing network. Creating a manageably small number of shares and relying on file-level security rather than share-level security when possible will provide you with greater security and flexibility. Auditing files when necessary can help you identify users who tread where they shouldn't or who may not understand the implications of their actions on other users.

The distributed file system provides a powerful way to increase the complexity of a network while maintaining the illusion of a single coherent interface. Dfs works by simulating a single, large directory hierarchy, called a tree, using multiple Windows NT servers, workstations, or Windows 95 clients.

Directory replication provides an easy way to distribute documents to servers in the network. By copying files only when they change, directory replication uses the minimum possible bandwidth to perform this distribution service.

Review Questions

1. File service is the primary function of most network servers.

   A. True

   B. False

2. When moving a file within a volume, Windows NT simply copies the file to a new location and deletes the original.

   A. True

   B. False

3. When you copy a file within the same volume, the new file inherits file permissions from the destination directory.

   A. True

   B. False

4. When you move a file within the same volume, the new file inherits file permissions from the destination directory.

   A. True

   B. False

5. When you copy a file between different volumes, the new file inherits file permissions from the destination directory.

   A. True

   B. False

6. When you move a file between different volumes, the new file inherits file permissions from the destination directory.

   A. True

   B. False

7. Files in copy and move operations always inherit directory permissions except when the file moves within the same volume.

   A. True

   B. False

8. The Server tools for Windows NT Workstation are the same tools provided with Windows NT Server.

   A. True

   B. False

9. Windows NT comes with a comprehensive suite of SNMP management tools.

   A. True

   B. False

10. Share permissions work no matter what the shared file system is.

   A. True

   B. False

11. The replication service cannot copy open files.

   A. True

   B. False

12. When you have both share and file permissions on a directory, Windows NT uses only the file permissions because they are more restrictive.

   A. True

   B. False

13. Users logged on locally are not limited by share-level security.

   A. True

   B. False

14. For security reasons, you should enable file auditing on all files at all times.

    A. True

    B. False

15. The distributed file system allows you to create a single, unified hierarchy that actually consists of shares on many different machines.

    A. True

    B. False

16. You can install Server tools on _____ and _____ client computers.

17. The _____ server logs on to the _____ server to copy files in the Directory Replication Service.

18. The status _____ means that although the Directory Replication Service has received updates in the past and can connect to the export server, it is not receiving them at the moment.

19. You can use the _____ to manage NTFS security after you've installed Server tools for Windows 95.

    A. Server Manager

    B. Policy Editor

    C. User Manager for Domains

    D. Windows 95 Explorer

    E. Event Viewer

20. Enabling Audit policy is performed through the:

    A. Server Manager

    B. Security Manager

    C. User Manager for Domains

    D. File Manager

    E. Explorer

Remote Access Service

THE LOCAL AREA network centralizes data in your organization, expedites the exchange of information, provides security, and allows the sharing of expensive equipment and software. When you are away from your office (for example, at home or traveling), you obviously cannot connect your computer directly to the LAN. Unless you have some other way to participate in the network, you are cut off from the many advantages a network provides your organization.

The Remote Access Service (RAS) in Windows NT allows you to participate in your organization's network even when you are away from the physical location of your network. RAS allows you to use modems and telephone lines as a slow network connection. This chapter starts with an overview of how RAS works and then shows you how to install and configure RAS on your network. You will learn how to make RAS secure, connect client computers to a RAS server, and troubleshoot RAS connections.

Remote Access Service Overview

THE PURPOSE OF RAS is to provide temporary network links over regular telephone lines. You can also set up RAS to use other types of connections such as ISDN and X.25. However, in most networks RAS controls a bank of modems attached to telephone lines so that remote users can dial in and access network files, such as word processing documents and spreadsheets, and use network services, such as e-mail and group scheduling. Figure 11.1 illustrates a typical RAS setup.

The client computer can also use RAS client software to connect to the Internet or to networks other than your organizational network. Another book in this series, MCSE: NT Workstation Study Guide, *explains how to connect to other networks and to the Internet using RAS.*

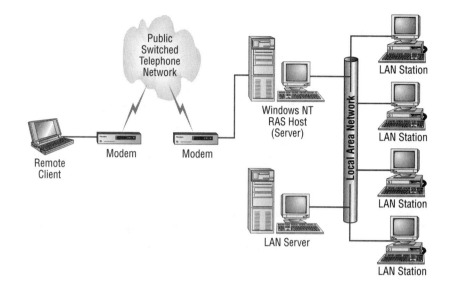

FIGURE 11.1

In a typical RAS setup, remote client computers connect to a central network via RAS and the telephone lines.

RAS Clients

In order for you to use RAS in a client computer, you must have networking installed on that computer. You do not need a network interface adapter (such as an Ethernet or a Token Ring card), but you do need a transport protocol such as TCP/IP, NWLink, or NetBEUI. You also need the components that use networking such as the Workstation component in Windows NT Workstation and the Client for Microsoft Networks component in Windows 95.

RAS on the client computer allows you to use the modem to dial to and establish a connection with a RAS server on your organization's network. Then RAS emulates a network interface adapter for the transport protocol and allows the network services component to operate as if your client computer were directly connected to the network. The network connection, however, will be slower than a direct connection would be because most network adapters are much faster than modems.

A regular Ethernet adapter can (theoretically) transmit 10 megabits of information in one second. Modems can (theoretically) transmit 56 kilobits of information in one second, which makes Ethernet almost 200 times faster than the fastest modems. However, Ethernet networks seldom achieve more than 50 percent of their theoretical limit, so in practice Ethernet is only 100 times faster than the fastest analog modems.

The RAS Server

The RAS server, which usually runs on a Windows NT server, uses modems attached to the server computer to accept connections from client computers and to exchange network data over those connections. You can configure the RAS server to allow the client to access resources on the RAS server only, or you can configure it as a router or gateway so that the client computer can access any of the resources on the network. RAS supports the TCP/IP, Net-BEUI, and IPX/SPX transport protocols.

To the server computer, the RAS server modems look like network interface adapters. A RAS server, like a RAS client, must have networking components installed in order to use RAS.

You can also use RAS servers to link networks together. For example, if you have a main office downtown and you have several branch offices in other neighborhoods, you can connect the networks at each site using modems and telephone lines. The RAS servers on each network will route network traffic destined to another network correctly and will not send transmissions that are meant for computers on the local network. This arrangement minimizes the amount of information that has to be sent over the slow modem lines.

However, using RAS to link networks is not a feasible long-term solution because a phone line that is constantly connected to another location can be expensive (especially if the call is long distance). Permanent links between networks are more often made with dedicated digital hardware (unlike the analog technology used in regular modems) and telephone lines that are leased from the telephone company.

Analog Modems or ISDN?

What is the difference between an analog modem (or Public Switched Telephone Network [PSTN] modem, the type that is in most common use today and that you are probably most familiar with) and an Integrated Services Digital Network (ISDN) modem? The best way to explain the difference is to describe what a modem does, how the telephone company works, and why modems are inefficient. Then we'll explain how ISDN makes networking via telephone lines more efficient.

How Modems Work

Modem stands for MODulator/DEModulator, and modems traditionally have operated by converting the serial data from your computer's serial port (digitally encoded using the RS-232 serial communications standard) to an analog signal in the acoustic range that can be transmitted over the public telephone system. Most modem communications involve two modems—one at either end of a telephone call. The modem at the other end of the call takes the analog signal and converts it back to a digital signal (RS-232) that is sent to the receiving computer's serial port.

How Telephone Companies Work

In early telephone technology someone making a phone call was physically patched through to the receiving party by an operator who made the connection with patch cords. The two parties of the phone call would then have a circuit over which the analog electrical signal of their voices could travel. Later the telephone companies automated the connection process with relays, allowing people to establish their own connections. The relays replaced the operators. With the advent of digital communications, the phone companies found they could digitize the analog signals and use digital electronics to squeeze more phone calls into the telephone lines between branch offices (for instance, in New York and Chicago). Because digital data can be switched by solid state integrated circuits (essentially making the phone company a vast computer network), there is no need for physically moving relays.

Why Modems Are Inefficient

When you use a regular (i.e., PSTN) modem to communicate with another computer, the modem encodes the digital serial signal from your computer into analog form. These are the sounds that you hear when your modem connects. Your telephone company is encoding that analog signal into digital form. The telephone company branch office (called a central office by the telephone company) at the other end of the call decodes that digital signal back to analog form, and the resulting analog signal is encoded back to the original serial digital signal sent by your computer. That serial signal finally enters the serial port of the receiving computer. Data flowing the other way undergoes the same process.

How ISDN Works

Although many vendors refer to ISDN adapters as "modems," they really aren't modems because they don't modulate or demodulate. The correct term is ISDN adapter.

An ISDN adapter does not modulate or demodulate a signal. Instead it delivers the serial digital signal from your computer's RS-232 port in its original form to the telephone company. (This process requires a special phone connection.) The phone company routes the digital information through its digital network to the other phone company branch office, which provides the signal to the ISDN adapter at that end of the connection. That ISDN adapter sends the digital signal to the receiving computer's serial port. Figure 11.2 illustrates the difference between regular modems and ISDN adapters.

FIGURE 11.2

Modems use analog phone lines; ISDN adapters use digital phone lines.

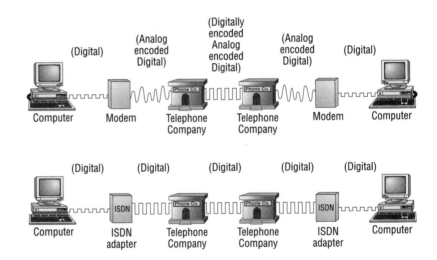

ISDN adapters allow you to take advantage of the phone companies' digital networks to send digital information. ISDN is faster than regular analog modems because none of the capacity of the telephone line is wasted by less than 100 percent efficient encoding schemes. Many ISDN connections are even faster than the optimal analog modem encoding schemes because the telephone company allows you to use additional voice channels to transmit information. (Essentially, you are using two telephone lines to send your data.)

Unfortunately ISDN is not available to every telephone company customer. Some telephone company installations have not upgraded to equipment capable of accepting ISDN connections. In other places ISDN is prohibitively expensive. ISDN is, however, both available and affordable in many areas of the United States. Check with your local phone company.

RAS Capabilities and Limitations

RAS performs both dial-out and the dial-in service. RAS can host clients from many operating systems and can support all Windows NT interprocess communications mechanisms. RAS supports all TDI-compliant protocols loaded on your machine and is capable of operating over any dial-up public network medium. RAS supports software compression to maximize bandwidth over low-speed connections.

Supported Dial-in Operating Systems

RAS can host any computer running the following operating systems:

- LAN Manager

- Windows For Workgroups

- Windows NT 3.1 and higher

- Windows 95

- PPP-based TCP/IP clients

In addition to the Windows-based operating systems capable of using NetBEUI or NWLink, RAS can support any computer using a TCP/IP protocol stack and capable of dialing in via Point-to-Point Protocol (PPP), such as personal digital assistants, mainframes, UNIX X-terminals, and remote data acquisition devices. However, these clients will not be able to use domain resources such as print and file services. Although Windows NT Server can dial out to SLIP servers, it provides connections only to client computers using the PPP protocol.

Supported Network Interfaces

RAS supports all Windows NT interprocess communications mechanisms. Therefore, the client side of any client/server application capable of running under Windows NT can run over a RAS connection. These mechanisms include

- Windows Sockets

- NetBIOS

- Mailslots

- Named Pipes

- Remote Procedure Call (RPC)

- Win32 and LAN Manager APIs

Supported Protocols

RAS supports all TDI-compliant protocols via the PPP serial protocol. RAS also supports dialing out to SLIP servers, but Windows NT RAS hosts will only answer PPP.

- NWLink

- TCP/IP

- NetBEUI

IPX-Supported WAN Connections

RAS currently supports wide area network (WAN) connections over the following media:

- PSTN

- ISDN

- X.25 (a protocol commonly used with leased-line frame relay and WANs prior to the Internet)

ISDN and X.25 interfaces are often treated as network adapters rather than as modems by Windows NT.

RAS also supports certain other WAN interfaces such as asynchronous transfer mode (ATM). The component-based architecture of Windows NT allows the technology-dependent aspects of the WAN (such as the connection protocol for ATM and the packet nature of X.25) to be isolated in a WAN wrapper. This design means that the upper-level services (the transport protocols and RAS itself) do not have to be modified to support new WAN technologies. (A *wrapper* is simply a shell around a protocol to make all the adapter drivers look the same to higher-level protocols.)

RAS Limitations

RAS for Windows NT Server supports up to 256 simultaneous inbound sessions. Setting RAS to receive calls will dedicate the COM port and modem you are using. The port will not be available for non-RAS communication software such as terminal emulators or fax software. However, you can stop the RAS service through the Services control panel if you need to dial out using the COM port that RAS dedicates. When finished, simply restart the RAS service to again receive RAS calls.

Installing RAS

NSTALLING RAS IS no more difficult than installing any other service in Windows NT. Because the purpose of RAS is to connect computers over a low-speed, dial-up line, you should have access to another computer running RAS or RAS client software (such as Windows NT Workstation or Windows 95) and using the same transport protocol (such as TCP/IP or NWLink).

Without access to another computer to which you can attach, you will have difficulty understanding the operational nuances of RAS. You really need to *use* the software in order to understand it.

Before you install RAS you need to have modems or other WAN connection adapters (such as ISDN or X.25) installed for RAS to use. If you have two computers right next to each other, you can select the Dial-Up Networking serial cable between 2 PCs option in the RAS device selector. You can also select this option if you want to install RAS but don't yet have a modem for it because RAS requires you to select a device when you install it. Next we explain how to install a modem in Windows NT, then we show you the more complicated process of configuring an ISDN adapter, and finally we guide you through the steps of installing and configuring RAS.

RAS and PSTN Modems

If you have a modem, but have not installed it through the Modem control panel, do so now. You also need to identify a free COM port in your computer and configure the modem to use that port. Use Exercise 11.1 to perform this step if you have an internal modem. (If you are using an external modem or if your modem is already installed in the Windows NT system, you can skip Exercise 11.1.)

Check your modem documentation for the correct COM and IRQ settings. (If you are using an external modem, you just need the COM port number.)

EXERCISE 11.1

Finding an Available COM Port

1. Select Start ➤ Programs ➤ Administrative Tools ➤ Windows NT Diagnostics.

2. Select the Resources tab.

3. Click the IRQ button.

4. Note the state of interrupt requests (IRQ) 03 and 04. If either does not appear in the list, you need to configure your modem to use that IRQ.

5. Select a free IRQ.

- If IRQ 04 is available (not in the resource list), set your modem to use IRQ 04 and COM 1.

- If IRQ 03 is available, set your modem to use IRQ 03 and COM 2.

- If both are in use, you will need to set your modem to use another unused IRQ. Check your modem documentation to see if it supports IRQ 05, 07, or 09. Set the modem IRQ to any IRQ your modem supports that is not shown in the resource list.

6. Set your modem to use either COM 3 or COM 4. Make sure that no other serial port in your system is using the COM port you select.

7. Shut down your Windows NT server and physically install the modem. When you restart, your modem should be available for use. If you have any difficulties or encounter new error messages, call the technical support number provided by your modem manufacturer for assistance.

Once your modem is in place, you need to tell Windows NT about it. Follow Exercise 11.2 to make your modem available to Windows NT. Before going through this exercise, make certain that your modem is physically installed on a free COM port and IRQ.

EXERCISE 11.2

Modem Installation

1. Double-click the My Computer Icon on the Desktop.

2. Double-click Control Panel.

3. Double-click the Modems control panel.

4. Click the Next button to detect your modem. Letting Windows NT automatically detect allows you to confirm that your modem is answering as it should. Detecting will take up to five minutes, depending upon the speed of your computer.

5. Accept the settings shown in the detected modem window by clicking the Next button unless you are absolutely certain they will not work with your modem. Windows NT will usually work correctly with a modem it has identified, even if the model shown in the window doesn't match the brand name of the modem.

6. Click Finish to complete the installation process.

7. Click the Dialing Properties button in the Modem Properties dialog box.

8. Enter the country and area code information that is appropriate for you.

9. Add the appropriate information if you need to add outside-line access or disable call waiting. If you have call waiting and someone calls while a RAS session is active, your RAS connection can be abruptly terminated.

10. Click OK.

11. Click the Close button.

Your modem is now available to Windows NT programs such as RAS.

IRQ conflicts can appear as a number of different problems under Windows NT. If you suddenly begin having problems with your Windows NT installation, remove your modem and verify that the COM port and IRQ are indeed free. Check that no other service (for instance, a fax monitor) is attempting to use the same modem. Check the Event Viewer for serial events occurring during startup.

RAS and ISDN Adapters

Some ISDN adapters connect to your computer through the regular serial port on the back of your computer and will appear to your computer as a regular PSTN modem. You can find drivers for many of these ISDN adapters in the Modems control panel. Other ISDN adapters (usually adapters that are installed internally to your computer) establish a new serial interface in your computer separate from the familiar COM1 or COM2. Windows NT treats these ISDN adapters as normal network interface adapters, just like Ethernet and Token Ring cards. You can install the ISDN drivers for these adapters from the Adapters tab of the Network control panel.

Configuring an ISDN adapter is a bit more complicated than connecting a regular modem to your phone line. Here are some issues to consider:

- Physical changes must be made to your phone line (or a new, different phone line must be installed) so that the telephone company will exchange digital signals with your ISDN equipment rather than exchange analog signals with your telephone.

- You may need to have a network termination device (NT-1) to connect your ISDN adapter cards to the ISDN phone line. Some network adapter cards have an NT-1 built in; others do not.

- Not all ISDN services provide the same transmission speeds. Some phone companies provide data channels in increments of 64Kbps transmission speeds, and others provide them in increments of 56Kbps.

- Your local telephone company may use the N11 switch protocol, or it may be another type, such as that used by AT&T 5ESS switches or Northern Telecom DMS100 switches. You must configure your adapter to use the appropriate switch protocol.

- You should configure your ISDN connection to be multipoint. This setting allows you to use each ISDN channel (ISDN basic rate allows two channels) independently, or you may combine the ISDN channels to provide greater bandwidth to a single connection.

- To take full advantage of the multipoint capabilities of ISDN, you should set the number of Service Profile IDs (SPIDs) for ISDN basic rate to two and install two telephone numbers for your ISDN line. SPIDs identify the services and features the telephone company provides to you. The format of the SPID is usually the ten-digit phone number of the ISDN line plus a prefix and a suffix that are sometimes used to identify features on the line.

The installation process for ISDN adapters varies by type and model of ISDN adapter. Exercise 11.3 shows you how to configure a typical adapter (the U.S. Robotics Sportster ISDN adapter inserted in an ISA slot). You can perform this exercise without actually having an ISDN adapter in your computer—you will not be able to use the (nonexistent) adapter when you are done, of course.

EXERCISE 11.3

Configuring an ISDN adapter

1. Select Start ➤ Settings ➤ Control Panel ➤ Network.

2. Select the Adapters tab in the Network window and then click the Add button.

3. Select the U. S. Robotics Sportster ISDN adapter.

4. Enter the location of your Windows NT Server CD in the input box and click Continue.

5. Select ISA. If you have more than one bus in your computer (for example, you might have both ISA and PCI cards in your computer), you must select the bus that the adapter uses.

6. Select the I/O base address and interrupt for the ISDN adapter as installed in your computer (or accept the defaults if you do not actually have an adapter installed).

7. Select the Telco Switch option that matches your local telephone company or accept the default setting.

8. Set the number of terminals to two unless you are limited by your local telephone company to one ISDN channel.

9. Set the phone numbers and SPIDs of your ISDN channels in the Terminal 1 and Terminal 2 areas. (Your telephone company will give you this information.) If you are just following along with the example, enter 1, 2, 3, 4...; the numbers don't matter because you don't actually have an ISDN adapter installed.

10. Click the OK button.

11. Press OK when you are notified that the ISDN installation process is complete. Now you are ready to configure RAS to use the ISDN adapter.

Installing the RAS Service

Installing the RAS server is similar to installing all other network services. If you are using X.25 or an ISDN connection, follow the device manufacturer's instructions to install those adapters before proceeding with the RAS installation. Rather than selecting the modem settings, you will use the X.25 PAD button in the RAS Setup dialog box or the Settings window for the ISDN adapter in the Network control panel. Exercise 11.4 shows the standard procedure for installing a RAS server with a regular modem. (You should already have installed your modem to work with Windows NT through the Modems control panel.)

EXERCISE 11.4

Installing the Remote Access Server

1. Right-click the Network Neighborhood icon on the desktop.

2. Select the Properties menu item to open the Network control panel.

3. Click the Services tab.

4. Click the Add button.

5. Select Remote Access Service from the Services list.

6. Click OK.

7. Enter the path to your Windows NT Server CD-ROM and the directory containing the source files for your microprocessor. For most users, this path is D:\i386.

8. Select the modem you wish to use for RAS and click OK in the Add RAS Device dialog box. If your modem does not appear in the modem list, click the Install Modem button and follow the prompts to install your modem.

9. Click Configure.

10. Select the Dial Out and Receive Calls option if you wish to also be able to dial out using the modem line (this option is required for later exercises); otherwise, select Receive Calls Only and click OK.

11. Click Add and then repeat steps 8 through 10 if you want to configure another modem or serial port for RAS.

---

12. Click Continue when you are finished adding your modem(s). We will accept the default protocols for now and show you how to choose specific transport protocols in Exercise 11.5.

13. Close the Network dialog box.

14. Answer Yes when asked if you want to restart your computer.

Configuring Network Protocols for RAS

In Chapter 6 you learned how to configure and install networking protocols for Windows NT. RAS can use any of the three primary Windows NT communications protocols to provide network services over a dial-up connection. The protocol must be installed for Windows NT before you can use it with RAS.

RAS uses one of two different framing protocols (SLIP and PPP) to provide a network layer protocol in addition to the transport protocols also used for LAN communication. SLIP and PPP perform the same function in a dial-up networking connection that Ethernet or Token Ring perform in a LAN environment; that is, they provide a media access protocol that the communications protocol (TCP/IP, NWLink, or NetBEUI) uses to transport information.

For each device you configure for use with RAS (usually a modem), you can select the communications protocols you want to use. For example, you can configure one modem to use TCP/IP to connect your network to the Internet and configure several more modems to use NWLink. This technique enables remote Windows clients to connect to your network with less communications overhead because NWLink is more bandwidth efficient than TCP/IP is.

You set the protocols a modem will use from the RAS item in the Services tab of the Network control panel. You can enable or disable TCP/IP, NWLink, and NetBEUI for a modem that dials out and receives calls. For example, this option allows the same modem to use NetBEUI for incoming calls from remote network clients and TCP/IP to connect to an Internet service provider.

Each protocol is configured for dial-in in a slightly different manner. When you click the Configure button for a protocol, a window prompts you for the specific settings for that protocol. The next section of this chapter takes you on a tour through the settings for each protocol, and Exercise 11.5 explains how to configure each protocol for a typical RAS installation.

TCP/IP

TCP/IP is the transport protocol of the Internet. You can also use TCP/IP, which is a very robust protocol, to connect remote computers to your network. If you cannot guarantee that the telephone connection will be free of extraneous noise, then the error detection and correction characteristics of TCP/IP may make it more suitable for this purpose than faster transport protocols such as NWLink and NetBEUI.

With TCP/IP you can allow an incoming call to access only the RAS Server computer, or you can allow the computer making the incoming call to access the rest of the network as well. You can also configure the incoming connection to be given an IP address via the dynamic host configuration protocol (DHCP) or from a pool of addresses maintained on the RAS server. Another option is to allow the incoming connection to request its own IP address. Figure 11.3 shows the RAS Server TCP/IP Configuration window.

FIGURE 11.3

You configure TCP/IP dial-up settings from the RAS Server TCP/IP Configuration window.

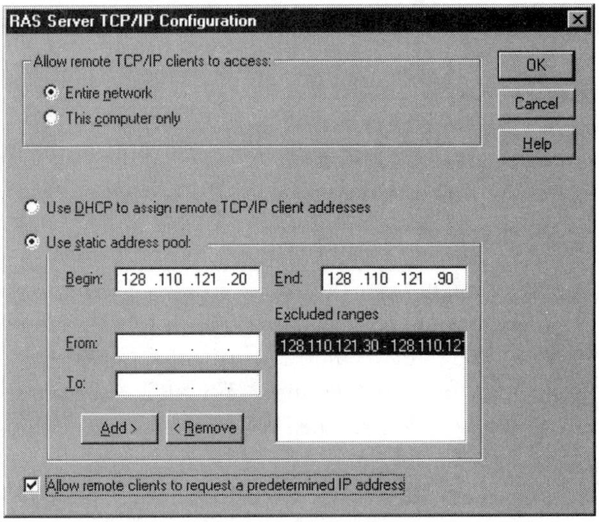

RAS AND SLIP Serial Line Internet Protocol (SLIP) is an early protocol for the transfer of Internet packets (IPs) over serial connections such as modems and T1 leased lines. Until recently SLIP was the most common method of making a modem connection to an Internet service provider. PPP is now more popular than SLIP.

Although you can configure RAS to dial out and make a connection to another computer using the SLIP protocol, you cannot configure RAS to accept a connection using SLIP. Consequently, you cannot use SLIP to connect two computers running RAS, nor can you use SLIP to connect a client computer running another operating system such as Windows 95 to your RAS server. Instead you will have to use PPP.

RAS AND PPP PPP stands for Point-to-Point Protocol. PPP addresses some deficiencies in the SLIP protocol. For example, it provides mechanisms for encrypting logon requests and for supporting transport protocols other than TCP/IP. PPP is optimized for low-bandwidth communications and conveys data between communicating computers more efficiently than SLIP does.

PPP is the default method of making connections to and from a RAS server. PPP is automatically installed when you install the RAS server component, and you can do very little to directly configure how RAS uses PPP. You do, however, indirectly configure PPP when you select and use PPP security options (as explained in the section on security).

NWLink

NWLink (also called IPX because it uses the IPX/SPX protocols made popular by NetWare) is a fast and efficient network transport protocol. If you have NetWare servers in your network, you might standardize on NWLink for both LAN communications and dial-up connections so that you do not have to configure computers to support more than one networking protocol.

You can configure NWLink to allow the connecting computer to access only the RAS server computer or to access the whole network. In addition, the NWLink dial-in configuration window allows you to allocate network numbers automatically or to allocate them starting at a number you specify. You can also set NWLink to assign the same network number to all IPX clients, and you can set it to allow remote clients to request an IPX node number. Figure 11.4 shows the RAS Server IPX Configuration window.

NetBEUI

NetBEUI is the simplest of the network transport protocols, and it is also the most efficient. Microsoft suggests that if you do not require features of either NWLink or TCP/IP, then you should use NetBEUI to make dial-up connections to your RAS server. The result is that the maximum amount of bandwidth remains available for use in programs rather than being tied up in protocol overhead.

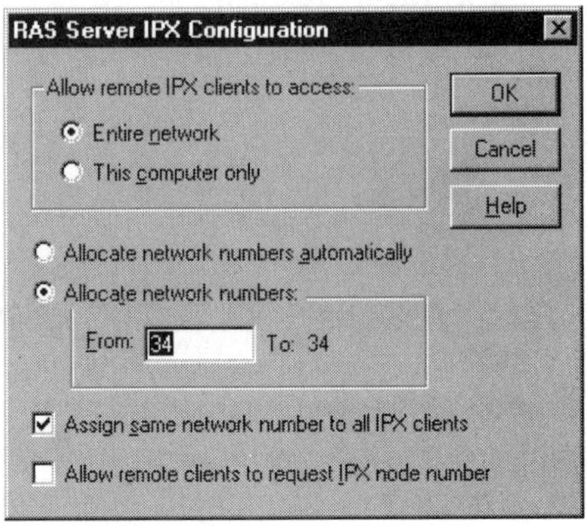

FIGURE 11.4

You configure NWLink dial-up settings from the RAS Server IPX Configuration window.

The only setting you can configure from the NetBEUI Setup button is whether NetBEUI dial-up clients can access the rest of your network or whether they are limited to accessing only the RAS server computer. Figure 11.5 shows the RAS Server NetBEUI Configuration window.

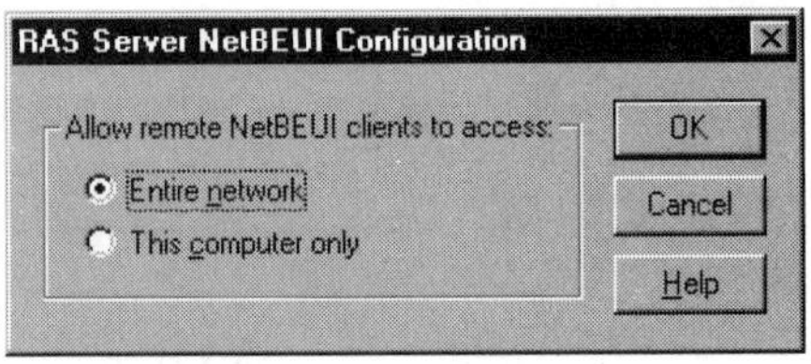

FIGURE 11.5

You configure NetBEUI dial-up settings from the RAS Server NetBEUI Configuration window.

Configuring the Protocols for RAS

Windows NT automatically provides settings for the protocols that should work properly in most dial-in situations. In most cases you can simply accept the values and selections that appear in the configuration windows. In Exercise 11.5 you will configure your RAS server to allow access to your network via RAS using any of the supported protocols.

RAS Security

Before RAS connects your remote client computers to your network, it must ensure that the client computers are not intruders masquerading as regular client connections. RAS security features, including permissions, callback, encrypted passwords, and PPTP, protect your RAS connections against intrusion and eavesdropping.

EXERCISE 11.5

Configuring RAS Protocols

1. Select Start ➤ Settings ➤ Control Panel.

2. Double click the Network Control Panel program.

3. Select the Services Tab.

4. Select the Remote Access Services entry from the list and then click the Properties button.

5. Select the modem you wish to configure protocols for and then click the Network button.

6. Check NetBEUI, TCP/IP, and IPX in the Allow remote clients running section.

7. Click the Configure button next to NetBEUI and select Entire network. Click OK.

8. Click the Configure button next to TCP/IP. Select Entire network. Select Use DHCP and select Allow clients to request a predetermined IP address. Click OK.

9. Click the Configure button next to IPX. Select Entire network and Allocate network numbers automatically. Click OK.

10. Click OK in the Network Configuration window and then click Continue in the Remote Access Setup window.

11. Click Close in the Network window. You must restart your computer before the changes take effect, so select Yes to restart your computer.

Permissions

If your network is not connected to the Internet and if it does not provide dial-up connections, then you do not have to be concerned about electronic intrusion. Your primary security concerns will be unauthorized physical access to your network and network users who may exceed their authority to read or modify network data.

If, however, you do provide dial-up lines (or Internet connections), then you must ensure that only authorized users access your network. Internet security will be discussed in the next chapter. Figure 11.6 shows RAS permissions for users of dial-up connections.

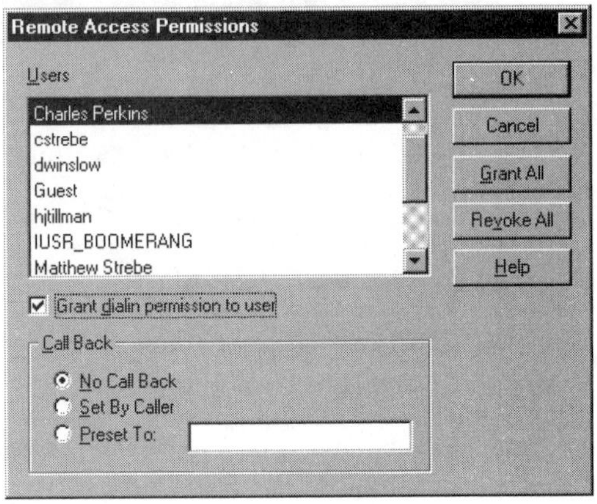

FIGURE 11.6

You can set dial-up permissions to specific users in the Remote Access Permissions window of the Remote Access Admin program.

You can also set dial-in permissions with the Dial-up button in the User Manager for Domains.

The RAS permissions you establish for dial-up connections are your first line of defense against network intruders. You should pay careful attention to how you set up the dial-in permissions of your RAS server so that only users that should access your network over dial-up lines can do so. In addition, if your network contains sensitive information, you should consider disallowing dial-up access for user accounts with extensive permissions to the system (such as the Administrator account). If the users of those accounts require dial-up access, they can use an account with fewer privileges when connecting via RAS.

You may notice that when you first start the Remote Access Admin program, you see only user accounts local to the server that RAS is running on, not domain accounts (which, if you organized your domain as described in this book, is where most of your user accounts are located). In order to view and set permissions for domain users, you must click Server ➤ Set Domain or Server from within the Remote Access Admin window and then select the domain (not a server within the domain) that you wish to view. This procedure displays the users for the domain as a whole.

You can set permissions only for individual users, not for groups.

Network intrusion is a serious threat to any network that is connected to the Internet or that allows dial-up access via telephone lines. Chapter 12 introduces the concept of firewalls for Internet security and outlines steps you should take to protect your network from unauthorized access from the Internet.

Callback

The RAS callback feature provides additional security to your network by verifying the phone number given by the calling computer or ensuring that the calling computer is at a predetermined number configured from RAS.

Callback simply calls back the client computer after the client computer calls the RAS server and requests a network connection. You use the Remote Access Permissions window (shown in Figure 11.6) to enable callback in your system. Just as you set dial-in permissions for each user, you also set callback features for each user account that has dial-in permissions. You do not set callback features for groups of users or for specific modems.

Encrypted Passwords and Data Encryption

When you log on to your network using RAS, you must provide a username and a password. That password must travel over the telephone lines to your RAS server so that the RAS server can determine if that username has dial-in privileges and if the connection must be made using the RAS callback feature.

The way the RAS client and the RAS server exchange the username and password (and some other information such as the temporary network address allocated to the client) is called the *authentication protocol*. RAS supports only PPP for dial-in connections, and it supports three authentication protocols for PPP:

- Password Authentication Protocol (PAP)

- Challenge Handshake Authentication Protocol (CHAP)

- Microsoft extensions to CHAP (MS-CHAP)

REQUIRE MICROSOFT ENCRYPTED AUTHENTICATION The default setting for RAS password authentication is Require Microsoft encrypted authentication. When you enable this option for a RAS device (such as a particular modem or ISDN adapter), the clients connecting via that device must encrypt the password with the MS-CHAP protocol. With this option only Microsoft clients (such as Windows 95, Windows NT Workstation, or other Windows NT

Server computers) can connect to your RAS server. MS-CHAP implements the RSA Data Security Message Digest Four (MD-4) algorithm over PPP.

REQUIRE DATA ENCRYPTION If you use the MS-CHAP protocol, then you can also set the RAS device to Require data encryption. This option encrypts the data exchanged between the RAS server and client as well as the password exchanged to establish the connection. Windows NT handles the details of establishing the encrypted communications channel, such as selecting and exchanging encryption keys.

REQUIRE ENCRYPTED AUTHENTICATION If you want to allow computers running other operating systems (such as UNIX) to connect to your RAS server but you also want to require encrypted passwords, then select Require encrypted authentication. This option enables the CHAP authentication protocol. CHAP implements the RSA Data Security MD-5 algorithm over PPP.

ALLOW ANY AUTHENTICATION INCLUDING CLEAR TEXT Some client operating systems do not support encrypted password authentication. For these computers you can select Allow any authentication including clear text. This option allows users to connect using the PAP protocol, which does not require encryption.

Multilink

Multilink combines multiple serial data streams into one aggregate bundle. The most common use of Multilink is to combine the multiple ISDN channels into one aggregate total, but it can also combine regular modems. For instance, if you have two 14.4Kbps modems with Multilink enabled, your bandwidth could be aggregated to 28.8Kbps. To use Multilink, both the server and client must be Windows NT computers and both must have Multilink enabled.

In ISDN jargon *Multilink* is sometimes referred to as "bonding" because you are bonding multiple data streams together.

Point-to-Point Tunneling Protocol

A new feature of Windows NT 4 is RAS support for the Point-to-Point Tunneling Protocol (PPTP). PPTP allows you to exploit the Internet to allow secure connection to your RAS server from anywhere you can get an Internet connection.

PPTP uses a two-step process to connect the client computer to your RAS server.

1. Connect the client computer to the Internet (usually by making a regular connection to an Internet service provider).

2. Use the PPTP service on the client to make an encrypted link to the RAS server on your network.

The RAS server must be connected to the Internet; otherwise, the client would not be able to make a connection to it.

The RAS server will encrypt the traffic that it would normally send over a modem connection to the client and instead send it over the Internet to the client. The client and the RAS server can continue to exchange information in this manner, tunneling the stream of information through the Internet.

You enable PPTP access via the Services tab of the Network control panel. Exercise 11.6 sets up PPTP for RAS.

EXERCISE 11.6

Configuring PPTP for RAS

1. Select Start ➤ Settings ➤ Control Panel.

2. Double-click the Network control panel program.

3. Select the protocols Tab.

4. Click the Add button.

5. Select Point to Point Tunneling Protocol and then click OK.

6. Enter the location of the Windows NT Server setup files. (If the CD is in drive F and you are running Server on an Intel-based computer, then you would enter `F:\I386\`.)

7. Accept 1 as the number of virtual private networks and then click OK. The setup process will invoke RAS so that you can configure it to accept PPTP connections. Click OK.

8. Click the Add button and then select VPN1 - RASPPTPM from the list of RAS capable devices. Click OK to continue.

9. Click Continue and then click Close at the Network window.

RAS Clients

THE PREVIOUS SECTION showed you how to set up a RAS server, which solves half the problem of enabling remote access to your network. The other half entails the configuration of clients to connect to your RAS server.

RAS supports the connection of any operating system that supports PPP, one of the three authentication protocols (PAP, CHAP, or MS-CHAP), and one of the three communications protocols (TCP/IP, NWLink, or NetBEUI). If the client is going to access services on the Windows NT Server, then the client must support a service protocol of Windows NT (such as NetBIOS for file access or HTTP for access to Internet Information Server Web pages).

The above "limitations" effectively mean that just about any computer can connect to your network via Remote Access Services. Each operating system has its own methods of configuring the various protocols it supports. *MCSE: NT Workstation Study Guide* explains how to connect Windows NT Workstation computers to RAS in detail. You can connect Windows NT Server as a client to another Windows NT Server using RAS exactly the same way you connect Windows NT Workstation. The following section describes how to use RAS as a client to connect a Windows NT computer to a RAS server on another computer.

Installing RAS Client Software

On a Windows NT Workstation computer or on a Windows NT Server computer that does not already have RAS loaded to allow RAS dial-in connections, you may need to install RAS services in order to connect to a RAS server. If you already have RAS configured for dial-in, you do not have to install it again for dial-out. You can simply check the Dial Out and Receive Calls or the Dial Out Only options from the Configure Port Usage window.

(Refer to Exercise 11.4 to review the process of installing RAS on a Windows NT Server or Workstation computer.)

Creating a Dial-Up Connection

After installing RAS, you will need to create a dial-up network connection in the RAS phone book that contains the dialing and network information for each dial-up server to which you will attach. This process is basically the same for Windows RAS servers and UNIX/Internet servers. Follow Exercise 11.7 to create a dial-up networking connection. Repeat this process for each dial-up server you want to access. The RAS Edit Phonebook entry screen appears in Figure 11.7.

EXERCISE 11.7

Creating a Dial-Up Networking Connection

1. Double-click the My Computer icon on the Desktop.

2. Double-click the Dial-Up Networking icon.

3. Click OK to pass the Phonebook Is Empty notice if it appears. If it does not appear, you already have at least one RAS entry. Click New to display the New Phonebook Entry Wizard dialog box.

4. Type the name of the new phone book entry, check the I know all about phonebook entries box, and click the Finish button. (If you choose to enter the phone book information without the wizard, you must use More ≻ User Preferences ≻ Appearance ≻ Use Wizard to Create New Phonebook Entries to use the wizard again.

5. Enter the name of the server to which you will be attaching in the Entry name text box.

6. Select your modem in the Dial Using drop-down box. If you are using a null modem cable to connect two computers, select Dial-Up Networking Serial Cable between 2 PCs on the appropriate COM port.

7. Click the Use Telephony dialing properties option.

8. Enter the area code and phone number of your RAS server in the Phone number input lines. If you are using a null modem cable, leave these lines blank.

9. Click the Alternates button if your RAS server has alternate phone numbers. Add the alternate phone numbers.

10. Click the Server tab.

11. Select the protocol used by your RAS server network (TCP/IP, NetBEUI, or NWLink).

12. Click the Security tab.

13. Select Allow any encryption including clear text.

14. Click OK to accept your settings.

15. Click Close. Restarting your computer is not necessary after adding dial-up servers.

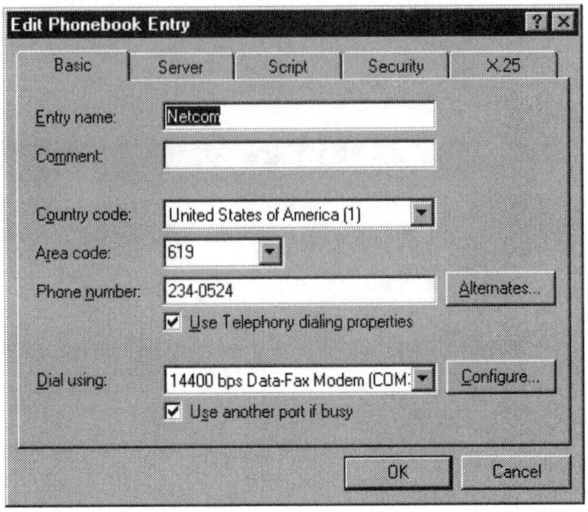

FIGURE 11.7

The RAS Edit Phonebook Entry screen.

Client Protocols

When you dial into a network, you must use a protocol that the remote server supports. For a Windows NT RAS server, this protocol will be TCP/IP, NWLink, or NetBEUI. Each protocol has its advantages and disadvantages. The utility of each protocol for dial-up purposes is discussed earlier in this chapter in the section "Configuring Network Protocols for RAS"; a general discussion of the protocols appears in Chapter 6.

You can select a different protocol or set of protocols for each phone book entry, and you can have two phone book entries for the same RAS server, differing only by protocol. You could use this feature, for instance, to select TCP/IP when telephone service is bad and NWLink otherwise. TCP/IP is far more forgiving of dropped packets than NWLink is, but NWLink can be much faster when line conditions are good. You can change the protocols a phone book entry uses by clicking My Computer ➤ Dial-up Networking, clicking the phone book entry, and then selecting the Server tab. Figure 11.8 shows the Server tab of the phone book entry.

Security

The RAS client complement to the RAS server security options resides in the Security tab of the phone book entry. From there you can specify what kind of dial-up authentication you will use to connect your RAS client computer

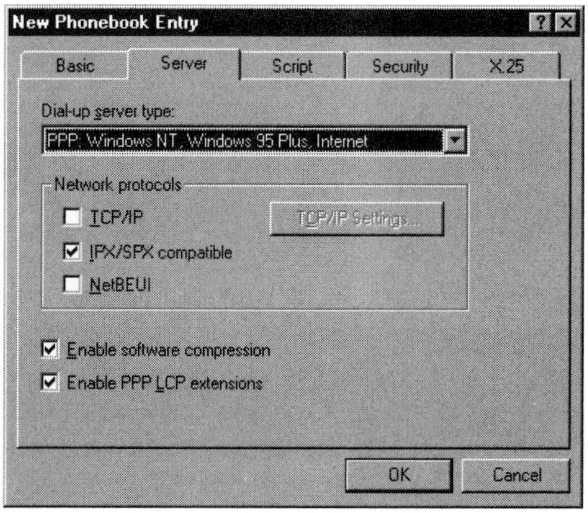

FIGURE 11.8

You can select TCP/IP, IPX, or NetBEUI as the transport protocol of your dial-up connection.

to the remote server. The same options are available from both the client and server side.

- **PAP:** allow any authentication including clear text

- **CHAP:** require encrypted authentication

- **MS-CHAP:** require Microsoft encrypted authentication

You can also specify that data passing over the RAS connection will be encrypted if you select the MS-CHAP protocol.

The security you select must almost always match the security selected on the remote server. The exception is if either side selects Allow any authentication including clear text; then it doesn't matter which protocol the other uses (except from a security standpoint).

Multilink

You can select Multiple Lines in the Dial Using selection box of the Basic tab of the phone book entry screen. The Configure button then will allow you to check each modem you want to use for the Multilink connection. You can use several modems to connect to the same RAS server, providing you with more bandwidth for your dial-up connection. Your RAS server must be configured to accept Multilink connections in order for you to use this feature.

Scripting

Windows NT Server and Workstation version 4 include a powerful new scripting language, which you can use to automate connections to non-RAS dial-up servers. (The scripting language is not necessary for connecting to RAS servers because the authentication protocols already do all the work of connecting the client to the RAS server.)

Using the scripting language is not difficult, but it is beyond the scope of this book to show you how to program in it. Look at the examples provided with the Windows NT Server CD-ROM and read the documentation about the scripting language (`<Winnt>\system32\ras\Script.doc`) in order to see how it works.

Testing a RAS Installation

Testing a RAS installation requires two computers running a compatible dial-up service such as Microsoft RAS. You may need to ask your network administrator for the phone number of your company's RAS server and what protocols it supports. You can test both a client and a server installation using the procedure shown in Exercise 11.8.

EXERCISE 11.8

Testing a RAS Connection

1. Double-click the My Computer Icon on the Desktop.

2. Double-click the Dial-Up Networking Icon.

3. Check whether the server you entered in the previous section appears as the default phone book entry. If it does not appear, select the entry from the list box. If it does not appear in the list box, repeat Exercise 11.6 to add a phone book entry.

4. Click the Dial button.

5. Enter your username, password, and domain for the remote server in the Connect to window. Click the Save Password checkbox.

6. Click OK.

7. Listen for the modem to dial and connect. RAS will beep if the connection goes through correctly.

After running this procedure, you are connected to the remote server. You will have access to all the resources on the remote network that your security permissions allow.

Disconnecting a RAS session

You can disconnect a RAS session through the RAS session dialog box. Exercise 11.9 shows this simple procedure.

EXERCISE 11.9

Disconnecting a RAS Session

1. Right-click the RAS monitor next to the Time in the Taskbar. (If you already changed the icon into a status window, right-click on the window.)

2. Select the Hang up connection option.

3. Select the name of the server or service provider from which you wish to disconnect.

4. Answer Yes to the Disconnect dialog box.

5. Listen for a beep to confirm the disconnect.

Troubleshooting RAS Connections

RAS IS EASY to set up, but it sometimes can be difficult to troubleshoot because any of a number of incorrect settings can cause your RAS connection to fail. The most important part of troubleshooting RAS, like troubleshooting any other part of Windows NT, is knowing where to start. As with most other troubleshooting situations, you should check your cables first. Exercise 11.10 highlights steps that will help you find the trouble spot in a failed RAS communication.

EXERCISE 11.10

Troubleshooting RAS Connections

1. Check your telephone cord and make sure that it is securely connected to the telephone outlet and to your modem.

2. Check the modem cable (for external modems) and make sure it is securely fastened to both the modem and the serial port of your computer.

3. Plug a regular telephone into the telephone jack of the modem if it has one. Most do—if yours does not, plug the telephone into the phone jack in your wall for testing purposes and then replace the modem phone line. If you do not hear a dial tone through the telephone handset, then you have either a telephone service problem (contact the telephone company) or a wiring problem at your location.

4. Make sure that the modem (internal modems only) is securely fastened in the expansion slot of your computer.

5. Verify that the modem is working properly and that the IRQ and port address settings of the modem are reflected in the Windows NT Modem Properties settings.

6. Do one of the following:

- If you are using an external modem, ensure that the COM port that the modem is using is enabled in the BIOS of your computer.

- If you are using an internal modem, verify that the IRQ and port address of your modem do not conflict with other devices in your computer, including the built-in serial ports of your computer.

7. Verify that RAS is installed in your computer and that it is configured to use your modem as a RAS device.

8. If you expect to place calls only, verify that Dial Out Only is selected in the RAS configuration panel of the Network control panel program. If you expect to receive RAS calls only, verify that Receive Calls Only is selected. If you want to do both, verify that Dial Out and Receive calls is selected.

9. Verify that you are have installed the same transport protocols on both the client computer and the RAS server computer and that both computers are configured to use those protocols from within RAS.

EXERCISE 11.10 (CONTINUED FROM PREVIOUS PAGE)

10. Verify that both computers allow the same type of authentication or that the server has selected Allow any authentication including clear text.

11. Verify that the user account you will be using to connect to the RAS server has dial-in privileges and that the call-back feature is properly set.

12. Verify that you are using the correct username, password, and domain name when making the connection.

The RAS Monitor

THE RAS MONITOR is a useful way to keep track of the occasionally unreliable status of modem connections over the public network. The RAS monitor appears by default in the Taskbar, but you can change it to a window that constantly shows the connection status, as explained in Exercise 11.11. If you use Exercise 11.11 to change the RAS monitor icon to a window, remember that clicking the window has the same effect as clicking the icon. Figure 11.9 shows the Dial-Up Networking Monitor screen.

EXERCISE 11.11

Checking the Status of a RAS Connection

1. Establish a RAS session using the procedure shown in Exercise 11.7.

2. Double-click the RAS monitor icon next to the time system tray on the Taskbar.

3. Notice the count of incoming bytes and frames in the status page.

4. Select the Preferences tab.

5. Select the As a window on the desktop in the Show status lights control group.

6. Check Display the windows title bar.

7. Check Always on top.

8. Click OK.

9. Notice that the RAS monitor now shows up as a window on the desktop.

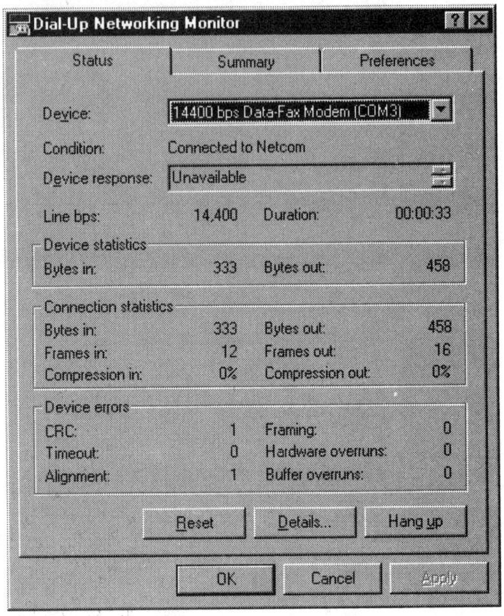

FIGURE 11.9

The Dial-Up Networking Monitor screen controls the RAS monitor.

Summary

THE REMOTE ACCESS Service for Windows NT extends the advantages of networking to computers that cannot be directly connected to your network. RAS uses modems or other devices that attach to telephone company lines to share files and services.

Regular Ethernet can transfer data 100 times faster than can the fastest regular modems. Fast Ethernet (which can be 10 times faster than regular Ethernet) can transfer data 1,000 times faster than regular modems can.

A RAS server can support any of the three primary transport protocols of Windows NT (TCP/IP, NWLink, and NetBEUI). It supports PPP for dial-in and supports both SLIP and PPP for dial-out. It supports PAP, CHAP, and MS-CHAP for password authentication, and if you use MS-CHAP, you can also encrypt the data transferred over a RAS link.

RAS can link networks together, but a constantly connected regular phone line can be prohibitively expensive, especially if the phone call is long distance. Such constantly connected wide area links are usually made with dedicated equipment and special telephone lines that are leased from the phone company.

Regular analog (or PSTN) modems encode the serial digital signal from your computer into an analog signal that can be sent over telephone lines to the phone company. The phone company digitizes the analog signal and sends it to another location, at which the analog signal is re-created. The modem at the other end decodes the analog signal and sends the resulting serial digital signal to the receiving computer.

ISDN skips all of the encoding and decoding by delivering the digital serial signal directly to a digital telephone company interface. That digital signal is routed to the destination digital telephone company interface, where it is given to the receiving ISDN adapter, which then gives the digital signal to the serial port of the receiving computer.

RAS supports the connection of any computer that supports PPP as a serial line protocol; PAP, CHAP, or MS-CHAP as an authentication protocol; and IPX, TCP/IP, or NetBEUI as a transport protocol. If the client computer will access services on the RAS server, then the client must also support a protocol that the RAS server also supports, such as NetBIOS or HTTP.

RAS permissions are established on a per user basis and include a callback feature. You cannot assign RAS permissions by groups.

The Multilink protocol allows you to use more than one modem for the same dial-up connection. Using multiple modems allows you to transfer data faster than using only one modem. The Point-to-Point Tunneling Protocol allows remote clients to access your network in a secure manner over the Internet using an Internet service provider.

Protocols are selected for dial-out from the phone book entry for that dial-out connection, as is the authentication that the connection will use. RAS also allows you to write a script to automate connection to non-RAS servers.

Review Questions

1. The purpose of RAS is to provide permanent network links over telephone lines leased from the phone company.

   A. True

   B. False

2. You do not need a network interface adapter to use RAS.

   A. True

   B. False

3. You do not need a transport protocol to use RAS.

   A. True

   B. False

4. With RAS you can use a transport protocol that is not installed as one of the networking protocols in the Protocols portion of the Network control panel.

   A. True

   B. False

5. Regular modems are much slower than regular Ethernet.

   A. True

   B. False

6. RAS supports AppleTalk.

   A. True

   B. False

7. RAS looks like a network interface adapter to Windows NT networking components.

   A. True

   B. False

8. ISDN is more efficient than regular PSTN modems.

    A. True

    B. False

9. RAS provides dial-in capability only. You must use the Dial Up Networking (DUN) service to dial out to a RAS server.

    A. True

    B. False

10. RAS supports SLIP for remote client dial-in.

    A. True

    B. False

11. RAS supports X.25 for wide area networking.

    A. True

    B. False

12. ISDN adapters can be installed only from the Modems control panel.

    A. True

    B. False

13. SLIP is a recent improvement on the PPP protocol.

    A. True

    B. False

14. RAS permissions are set per user rather than per RAS device.

    A. True

    B. False

15. You can use PPTP to allow remote clients to make secure connections to your RAS server using the Internet.

    A. True

    B. False

16. RAS stands for _____ _____ _____.

17. In practice, Ethernet is about _____ times faster than the fastest analog modems.

18. PSTN stands for _____ _____ _____ _____.

19. ISDN stands for _____ _____ _____ _____.

20. If you will connect to the Internet via RAS, you must use the _____ protocol.

21. SLIP stands for _____ _____ _____ _____.

22. PPP stands for _____ _____ _____.

23. _____ is the simplest network transport protocol.

24. You modify RAS permissions in the _____ _____ _____ program.

25. _____ functions by calling back the client computer after the client computer calls the RAS server and requests a network connection.

26. The Require Microsoft encrypted authentication option uses the _____ authentication protocol.

27. The Require encrypted authentication option uses the _____ authentication protocol.

28. The Allow any authentication including clear text option uses the _____ authentication protocol.

29. _____ allows the combination of multiple serial data streams into one aggregate bundle.

30. PPTP stands for _____ _____ _____ _____.

Internet and Intranet

12

HE INTERNET IS big. Really big. You just won't believe how vastly, hugely, mind-bogglingly big it is. You may think a campus computer network linking sites with hundreds of personal computers is big, but that's just peanuts compared to the Internet.

The Internet is the sum of all private networks connected to it. It is organized like a massive city of information, with sites dedicated to commercial, academic, and personal pursuits. Each site has an address, much the way a building has a street address. Each attached network "owns" a range of addresses, the same way a zip code refers to a certain area.

The Internet originally connected government facilities and universities so they could share research information. Although the U.S. government and major universities funded much of the research that developed the Internet protocols, no single organization owns the Internet, or even a very large portion of it. Portions of the backbone of the Internet are owned by major Internet service providers (ISPs), such as PSInet, Cerf-net, UU-Net, and all the other companies whose name ends with net, and by the large telephone companies, such as AT&T, MCI, and Sprint, that also act as major Internet service providers.

The Internet operates primarily over telephone lines and trunks, according to the following scheme:

- Home users use modems to call their Internet service providers over standard telephone lines.

- Local Internet service providers lease high-capacity telephone trunk lines from regional telephone companies to connect their own networks.

- Smaller regional Internet service providers connect their networks to national Internet service providers, which are sometimes owned by long distance telephone companies.

- National Internet service providers, through mutual agreement, connect their networks at regional sites where vast telephone capacity is available, usually in major metropolitan areas. The maintenance of these network access points is divided equitably among the participating national Internet service providers.

Because each Internet service provider leases its own lines, quite a bit of redundancy exists in Internet connections. The map in Figure 12.1 shows how the Internet links come together at the top tier—in fact, there are vastly more telephone trunk lines than shown here.

FIGURE 12.1

The Internet is configured as a hierarchy of stars. TCP/IP routers connect the Internet links at the central points of the stars.

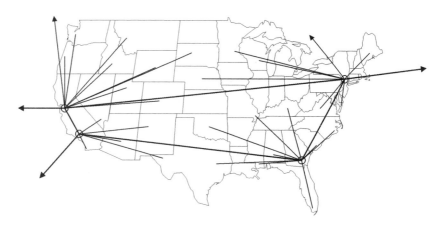

In the Internet's early years, you had to know the exact location of information in order to retrieve it—no indexes existed. A few attempts at organizing information using higher-level protocols with arcane names like Archie, Veronica, and Gopher worked rather well, but they were not easy to use.

Then the World Wide Web (WWW, but referred to as the Web) made the Internet accessible to people with social lives. The Web uses a higher-level protocol called Hypertext Transport Protocol (HTTP) to send documents containing text, graphics, and links to other Web documents (called *pages*) to users with Web browser applications. Users can simply click a link to retrieve the document referred to by the link.

Because the most useful protocol on the Internet is HTTP (the foundation of the World Wide Web protocol), many people use the terms Internet and Web interchangeably. This usage is not entirely correct as many other useful Internet protocols exist.

The tremendous utility of an easy to use information retrieval system was an instant hit, and the rush to become connected to the Internet began in 1994. Within two years, most medium to large organizations started Web sites, and millions of typical computer users began dialing into the Internet on a regular basis. The Internet rapidly became a major global communications medium and is beginning to rival radio and television in its social impact and importance.

Netspeak: The Internet

- **Internet**   The public global interconnection of networks based on the TCP/IP protocol suite.

- **Intranet**   A privately owned network based on the TCP/IP protocol suite.

- **Host**   An Internet server. Hosts are always connected to the Internet.

- **Dial-up client**   A computer with a temporary connection to the Internet that cannot act as a server because its IP address is temporary.

- **Domain name**   The textual identifier of a specific Internet host. Domain names in the form `server.organization.type` (e.g., `www.microsoft.com`) are resolved to Internet addresses by Domain Name Servers.

- **Domain Name Server**   An Internet host dedicated to the function of translating fully qualified domain names into IP addresses.

- **Request for Comment (RFC)**   The standards describing each Internet protocol developed by the Internet Engineering Task Force (IETF) and other Internet related-topics. They are freely available on the Internet at many Web sites.

Windows NT jumped on the Internet bandwagon with the release of Windows NT 4. Unlike earlier versions of Windows NT, which supported TCP/IP as a transport protocol mainly to allow the interconnection of larger networks, NT Server 4 ships with a number of services and applications specifically designed to provide the functionality of an Internet host, including

- **Internet Information Server** (IIS) serves Internet higher-level protocols such as HTTP and FTP to clients using Web browsers.

- **Domain Name Server** (DNS) resolves fully qualified domain names such as `www.microsoft.com` to the TCP/IP address that identifies the computer serving Microsoft's home page.

- **FrontPage** helps you make complex Web pages and link them to form a useful Web site.

- **Internet Explorer** is a leading Web browser that lets you take full advantages of all popular Internet protocols. Internet Explorer supports the use of modular components so you can add new protocols (like voice and multimedia support) without upgrading.

UNIX is the traditional operating system of the Internet, but Microsoft Windows NT Server, IBM OS/2, Apple Macintosh OS, and Novell IntraNetware are also commonly used as operating systems on Internet servers. Many older mainframes are being migrated to the role of powerful Internet servers.

Requests for Comment Recommended Reading

- **RFC 1580** discusses in detail the operation of all the client/server Internet tools, including Gopher and the World Wide Web.

- **RFC 1392** is a very complete glossary of Internet terms.

- **RFC 1739** is a primer on TCP/IP, the Internet, and Internet tools.

In this chapter we describe the Internet tools provided with Windows NT and explain the installation and function of each one. The first section covers the Internet Information Server (IIS), which provides a foundation for serving Internet information. We then look at the major Internet client/server protocols.

Internet Information Server

MICROSOFT INTERNET INFORMATION Server (IIS) is a package of services that form a fully functional Internet host. The Internet protocols function as client/server applications. Internet Information Services provides the server portion of this application; Internet Explorer and other Web browsers provide the client portion.

Internet Information Server supports three Internet protocols:

- **Hypertext Transfer Protocol** (HTTP) serves Web pages consisting of text, graphics, and links to other Web pages.

- **File Transfer Protocol** (FTP) serves files regardless of operating system type.

- **Gopher** serves text and links to other Gopher sites. Although Gopher predates HTTP by about a year, the richer format of HTTP has made Gopher obsolete.

Internet Information Server is part of Windows NT Server 4. Prior to Internet Information Server, serving Internet sites required either expensive preconfigured servers or an intimate knowledge of UNIX and a constant maintenance effort. Microsoft has included these services to make Windows NT Server even more competitive and entice network administrators to move to it from competing operating systems.

Comparing the Internet and Intranets

Once the World Wide Web took off and many organizations began publishing information on the Internet, the utility of low-cost, low-bandwidth information publishing and e-mail for internal use with private information became obvious. Network managers began creating Web sites on file servers inside the organization that didn't have the stringent security requirements necessary on the public Internet. They could use sophisticated interactive scripts and interactive Internet applets written in new computer languages like Java on these networks without worrying about the effect of transferring data over data links. Soon after, somebody coined the term *intranet* to refer specifically to private networks utilizing the Internet protocols, especially HTTP.

The only differences between Internet servers and intranet servers are where and how they are used. Both servers perform exactly the same functions, but they have different audiences. Whenever we use the term *Internet servers* in this book, you can assume the information applies to intranet servers as well.

Many organizations that don't have or need a presence on the Internet use intranets because the software is inexpensive and because they can use very simple, inexpensive computers (called NetPCs) that have no local hard disk storage as clients to powerful intranet servers. Databases that support this sort of solution already exist, and word processors and spreadsheets will soon be available.

Internet Client Tools

ICROSOFT ROUNDS OUT its Internet tools with a complete set of client applications. All these client tools are installed automatically when you install Windows NT. Windows NT ships with the following Internet client tools:

- **Internet Explorer** is a full-featured Web browser, second only to Netscape Navigator in popularity.

- **Exchange** e-mail package can be configured to send and receive e-mail over the Internet via the SMTP and POP protocols.

- **FTP** is a command-line utility useful for downloading files via the FTP protocol when you can't or don't want to use Internet Explorer. RFC 765 describes the FTP protocol in detail.

- **telnet** provides a command-line interface to remote Internet hosts via the TCP/IP directly.

- **finger** looks up information about users of remote systems.

- **ping** troubleshoots connections between your computer and any computer on the Internet.

- **nslookup** resolves domain names to Internet protocol addresses.

- **rsh** runs commands on remote UNIX hosts running the rsh service.

- **tftp** (trivial FTP) allows you to upload and download files between two computers on a network with a command-line only interface. The complete functionality of tftp and more is provided by FTP, so it is obsolete except in extremely memory limited systems. RFC 1350 describes tftp.

- **tracert** allows you to trace the route and count the "hops" or number of router packet exchanges between your computer and any Internet host.

Internet users use some of these tools (e.g., Internet Explorer and Exchange) on a daily basis. Other tools, such as ping and tracert, are invaluable for debugging; you should become familiar with them. Others (e.g., rsh, tftp, and finger) are obsolete or arcane; Microsoft provides them as a convenience for interoperating with UNIX hosts or so old UNIX administrators won't have to learn new tricks with Windows NT. Figure 12.2 shows how the trace route (tracert) tool can help you determine how many hops, or router exchanges, the data in a TCP/IP connection is subject to. Exercise 12.1 shows how to use the FTP tool to download software.

FIGURE 12.2

Tracert shows the routers between two computers on the Internet.

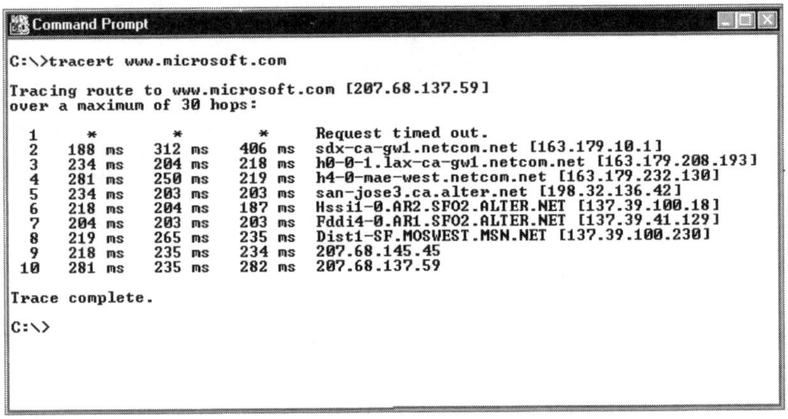

```
Command Prompt                                                              _ □ ✕

C:\>tracert www.microsoft.com

Tracing route to www.microsoft.com [207.68.137.59]
over a maximum of 30 hops:

  1     *        *        *      Request timed out.
  2   188 ms   312 ms   406 ms  sdx-ca-gw1.netcom.net [163.179.10.1]
  3   234 ms   204 ms   218 ms  h0-0-1.lax-ca-gw1.netcom.net [163.179.208.193]
  4   281 ms   250 ms   219 ms  h4-0-mae-west.netcom.net [163.179.232.130]
  5   234 ms   203 ms   203 ms  san-jose3.ca.alter.net [198.32.136.42]
  6   218 ms   204 ms   187 ms  Hssi1-0.AR2.SFO2.ALTER.NET [137.39.100.18]
  7   204 ms   203 ms   203 ms  Fddi4-0.AR1.SFO2.ALTER.NET [137.39.41.129]
  8   219 ms   265 ms   235 ms  Dist1-SF.MOSWEST.MSN.NET [137.39.100.230]
  9   218 ms   235 ms   234 ms  207.68.145.45
 10   281 ms   235 ms   282 ms  207.68.137.59

Trace complete.

C:\>
```

EXERCISE 12.1

Using the File Transfer Protocol

1. Establish a connection to your Internet provider. If you are on a network connected to the Internet, skip to step 2. Otherwise, use RAS as covered in Chapter 11 to connect to the Internet.

2. Select Start ➤ Programs ➤ Command Prompt.

3. Type **ftp ftp.microsoft.com** at the command prompt.

4. Type **Anonymous** at the user prompt.

5. Type your e-mail address in at the password prompt. Type **none** if you don't have an e-mail address.

6. Type **?** at the FTP prompt to see a listing of FTP commands.

7. Type **ls** at the ftp prompt to see a directory listing of the root directory.

8. Type **cd msdownload** to change to the business systems directory.

9. Type **cd iis** to change to the Windows NT directory.

10. Type **cd activeserver.**

EXERCISE 12.1 (CONTINUED FROM PREVIOUS PAGE)

11. Type **cd i386** (or the directory indicating your microprocessor).

12. Type **binary** to set FTP into binary transfer mode.

13. Type **hash** to turn on hash mark printing.

14. Type **get asp.exe** to begin transferring the new (3.0) version of Internet Information Server to your hard disk. If you don't want to download `asp.exe` (the file is 10MB, so downloading takes some time), skip this step.

15. Type **Close** to close the connection to `ftp.microsoft.com`.

16. Type **Bye** to end your FTP interactive session.

Overview of Internet Protocols and Services

I NTERNET COMMUNICATION PROTOCOLS such as HTTP allow browsers to request information from servers and servers to respond to those requests. For example, when you click on a Hypertext link in a Web page, you are actually making a request for the Web page referred to by the link from the server that stores it. Here's the entire process:

1. User clicks on Hypertext link.

2. Browser translates uniform resource locator (URL) embedded in the link into a fully qualified domain name and a path to the document.

3. Browser requests resolution of the domain name from the domain name server (DNS) indicated by your Internet service provider when you established your connection or as indicated in the Network control panel.

4. Browser checks cache. If document exists in the browser cache, skip to step 8. Cached version may not be recent unless you click the Reload button.

5. Sockets service establishes a TCP/IP connection to the IP address returned by the DNS server, naming the Web server in the URL.

6. Browser requests the document indicated by the path in the URL from Web server.

7. Web server transmits HTML document at the path indicated in the URL to browser.

8. TCP/IP connection to Web server is disconnected. Each page request makes a unique temporary TCP/IP connection.

9. Browser formats HTML data and presents it to user.

10. Browser repeats steps 4 through 8 for each embedded object such as graphics and frames. One HTML page may contain many embedded objects and therefore may instantiate many TCP/IP connections to the Web server.

HTTP is a client/server communication protocol dedicated to the service of HTML documents. All Internet protocols work in a similar fashion, varying only in the duration of the connection they establish and the type of documents they exchange.

Each Internet client/server protocol has three components:

■ A server service that runs on an Internet host

■ A client application that runs on the user's computer

■ A protocol that connects the two

HTTP and the Web

The World Wide Web is the most important Internet client/server protocol because it delivers the richest content and is the easiest to use. Hypertext Markup Language (HTML) delivers embedded links to other pages along with text and graphics from Web servers to Web browsers. This process allows users to receive information and follow their own trains of thought through the presentation of that material by choosing the links most relevant to their needs. New search engines that index the contents of all the Web pages they find make a convenient starting point for any information search on the Internet.

Netspeak: The Web

- **World Wide Web (Web)**   A collection of rich content documents maintained by millions of Internet servers around the world.

- **Hypertext Transfer Protocol (HTTP)**   The client/server interprocess communication protocol served by Internet servers and requested by Internet browsers.

- **Hypertext Markup Language (HTML)**   The syntax of Web documents. A human-readable language describing both the presentation characteristics and content of Web documents.

- **Uniform resource locator (URL)**   Information embedded in a Hypertext link that uniquely identifies a resource on the Internet. URLs contain the domain name of the Internet host serving the resource, the path to the resource, and the resource name. URLs are defined in RFC 1738.

- **Web page**   Any HTML document on an HTTP server.

- **Home page**   The default page returned by an HTTP server when a URL containing no specific document is requested.

- **Web browser**   An application that makes HTTP requests and formats the resulting HTML documents for the users. Web browsers are the preeminent Internet client, and most of them understand all standard Internet protocols.

- **Site**   A related collection of HTML documents at the same Internet address, usually oriented toward some specific information or purpose.

- **Search engine**   Web sites dedicated to responding to requests for specific information, searching massive locally stored databases of Web pages, and responding with the URLs of pages that fit the search phrase.

- **Web crawler**   Programs that search the Internet for Web servers, retrieve all the pages they can find, index those pages word by word, and store the results in the databases used by search engines.

- **Surf**   1. To browse the Web randomly looking for interesting information. 2. To bob in ocean randomly looking for an interesting wave.

Windows NT Server 4 provides all the software you need to create both the client and the server portion of the World Wide Web.

- **Internet Information Server** creates Internet hosts by serving the HTTP protocol over TCP/IP.

- **FrontPage** creates HTML documents with Hypertext links.

- **Internet Explorer** browses Web sites.

The creation of HTML documents is beyond the scope of this book, but many manuals of procedure and style exist to help you author them. We focus on the protocols and services used to create Internet and intranet hosts. Exercise 12.2 shows you how to surf the Web.

EXERCISE 12.2

Surfing the Web

1. Establish a connection to the Internet using RAS if your network is not directly attached. See Chapter 11 for details on RAS.

2. Double-click the Internet Explorer icon on your desktop.

3. Enter the following URL in the Address input box:

```
www.altavista.digital.com
```

4. Press Enter. Wait while the Web page appears in the document window.

5. Enter the following criteria in the AltaVista search text box:

```
+"windows nt server"+"internet information server"
```

6. Browse the list of page responses. If you find an interesting link (links are identified by a blue underlined phrase), click it.

7. Follow these Hypertext links around for a while. Every time the content screen changes, you are looking at a new Web page.

8. Surf until tired and then close Internet Explorer.

9. Hang up your RAS connection if necessary.

Gopher

Gopher is essentially an interactive text-document indexing and retrieval system. Gopher presents a directory wherein each element is either a document or a link to another directory, similar to a file system hierarchy. Because the functionality of Gopher is far more limited than the functionality of HTTP, Gopher is obsolete.

FTP

File transfer protocol is a way to upload and download files to FTP sites or to Internet hosts with large file libraries. The FTP protocol provides both a security interface to prevent anonymous users from accessing all areas of the Internet host and all other necessary functions to transfer files between clients and Internet hosts.

Netspeak: Files

- **File Transfer Protocol (FTP)**   A client/server protocol for logging into Internet servers and retrieving files. Most Web browsers support FTP as well as HTTP, obviating the need for a separate FTP client.

Windows NT includes an FTP command-line utility. If you prefer to work with a graphical interface, you can use the Internet Explorer to access FTP sites and download files.

telnet

telnet provides a command-line interface to Internet hosts running the telnet service. With telnet, you can establish a remote session with an Internet host and control it as if you were sitting at its console. telnet is useful for the remote administration of Internet hosts over the Internet.

Most routers are actually high-speed RISC computers running small UNIX-like kernels. You can use the telnet utility to administer these routers.

Net News Transport Protocol (NNTP) and Usenet News

Usenet news browsers allow you to browse the Internet newsgroups and post messages. Newsgroups are broken into hierarchies that start with vague encyclopedic topics and become more focused as you traverse the hierarchy. Newsgroups are especially useful for exchanging professional information with colleagues around the world through the Net News Transport Protocol (NNTP). Internet Information Server does not come with an NNTP server because few organizations are large enough to justify the necessity of a direct Usenet feed that copies all the discussion groups to your server on a daily basis.

Scan every file you download from the Internet with a virus scanner before installing any software.

Netspeak: Usenet News

- **Usenet** A massive online bulletin board containing indexed topics of discussion. Because many professionals use Usenet, it has become a valuable way for people who don't know each other personally to exchange information and ideas on almost any topic.

- **Net News Transfer Protocol (NNTP)** An Internet protocol that distributes Usenet news to news servers and responds to client requests for news.

- **Newsgroup** A Usenet discussion on a specific topic. Newsgroups may be moderated by editors who sort through posts to determine relevance and professionalism; unmoderated newsgroups allow anyone to post information.

SMTP, POP, and E-Mail

You can use Internet mail to send e-mail messages anywhere in the world. If you have a dedicated Internet connection and your LAN e-mail package is set up to route e-mail to the Internet, you do not have to do anything special to send Internet mail. In fact, you may not even need to have TCP/IP installed on your workstation if another computer does the e-mail conversion.

If you are using Microsoft Exchange as your e-mail package, you can use Microsoft Exchange Server to route your e-mail to the Internet. If you checked the Internet option when you installed Exchange, you can send mail directly to the Internet from your workstation.

Netspeak: E-Mail

- **Electronic Mail (e-mail)** Text messages sent between users of the Internet (and other networks) that are stored in a receiving buffer for perusal at the convenience of the receiver. Some Web browsers support both SMTP and POP. Some LAN e-mail packages support POP and SMTP for the forwarding of local e-mail to the Internet.

- **Simple Mail Transfer Protocol (SMTP)** An Internet protocol for transferring mail between Internet hosts. SMTP can upload mail directly from the client to an intermediate host but can receive mail only on computers constantly connected to the Internet.

- **Post Office Protocol (POP)** A client/server protocol for the management and transfer of stored e-mail between a client and an Internet host acting as a POP server. The POP server is constantly connected to the Internet so it can receive messages as they arrive via SMTP and buffer them for clients.

E-mail messages are addressed to individuals by entering their e-mail account name followed by the @ symbol followed by the Internet host that serves their post office account; for example, MCSESVSG40@aol.com. MCSESVSG40 is a user known to the aol.com SMTP or POP server. If the server doesn't recognize the user's name, it will bounce the message back with a note that says so.

In Exercise 12.3 you will send an e-mail message over the Internet using Microsoft Exchange.

Configuring the Microsoft Exchange Server (not included in the Windows NT Server 4 package) is the topic of the companion Network Press book *MSCE: Exchange Server Study Guide*.

EXERCISE 12.3

Sending an Internet E-Mail Message Using Microsoft Exchange

1. Establish a connection to the Internet using RAS. (Skip this step if you are on a network that is constantly connected to the Internet.)

2. Start Microsoft Exchange.

3. Select New Message from the Compose menu.

4. Type the address **MSCESVSG40@aol.com** in the To: box.

5. Type **Exercise 12.{sendmail}** in the Subject: box.

6. Type **Exercise 12.{sendmail} completed. I will be a Microsoft Certified Systems Engineer soon.** in the text area of the window.

7. Select Send from the File menu.

8. If you are working offline (check your configuration and refer to step 1), select Tools ➢ Deliver Now Using ➢ Internet Mail in the Inbox - Microsoft Exchange window.

9. Select File ➢ Exit and Log Off.

Installing Internet Information Server

INSTALLING INTERNET INFORMATION Server is straightforward and is usually performed during the installation of the operating system, especially if your server's primary function will be Internet or intranet service. In Chapter 3 when we installed Windows NT Server 4, we skipped this portion of the installation so that we could cover it in depth in this chapter.

When Internet Information Server is installed, the WWW, FTP, and Gopher services start by default. Exercise 12.4 shows how to install Internet Information Server.

EXERCISE 12.4

Installing Internet Information Server

I. Insert the Windows NT Server 4 CD-ROM in your CD-ROM drive.

2. Double-click My Computer.

3. Right-click your CD-ROM drive and select Open.

4. Double-click the I386 directory (or the installation directory for your processor).

5. Double-click the Inetsrv folder.

6. Double-click the Inetstp program.

7. Click OK to continue installing.

8. Check all available options and click OK.

9. Accept default directory assignments and click OK.

10. Click OK if you see the *Domain name necessary for Gopher services* message.

I I. Select SQL Server and click OK in the ODBC connectivity dialog box.

12. Click OK to acknowledge completion of the installation.

Your server is now able to serve HTTP, FTP, and Gopher requests.

Internet Service Manager

The Internet Service Manager is the utility that customizes and administers your Internet services. Internet Information Server is configured by default for the most common set of services and the most common security requirements, so you may never need to use the Internet Service Manager. Figure 12.3 shows the Internet Service Manager. Exercise 12.5 shows how to launch and use the Internet Service Manager.

Perhaps the most important function of the Internet Service Manager is troubleshooting. For example if your clients can see other normal Windows NT shares, but not your Web page, you should first check to see if your TCP/IP settings are working with the ping command. If they are, launch the Internet Service Manager and verify that all your Internet services are running properly. Exercise 12.5 shows some important settings to check.

FIGURE 12.3

The Internet Service Manager.

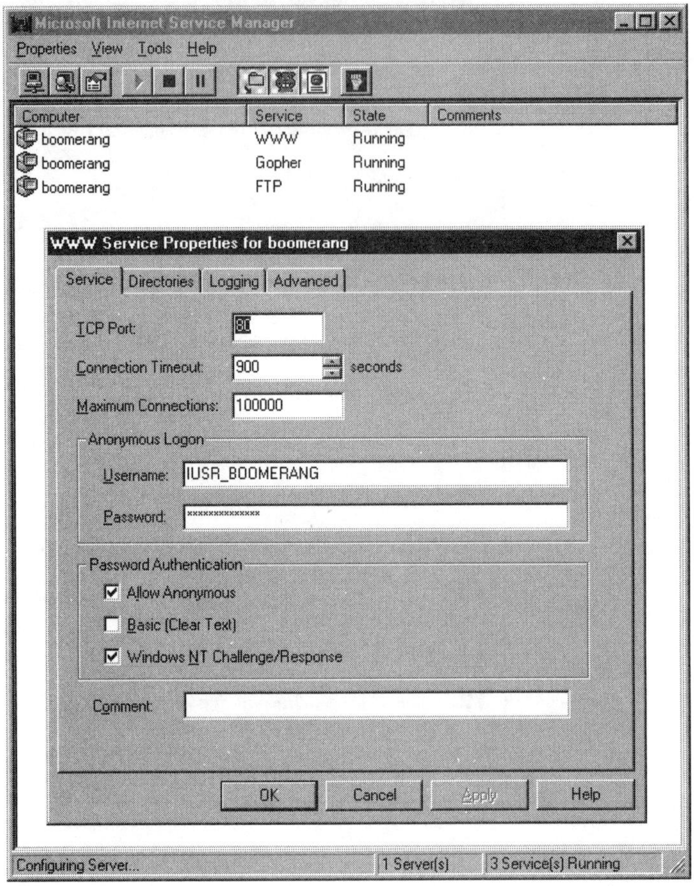

Microsoft Internet Service Manager

Properties View Tools Help

Computer	Service	State	Comments
boomerang	WWW	Running	
boomerang	Gopher	Running	
boomerang	FTP	Running	

WWW Service Properties for boomerang

Service | Directories | Logging | Advanced

TCP Port: 80

Connection Timeout: 900 seconds

Maximum Connections: 100000

Anonymous Logon

Username: IUSR_BOOMERANG

Password: **************

Password Authentication

☑ Allow Anonymous

☐ Basic (Clear Text)

☑ Windows NT Challenge/Response

Comment:

OK   Cancel   Apply   Help

Configuring Server...   1 Server(s)   3 Service(s) Running

You may not be able to ping Web sites that are reachable via HTTP if a firewall that restricts TCP/IP access exists between you and the Web server. Many firewalls do allow HTTP and FTP requests through, but not lower-level TCP/IP requests made by tools such as ping.

EXERCISE 12.5

Troubleshooting Tour of the Internet Service Manager

1. Select Start ➤ Programs ➤ Microsoft Internet Server > Internet Server Manager.

2. Check to see that the service you are troubleshooting is running in the Service Condition list box.

3. Double-click the service you are troubleshooting. Make sure the TCP/IP port is correct for the service you are running. WWW should be port 80, Gopher should be 70, and FTP should be 21.

4. Perform this step only if you are allowing anonymous logon. Check to be sure the user listed in the Anonymous users Logon as input line is a valid user with the correct security settings for your security environment. IIS creates a user with a random password for anonymous logon when you install it. You should change this user only if your organization's security requirements are more stringent than those provided automatically.

5. Set your Internet e-mail address (if you have one) in the service administrator's e-mail address input line. This information allows users using the finger and DNS services to identify the person in charge of your Internet host.

6. Make sure the maximum connections value is appropriate for your server and network. The default settings are pretty good, but if you have a busy public Internet host, you may want to limit the connections to increase responsiveness to connected users.

7. Check the password authentication settings. Public Internet servers need to have the Allow Anonymous connections checked or users will see Access Denied. Secure intranets should not allow anonymous access.

8. Click the Directories tab. Make sure the directories shown in the directories list box match the directories where your Internet files are stored. Check permissions on those directories to make sure they're available to the Internet anonymous user.

9. Click Advanced. Check the default access settings. Public servers should allow access by default and exclude only computers or domains known to cause security problems. Private intranets should deny access by default and allow access only to computers on the local or trusted domains.

If your server is frequently swamped by users on fast connections, you can limit network use. This method is commonly called "throttling" because you can specify the maximum service speed to each connection, thereby keeping users on T1 lines from sucking up all the bandwidth your server can provide.

Remote Internet Service Manager

Windows NT provides a second version of the Internet Service Manager. This version is actually a set of HTML documents that you can use to administer your site from remote locations. However, you cannot start or stop Web services with the HTML version of the Internet Service Manager. You can browse through an HTML version of the Internet Information Server Installation and Administration Guide from the HTML version of the Internet Service Manager by clicking the documentation hypertext link. Figure 12.4 shows the HTML version of the Internet Service Manager running inside Internet Explorer. Exercise 12.6 shows you how to launch the HTML version of the Internet Service Manager and how to browse through the IIS documentation in HTML.

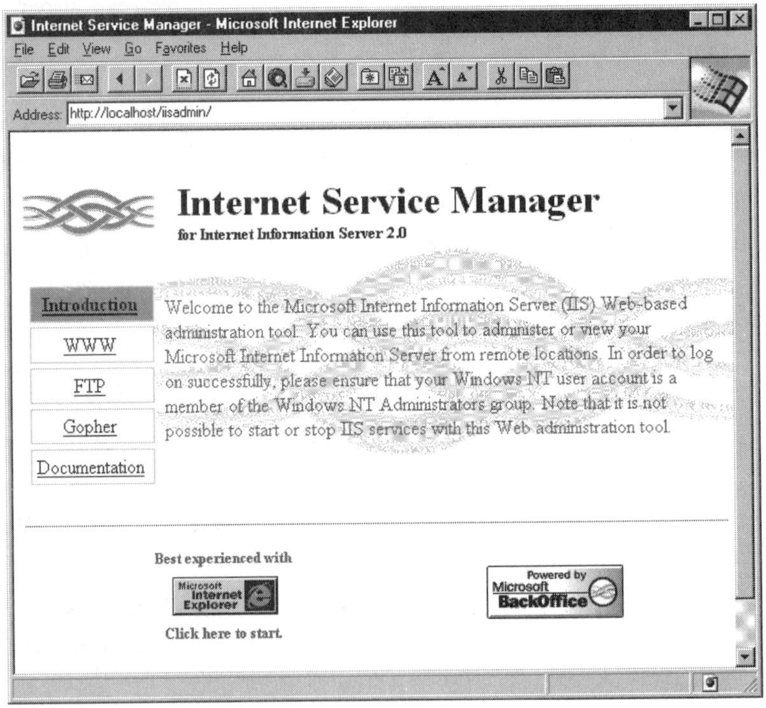

FIGURE 12.4

HTML version of the Internet Service Manager.

EXERCISE 12.6

Using the HTML Version of the Internet Service Manager

1. Select Start ➤ Programs ➤ Microsoft Internet Server ➤ Internet Service Manager (HTML). Internet Explorer (or your registered Web browser) will open with the HTML Internet Service Manager showing.

2. Click WWW. Browse through the links at the top corresponding to the tabs in ISM and notice the similarity between the two versions of the Internet Service Manager.

3. Click the Documentation link.

4. Click How to Navigate the Product Documentation and read through the instructions.

5. Browse through the product documentation. Notice how much faster Web pages run on local servers than they do over the Internet. The HTML Internet Service Manager is an example of what is possible with intranets running Internet protocols. Can you think of any function in your organization that could benefit from a client/server solution based on HTML?

6. Close the Internet Explorer when you finish.

Logging

The most important feature controlled in the Internet Service Manager is the logging feature, which tells you how your server is used. You can use this information to determine how many "hits" (or how popular) your site is. You can log to a text file or to a database and select how often you want to clear the log. Logging to an ODBC database is more difficult to set up but makes working with the information generated far easier. Logging to a text file is useful only if you will be importing the text into a database manager or spreadsheet or if you are looking for details on a specific access attempt.

By default, a new log file is created each day your Internet site operates. Each connection to your Internet server is recorded in the log file or database you specify. The log information includes the TCP/IP address of the connected user and the e-mail address for anonymous FTP. You can use this information to determine how many people visit your site and with what frequency and to identify the heavy users. The default location for the log files is the \system32\logfiles directory in the Windows NT system folder.

Serving for the World Wide Web

Once you've installed Internet Service Manager, services for the World Wide Web are installed and running. To access Microsoft's default Web for IIS, simply launch Internet Explorer from any computer on your LAN and enter the name of your IIS server in the URL location (without any slashes, periods, or colons). You can use FrontPage, which comes with Windows NT Server 4, to modify this Web site or replace it with your own.

Serving for File Transfer Protocol

Serving for FTP is automatic once you've installed the IIS. Simply copy the files or directories you want to make available via FTP into the `\InetPub\FTProot` directory of your system drive or the location you've specified as the FTP root in the Internet Service Manager.

Because using the file services of Windows NT is far easier than using FTP, it generally is not used for intranets. Public FTP sites nearly always allow anonymous logon and ask users for their e-mail address as the password. These e-mail addresses are available in the log file setup under the Logging tab in the IIS.

Do not put files you don't have the right to publish or distribute, including copyrighted software, in FTP roots on servers that allow anonymous logon. You may be liable for copyright violation or software piracy if you do. As a general rule, the only files you can serve via FTP are files created by your organization.

Serving Gopher

Serving Gopher files is similar to serving FTP or WWW files. Simply copy the files you want to appear to Gopher clients into the `\Inetpub\Gophroot` directory of your system drive. You can find more information about Gopher in the Internet Requests for Comment.

You should consider using Web protocols (such as HTTP) to serve information rather than Gopher. The Web allows much richer content, and many more people are familiar with it.

Internet Information Server and the Domain Name Service

M OST OF THE network services that come with Windows NT Server are designed to work with any transport protocol that Windows NT supports. Windows NT provides features such as network browsing and name resolution that are independent of the transport protocol. This system works just fine because most Windows NT services use universal naming convention (UNC) names, which describe computers and resources in a protocol-independent fashion.

Internet resources, however, are not presented in a protocol-independent fashion. Web pages, Gopher sites, and FTP servers are specified instead with textual Internet names that your computer must convert into numerical Internet addresses. The service that does this conversion is called the *Domain Name Service*, or DNS for short.

DNS is easy to install and configure. The next two sections walk you through installing the service, creating zones, and adding host records. DNS allows other computers on your network to use your DNS server to resolve Internet names. Note, however, that for other computers on the Internet to be able to resolve Internet names on your network, it must be

- Connected to the Internet

- Configured in the DNS service of your Internet service provider

Installing the DNS service

Installing DNS is simple. You install this service the same way you install any other networking service in Windows NT—from the Services tab of the Network control panel. You will have to reboot your server after you install the service in order for the changes to take effect. Exercise 12.7 shows you how to install the DNS service.

EXERCISE 12.7

Installing the DNS Service

1. Open the Control Panel and double-click the Network icon.

2. Click the Services tab.

3. Click the Add button.

4. Select Microsoft DNS Server and click the OK button.

5. Give the path to the installation files and click the Continue button.

6. Restart the computer after the DNS server is installed.

Using the DNS Manager

Once you have installed the DNS manager, it will start automatically, but before it can do anything useful you have to install some DNS zones. In particular, you should create two primary DNS zones—one to hold host records for your domain and one to hold reverse mappings for those hosts. (A *reverse mapping* allows a computer to ask which Internet name goes with an IP address.) Exercise 12.8 shows you how to create these zones.

EXERCISE 12.8

Creating a Primary and a Reverse DNS Zone with the DNS Manager

1. Start the DNS manager.

2. Select New Server from the DNS menu.

3. Enter the host name for the computer that will be the DNS server.

4. Select the server that you have just created. (Click it.)

5. Select New Zone Item from the DNS menu.

6. Select Primary and click Next.

7. Enter the name for your zone (the name for your domain, such as OEADM.ORG) and click Next.

EXERCISE 12.8 (CONTINUED FROM PREVIOUS PAGE)

8. Select your server again.

9. Select New Zone Item from the DNS menu (again).

10. Select Primary and click Next.

11. Type in the IN-ADDR.ARPA name for your zone. For example, if your zone (class C) network address is 192.5.212(.0), then you would type **212.5.192.IN-ADDR.ARPA**; then click Next.

12. Click Finish.

Once you have created zones you can start adding host records. These records map Internet names to IP addresses (such as bob.oeadm.org to 192.5.212.32). You should start with the computer that is hosting the DNS service. Exercise 12.9 shows you how.

EXERCISE 12.9

Adding a Host Record

1. Start the DNS manager.

2. Select New Host from the DNS menu.

3. Enter the host name (but not the network name). For example, if you have a computer with the Internet name of bob.oeadm.org on the zone oeadm.org, you would type in **bob** as the host name.

4. Enter the IP address of the host.

5. Select the Create Associated PTR Record checkbox. (You must have created the reverse mapping in the previous exercise to do this step.)

6. Click OK.

You can, however, do many more things with DNS than just create zones and host records. For example, you can (and should) set up mail records so that Internet mail will be routed to the right computer, and you can set up subnets and other DNS servers that will resolve addresses for portions of your network. DNS is a complex and powerful service. This, information should be enough to get you started.

Internet Security

MILLIONS OF PEOPLE use the Internet every day, and not all of them are nice. Hackers have flocked to the Internet in droves, abandoning their attacks on dial-up mainframes and bulletin board services for the easy pickings on the Internet. The Internet protocols were created without an emphasis on security because the people who created them had no idea they would form the basis of a public global network. Hackers and legitimate security experts (a.k.a. former hackers) have found and exploited numerous holes in TCP/IP and the Internet protocols through which they can access and extract information from Internet servers. They can also propagate insidious software like viruses, worms, and Trojan horses to unsuspecting, innocent victims. The resulting security breaches and data loss, including information sabotage, lost revenue, and loss of competitive information, can cause irreparable harm to businesses.

Increasingly, businesses with an Internet presence are being attacked by hackers with a specific purpose: to find and sell proprietary information. This information makes its way through a seedy chain of don't-ask-don't-tell consulting and contracting arrangements until it winds up in the hands of the competition, who may not even be aware of the illegal methods used to glean the information.

Hackers are even able to attach to your computer when you are browsing the Web through RAS, especially if you have file sharing active. This type of attack is uncommon and unlikely, however, because your TCP/IP address is usually unique every time you attach.

The only way to completely secure your network from attack via the Internet is not to attach it to the Internet. This approach also forces your organization to forgo the myriad of benefits provided by the Internet and keeps your network an information island unto itself. Firewalls are the next most secure method of thwarting attack. Firewalls are security gateways that sit between the Internet and your network. They hide internal IP addresses from exposure to the Internet and filter all the higher-level protocols to ensure they should be passed between the private network and the Internet. Firewalls also filter packets to prevent clients from the Internet from contacting internal servers and can prevent the use of TCP/IP ports other than those specifically enabled—thus allowing only traffic of a certain type, such as HTTP, to pass.

Firewalls must run on machines dedicated to the firewall function—otherwise hackers may be able to exploit bugs in other software applications to bypass the firewall completely. Most firewalls remove all other services running on their host machine. Figure 12.5 shows how firewalls secure private networks while allowing Internet service to continue.

FIGURE 12.5

An Internet firewall protecting a private network.

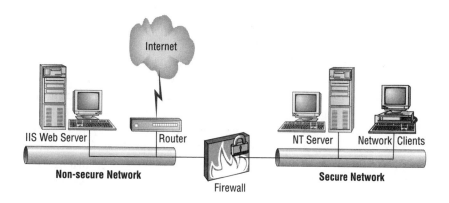

Many large Internet service providers have responded to the security threat on the Internet by providing Internet firewalls on their end of the leased-line connection to the Internet, thus reducing the up-front costs of firewall software and a gateway server. By using your Internet service provider's firewall services and Web-site hosting services, rather than hosting files with an IIS server on your network, you can make your network very secure.

Internet firewalls are very complex. Windows NT Server does not contain firewall software, but a few very strong firewalls do run under Windows NT. However, because the firewall must run on its own machine, you are free to use firewalls running the UNIX operating system even in a Windows NT environment.

Summary

INDOWS NT SERVER 4 includes a variety of server and client tools that enable you to serve information to the Internet, access the Internet as a client, and easily create client/server solutions for your own private network.

Internet protocols like Hypertext Transfer Protocol use the client/server model to distribute information. Servers called Internet hosts accept requests from clients running Web browsers contained in uniform resource locators and return the HTML document requested to the Web browser. The Web browser interprets the HTML commands and presents them graphically to the computer user.

Internet Information Server is the primary tool used in Windows NT Server to provide services to Internet clients. With IIS, you can publish Web pages, create a complete Web site, serve FTP files, and serve Gopher indexes and documents. Windows NT Server also comes with FrontPage to help you create Web pages and Internet Explorer so you can browse them.

Other common Internet utilities such as an FTP client, ping, and tracert are also included with Windows NT Server 4. These utilities are less commonly used but serve important troubleshooting and interoperability needs.

Internet security is a major issue facing companies connecting to the Internet. The best way to balance security with connectivity to the Internet is to use Internet firewalls. Firewalls are security gateways that filter packets, act as proxies to hide internal IP addresses, and filter higher-level Internet protocols to prevent unauthorized access. Some Internet service providers offer firewall services on their end of the connection to reduce the risk of intrusion from the Internet.

Review Questions

1. The Internet and the Web are two names for the same thing.

   A. True

   B. False

2. The Internet is the largest network in the world.

   A. True

   B. False

3. The Internet is run by the U.S. government.

   A. True

   B. False

4. The only difference between an Internet server and an intranet server is where and how they are used.

  A. True

  B. False

5. An intranet is a private network running Internet protocols.

  A. True

  B. False

6. _____ _____ _____ are standards describing the Internet protocols.

7. Internet Information Server is administered using the _____ _____ _____ tool.

8. The World Wide Web is based on which protocol:

  A. HTTP

  B. HTML

  C. FTP

  D. SMTP

  E. PPP

9. You can use the _____ tool to create Web pages for the Internet.

  A. Internet Explorer

  B. Internet Information Server

  C. Domain Name Server

  D. FrontPage

10. The term *host* refers to

  A. A RAS server that hosts dial-up clients

  B. A terminal server that hosts dial-up clients

  C. A file that resolves domain names

  D. An Internet server

  E. A Domain Name Server

11. The traditional operating system of the Internet is

    A. Windows NT Server

    B. UNIX

    C. MacOS running Apple Internet Server

    D. OS/2 Warp Server

    E. NetWare for TCP/IP

12. HTTP stands for

    A. High Speed Text Transfer Protocol

    B. Hierarchical Text Transfer Protocol

    C. Hypertext Transfer Protocol

    D. Host-to-Terminal Text Protocol

    E. None of the above

13. Internet Information Server serves the following Internet protocols (choose all that are correct):

    A. HTTP

    B. SMTP

    C. FTP

    D. Gopher

    E. NNTP

    F. POP

Interoperating
with NetWare

MORE FILE SERVERS run Novell NetWare than run all other server operating systems combined. Consequently, NetWare is both the most important server operating system to be compatible with and the biggest competition for other network operating systems such as Microsoft Windows NT Server 4.

Few network administrators are willing to risk their jobs on a massive upgrade to a new operating system. Even if all the server upgrades go smoothly, installing new client software throughout an organization can take weeks, and months might pass before users are comfortable with the new system. Because lost productivity in some organizations can be tremendously expensive, many simply won't take the risk.

Microsoft wisely decided to avoid the migration problem entirely by making Windows NT interoperate very closely with NetWare. For example:

- Windows NT can act as a NetWare client just like any other operating system, so you can install Windows NT workstations and servers in a NetWare network and gain access to resources stored on NetWare servers.

- Windows NT Server can emulate a NetWare server with inexpensive additional software from Microsoft that allows Windows NT Server to login NetWare clients and trade user account information with NetWare servers.

- Windows NT comes with a tool to migrate shared resources on Net-Ware servers to Windows NT servers automatically.

- Windows NT can act as a gateway to NetWare so that computers not running NetWare client software (called NetWare requesters) can access shared resources on NetWare servers.

Login *is NetWare parlance for the Windows NT term* logon.

These compatibility tools exist both to make your job as a network integrator easier and to smooth the migration from NetWare to Windows NT Server. Microsoft has made that transition as easy as possible. Directories on NetWare servers and directories on Windows NT servers are equally accessible to Windows clients. The screen shot in Figure 13.1 shows a NetWare 4.1 NDS tree as viewed from a Microsoft Windows NT server.

FIGURE 13.1

The NDS tree structure of NetWare 4.1 viewed from a Windows NT server.

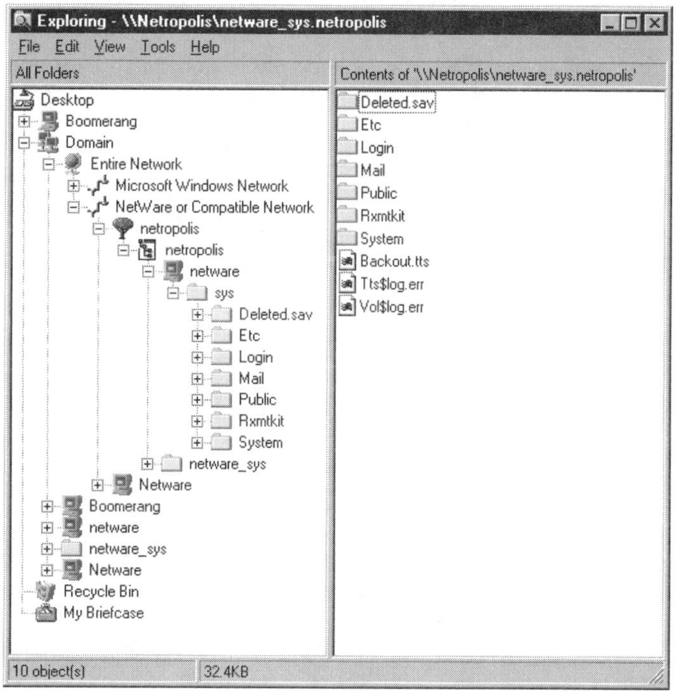

NetWare uses the IPX/SPX transport protocol developed by Novell. Microsoft provides the NWLink transport protocol, an IPX/SPX compatible protocol, to support communication with NetWare clients and servers.

This chapter discusses the following topics:

- The three major phases of migration from NetWare to Windows NT

- The software necessary to implement each migration phase

- How to install Gateway Services for NetWare (GSNW)

- How to attach to NetWare 3.12 and 4.1 servers

- How to provide the gateway to NetWare servers for Microsoft network clients

- How to migrate NetWare servers to Windows NT

The software loaded on client computers to allow them to attach to NetWare servers is called the NetWare requester. The Client for Microsoft Networks software that is built into most versions of Windows (and comes on the Windows NT Server CD-ROM for MS-DOS and early versions of Windows) provides the same function for Windows NT.

12 Steps to Windows NT

MICROSOFT HAS MADE moving from NetWare to Windows NT very easy. The steps outlined here allow you to migrate from NetWare to Windows NT Server painlessly and at your leisure. Here's a preview:

- During step 1 Windows NT servers run in a NetWare environment.

- At the end of step 2, NetWare and Windows NT servers are active on the network.

- At the end of step 4, NetWare servers run in a primarily Microsoft networking environment.

- At the end of step 9, no traces of NetWare remain.

Now for the details of our 12 step plan:

1. Install Windows NT machines running Microsoft Services for NetWare and the NWLink protocol to simulate NetWare servers. This step allows Windows NT servers to interoperate with NetWare servers and clients with no software changes on existing servers or clients.

   or

   Install Windows NT machines with GSNW to provide gateways to NetWare resources for Microsoft network clients. This step allows your clients to access the same NetWare resources when they are migrated individually from the NetWare requester to the Client for Microsoft Networks.

2. Copy NetWare user account information to your Windows NT domain.

3. Create a Distributed File System (DFS) tree to match your NetWare Directory Services (NDS) tree if you are running NetWare 4.1. DFS is discussed in Chapter 10.

4. Add the Microsoft redirector to all clients running Windows, Windows 95, OS/2, and Windows NT. Enable Services for Macintosh for any MacOS computers at your site. Do this step at your leisure because your clients already have access to Windows NT Servers as NetWare clients or through the GSNW gateway.

5. Migrate shared resources on NetWare servers to Windows NT servers using the migration tool or set up your Windows NT servers to act as gateways to NetWare servers. Again, you don't have to rush because your clients can access both systems.

6. Change MS-DOS NetWare clients to Microsoft Windows NT client software. DOS clients are generally too limited to run both the NetWare requester and the Microsoft network client for DOS simultaneously.

7. Remove NetWare client software from client stations. All shared resources are now served by Windows NT machines and gateways.

8. Complete the migration of resources remaining on NetWare servers to NT servers.

9. Configure the Windows NT Server Multi-Protocol Router to replace any NetWare servers acting as routers in your network.

10. Remove Microsoft Services for NetWare and GSNW from NT servers. Clients at this point no longer have any access to NetWare servers. If your organization is part of a larger organization that is still using Net-Ware, you may have to continue to run these servers.

11. Bring down NetWare servers. Install Windows NT Server 4 on these computers or migrate them to client status.

12. Sell your NetWare software to unsuspecting Certified NetWare Engineers.

That's it! You can also easily migrate from NWLink to TCP/IP by adding TCP/IP support, first to servers and then to clients. Then remove NWLink, first from clients and then from servers. NWLink is a faster transport protocol than TCP/IP is, however, so you should consider keeping NWLink as your primary transport, especially if you are using IPX routers in your network.

The Migration tool for NetWare requires two servers—a Windows NT server to receive data from a NetWare server and a NetWare server to send it. At first glance this requirement might suggest that migrating your network will require you to double your current number of servers. However, this assumption isn't accurate. As long as your NetWare servers run hardware compatible with Windows NT (most Pentium-class machines and higher will have no problems), you can simply migrate your servers one at a time. After a NetWare server is migrated to Windows NT, you can install Windows NT on that newly free server and use it as the receiver for the next NetWare server in line. Figure 13.2 shows this process.

Migrate your NetWare users and groups to the Windows NT primary domain controller first. Then migrate files and applications among the various servers in your organization.

FIGURE 13.2

NT migration performed
one server at a time.

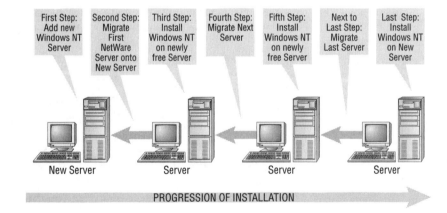

Managers of larger networks may hesitate to switch to Windows NT Server because the directory services in NetWare 4.1 make managing massive networks easier. Have no fear. The Distributed File System (DFS) for Windows (available from Microsoft at `www.microsoft.com`) provides a similar level of domain control by making all domain shared resources—even resources on

Windows 95 clients—visible from a single hierarchical root. This tool enables you, for example, to back up the shared resources of an entire network in a single step, to move large shares between servers transparently, and to browse all domain shared resources easily. Refer to Chapter 10 if you don't know how to use DFS to manage shared resources on larger machines.

NT Servers in NetWare Networks

NETWARE HAS BEEN the top-selling network operating system for more than a decade; millions of NetWare servers and hundreds of thousands of NetWare networks are running in offices around the world. Microsoft is determined to be a part of that huge market. Windows NT servers can participate in NetWare networks in various ways.

Services for NetWare

With the addition of the Microsoft Services for NetWare, which includes the formerly separate products File and Print services for NetWare (FPNW) and Directory Service Manager for NetWare (DSMN), Windows NT servers can share user account information in NetWare NDS networks and can act as NetWare servers to log in users running NetWare client requesters. Services for NetWare is a separate but inexpensive product from Microsoft.

Services for NetWare allows Windows NT servers to exist in NetWare networks without changing anything about the network from the perspective of NetWare. From the perspective of NetWare servers and clients, Windows NT machines running Services for NetWare are simply NetWare servers.

If you aren't going to use the additional features of Windows NT, why not just buy another NetWare server? There are three primary reasons:

- Windows NT is considerably less expensive than NetWare, coming in at about half the price when you include client access licenses for equivalent packages. That's a lot of money in large networks.

- Windows NT is more stable than NetWare networks, especially if servers must run third-party software. NetWare 4.1 does include a level of crash protection, but it is less extensive than Windows NT.

- You can introduce Windows NT servers slowly and then migrate your network quickly once you reach a critical mass of NT servers in the organization.

MS-DOS clients may not have enough available memory to run two requesters because the Microsoft requester for MS-DOS is a memory hog compared to the requester for NetWare. If you have a limited amount of MS-DOS memory and cannot run both requesters, you have two options:

- You can wait until you migrate shared resources to NT servers before switching DOS clients from the NetWare requester to the Microsoft requester.

- You can use the GSNW to serve NetWare files to DOS clients using the Client for Microsoft Networks so those clients don't have to run the NetWare requester.

Strangers in a Strange Land

Windows NT servers can also perform many useful roles in NetWare networks without using Services for NetWare. However, client computers must use the Client for Microsoft Networks for the operating system they are running to attach to a Windows NT server. Client for Microsoft Networks comes with Windows NT, Windows 95, and Windows 3.11 for Workgroups. Each of these operating systems supports being attached to at least two different network types, so operating them with access to both Windows NT and NetWare is easy. The MS-DOS Client for Microsoft Networks is included on the Windows NT Server CD-ROM. However, setting up both the Client for Microsoft Networks and the NetWare requester on the same DOS client is difficult and uses a large portion of the memory available to DOS. See Chapter 15 for more information on supporting clients for Windows NT Server.

Windows NT servers can still perform many functions in NetWare networks even if you don't install the Client for Microsoft Networks on any client computers. For instance, Windows NT servers can act as any of the following:

- RAS servers on a NetWare network. Installing RAS on NT is easier than installing NetWare Connect on NetWare, and RAS is free with the operating system.

- Archive servers. Freeing NetWare servers from the troublesome and crash-prone process of tape backups using third-party NLMs, especially if you want to back up to media such as magneto optical disk. Note that network backups to a Windows NT server cannot include the NetWare Bindery (which serves the same purpose as the security accounts portion of the Registry in Windows NT).

- Application or messaging servers.

- Internet/intranet servers.

None of the preceding uses requires that clients use the Client for Microsoft Networks.

Gateway Services for NetWare (GSNW)

Gateway services for NetWare expands the Client Services for NetWare provided with Windows NT Workstation to implement the service of "re-sharing" NetWare volumes. Basically, you can set up GSNW to provide shared resources from a NetWare server to Windows NT Server clients that are not running the NetWare requester or even an IPX/SPX-compatible protocol. Re-sharing is possible because GSNW acts as an agent for Windows NT Server clients by attaching to a NetWare server as a client and then serving the resources to which it has access. Figure 13.3 shows the GSNW control panel.

The two current versions of NetWare are 3.12 and 4.1. NetWare 3.12 is an older, simpler version suited to small, single-server networks, whereas NetWare 4.1 is designed for large, multiserver networks. The two versions have different requesters, but the 4.1 server can respond to 3.12 clients if bindery emulation is enabled and the client for 4.1 knows how to talk to 3.12 servers.

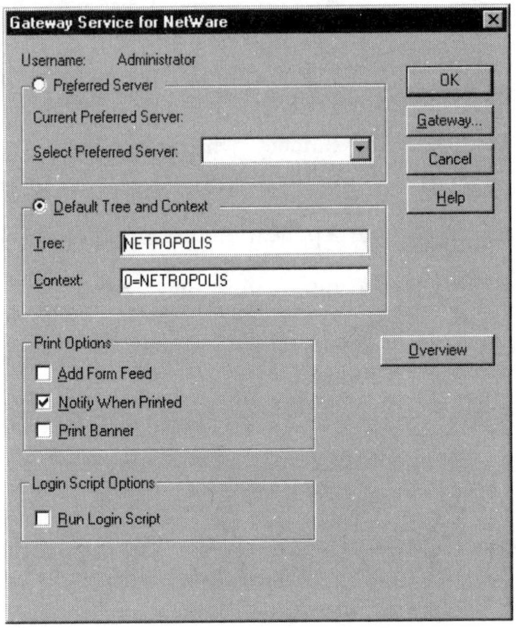

FIGURE 13.3

Gateway Services for
NetWare.

Activating the NetWare Gateway requires five steps:

1. Install GSNW on a Windows NT server.

2. Create a group called NTGATEWAY on the NetWare server or NDS tree that has trustee rights to the resources you want to re-share.

3. Create a user on the NetWare server or NDS tree that is a member of that group. Windows NT will use this account to login to the NetWare server or NetWare tree.

4. Configure GSNW to attach to that preferred server (NetWare 3.1x) or default tree and context (NetWare 4.x).

5. Add the server or tree shared resources to the GSNW service.

Exercise 13.1 shows you how to install the GSNW to allow Windows NT servers to attach to NetWare servers. This exercise assumes that the NWLink transport protocol is already installed on your computer. If it is not, it will be installed during the GSNW installation process.

EXERCISE 13.1

Installing Gateway Services for NetWare

1. Right-click the Network Neighborhood icon on the desktop and select the Properties menu item.

2. Click the Services tab.

3. Click Add.

4. Select Gateway (and Client) Services for NetWare.

5. Click OK.

6. Enter the path to your Windows NT CD-ROM.

7. Click OK. Windows NT will copy the GSNW files.

8. Click Close.

9. Create the NTGATEWAY group and a user that is a member of that group on your NetWare server or tree.

10. Click Yes to restart your computer.

11. Enter the user account you created that is a member of the NTGATEWAY group when your server restarts. GSNW is now operational.

After installing GSNW, Windows NT will be able to attach to NetWare servers as a client and serve NetWare shared resources to clients for Microsoft networks.

NDS trees are roughly analogous to Windows NT domains.

Attaching to a NetWare 4.1 Server as a Client

Attaching to a NetWare 4.1 server is slightly more complex than attaching to a NetWare 3.12 server because of the additional complexity of the NetWare Directory Services implemented in NetWare 4.1. To attach to a NetWare 4.1 server, you must enter the default tree and context where your user account exists. Exercise 13.2 shows you how to attach to a NetWare 4.1 server. Figure 13.4 shows a NetWare server among Windows NT servers in a heterogeneous network environment.

FIGURE 13.4

NetWare and Windows NT servers in the same network.

EXERCISE 13.2

Attaching to a NetWare 4.1 Server

1. Select Start ➤ Settings ➤ Control Panel.

2. Double-click GSNW.

3. Select Default Tree and Context.

4. Enter the tree name of your NetWare 4.1 server in the Tree input box.

5. Enter the context of your user account in the context input box.

6. Click OK.

Attaching to a NetWare 3.12 Server as a Client

Attaching to a NetWare 3.12 server is similar to attaching to a NetWare 4.1 server except that in the former you enter a preferred server rather than a default tree and context. Note that *attaching to* a server is not the same as *logging in*. Windows NT will attempt to log you in when you open a NetWare resource for the first time. If you are not already logged in, Windows NT will open a Login dialog box. Exercise 13.3 shows you how to attach to a NetWare 3.12 server.

EXERCISE 13.3

Attaching to a NetWare 3.12 Server

1. Select Start ➢ Settings ➢ Control Panel.

2. Double-click GSNW.

3. Select Preferred Server.

4. Select the server from the drop-down list or type in the server name if it does not appear in the list.

5. Click OK.

Using NetWare Resources

Attaching to a NetWare resource under Windows NT is exactly the same as attaching to a Windows NT resource except that in the former you browse through NetWare resources using the NetWare or compatible Network rather than the Microsoft Network resource hierarchy. Because the NetWare NDS resource hierarchy is more complex than the Microsoft Network hierarchy, you will have to search through a few more levels.

Exercise 13.4 shows you how to map a NetWare volume as a local drive. Notice the similarity to the process for mapping a regular shared Windows NT volume.

EXERCISE 13.4

Mapping NetWare Resources

1. Double-click Network Neighborhood. If the NetWare server to which you wish to attach appears in the list of servers, skip to step 6.

2. Double-click Entire Network.

3. Double-click NetWare or Compatible Network.

4. Click the tree containing the server to which you are attaching. If the server appears in this list, skip to step 6.

5. Click the context containing the server to which you are attaching.

6. Click the server to which you are attaching.

EXERCISE 13.4 (CONTINUED FROM PREVIOUS PAGE)

7. Right-click the volume you want to map.
8. Select Map Network Volume.
9. Enter a valid NetWare account name in the Connect As input box. (You can skip this step if a user account with the same name and password exists in the NetWare network.) If you are not logged in to the NetWare server, a dialog box may appear asking for your account name and password. Enter them and click OK.

A window will open showing the contents of your newly mapped drive.

Sharing NetWare Files

Windows NT servers can act as a gateway for Microsoft Network clients that need access to resources on NetWare file and print servers. When operating as a NetWare gateway, an NT server attaches to a NetWare server as a client through a single logged in account. It then shares the resources it has access to on the Microsoft network. Figure 13.5 shows the GSNW Gateway configuration panel.

FIGURE 13.5
GSNW Gateway configuration panel.

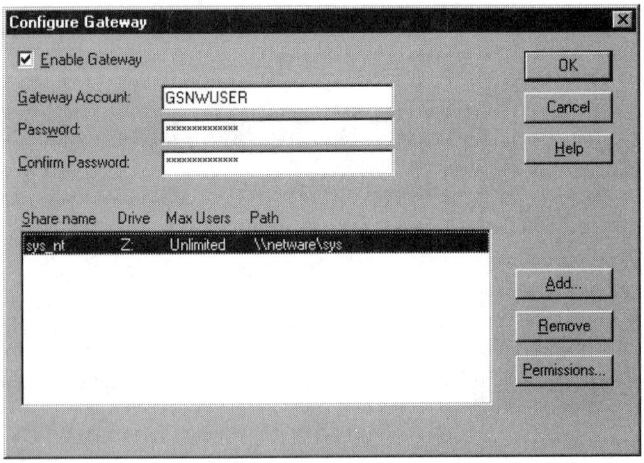

Providing a gateway has five primary advantages over simply using the Client for Microsoft Networks and a NetWare requester on each computer.

- Clients only need to log on to the Microsoft network.

- The gateway counts as only one logged in NetWare user but can share to many users, thus legally expanding access to the NetWare server without additional NetWare client licenses.

- Clients require only one client software package, which saves memory especially in memory-limited MS-DOS systems.

- Reduces administrative burden by eliminating the need to support multiple client requesters.

- Allows you to migrate NetWare clients over to Microsoft network clients gradually without creating two copies of data or worrying about synchronizing files.

Exercise 13.5 shows you how to set up a file share through a Windows NT-to-NetWare gateway. This exercise assumes that you know how to administer your NetWare server to create users and groups and assign trustee rights to directories.

EXERCISE 13.5

Creating a NetWare Gateway Share

1. Create a group called NTGATEWAY on the NetWare file server. On NetWare 3.12 or earlier servers, you will use the SYSCON utility to perform this step. On NetWare 4.0 or later servers, you will use the NWADMIN (Windows) or NETADMIN (DOS) utility.

2. Give the NTGATEWAY group trustee rights to the directory(ies) you wish to share.

3. Create a user for the gateway called GSNWUSER (or any name you want) and make this user a member of the NTGATEWAY group.

4. Attach to the NetWare server as a client as shown in Exercise 13.4 on the Windows NT server that will act as a gateway.

5. Select Start ➢ Settings ➢ Control Panel.

6. Double-click the GSNW control panel.

EXERCISE 13.5 (CONTINUED FROM PREVIOUS PAGE)

7. Click Gateway.

8. Check Enable Gateway.

9. Enter GSNWUSER (or the name of the user you created in step 3) into the Gateway Account input box.

10. Enter the password for the NTGATEWAY user in the Password input box and confirm it in the Confirm Password box.

11. Click Add.

12. Enter a name you will use for the NT share. This name should be somewhat similar to the NetWare directory name.

13. Enter the UNC path to the NetWare directory you wish to share. If you browse to that share using Network Neighborhood, the UNC path will be showing in the title bar.

14. Enter an unused drive letter in the Use Drive pick list.

15. Click OK. The new gateway share appears in the Gateway shares list box.

If you get a warning that a gateway share could not be created, make sure your NetWare server has fewer than the maximum number of users logged in. You may also want to try using an account name that exists on both the NetWare and NT servers with the same password. This technique enables Windows NT to log you in to NetWare resources without asking for an account name or password.

Migrating Clients from NetWare to NT

Performing a large migration is troublesome if you can't convert all your clients at the same time. Typically, you would bring a new server online and connect it to the legacy system as a client, migrate account information, copy shared files to the new system, and begin migrating clients from the old system to the new.

The problem occurs when users attached to the new system make changes to copies of files that users on the old system have also changed, thus creating two versions of the same file. These problems are referred to as *version control* problems, and they are quite common when multiple copies of the same data exist. Figure 13.6 shows a network using two copies of the same files.

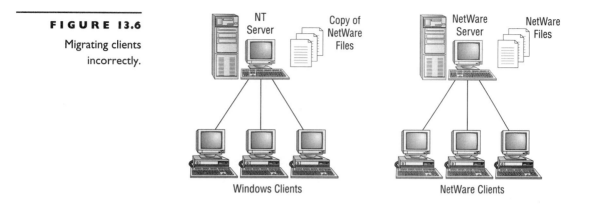

FIGURE 13.6

Migrating clients incorrectly.

Gateway services allows you to use one coherent set of files on the NetWare server during your migration when you will have both Microsoft network and NetWare clients at the same time. You can move the files to the Windows NT server when all the clients have been migrated from NetWare to Windows NT server. Figure 13.7 shows how the gateway service allows two types of clients to use the same files simultaneously.

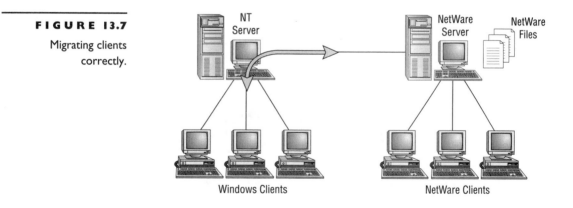

FIGURE 13.7

Migrating clients correctly.

Sharing NetWare Printers

Providing a gateway to NetWare printers (called "print queues" in NetWare terminology) is just as easy as providing a gateway to files, but it's done through the Printers settings rather than through the GSNW control panel. You must configure the gateway as shown in Exercise 13.6 before you can share a NetWare printer queue. Figure 13.8 shows a NetWare print queue being shared by a Windows NT server.

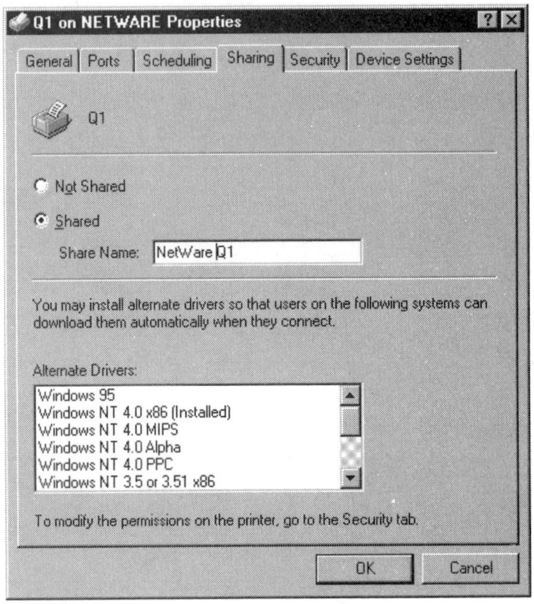

FIGURE 13.8

Sharing a NetWare print queue.

Q1 on NETWARE Properties

General | Ports | Scheduling | Sharing | Security | Device Settings

Q1

○ Not Shared

● Shared

Share Name: NetWare Q1

You may install alternate drivers so that users on the following systems can download them automatically when they connect.

Alternate Drivers:

Windows 95
Windows NT 4.0 x86 (Installed)
Windows NT 4.0 MIPS
Windows NT 4.0 Alpha
Windows NT 4.0 PPC
Windows NT 3.5 or 3.51 x86

To modify the permissions on the printer, go to the Security tab.

OK | Cancel

Once you've enabled the GSNW gateway, you can share a NetWare print queue the same way you would share any local or network printer from the Windows NT printers control panel.

Print queues *is NetWare parlance for the Windows NT term* printers.

EXERCISE 13.6

Gateway Services for NetWare Printers

1. Select Start ➢ Settings ➢ Printers.

2. Double-click Add Printer.

3. Select Network Printer Server.

4. Click Next.

5. Browse the Share Printers list box and double-click the NetWare printer you want to service.

6. Click Yes to install a print driver if Windows NT tells you that the server on which the printer resides does not have a suitable print driver installed. Select the driver from the list as shown in Chapter 14.

7. Select No when asked if you want to make this printer your default printer.

8. Click Next.

9. Click Finish.

10. Right-click the printer you wish to share.

11. Click the Sharing tab.

12. Click Shared.

13. Click OK to accept the default share name, which is equal to the NetWare queue name.

When the Gateway Service for NetWare shares a NetWare printer, it treats that printer as a normal network printer. The printer management when printing through the gateway occurs on the NT Server, not on the NetWare server. The NetWare server still controls the use of a NetWare client's printer.

Moving from NetWare

ONCE YOU HAVE a few Windows NT servers running in your NetWare network, you can add client services for Microsoft networks to a few of your power user's Windows installations and promise them "their own server" to play with for a while. Create shares (which will not be visible to NetWare clients) for these users as an incentive to begin using the new server. Once a few of your users become familiar with the differences between NetWare and Windows NT Server from the client perspective, you'll know exactly how to tackle adding the client software for Windows, OS/2, and Macintosh users in the rest of your organization.

Macintosh users will be early adopters of Windows NT in your organization because Windows NT Macintosh services are far superior to those provided by NetWare. Unlike NetWare, Windows NT comes with software that emulates an Appleshare server (the previous competitor Windows NT decided to take out) so perfectly that no client software is required for Macintoshes. Apple Computers builds client access software into Macintoshes. Therefore, you can set up a Windows NT server with services for Macintosh and it will automatically be available to Macintosh users without installing software on the client side.

Migration Tool for NetWare

When all your users are running clients for Microsoft networks and no longer logging into NetWare servers, or if you are brave and simply want to migrate everything in a weekend, you're ready to perform the final step: migrating a server from NetWare to Windows NT. The migration process requires two servers: the destination Windows NT server and the source NetWare server. You will perform the migration with the Migration Tool for NetWare that is installed automatically when you install GSNW. Figure 13.9 shows the Migration Tool for NetWare.

FIGURE 13.9

The Migration Tool for NetWare.

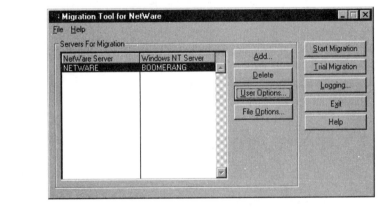

Windows NT can't migrate passwords from the NetWare server, so you'll have to set a password for them before the migration. Users can then change their password when they log on to the network for the first time.

Most options in the User Options dialog box are rather obvious and don't merit further discussion. The Use Supervisor Defaults option under the Defaults tab is strangely named, however, and does not seem to indicate its true purpose. If this option is selected, it migrates the account policy from NetWare. Account policy determines such settings as password length and expiration. If you clear this option, account policies will not be transferred from NetWare. NT Domain account policy defaults will be used instead. Figure 13.10 shows the Migration Tool Defaults tab under User and Group Options.

FIGURE 13.10

The Migration Tool
Defaults tab.

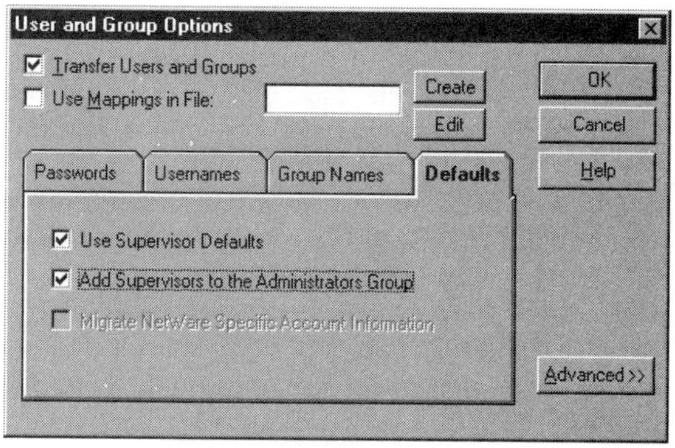

Exercise 13.7 shows you how to migrate a NetWare server to Windows NT server. Figure 13.11 shows a NetWare migration in progress.

FIGURE 13.11

Migrating from NetWare.

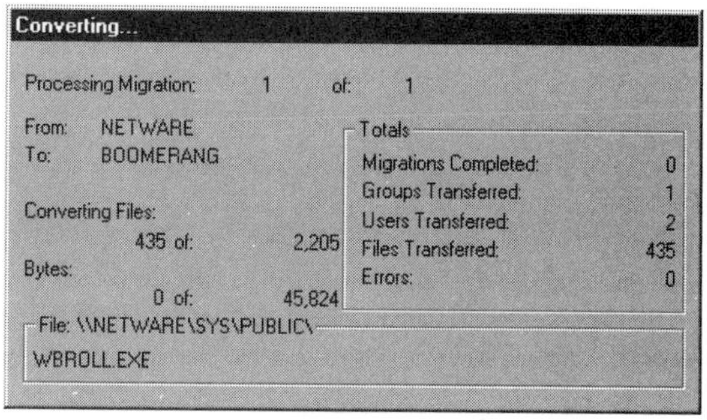

EXERCISE 13.7

Migrating a NetWare Server to Windows NT Server

1. Select Start ➢ Programs ➢ Administrative Tools ➢ Migration Tool for NetWare.

2. Click the ... button next to the From NetWare Server input box to select the source NetWare server.

3. Select the name of the server you wish to migrate from in the server selection list.

4. Click the ... button next to the To Windows NT Server input line.

5. Browse the network list and select the Windows NT Server you will be migrating to.

6. Click OK.

7. Enter the administrative username and password for the NetWare server if necessary.

8. Click User Options.

9. Check Transfer Users and Groups.

10. Select Passwords Tab.

11. Select the Password is Username option.

12. Select the Usernames tab.

13. Select Add Prefix.

14. Type **nw_** in the Add prefix input box.

15. Select the Group Names tab.

16. Select Add Prefix.

17. Type **nw_** in the Add prefix input box.

18. Check Add Supervisors to the Administrators Group.

19. Select the Defaults tab.

20. Uncheck the Use Supervisor Defaults checkbox.

21. Click OK.

22. Click File Options.

23. Click Modify.

24. Check the volumes and subdirectories you wish to migrate. Consider not migrating (unchecking) the SYS:ETC, SYS:LOGIN, SYS:MAIL, SYS:PUBLIC, SYS:SYSTEM directories, as they contain NetWare-specific software that will not be necessary in Windows NT.

25. Click OK.

26. Click OK.

27. Click Trial Migration. This option goes through the migration without creating files to verify that no gnarly errors occur. You can also make certain that you have enough space on the destination server to hold the migrated files. Trial migrations do not take very much time, so you should always perform a trial migration before an actual migration.

EXERCISE 13.7 (CONTINUED FROM PREVIOUS PAGE)

28. Click View Log Files.

29. Select the Summary.LOG.

30. Scroll down to the Bytes Transferred entry and verify that your destination server has room for the migration.

31. Close the Log Viewer application.

32. Click OK.

33. Click Start Migration. Go to lunch now because this procedure will take some time.

34. Click OK when the migration process completes. Close the Migration Tool.

After migrating the share, you can simply remove the gateway share and replace it with a Windows NT share of the same name. This step saves your users the trouble of having to map a new network drive when they can no longer access the NetWare server. You can take this shortcut because, unlike users and directory security assignments, directory share paths do not have unique security identifiers. Exercise 13.8 shows you how to make a Windows NT share look just like a previous gateway share.

EXERCISE 13.8

Changing a Gateway Share to a Migrated Share

1. Select Start ➢ Settings ➢ Control Panel.

2. Double-click the GSNW control panel.

3. Click Gateway.

4. Select the gateway share you just migrated.

5. Click Remove.

6. Click OK.

7. Close the GSNW control panel. You have disallowed access to the share on the NetWare file server.

8. Right-click the directory to which you migrated the NetWare file server. You may have to browse to it with the Explorer.

9. Select Sharing.

10. Click Shared As.

11. Enter the share name used formerly by the gateway share in the Share Name directory.

12. Click OK. Your users will now be able to access the files moved to your NT server just as they did when it was a gateway share. They will not notice that the NetWare server is no longer available.

A NetWare migration will create a serious load on your network. You should not attempt this process while other users are accessing the same network segment. Consider starting the migration as you leave work for the evening and letting it run overnight.

When you finish migrating all your gateway shares to Windows NT servers, you are ready to pull the plug on your NetWare server. Before doing so, remember to test access from your clients to make certain that no problems occur and that all the necessary files have been transferred. Then shut down your NetWare server, insert the Windows NT Setup Boot disk, and boot it.

Summary

WINDOWS NT COMES with a variety of tools to support interoperating with NetWare. Windows NT Server can act as a client in NetWare networks, and can share NetWare resources with Microsoft network clients. With additional software, Windows NT can emulate a NetWare server completely to provide seamless integration in networks in which NetWare is installed on most clients.

GSNW provides all the services of Windows NT Workstation's CSNW and can also share file and print resources on NetWare servers with Microsoft network clients. This functionality allows you to migrate clients slowly without worrying about version control problems inherent in most migrations in which servers cannot be cut over to the new operating system immediately.

Windows NT Server also includes a Migration Tool for NetWare that makes moving shared resources with security settings and account objects such as Users, Groups, and certain policies to Windows NT networks easier. After migration, a Windows NT server will be able to serve the same files to the same users with the same level of security as the NetWare server served.

These tools make migrating from NetWare to Windows NT seamless and hassle free. They allow network administrators to operate with both NetWare and Windows NT at the same time and to move clients from one operating system to the other as needed.

Review Questions

1. Microsoft Windows NT Server has the largest installed base of servers of any network operating system software.

A. True

B. False

2. Windows NT is more expensive than NetWare.

A. True

B. False

3. Microsoft Windows NT comes with software to make it look like a NetWare server.

A. True

B. False

4. If you use a Windows NT server running GSNW to provide access to NetWare resources to Microsoft network clients, you must have as many client access licenses for Windows NT Server as you have Microsoft clients simultaneously accessing the NetWare resources.

A. True

B. False

5. NetWare 4.1 provides a higher level of crash protection than Windows NT.

  A. True

  B. False

6. If you use a Windows NT server running GSNW to provide access to NetWare resources for Microsoft network clients, you must have as many client access licenses for NetWare as you have Microsoft clients simultaneously accessing the NetWare resources.

  A. True

  B. False

7. The Client for Microsoft Networks is built into all versions of Windows since 3.11 for Workgroups.

  A. True

  B. False

8. Without GSNW or Services for NetWare, Windows NT servers would be useless in a NetWare network.

  A. True

  B. False

9. GSNW must be enabled before you can share NetWare print queues.

  A. True

  B. False

10. You can't use the same share name to refer to a Windows NT server share that used to be a gateway share because the security identifiers (SID) for the share name won't match.

  A. True

  B. False

11. GSNW provides all the functions of the CSNW included in Windows NT Workstation.

    A. True

    B. False

12. Although Windows NT can attach to NetWare 4.1 servers, it cannot browse the NDS tree structure.

    A. True

    B. False

13. The _____ _____ _____ service can make Windows NT computers act just like NetWare file servers.

14. The NetWare _____ performs the same function as the Client for Microsoft Networks.

15. Services for NetWare includes which of these formerly separate products (choose two):

    A. File and Print services for NetWare (FPNW)

    B. Directory Services Manager for NetWare (DSMN)

    C. Gateway Service for NetWare (GSNW)

    D. NetWare Directory Services (NDS)

    E. Distributed File System (DFS)

16. GSNW provides which of the following functions (choose two):

    A. Makes Windows NT look like a NetWare server to clients running the NetWare Requester

    B. Allows Windows NT server to attach as a client to NetWare servers

    C. Allows Windows NT servers to trade user account information with NetWare servers

    D. Allows Windows NT servers to request NetWare files and serve them to clients for Microsoft networks

17. Services for NetWare provides which of the following functions (choose two):

   A. Makes Windows NT look like a NetWare server to clients running the NetWare requester

   B. Allows Windows NT server to attach as a client to NetWare servers

   C. Allows Windows NT servers to trade user account information with NetWare servers

   D. Allows Windows NT servers to request NetWare files and serve them to clients for Microsoft networks

Printing

WINDOWS NT SERVER gives you flexible and powerful printing support. You can attach printers directly to your server computer, or you can print to printers over the network. Windows NT supports many different types of printers from many different printer manufacturers. Some of the features of Windows NT printing are local and remote printing, print spooling with print job monitoring and forwarding, printer security, and foreign client support for operating systems such as Macintosh and UNIX.

This chapter introduces the basic concepts of local and network printing; describes the Windows NT print model; shows you how to use the print manager and how to set up printers; guides you through the process of connecting to remote, foreign, and network printers; discusses printer pools; and shows you how to troubleshoot common printer problems.

Introduction to Printing

MANY COMPANIES MANUFACTURE printers, and each manufacturer makes printers that are a little different from all the others. There are many ways of making marks on paper, which is, after all, what printers do. Some manufacturers introduce new technology to increase the resolution, color capacity, or pages per minute of their printers. Other manufacturers wait a while to see which technologies will be prove to be popular and then implement the features that are most cost effective in their niche of the printer market. The result is that almost any printing technology is implemented on some manufacturer's printer.

Every operating system's printing system has three components:

- The printing devices themselves and how they are attached to the computers

- The printing software that translates print requests from application software into a form the printing devices will understand

- The way the operating system accomplishes printing over networks.

A very cost-effective approach in a network environment is to attach a printer to the file server, rather than to give each user his or her own printer. If many users on the network do a lot of printing, you can attach several printers to your file server or dedicate a computer to be a print server.

Windows NT supports printing over a network, which means some parts of the printing process may occur on a computer other than the one that submits the print job (i.e., the one running the application from which the user selects Print).

Before explaining how Windows NT prints documents, we need to define a some terms and introduce a few concepts that pertain to the following topics:

- Printing devices

- Printing software

- Printing and networks

Printing Devices

The *printing devices* are the physical parts of the printing system, the components that make the black or colored marks on the paper. These units are commonly called *printers,* but in Windows NT terminology they are called *printing devices* because application software never directly communicates with a printing device. The "printer" that a Windows application sees is a software construct that translates print requests and forwards the resulting print job to the appropriate printing device.

A printing device is usually connected to a computer via a serial or parallel cable, but printing devices can be connected to computers in other ways, such as directly via the computer's expansion bus or through a SCSI interface. Sometimes printers are connected directly to a network without an intervening general-purpose computer.

Some printing devices do not print directly to paper. For instance, a Post-Script slide maker prints directly to 35mm slides for use in presentations. A fax modem, connected via a serial cable or installed in an expansion slot in your computer, can be configured as a printer, making it possible for you to print directly from your word processor or other application to a fax machine anywhere in the world. If the device you are "printing to" is actually a fax modem, the document may never be printed. Figure 14.1 illustrates several printing devices.

FIGURE 14.1

Laser printers, ink-jet printers, fax modems, slide makers, and plotters are all printing devices.

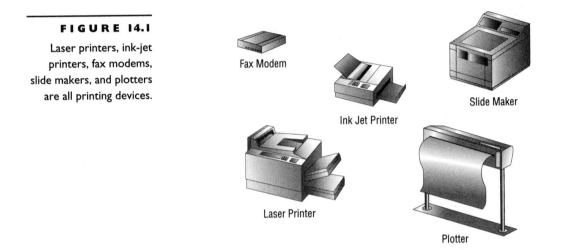

Fax Modem

Slide Maker

Ink Jet Printer

Laser Printer

Plotter

Printing Software

You cannot expect your word processor or spreadsheet to understand the printing languages and features of every printing device you can attach to your computer. The variety of printing devices and printing languages is too great, and if the applications contained routines for accessing printing devices, then you would have to update your applications whenever you attached a new printer with new options to your computer. This method was how applications and printers worked in early operating systems such as MS-DOS.

Windows NT, like many other modern operating systems, frees the application from the requirement of having to speak the printer's native printing language. A middle layer of software between the printing device and the application software converts the application's print requests into a form that the user's printer can understand. This middle layer in Windows NT is the set of software components described in the "NT Print Model" section later in this chapter.

The *printer,* in Windows NT terminology, is a software component, not the physical device that produces documents on paper. When you select a printer from within an application, you are selecting the software component that will translate the application's print requests into a form that the printing device can understand. If your printing device is versatile, you might have several printer software components for one device, one for each mode of printing that the device supports. For instance, if you have a printer that supports both the HPGL/2 printing language and the PostScript printing language, you might have two printer icons and two printer options within your application but only one physical printer. Or if you have two identical printers, you might have just one printer (software component) that operates both of the printing devices; whichever one is free prints the current document.

When one printer services more than one printing device, the printing devices form a *printer pool*. All the printing devices in the printer pool must be of the same type, and the printer will assign documents to be printed to whichever printing device is free in the printer pool.

Some network operating systems (NetWare, for example) use the term queue *to refer to what Windows NT calls printers.*

Figure 14.2 shows the relationship between applications, printers, and printing devices.

FIGURE 14.2

A printing device may be associated with more than one printer (application visible software component), and a printer may be associated with more than one printing device.

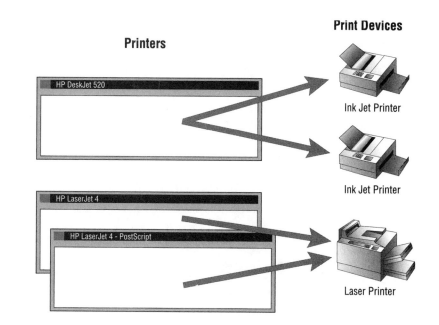

Print Devices

Printers

HP DeskJet 520

Ink Jet Printer

Ink Jet Printer

HP LaserJet 4

HP LaserJet 4 - PostScript

Laser Printer

Printing and Networks

One of the most common network functions is printer sharing. In the Windows NT print model, an application program doesn't care whether a printing device is connected directly to the computer the application is running on or resides elsewhere on the network.

If the printing device is attached to another computer over the network, the networking software redirects the print request to the computer to which the printing device is attached. That computer presents the print request to the printing device.

One computer can provide printing services for many different types of computers. For instance, Windows NT Server can provide printing services for Windows, UNIX, Apple Macintosh, and MS-DOS computers.

NT Print Model

WINDOWS NT HAS a modular print architecture. Each portion of the Windows NT printing system has a specific purpose and well-defined interfaces to other components of the system. The modular architecture makes Windows NT printing flexible; different versions of the modules can be installed for different purposes, and only the versions of the modules that are needed must be loaded. The software and hardware components that make up the print model are as follows:

- Graphics Device Interface (GDI)

- Print driver

- Print router

- Print provider (spooler)

- Print processor

- Print monitor

- Network printing devices

Figure 14.3 illustrates the Windows NT print model.

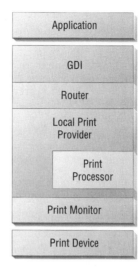

FIGURE 14.3

Software components in the Windows NT print model cooperate to provide a sophisticated and powerful printing system.

Graphics Device Interface (GDI)

The Graphics Device Interface (GDI) provides Windows programs with a single unified system for presenting graphical information to the user. Therefore, the program can ignore the specific details of a device's resolution, color depth, coordinate system, bits per pixel, available fonts, and so on. The GDI translates the application's generic print requests into device driver requests that are specific to the printing characteristics of that device.

The GDI does not make a special case of either drawing on the screen or printing to a printer; both are merely graphical devices that vary somewhat in characteristics. The screen, for instance, is usually a much lower-resolution printing device than a printer is, but the screen usually supports many more colors.

The GDI translates application print requests and into Device Driver Interface (DDI) calls. DDI calls are specific to the drawing characteristics of a printer, but they are not specific to an individual printing device.

When an application prints a document using the GDI interface and the device driver for the printer, the GDI and device driver produce a file called a print job. The *print job* contains one of the following:

- **A raw print job:** the sequence of instructions for the printer that will produce the printed document

- **A journal file print job:** a list of the DDI calls that would produce a raw print job

The GDI produces a journal file print job when the printing device is local (directly connected to the computer instead of over the network). The GDI produces a journal file more quickly than it produces a raw print job, which means that the GDI can return control to the application more quickly. The DDI calls stored in the print job must still be performed in order for the document to be printed. However, the print processor performs each DDI call in order, in the background, producing the raw print job that will be sent to the printing device.

Print Driver

The print driver is the software component that translates the printer-generic DDI calls into the printer-specific commands that are passed to the actual printer. You must have a print driver for the type of printer your server is connected to when you print. The print driver may be downloaded from a remote print server automatically. The printer manufacturer usually supplies the printer driver software.

The printer driver consists of three parts:

- **Printer Graphics Driver** does the actual DDI-to-printer-language conversion. Windows NT includes three printer graphics drivers: `PSCRIPT.DLL` (for PostScript printers), `RASDD.DLL` (for raster-based printers), and `PLOTTER.DLL` (for HPGL/2-based printers).

- **Printer Interface Driver** provides the user interface in Print Manager in which you configure the printer. The printer interface for the above mentioned printer graphics drivers are `PSCRIPTUI.DLL`, `RASDDUI.DLL`, and `PLOTUI.DLL`.

- **Characterization Data File or Mini-driver** isolates the make- and model-specific characteristics of a printer for the printer graphics driver.

Some printer manufacturers supply all three components of the printer driver. However, the only part that the manufacturer needs to provide is a mini-driver for one of the three Microsoft-supplied printer graphics and printer interface drivers.

Print Router

The print router directs the print job to the appropriate print provider. The router can also download a printer driver for the printer if the printer is on a remote computer and the remote computer is configured to provide a printer driver for the type of computer on which the router is running.

Print Provider (Spooler)

Each printing device configured for use in your Windows NT Server has a print provider. A print provider may accept print jobs from the router for a local printer, or it may accept print jobs to be printed on a remote printer. An application sees this printer when it prints.

A print provider for a local printer accepts print jobs from the router, calls the print processor to perform any final modifications to the print jobs, and then transfers the jobs one by one to the print monitor. Print providers can accept print jobs while a print job is printing. Print jobs that are waiting to be printed are stored in memory or on disk as spool files.

The print provider also adds separator pages to print jobs if the user has requested them in the Print Manager.

A print provider for remote printers locates the network print server that is the destination of the print job and transfers the print job to that print server. Remote print providers do not spool the print job—they transfer the print job to the destination, where it may be spooled.

Do not confuse a remote print provider with a remote printer. The remote print provider is the printer on the client, which transfers the print job to the remote printer on the print server, which spools the job to the print device.

Print Processor

The print processor performs any modifications to the print job before passing the print job to the print monitor. Windows NT supplies two print processors: the Windows print processor and the Macintosh print processor.

In the Windows print processor, if the print job is a journal file, the print processor creates the raw type of print job by performing each of the DDI print driver calls.

The print processor may perform print processing on two types of raw print jobs: Raw FF Auto or Raw FF Appended.

- In Raw FF Auto jobs, the print processor always appends a form feed to the print job, which causes the printer to eject the printed page.

- In Raw FF Appended jobs, the print processor appends a form feed if one is not already present.

These two options are useful for older programs that send ASCII text to the printer, never or seldom appending a form-feed character.

The print processor does not process a normal raw print job (the kind of print job produced by Windows programs when they do not produce journal files).

The Windows print processor handles all print jobs from Macintosh computers to PostScript printers attached to a Windows NT computer and from UNIX, Windows 95, older versions of Windows, and DOS.

The Macintosh print processor processes print jobs that a Macintosh computer sends to a non-PostScript printer connected to a Windows NT computer. The Macintosh print processor interprets the PostScript language in the Macintosh PostScript print job and prepares a raw print job for non-PostScript printers.

Print Monitor

The print monitor is the software component that transmits the print job (by now transformed into the language of the printer) to the printing device. Windows NT supplies several print monitors, the most important of which are `LOCALMON.DLL`, `HPMON.DLL`, and `LPRMON.DLL`.

- The local print monitor communicates with the printing device through serial and parallel ports, remote print shares, and Named Pipes and can store the print job in a file instead of sending it to a printer.

- The HP print monitor sends the print jobs to an HP printer that is connected directly to the network instead of attached through a computer.

- The LPR (which stands for Line Printer, a type of printer that early UNIX computers often used) print monitor sends the print job to a UNIX LPD (Line Printer Daemon) print server.

The print monitor can also report the condition of the printing device (busy, offline, ready, out of paper or toner, etc.), detect printing errors, and restart a print job if necessary.

Network Print Devices

Network print devices are print devices that are connected directly to your network cable through a special-purpose adapter, rather than being connected to a computer (such as a server or workstation) on the network.

Two common types of network print devices are HP printers with Jet Direct network interface adapters and devices confusingly called network print servers. They usually implement an LPD interface and allow you to connect almost any print device to them.

Remember: Even though HP thinks it makes printers, in Microsoft's lexicon HP makes print devices.

Most HP network print devices support the LPR protocol as well as the DLC protocol. See the section "Creating an LPR Printer" for instructions on how to attach to an LPR print server.

Network print servers allow you to attach a print device to the network. Print servers are computers that accept print requests from other computers over the network. A print server in an NT network accepts print requests from other computers over the network and may send the resulting print jobs over the network to a physical network print server.

Local Printers

ROM THE SERVER'S point of view, any printer directly attached to the server computer is a local printer. A printer attached to a computer elsewhere on the network (such as on another server or on an NT Workstation computer or a Windows 95 computer) is a remote printer. A print device that is attached directly to the network through a special purpose adapter is a network print device.

From the server's point of view, a print device directly attached to the server is a local printer. However, from a client computer's point of view (such as that of a Windows 95 or a Windows NT Workstation computer elsewhere on the network), that very same print device is a remote printer. Whether a print device is a local printer or a remote printer therefore depends on your point of view—if it is directly connected to the computer you are at, then it is a local printer; otherwise, it is a remote printer.

Creating, configuring, and managing printers is a simple process in Windows NT. You can also perform most printer management functions over the network. This section explains how to create, configure, and manage a *printer* (i.e., a software construct that controls a print device).

Creating a Local Printer

Before you can use a print device that is directly attached to your computer, you must create a printer within the Printers control panel program. Exercise 14.1 outlines the steps for creating a local printer.

Creating a printer installs the printer driver for the printer and configures Windows NT applications and the Windows NT operating system to be able to print to the printer.

When you create the printer, you can also select printer drivers for other operating systems to be downloaded when the printer is installed on client computers that will be attaching to your shared printer. By including these printer drivers when you create the printer, clients won't have to keep their OS installation CD-ROMs around just because they've attached to your printer.

EXERCISE 14.1

Creating a Local Printer

1. Log on as an administrator.

2. Select Start ➤ Settings ➤ Printers to display the Printers window (see Figure 14.4).

3. Open the Add Printer icon by double-clicking it. This step starts the Add Printer Wizard.

4. Make sure that the My Computer option is checked.

5. Click the Next button at the bottom of the window. The Add Printer Wizard window shows you a list of available ports (see Figure 14.5).

6. Select the port that the printer is attached to (a parallel printer will most likely be attached to LPT1:) and then click the Next button at the bottom of the window.

7. Select the manufacturer of your printer from the first list and then select your printer model from the other list. Click Next.

8. Enter a name for the printer. If you wish this printer to be the default printer for use with Windows programs, select the Yes option; otherwise, select No. Click Next when you are ready to continue.

9. Select the Shared option and enter a name by which the printer will be recognized on the network if you wish to allow other computers on the network to print to this printer. Hold down Ctrl and click on any other operating systems you wish to support for this shared printer. Click Next to continue (see Figure 14.6).

EXERCISE 14.1 (CONTINUED FROM PREVIOUS PAGE)

10. The Add Printer Wizard window will allow you to print a test page.
11. Select Yes to print a test page and then click Finish.
12. Insert the operating system installation media (the Windows NT CD-ROM) if you are asked to do so. Follow the instructions in the dialog boxes so Windows NT can load the drivers it needs to control the printer.
13. Notice that a new icon appears in the Printer window. In addition, the Properties window for the icon will open for you to configure the printer you have just installed.
14. Click OK to close the window.

FIGURE 14.4

The Printers window shows you the printers you have configured in your server.

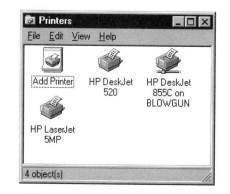

FIGURE 14.5

You can select one or more local ports for the printer to send documents to. If you select more than one, the printing devices on each port must be of the same type.

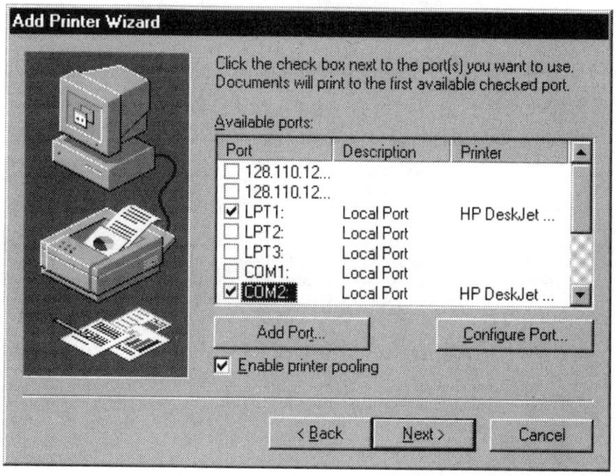

Creating an LPR Printer

When you connect to a network print device using the LPR protocol, you must take several additional steps between steps 5 and 6 in Exercise 14.1. These steps create a local printer port that corresponds to the network print device. After that port is created, you can select it (step 6) and continue with the printer creation.

To create an LPR printer, you must install the Microsoft TCP/IP Printing service in the Networking control panel. When you subsequently create the printer, the Add Port button will display another type of port called an LPR port. You can select the LPR port, give the TCP/IP address of the LPR printer, and then continue with the process of creating a printer.

Exercise 14.2 shows you how to install Microsoft TCP/IP printing (a) and create a port corresponding to an LPR printer (b).

Local Printer Configuration

Once you have created a printer you should configure that printer for the way you will use it on your network. You can set such options as whether or not it will print a cover page on each document (and what will be on that page), which ports the print devices are connected to (you will learn how to have a single printer process jobs for more than one print device in a pool later in this chapter), how the printer is scheduled and shared on the network, and who may use the printer.

EXERCISE 14.2

(a) Installing Microsoft TCP/IP Printing

1. Select Start ➤ Settings ➤ Control Panel.

2. Open the Network icon.

3. Select the Services tab.

4. Click the Add button.

5. Select Microsoft TCP/IP Printing and click OK.

6. Enter the location of the Windows NT Server CD-ROM files and click OK.

7. Click Close. You will have to restart your computer in order for the changes to take effect. Click Yes to do so.

(b) Creating an LPR Port

1. Perform steps 1 through 5 in Exercise 14.1. Select Add Port in the Ports tab.

2. Select LPR Port and then click the New Port button.

3. Enter the IP name or IP address of the LPR network print device.

4. Enter the name of the network print device and click OK.

5. Click Close in the Ports tab. The LPR print device will now appear as a selectable port from the Ports tab.

6. Resume Exercise 14.1 at step 6.

You configure the printer from the Properties window for that printer, which you can reach from the Printers window. (Right-click the Printer icon and then select Properties or click the Printer icon once to select it, select the File menu option in the Printers window, and then select Properties.)

The Printer Properties window has six tabs across the top, and each tab allows you to modify one aspect of the printer's operation. The tabs are

- General

- Ports

- Scheduling

- Sharing

- Security

- Device Settings

General

From this tab you can enter a comment about the printer, describe the location of the printer, and select the print driver for the printer (see Figure 14.7). Across the bottom are three buttons:

- **Separator Page:** This button allows you to place a separator page between each document printed on the printer. Exercise 14.3 outlines the steps of selecting a separator page for a printer.

- **Print Processor:** This button allows you to select a print processor for this printer. When a printer has a print processor, it can accept print jobs from other operating systems such as UNIX or Macintosh. (Refer to the section on Windows NT printing architecture earlier in this chapter.)

- **Print Test Page:** This button prints a test page so that you can be sure the settings for the printer are correct.

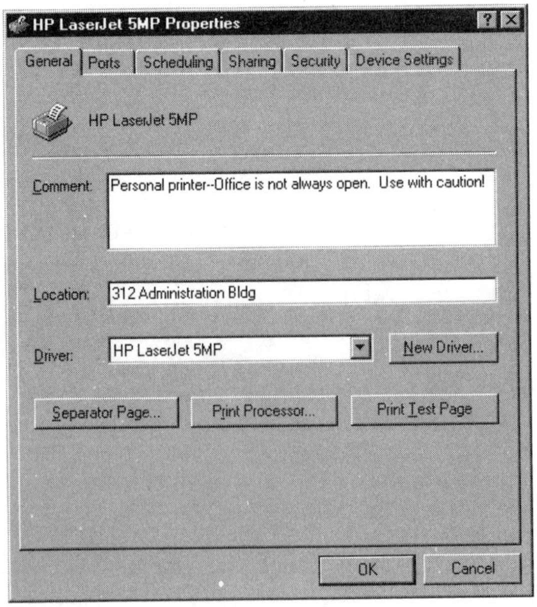

FIGURE 14.7

The Properties window for your printer has six tabs. The general tab allows you to describe the printer to network users, print a test page, and set the separator page and print processor options.

EXERCISE 14.3

Selecting a Separator Page

1. Select Start ➤ Settings ➤ Printers.

2. Select the printer from the Printers window (click the printer one time).

3. Select File ➤ Properties from the Printers window.

4. Make sure that the General tab is selected and then click the Separator Page button.

5. Click Browse.

6. Select the file `sysprint.sep` and then click Open.

7. Click OK.

8. Click OK to close the Properties window.

Ports

The Ports tab shows you a list of ports that this printer selection can print to. If you can have more than one printing device attached to your computer, configure this printer selection to print to whichever is not busy. Several printing devices that work together are called a *print pool*. All printers in a print pool must be the same type.

Print pools are an important part of the Windows NT printing architecture and are useful for solving many printer congestion problems on a network. See the section "Print Pools" later in this chapter for a closer look at print pools.

The buttons at the bottom of the window allow you to add, delete, and configure ports. You can also enable bidirectional printing if your printer supports it.

You can redirect the output of the printer to a file, which you might do if you needed a file containing the printing-device specific commands, for example, to send output for printing on a large or high-resolution printing device.

Exercise 14.4 shows you how to redirect printer output to a file.

EXERCISE 14.4

Redirecting Printer Output to a File

1. Select Start ➢ Settings ➢ Printers.

2. Select the printer from the Printers window (click the printer one time).

3. Select File ➢ Properties from the Printers window.

4. Select the Ports tab.

5. Remove the check mark from the currently checked ports.

6. Click Add Port and then select Local Port from the Printer Ports window.

7. Click the OK button at the bottom of the window. In the Port Name window, enter the path and filename that this printer will print to. Click OK and then click Close. The name you entered will appear in the Ports list.

8. Click the checkbox for that entry to enable printing to the file.

9. Click the OK button at the bottom of the window.

Scheduling

The Scheduling tab (see Figure 14.8) controls the availability of the printer and how print jobs are presented to the printer. You can set the printer to be always available or to be available for certain hours of the day. If you limit the availability of the printer, you must enter the start time and stop time of the printer's operation. Exercise 14.5 shows you how to limit the hours of operation of a printer.

EXERCISE 14.5

Limit the Hours of Operation of a Printer

1. Start ➢ Settings ➢ Printers.

2. Select the printer from the Printers window.

3. Select File ➢ Properties from the Printers window.

4. Select the Scheduling tab.

5. Go to the top of the window. After Available: select the From: option. Enter the start time (9:00 AM, for example) and the end time (5:00 PM).

6. Click the OK button at the bottom of the screen.

You can set the priority of print jobs from this printer (represented by an icon) in the Priority section of the window. If you have created more than one printer icon for one printing device, and therefore more than one logical printer, the print jobs from the printer with the highest priority print first. The priority for this printer can be set to any number from 1 to 99.

The Spooling Options in the middle of the window allow you to set the printer either not to spool, which pauses the printing program until the print monitor can accept the print job, or to spool the jobs to disk, which stores jobs on the hard disk until the print monitor is ready to accept them. If you enable spooling, you can set the spooler either to begin sending the print job to the print monitor immediately or to send the print job when the whole job has been received by the spooler. The three checkboxes at the bottom of the window allow you to hold mismatched jobs in the spooler, which checks to ensure that the type of print job matches the type of printer and holds the mismatched documents, or to print spooled jobs first, which gives documents that have been spooled to disk priority, or to keep documents after they have been printed, which you might enable if you needed an electronic copy of every document printed on a printer.

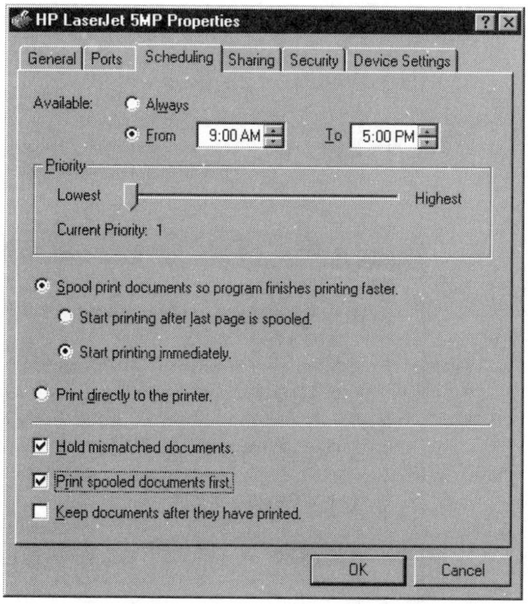

FIGURE 14.8

The Scheduling tab governs the availability of the printer and its print-spooling characteristics.

Sharing

From the Sharing tab you control the availability of your printer on the network. By selecting the Not Shared option, you restrict printing to that printer to your computer.

If you enable sharing by selecting the Shared option, you must give a network name for the printer in the Share Name field.

You may also wish to configure your server to automatically download print drivers to computers that access your printer over the network. You will need to load the print drivers for these client computers onto your Windows NT Server computer so that they can be downloaded automatically to the client. You must have the media containing the client operating system to install the device drivers. The remainder of the window allows you to select the client operating systems for which your server will provide print drivers.

Windows NT's ability to automatically download print drivers to client computers that need them vastly simplifies supporting printing on a large network. Instead of installing the print driver on each client computer on the network, you have to install it only once on the print server computer for each type of client operating system on the network. This feature works only with operating systems that support the automatic download mechanism. Currently only Windows NT Server, Windows NT Workstation, and Windows 95 support the feature.

In Exercise 14.6 you will add Windows 95 client support to the printer you created in Exercise 14.1.

EXERCISE 14.6

Adding a Downloadable Print Driver

1. Select Start ➢ Settings ➢ Printers.

2. Right-click the printer you defined in Exercise 14.1 and then select Properties. Select the Sharing tab.

3. Select Windows 95.

4. Click OK.

5. Give the path to the Windows 95 CD-ROM and click OK.

You may have to provide a driver disk that came with the printer instead of the Windows 95 CD-ROM if the driver for the printer you created in Exercise 14.1 was not on the CD.

Security

The Security tab contains three buttons: Permissions, Auditing, and Ownership.

- **Permissions** displays a window from which you set user permissions for printing and managing documents. Exercise 14.7 leads you through the process of restricting a printer so that only administrators can print to it.

- **Auditing** displays an auditing window, which allows you to track the printing activities of users and groups for this printer.

- **Ownership** allows you to take ownership of the printer, although we do not recommend this step.

EXERCISE 14.7

Restricting Access to a Printer

1. Select Start ➤ Settings ➤ Printers.

2. Select the printer from the Printers window.

3. Select File ➤ Properties from the Printers window.

4. Select the Security tab and then click the Permissions button to display the Printer Permissions window.

5. Click once on the Everyone item in the Name: list.

6. Click Remove.

7. Click once on the Power Users item in the Name: list.

8. Click Remove.

9. Click the OK button in the Printer Permissions window and then click OK in the Printer Properties window.

Device Settings

The Device Settings tab contains a hierarchical view of device-specific settings such as default tray assignment, printer fonts loaded, and printer memory available. Although you can change device settings from this tab, the Printer Properties window (available from the Print dialog box by clicking Properties when you print from an application) is a better place from which to change these settings.

Managing Print Jobs

Within the Printers folder is an icon for each printer you have installed or connected to your server. Opening the icon for a printer (double-clicking the icon) shows you the status of the printer (see Figure 14.9). Each printer has a separate window, showing only print jobs for that printer.

FIGURE 14.9

Opening the Printer icon shows you the jobs in that printer's queue and allows you to control the printer and manage those jobs.

Document Name	Status	Owner	Pages	Size	Subn
Microsoft Word - 1973c13.doc	Spooling	Administrator		86 bytes	7:41:
VISIO-F1303.vsd	Printing	Administrator	1	6.62KB/6.62KB	

HP DeskJet 520
Printer Document View Help
2 document(s) in queue

Print job entries appear in the list in the middle of the window and persist until the document is printed or until the print job is removed from the queue. You can modify a print job's status while it is in the queue.

If you have sufficient permission, you can pause, resume, restart, and cancel print jobs. You perform any of these actions by clicking the print job name and then selecting the operation (e.g., pause) from the Document menu in the Printers window.

From the Printer menu in the Printers window, you can do the following:

- Pause all printing for that printer

- Cancel all print jobs on that printer

- Set the printer to be the default printer

- Start and stop sharing of the printer

- Select the default document properties (page size, paper tray, etc.)

- Reach the Properties window for that printer

The Properties window is described in the "Printer Configuration" section later in this chapter.

Deleting Print Jobs

You will surely find many occasions when you want to delete a print job. For example:

- You (or another user) selected multiple copies and then realize you need only one.

- You sent the wrong document to the printer.

- You realize that the document must be revised (again).

Exercise 14.8 shows you how to delete a print job from a printer. This exercise assumes that your user account has sufficient privileges to manage the printer.

EXERCISE 14.8

Deleting Print Jobs

1. Open the print device. (Select Start ➢ Settings ➢ Printers and then double-click the icon corresponding to the printer.)

2. Select Printer ➢ Pause Printing. A check appears beside Pause Printing, and print jobs will be held instead of being sent to the print device.

3. Open the Notepad. (Select Start ➢ Programs ➢ Accessories ➢ Notepad.)

4. Type **I will be an MCSE.** in the Notepad.

5. Select File ➢ Page Setup and then press the Printer button.

6. Go to the Name: field. Select the printer that you paused in step 2. Click OK two times.

7. Select File ➢ Print. Your print job appears in the printer window. Because the printer is paused, it will wait for you to do something to allow it to print.

8. Select the printer window. Click the printer window, click the printer icon in the Taskbar, or press Alt+Tab until you get to the printer window.

9. Select that print job in the printer window and then select Document ➢ Cancel.

10. Select Printer ➢ Pause Printing to allow printing to the print device to resume. The check beside Pause Printing disappears.

Pausing, Resuming, and Restarting Print Jobs

Sometimes you need to control the exact time that a print job is printed; for example, you need to load special bond paper. You can pause the printer so that jobs are held until you release the printer. You can also pause individual print jobs; for example, you might want to send a small print job to the print device before a larger job.

Sometimes a print job may halt in the middle of printing, for example, when a piece of paper becomes jammed in the print device. You can instruct the printer to resume printing print jobs, but before you do so, you may want to instruct the printer to restart the print job that was interrupted so that all its pages are printed.

- **Resuming** continues printing from the point at which the document was paused.

- **Restarting** starts printing the document again from the beginning.

Exercise 14.9 shows you how to pause, resume, and restart individual print jobs and the printer as a whole.

EXERCISE 14.9

Pausing, Resuming, and Restarting Print Jobs and the Printer

1. Open the print device. (Select Start ➢ Settings ➢ Printers and then open the icon corresponding to the printer.)

2. Select Printer ➢ Pause Printing. A check appears beside Pause Printing, and print jobs will be held instead of being sent to the print device.

3. Open the Notepad. (Select Start ➢ Programs ➢ Accessories ➢ Notepad.)

4. Type **This is the first document.** in the Notepad.

5. Select File ➢ Page Setup and then click the Printer button.

6. Go to the Name: field. Select the printer that you paused in step 2. Click OK two times.

7. Select File ➢ Print. Your print job appears in the printer window. Because the printer is paused, it will wait for you to do something to allow it to print.

8. Change the text in the Notepad window to **This is the second document.**

9. Select File ➢ Print.

10. Select the printer window. (Click the printer window, click the printer icon in the Taskbar, or press Alt+Tab until you get to the printer window.)

11. Select the first print job in the printer window and then select Document ➤ Pause. Do the same for the second print job in the printer window.

12. Select Printer ➤ Pause Printing to allow printing to the print device to resume. (The check beside Pause Printing disappears.)

13. Select the Notepad window. (Click the Notepad window, click the Notepad icon in the Taskbar, or press Alt+Tab until you get to the Notepad window.)

14. Change the text in the window from This is the first document to **This is the third document.**

15. Select File ➤ Print. Your printer will print the third document.

16. Select the printer window. (Click the printer window, click the printer icon in the Taskbar, or press Alt+Tab until you get to the printer window.)

17. Select the first document in the printer window. Select Document ➤ Resume. Your printer will print the first document.

18. Select the last document in the printer window. Select Document ➤ Restart. Your printer will print the second document.

Moving Print Jobs to Other Servers

Sometimes you may need to redirect print jobs from one printer to another printer or from one print server to another print server. For example, users who don't know that a print device is unavailable (perhaps it is being serviced) may attempt to print to it anyway. You can delete the print jobs (as described in Exercise 14.8) and inform the users that they must print to another printer. Alternatively, you can simply redirect the port that the printer is using either to another local port or to a port on an other print server and inform the users of the change.

You will usually want to redirect the print jobs to another print device when a print device is temporarily removed from service. When the print device is again ready to service print jobs, all you have to do is set the printer's port back to the original location. Your network users do not have to modify their work habits (other than to pick up their documents from a different print device) or their software settings. Exercise 14.10 shows you how to redirect a printer to another print server on the network.

EXERCISE 14.10

Moving Print Jobs to Another Print Server

1. Select Start ➢ Settings ➢ Printers.

2. Select the printer to Redirect.

3. Select Printer ➢ Properties.

4. Click the Ports tab and then click Add Port.

5. Select Local Port and then click New Port.

6. Enter the network share path of the printer you will redirect the print jobs to (for example, if you are redirecting to the printer HP on the server BOOMERANG, type **\\BOOMERANG\HP**) and then click OK.

7. Click Close and then click OK.

When you redirect print jobs from one print device to another in the manner described here, the print devices must be identical.

Remote Printers

A *remote printer* is a printer that is attached to another computer on the network. (Refer to the Note in the "Local Printers" section.) Your computer must send print requests to the remote computer, which will then spool the print job to the print device. (The printer must be shared by the other computer in the manner described previously in order for you to be able to print to it.)

Depending on the client operating system you run and whether the remote computer has installed client print drivers for you to download, you may be able to automatically download the print driver for your computer. Windows NT Server, Windows NT Workstation, and Windows 95 support this feature. (Installing print drivers for this purpose was also discussed in the section on sharing earlier in this chapter.)

The following section explains how to connect to a remote printer and then points out how the process of configuring and managing a printer is similar for both remote and local printers.

Connecting to a Remote Printer

When a printer is not directly attached to your computer, but is instead attached to another computer over the network, you must connect your server to that printer before you can print to it. The printer attached to a computer over the network is called a *remote printer*. To the other computer, however, the remote printer is a local printer. (Refer to Exercise 14.1 to create a local printer for the remote computer.) Exercise 14.11 and Figure 14.10 show you how to connect to a remote printer.

Exercise 14.11 explains the preferred method of connecting to a remote printer. You can also connect to a remote printer by creating a local printer of the same type as the remote printer and then changing the port setting of the printer to point to the remote location, rather than to LPT 1 as follows: \\remote_computer_name\printer_name. *This statement will cause the print job to be spooled on both the local and remote computers.*

EXERCISE 14.11

Connecting to a Remote Printer

1. Select Start ➤ Settings ➤ Printers to display the Printers window.

2. Open the Add Printer icon by double-clicking it. This step will start the Add Printer Wizard and display a network browse window.

3. Make sure that the Network printer server option is checked. Click Next.

4. Browse the network to find the printer that you wish to attach to. Figure 14.10 shows a remote printer being selected.

5. Select the printer you want to attach to and click OK in the Connect to Printer window. You may be asked to install a printer driver if the printer cannot download a driver for your operating system. Follow the print driver installation procedure for your operating system in this case. You will be asked if this printer should be the default printer for use with Windows programs.

6. Select the Yes option to make it the default printer; otherwise select No. Click Next when you are ready to continue.

7. Click Finish to allow Windows NT to complete the installation of the remote printer in your server.

FIGURE 14.10

The Add Printer Wizard
helps you connect to
remote printers.

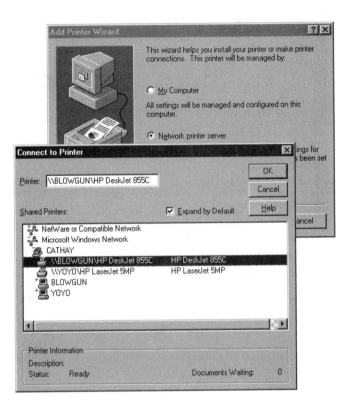

Remote Printer Configuration and Management

You usually configure a printer from the computer that the print device is local to because you must be at that computer to install the printer. However, when you right-click a remote printer on another Windows NT computer, all the printer properties tabs that you saw when you installed and configured the printer on the other machine are still available for you to set or change, including options such as which port the printer is connected to and the print driver it is using.

This flexibility can be disconcerting if you are used to operating systems that require you to be at the computer to change its hardware parameters. You should embrace this feature, however, because it greatly enhances your ability to administer a large network of computers with many printers connected to Windows NT computers located throughout your organization. You must take care to establish proper security permissions, however, to ensure that printers are not reconfigured without your supervision.

In Exercise 14.12 you will change the printer port of the remote printer you connected to in Exercise 14.11, verify the change, and then change it back from the other computer.

EXERCISE 14.12

Remote Printer Configuration

1. Log on using the Administrator account.

2. Select Start ➤ Settings ➤ Printers.

3. Right-click the printer that you connected to in the previous exercise.

4. Select Properties and then select the Ports tab of the Printer Properties window.

5. Deselect the port the printer is configured to use and select the LPT2: port instead. (Remember the previously selected port for later in this exercise.)

6. Click the OK button.

7. Go to the computer to which the printer is directly attached and log on using the Administrator account.

8. Select Start ➤ Settings ➤ Printers.

9. Right-click the printer to which you connected from the other computer in Exercise 14.11.

10. Select Properties and then select the Ports tab of the Printer Properties window.

11. Verify that LPT2: is checked. Deselect LPT2: and then select the port the printer was configured to use before step 5.

12. Click the OK button.

NetWare Printers

FROM WINDOWS NT, connecting to a printer on a NetWare network is as easy as connecting to a printer that is connected to a Windows NT or Windows 95 computer. In the previous chapter you learned how to set up Gateway Services for NetWare (GSNW), which is required for you to connect your Windows NT server computer to a NetWare print server.

In order for you to print to NetWare print queues, you must have GSNW installed on your Windows NT server. Refer to Chapter 13 for instructions on installing GSNW.

Once you are connected to the printer, you will be able to configure how your server uses that printer from a properties window that looks just like the properties window of a local or remote Windows NT printer. You will also be able to manage that printer just as you would any other printer on an NT network.

Note, however, that when you change the properties of the printer from your Windows NT server, you are changing those properties only for the server, not for other NetWare clients on the NetWare network.

Apple PostScript Printers

SERVICES FOR MACINTOSH, which comes with Windows NT Server, includes the AppleTalk protocol and allows Macintosh computers to participate in a Windows NT network. One part of the functionality in the Services for Macintosh package is support for the printing protocols that Macintosh computers and printers use. With these protocols you can print to AppleTalk printers and also allow Macintosh computers to print to printers attached to computers on the Windows NT network (which is discussed in Chapter 15).

To print to Macintosh printers, you must have Services for Macintosh installed on your Windows NT server. Refer to Chapter 15 for installation instructions.

Print Pools

ONE OF THE most useful features of the Windows NT printing architecture is the ability to pool print devices into print pools. Earlier in this chapter we explained that one printer can control more than one print device. All the print devices must be of the same type, and when the printer is given a job to print, the printer will send the print job to the next available print device in the print pool.

This technique is useful because it automatically balances the network printing load among the available print devices. If you pool your print devices, no one print device will sit idle while print jobs stack up to be printed on another print device.

All the print devices in a print pool should be in the same location. The print job may be given to any one of the print devices in the print pool—even if that print device is located far away from the computer that sent the print job. Users will quickly tire of running from printer to printer searching for their documents—they may even secretly plot your demise.

You use the Ports tab in the Printer Properties window to establish a print pool for the printer. In Exercise 14.13 you will add print devices to the original printer you created in Exercise 14.1, thereby forming a print pool.

EXERCISE 14.13

Establishing a Print Pool

1. Select Start ➤ Settings ➤ Printers.

2. Right-click the printer that you created in Exercise 14.1.

3. Select Properties and then select the Ports tab of the Printer Properties window.

4. Check the Enable printer pooling option.

5. Check the ports that also have printers of the same type attached to them. For example:

- If you have similar print devices connected to COM1: and COM2: as well as the original printer on LPT1:, then check COM1: and COM2:.

- If you have three identical printers connected to network LPR ports created as described in the previous sections on remote printers, then select each network printer port.

6. Click OK.

Printer Priorities

ANOTHER USEFUL FEATURE of the Windows NT printing architecture is the ability to establish the priority among several printers that control the same print device. You may recall that several printers can share control of one device. When each printer has a print job for the print device and the print device is ready to accept another job, the printer with the higher priority will be allowed to submit the job to the print device.

You can use this feature to establish high-priority printers and low-priority printers, as well as printers that accumulate large documents and then print them at a specified time, such as after business hours when demand for the print devices is light.

You use the scheduling tab in the Printer Properties window to establish the printing priority for that printer. You also use that tab to establish the hours of availability of that printer. In Exercise 14.14 you will create two new printers alongside the original printer you created in Exercise 14.1, one for high-priority print jobs and another for print jobs that will be held for printing after 5:00 p.m.

EXERCISE 14.14

Creating Printers with Different Priorities

1. Create two new printers that connect to the same print device that you used in Exercise 14.1. (Refer to Exercise 14.1 if you need help creating the printers.)

2. Open the first of the two new printers you created. (Select Start ➤ Settings ➤ Printers and then double-click the appropriate printer icon.)

3. Select Printer ➤ Properties and then select the Scheduling tab.

4. Change the priority of the printer to the highest setting.

5. Click the OK button.

6. Open the second of the two new printers you created. (Select Start ➤ Settings ➤ Printers and then double-click the appropriate printer icon.)

7. Select Printer ➤ Properties and then select the Scheduling tab.

8. Change the time that the printer is available from Always to From 5:00PM to 8:00PM.

9. Click the OK button.

Troubleshooting Printing Problems

P RINTING PROBLEMS CAN be especially difficult to solve because they can reside in any part of your computer or network, including

- The application that originates the print job

- The operating system software of the computer (or computers and network)

- The eventual print device's mechanical components

Fortunately, you can deduce the nature of the print problem and close in on its actual cause by observing the nature of the problem and watching for other problems in related computer components.

For example, if you can't print to a network printer and you also can't see any file servers or peer computers on the network, then the problem probably resides with the networking components of your computer or your computer's software. In this case printing should resume when network access resumes.

This section concentrates on fixing problems that specifically have to do with printing from your Windows NT server computer. We examine intermittent printing problems (i.e., a printer does not print reliably after formerly printing just fine) and consistent printer failure (i.e., a printer no longer prints).

Printer Sometimes Does Not Work

If you can sometimes print and sometimes not print, or if you were able to print before and suddenly you cannot (but you have not changed the configuration of your computer), try stopping and restarting the spooler service. Sometimes a print job can cause the spooler service to be confused. Restarting the spooler service clears its state and allows it to resume the printing process on your computer.

Stopping and Starting the Spooler Service

If you are not able to print and printing seems to be correctly configured on your server, you should stop and then restart the spooler services. In many cases this step will fix the printing problem. To stop and restart the spooler service, perform the steps in Exercise 14.15.

EXERCISE 14.15

Stopping and Restarting the Spooler Service

1. Select Start ➤ Settings ➤ Control Panel.

2. Open the Services icon. Select the Spooler item in the services list.

3. Click the Stop button and then confirm that you wish to stop the spooler service by clicking Yes.

4. Click the Start button.

5. Click the Close button.

Printer Does Not Work

No set of guidelines can solve every printing problem. However, you can resolve many printing problems by checking a few basic failure points of printers and printing systems.

Follow the steps outlined in Exercise 14.16 if you have difficulty printing to your printer and restarting the print service does not fix the problem. Each step checks a potential printing problem. Check to see if the problem has been solved after each step.

EXERCISE 14.16

Resolving Simple Printing Problems

1. Make sure that the printer is plugged in and turned on.

2. Make sure that the printer is online. If the printer is not online and is reporting an error condition, consult the printer manual to determine the cause of the error and then fix the problem.

3. Make sure that the printer cable is attached securely to both the printer and the computer.

4. Check the printer driver. Is it installed properly, and is it the correct version for the printer? If not, install the correct printer driver.

5. Make sure that when you attempt to print, you are selecting the printer driver you verified in step 4.

6. Check to see if you have sufficient hard disk space for the print driver to create temporary print files. Without sufficient space, the print driver will not be able to create a print job to send to the printer. If space is low, delete some files, archive some files to floppy or backup tape, or add hard disk space.

7. Check to see if you can print from other applications within Windows NT. If so, you may have to troubleshoot the printing options of the application you are using. If you can print from Win32-based applications but not from a DOS, Win16, or POSIX application, you may have to troubleshoot that subsystem of your Windows NT operating system configuration.

8. Print to a file and then copy the output of the file to the printer port. If you get a printed document using this method, then the spooler or data transmission may be the source of the problem. Otherwise, the driver or application is probably at fault.

Summary

WINDOWS NT PROVIDES Windows programs with a flexible and powerful printing system. Windows NT supports local and remote printers, print pools, sophisticated printer and print job management, and sharing printers attached to a Windows NT computer with computers of other operating systems such as UNIX and Macintosh.

In Windows NT terminology, the *printing device* is the physical machine that produces the document. A *printer* is the software component to which the application sends print jobs. You may have more than one printer for a single printing device and more than one printing device for a single printer. In the latter case, the printing devices are collectively called a printing pool.

The Windows NT print model splits the software that provides the printing services to the applications into several components: the GDI, the printer driver, the router, the print provider (or spooler), the print processor, and the print monitor.

An icon in the Printers window represents each printer. Opening the icon shows the print jobs in that printer's queue and allows you to manage those print jobs. It also allows you to start and stop that printer.

Opening the properties of that icon allows you to modify the settings for that printer. Settings that you can change include the destination port, user permissions, hours of operation, spooling characteristics, separator pages, which print processor it uses, and default tray settings.

Troubleshooting printing problems requires patience and experience, but you can resolve common printing problems by carefully confirming the correct operation of each hardware component (such as the cables and print mechanism) and of each software component (such as the print drivers loaded and the printer selected) of the printing system.

Review Questions

1. In Windows terminology a printer is not a physical device that produces printed pages.

   A. True

   B. False

2. A fax modem can be a print device.

   A. True

   B. False

3. You can have more print devices than you have printers.

   A. True

   B. False

4. You can have fewer print devices than you have printers.

   A. True

   B. False

5. Windows NT Server can provide printing services for Windows, UNIX, Apple Macintosh, and MS-DOS computers.

   A. True

   B. False

6. The GDI translates application print requests into DDI calls to the printer driver.

   A. True

   B. False

7. DDI calls are specific to the drawing characteristics of a printer.

   A. True

   B. False

8. A journal file print job contains DDI calls that must be made to the device driver to produce a raw print job.

   A. True

   B. False

9. The GDI will produce a journal file for a print job destined for a remote printer.

   A. True

   B. False

10. You may not need to install a print driver in your computer if you are connecting to a remote printer to print.

   A. True

   B. False

11. Windows NT can send print jobs to HP network printers and to UNIX printers.

   A. True

   B. False

12. The print provider is also known as the spooler.

   A. True

   B. False

13. Windows NT supports printing to Macintosh PostScript printers on an AppleTalk network.

    A. True

    B. False

14. You can schedule several times during the day when a printer is available and is not available from within the Printer Properties window.

    A. True

    B. False

15. You must install Gateway Services for Netware in your Windows NT server in order to connect to NetWare print queues from your Windows NT server.

    A. True

    B. False

16. You must use the Remote Printer Management tool to manage remote printers.

    A. True

    B. False

17. The _____, in Windows terminology, is a software construct that translates print requests from applications and forwards the resulting print job to the appropriate printing device.

18. A _____ _____ consists of several printing devices fed by one printer.

19. GDI stands for _____ _____ _____.

20. DDI stands for _____ _____ _____.

21. A _____ print job contains the sequence of instructions for the printer that will produce the printed document.

22. The _____ _____ is the software component that translates the printer-generic DDI calls generated by the GDI system into the printer-specific commands that are passed to the actual printer

23. The _____ _____ modifies the print job before it passes the print job to the print monitor.

24. The _____ _____ is the software component that transmits the print job (by now transformed into the language of the printer) to the printing device.

Supporting Network Clients

N THE CHAPTERS leading up to this one, you learned to install, configure, and manage a Windows NT server computer. The server, however, was not designed to operate alone; it is meant to be the focus of the network activities of client computers. A network administrator may spend relatively little time administering the server because networks usually have many more client computers than servers.

Just as you can facilitate server administration with careful planning, you can make the job of supporting network clients much easier by choosing support options that minimize support and administration hassle.

Even in a small network, the number of client computers will greatly outnumber the number of server computers. You do not need to spend all your time supporting network client computers, however, if you abide by two general principles: plan for support and use the capabilities of your NT server to manage clients and client software.

Plan for Support

N CHAPTER 2 you designed your network for optimum performance and ease of administration. In Chapter 3 you did the same for your server hardware. Here are some things you can do to make your network clients much easier to support:

- Standardize client hardware.

- Use uniform hardware configurations.

- Standardize client software.

- Store client software on the file server.

- Store user files on the file server.

- Implement roaming profiles.

Standardize Client Hardware

The most important thing you can do to make managing your network clients easier is to standardize the client hardware. For example, managing 100 identical PC-compatible computers and 50 identical Macintosh computers is much easier than trying to manage 150 network clients that include a dozen different types of PC-compatible computers and Macintoshes bought at different times in different numbers from different manufacturers, each with different hardware components included or added over time.

A network composed of identical computers is easier to manage because you can expect one computer to perform much like the next. You can be assured that a hardware or software configuration that works for one computer in the network will work on any computer in the network. Diagnosing hardware problems in one computer is easier when you can compare it to another computer with identical hardware that is working perfectly.

Standardizing on exactly the same client hardware throughout your organization may not be feasible because of the cost associated with replacing or upgrading all the units at the same time. Therefore, you should consider dividing the client computers into three or four pools and upgrading one pool at a time. This system allows you to minimize hardware differences (with only three or four types of computers in use at one time) and spread out the cost of upgrading.

Use Uniform Hardware Configurations

The next thing you can do to make your network clients easier to support is to standardize the hardware configurations of the client computers as far as possible. If you have a number of identical client computers, you should configure them identically—use the same network adapter cards, video cards, and so on. Also set them to the same interrupt numbers, memory addresses, DMA numbers, and so forth. If you have serial mice, use them all on the same serial port. If you have modems, install them all on the same COM port.

Uniform hardware configurations mean that when you sit down at a client computer to configure software (or, more ideally, configure software for a number of client computers remotely), you already know exactly how to configure the software for that computer. A uniform configuration scheme also eliminates special batch configurations.

You can frequently establish uniform hardware configurations even among computers that come from different manufacturers. For example, you can configure all computers with ISA Ethernet cards to use IRQ 5, port 320, and

DMA 6, even if the computers come from Dell, Micron, and IBM and the adapters come from SMC, Allied Telesyn, and Accton. Similarly, you can configure most internal modems to use COM4. Establishing standards for settings that can be standardized across hardware types greatly expedites computer configuration, troubleshooting (you don't have to guess what the sound card is set to use because you know what it should be), and software installation.

List the port, IRQ, and DMA assignments of each client computer on a note card and tape it to the bottom of the computer. Update the card each time you change or add any hardware. This card makes a handy reference any time you are dealing with drivers or configuration issues, and it can help you quickly determine which resources are free when you install new hardware. This low-tech source of information is especially important when you use client operating systems that cannot report all the hardware resources in use.

Standardize Client Software

You can reduce the burden of client administration (and software costs as well) by standardizing the software used on client computers in your network. Installing and configuring the same word processor on all the client computers and upgrading the software on all client computers simultaneously is much easier than trying to handle a network that contains several versions of two or three brands of word processors.

Maintaining several software packages of the same type on a network is difficult because you must learn the hardware requirements, computer environment needs (such as search paths, environment variables, and write permissions on certain directories), and operating quirks of many packages. Because the network administrator is frequently the de facto computer trainer, he or she must be familiar with the features and capabilities of multiple software packages as well.

Standardizing software is especially important for applications that interact with the network and other applications. E-mail is an example of such an application. It must be able to communicate with other e-mail packages on other client computers, with the e-mail server or gateway on a server, and with e-mail-enabled applications on the client computers. Conflicts and incompatibilities among e-mail packages can be especially difficult to solve, so your best plan is to prevent problems by only using one package.

You can also realize a software savings by purchasing software in bulk. Many software manufacturers offer discounts when you buy multiple software licenses at one time. In many cases you buy one set of distribution disks, or a CD-ROM, and a number of licenses. You are allowed to install from the installation disks to the number of computers for which you have purchased licenses. The savings can be considerable when the network has many computers, such as on a college campus or in a large corporation.

One circumstance in which you might wish to violate the principle of only one software package per type of software is when you upgrade from one version to another or when you switch from one package to another. During the transition you may wish to have both versions available so that users can learn the idiosyncrasies of the new package and so that you can ensure that the new package is stable and operates as advertised.

Store Client Software on the File Server

One way to make network administration easier and reduce the cost of computers on the network is to install the client software on the file server. Because the client software occupies disk space only on the file server, you have to buy just enough disk space for one copy of the software, instead of having to include enough disk space for the software in each client computer on the network. This configuration can produce significant savings in large networks.

Because the software is physically located in only once place, you need to perform only one installation. You may need to perform ancillary configurations on the client computers (for example, put icons on the desktops pointing to the server-installed application), but most of your configuration effort goes into the server.

When you implement roaming profiles and teach your users to store their files on the server, each user can have his or her entire computing environment on any client computer they log on to.

Another advantage of storing client software on the file server is that you can make better use of the number of client licenses you purchase for the software. Software licenses vary from manufacturer to manufacturer, but in most cases when you install software on the client computers, you may install the software on only as many client computers as you have software licenses. If your software license allows it, storing the software on the server and allowing client computers (up to the number of licenses you have) to connect to the server and use the software is a much more economical arrangement. Different groups of clients may be connected to the software at different times. Therefore, you are limited to the number of clients that can use the software simultaneously, rather than the set number of computers that have the software on their hard disk drive, many of which will be doing something else or even sitting idle at any particular time.

One drawback to loading applications from a file server is increased network traffic. Make sure your network has plenty of spare capacity before moving locally installed applications to a file server.

Implement Roaming Profiles

Roaming profiles allow users to work at many computers without giving up their personalized working environments. Unfortunately, the current implementation in Windows NT 4 is half-baked—much of the functionality of roaming profiles depends on the computers being configured exactly the same. Most of the application software installed on your computers must be the same and located in the same place, or roaming profiles will be confused. Roaming profiles have no local aspect, so they don't know anything about the machine upon which they run. If, for instance, you install MS-Word in the \office95\word directory on one computer and in the \word directory on another computer, the shortcuts stored in the profile will not work on both computers. Since very few installations have uniform software installations throughout, you may find that you cannot implement roaming profiles effectively. Roaming profiles currently work only in Windows NT—Windows 95 users cannot benefit from them. This limitation is another serious drawback because few organizations use Windows NT throughout. As time goes by, Microsoft is likely to correct these problems, and Windows NT is likely to supplant Windows 95 as the most common operating system installed on new computers, so these problems should go away eventually.

Despite these drawbacks, you should implement roaming profiles on your network for users of Windows NT. Implementing roaming profiles actually takes more effort than leaving profiles to their default (nonroaming) status, but using roaming profiles enables you to do other tasks (such as store client software on the server) more effectively. In addition, a uniform environment for your users is easier to troubleshoot than one in which the environment changes from one computer on the network to another. Exercise 15.1 shows you how to implement roaming profiles. Note that you cannot make roaming profiles for the built-in accounts Administrator and Guest.

EXERCISE 15.1

Implementing Roaming Profiles

1. Double-click My Computer on your primary domain controller.

2. Double-click your boot drive (usually C).

3. Select File ➢ New ➢ Folder.

4. Type **Profiles** to name the folder and press Enter.

5. Right-click the Profiles folder.

6. Select Sharing.

7. Select Shared As:.

8. Click OK to accept the default permissions of Full Control for Everyone.

9. Select Start ➢ Programs ➢ Administrative Tools ➢ User Manager for Domains.

10. Double-click a username other than the built-in accounts Administrator and Guest.

11. Click Profile.

12. Type **\\servername\Profiles\username** in the User profile path substituting {servername} for the name of your server and {username} for the account name of the user you selected.

13. Click OK.

14. Click OK.

Repeat steps 10 through 14 for each user in your domain.

Exercise 15.1 only tells Windows NT where to find profiles; it does not create them. If you point to the Profiles directory when you create your user accounts, a profile will be created for them. If, however, a user already has a profile that he or she knows and loves on the current machine, you can copy that profile to the Profiles directory. Exercise 15.2 shows you how.

EXERCISE 15.2

Copying User Profiles to the Profiles Share

1. Log on as the administrator to the computer where the user's profile is stored locally, which is normally that user's computer.

2. Select Start ➤ Settings ➤ Control Panel.

3. Double-click the System control panel program.

4. Select the User Profiles tab.

5. Select the account you want to copy.

6. Click Change Type if the account type is listed as local. Select Roaming Profile and click OK.

7. Click Copy To.

8. Enter the UNC path to the profiles share, followed by the user account name; for instance: **\\servername\profiles\accountname**.

9. Click OK. The profile is now being transferred to the Profiles directory.

10. Click OK to close the System control panel program.

Store User Files on the File Server

Storing user files (and all files except the client computer operating system files) on the file server not only simplifies backing up the files but also allows you to repair or replace the hard drive of the client computer without having to sort through the contents of the hard drive for user files. At most you would have to reinstall the operating system for the client computer.

Another advantage is that if the client computer malfunctions you can give the user another computer while the client computer is being fixed. The user will be able to resume work with all the user files still available. If you have implemented roaming profiles, the user may not even notice that the client computer has been replaced.

Upgrading computers is also much easier when you store user files on the server. More powerful computers can be installed in locations where users need the additional computing power, and the displaced client computers can be moved to locations where computer use is less sensitive to computer performance.

Use the Administration Capabilities of Your NT Server

Windows NT Server can help you support a large number of client computers. Windows NT Server can also support many different types of client computers such as Windows 95 clients, DOS clients, Macintosh clients, and OS/2 clients at the same time. Windows NT Server can be a part of several non-Microsoft network environments, including NetWare networks, AppleTalk networks, and UNIX (TCP/IP) networks.

Many network administrators are configuring their networks to use TCP/IP for several reasons, including connecting to the Internet, interoperating with UNIX workstations, and developing organization-centric intranets. They are using TCP/IP because it is flexible and because it is the protocol of the Internet.

 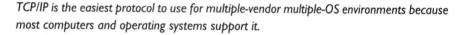

TCP/IP is the easiest protocol to use for multiple-vendor multiple-OS environments because most computers and operating systems support it.

The price of TCP/IP's flexibility, however, is its complexity. Every computer must be configured with an IP address, subnet mask, gateway address, DNS address, WINS address, etc., and each setting must be correct for the computer to fully participate in the network. DNS and WINS services should also be provided on all but the simplest networks.

You should also provide server-based services such as e-mail and license management. A user on one computer has to be able to send mail to another user on another computer even when that other user is not logged on to the network and when that other computer is turned off. A post office on the file server holds the mail until the user accesses it. A post office also can route mail between different mail packages on different client operating systems, such as Windows 95, Macintosh, and UNIX, or to and from the Internet.

To use the tools that Windows NT provides to make managing your network easier, you should:

- Use automatic network configuration mechanisms such as DHCP, DNS, and WINS.

- Set up an e-mail post office.

- Use the License Manager.

- Use Services for Macintosh.

- Use the Network Client Administrator.

Use Automatic Network Configuration Mechanisms

Network clients that use TCP/IP are much easier to administer when you also implement DHCP, DNS, and WINS. The Windows NT Server operating system provides services called servers for each of the three protocols.

Dynamic Host Configuration Protocol (DHCP)

DHCP is the preferred way to configure TCP/IP settings for client computers on Windows networks. A DHCP server maintains a list of available IP addresses, and when a client computer asks for one (using a special DHCP packet), the DHCP server sends the IP address along with other TCP/IP information such as the DNS address and subnet mask to the client. The client computer, configured with that information, can then participate in the TCP/IP network.

Why bother with DHCP when you can assign permanent TCP/IP addresses? Because DHCP assigns TCP/IP addresses only to computers that are active on a TCP/IP network. Consequently, any computers not active on the TCP/IP network are not reserving a TCP/IP address. Because many organizations are limited to 254 simultaneous TCP/IP addresses, DHCP can help them conserve. DCHP also simplifies setting up clients. Instead of your having to remember which addresses you've assigned and which ones are free, you simply set the client to use DHCP; you don't have to worry about a thing.

You install DHCP from the Services tab of the Network control panel, but once it is installed, you configure and manage it from the DHCP Manager. (Start ➤ Programs ➤ Administrative Tools ➤ DHCP Manager). Figure 15.1 shows the main window of the DHCP Manager.

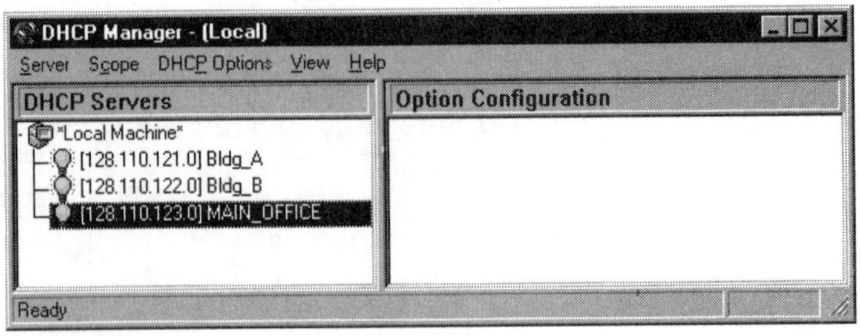

FIGURE 15.1

You can automatically assign IP addresses to client computers in IP subnets of your network using the DHCP Manager.

INSTALLING DHCP DHCP is simple to install. Because it is just another network service, you use the Network control panel to add it to the services already installed in your server.

One complication is that a DHCP server cannot rely on DHCP to configure its own network adapter cards. After installing the DHCP service, you may be asked to enter the IP addresses of the network adapter card(s) in your server. If you specified these values explicitly when you installed TCP/IP, rather than relying on DHCP, you will not have to do so at this time.

Exercise 15.3 shows you how to install DHCP. This exercise assumes that you did not configure the adapters in your server to use DHCP when you installed TCP/IP.

EXERCISE 15.3

Installing DHCP

1. Select Start ➤ Settings ➤ Control Panel.

2. Open the Networking control panel and select the Services tab.

3. Click Add.

4. Select Microsoft DHCP Server from the list of services and then click OK. If you have adapters configured to use DHCP, enter static IP addresses for them.

5. Click OK.

6. Click Close.

7. Click Yes to restart your computer and activate the changes.

CONFIGURING DHCP Configuring DHCP consists primarily of creating scopes and modifying options of existing scopes. Scopes usually correspond to IP subnets, and a single DHCP server can respond to DHCP requests for multiple subnets if the routers in the TCP/IP network are correctly configured.

Configuring Windows NT Server for large networks, including networks with multiple subnets, is covered in the book MCSE: NT Server 4 in the Enterprise Study Guide.

The DHCP Manager controls all aspects of the DHCP service. You can run the DHCP Manager from any NT computer in your network (that has the DHCP Manager program installed), even from a computer that is not providing IP addresses to client computers on the network. To understand the DHCP Manger, you will need know these new terms:

- **DHCP**—Dynamic Host Configuration Protocol is the protocol by which client computers on Windows NT networks discover their IP address.

- **DHCP server**—A Windows NT Server computer providing the DHCP service. This computer answers DHCPDiscover requests for IP addresses.

- **DHCP client**—A computer that sends a DHCPDiscover packet requesting an IP address from a DHCP server.

- **Scope**—A scope in DHCP encompasses a range of IP addresses in a TCP/IP subnet. Local options can be set for a scope, and global options can be set for all scopes managed by the DHCP server.

- **Global options**—IP configuration settings such as DNS Server addresses and the domain name that apply across all scopes managed by the DHCP server.

- **Scope options**—IP configuration settings such as the router (equivalent to gateway) address and many other optional elements of information.

- **Lease**—A period of time for which a client computer may use an assigned IP address.

- **Default gateway or router**—The location on the IP subnet that a client can use and expect to relay packets beyond the IP subnet.

- **Domain name**—The human-readable Internet name of your IP domain.

- **DNS server**—Domain Name Service server is the computer that resolves human-readable Internet names into numerical IP addresses, and vice versa.

- **WINS server**—Windows Internet Name Service server is the computer that resolves Windows network UNC computer names into numerical IP addresses, and vice versa.

ESTABLISHING A SCOPE Once you have installed the DHCP service in your Windows NT Server, the service will start automatically when you boot the computer. It will not give out IP addresses to client computers, however, until you establish a scope for your subnet and thereby give it a range of addresses to dispense. You must use the DHCP Manager to create the scope(s).

The usual configuration of DHCP in a small network is for one DHCP server to establish one scope for one IP subnet (which is usually the whole local area network in a single server or in a single-domain, multiple-server network). To implement redundancy in a single-domain network, you may wish to have two DHCP servers, each on a different computer, each dispensing from a disjoint set of numbers for the same IP subnet. For larger networks, you may wish to have a pair of central DHCP servers, or you may wish to establish DHCP servers in each IP subnet of your larger campus-area network. For other issues concerning DHCP in larger networks and for instructions on how to use DHCP in large networks, see the book *MCSE: NT Server 4 in the Enterprise Study Guide*.

You must configure several settings when you establish a scope. Figure 15.2 shows the Create Scope (Local) window.

FIGURE 15.2

The DHCP Create Scope window.

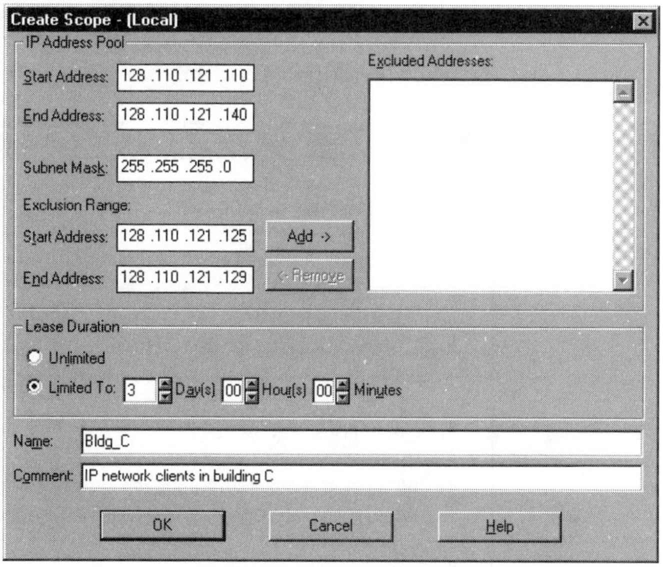

The settings in the DHCP Create Scope window are as follows:

- Start Address—Each scope has a range from which IP addresses will be allocated for DHCP client use. This setting is the start address for the range.

- **End Address**—This entry is the last address in the pool of IP addresses for allocation.

- **Subnet Mask**—This setting (described in Chapter 6) configures the client for the size of the IP network and allows the client to determine which computers are on the same network and which computers must be reached via the gateway (or router).

- **Excluded Addresses**—The pool of addresses defined by the start and end addresses excludes these addresses. If you have computers (such as a DNS or WINS server and the DHCP server itself) that have set IP addresses between the start and end address, you should exclude those addresses.

- **Lease Duration**—When a client requests an IP address, it is given that address for permanent use only if you check the Unlimited option. Otherwise, the lease on the IP address is set to expire after a period of time, after which the client computer must have received an extension on the lease or another IP address to use. The default lease is three days.

- **Name**—This entry is the name for the scope. You should select a short name that is easy to view in lists.

- **Comment**—This entry describes the scope.

Exercise 15.4 shows you how to establish a scope for an IP subnet and set a range of IP addresses for the scope.

EXERCISE 15.4

Establishing a Scope

1. Select Start ➤ Programs ➤ Administrative Tools ➤ DHCP Manager on the DHCP Server computer.

2. Double-click Local Machine. The title bar for the window will change to include the word Local.

3. Select Scope ➤ Create.

4. Enter the starting and ending IP numbers in the Create Scope (Local) window (refer to Figure 15.2).

5. Enter the subnet mask.

6. Exclude addresses. If some of the computers in the network have static (permanently assigned) IP addresses between the start and end addresses you selected, you should exclude these addresses from the scope. Enter a start and end address for the exclusion range and then click Add.

7. Click the OK button. DHCP Manager will inform you that the scope has been created but that it has not yet been activated. Click Yes to activate the scope.

SETTING GLOBAL AND SCOPE OPTIONS Once you have created a scope and activated it, the DHCP server will begin automatically dispensing IP addresses to requesting DHCP client computers. Although this process gives the client computers enough information to participate on the local IP subnet, you may wish to set some additional information in the DHCP server so that client computers will be able to communicate with other computers beyond your subnet and beyond your network (i.e., over the Internet).

You give client computers additional information (such as the domain name, DNS addresses, and the gateway address) by setting global and scope options. *Global options* apply to all scopes managed by the DHCP server, and *scope options* apply to a single scope.

DHCP supports many more options than Windows DHCP clients use. For example, you will probably never set global option 048, which configures the X Window System Font in UNIX environments. You will find some default settings that you should not change, even though you can, because they are optimized for best performance under Windows. Some settings that you may find useful to configure, however, include:

- Global options
    - Domain name
    - DNS server
    - WINS server (called a WINS/NBNS server in DHCP)
    - WINS/NBT node type
- Scope options
    - Default gateway (called Router in DHCP)

If you fail to provide the Router scope option containing the IP address of the router local to your client, that client will not be able to communicate with computers outside its IP domain.

You can set many of the options either globally or in a scope. For instance, you will be placing separate DNS and WINS servers in each IP subnet (for performance or for reliability purposes), then you may set these options in each scope rather than globally. You reach the global and scope options from the DHCP Options menu, from which you can also set default DHCP options. Exercise 15.5 guides you through the process of setting global and scope options for an IP subnet.

EXERCISE 15.5

Setting Global and Scope Options

1. Select Start ➤ Programs ➤ Administrative Tools ➤ DHCP Manager.

2. Select DHCP Options ➤ Global.

3. Select DNS Servers from the Unused Options list and then press Add.

4. Click Value and then click Edit Array.

5. Enter the IP address of the DNS servers in your network by entering each server's address in the New IP Address field, clicking Add, and then clicking OK.

6. Select Domain Name from the Unused Options list and then click Add. The Value window should still be visible.

7. Enter the domain name for your domain.

8. Select WINS/NBS from the Unused Options list and then click Add.

9. You will be informed that you must also set the WINS/NBT option. Click OK.

10. Enter the WINS/NBT server addresses as you did in steps 4 and 5.

11. Select WINS/NBT from the Unused Options list and then click Add.

12. Type **0x08** in the value field.

13. Click OK.

14. Select DHCP Options ➤ Scope.

15. Select Router from the Unused Options list and then click Add.

16. Enter the IP address of the router(s) in your network as you did in steps 4 and 5.

17. Click OK.

CONFIGURING CLIENTS TO USE DHCP Each client operating system has a different method of DHCP configuration. You should review the documentation for the client operating system to determine how to configure your client computers. For Windows NT and Windows 95, the process is simple, as is shown in Exercises 15.6 and 15.7.

EXERCISE 15.6

Configuring Windows NT Workstations and Windows NT Servers to Use DHCP

1. Select Start ➤ Settings ➤ Control Panel.

2. Open the Network icon.

3. Click Protocols and then double-click the TCP/IP protocol.

4. Click the Obtain an IP address from the DHCP server radio button.

5. Click OK and then click OK again. Click Yes to reboot your computer.

EXERCISE 15.7

Configuring Windows 95 to Use DHCP

1. Select Start ➤ Settings ➤ Control Panel.

2. Open the Network icon.

3. Select that networking adapter for each TCP/IP-to-networking adapter, click Properties, then select Obtain IP address automatically, and click OK.

4. Click OK. Click Yes to reboot your computer.

Domain Name Service (DNS)

Domain Name Service (DNS) is the standard way that TCP/IP computers transform human-readable Internet names (such as www.oeadm.org) into IP addresses (such as 128.110.121.42). DNS, like DHCP, is a client/server protocol, which means that clients request the domain name information from DNS servers.

Don't confuse the word Domain *in DNS with a Windows NT security domain. In TCP/IP parlance the term* domain *refers to a TCP/IP subnetwork.*

A DNS server maintains a list of the Internet names of computers on the TCP/IP network and their associated IP addresses. It can also record other information, such as alternate names (aliases) and mail addresses, for the domain as a whole. The DNS server stores this information in many types of records. The types you are most likely to use follow.

- **A** (Address record): Allows DNS to translate an Internet name into an IP address. You should have an A record for each computer on your network that has a static (permanently assigned) IP address.

- **CNAME** (Alias, or Canonical Name record): Allows your computers to have additional names so that one computer can perform several roles, such as name server, FTP server, Web server, under various names. You can move these roles to other computers simply by changing the CNAME record (and by moving the service itself, of course).

- **HINFO** (Host Information record): Stores information about the computer, such as its CPU type and operating system.

- **MX** (Mail Exchanger record): Specifies the mail exchange server that handles Internet mail reception for the specified computer. You can have one computer (usually a mail server on an NT or UNIX computer) receive all mail for your network and hold it for clients to access.

- **NS** (Name Server record): Describes DNS servers for a domain. If you have several name servers in your network (each serving a part of it), you may have a top-level server that contains records for each.

- **RP** (Responsible Person record): Identifies the responsible person for mail service.

INSTALLING DNS You install the Microsoft DNS Server the same way you install the DHCP server, from the Services tab of the Networking control panel. Exercise 15.8 guides you through the process.

EXERCISE 15.8

Installing Microsoft DNS Server

1. Select Start ➤ Settings ➤ Control Panel.

2. Double-click the Network control panel program.

3. Click the Services tab and then click Add.

4. Select Microsoft DNS Server from the list of services and then click OK.

5. Click OK.

6. Click Yes to restart your computer.

CONFIGURING DNS Once you install the DNS server, it will start automatically whenever you boot that Windows NT server computer. Like the DHCP server, you do not configure DNS from the Network control panel; instead, you configure it from an administrative tool. The tool in this case is the Microsoft DNS Manager (see Figure 15.3).

FIGURE 15.3

The Domain Name Service Manager.

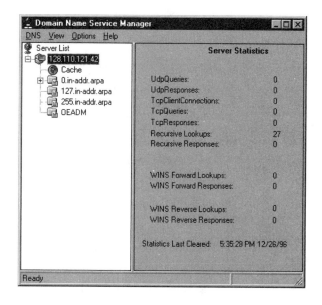

The first thing you must do to configure DNS is to connect to the DNS server. (You can run the Microsoft DNS Manager on a different computer than the one that is running the actual DNS service.) The first time you connect to the server, you should create a new zone. This zone will contain the records describing your TCP/IP network and the IP addressed computers within it.

Once you have created a zone, you should create DNS entries for those computers with statically assigned IP addresses in your network. You don't have to create entries for the IP addresses dynamically assigned by DHCP if you configure DNS to look up those addresses using WINS (described in the next section).

You usually create an A record for each computer with a statically assigned IP address, and in many cases (especially when connecting your network to the Internet), you also create MX records in the in-addr.arpa zones of your DNS server. (Refer to the *MCSE: TCP/IP Study Guide* to learn how to configure DNS and other TCP/IP protocols so that your computers are visible on the Internet.) Exercise 15.9 guides you through a simple configuration of the Microsoft DNS Server.

EXERCISE 15.9

Configuring Microsoft DNS Server

1. Select Start ➤ Programs ➤ Administrative Tools ➤ Domain Name Service Manager.

2. Select DNS ➤ New Server.

3. Enter the IP address of your DNS server and click OK.

4. Select the address of your DNS server in the list of servers.

5. Select DNS ➤ New Zone.

6. Select Primary Zone and then click Next.

7. Enter a zone name (which may be the same as your domain name if you have one DNS server for your whole domain) and then press the Tab key to automatically fill in the Zone file. Click Next.

8. Click Finish. You will now have a new zone in the Domain Name Service Manager window.

9. Select the zone you just defined by clicking it once.

10. Select Add Host for each computer that has a static IP address. Enter the computer name (without the domain name, for example, for `mu.law.utah.edu` you would enter `mu`) and the IP address. Click the Add Host button.

11. Click Done when you have added all of the computers with static IP addresses on your network.

12. Select the zone you are adding hosts to. Right-click and select Properties from the menu.

13. Click the WINS lookup button and select Use WINS resolution.

14. Enter the address of the WINS server on your network and click Add.

15. Repeat step 14 for as many WINS servers as you have on your network.

16. Click OK.

CONFIGURING CLIENTS TO USE DNS Fortunately, configuring client computers to use DNS is easy. Either the client computer will be set up to automatically use the correct DNS server by DHCP or you explicitly enter the IP addresses of the DNS servers in your network (in the TCP/IP protocol configuration of the client computer). In Windows NT Workstation and Windows NT Server, you enter these values in the Protocol tab of the Networking control panel. In Windows 95 you enter these values in each of the TCP/IP-to-network-adapter entries in the Networking control panel.

Windows Internet Name Service (WINS)

The final component of the Windows TCP/IP networking suite of services is the Windows Internet Name Service (WINS). WINS translates Windows networking UNC names to and from IP addresses, much like DNS translates Internet names to and from IP addresses. WINS, however, is much easier to configure.

INSTALLING WINS You install the Windows Internet Naming Service the same way you install the DHCP server, from the Services tab of the Networking control panel. Exercise 15.10 guides you through the process.

EXERCISE 15.10

Installing Microsoft Windows Internet Naming Service

1. Select Start ➤ Settings ➤ Control Panel.

2. Double-click the Network control panel program.

3. Click the Services tab and then click Add.

4. Select Windows Internet Naming Service from the list of services and then click OK.

5. Click OK.

6. Click Yes to restart your computer.

CONFIGURING WINS The WINS administrative tool is called WINS Manager, and you reach it from Start ➤ Programs ➤ Administrative Tools ➤ WINS Manager. WINS is much easier than DHCP or DNS to administer. The only thing that you really need to do is give it a list of the computers with statically assigned IP addresses in your network.

By this point in the chapter you may have noticed how many times you have to enter statically assigned IP addresses into various IP management tools. Therefore, we suggest that you use statically assigned IP addresses as little as possible. You will have to use them for the DHCP servers, DNS servers, gateways, and WINS servers, but for a small network, the same computer may perform all the functions. Use DHCP to automatically assign the addresses to everything else.

To add mappings, select Mappings ➤ Add Mappings and then click the Add Mappings button. Enter as many unique mappings as you have statically assigned IP addresses.

CONFIGURING CLIENTS TO USE WINS Configuring network clients to use WINS is just as easy as configuring them to use DNS. If the client supports WINS, you will be given an option when configuring TCP/IP to enable WINS lookups and you will be able to enter the IP address of the primary and secondary WINS server. If the operating system supports DHCP and your network has DHCP configured, then you may be able to skip this step.

For Windows NT Server and Windows NT Workstation, you configure TCP/IP to use WINS from within the Protocol tab of the Networking control panel. For Windows 95 you configure each TCP/IP-to-adapter item in the Networking control panel to use WINS.

Set Up an E-Mail Post Office

Windows NT comes with software that allows it to be a simple mail post office. Other more complex and feature-filled packages are also available for purchase, such as Microsoft Exchange Server that, in addition to simple storage of e-mail, can also route it to and from other networks and the Internet; convert mail formats; and more. The Microsoft Mail Postoffice control panel simply sets up your server to store mail and to allow network clients to access their stored mail.

The Microsoft Mail Postoffice Control Panel Program

The first time you attempt to use the Postoffice control panel, you will be prompted either to connect to an existing post office or to create a new post office on your network. Exercise 15.11 explains how to create a new post office.

Exercise 15.11 assumes you have Windows Messaging installed. (It is installed by default.) You may need to use the Add/Remove programs control panel program to install the messaging option if the Microsoft Mail Postoffice program does not appear in your Control Panel.

EXERCISE 15.11

Creating a New Post Office

1. Select Start ➤ Settings ➤ Control Panel ➤ Microsoft Mail Postoffice.

2. Select Create a New Workgroup Postoffice and then click Next.

3. Enter the location of a directory on the network for the post office to occupy and then click Next. If the location is on another computer, you can give the UNC path to the location.

4. Click Next to confirm the location of the new directory.

5. Enter a name, mailbox name, and password for the Administrator account. Click OK to continue. You will be informed that for other users on the network to access the post office, the directory for the post office must be shared. Click OK.

6. Open the My Computer icon on the desktop.

7. Find the directory that was created for the mailbox (for example, if the mailbox was created on drive E as `wgpo0000`, then double-click the E: icon and select `wgpo0000`.

8. Right-click the post office folder and select Sharing from the menu.

9. Click the Shared As button and then click OK.

After you have created a post office on the network, you can use the control panel to connect to it and create additional e-mail accounts for the users on the network.

Unfortunately, Microsoft Mail Postoffice that comes with Windows NT Server does not automatically create post office accounts for users that you create on the network with the User Manager for Domains program. Therefore, you will have to create every mail account as well as every user account. Other mail packages usually take the list of users from the NT accounts database so you don't have to perform this chore.

Exercise 15.12 shows you how to create additional mail accounts. (You created the account for the administrator when you created the post office.)

EXERCISE 15.12

Creating Post Office Accounts

1. Select Start ➤ Settings ➤ Control Panel.

2. Open the Microsoft Mail Postoffice icon.

3. Select Administer an Existing Workgroup Postoffice.

4. Click Next. Your post office should appear as the location of the post office. If it is incorrect, enter the correct location of the post office.

5. Click Next. The administrator mail account name should appear in the Mailbox field.

6. Enter the administrator mail account password in the password field and click Next.

7. Click Add, enter the person's name, enter the person's mailbox name, and enter a password; then (optionally) enter additional information such as the individual's phone number(s), office number, and so on. Click OK.

8. Repeat step 7 for each user that requires a post office box.

9. Click Close.

Connecting to the Post Office as a Client

Once you have created the post office, you must connect to it as a client. (What good is a post office if nobody ever checks the mail?) The easiest way to make this connection in Windows NT and Windows 95 is from the Inbox icon on the desktop. When you open the Inbox for the first time, it will recognize that it has not been configured and will provide a wizard to prompt you through the configuration process. Exercise 15.13 uses this method of configuring your Windows NT computer to access the post office.

EXERCISE 15.13

Connecting to the Microsoft Mail Postoffice

1. Open the Inbox on the desktop.

2. Select only Microsoft Mail (deselect Internet Mail). Click Next. (This screen will not appear if you've already installed Microsoft mail—instead, the Microsoft Messaging client will open.)

3. If the post office does not appear, click Browse to find the post office or enter the location of the post office in the field. Figure 15.4 shows browsing to a network post office share. Click Next when the location of the post office is in the field.

4. Select your name from the list of post office mail accounts and press Next.

5. Enter the password for the name you selected and click Next.

6. Allow the wizard to create your personal address book (click Next) and your personal folders (click Next.)

7. Click Finish.

FIGURE 15.4

You can browse and connect to a post office elsewhere on the network.

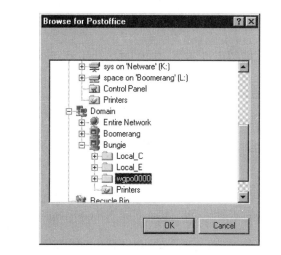

The Mail Control Panel

Once you have connected to the post office, you can modify your post office configuration either through the Mail control panel or by right-clicking the Inbox icon on the desktop and selecting Properties. Both methods take you to the Mailbox Properties window.

Each user receives his or her own mailbox configuration, so when you log out as Administrator and log on as another (regular) user, you will have to go through the mailbox connection process (Exercise 15.13) again. Each user will have to repeat this routine.

Microsoft Exchange Server is a powerful software package that allows you to do much more than just store mail on your file server. The book MCSE: NT Server 4 in the Enterprise Study Guide *shows you how to route mail to non-exchange clients, route to and from the Internet, and more.*

Using License Manager to Monitor Application Use

The License Manager is an excellent tool to help you monitor how many simultaneous copies of certain Microsoft products are in use. This tool enables you to buy only the number of licenses you actually need, rather than purchasing one license per computer or user, which would be the only way you could really ensure compliance with Microsoft's licensing requirements otherwise.

Software licensing can be confusing, but here's a fairly simple explanation. Software is licensed like a book, which means that you don't have to have one copy of a software title per computer, nor do you have to have one copy per user. Rather, you need only as many copies as are in use simultaneously. In other words, if 25 people in your office occasionally use Microsoft Systems Management Server, you don't need 25 copies of it. You need only as many as are ever in use at any one time—which might be 1, 3, 5, or 20, depending upon your environment.

Therein lies the licensing problem—you have to be able to verify the greatest number of copies that have ever run simultaneously, or you are open to claims of software piracy. Without a network running the License Manager or a similar product to track usage, you would have no way to determine how many licenses you actually need.

The License Manager does not prevent you from exceeding the number of copies you've told it you have. But it warns you when you've exceeded the limit and tells you how many additional licenses you need to purchase.

As explained in Chapter 2, two licensing modes exist. In per seat licensing, you buy one client access license for the product for each client computer you have in your environment. This mode allows you to attach to any number of servers from any number of clients without worrying about licensing. Per server licensing allows a certain number of clients to attach to a specific server. This mode is best used in single-server environments.

Not all applications work with the License Manager. Currently, only Microsoft BackOffice applications are supported. Supported applications will automatically appear once you've installed them. Exercise 15.14 shows you how to run the License Manager, view and add licenses, and revoke them if necessary. Figure 15.5 shows the License Manager running.

EXERCISE 15.14

Using the License Manager

1. Select Start ➤ Programs ➤ Administrative Tools ➤ License Manager.

2. Select License ➤ New License.

3. Select Windows NT Server in the Product pick box of the New Client Access License dialog box.

4. Type 1 in the Quantity text box.

5. Click OK.

6. Check to indicate compliance with the terms of Microsoft's licensing agreement.

7. Click OK.

8. Verify that the license you just added shows up in the Purchase History list box.

9. Click Products view.

10. Note the number of Windows NT licenses it now shows.

11. Double-click Windows NT Server in the Product pick box.

12. Double-click the Administrator user in the Windows NT Server list box.

13. Select the client access license you just created and click Revoke.

14. Click OK.

15. Click OK.

16. Click the Purchase History tab to view the changes to the license history for this server.

17. Close the License Manager.

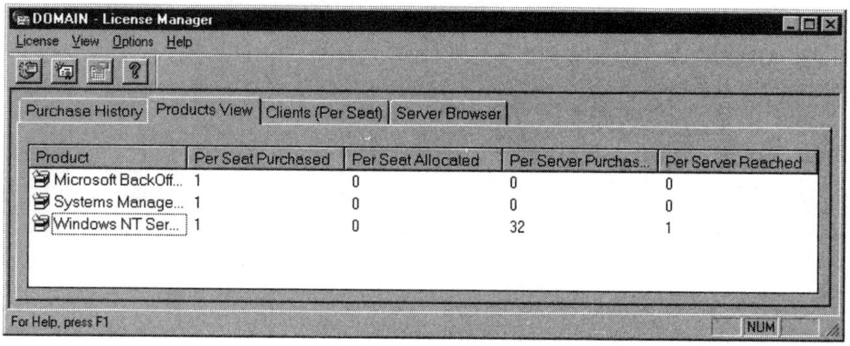

FIGURE 15.5

The License Manager.

DOMAIN - License Manager

License   View   Options   Help

| Purchase History | Products View | Clients (Per Seat) | Server Browser |

Product	Per Seat Purchased	Per Seat Allocated	Per Server Purchas...	Per Server Reached
Microsoft BackOff...	1	0	0	0
Systems Manage...	1	0	0	0
Windows NT Ser...	1	0	32	1

For Help, press F1   NUM

When your network usage exceeds the number of installed licenses for a specific product, a yellow exclamation point icon appears next to the product. You must buy the number of licenses in deficit to maintain legal compliance.

Providing Services for Macintosh Clients

Windows NT Server includes very strong support for Apple Macintosh client computers—stronger even than support for Novell networks. Windows NT Server looks exactly like an AppleShare server (because it is) to Macintosh clients. They can use the AppleShare network redirector built into every MacOS computer. You won't have to install any extra software on the Macintoshes to allow Windows NT Server to support them.

Windows NT File System (NTFS) also supports the multiple-fork file system structure used by the Macintosh Hierarchical File System (HFS) to store resource information for applications such as icons, window positions, fonts, and code resources. This feature makes Windows NT Server fully compatible with Apple Macintosh computers.

PC clients on your network will be able to use the data forks of documents that are shared between Macintosh users and PC users, such as Microsoft Word documents, without disturbing the data in the resource fork.

Support for Macintosh clients is added using Services for Macintosh, which installs the AppleTalk network transport. (This transport is not TDI compliant, so it does not show up in the Transports tab of the Network control panel.) Once MacFile is installed, you will use the Server Manager or WinFile (remember the File Manager from Windows NT 5.31?) to manage your Macintosh-accessible volumes.

Desktop Explorer does not support MacFile services, so you must use either the Server Manager or WinFile to manage Macintosh volumes on your Windows NT Server.

Services for Macintosh

You need to perform two steps to make file services available to Macintoshes on your network.

1. Install the Services for Macintosh service, as shown in Exercise 15.15.

2. Add any volumes you want to make available to Macintosh clients to the MacFile service through the Server Manager as shown in Exercise 15.16.

EXERCISE 15.15

Installing Services for Macintosh

1. Right-click Network Neighborhood.

2. Select Properties.

3. Click the Services tab. Click Add.

4. Select Services for Macintosh from the scrolling list. Click OK.

5. Enter the correct path to your Windows NT Server 4 CD-ROM.

6. Click Continue.

7. Click Close.

8. Select the network adapter connected to the subnetwork on which the majority of your Macintosh clients appear.

9. Enter a default Zone (a Macintosh analogy to the Domain concept in Windows NT) for your Macintosh computers. Most users will leave this blank.

10. Click Close. Answer Yes to restart your computer.

EXERCISE 15.16

Creating Macintosh-Accessible Shares

1. Select Start ➤ Programs ➤ Administrative Tools ➤ Server Manager.

2. Select MacFile ➤ Volumes.

3. Click Create Volume.

4. Enter a name for the volume in the Volume Name input box. This name is somewhat similar to a share name in regular windows networking.

5. Enter the path to the volume in the Path box.

6. Click OK.

7. Click Close. You will notice disk activity in the background for some time as the volume is prepared for Macintosh users.

8. Close the Server Manager.

If you need to enable AppleTalk protocol routing (if you have Macintosh computers on networks serviced by different network adapters in your server), check Enable Routing. You can add default Zones if necessary by checking the Use this router to seed the Network option. Most users will not need to do this. Consult the Macintosh networking documentation that came with your Apple Server if you need to configure these options.

Once you've installed Services for Macintosh, you'll notice two new services running in the Services control panel (File Server for Macintosh and Print Server for Macintosh) and a new control panel called MacFile. The MacFile control panel is very similar to the Server control panel. It lets you see how many users are connected using the File Server for Macintosh, view Macintosh accessible volumes, see files in use, and change miscellaneous AppleShare server settings such as the server name, authentication requirements, and log on message. Figure 15.6 shows the MacFile control panel.

FIGURE 15.6

The MacFile control panel.

MacFile Properties on BOOMERANG

Usage Summary

Active AppleTalk Sessions:	0
Open File Forks:	0
File Locks:	0

Close · Help

Users · Volumes · Files · Attributes

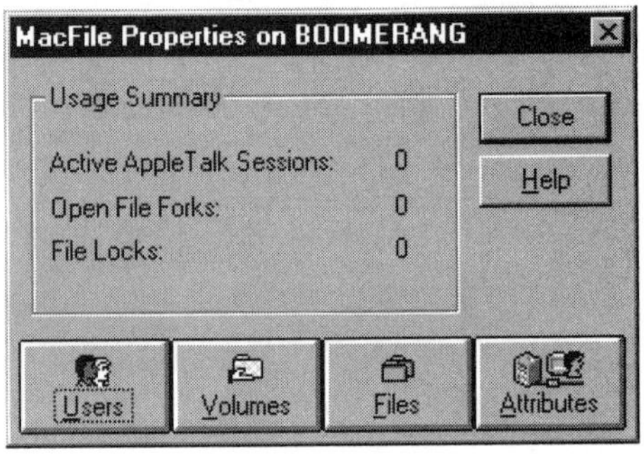

The Server Manager controls how Macintosh clients access the shared volumes on your server. A Macintosh-accessible share was created in the Microsoft UAM Volume folder in your Windows NT boot volume when you installed services for Macintosh. If you want to provide access to other volumes, use the procedure shown in Exercise 15.16.

MacFile will not allow you to create new AppleShare volumes inside other AppleShare volumes, nor will it allow you to share a volume containing an AppleShare volume. For instance, you won't be able to share the root directory of your system volume because the Microsoft UAM volume created by default when you installed MacFile is already shared. To get around this restriction, select the conflicting AppleShare volume and select MacFile ➤ Remove Volume (no files will be deleted). Then select the volume you wish to share and select MacFile ➤ Create volume.

You can use the MacFile menu in WinFile to change permissions on Macintosh-accessible volumes as well. Explore the features of the MacFile menu. Then log on to the Windows NT Server as a Macintosh client to see the effects of the changes you make. Figure 15.7 shows the Volume Permissions dialog box for a Macintosh accessible volume.

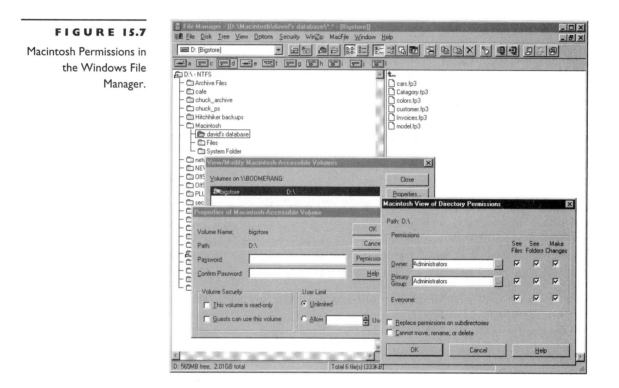

Printing

Windows NT also includes strong support for AppleTalk printers and Macintoshes clients printing to PC printers. Essentially, Windows NT allows any clients on the network to print to any printers on the network, regardless of their normal affiliation. Windows NT will even convert raster documents to PostScript documents so you can continue to use your expensive AppleTalk printers when you migrate to Windows NT.

Printing support is automatically installed when you install Services for Macintosh. All printers normally available to PC clients will be made available to Macintosh clients as part of the boot process. You can check MacPrint messages in the Application log available from the Event Viewer to see when Macintosh printers become available.

You need an AppleTalk printer driver for any printers you wish to use from a Macintosh on your network. Install this printer driver on each Macintosh client on your network to access printers shared by Windows NT. Once you have installed the printer driver, you should be able to use the AppleTalk printer for your Macintosh clients. It will appear the same way any shared Macintosh printer appears.

Install Clients with Client Administrator

The Network Client Administrator is a powerful utility for bringing clients online in a new network installation. To install network client software from many network operating systems, you must do the following:

1. Individually configure each computer in software by determining which drivers, transports, and requester or client files are necessary for that client to attach to the network.

2. Create configuration files to configure these drivers and transports

3. Write a batch file to load the network files in the proper order.

4. Manually modify the boot files of the operating system to load all these various files correctly.

If this job sounds complicated for one operating system, try remembering how to bring up a client on three or four different client platforms.

You will use two major options to install client computers with the Network Client Administrator:

- **Make Network Installation Startup Disk** creates a single unique floppy disk for each client you want to install. You can boot this floppy to automatically install all necessary client software directly from the server without user intervention on the client side. Use this option when you have only a few client computers to install and prefer to enter client configuration information at the time you create the disks.

- **Make Installation Disk Set** creates a set of floppy disks you can use to install any number of clients for the specific operating system you select. Client configuration information is entered at the client computer during the installation. Use this option when you have many client computers to install.

The Make Installation Disk Set option is generally more useful. You can create a single set of installation disks once and use these disks as many times as you like. The Make Network Installation Startup Disk option is used only when you install the specific client for which the disk was created.

The Network Client Administrator makes this job easy by automatically creating installation disks that contain all the files necessary to bring a computer online without manual configuration. The Network Client Administrator also has a function that copies server tools to the server's hard disk and shares the directory so you can connect to and use the administration tools from any computer on your network. The Network Client Administrator can make installation disk sets for the following client platforms:

- Client for Microsoft Networks for MS-DOS and Windows 3.0 or 3.1

- Windows for Workgroups 3.11 (adds TCP/IP support)

- LAN Manager v2.2c for MS-DOS

- LAN Manager v2.2c for OS/2

- Windows 95

- RAS Client for MS-DOS

The Network Client Administrator can make Network Installation Startup Disks for the following clients:

- MS-DOS and Windows

- Windows 95

Windows 95, Windows NT, versions of OS/2 since 2.0, and Macintosh clients do not need installation disk sets because networking support is built into these operating systems. Windows for Workgroups includes built-in networking, but cannot use the TCP/IP protocol stack unless it is installed. Although you can make a network installation startup disk for Windows 95, attaching a Windows 95 computer to a Windows NT network is so easy, using the Network Client Administrator would probably be more trouble.

Despite the multitude of options available, the Network Client Administrator is provided chiefly to make attaching MS-DOS and Windows clients to your network easy.

Unfortunately, the Network Client Administrator works only with network adapters included on the Windows NT CD-ROM. There is no Have Disk option to include a driver from floppy disk. This limitation prevents you from using the Network Client Administrator installation disks with network adapters not included in the Windows NT Server CD-ROM.

Exercise 15.17 shows you how to use the Make Installation Disk Set option of the Network Client Administrator.

EXERCISE 15.17

Making MS-DOS Installation Disk Sets with the Network Client Administrator

1. Select Programs ➤ Administrative Tools ➤ Network Client Administrator.

2. Select Make Installation Disk Set.

3. Click Continue.

4. Select Copy Files to a New Directory. Select Share unless you performed this step earlier. If you have, select Use Existing Shared Directory, enter the server and share names, and skip to step 7.

5. Put the Windows NT Server CD-ROM in your CD-ROM drive and enter the path to the \clients directory on the CD-ROM in the Path input box.

6. Click OK. The Network Client Administrator copies the client installation files to your server and automatically shares the directory.

7. Select Network Client v3.0 for MS-DOS and Windows.

8. Check Format Disks. If your 3 1/2-inch floppy disk drive is not A, select the correct drive in the Destination Drive pick box.

9. Click OK.

10. Insert the first blank disk and click OK. This disk will become the Network Client v3.0 for MS-DOS installation disk 1.

11. Click Yes to quick format the floppy disk.

12. Remove disk 1, insert disk 2, and click OK when prompted.

13. Click Yes to quick format the floppy disk.

14. Remove disk 2 when finished. You are now ready to use the installation disk set to quickly configure MS-DOS and Windows clients with the necessary network drivers, transport protocols, and files to allow access to your Windows NT server.

Once you've created an installation boot disk for MS-DOS, using the installation disks to bring up an MS-DOS client is rather simple. The one thing you should know that isn't obvious is that you can use the Tab key to switch between the Driver, Transport, and Configuration windows.

Summary

Y OU CAN MAKE your network a lot easier to administrate if you plan how you will install, configure, and manage the client computers on your network. You should:

- Standardize client hardware

- Use uniform hardware configurations

- Standardize client software

- Store client software on the file server

- Store user files on the file server

- Implement roaming profiles

You should also use the capabilities of Windows NT Server to support administration. If you use TCP/IP in your network, you will find that the DHCP, WINS, and DNS servers that come with Windows NT will automate the configuration and speed the operation of TCP/IP-based clients.

The Microsoft Mail Postoffice that comes with Windows NT is easy to set up, but you will find that it doesn't have many administrative tools and is very limited in its functionality. It is perfectly adequate for simple e-mail in a small network. If you grow beyond the capabilities of this simple post office, you can install more powerful e-mail products such as Microsoft Exchange Server.

Windows NT 4 includes strong support for Macintosh file and print services, allowing Macintosh clients to log on without additional client software and experience the same level of support as PC clients. Windows NT can make cross-platform environments easy to manage by eliminating the need for separate servers for each type of client in your network.

Review Questions

1. Storing client applications on the server has no drawbacks.

  A. True

  B. False

2. TCP/IP is the easiest protocol to use.

  A. True

  B. False

3. TCP/IP is more difficult to configure than any other protocol included with Windows NT Server.

  A. True

  B. False

4. The Microsoft Mail Postoffice must reside on a domain controller.

  A. True

  B. False

5. You must use the License Manager to maintain compliance with software copyright laws.

  A. True

  B. False

6. The License Manager will keep you from exceeding the legal licensed limit for some software you have installed.

  A. True

  B. False

7. AppleTalk is a TDI-compliant network transport.

  A. True

  B. False

8. Services for Macintosh will allow PCs to print to AppleShare PostScript printers.

   A. True

   B. False

9. Because desktop explorer does not support Services for Macintosh, you must use _____ _____ or _____ to manage Macintosh accessible volumes.

10. The most effective way to reduce your client support burden is to

   A. Use the License Manager

   B. Standardize client hardware

   C. Standardize client software

   D. Use DCHP to automatically assign IP addresses

11. DHCP stands for

   A. Domain Host Configuration Protocol

   B. Domain Host Connection Protocol

   C. Dynamic Host Configuration Protocol

   D. Dynamic Host Connection Protocol

12. The DNS service:

   A. Translates Microsoft network names into IP addresses

   B. Translates fully qualified Internet names into IP addresses

   C. Translates Domain security ID numbers into IP addresses

   D. Serves Web pages on the Internet

13. The WINS service:

   A. Translates Microsoft network names into IP addresses

   B. Translates fully qualified Internet names into IP addresses

   C. Translates Domain security ID numbers into IP addresses

   D. Serves Web pages on the Internet

Performance
Tuning

WINDOWS NT IMPLEMENTS a number of automatic performance optimizations that ensure good performance from just about any Windows NT Server–based network.

However, as with any complex system, understanding how and why resources of the system function (and knowing how to measure their performance) will help you tune your servers and your network for optimal performance.

Performance tuning is finding the resource that slows your network the most, speeding it up until something else has the most impact on speed, and then starting over by finding the new slowest resource. This cycle of finding the speed-limiting factor, eliminating it, and starting over allows you to reach the natural performance limit of your network in a simple, methodical way.

In this chapter we first cover the automatic optimizations that Windows NT performs to ensure that a server will operate smoothly and respond quickly to client requests at almost any load level. Then we dig into performance-tuning theory and definitions, explaining how various software and hardware resources interact to achieve the smooth, responsive system performance you expect from Windows NT.

Next we cover the performance monitor, the tool used to assist with most performance tuning in Windows NT. After you understand how the performance monitor works, we show you how to ferret out processor, memory, and hard disk bottlenecks in your server.

Then we will cover network monitoring and performance tuning to make sure your servers can meet the demands of the clients on your network and to make sure your network data link technology is not a limiting factor in the overall speed of your network.

Overview of Network Performance

BECAUSE THE SPEED at which network clients can work is usually tied to the speed at which they can access the network, the speed of the network limits the speed of every computer attached to it. Many factors affect the responsiveness of a network from the point of view of client computers, but the two that have the most impact are the availability of network bandwidth and the responsiveness of network servers.

Bandwidth *refers to the amount of information that can be transferred in a certain period of time, usually one second. For instance, 100MB of bandwidth refers to the capacity to transfer 100 million bytes of data in one second. The term comes from the early days of data transmission over radio; different channels are referred to as bands, and the width of a band in hertz determines its data carrying capacity. With standard modulation techniques one bit of digital data can be transmitted in 1 hertz.*

If too many computers are competing for a single shared media subnetwork, if the computers are able to process data faster than the data rate (or bandwidth) supported by the network data link, or if the network servers are too loaded down to respond quickly, then the network will limit the speed of network clients. Conversely, if the network is usually immediately available, if the data link bandwidth is greater than the amount of data that the client can process, and if the servers are able to quickly respond to client requests, then the speed of the network will not limit the clients.

Therefore, a fast network requires the following conditions:

- The data rate of the data link technology must exceed the ability of the clients to process data.

- The competition to access shared media networks must not be excessive.

- The servers must be fast enough to respond to all simultaneous client requests.

The next two sections cover speed, first as it relates to individual Windows NT servers and then in terms of network performance.

Bottlenecks

BOTTLENECKS ARE FACTORS that limit performance in a computer. For instance, slow memory limits the speed at which a processor can manipulate data—thus limiting the computer's processing performance to the speed that the processor can access memory. If the memory can respond faster than the processor, the processor is the bottleneck.

The terms processor, microprocessor, *and* central processing unit *(CPU) are synonymous throughout this book.*

System performance is always affected by a bottleneck. You may not notice it because your computer may run faster than the work you perform requires. Chances are, if you use your computer only for word processing, the speed of your machine has never limited how fast you can work. On the other hand, if you use your computer as a CAD workstation or to compute missile trajectories, chances are you've spent a lot of time waiting for the computer to catch up to you.

Users of client computers in your network should be the bottleneck in your network. To achieve performance nirvana, their computers must be more responsive than they need to be, the network data link must be more responsive than the clients attached to it, and the servers must be more responsive than the networks to which they are attached.

Performance tuning in both individual computers and networks is the systematic process of finding the resource experiencing the most load and then relieving that load. You can almost always optimize a server to make it more responsive. Understanding how Windows NT Server achieves its performance and how you can increase its performance is important. Even if you don't need to make your servers any faster, understanding performance tuning can help you diagnose many problems.

Before we get too far into discussing computer performance, you should understand a few of the terms we will be using in the context of performance tuning.

- **Resources** are hardware components that provide some quantifiable work capacity in the context of performance tuning. Software processes load down hardware resources.

- **Bottlenecks** are resources with performance limitations that affect the responsiveness of a computer. When used singularly, bottleneck refers to the single most-limited component of the system.

- **Load** is the amount of work that a resource has to perform. For example, the network is under heavy load if it is constantly transmitting data. The microprocessor is said to be under heavy load if it is performing a number of complex math operations.

- **Optimizations** are the measures taken to reduce the impact of a bottleneck on performance. Optimizations may include eliminating unnecessary loading, sharing loads across devices, or finding ways to increase the speed of a resource.

- **Throughput** is the measure of information flow through a resource. For instance, disk I/O throughput is the measure of how much data can be read from or written to a disk in a given time period, usually one second.

- **Bandwidth** is synonymous with throughput.

- **Processes** are software services running concurrently on your computer that perform a certain function. Drivers and file systems are processes. A process has its own address space and is therefore protected from other processes in Windows NT.

- **Threads** are software chains of execution that run concurrently to perform the functionality of a process within the address space of that process. A process is one or more threads. Threads are the basic units of division among processors in multiprocessing environments.

The term bottleneck comes from the observation that the neck of a bottle limits the flow of water through it. Imagine the difference between turning over a cup of water and turning over a bottle of water to visualize why that term is used.

Exercise 16.1 will help you see the difference between threads and processes by introducing the task manager. If you are running any other applications, you can leave them running, but you will have more information showing in the task manager than the exercise describes.

EXERCISE 16.1

Viewing Applications, Processes, and Threads

1. Select Programs ➢ Accessories ➢ Paint from the Start menu.

2. Select Programs ➢ Accessories ➢ WordPad from the Start menu.

3. Simultaneously press Ctrl+Alt+Del.

4. Click Task Manager.

5. Select the Applications tab.

6. Notice the number of applications running. You should see Paint and WordPad in the Task list box.

7. Select the Processes tab.

8. Notice how many processes are running. Find the mspaint.exe and wordpad.exe processes in the list. In this case each application has only one process. The other processes you see are system processes that run all the time.

9. Select the Performance tab.

10. Notice how many threads are running in the totals box.

11. Close the Windows NT task manager.

Now that you understand the terminology, we can discuss how performance tuning works. A slow hardware resource, such as a hard disk drive, causes the microprocessor and system RAM (both fast) to wait for it to complete I/O requests. Thus during disk I/O, the speed of the hard disk is the speed of the computer.

Although you cannot make your hard disk faster (except by replacing it with a faster one), you may be able to reduce the number of times the computer needs to access it or to limit the amount of information transferred. You may also be able to spread the load across many hard disk drives, thus dividing the time you spend waiting for drive access by the number of drives available.

Eventually, you will find a limitation that you cannot overcome. This point is the natural limit of your machine, and finding it is the ultimate goal of performance tuning. If you need speed beyond the natural limit of your machine, you will need to upgrade the hardware resource causing the limitation.

Finding Bottlenecks

Ferreting out bottlenecks involves a little understanding of how computers and networks work, and it requires some software. Even the best system engineers can only guess at what causes a complex system to run slowly unless they have proper monitoring tools. Windows NT provides a comprehensive set of tools for finding and eliminating bottlenecks in both servers and networks.

To find a bottleneck, you must be able to measure the speed of the different resources in your system. Measurements enable you to find the one resource that is performing at its peak and therefore causing the bottleneck.

Hardware resources operating at their maximum performance level are the bottlenecks.

Different resources require different measurements. For example:

- Network traffic is measured as a percentage of utilization.

- Disk throughput is measured in megabytes per seconds.

- Interrupt activity is measured in interrupts per second.

To compare resources, you must use measurements that are equal. In most cases, Windows NT provides a basic "percentage of processor time spent doing this" metric that you can use to compare unlike resources.

To find a bottleneck in a network, you use the network monitor to determine whether your data link layer is sufficient for the number of computers on it. With an Ethernet or Fast Ethernet network, a sustained network utilization of 30 percent or more is an indication that you need to consider splitting that subnetwork into two or more subnetworks or moving to a faster data link technology. If your network is not experiencing excessive utilization, servers that are too loaded to respond to client requests quickly may be causing slow performance. Perhaps the servers are not optimized for their tasks or perhaps they simply aren't powerful enough to handle their duties for the number of clients attached.

To find a bottleneck in a server, you first run the performance monitor application that we discuss later in this chapter. You then have to put your server under the load that causes it to perform more slowly than you want. Attach multiple clients to your network file server and start copying files. Run SQL Server and put it under load by generating complex queries. Do whatever normally makes your server slow.

The performance and network monitors will suggest a few broad measures that will show you where to search more deeply to find the exact bottleneck. For example, if after showing processor time and disk time you see that the disk is running at its peak, you know to concentrate on disk-related measurements. Or if the network monitor shows that the network is under excessive load, try to find the clients that are transmitting excessively and determine if their traffic is appropriate. If it is, you should try splitting your subnetworks further or upgrade to a faster data link technology.

Make certain you've found the bottleneck before concentrating on detailed performance monitoring. Since performance-limited resources hide behind other, slower resources, you won't be able to see the difference if you make changes to objects that are not truly the bottleneck.

Eliminating Bottlenecks

Finding a bottleneck is only half the battle. Eliminating it (making it fast enough that something else becomes the primary bottleneck) may involve changing a Control Panel setting, or it may involve replacing every cable in your network and the devices that connect to them. You will have to determine how to relieve the load placed on the resource.

Usually, you will be able to look at more detailed measurements to determine the specific activity that is loading down your network. For instance, if you determine that your network utilization is high, you should then use the network monitor to determine which computers are generating that load and why. You may find that you have a malfunctioning device on your network that is generating spurious traffic or that your replication or backup scheme is generating far more network traffic than you suspected. These problems are easy to correct. Sometimes, however, you'll find that your network simply isn't fast enough, and major architectural changes are in order.

When troubleshooting, make only one change at a time. Otherwise, you will not be able to tell which change fixed the problem.

The Perpetual Cycle

Achieving maximum performance from your network is a continuing process. Once you've eliminated the major bottleneck in your system, you start over and eliminate the next new bottleneck. Your system will always have a bottleneck because one resource will always cause other resources to wait for it.

You want to eliminate bottlenecks until

- You make your computer so fast that you never need to wait for it.

- You find the component to replace or upgrade.

- You realize that you can't afford to buy any more new components and settle for what you have.

Improving Network Performance

W HEN NETWORKS BEGIN to run slowly, speeding them up can be very difficult. Here are three ways to improve network performance:

- **Reduce traffic.** This option is best when circumstances permit because it works regardless of your current network architecture and does not require any physical changes. Reducing traffic may mean localizing servers inside departmental subnetworks or migrating network applications to lower bandwidth Internet client/server protocols.

- **Increase the number of subnetworks.** This option is the next best. This approach is equivalent to building more roads to relieve traffic congestion, rather than simply raising the speed limit.

- **Increase speed.** This option works very well, but it is also very expensive because it requires the replacement of every data link device on the network. This option should be regarded as a major network architectural change and implemented slowly over a period of time.

Reducing Traffic

There is no systematic way to reduce network traffic—you must monitor your network using the tools discussed later in this chapter and decide whether you can relieve the traffic load on your network. However, you can look for a few problem areas.

- Users who generate excessive traffic (compared to their peers). Find out why. If they don't have a valid work-related reason, encourage them to stop.

- Diskless workstations running Windows. These stations generate an enormous load on networks. Hard disks are very inexpensive compared to the cost of a network upgrade, so consider adding hard disks to these machines and booting the operating system locally.

- Network loading of applications that could be stored locally. Although we recommend in Chapter 15 the central installation of applications for ease of administration, decreasing the load on your network may be a higher priority for you. This trade-off is typical of the many cost, performance, and ease-of-use compromises you will make.

- Inefficient client applications that rely on data stored on the network with true client/server application. An example would be migrating an Access database stored on a server to a client/server database using an Access front end and an SQL server back end.

IDENTIFYING TOP TALKERS Reducing your network load usually involves identifying which computers generate the most load, determining why, and reducing the load generated by that specific computer if possible. Repeating this process until you can't relieve the load any further will reduce traffic to the extent possible.

Routers, bridges, and servers normally generate the most load on the network. Servers usually respond to each client request, so they normally generate about 50 percent of the load on a network. Bridges and routers are actually forwarding data from other networks, but their Media Access Control (MAC) addresses will appear in the network monitor as the source of the traffic.

If you are using a packet sniffer such as the network monitor to monitor network traffic and you see multiple IP addresses coming from a single MAC address, the traffic is coming through a bridge or router.

Splitting Networks

Unless your network is far behind your traffic requirements, you will be able to get a lot of mileage out of simply splitting your shared media networks into multiple subnetworks joined by bridges, routers, or servers performing the routing service.

In our highway analogy, splitting networks is the same thing as building more highways. In theory, doubling the number of collision domains cuts the traffic on each in half. However, that method works only when you can guarantee that both sides of the conversation are on the same subnetwork. For instance, if you split your network but two computers that spend most of their time communicating on the network are on different subnetworks, you haven't solved the problem. Their traffic will simply be retransmitted on both subnetworks.

Putting an Ethernet switch at the center of many Ethernet subnetworks is an easy and hassle-free way to split and reconnect networks without spending a lot of time changing the network architecture. Make sure you put servers in the subnetworks where they are used most for the best efficiency.

You have to make sure you've isolated computers that spend time talking to each other on the same subnetworks, which is why basing subnetworks on some real grouping of individuals, such as by department, usually works well. These users, and by extension, their computers, will spend most of their time communicating internally.

The vast majority of all network traffic in client/server local area networks is between clients and servers. Peer-to-peer networks may be communicating with any other computers on the network, which makes splitting subnetworks difficult. However, because most clients spend the majority of their time communicating with a single server, you can usually simply make the server a part of each subnetwork. Figure 16.1 shows a network that puts a single server on each subnetwork, thus efficiently multiplying the total bandwidth to the server without upgrading to a higher-speed network.

FIGURE 16.1

A central server on multiple subnetworks.

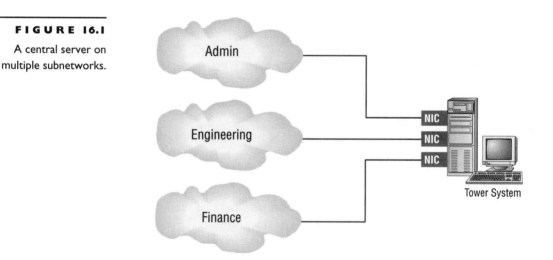

This solution isn't quite as easy when you have more than one server, but you can still identify the server that each client usually talks to and put that client on the same subnetwork as that server. Then, by attaching all your servers to a single high-speed subnetwork, you can route any traffic for other servers over a higher-speed link rather than upgrading the link technology of your entire network. The configuration in Figure 16.2 shows a high-speed backbone between servers localized to subdomains.

FIGURE 16.2

Many departmental
servers on a high-speed
backbone.

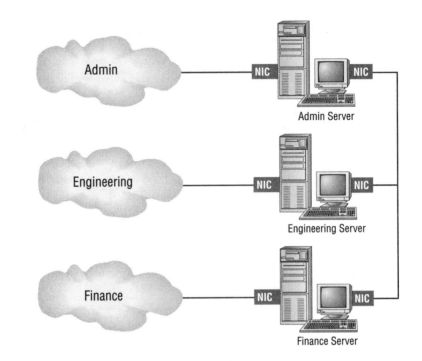

When clients must access many different servers without preference (this is rare), you may need to implement servers on a high-speed backbone, using dedicated routers to attach client subnetworks. This architecture has the disadvantage of requiring expensive routers to attach to the backbone. It also means that every packet transmitted to a server must traverse the backbone, forcing the backbone to deal with the vast majority of all the traffic on the network. Figure 16.3 shows servers on a high-speed backbone.

In some situations clients must access not only their departmental server but also many other servers (for example, an intranet server, a messaging server, and an Internet gateway). An obvious solution would be to simply put all the servers on a backbone and route to them, but that configuration might not be the best. Even if the clients spend only 25 percent of their network time communicating with their departmental server, you're better off attaching them to the server directly and using it to route to a backbone containing the other servers. Remember that every packet you keep off the backbone makes the backbone faster. For instance, a network with four departmental servers that are able to deal with 25 percent of their client's requests without forwarding them to the backbone will cut backbone traffic in half. That load reduction can stave off migrating to a higher-speed network technology for years.

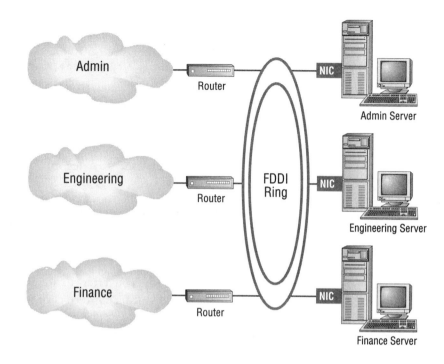

FIGURE 16.3

Many servers on a high-
speed backbone.

Routing can be a significant performance hit for servers, however. When-ever you configure servers to perform a routing function, you should monitor them periodically to ensure they are not causing a significant network bottle-neck. If they are, you should move the server inside the department and use a dedicated bridge or router to perform the routing function.

Routers are simply high-speed servers designed to route packets very efficiently and with as little delay as possible.

Increasing Speed

If you can no longer reduce traffic or efficiently divide subnetworks, you will have to upgrade the physical data link network protocol. Usually, this upgrade means moving from Ethernet or Token Ring to Fast Ethernet or Fiber Distributed Data Interface (FDDI).

Remember that you may not have to upgrade your entire network. You may be able to simply upgrade your backbone technology, the links between servers, or certain subnetworks or users to higher speed networks. Use the net-work monitor to identify top talkers on your network and migrate those users to faster protocols first.

FAST ETHERNET Fast Ethernet is simply regular Ethernet at ten times the raw throughput. Fast Ethernet runs at 100 megabits rather than at 10. The two major varieties of Fast Ethernet are 100Base-X, which is regular Ethernet at a higher speed, and 100Base-VG (AnyLAN), which uses a similar but incompatible access method that can guarantee throughput even in heavily loaded networks, making applications such as real-time voice or video possible over the network.

Three varieties of 100Base-X fast Ethernet exist:

- 100Base-TX runs over standard category 5 twisted-pair wiring on two pairs.

- 100Base-T4 runs over category 3, 4, or 5 twisted-pair wiring on all four pairs.

- 100Base-FX runs over one pair of multimode optical fibers.

You must use special media converters to adapt from any one cable type to another. Some hubs include media converters or transceivers that do the job for you. Most 100Base-FX adapters and some 100Base-TX adapters can operate in a special mode called "full duplex," which allows them to simultaneously transmit and receive data and eliminates collisions on the wire. Collisions still occur inside hubs, however. This technology not only doubles the capacity of Fast Ethernet to 200Mb/s but also extends the distance limitation of 100Base-FX from 400 meters to 2,000.

FIBER DISTRIBUTED DATA INTERFACE (FDDI) FDDI is essentially 100-megabit Token Ring over fiber optic cable with a second counter-rotating (the data flows in the opposite direction) ring that provides a measure of fault tolerance in case of cable faults. A copper variant called CDDI runs over the same category 5 twisted-pair wiring that fast Ethernet runs over.

FDDI is the oldest high-speed network technology in common use. Early problems with fault tolerance features were solved long ago, and although it remains expensive, FDDI is very stable and can support operations at metropolitan-area distances.

ASYNCHRONOUS TRANSFER MODE (ATM) ATM is the new telephony standard for wide-area telecommunications links. Because it supports different guaranteed levels of service for voice, video, and data networking at very high data rates, ATM has become a compelling new option for campus-area transports. ATM standards using the same frame technology have been defined for the following data rates:

- ATM-25 runs at 25Mb/s and is intended as a competitor to Fast Ethernet in local area networks.

- STS-3 runs at 155Mb/s over fiber or category 5 twisted-pair wiring as an alternative to Fast Ethernet or FDDI in high-speed workstations or network backbones.

- STS-12 runs at 620Mb/s over fiber as a campus area transport.

- STS-48 runs at 2.2Gb/s over fiber as a metropolitan area transport. Few computer networks will implement this speed, but they may be attached to telephone networks operating at this speed.

- STS-192 runs at 8.8Gb/s over fiber as a long-distance intercity transport. Only telephone companies will install this grade of ATM.

The compelling factor in ATM is that the same frame technology can be switched among any of the data rates listed above by relatively simple switches. Unfortunately, the ATM standards are still not completely defined, and you may have trouble getting devices from different manufacturers to communicate properly. Be certain to choose equipment that the manufacturers guarantee to be compatible before buying any ATM equipment.

FIBERCHANNEL FiberChannel was developed as a high-speed peripheral interconnection bus for disk arrays and mainframe computers, but its very high data rate (256Mb/s or 1Gb/s) make it compelling as a point-to-point, full-duplex, server-to-server connection. It is the least expensive gigabit networking technology available.

GIGABIT ETHERNET Gigabit Ethernet encapsulates regular Ethernet frames inside the data payload of FiberChannel frames, which makes the endpoints of a FiberChannel network work like an Ethernet bridge. Gigabit Ethernet will probably be the least-expensive high-speed backbone technology available for quite some time, especially for networks using Ethernet or Fast Ethernet.

Windows NT Self-Tuning Mechanisms

Y ou may never have to deal with manual performance tuning because Window s NT tunes itself very well for most users and most situations. Unlike many operating systems, Windows NT does not require you to manually adjust arcane environment variables to improve its performance. Windows NT takes care itself. The tuning you will do to optimize Windows NT performance involves determining which hardware resources are under the greatest load and then relieving that load. Windows NT comes with some very powerful tools to assist you, but because of the self-tuning nature of Windows NT, you may never have to use them.

Windows NT implements a number of automatic performance optimizations. They are

- Symmetric multiprocessing

- Avoiding physical memory fragmentation

- Swapping across multiple disks to increase performance

- Prioritizing threads and processes

- Caching disk requests

Multiprocessing

Multiprocessing divides the processing load across several microprocessors. Windows NT uses *symmetric multiprocessing*, a technique in which the total processor load is split evenly among processors. Simpler operating systems use *asymmetric processing*, which splits the processing load according to some non-load-based metric. Usually, those operating systems put all system tasks on one processor and all user tasks on the remaining processors.

Windows NT Server ships with support for four microprocessors. If you have a computer that uses more than four microprocessors, contact your OEM vendor for the support files for your server.

Scheduling and resource assignment between processors takes computing time, which means that two processors are not twice as fast as one processor. Windows NT with two processors generally runs at about 150 percent of the speed of a one-processor system, depending upon the type of programs run. An application that has only one thread cannot be run on more than one processor.

In many computing problems, threads depend on results provided by other threads. This circumstance is like a baton race in which a runner (thread) must wait for the baton (results) before starting. Obviously, splitting these threads among processors doesn't make the application run any faster. Multiprocessing works best with large computing data sets that can be broken into chunks and solved independently.

Memory Optimizations

Windows NT performs a number of optimizations to make the most effective use of random access memory (RAM). In Windows NT, memory is divided into 4KB chunks called pages. Each page can be used by only one thread. A thread may be stored in any number of pages. Consequently, a 13KB thread actually takes 16KB of physical RAM because the remaining 3KB in the last page cannot be used by anything else.

Some operating systems use 64KB page files to maximize swapping speed (64KB is the maximum size of a single block transfer to SCSI and IDE hard disks). Unfortunately, this optimization forces each thread to use a minimum of 64KB. If the average size of an executing thread is 96KB, 25 percent of physical RAM would be wasted on unusable excess storage. Windows NT loses the performance benefit of 64KB page sizes in order to leave more physical memory available to reduce the necessity for swapping.

The system must have enough memory to store all the executing threads. If the amount of memory is insufficient, Windows NT uses a portion of the hard disk to simulate memory by swapping memory pages not currently in use to a special system file called the virtual memory swap file (`pagefile.sys`). When the system needs the pages that were swapped to disk, Windows NT trades pages in RAM for pages on the hard disk. This process is completely hidden from the threads, which do not need to know anything about memory swapping.

The more memory you have, the less time the system spends on page swapping. Windows NT systems with less than 32MB of memory spend a significant amount of time swapping pages to the virtual memory page file, especially if they are running more than one application at a time. This swapping activity slows the computer dramatically because hard disks are very slow (but very cheap) compared to physical RAM.

The faster page swapping happens, the lower its impact on system responsiveness. To speed up this process, Windows NT supports simultaneous writing to more than one hard disk for its virtual memory paging file. Since physical drives can operate simultaneously, splitting the virtual memory swap file among different disks allows Windows NT to divide the time spent processing virtual memory swaps by the number of physical disks. Exercise 16.2 shows you how to split your swap file among more than one disk. Note that you must have more than one hard disk drive to perform this exercise.

Windows NT allows you to split your swap file among volumes on the same physical disk, but there is no performance-related reason to do so. In fact, this configuration increases swap time by forcing the drive head to move a great deal more than normal during swapping. You should set only one swap file per physical disk.

EXERCISE 16.2

Splitting the Swap File among Disks

1. Select Settings ➤ Control Panel from the Start menu.

2. Double-click the System control panel.

3. Select the Performance tab.

4. Click Change in the virtual memory area.

5. Select the primary volume on the first physical disk.

6. Set the Page file Initial size to 16MB.

7. Set the Page file Maximum size to 48MB.

8. Click set.

9. Repeat steps 5 through 8 for the primary volume on each physical disk.

10. Click OK.

11. Click Close.

12. Answer Yes to restart your computer.

Prioritizing Threads and Processes

In a multitasking operating system, if each thread of each process got equal processor time round-robin fashion, the computer would respond to user requests very slowly. System processes such as moving the mouse cursor or updating the screen must happen all the time—far more often than most other system processes.

Windows NT prioritizes each thread based on its importance to system responsiveness or any requirements it may have to respond to external (real-time) events in a timely fashion. Windows NT does a good job of setting thread priorities by default, but Microsoft cannot predict exactly how you will use your computer, so it leaves you the ability to tune priorities.

Processes start with a base priority of 7 on a scale of 0 to 31. Each thread of a process inherits the base priority of the process. Windows NT can vary priority levels up to two priorities higher or lower automatically as the system runs, allowing the system to prioritize as it sees fit. Users can also start processes with higher-than-normal priorities. Figure 16.4 shows the Windows NT thread priority scale.

Extremely high-priority threads are called "real time" threads because they usually must respond to some "real" (i.e., non-computer-generated) event within a certain period of time. For instance, if a computer is polling an input for an event that can occur within a fraction of a second, the computer must check every fraction of a second to see if that event occurred. Missing the time frame for the event could mean missing the event entirely.

FIGURE 16.4

Thread priorities in Windows NT

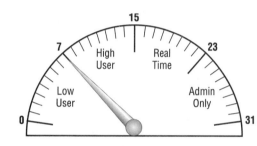

Real-time applications are started with priorities higher than 23. These real-time processes require processor time quite frequently to ensure that they can respond to external real-time events. Drivers, which must respond to hardware events very close to the time the device demands attention, run in these priority levels.

Only administrators may start processes with a priority higher than 23. These processes demand so much processor time that they can make all other processes run very slowly. Starting a regular application with a priority this high will make even moving the cursor slow and laborious. Starting processes with other-than-normal priorities is shown in Exercise 16.15 in the "Application Performance" section of this chapter.

You can also increase the priority of an already running program through the task manager. This step will normally not be necessary, but it is a good way to test the demands a process will make on the system at different priority levels.

Caching Disk Requests

Windows NT uses disk caching to reduce the amount of input/output traffic to the hard disk drive. Caching works by reserving a portion of memory as a staging area for hard disk reads and writes. When data is read from the disk, it is stored in the cache. If the same data needs to be read again, it is retrieved from the very fast memory cache, rather than from the disk.

In this book the term memory *is synonymous with* random access memory (RAM), *not with hard disk space.*

Actually, disk read operations don't just bring in the data requested. Entire clusters are transferred from the hard disk to the memory cache because read and write operations are most efficient at the cluster size. Consequently, a good portion of the data on the hard disk located immediately after the data that is requested also comes into the memory cache. Because read accesses tend to be sequential, the next read request is likely to be in the cache.

The disk cache is also used for write operations. The Windows NT file system (NTFS) doesn't write data to the hard disk immediately. It waits for system idle time so as not to affect the responsiveness of the system. Data writes are stored the memory cache until they are written to disk. Often, especially in transaction-oriented systems like databases, new changes supersede data writes in the cache even before it is written from the cache to the hard disk. Consequently, the write cache has eliminated the need to write that data to disk.

Data writes waiting in the cache can also be read back if they are subsequently requested, which allows yet another cache-related optimization. The type of caching used in Windows NT is called *write-back caching,* as opposed to *write-through caching,* which immediately writes data to the disk while preserving it in the cache for subsequent rereads. Write-through caching is used in operating systems that cannot otherwise guarantee the integrity of data on the disk if power is lost while data is in the cache waiting to be written to disk.

Caching is analogous to using your refrigerator to store food rather than going to the grocery store each time you need an egg or a glass of milk. By estimating your future needs, you are able to make one trip out to the slow resource (the grocery store) and store the data (food) you need very close to you in the cache (refrigerator). Don't try to extend this analogy to write-back caching though.

The caching schemes used in hardware to make your microprocessor run faster operate on exactly the same cache theory as presented here.

Windows NT uses all the memory that remains free after the running processes have the memory they need. Windows NT dynamically changes the amount of memory assigned to the disk cache as new processes are started to ensure the optimal performance boost from caching. Windows NT balances the amount of disk cache and the amount of virtual memory page swapping to optimize the use of physical memory.

Although you cannot change any software parameters to affect caching performance, you can add more memory, up to the limit your motherboard will support. Windows NT Server runs best when used with at least 24MB of RAM. Windows NT can make good use of all the RAM you give it.

Performance Monitoring

THE WINDOWS NT performance monitor is an amazing tool, unique to the Windows NT operating system, that provides the ability to inspect the performance of just about every process and resource that occurs in your computer (see Figure 16.5). The performance monitor allows you to determine the exact cause of every performance-related problem your computer experiences.

FIGURE 16.5

The Performance Monitor window displaying some processor and disk activity.

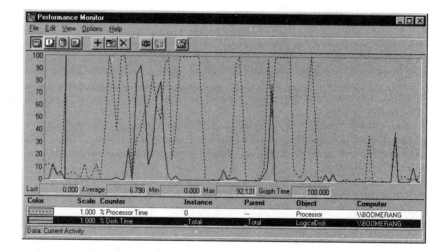

Performance and the performance monitor are broad topics. An entire book could be dedicated to the various features and the work flow theory used to discern where and why bottlenecks occur. Windows NT automatically makes most adjustments for you though, so that level of detail is not required to make your computer run well for most tasks.

This section explains how the performance monitor works and tells you which indicators to watch to quickly narrow down performance problems. You cannot harm your system by experimenting with the performance monitor, so feel free to see the effect of the different low-level indicators.

Heisenberg's uncertainty principle states that to measure quantum phenomena is to change them. This principle is also true of performance monitoring. Running the performance monitor takes a small amount of CPU time, and enabling disk monitoring also slows input/output requests slightly. Therefore, you cannot measure system performance without causing the performance to change slightly. In almost every case, this change in performance is slight and will have no real effect on your measurements or the validity of your conclusions, but you should be aware that it is happening.

The performance monitor doesn't actually measure anything. It is only a graphical tool used to inspect the measurements that occur constantly throughout the running processes in Windows NT.

Be sure to let your computer finish the various logon processes before using the performance monitor to measure performance. A number of services are started in the background after logging on that will affect performance measurements taken right after booting.

Exercise 16.3 shows how to start the performance monitor. The remaining exercises in this chapter assume that the performance monitor is already loaded.

EXERCISE 16.3

Starting the Performance Monitor

1. Select Start ➤ Programs ➤ Administrative Tools ➤ Performance Monitor.

2. Size the Performance Monitor window so that it takes up about one-quarter of your screen.

3. Select Add to Chart in the Edit menu.

4. Click Add when the drop-down box opens with %Processor Time selected.

This value is the measure of how busy the microprocessor is. Leave this measurement running throughout the remaining exercises.

Object Counters

Each Windows NT software object is associated with counters that are incremented each time that object performs a function. For instance, each time a network device driver reads a packet, the device driver increments the packet's read counter by one and the byte's read counter by the size of the packet. Or each time the processor switches threads, it updates the time spent in that thread in a counter used for that purpose.

Counters permeate all Windows NT objects, and they allow meaningful measurement to occur by accounting for everything that happens. Windows NT uses many of these counters to measure performance for its own automatic optimizations and is the first PC operating system to include this level of support for performance monitoring. Table 16.1 shows the objects that you can monitor with the performance monitor.

TABLE 16.1 Windows NT Object Counters	OBJECT	PURPOSE
	Cache	Microprocessor level 2 cache performance
	Logical disk	Mass storage performance, including network storage
	Memory	Memory performance and usage
	Objects	Process and thread counts
	Paging file	Virtual memory usage
	Physical disk	Hard disk drive performance
	Process	Executing process performance
	Processor	Microprocessor performance
	System	Windows NT performance
	Thread	Individual thread performance

You will also see objects for each network service you have installed. Any software can be written to register performance monitoring counters with the system, so you may see even more counters than are shown here.

Processor Performance

The microprocessor is generally the fastest component in a computer. In Pentium class and higher computers, the microprocessor is rarely the cause of a bottleneck unless you are running scientific, mathematical, or graphical software that puts a heavy load on the floating-point unit of the microprocessor.

Windows NT was designed to run on fast microprocessors. If you are using a computer with a processor slower than a Pentium, you may be experiencing processor bottlenecks routinely.

Monitoring Processor Performance

As with all performance objects, a few measurements will give you a good idea of whether the processor is a bottleneck in your system. Important processor-related counters are

- Processor: %Processor Time

- Processor: Interrupts/sec

- System: Processor Queue Length

PROCESSOR: %PROCESSOR TIME The microprocessor does not become a bottleneck until you see a sustained 80 percent or better level of utilization when watching the Processor:%Processor Time counter in the performance monitor. If after tuning your computer to eliminate processor bottlenecks, it still runs in this zone, you need to upgrade to a faster (or another) microprocessor. This counter shows how busy the microprocessor is. The processor will spike to 100 percent at times—this spike is normal and does not indicate a bottleneck. As long as the processor normally runs somewhere between 0 and 80 percent, your processor is sufficient for the work load. Exercise 16.4 shows you how to add this counter to the performance monitor.

After adding this counter, let the computer idle for a moment. Now move your mouse around on the screen and notice the effect on the Processor: %Processor Time measure. Dramatic, isn't it?

EXERCISE 16.4

Adding Processor: %Processor Time to the Performance Monitor

1. Click + in the Performance Monitor tool bar.

2. Select Processor in the Object drop-down list.

3. Select % Processor Time in the Counter drop-down box.

4. Click Add.

5. Close the Add to Chart window.

PROCESSOR: INTERRUPTS/SEC Processor: Interrupts/sec measures the rate of service requests from peripheral devices. An unusual amount of activity on this counter without a corresponding increase in computer activity indicates that a hardware component is malfunctioning and is sending spurious interrupts. This counter should operate continuously between 100 and 1,000, but spikes up to 2,000 are acceptable. Exercise 16.5 shows how to use the Interrupts/sec performance counter.

EXERCISE 16.5

Adding Processor: Interrupts/sec to the Performance Monitor

1. Click + in the Performance Monitor tool bar.

2. Select Processor in the Object drop-down list.

3. Select Interrupts/sec in the Counter drop-down box.

4. Select 0.1 in the Scale drop-down list.

5. Click Add.

6. Close the Add to Chart window.

SYSTEM: PROCESSOR QUEUE LENGTH System: Processor Queue Length counts the number of threads waiting for attention from the processor. Each thread requires a portion of microprocessor time. Many threads running simultaneously may exceed the supply of processor time, causing the microprocessor to become a bottleneck. A sustained thread queue greater than two indicates a processor bottleneck; too many threads are standing in line awaiting execution, which bogs down the processes that rely upon those threads.

If you try to watch the processor queue length indicator only, you will notice that it always sits at zero. This reading occurs because the performance monitor must be monitoring a thread-related counter to determine how many threads are awaiting execution. To see the true value of the processor queue length counter, you must also be monitoring a thread counter of some sort. Exercise 16.6 shows how to monitor the processor queue length.

EXERCISE 16.6

Adding System: Processor Queue Length to the Performance Monitor

1. Click + in the Performance Monitor tool bar.

2. Select System in the Object drop-down list.

3. Select Processor Queue Length in the Counter drop-down box.

4. Click Add.

5. Select Thread in the Object drop-down list.

6. Select Context Switches/sec in the Counter drop-down box.

7. Leave Total selected in the Instance drop-down box.

8. Close the Add to Chart window.

Remember that to monitor the processor queue length, you must also be monitoring a thread-specific counter. Context Switches/sec shows how many thread switches occur each second.

Troubleshooting Processor Performance

If you have determined that your processor is truly a bottleneck, you may not be able to find an inexpensive way to fix your problem. Before you run out and buy a new processor, check your computer for the following common problems:

- Do you have sufficient external processor cache?

- Are your internal and external caches enabled?

- Is the BIOS processor startup speed setting set to Fast?

SUFFICIENT PROCESSOR CACHE Do you have sufficient level 2 cache? Reboot your computer and enter the BIOS. Find the area that describes the amount of external cache your computer uses. Your system should have at least 256K external cache. Some Pentium-class computers ship with less than this amount. If your computer does not have at least this much cache memory, you need to increase it.

Some computers ship with EDO RAM (which is faster than normal memory) to eliminate the necessity for an external cache. Unfortunately, EDO RAM does not speed up your computer as much as a 256K external cache does. Even if you have EDO RAM in your computer, you should add an external cache if you can.

ENABLING CACHES Are your processor level 1 and level 2 caches enabled? Using the manual that came with your computer or motherboard, enter the BIOS settings when you reboot your computer and verify that both the CPU internal cache and the external (or level 2) cache are enabled. If they are not, enable them.

Changing settings in your BIOS without knowing exactly what the setting does may cause your computer to become erratic or fail to work. If you are not comfortable with the BIOS, have an experienced PC technician make these changes for you.

DECIDING WHAT TO UPGRADE If you determine that your processor is the bottleneck, you will need to upgrade to a newer microprocessor or computer. If you can't get a microprocessor that is twice as fast to work in your computer, don't bother upgrading the microprocessor. Upgrade the entire computer.

Disk Performance

Disks are the biggest single bottleneck in your computer. Booting, application loading, data storage and retrieval, and swap file performance are all tied to the speed of your disk because disks are so much slower than the processor or memory. For these reasons, the speed of your disk(s) affects the overall speed of your computer.

As with all performance monitoring in Windows NT Server, you can use the disk monitor to profile your disk activity. However, your computer also comes with a performance indicator that works in any operating system: the hard disk drive light. If your disk light is on most of the time under normal working conditions, you need to add RAM. You can't avoid this solution, and all the performance monitoring on the planet isn't going to uncover a different answer.

Physical versus Logical Disk Performance

In Table 16.1 you'll notice two disk-related objects: logical disk and physical disk. Logical disk is used to measure performance at a higher level than physical disk.

The logical disk object can measure the performance of network connections that are mapped as drives and the performance of volume sets and stripe sets that cross physical disks. You will use the logical disk object to uncover bottlenecks initially and then move to the physical disk object to uncover the reasons why that bottleneck is occurring.

Physical disk measures only real transfers to and from actual hard disk drives (or a RAID set in the case of RAID controllers, discussed later in this chapter). These measures isolate performance differences between disks in your system and provide detailed information about the specific performance of a certain disk.

High-Impact Counters

Disk counters cause a measurable performance degradation by distracting the processor at critical input/output periods. These counters are disabled by default. If you attempt to monitor physical or logical disk performance without enabling these counters, you will not see any disk data.

On Intel i386-based computers, the disk counters cause about a 2 percent degradation in overall performance. You should enable them only when you need to monitor disk performance (and disable them when you are finished). Enabling the disk counters is shown in Exercise 16.7.

EXERCISE 16.7

Enabling the Disk Performance Counters

1. Select Start ➤ Programs ➤ Command Prompt.

2. Type **diskperf -y** in the input line and press Enter. A message indicates that disk performance counters on the system are set to start at boot time.

3. Restart your system.

When you have finished monitoring disk performance, remember to disable the disk performance monitors. Leaving them enabled serves no purpose and slows your machine down. Exercise 16.8 shows how to disable them.

EXERCISE 16.8

Disabling the Disk Performance Counters

1. Select Start ➤ Programs ➤ Command Prompt.

2. Type **diskperf -n** in the input line and press Enter. A message will confirm the change.

3. Restart the system.

Monitoring Disk Performance

Once you've enabled the disk performance monitors as shown in Exercise 16.7, you'll be able to make meaningful disk throughput measurements.

Important counters you'll want to watch are

- Memory: Pages/sec

- % Disk Time

- Disk Bytes/Transfer

- Current Disk Queue Length

MEMORY: PAGES/SEC. A memory indicator is part of the disk performance section because the pages swapped in this indicator are written to disk. Leave this counter showing in the performance monitor while watching the % Disk Time to see how dramatically page file performance affects your overall performance. Add Memory: Pages/sec to your performance monitor graph using Exercise 16.9.

EXERCISE 16.9

Adding Memory: Pages/sec to the Performance Monitor

1. Select Start ➤ Programs ➤ Administrative Tools ➤ Performance Monitor.

2. Click + in the Performance Monitor tool bar.

3. Select Memory in the Object drop-down list.

4. Select Pages/sec in the Counter drop-down box.

5. Click Add.

6. Close the Add to Chart window.

% DISK TIME This counter shows how much processor time is spent servicing disk requests. It is a good broad indicator for determining whether your hard disk drive is a bottleneck during activities when you would not normally expect to wait for your hard disk drive. Note that this counter is a processor metric, not a physical disk metric. Measure this counter against Processor: % Processor Time to see if disk requests are eating up all your processor time. Use Exercise 16.10 to measure the amount of time used servicing disk requests.

EXERCISE 16.10

Adding Logical Disk: % Disk Time to the Performance Monitor

1. Click + in the Performance Monitor tool bar.

2. Select Logical Disk in the Object drop-down list.

3. Select % Disk Time in the Counter drop-down box.

4. Click Add.

5. Close the Add to Chart window.

DISK BYTES PER SECOND This counter shows how fast your hard disks are transferring data. Turn on this counter and then copy a large directory of files between disks to get a good baseline of the speed at which your disk(s) runs. Exercise 16.11 shows how to monitor this counter.

EXERCISE 16.11

Adding Logical Disk: Disk Bytes/sec to the Performance Monitor

1. Click + in the Performance Monitor tool bar.

2. Select Logical Disk in the Object drop-down list.

3. Select Disk Bytes/sec in the Counter drop-down box.

4. Click Add.

5. Close the Add to Chart window.

AVERAGE DISK BYTES PER TRANSFER This metric shows the size of the average transfer. Larger average transfers make more efficient use of disk hardware and execute faster; smaller transfers cause the computer to work too hard to write them to disk. Perform Exercise 16.12 to monitor this counter.

EXERCISE 16.12

Adding Logical Disk: Average Disk Bytes per Transfer to the Performance Monitor

1. Click + in the Performance Monitor tool bar.

2. Select Logical Disk in the Object drop-down list.

3. Select Avg. Disk Bytes/Transfer in the Counter drop-down box.

4. Click Add.

5. Close the Add to Chart window.

CURRENT DISK QUEUE LENGTH The Current Disk Queue Length shows how much data is waiting to be transferred to the disk. Many processes must wait for disk requests to be serviced before they can continue. A long disk queue indicates that many processes are being delayed by disk speed. Exercise 16.13 shows how to monitor this counter.

EXERCISE 16.13

Adding Logical Disk: Current Disk Queue Length to the Performance Monitor

1. Click + in the Performance Monitor tool bar.

2. Select Logical Disk in the Object drop-down list.

3. Select Current Disk Queue Length in the Counter drop-down box.

4. Click Add.

5. Close the Add to Chart window.

Troubleshooting Disk Performance

The best way to eliminate disks as bottlenecks is to use them as little as possible. Adding a lot of RAM to your computer to increase the size of your disk cache and reduce the need for swapping pages to disk will improve the overall performance of your computer more than any other optimization.

If you cannot add more memory or if your computer already has all it can use, you will need to take other measures to improve disk performance. Your options are

- Use a newer, faster, or higher capacity hard disk.

- Move to a faster hard disk controller interface.

- Create stripe sets across multiple disks.

- Use a redundant array of inexpensive disks (RAID).

UPGRADING YOUR DISK If your hard disk is more than two years old, you can probably increase your performance by upgrading it. New hard disk drives, especially hard disks larger than 1GB, transfer data quite a bit faster than the drives of just a few years ago. However, if your disk is relatively new, replacing it won't speed up overall performance very much. Good, fast hard disk drives can transfer data at between 1.5MB and 2MB per second. This speed is generally faster than a single hard disk controller, but two or more fast hard disks running on a slow controller can easily swamp it, causing the controller to become the bottleneck.

FASTER HARD DISK CONTROLLERS Hard disk controllers affect the speed at which data can be transferred from your hard disk. Original SCSI and IDE both have a maximum limit of 5MB per second per controller bus. New hard disks can exceed this limit. Synchronous SCSI runs at 10MB per second for devices that support it.

Hard disk controllers running in ISA slots also have a hard limit of about 8MB per second. Also, because ISA controllers can address only the bottom 16MB of RAM, the processor must move disk requests from regions higher in memory, creating an additional load.

If you have a SCSI or IDE controller running in an ISA slot and you have an open PCI slot, you should replace the ISA controller with a PCI controller.

Finally, if you are using a PCI controller and you need more speed, consider moving to wide or ultra SCSI. These technologies transfer more data by increasing the width of the SCSI bus from 8 bits to 16 or 32, which doubles the amount of data that can be transferred on the bus. Your disk must support wide or ultra SCSI to benefit from this change. Table 16.2 shows the performance maximums for hard disk controllers of different types. Note that in all cases the hard disk drives run slower than the maximum speed of the controller; however, the controller can be loaded at the sum of the sustained transfer rates of all attached drives.

TABLE 16.2
Hard Disk Controller Technologies

CONTROLLER TECHNOLOGY	MAX TRANSFER RATE	DEVICES
BIOS Hard disk (MFM, RLL, ESDI)	8MB/s*	2
IDE	5MB/s	2
SCSI	6MB/s	7
SCSI-2 Fast	10MB/s	7
SCSI-2 Wide	20MB/s	7
SCSI-2 Fast & Wide	40MB/s	7
Ultra SCSI	80MB/s	15

*This rate is the theoretical maximum for a BIOS controlled hard disk running in an ISA slot. In practice, you will not achieve this result. Controllers running in local bus slots may achieve higher burst throughput, but drives of this age will have sustained transfer rates less than 1MB/s.

STRIPE SETS Stripe sets increase the speed of a logical disk by splitting it across many physical disks. Since disks can operate simultaneously, striping allows you to multiply the speed of a logical drive by the number of physical drives it comprises up to the maximum speed of a shared bus. Figure 16.6 shows how Windows NT splits data across physical drives to improve performance. Creating stripe sets is covered in detail in Chapter 5 under the section on the disk administrator utility.

FIGURE 16.6

A stripe volume across three disks.

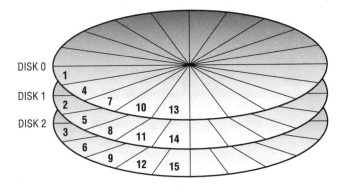

RAID RAID works on the same theory as stripe sets. The difference is that a RAID controller replaces your regular SCSI controller and makes the stripe set look like one physical disk to Windows NT.

RAID controllers include a microprocessor that handles breaking up and recombining the disk data so that the computer's microprocessor doesn't have to. Most RAID controllers also use some RAM as a cache to increase the speed of transfers to and from the controller. This cache works the same way as the Windows NT cache described in the memory optimization section.

RAID controllers essentially perform the same service as stripe sets, but because they relieve the computing burden of stripe sets from the processor and add a memory cache dedicated to disk transfers, they can help relieve processor bottlenecks. Unfortunately, RAID controllers can be very expensive. RAID controllers are generally used only in servers. RAID is covered in depth in Chapter 5.

The Network Monitor

THE NETWORK MONITOR monitors data sent over the network. Data moves through the network in frames or packets, each containing header information that identifies the protocols being used to send the frame, a destination address, a source address, and the data.

Specifying a transport protocol—for example, Transmission Control Protocol (TCP), Server Message Blocks (SMB), or NetBIOS over TCP (NBT)—in the header is somewhat similar to deciding whether to send a package by UPS, Federal Express, or USPS. Each package must also contain a source and destination address to be delivered correctly.

Most people don't make a habit of opening packages not addressed to them. The network is the same way. By default, a network card will ignore any packet that is not addressed to its computer. On the other hand, network monitors really don't care to whom a packet is sent. They are able to capture all packets on the network.

Network monitors use a special mode supported by most modern network cards called promiscuous mode. *Promiscuous mode* allows the network adapter to capture all the data packets on the network. Special promiscuous mode drivers work by capturing the data of every packet, as opposed to capturing only packets that are addressed to the computer network card.

The network monitor that ships with NT Server 4.0 is not a fully functional network monitor. It is a limited version of the network monitor that ships with SMS (a Microsoft BackOffice application that can be purchased separately). Instead of being able to capture all the network packets, this version of network monitor can capture only:

- Frames sent from the server

- Frames sent to the server

- Broadcast frames

- Multicast frames

Because the network monitor that ships with NT Server 4.0 is not fully functional and does not capture every network packet, the server's network card driver does not have to run in promiscuous mode. Network monitor is able to use the network driver interface specification (NDIS) 4.0 that your network card uses. The frames that are detected are then copied to the server's memory in a capture buffer. Using the NDIS 4.0 standard instead of using promiscuous mode reduces the CPU load up to 30 percent.

The limited version of the network monitor that ships with Windows NT Server 4 does not support promiscuous mode. Therefore, it can capture only packets sent to the server or to all stations. The online documentation that comes with NT Server states that the network monitor is limited for "security" reasons, but it is more likely limited for marketing reasons.

In contrast, the network monitor that ships with the SMS product is able to capture all packets on the network, regardless of the source or destination computer address. The SMS Server must use a promiscuous mode network driver.

Installing Network Monitor

Installing the network monitor is similar to installing any service in Windows NT Server 4. Exercise 16.14 shows you how to install the network monitor.

EXERCISE 16.14

Installing the Network Monitor

1. Right-click Network Neighborhood.

2. Select Properties.

3. Click the Services tab.

4. Click the Add button and choose Network Monitor Tools and Agent.

5. Click OK.

6. Enter the path for the NT Server CD or the source files and click OK.

7. Click Close on the Network dialog box.

8. Click Yes when the Network Settings dialog box prompts you to restart your computer so that the changes can take effect.

Once the network monitor has been installed, you will notice a new control panel for the Monitoring Agent and the Network Monitor Tool will appear in Administrative Tools.

Using the Network Monitor

In this section you will learn how to manually initiate a data capture with the network monitor, view information generated by a data capture, and save captured data. (Note that you can capture only as much data as will fit into system memory.) Figure 16.7 shows the network monitor.

You can manually capture data at any time by running the network monitor and choosing to start a capture. When you are done capturing data, you can simply stop the capture and view the data later. You can also stop and view the data within a single menu choice.

Information Captured by the Network Monitor

The network monitor can provide both real-time information and cumulative, saved data. In Figure 16.7, notice that the network monitor user interface has four main sections:

- **Bar graphs** provide information on real-time network activity. The bar graphs show network utilization, frames per second, bytes per second, broadcasts per second, and multicasts per second. The utilization statistic shows you how much traffic to and from the server is affecting segment performance.

- **Session statistics** show the conversations that are taking place on the network. This information is real time and cumulative for the capture session. Because of the limitations placed on this utility, you will only see sessions that include the NT Server.

- **Station statistics** are a cumulative number and provide information on the network conversations. You can see the network address, frames sent, frames received, bytes sent, bytes received, directed frames sent, multicasts sent, and broadcasts sent.

- **Summary statistics** are cumulative statistics and include network statistics, captured statistics, per second statistics, network card (MAC) statistics, and network card (MAC) error statistics.

During the network capture, all packets that the server sends or receives are saved in the server's memory buffer. To see the frames that have been captured, select Capture ➤ Display Captured Data from the Network Monitor dialog box. To see specific information regarding a packet (see Figure 16.8), double-click the packet.

Notice in Figure 16.8 that each frame detail screen consists of three sections:

- Top section: Summary pane

- Middle section: Detail pane

- Bottom section: Hex pane

The Summary pane lists all the frames in the current capture. By highlighting specific frames, the information in the Detail pane and Hex pane reflects the information in the highlighted frames. The Summary pane lists columns for the frame number, the time (relative to the capture process), the source MAC address, the destination MAC address, the protocol used to transmit the frame, and a description that summarizes the frames' contents.

FIGURE 16.8

Network monitor information for a packet.

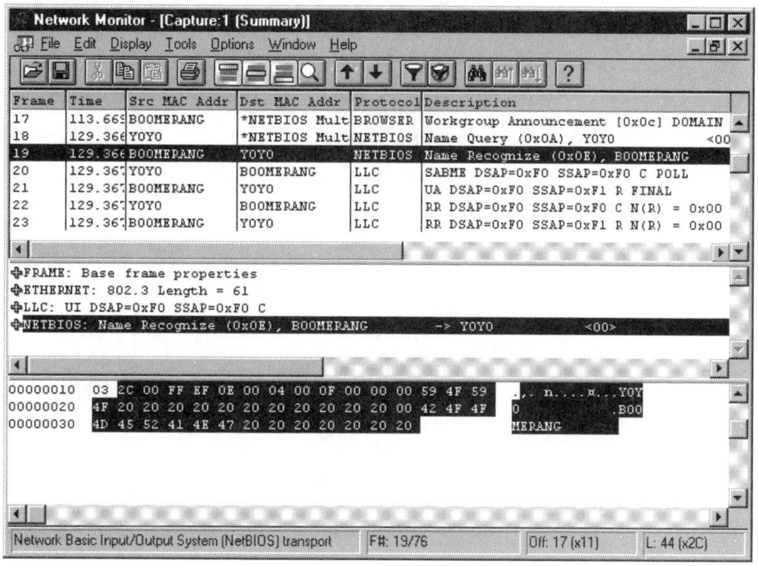

The Detail pane shows all the protocol information associated with the specific frame. If a + sign appears to the left of the protocol, you can click the protocol for more detailed information.

The Hex pane shows the hexadecimal information associated with the selected frame. The hex values appear to the left of this pane, and the corresponding ASCII characters appear to the right.

This information assumes that you have an understanding of protocol analysis. Entire books have been written on this topic, and it is beyond the scope of this book.

Saving Captured Data

You can save captured data to a file for archiving purposes or to be analyzed by another source. By default, captured data is saved in the root directory in which NT Server has been installed under \SYSTEM32\NETMON\CAPTURES, and the file is saved as a CAP file. Exercise 16.15 shows you how to capture, view, and save data with the network monitor.

If you save captured data on a regular basis, you may want to use the date as your file name, so that you can easily identify the captured frames' data files.

EXERCISE 16.15

Manually Initiating a Data Capture

1. Select Start ➤ Programs ➤ Administrative Tools ➤ Network Monitor.

2. Select Start from the Capture menu.

3. Allow the capture to run for one or two minutes.

4. Select Capture ➤ Stop.

5. Select Capture ➤ Display Captured Data.

6. Select a frame from the Capture dialog box and double-click anywhere on the frame. You should see something similar to Figure 16.8.

7. Select File ➤ Save As.

8. Type **TESTCAPT** in the Save Data as text box and click OK. Your captured data has now been saved.

Filtering Captured Data

You can very easily accumulate a large amount of data in a very short time during data captures. Capturing data on a heavily loaded server over an extended time tends to produce copious amounts of data that can be difficult to store and wade through. Looking for specific information can be as challenging as looking for a needle in a haystack. Luckily, the network monitor enables you to filter frames that are displayed based on transport protocol, computer address, and protocol properties.

By default the filter is not set and displays all protocols, all computer addresses, and all protocol properties.

To filter network data, choose Display ➤ Filter. Then configure the filter to display frames that match the values that you specify in the Expression input box (see Figure 16.9).

The following examples illustrate situations in which you might want to filter data. Assume that you suspect that the network card in Pam's machine is failing and is causing excessive network traffic to the server even though Pam

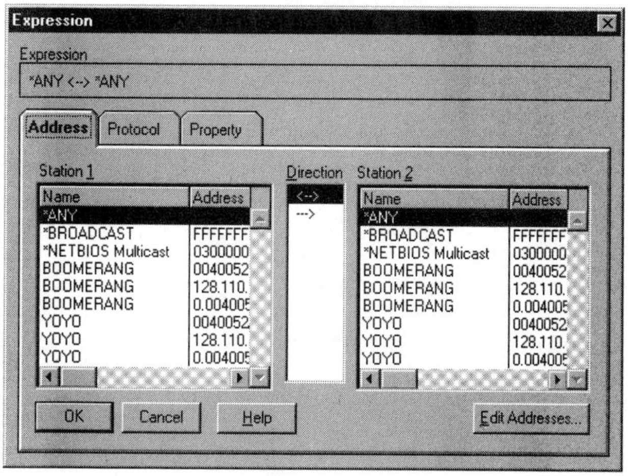

FIGURE 16.9

Network monitor display
filter wiindow.

FIGURE 16.9

Network monitor display
filter wiindow.

is not currently using her machine. You can filter and view all the packets that are being sent from Pam's network card by choosing her network address.

We've also seen documentation that tells you to install all protocols (TCP/IP, NWLink IPX/SPX, and NetBEUI) if you're not sure which protocol to use. (We don't advocate this approach!) If you follow this advice and want to see the impact of each protocol on server traffic, you could create a filter for each specific protocol and see how many packets each protocol generates.

Network Monitor Security

As previously noted, the network monitor allows you to view network packets that are transmitted or received by the NT Server. These packets could potentially contain sensitive data that you want to protect. The network monitor provides two security features to help protect against unauthorized use of the network monitor: password protection and detection of other network monitor installations.

Password Protection

Before the network monitor can capture packets, the network monitoring agent must be running. The network monitoring agent is capable of using dual-level passwords to control who can view captured data and who can capture and view captured data files. Exercise 16.16 shows how to set network monitoring passwords.

EXERCISE 16.16

Setting Network Monitor Passwords

1. Select Start ➤ Settings ➤ Control Panels.

2. Double-click Monitoring Agent.

3. Click Change Password.

4. Enter passwords in the Change password text box.

The network monitor and monitoring agent do not have default passwords. Therefore, anybody running network monitor can connect to your server and capture and view your frames.

Detection of Other Network Monitor Installations

Network monitor enables you to detect whether other instances of network monitor are running (through SMS or NT Server's network monitor). If other instances of network monitor are running, you will see:

- The computer name from which network monitor is being run

- The user who is currently logged on to the computer running network monitor

- The MAC address of the computer running network monitor

- The state of network monitor (running, capturing, or transmitting)

- The version of network monitor

To learn whether other instances of network monitor are currently running, access network monitor from the Administrative Tools group and select Tools ➤ Identify Network Monitor Users.

Summary

WINDOWS NT PROVIDES low-level support for performance monitoring by including counters in every object that can be meaningfully measured. Windows NT uses these counters to perform a number of automatic optimizations, such as multiprocessing, virtual memory swap files spread across multiple disks, prioritization of threads, and disk caches.

Windows NT also provides a performance monitor tool that enables you to measure system performance through object counters. You can use the performance monitor to find bottlenecks, or performance-limiting resources, in your server. The performance monitor enables you to inspect the value of the object counters in real time so you can see how various activities affect the resources of your server.

To effectively find bottlenecks, you must look at the overall performance of your computer under a typical load. Using more general counters and averages will give a good indication of where to look for specific bottlenecks. Processor performance, memory performance, and disk performance are the three major capacities that you should check.

The network monitor can capture packets, broadcasts, or multicast frames being sent to or from NT Server. It is a limited version of the network monitor that ships with SMS and can capture network packets from the entire network. You can filter captured data based on protocol used, computer address, and protocol properties. Filtering allows you to take a large amount of information and display only the frames that match your criteria.

Tuning a network's performance is the perpetual cycle of finding performance bottlenecks, eliminating them, and starting over with the next most-limiting factor. When a system can no longer be tuned for greater performance, it is at its natural performance limit.

By using the performance monitor to tune the performance of individual servers and the network monitor to tune the performance of your network, you can increase the speed of your network and stave off major hardware upgrades until the system reaches its natural limit.

Review Questions

1. Running the performance monitor does not affect the performance of the computer.

   A. True

   B. False

2. The performance monitor measures system performance.

   A. True

   B. False

3. Upgrading your hardware is one way to eliminate bottlenecks.

   A. True

   B. False

4. Bottlenecks are components that are not operating at peak performance.

   A. True

   B. False

5. Even the fastest computers have bottlenecks.

   A. True

   B. False

6. Windows NT can vary priority levels up to _____ priorities higher or lower automatically.

7. _____ performance counters are disabled by default to increase overall operating speed.

8. _____ are the measures taken to reduce the impact of a bottleneck on performance.

9. _____ are the basic units of division among processors in a multiprocessing environments.

10. Windows NT supports which type of multiprocessing?

A. Symmetrical

B. Asymmetrical

C. Both symmetrical and asymmetrical

D. Windows NT supports Multitasking instead.

11. Windows NT provides which tool for optimizing Windows NT performance?

A. Microsoft Diagnostic tool (WinMSD)

B. The performance tuner

C. Windows NT Diagnostics (NTD)

D. The performance monitor

E. The task manager

12. Which performance optimization is not implemented in the Windows NT operating system?

A. Symmetric multiprocessing

B. Swapping across multiple disks to increase performance

C. Prioritizing threads and processes

D. Caching RAM in the external processor cache

E. Caching disk requests

13. In Windows NT, memory is divided into pages of what size?

A. 4KB

B. 16KB

C. 64KB

D. 256KB

14. NTFS uses which type of caching to improve performance?

   A. Write through

   B. Write back

   C. Write now

   D. Write optimization

   E. Buffered

15. The biggest single bottleneck in most computers is _____ .

   A. the processor

   B. memory

   C. disks

   D. networks

16. The best way to eliminate disks as bottlenecks is to _____ .

   A. create a stripe set

   B. use them as little as possible

   C. install a RAID controller

   D. use Ultra SCSI drives and controllers

17. Which of the following can the network monitor in NT Server track? (Choose all that apply.)

   A. Any packet sent over the local network

   B. Any packet sent over the network, even packets across a router

   C. Packets sent to or from the server

   D. Broadcast packets

18. If you want to use a fully functional network monitor, which additional package should you purchase?

A. SQL

B. SMS

C. Network Monitor v2.0

D. Network Monitor v3.0

19. Assuming that NT Server has been installed to drive C in the WINNT directory, which directory does the network monitor use (by default) to save captured data?

A. `C:\WINNT\SYSTEM32\NETMON\CAPTURES`

B. `C:\WINNT\NETMON\CAPTURES`

C. `C:\WINNT\SYSTEM32\REPL\NETMON\CAPTURES`

D. `C:\NETMON\CAPTURES`

20. Which properties can be filtered through the network monitor filter process? (Choose all that apply.)

A. Hex strings

B. Protocols

C. Computer address

D. Protocol properties

Troubleshooting

ETWORKS ARE INCREDIBLY complex. Network software is even more complex than network hardware and computers, and network operating systems are the most sophisticated pieces of software that programmers can create. Making such complex and sophisticated program elements foolproof is virtually impossible, so although Windows NT is as robust an operating system as you will encounter, you will occasionally need to fix problems with your servers. Because network problems often look like server problems, you need to learn to quickly determine what components are likely to cause various fault conditions.

Troubleshooting is a skill like any other. You can apply certain general principles to any troubleshooting situation, but you must know how the specific system you are troubleshooting works if you want to be able to diagnose faults. As with any other skill, you get better at troubleshooting with practice.

This chapter introduces you to some general computer troubleshooting principles and then shows you how to troubleshoot computer hardware, Windows NT operating system software, and network connections.

Principles of Troubleshooting

ROUBLESHOOTING IS THE methodical process of eliminating faults from a system. Although troubleshooting a computer is difficult, you can quickly isolate the faulty by following a few basic rules that allow you to focus your troubleshooting efforts on components more likely at fault.

Troubleshooting a network involves determining the component that is at fault, changing the hardware or software configuration of suspect components, and then testing to see whether the configuration change has eliminated the fault.

If a hardware failure caused the fault, you will have to find and replace the failed component. If a software configuration causes the fault, you will have to reconfigure your system to eliminate the fault. In some cases you may not be able to reconfigure your system because the configuration problem involves the denial of some service that is required to reconfigure the faulty component. If you run into this catch 22, you may have to reinstall the operating system on the server or client that is faulty.

Working on electronic devices such as computers can be dangerous. You should attempt to troubleshoot a computer only if you are very familiar with electrical safety, electronic equipment, and computer hardware.

Microsoft has thoroughly debugged Windows NT software. Windows NT runs well and all of its services operate properly. If you have a persistent problem with a Windows NT server, the most likely cause is less-than-compatible hardware or improperly configured software. However, bugs exist in all nontrivial software, especially in the less frequently used areas.

Bugs are most likely to exist in rarely executed code.

Windows NT is very specific about which hardware it will work with. Early in NT's design cycle, Microsoft chose not to support every possible peripheral device for two reasons:

- DOS mode drivers allow security holes.

- Writing drivers for all existing PC-compatible hardware is impossible.

If you are having a problem with a new Windows NT installation, you are probably using hardware that does not appear on the Windows NT hardware compatibility list (HCL).

Bugs are more likely the fault of a third-party driver than of Windows NT standard components. Consider these drivers primary suspects when troubleshooting.

Focus is important in troubleshooting. Making changes randomly in a system hoping something will work is a good way to waste a lot of time and to create more problems with untracked changes. Focus on a specific component. Test it thoroughly. If you are not able to correct the fault, restore the original configuration before moving on to another component.

Troubleshooting is relatively easy when you are dealing with only one fault, as is generally the case with a hardware failure. Software failures, however, are usually more complicated. You may have a situation in which two or more simultaneous problems are causing a fault. Correcting only one fault at a time will change the symptoms, but will not correct the problem. For instance, suppose your modem doesn't work. You have a hardware conflict because your modem is set to the same IRQ as your LAN adapter, which caused your modem software to automatically detect the wrong modem. In fact, you have two problems (a hardware setting and a software configuration) to fix before you can operate your modem. Correcting one or the other problem does not allow you to use your modem.

Partial troubleshooting success or rotating symptoms usually indicates the presence of more than one problem.

The rest of this section covers the general principles of troubleshooting. Following these guidelines will help you quickly determine what is at fault in your system. However, no book or set of rules will really help you find a problem unless you understand the system you are troubleshooting. That's why we put this section at the end of the book. We hope that by performing the exercises and taking the tests in the first 16 chapters you've gained the requisite knowledge to effectively troubleshoot Windows NT Server 4.

New Computers

The troubleshooting procedures presented here assume that the computer you are troubleshooting has operated correctly under Windows NT in the past. Troubleshooting a newly built computer is beyond the scope of this book.

If you are building a computer from scratch, save yourself a lot of time by getting it to work correctly under MS-DOS or Windows 95 before trying to install Windows NT. Better yet, save yourself even more time by buying a complete computer with Windows NT factory installed. If you can't buy Windows NT preinstalled, check the Microsoft Web site (at www.microsoft.com) for computers listed on the Windows NT hardware compatibility list. Microsoft has certified that these computers will run Windows NT properly.

Microsoft will not certify individual components for use with Windows NT—it certifies only complete computers. Therefore, you can't be sure that all your hardware will work correctly under Windows NT if your computer is custom built. For these reasons, even the most experienced PC technician should think twice before building a Windows NT machine from components.

If you are determined to build your own computer, study the Windows NT Knowledge Base on the Microsoft Web site so you can avoid buying hardware that is known to cause problems under Windows NT. Pay special attention to the specific type of SCSI adapter and motherboard you purchase.

New Windows NT Installations

Make absolutely certain you don't have any interrupt, DMA channel, or memory port conflicts before attempting a Windows NT installation. Windows NT only allows interrupt sharing for PCI devices, not for devices like serial ports. Modems and sound cards are especially likely to share interrupts under less-sophisticated operating systems such as MS-DOS or Windows 95.

If you have a hardware conflict, turn off PCI Plug-and-Play compatibility (if your BIOS allows you to) and manually assign interrupt settings to hardware. Record these settings so you know what they are. Remove any hardware that is not necessary for the operation of the computer, such as modems, sound cards, and (if possible) your network adapter. This step reduces possible sources of conflict when you install Windows NT. You can add these components one at a time to be certain they are configured correctly once the operating system is running.

If you are using SCSI devices, be aware that many popular SCSI adapters have compatibility issues running under Windows NT. Search under SCSI Adapters in the Windows NT Knowledge Base for a run down of the compatibility issues of certain controllers. Also, with some SCSI controllers, the NT loader can have a hard time finding your boot drive if you have an active IDE bus and SCSI devices set on ID 0.

Axioms of Troubleshooting

Finding the component at fault is the primary purpose of troubleshooting. Once you know exactly what is wrong, fixing the problem is usually trivial. We've compiled a list of axioms for general troubleshooting that will help you quickly isolate and repair hardware and software faults in Windows NT.

- Be patient.

- Know the system.

- Isolate the fault.

- Check the most recent change.

- Check the most common failure point.

- Check things that have a history of failure.

- Perform easy tests first.

- Make assumptions to guide your troubleshooting.

- Use what you know.

- Change only one setting at a time.

- Track the changes you make.

- Try to make transient failures repeatable.

- Try to isolate individual faults in multiple-fault malfunctions.

- Resort to permanent changes last.

Be Patient

Patience is not just a virtue when troubleshooting; it's an absolute necessity. If you are under time pressure to get a system working, you are better off using another computer if possible. If you can't, you will just have to forget about your deadline because rushing through the troubleshooting process usually doesn't work. You will save yourself more time in the long run by taking your time to troubleshoot than by frustrating yourself with rushed efforts that don't work and may introduce additional faults. Most troubleshooting efforts take hours!

Know the System

You can't troubleshoot unless you know your system. Troubleshooting is the process of diagnosing symptoms, postulating causes, and testing your hunch by making configuration changes. If you don't understand the symptoms you see, you will be unable to make a reasonable diagnosis.

If you are reading this chapter first because you have a Windows NT computer that isn't working, you should turn back to page one and start reading there. The knowledge you gain about the inner workings of NT from the rest of this book will help you diagnose your problem.

Isolate the Fault

The fastest way to isolate a fault in a malfunctioning computer is to remove what you know works from the list of suspect components. Narrowing your search helps you focus on components that could be at fault and keeps you from making changes in other working portions of the system. For instance, if you can reliably see information on the screen, most of the hardware in your computer is working properly. You can eliminate the processor, motherboard, RAM, video card, and monitor from your list of suspect components.

In many cases, you will be able to quickly isolate a component by validating many components at one time. For instance, a computer that boots completely probably does not have any failed hardware components.

Check the Most Recent Change

If you've just changed something and your computer no longer works properly, it doesn't take a rocket scientist to figure out that the most recent change caused the problem (or exacerbated an existing unexpressed problem). This logic would normally go without saying, but when you are challenged by a malfunctioning computer, it's easy to forget.

In addition, a fault might not show up immediately, and you may have to think about what you changed last. Or someone else might have changed something on the computer that you are not aware of.

Often users accidentally break something when they try to make a change to their system and then pretend not to know what is wrong to avoid embarrassment or liability. You should try to foster an environment in which users are not afraid to come clean with this information. You will spend a lot more time trying to get to the bottom of a fault if you don't know about recent changes.

Here are some suggestions to facilitate troubleshooting in a corporate environment.

- Implement security on workstations to prevent users from being able to incorrectly configure a system.

- Try to change policies that hold your coworkers liable in some way for accidental damage to a computer, or they will never help you troubleshoot anything.

- Make sure your clients understand that your ability to work quickly will save them money.

Check the Most Common Failure Point

This point is also rather obvious, but it is an important axiom of trouble-shooting. Although newer hard disks are very reliable, they are still the third most-likely-to-fail component in a computer, after the monitor and the floppy disk drive. Unlike monitors and floppy disk drives, however, a crashed hard disk will quite probably make your computer useless. Hard disks are also complicated enough that the failure might not be obvious. In addition, some software problems look like hard disk problems.

Connectors and cables are also common failure points. Cables inside computers can become loose if a computer is moved or subject to vibration. PCI bus card edge connectors are very sensitive to movement (compared to ISA bus cards), and single inline memory modules can also loosen easily. Check all these components when you have a mysterious hardware failure that keeps your computer from booting.

Peripherals that rely on jumpers for option settings are susceptible to loose jumpers. Check to make sure no jumpers are missing and that they are firmly seated in their correct positions if you suspect a component is faulty.

Most computers also have cooling fans that are likely to eventually fail. When a processor cooling fan fails, the computer will begin to lock up randomly when it has been on for a short time. If the power supply cooling fan fails, your computer is likely to blow a fuse and not work at all. Case-cooling fans don't cause specific problems, but components such as hard disk drives will run hotter and therefore fail sooner without them.

Check Things That Have a History of Failure

If you have a component that has failed or disconnected in the past, chances are it will do so again. If you are experiencing the same sort of failure symptoms as you have in the past, the first thing to check is the component that failed before.

If you find that a recently replaced component has failed again, some other component may be causing that component to fail.

Perform Easy Tests First

If you don't have any idea what might be wrong, you should start by checking components that are easy to test. This process is most easily accomplished if you have a known working computer configured similarly. You can swap easily removable components between the two computers to see if the fault moves with a component.

Check BIOS settings if you have a problem with any hardware embedded on the motherboard.

You should perform quick software reconfigurations before making more lengthy or sweeping changes, such as reinstalling the operating system or swapping out a hard disk.

Make Assumptions to Guide Your Troubleshooting

When troubleshooting, you will refine or redefine your initial diagnosis as you work. This diagnosis will lead in the direction of failed components. For instance, if your computer boots but does not come up on the network, you can make any of these assumptions:

- The network software is configured incorrectly.

- Another piece of hardware conflicts with the network adapter.

- The network adapter has failed.

- The network adapter cannot reach the network because of a cable fault.

- The server is down and not responding.

Use What You know

You might know the events that precipitated a failure without realizing it. In the network scenario described above, you can use your knowledge of the computer's environment to guide your troubleshooting. For example:

- If the computer used to work fine on the LAN but stopped networking after a new sound card was installed, the LAN adapter and the sound card are conflicting.

- If the computer stopped networking after a recent remodel, perhaps a cable was broken or unplugged during the construction.

- If a network administrator has been reading this book and performing the exercises, there's a chance the networking software is no longer configured correctly for your network.

Change Only One Setting at a Time

This axiom is very important. Often, especially with software configuration troubleshooting, you are tempted to try something, see if it works, then try something else, and see if that works. Unfortunately, this haphazard process causes you to unwittingly change configuration information that may, in turn, produce another fault. You can easily fix the original fault but introduce another without even realizing it.

If a change does not correct the problem, always *restore the original settings* before continuing to the next test.

Track the Changes You Make

Write down each change you make in a change log. You need a way to keep track of the multiple changes you implement simultaneously in an effort to solve a complex problem. A change log also allows you to update the computer configuration report you keep on all your computers.

Try to Make Transient Failures Repeatable

Transient failures indicate either an environmental variable failure, such as a loose connection, or conflicting software that causes the fault under certain conditions.

If you suspect an environmental fault, try to exacerbate the condition to make the fault stable. If you suspect a software fault, try stopping services and unload running applications until the fault disappears. Then begin restarting services until you can get the fault to reappear.

Try to Isolate Individual Faults in Multiple-Fault Malfunctions

Unusual symptoms (those you don't see in this chapter) usually occur because more than one fault is present. To get a computer up in a multiple-fault malfunction, you may have to correct all faults simultaneously if the faulty components depend on each another. Troubleshooting multiple faults is exponentially more difficult than troubleshooting single faults. If you can isolate a fault by removing a hardware component or stopping a software service that allows you to determine one of the factors in the malfunction, you will be able to concentrate on that factor until it works correctly.

If you cannot isolate an individual fault in a multiple-fault situation, you should start with the basic troubleshooting procedures of validating the proper performance of your hardware and then reducing the complexity of your software by stopping unnecessary services and unloading running software. This approach reduces the complexity of the environment and fine-tunes the list of suspect components. When you have reduced the software environment to the minimum level required to operate, reintroduce the components until the fault appears again.

Resort to Permanent Changes Last

Permanent changes, such as replacing hard disk drives, reinstalling the operating system, or deleting files should be your last resort. All these repairs take a long time to implement and require you to reset your security permissions, shares, and network names. Be certain you are replacing the component at fault before making these drastic repairs.

Troubleshooting Networks

THE FAILURE OF a single component is responsible for most network problems. Networks never completely fail unless acted upon by an external factor such as power loss or flooding. And when external factors cause multiple faults, the cause is usually quite obvious (e.g., you are or were working in the dark; the carpet is wet).

Because networks tend to fail one piece at a time and because the voltages transmitted on normal network cables are so low that even a malfunctioning device won't damage other devices attached to the cable, you can usually be certain that once you've found the problem, you'll be able to fix it. So the trick to troubleshooting networks is to quickly isolate the failed component and then troubleshoot that component.

Lightning strikes can cause power surges on network cables, thus causing all the equipment attached to the affected cable to fail—but again, that's usually pretty obvious.

Network failures can be divided into four categories:

- **Client problems** affect only a single client. Other computers will work normally on the network.

- **Server problems** may deny access to the server to everyone on the network and can, therefore, be confused with data link problems. Try to connect one peer to another without involving the server to validate the cable plant and data link equipment.

- **Data Link faults** occur with hubs, bridges, routers, switches, and network interface adapters. They fall into common categories such as addressing problems, incompatible frame types, and outright component failures.

- **Cable faults** are breaks, shorts, grounds, or loose connections that cause spurious faults. Most difficult network faults that involve random numbers of computers, partial or temporary loss of servers, or other non-deterministic faults are cable faults.

Client Problems

Identifying a client problem is easy. If the problem affects only a single station on your network, it's a client problem. Use the following steps to find the fault in a client-based problem:

1. Validate the cable running to that client by attaching another known good client to the same outlet and jumper cable.

2. Make sure the network interface adapter is installed correctly and is not conflicting with another device in the computer.

3. Make sure the correct driver is installed and configured to work with the hardware resource settings of the network interface adapter.

4. Make sure the proper transport protocols are installed and that any addresses, frame types, or network numbers are set correctly.

5. Use the ping tool in TCP/IP networks, or the IPXPING tool in NWLink networks, to see if the server is reachable from the client.

6. Make sure the client software is properly installed and configured and that the client computer has been properly named and identified as a member of the correct domain or workgroup.

7. Try adding the NetBEUI protocol to two computers on the same subnetwork to see if you can share resources over that protocol if you are having problems with NWLink or TCP/IP. NetBEUI is automatically configured correctly.

If more than one workgroup shows up in your domain browser, at least one of your computers is on that other workgroup. If you only have a single workgroup in your organization, that computer won't be accessible.

Server Problems

Server problems are just like client problems, but they affect the one computer everyone is trying to talk to. Therefore, nothing happens on your network. For this reason, they may look like data link problems. When running through server problems, first check all the steps shown in the client troubleshooting steps. Then try these steps:

1. Change two client computers to the same workgroup and share a resource from one to the other. If it doesn't work, move to data link troubleshooting.

2. If you have another server available, verify that clients can attach to it. If they can't, move to data link troubleshooting.

3. Troubleshoot the computer hardware to validate that the server is operating correctly.

4. Replace the network adapter with an adapter of a different manufacture using a different driver.

5. Use RDISK to create an emergency repair disk and reinstall Windows NT Server using the Repair option. Remove all third-party drivers and services except those absolutely necessary for server operation.

Data Link Problems

Data link problems occur when a device that connects the network physically or logically fails. These faults are relatively common, especially in larger networks having many data link devices. Data link faults usually affect entire subnetworks, generally denying the network access or access to other subnetworks, depending upon the function of the specific device. Use the following steps to validate your data link equipment.

1. Put a client next to your server and attach it via a single cable to the server (it must be a crossover cable for UTP or fiber networks) and try to log on from there.

2. Take each hub in the affected areas of your system and verify with your co-located client and server that you can attach to the server through each port of each hub. This test will quickly validate the proper operation of your hubs.

3. If you have two subnetworks that cannot connect to each other, replace the bridge between them.

4. If you suspect a router may be at fault, reboot it. Some routers allow you to use the telnet tool to check their configuration.

The ping utility enables you to check both your TCP/IP configuration and all of the hardware between clients and servers. If you can ping the IP address of your server from the client, all your hardware, the software network adapter drivers, and TCP/IP services are working correctly. Your problem must be with higher-level services.

Cable Faults

Cable faults are also rather common in network environments. Jumper cables that attach computers to wall outlets are always underfoot, so they often get run over by office chairs or pulled out of their sockets. Contractors working in ceiling areas may accidentally cut or kink network cables, and cables that are under stress may eventually break. Unfortunately, most installations have no way to fix damaged cable. All you can do is determine that the problem is in fact a bad cable and call in a cabling contractor to fix it. We put this section last because you should exhaust all the possibilities you can correct before assuming that you have a cable fault. Use the following steps to identify cable faults:

1. Determine how many computers are affected, and in what areas. Since cable faults generally affect only a single cable, check the one cable that the affected computers rely on.

2. Try using another computer at the failed station location to determine if you really have a cable fault. If a known good computer doesn't work at that location, it's probably a cable fault.

3. Validate the data link devices between the failed station and the server using the steps explained for troubleshooting client problems and data link problems.

4. Disconnect the cable on both ends of the link. Use a cable tester to check for continuity, shorts, or grounds.

5. Run a temporary long jumper between the computer and the closest hub or other data link device. If the computer starts working with the long jumper, you have a cable fault.

6. Call in a cabling contractor to repair the damaged cable.

Troubleshooting Computer Hardware

I N ORDER FOR your software to run correctly, the hardware in your computer must be operating correctly. Whenever a hardware component is possibly at fault in a malfunctioning computer, you should validate its correct operation before attempting to correct software faults.

The few simple troubleshooting techniques presented here help you isolate common hardware problems quickly. These techniques are not all inclusive, nor do they in any way replace the general techniques presented in the previous section. These techniques are simply the culmination of a great deal of troubleshooting experience.

Night of the Living DOS

Windows NT requires a completely functional hardware and software environment from a computer just to boot. Windows NT probes hardware and exercises the entire system as it comes online. Consequently, any number of faults will prevent Windows NT from starting at all. Simpler operating systems, such as MS-DOS, can operate on a computer that is significantly degraded. Consequently, a floppy disk that boots a simple operating system can be an invaluable troubleshooting tool.

In addition, quite a few DOS-based hardware validation tools are available. You can use these tools to inspect hardware, check for hardware conflicts, and validate the proper operation of a number of computer components. You can run these tools from a floppy disk on a system that doesn't boot Windows NT at all.

Remember, however, that MS-DOS will not have access to NTFS file system partitions. The DOS partition and format tools will not be able to modify an NTFS partition. Because NTFS creates partitions in larger boundaries than the FAT file system, you are likely to find 1 or 2MB of free space after the end of an NTFS partition that can be partitioned and formatted for MS-DOS. You can use this area to verify the physical operation of a hard disk drive by checking to see if you can read and write to it. You can also store MS-DOS utilities and Plug-and-Play software configuration tools for the hardware in your computer.

Finding Hardware Faults

The following is a short list of components to consider suspect under a range of troubleshooting issues. Check these in order to progressively narrow your search. Remember that complex faults (those involving more than one specific failure) may not fit into any one category. Also, many software problems can look like hardware faults until you test the component under a different operating system like MS-DOS.

Power

If nothing happens when you turn the computer on, check the power cords and switches. Even in the worst failure situation, you should at least hear the fan spinning in the power supply. If you hear the fan in the power supply, check to see if the microprocessor fan is spinning. If it is, you probably don't have a power supply problem. See if you can hear hard disks spinning.

Never install or remove anything while your computer is powered on. Dropping a screw onto a powered motherboard will probably destroy it and some of your peripheral cards.

Motherboard, Processor, RAM, and Video

The computer's motherboard, processor, RAM, and video adapter must all be operating correctly for the computer to complete the power on self-test (POST) the BIOS performs each time you turn it on. If after turning on your computer you see the normal boot screen, all these components are probably working correctly. If they are not, you may hear a few beeps (POST codes) or there may be no activity at all. Some computers can operate with a bit of failed RAM. These computers will either give an error message while testing RAM or will not count up to the entire compliment of memory.

If you suspect a problem with any of these components, remove and reseat the video card and memory modules. Processor failures are very rare. The only way to test for a processor failure is to swap in a known good processor of the same brand, model, and speed rating. Motherboard failures are also rare and are very difficult to validate. Verifying the processor, RAM, and video adapter in another computer of exactly the same make is usually easier than swapping out the motherboard.

BIOS Configuration Problems

With many computers, it is possible to set BIOS information incorrectly. The BIOS determines such critical parameters as how fast RAM memory is accessed, what type of hard disk drive is attached, and how interrupts are assigned to PCI slots. Incorrectly configuring your BIOS can very likely degrade its performance or keep it from working at all.

If you don't understand a BIOS setting's purpose, don't change it without recording its present value so you can change it back.

When you suspect a hardware conflict or a problem with the video, memory, processor, or the motherboard, check your BIOS parameter settings before you replace anything. The manual that came with your computer or motherboard should show the proper settings for your computer. If it does not, check with the manufacturer's technical support.

Failing all else, you can usually use the default settings option to get your computer working, although generally at a lower-than-optimal speed. Use this setting to verify that you are having a BIOS configuration problem and then tune parameters to increase the speed.

Hardware Conflicts

Hardware conflicts are by far the most common problem in PCs running any operating system. Hardware conflicts occur when two peripherals are configured to use the same interrupt, DMA channel, port address, or buffer memory. Windows NT is especially sensitive to hardware conflicts because it does not allow devices to share resources, as MS-DOS and Windows 95 do. Therefore, a computer that worked fine under MS-DOS or Windows 95 operating systems may malfunction under Windows NT.

You troubleshoot these problems by removing all peripheral cards that are not absolutely essential to boot the computer, such as modems, LAN adapters, sound cards, I/O controllers, secondary hard disk controllers, and CD-ROM controllers. Do not remove the video card or your primary (boot) hard disk controller.

If your computer goes through a normal start up process, reintroduce each peripheral card, starting with the secondary hard disk controller and adding each additional card in order of its importance to you. Power off the computer, install the card, and then check for a normal boot. If you have a diagnostic tool that shows the interrupt, DMA channel, and port assignments, use it to make sure a hardware conflict has not occurred. Repeat this process with each card until the problem reappears. When the problem reappears, the most recently installed card is either conflicting with an installed device, incorrectly configured, or has failed.

Hard Disk Controllers and Drives

Hard disk failures are the most damaging of all computer component failures because they contain the most recent set of all the data you store on your computer. Their loss means the loss of irreplaceable data. Hard disk problems fall into just a few categories:

- Power or connection problems

- Hardware configuration problems

- Incorrect Bios information

- Failed mechanisms

- Failed hard disk controllers

- Bad sectors

- Corrupted boot sectors

- Corrupted partition tables

- Corrupted file systems

- Viruses

Symptoms and solutions for each of these problems follow.

Backing up your data to other media, usually tape or magneto-optical disk, is the only way to recover completely from a total hard disk failure. If your data is important, you need to back it up daily.

POWER OR CONNECTION PROBLEMS Power or connection problems are easy to find. Check to make sure each hard disk drive is receiving power. If the hard disk is spinning, it is powered up correctly. On IDE drives, check to make sure the cables are securely and correctly installed. If you can't tell which way the cable should fit and the connector isn't keyed to prevent incorrect insertion, the side of the connector with two notches mates to the side of the hard disk port that has a notch in the center. Make sure the cable is attached to the motherboard/hard disk controller correctly by matching the red striped side of the cable to the pin labeled *1* on the circuit board.

SCSI is slightly more difficult. A SCSI bus must be properly terminated and the total cable length should be as short as possible. Proper SCSI termination is set when the devices at each end of the SCSI bus have termination enabled or a physical terminator is installed at the end of the bus. No device, including the controller card, should have termination enabled if it is not at the end of the SCSI bus. Often, one SCSI bus will have some internal components and some external components. In this case the last drive attached to the internal bus should be terminated, the SCSI controller should not be terminated, and the last device on the external bus should be terminated. Refer to your SCSI adapter manual for more information on SCSI termination.

HARDWARE CONFIGURATION PROBLEMS Drives can be incorrectly configured in ways that will prevent them from operating. Make sure that you don't have two devices on a SCSI bus with the same SCSI identification number. Make sure that you don't have two IDE devices both set to master or slave. If you have only one IDE device, it should be set to master. If you have an IDE CD-ROM and an IDE hard disk on the same bus, the CD-ROM should be set to slave.

Some SCSI drives must be set to have the SCSI controller issue a startup command before the disk will spin up. Make sure the controller is set to issue a startup command to these disks. If your controller can't issue startup commands, jumper the drive to start up at power on.

INCORRECT BIOS INFORMATION In the past you had to set the specific drive parameters for each hard disk in the BIOS so that operating systems knew how to partition and format the disk. Most modern controllers and motherboards automatically detect hard disk geometry. Some computers have

BIOS programs that are too old to recognize new large disks. In these cases you should upgrade to a hard disk controller that can recognize the full capacity of your disk.

Use the automatic hard disk geometry detection setting if it is available.

Many IDE and SCSI disks provide sector translation to allow operating systems that have a 1,024 cylinder limit to access an entire large disk. You may need to turn on this feature to complete the MS-DOS portion of the Windows NT installation if your primary disk has more than 1,024 cylinders. Once you have turn on sector translation, it must remain enabled for that drive.

FAILED MECHANISMS Failed mechanisms are the worst hard disk problem you can have. This problem is caused when the hard disk spindle or head assembly physically breaks. Unfortunately, you cannot recover from this situation, and you will lose the data on that hard disk.

Because you cannot prevent hard disk failures, back up regularly to another mass storage device to keep from losing your data.

Strange noises coming from your hard disk signal this fault. If your disk is "knocking" when you try to access it or if you hear strange grinding or scraping noises, it is usually too late. Sometimes the disk will bind and fail to spin at all. This symptom can make a physical disk failure seem like a power problem.

FAILED HARD DISK CONTROLLERS Hard disk controllers rarely fail, but they can conflict with other devices in your computer. Check these cards the same way you would check any other hardware conflict. If you seem to have no access whatsoever to your hard disk, or if during the BIOS phase of the boot process your computer tells you that you have a hard disk controller failure, check the seating and settings of your hard disk controller. Swap it with another hard disk of the same type if necessary. If your hard disk controller is embedded on your motherboard, disable it and install a peripheral card hard disk controller set to the same interrupt, port, and DMA channel.

BAD SECTORS Bad sectors are a fact of life in hard disks. As hard disks age, they gradually lose their ability to store information. This gradual loss shows up as bad sectors. Hard disks typically ship from the factory with bad sectors, so all operating systems are capable of marking sectors bad. Sectors will usually fail on a write operation rather than on a read operation, so the

NTFS hot-fixing feature described in Chapter 5 should keep you from having to worry about sector failure.

When you have a lot of sectors fail suddenly, you are about to experience a failed hard disk mechanism. The unexplained loss of hard disk space during the normal operation of Windows NT as NTFS marks more and more sectors out of use signals this failure. You may also experience unrecoverable read errors. Transfer data off the disk as soon as possible and replace the hard disk.

CORRUPTED BOOT SECTORS Corrupted boot sectors can occur when a power fluctuation interrupts a file system installation or by installing another operating system over Windows NT. This problem can be corrected using the MS-DOS fdisk utility and issuing the following command at the C prompt:

```
fdisk /mbr
```

The /mbr switch tells fdisk to write a new master boot record to the hard disk. You may also see this problem if you turn off sector translation in the BIOS of your hard disk controller. Try changing the sector translation setting before issuing the fdisk command. If you are unable to correct the problem by changing sector translation, change the translation setting back to its original setting and issue the fdisk /mbr command.

This command will have no adverse effect on your system even if it doesn't correct the problem unless you have changed the sector translation since the disk was originally formatted.

CORRUPTED PARTITION TABLES Corrupted partition tables usually do not happen unless you have tried to set a partition on your hard disk with an operating system that is not compatible with the IBM/Microsoft partitioning scheme. Some UNIX operating systems fall into this category. Unfortunately, this problem will probably cause you to lose data.

If you have not written anything to the disk since the partition problem occurred and you know how your disks were partitioned previously, you may be able to set the partition tables exactly as they were and recover the data on your hard disks. Probably, however, you will have to create new partitions, format the partitions, and reinstall Windows NT if you have this problem.

CORRUPTED FILE SYSTEMS NTFS has a number of built-in mechanisms to keep it from becoming corrupt. However, some problems, especially hardware configuration, can cause NTFS to become corrupted. NTFS checks for hard disk corruption each time you reboot your computer.

FAT file system volumes are very likely to become corrupt over time with normal usage. You should use the Microsoft Scandisk utility at lease once a month to detect and correct file system corruption.

VIRUSES Viruses are insidious programs that intentionally cause computer malfunctions and are capable of self-replicating among computers that share media. These programs can look like any sort of real malfunction. They may advertise their presence on your machine through some sort of message, usually during boot time.

So far no Windows NT viruses have appeared because the security permissions structure of Windows NT prevents User mode programs from writing to system files.

However, a boot sector virus may exist on your disk if you previously used an operating system older than Windows NT, such as MS-DOS, on that computer. If you have any reason to suspect a virus infestation, run one of the many available virus detection software kits under MS-DOS to detect and eliminate the virus.

Troubleshooting the Windows NT Boot Process

AFTER YOU HAVE determined that the computer hardware is operating properly, you must be sure that Windows NT is being loaded correctly. This section will first show you some of the boot sequence errors and what they mean, teach you how to diagnose `boot.ini` problems, and then explain how to use Windows NT boot disks and emergency repair disks to repair the Windows NT boot process.

Boot Sequence Errors

The boot sequence is a complicated process. If one of the boot components is damaged or removed or if your `boot.ini` file is incorrectly configured, you may see one of the following messages (in which case you need to use a boot disk or an emergency repair disk to fix the boot sequence). For example, the following message indicates that the NTLDR file is missing or corrupt:

```
BOOT: Couldn't find NTLDR

Please insert another disk
```

If the next message repeats after you have selected the Windows NT operating system on the boot menu, then `NTDETECT.COM` is damaged or missing:

```
NTDETECT V1.0 Checking Hardware É

NTDETECT V1.0 Checking Hardware É
```

The following message indicates that the Windows NT operating system is damaged or missing or that the `boot.ini` file is missing and that Windows NT was installed in a directory other than `\WINNT` or that `boot.ini` directs the operating system loader to a location that does not contain a valid `ntoskrnl.exe`:

```
Windows NT could not start because the following file is
    missing or corrupt:

\<winnt root>\system32\ntoskrnl.exe

Please re-install a copy of the above file.
```

This problem can occur when you partition free space on your hard disk if the partition number that contains the Windows NT changes. Edit the `boot.ini` file to reflect the new partition number for the partition that contains Windows NT.

The following message indicates that the boot sector is missing or corrupt:

```
I/O Error accessing boot sector file

multi(0)disk(0)rdisk(0)partition(1):\bootsect.dos
```

The next message indicates that the Windows NT entry in `boot.ini` points to a missing or malfunctioning device or to a disk partition that does not contain a file system recognized by the Windows NT boot loader:

```
OS Loader V4.00

Windows NT could not start because of a computer disk
    hardware configuration problem.

Could not read from the selected boot disk. Check boot
    path and disk hardware.

Please check the Windows NTª documentation about hard-
    ware disk configuration and your hardware reference
    manuals for additional information.
```

This error occurs when the NT loader cannot access the hard disk upon which your Windows NT partition is stored or when NT loader is confused about which hard disk controller to consider the primary device:STOP: 0x000007E: Inaccessible Boot Device

Because a number of SCSI adapters do not conform to the complete SCSI standard, they may cause this problem.

The STOP message is also heralded by the infamous "blue screen" of Windows NT crash fame. Very rarely—and because of circumstances that Microsoft does not report until the problem has been corrected in downloadable service pack—these screens indicate a serious failure from which Windows NT was not able to recover. These problems are usually related to I/O, and the bug that crashed the computer probably resides in a driver. If you have a problem with a STOP message blue screen, log on to the Windows NT Knowledge Base and use search key STOP: to find the bugs Microsoft knows how to correct.

If you have just added a SCSI controller to a Windows NT computer that boots from an IDE hard disk, make sure that no SCSI device is set to id 0. Otherwise, disable bootable SCSI hard disks. This setting will prevent the SCSI controller from attempting to boot the disk and will prevent the NTDETECT portion of the boot loader from assigning the SCSI adapter a bus number of zero, thereby causing boot.ini to refer to the wrong partition.

The Windows NT Boot Disk

Your Windows NT Server will normally boot from its hard disk drive. You may have installed NT into the boot partition of your hard drive, in which case the boot files and the operating system all reside in the same volume, or you may have installed Windows NT on another partition, in which case the boot files will reside in the boot partition, separate from the operating system.

A third boot configuration is possible for Windows NT. You can create a floppy boot disk that contains the boot files necessary to start the Windows NT operating system. Booting from a floppy is slower than booting from a hard disk, but a floppy boot disk can be very useful when your computer is not booting properly. Exercise 17.1 shows you how to create a boot floppy.

If you are experiencing a problem booting NT because one of the boot files (`boot.ini`, `NTLDR`, `NTDETECT.COM` or `NTBOOTDD.SYS`) is missing or corrupt, you can boot NT with the boot floppy disk you have just created and then copy the files from the floppy disk to your boot drive (drive C). This process restores the missing or corrupted files and allows the boot to proceed normally.

EXERCISE 17.1

Creating a Windows NT Boot Floppy

1. Open My Computer and select the floppy icon.

2. Place a blank floppy disk in the disk drive.

3. Select File ➤ Format; click Start. You will be warned that formatting the floppy disk will destroy all data on the disk.

4. Click OK to continue.

5. Click OK when the format is complete and then close the Format window.

6. Open the icon for your boot drive in the My Computer window. (It will probably be drive C.)

7. Position the boot drive window so that you can also see the floppy disk icon in the My Computer window. (You will need to copy some files from your boot disk to your floppy disk.)

8. Copy the `boot.ini`, `NTLDR`, and `NTDETECT.COM` files to your floppy drive.

9. Copy the `NTBOOTDD.SYS` file if it resides in the root directory of your boot drive

10. Close the boot drive window and the My Computer window.

11. Reboot the computer with the floppy disk still in the disk drive.

The Emergency Repair Disk

However, the trouble you are experiencing may be more severe than simply missing or corrupted boot files. If any of the files that contain Windows NT Registry information become corrupt, Windows NT itself can become unstable, even to the point of making it impossible to fix the problem from within NT.

You can create an emergency repair disk to restore the Registry from the last time you performed an emergency repair disk update. The emergency repair disk includes the security account manager (SAM) database, disk configuration, and numerous other system parameters.

You can use the Windows NT RDISK.EXE utility to create and update an emergency repair disk. This utility has two options—update the repair information or create a new repair disk.

When you choose update repair information, RDISK.EXE copies the system hive, the security accounts manager, the security hive, the software hive, the default hive, and the CONFIG.NT and AUTOEXEC.NT files used when initializing a Windows NT virtual DOS machine into a directory off the Windows NT root directory called \REPAIR. The utility then asks if you want to create an emergency repair disk containing this information. (See Chapter 15 in the companion book *MCSE: NT Workstation Study Guide* for an explanation of NTVDM.)

The emergency repair disk is not a replacement for regular backups. The emergency repair disk stores only Registry configuration information, not your data.

The Create emergency repair disk option simply formats a floppy disk and copies the contents of the repair directory to it. Exercise 17.2 shows you how to run the rdisk utility to create an emergency repair disk. You should create a new repair disk each time you make a major change to security policy, add new users, or change the configuration of your Windows NT Server.

EXERCISE 17.2

Creating an Emergency Repair Disk

1. Click the Start menu and select Programs ≻ Command prompt.

2. Type **rdisk** at the command prompt and press Enter.

3. Click Update Repair Info.

4. Click Yes when asked if you want to overwrite the current repair information.

5. Click Yes when asked if you want to create an emergency repair disk.

6. Insert a new floppy disk into drive A and click OK.

7. Remove the emergency repair floppy for safekeeping.

8. Click Exit to close the rdisk program. Close the command prompt window.

Restoring Windows NT

The process of restoring a Windows NT installation that has somehow become damaged or corrupt is similar to reinstalling the operating system. In fact, you are reinstalling the operating system, but rather than using default information, you are restoring security and account information in the Registry from the emergency repair disk.

The restoration process checks the hard disk for errors and can verify the Windows NT system files. It restores some or all of the Registry information if you want it to.

You will need your Windows NT Setup boot disks, Server 4 CD-ROM, and emergency repair disk for this specific computer. The repair process will reinstall the security database from the last time you updated your repair disk. If your repair disk is very old or you can't remember the administrator password, you will be better off not reinstalling the Registry from the emergency repair disk. Exercise 17.3 shows you how to restore the Windows NT system settings.

EXERCISE 17.3

Restoring the Windows NT System Settings, Including the Registry

1. Boot the Windows NT Server Setup boot disk.

2. Insert Setup Disk #2 when prompted and press Enter.

3. Press R for Restore when prompted for the type of installation you want to perform.

4. Press Enter on each option you want to repair.

5. Move to Continue and press Enter.

6. Press Enter at the Detect Devices screen.

7. Insert Setup Disk #3 and press Enter.

8. Add drivers as necessary, using the Other Disk option and inserting driver disks as necessary. When finished, insert Setup Disk #3 again.

9. Press Enter.

10. Insert the emergency repair disk and press Enter.

11. Press Enter to select each Registry Hive you want restored.

12. Select Continue and press Enter.

13. Press A to replace all non-original files.

14. Insert any third-party driver disks requested by the Setup program.

15. Press Esc to skip using the DRVLIB disk if you do not have it.

16. Reboot your computer when the repair process is complete.

Troubleshooting a Running Windows NT Environment

I F YOU ARE sure that you have no hardware problems and your Windows NT Server boots properly, but you are still experiencing difficulties, you will need to troubleshoot the running operating system. Windows NT provides an excellent environment for troubleshooting. Microsoft provides tools with which you can view almost any aspect of the operating system. The tools you will most often use are the Event Viewer, which records problems detected by Windows NT, and the Windows NT diagnostic tool, which shows you how Windows NT is configured. You can also use the performance monitor to find programs that are using more resources than you might expect and degrading the performance of your machine.

Troubleshooting with the Event Viewer

Rather than reporting nonfatal error messages on screen during operation, Windows NT adds a record to the Event log. This technique keeps users from being bothered by annoying messages that they may not have the permissions to fix, and more important, keeps a written log of all error messages for you to review. If you've ever had a user call you to fix an error and then not remember what the error was, you'll appreciate the Event log. You can review the Event log with a program called the Event Viewer. Figure 17.1 shows the Event Viewer.

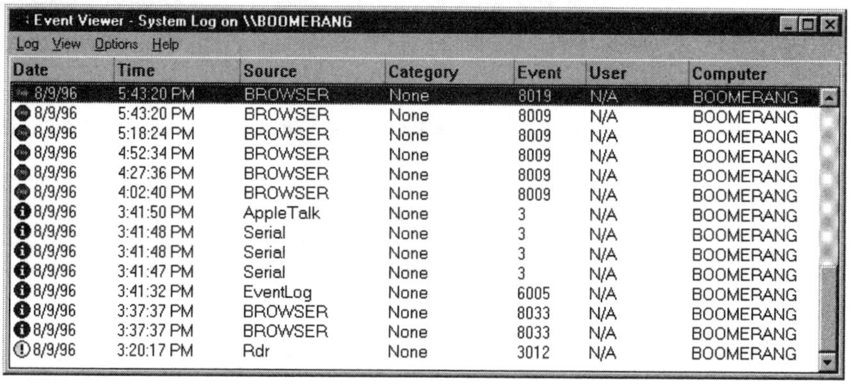

FIGURE 17.1

The Windows NT Event
Viewer.

Date	Time	Source	Category	Event	User	Computer
8/9/96	5:43:20 PM	BROWSER	None	8019	N/A	BOOMERANG
8/9/96	5:43:20 PM	BROWSER	None	8009	N/A	BOOMERANG
8/9/96	5:18:24 PM	BROWSER	None	8009	N/A	BOOMERANG
8/9/96	4:52:34 PM	BROWSER	None	8009	N/A	BOOMERANG
8/9/96	4:27:36 PM	BROWSER	None	8009	N/A	BOOMERANG
8/9/96	4:02:40 PM	BROWSER	None	8009	N/A	BOOMERANG
8/9/96	3:41:50 PM	AppleTalk	None	3	N/A	BOOMERANG
8/9/96	3:41:48 PM	Serial	None	3	N/A	BOOMERANG
8/9/96	3:41:48 PM	Serial	None	3	N/A	BOOMERANG
8/9/96	3:41:47 PM	Serial	None	3	N/A	BOOMERANG
8/9/96	3:41:32 PM	EventLog	None	6005	N/A	BOOMERANG
8/9/96	3:37:37 PM	BROWSER	None	8033	N/A	BOOMERANG
8/9/96	3:37:37 PM	BROWSER	None	8033	N/A	BOOMERANG
8/9/96	3:20:17 PM	Rdr	None	3012	N/A	BOOMERANG

You should begin all troubleshooting sessions by reviewing the Event log with the Event Viewer because this log frequently tells you exactly what is wrong. You can save yourself a lot of time by checking the Event log often. The Event Viewer allows you to view three types of events:

- **System events** are recorded by the Windows NT Kernel and drivers.

- **Security events** are recorded when security events as set by your audit and user policies occur.

- **Application events** are recorded by Windows NT User mode applications that are designed to use the Event log.

Events in the Event log are recorded with three priorities:

- A blue icon containing the letter *i* marks an informative message. These events do not affect the operation of your computer.

- A yellow icon containing an exclamation mark (!) records an alert. These events indicate that your computer is operating in a degraded condition or that some noncritical resource is not operating correctly.

- A red stop sign indicates a critical warning. Something serious is wrong with your computer or configuration that will cause denial of a service.

The Security section of the Event log has two event icons:

- A key shows an audit policy event that was passed.

- A padlock shows an audit policy event that was blocked by the system.

Exercise 17.4 shows you how to run the Event Viewer and how to view the different event types.

EXERCISE 17.4

Using the Event Viewer

1. Click the Start menu and select Programs ➤ Administrative Tools ➤ Event Viewer.

2. Notice the events in your log. System events are shown by default when you first run the Event Viewer.

3. Double-click on any event to see the entire event message. Click Close when you are finished viewing that event.

4. Select Security in the Log menu. If you don't have any audit policies set up, you might not see anything here.

5. Select Application in the Log menu. Again, if you haven't run any Event log–enabled applications, you may not see anything recorded here.

6. Select Clear All Events in the Log menu.

7. Answer No when asked if you want to save the log.

8. Answer Yes when asked if you are sure you want to clear the log.

You should check your Event log any time you suspect something isn't working correctly in your system. You should check it periodically (at least once a month) even when things are working fine.

You should clear your Event log before a troubleshooting session (after you've reviewed it, of course) to help you find events that relate to the current problem.

The Windows NT Diagnostic Tool

WinMSD is also called the Windows NT diagnostic tool. Through this tool, you can inspect everything Windows NT knows about your computer to verify that it works correctly. WinMSD is split into sections accessed by the tabs near the top of the WinMSD window. These sections are

- Version

- System

- Display

- Drives

- Memory

- Services

- Resources

- Environment

- Network

Exercise 17.5 explains how to load and use the Windows NT diagnostic tool. As you read through the rest of this section, move through the diagnostic tool to see the specific information it reports about your machine.

EXERCISE 17.5

Using the Windows NT Diagnostic Tool

1. Click start and select Programs ➢ Administrative Tools ➢ Windows NT Diagnostics.

2. Click the Resources tab.

3. Click IRQ. Note the interrupt level of each device.

4. Click I/O Port. Note the I/O ports used by each device.

5. Click DMA. Note the DMA status of each device.

6. Click Memory. Note the memory ranges used by each device.

7. Click Devices. Note the device drivers installed in your system.

8. Double-click the serial device driver.

9. Note how many serial device interrupts and port addresses your system uses. Click OK to close the Serial Properties window.

10. Click Print.

11. Click OK to print.

12. Click OK to close the Windows NT diagnostic tool.

The following sections describe how to use each Windows NT Diagnostic tab for troubleshooting. Figure 17.2 shows the Windows NT Diagnostic screen and its many options.

FIGURE 17.2

The Windows NT Diagnostic screen.

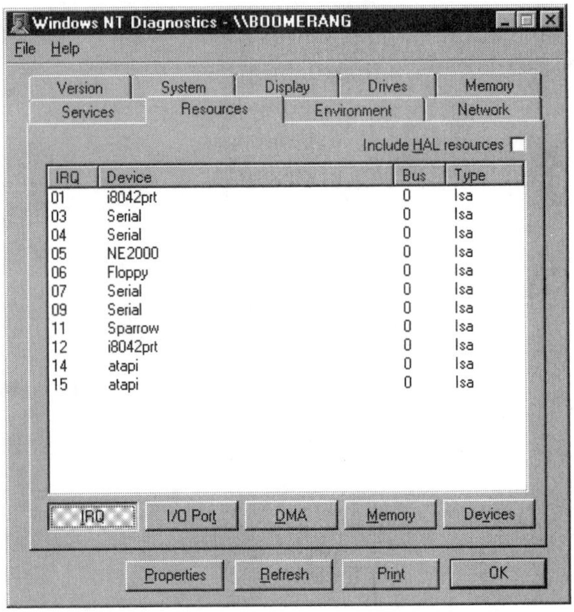

Version

Version tells you what version of Windows NT is running, what build of the operating system you have, how many processors are installed, and who this copy is registered to. This information is not of much value when troubleshooting.

System

System identifies what sort of motherboard and microprocessor you are using and displays BIOS date and manufacturer. This information is not of much value when troubleshooting.

Display

Display shows the BIOS date and revision for your video adapter, as well as the current settings. You should see the manufacturer of your video adapter and the type of digital-to-analog converter used. This information is not of much value when troubleshooting.

Drives

Drives shows all of the currently installed volumes, grouped by type such as removable drives, hard drives, CD-ROM, and network drives. Clicking on individual drives displays information about that drive, such as the file system time and how much data it contains. This tab is not available when viewing diagnostic information on a remote computer.

Memory

The Memory tab shows the system is using memory. In addition to showing the amount of physical RAM, this tab shows how much is being used by the Kernel and how much is being used by the page file. At the bottom of this screen, you can see how the page file is distributed across your physical disks.

The Memory tab also displays how many heap handles are allocated, how many threads are running, and how many processes are currently executing. This tab is not available when viewing diagnostic information on a remote computer.

Services

The Services tab displays the state of all loaded services and drivers. Click the Services button at the bottom of the screen to display the services and the Devices button to displays the devices.

When you double-click a service or device driver, a window shows the start type of the service or device driver and some other less useful information. You can click the Dependencies tab to show what services must be running for this service or device driver to operate.

Resources

The Resources tab is the most important part of the Windows NT Diagnostic screen. This tab shows the state of all hardware in the computer that Windows NT knows about. This tab will help you iron out hardware conflicts by showing the resource use for all devices installed in Windows NT.

You select the resource type you want to see by clicking the IRQ, I/O port, DMA, Memory, or Devices buttons located at the bottom of the Resource pane.

When you double-click a resource item in the display drop-down box, a window displays information about that resource line item. For the most part, useful information is shown only when viewing devices. In this instance, the window will show all the resources used for that device.

Before installing a new device in your computer, review the Resources tab of the Windows NT diagnostic tool to be certain other devices aren't already using the interrupt, DMA channel, and I/O port settings you intend to use for the new device. This step will prevent hardware conflicts and keep you from having to troubleshoot new hardware installations.

Environment

The Environment tab shows the environment variables that Windows NT uses to communicate simple information to applications about the Windows NT environment. Environment variables in Windows NT appear to applications the same way DOS environment variables do, so older applications can use them to find information or change their state based on the current system settings. You will probably not need to change or inspect any of these settings.

Network

The Network tab shows information about the current network session. Use this tab to determine which workgroup or domain you are logged onto, and under which account. This tab also shows the name of the logon domain and server.

Troubleshooting Security Problems

If a user cannot access a program or some data on a computer that he or she knows is there or can see, chances are the user does not have sufficient permissions to perform the action in question. To troubleshoot security problems, log on as the administrator and attempt the same operation. If you can perform the operation, the problem is a security problem. You can assign the user permissions to use the resource, or you can move the resource to an area where the user has sufficient permissions.

Sometimes even the administrator can't use or delete a resource that is visible. The reason is that the resource was created and assigned permissions under a previous installation of Windows NT that has been overwritten. Now the old administrator account that no longer exists is the owner. Because Windows NT assigns a new security ID to the new administrator during the new installation, no current user has permission to use or delete the resource.

Fortunately, Windows NT has a workaround for this problem. For any resource, the administrator can take ownership of the resource and then reassign permissions as necessary. Exercise 17.6 shows how to take ownership of a resource. Under normal circumstances, you would not take ownership of every resource on the computer as shown below. You would take ownership only of the specific files or subdirectories that had this security problem.

EXERCISE 17.6

Taking Ownership of a Resource

1. Log on as the administrator.

2. Double-click the My Computer icon on the desktop.

3. Right-click on drive C (or any other NTFS volume). Select Properties and then the Security tab.

4. Click Ownership.

5. Click Take Ownership.

6. Click Yes to take ownership of all files and subdirectories.

7. Click Yes to continue if a File in Use error occurs.

8. Wait while the security manager assigns each resource in the drive.

9. Click OK to close the window.

Troubleshooting Resources

ONCE YOU HAVE exhausted your own knowledge and skills and the diagnostic utilities provided by Microsoft give you no more useful information, you will need to turn to other resources for help. One of the best resources, the Windows NT Help files, exists right on your local hard drive. If you do not find the solution there, you can turn to the TechNET CD or the Microsoft Knowledge Base Library for more information. You can also ask others for help on the Internet or on online services such as Compuserve and America Online.

Windows Help Files

The Windows NT Help files are an excellent troubleshooting resource. These Help files are based on Microsoft's experience with customer support, so they include specific troubleshooting help for the problems reported to Microsoft most often. You stand a good chance of finding a Help file that can walk you through the steps for fixing software configuration problems. Use Exercise 17.7 to find specific Help files when you don't know what the help file's context normally is.

EXERCISE 17.7

Opening Help Files

1. Click Start and select Find ➢ Files or Folders.

2. Type ***.hlp** in the Name input line.

3. Check the Include subfolders option.

4. Make sure the root directory of the volume containing the Windows NT directory is showing in the Look In drop-down list.

5. Click Find now.

6. Double-click the `Regedit.hlp` file in the resulting list of help files.

7. Double-click the book titled "Changing keys and values."

8. Read the topic.

9. Close the Registry Editor Help file.

TechNET

Microsoft distributes the TechNET CD-ROM to technical support professionals who subscribe. The TechNET CD-ROM contains much of the same information that you can find on the Microsoft Web site, but it is far faster because your searches are not limited to the speed of your modem. The TechNET CD is especially useful for larger organizations that can absorb the cost of the subscription. You can subscribe to the TechNET CD-ROM service by calling 1-800-344-2121.

Internet

The Internet is by far the best troubleshooting resource for any computer problem. The cumulative experience of thousands of Windows NT experts is available through both Microsoft-sanctioned and private resources. Unless you are working with an experimental release of Windows NT, you can presume that someone else has had the same problem you are having. There's a good chance that your question has already been posted and answered on a newsgroup.

Most hardware manufacturers also maintain Web sites that contain current versions of their Windows NT drivers. If you are having a problem with a third-party driver, check the vendor's Web site for an updated driver. If you can't find the site, use AltaVista to search for it.

The Microsoft Knowledge Base

The Microsoft Knowledge Base is the official repository for support information about all Microsoft products including Windows NT. The Knowledge Base is an accumulation of answers to technical support questions received by Microsoft since Windows NT was first released. Figure 17.3 shows the Microsoft Web site.

FIGURE 17.3

The Microsoft Web site at
www.microsoft.com.

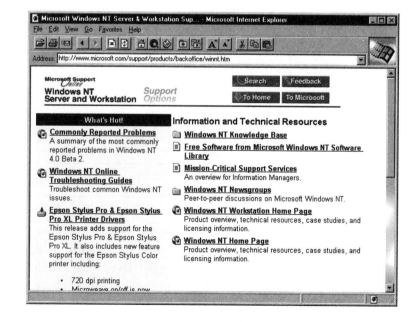

You can access this database at URL www.microsoft.com. You will need to have set up remote access service to connect to an Internet account, as explained in Chapter 12. Exercise 17.8 shows how to access and navigate the Knowledge Base.

Web sites change quickly. The exact steps to access the Knowledge Base may change, but you should be able to access the site easily from Internet Explorer.

EXERCISE 17.8

Accessing the Microsoft Knowledge Base

1. Double-click the My Computer icon on the desktop.

2. Double-click the Dial-up Networking icon.

3. Select your Internet service provider in the Dial-up service drop-down list.

4. Click Dial. Perform any post-connection logon procedures necessary to establish an Internet connection to your service provider.

5. Double-click the Internet Explorer Icon on the desktop.

6. Type www.microsoft.com in the Address input box and press Enter.

7. Click the Support link when the Microsoft home page appears.

8. Click the Search the Knowledge Base link.

9. Select Windows NT in the Microsoft Product list.

10. Type **SCSI Adapter** in the word search input line.

11. Click Go.

12. Select one of the articles and review it.

13. Leave Internet Explorer and the dial-up connection active for the next exercises.

World Wide Web Indexes and Search Engines

You can use many of the Web search engines and indexes to quickly find information about Windows NT and troubleshooting. Corporations that are interested in furthering the development of the Internet and the World Wide Web provide these free search engines. The largest index provider and the largest search engine provider are presented here. Many others exist, and you will find links to them through these providers.

YAHOO! Yahoo! is an Internet index. When you pull up the Yahoo home page, you will see a menu of general topics covering the spectrum of Web pages. You will successively narrow your search through Yahoo by choosing more specific links through each page. Figure 17.4 shows the Windows NT index at Yahoo!

FIGURE 17.4

Yahoo!

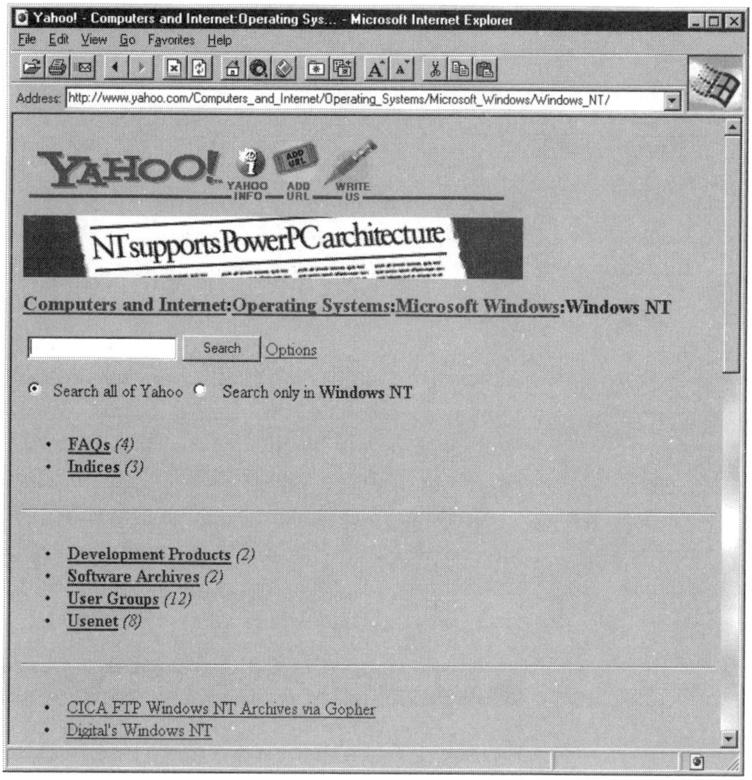

You can use Yahoo! when you can't think of a specific search phrase for a search engine or when your problem is a little too broad to express in a single search phrase. Exercise 17.9 shows how to use the Yahoo! Internet index to find troubleshooting support for Windows NT.

EXERCISE 17.9

Using Yahoo to Find Troubleshooting Support

1. Type www.yahoo.com in the Address input line of the Internet Explorer and press Enter.

2. Click the Computers and Internet link.

3. Click the Operating Systems link.

4. Click the Microsoft Windows link.

5. Click the Windows NT link.

6. Review the resources available to you at this site.

ALTAVISTA The AltaVista Web and Usenet search engine is a service provided by Digital Equipment Corporation. AltaVista works by constantly searching for new Web pages. When it finds new content, it sends the content back to the AltaVista site where it is indexed and stored in a huge database of indexed key words. When you enter a search phrase into the AltaVista main page, the engine searches the database of indexed key words and creates a new Web page containing the results of the search for you. You can select any of the links in the Web page simply by clicking on the corresponding link. Figure 17.5 shows AltaVista during a Windows NT–specific search.

Use AltaVista when you have a specific problem and you think you can narrow down a search with a single phrase. The AltaVista Web site has instructions on how to make your searches more efficient. Exercise 17.10 shows how to use AltaVista as a Windows NT troubleshooting resource.

EXERCISE 17.10

Using AltaVista to Find Troubleshooting Support

1. Type www.altavista.digital.com in the Address input line of the Internet Explorer and press Enter.

2. Type **+"Windows NT"+troubleshooting -course** in the Search input line.

3. Review the Web sites available from this search query.

4. Select Usenet in the Search Type pick list.

5. Type **+"Windows NT"+troubleshooting-jobs** in the Search input line.

6. Review the Usenet information available from this search query.

FIGURE 17.5

The AltaVista Web site.

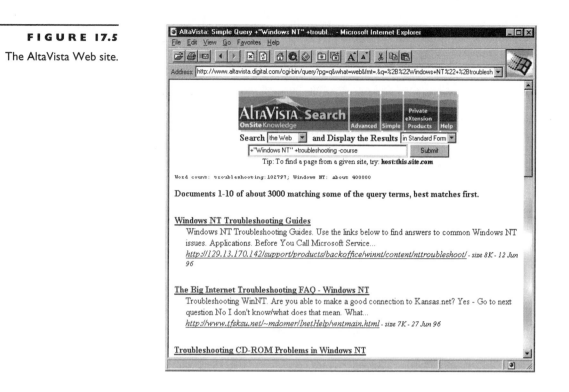

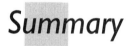

Summary

TROUBLESHOOTING IS A skill like any other. The basic principles used to troubleshoot Windows NT–based networks are universal and can be applied to any malfunction.

Hardware problems are common in servers, and Windows NT Server is especially sensitive to them. Therefore, you must solve hardware problems before attempting to troubleshoot software problems. MS-DOS is a valuable troubleshooting tool that you can use when a hardware problem prevents Windows NT Server from booting.

Networks are extremely sensitive to the configuration of software services. For instance, a misconfigured DHCP server can prevent properly configured client computers from operating on the network. So the primary rule when troubleshooting networks is to first identify the factors that explain all the failures that have occurred.

Windows NT provides a number of tools to assist in troubleshooting, including the Event Viewer, the Windows NT diagnostic tool, the performance monitor, and the network monitor. These tools will guide you to the source of a software configuration problem and help you prevent future hardware malfunctions.

The Internet is also a powerful troubleshooting resource. Microsoft provides free support via its Web site, which contains the Microsoft Knowledge Base. Internet indexes such as Yahoo! and search engines such as AltaVista can help you find private sources of information. Hardware manufacturers also provide updated Windows NT drivers via the Web.

Conclusion and Note from the Authors

We hope you've enjoyed reading this book as much as we enjoyed writing it.

Windows NT is a marvelous operating system, and our study guides really only scratch the surface of the power and flexibility it provides. We hope you'll use the information presented herein for good—not evil.

Taking and passing the MCSE exams provides you with a solid foundation upon which to learn. We hope that you will find this book a useful reference as you expand your knowledge of Windows NT and of networking. We suggest that you continue by studying the other books in this series and other materials on Windows NT such as the excellent reference materials produced by Microsoft and Sybex.

Those of you who will be using Windows NT as a platform for Internet services will enjoy our book titled *MCSE: Internet Information Server Study Guide*. It explores IIS and the Internet in much greater detail and will prepare you for Microsoft's Internet certification exams.

Thanks for Reading!

Matthew Strebe & Charles Perkins, 1 February 1997.

Review Questions

1. Release versions of Windows NT are bug free.

A. True

B. False

2. Windows NT runs on all computers capable of running Windows 95.

A. True

B. False

3. All Internet troubleshooting resources for Windows NT are maintained in the Windows NT Knowledge Base at the Microsoft Web site.

A. True

B. False

4. Microsoft does not certify hardware components as compatible with NT.

A. True

B. False

5. Recent changes are likely to be the cause of new malfunctions.

A. True

B. False

6. If you use Windows NT, you no longer have any reason to use MS-DOS.

A. True

B. False

7. The Microsoft Knowledge Base is the official repository for support information about all Microsoft products including Windows NT.

A. True

B. False

8. With MS-DOS you cannot access _____ volumes.

9. To create an emergency repair disk, use the _____ utility.

10. The _____ section of the Windows NT diagnostic tool is the most useful for troubleshooting.

11. The _____ is by far the best troubleshooting resource for any computer problem.

12. Which of the following is not good practice when troubleshooting?

    A. Be patient.

    B. Perform easy tests first.

    C. Change only one setting at a time.

    D. Make as many changes as possible.

13. The most common hardware problem in PCs is

    A. Bad memory

    B. Hardware conflicts

    C. Loose cables

    D. Power supply failure

14. Which of these failures is the most damaging of all computer component failures?

    A. Processor

    B. Memory

    C. Motherboard

    D. Hard disk

15. An emergency repair disk can restore

    A. Missing System files

    B. Damaged user files

C. Backup tapes

D. Registry information

16. To view the Event log, use the

A. Event Monitor

B. User Manager

C. Notepad

D. Event Viewer

17. If none of your clients can reach the file server, but you can share files through Windows 95 peer networking, the most likely problem is the:

A. Client configurations

B. Data link devices

C. Cable plant

D. Server

18. If none of your clients can reach the file server, and you cannot share files through Windows 95 peer networking, the most likely problem is the:

A. Client configurations

B. Data link devices

C. Cable plant

D. Server

19. If one of your clients cannot reach the file server, and you cannot share files through Windows 95 peer networking with that client, the most likely problem is the:

A. Client configurations

B. Data link devices

C. Cable plant

D. Server

20. If none of the clients in the building next door can reach the server in the main building right after a contractor dug a trench in the road between the two buildings, the most likely problem is the:

A. Client configurations

B. Data link devices

C. Cable plant

D. Server

Answers to Review Questions

Chapter I Answers

1. You would most likely use Windows NT Server to run application programs such as spreadsheets and word processors.

   A. True

   B. False

   Answer: B

2. Windows 95 is not a descendent of Windows NT.

   A. True

   B. False

   Answer: A

3. Windows NT will run every program that other versions of Windows and DOS will run.

   A. True

   B. False

   Answer: B

4. Windows NT can run some OS/2 programs.

   A. True

   B. False

   Answer: A

5. Windows NT 4 uses the Windows 95 interface.

   A. True

   B. False

   Answer: A

6. Normal users are allowed to install alternative device drivers in the kernel.

A. True

B. False

Answer: B

7. The Windows NT kernel provides a fault-tolerant environment for the execution of programs and services

A. True

B. False

Answer: A

8. Windows 95 is platform dependent because it runs on Intel-based computers only.

A. True

B. False

Answer: A

9. Windows NT Server can provide network services for DOS, Windows, Windows NT Workstation, OS/2, and the Apple Macintosh

A. True

B. False

Answer: A

10. Windows NT Server is a _____ operating system.

Answer: network

11. Windows NT Server as a _____ server provides a place for storing files for all of the client computers on the network

Answer: file

12. The _____ lies at the heart of the operating system and provides services to the programs running on the computer.

>   **Answer:** kernel

13. A _____ _____ kernel provides the illusion of many programs executing at once on the computer by dividing processor time between each program and ensuring that no program can monopolize the time of the processor.

>   **Answer:** preemptive multitasking

14. A _____ kernel supports the use of more than one microprocessor in the computer.

>   **Answer:** multiprocessing

15. NTFS does not use a _____ _____ _____ (FAT).

>   **Answer:** file allocation table

16. RAID stands for _____ _____ _____ _____.

>   **Answer:** redundant array of inexpensive (or independent) disks

17. TDI stands for _____ _____ _____.

>   **Answer:** Transport Driver Interface

18. One Windows NT Server becomes the _____ _____ _____ (PDC), which maintains the security database and controls various aspects of the network's operation.

>   **Answer:** primary domain controller

19. Windows NT Server also supports RISC microprocessors such as _____, _____ _____, and _____.

>   **Answer:** MIPS, Digital Alpha, and PowerPC

20. Microsoft maintains a list of computers and peripheral equipment that has been tested to work with Windows NT; the list is called the _____ _____ _____, or HCL.

>   **Answer:** Hardware Compatibility List

Chapter 2 Answers

1. You do not have to worry about supporting legacy systems, because the network will usually replace them.

A. True

B. False

Answer: B

2. Many older network operating systems require a separate login to each server.

A. True

B. False

Answer: A

3. Computers configured for domain security cannot participate in workgroups.

A. True

B. False

Answer: B

4. Organizational requirements are the same for all organizations.

A. True

B. False

Answer: B

5. Collecting servers in a central location reduces the administrative burden.

A. True

B. False

Answer: A

6. Collecting servers in a central location reduces traffic on the backbone.

   A. True

   B. False

     Answer: B

7. It is always better to distribute servers rather than to centralize them.

   A. True

   B. False

     Answer: B

8. Generally, you will choose the _____ security model.

     Answer: domain

9. The _____ security model governs the interactions of Windows and Windows NT computers in a peer network.

     Answer: workgroup

10. What is the most important part of setting up a network?

   A. Designing the physical plant

   B. Determining the client load

   C. Planning

   D. Calculating the number of licenses you will require.

     Answer: C

11. _____ are high-speed links that connect shared media networks

   A. Routers

   B. FDDI

   C. Backbones

   D. Bridges

     Answer: C

12. _____ is the most popular data link technology.

   A. Token Ring

   B. FDDI

   C. ATM

   D. Ethernet

   E. FiberChannel

   Answer: D

13. _____ wired physical plant architectures can simulate all other wiring architectures.

   A. Bus

   B. Star

   C. Ring

   D. Full-duplex

   Answer: B

14. The _____ is responsible for security in the Domain security model.

   A. application server

   B. security server

   C. domain security controller

   D. primary domain controller

   E. primary domain server

   Answer: D

Chapter 3 Answers

1. Servers use completely different architectures than typical PC computers use.

    A. True

    B. False

      Answer: B

2. The minimum requirements published by Microsoft to run Windows NT are sufficient for small servers.

    A. True

    B. False

      Answer: B

3. You can use any Windows NT application on any microprocessor supported by Windows NT.

    A. True

    B. False

      Answer: B

4. Servers use vastly different hardware depending upon the services they provide.

    A. True

    B. False

      Answer: A

5. Almost all servers perform more than one service role.

    A. True

    B. False

      Answer: A

6. Almost all servers provide file services.

   A. True

   B. False

   Answer: A

7. Almost all servers provide application services.

   A. True

   B. False

   Answer: B

8. File servers are rarely CPU bound.

   A. True

   B. False

   Answer: A

9. Application servers need more RAM than any other type of server.

   A. True

   B. False

   Answer: A

10. Because the Internet protocols are optimized for low speed, Internet servers do not need to be fast.

   A. True

   B. False

   Answer: A

11. Firewalls should be the only computer attached to both the secure and non-secure networks.

   A. True

   B. False

   Answer: A

12. Your firewall can safely do double duty as an Internet server.

    A. True

    B. False

      Answer: B

13. Your firewall can safely do double duty as an Internet router.

    A. True

    B. False

      Answer: A

14. RISC microprocessors are always faster than CISC microprocessors.

    A. True

    B. False

      Answer: B

15. A Pentium running at 200Mhz delivers twice the computing power of a Pentium running at 100MHz.

    A. True

    B. False

      Answer: B

16. Two processors deliver twice the performance of a single processor.

    A. True

    B. False

      Answer: B

17. An application server will not benefit from multiprocessing unless the application is written to support multiprocessing.

    A. True

    B. False

      Answer: B

18. Fault tolerance schemes such as mirroring and striping with parity allow your hard disk controller to fail without bringing down the system.

A. True

B. False

Answer: B

19. If you have a SCSI controller, you should not use IDE peripherals.

A. True

B. False

Answer: B

20. SCSI controllers should be embedded on the motherboard for maximum performance.

A. True

B. False

Answer: B

21. Hard drives wear out from normal use.

A. True

B. False

Answer: A

22. Windows NT supports _____ families of microprocessors.

Answer: four

23. _____ microprocessors are the fastest microprocessors supported by Windows NT.

Answer: Alpha

24. _____ microprocessors have the most applications available for use with Windows NT.

Answer: Intel

25. Windows NT uses the _____ method of multiprocessing.

> **Answer:** symmetrical

26. The only component whose failure is catastrophic in a server is
_____.

A. the microprocessor

B. RAM

C. a hard disk drive

D. the video adapter

> **Answer:** C

27. _____ is the fastest standard bus for the interconnection of mass storage
devices in typical servers.

A. PCI

B. SCSI

C. IDE

D. ISA

E. WORM

> **Answer:** B

28. The _____ is the brain of a computer.

A. microprocessor

B. motherboard

C. RAM

D. video adapter

E. hard disks

> **Answer:** A

Chapter 4 Answers

1. Any computer that can run DOS or Windows can run Windows NT Server.

A. True

B. False

Answer: B

2. You can read files on an NTFS partition from within the DOS and Windows operating systems.

A. True

B. False

Answer: B

3. You can configure your computer so that Windows NT Server will coexist with other operating systems such as Windows 95 and DOS.

A. True

B. False

Answer: A

4. You must have the floppy disks that came with the CD-ROM because that is the only way to install Windows NT Server.

A. True

B. False

Answer: B

5. If you perform an installation without a floppy disk, you must have a FAT file system on your computer's hard disk drive with sufficient free space to hold the Windows NT Server installation files.

A. True

B. False

Answer: A

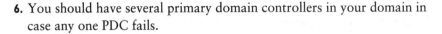

6. You should have several primary domain controllers in your domain in case any one PDC fails.

   A. True

   B. False

   Answer: B

7. The primary domain controller must be the first computer set up on the domain because it creates the domain.

   A. True

   B. False

   Answer: A

8. Backup domain controllers can authenticate log on requests.

   A. True

   B. False

   Answer: A

9. You can install a Windows NT Server as a member server or as a stand-alone server and later upgrade it to PDC or BDC status.

   A. True

   B. False

   Answer: B

10. Upgrading an earlier version of Windows NT is quicker and easier than installing from scratch.

   A. True

   B. False

   Answer: A

11. THE_SERVER is a good name for the server on your network.

   A. True

   B. False

   Answer: B

12. You should leave the domain name for your domain to its default, which is DOMAIN.

   A. True

   B. False

   Answer: B

13. Any version of DOS FDISK can remove NTFS partitions from your hard disk drive.

   A. True

   B. False

   Answer: B

14. You will use the _____ program with the /b option to perform an installation without a floppy disk of Windows NT Server from DOS or Windows.

   Answer: Winnt

15. You will use the _____ program with the /ox option to re-create the boot floppies from the CD-ROM from within Windows NT Workstation or Server.

   Answer: Winnt32

16. You can use the _____ _____ _____ program to create a network boot floppy that will attach to your file server so that you can install Windows NT Server from the network.

   Answer: Network Client Administrator

17. If you have a large number of similarly configured computers to which you must install Windows NT Server, you can use an _____ answer file to automate the process.

   Answer: unattended

18. The _____ _____ program helps you create files that automate the installation process.

   Answer: Setup Manager

19. A _____ _____ _____ or UDF contains unique information for each computer in automated installations of the Windows NT Server operating system.

Answer: uniqueness database file

20. The _____ utility records the difference between a normal Windows NT installation and an installation to which you have added files.

Answer: Sysdiff

21. PDC stands for _____ _____ _____.

Answer: primary domain controller

22. BDC stands for _____ _____ _____.

Answer: backup domain controller

23. Windows NT Server computers that are members of a domain and are not domain controllers are called _____.

Answer: member servers

24. Windows NT Servers that are not members of a domain are called _____ _____ _____.

Answer: stand-alone servers

Chapter 5 Answers

1. The FAT file system does not record security information such as the owner or file-sharing access permissions of a file or directory.

A. True

B. False

Answer: A

2. The FAT file system has more overhead than NTFS has for small volumes.

A. True

B. False

Answer: B

3. Under VFAT, names are not case sensitive, but they do preserve case.

    A. True

    B. False

       Answer: A

4. You must be careful when creating a partition because you might create a partition in a space occupied by an existing partition.

    A. True

    B. False

       Answer: B

5. Windows NT assigns a drive letter to each partition as you create it.

    A. True

    B. False

       Answer: A

6. The partitions combined into a volume set must be the same size and on the same drive.

    A. True

    B. False

       Answer: B

7. The system and boot partitions cannot be a part of a volume set.

    A. True

    B. False

       Answer: A

8. Volume sets provide fault tolerance to your file storage.

    A. True

    B. False

       Answer: B

9. Because of the way data is stored to a stripe set, stripe sets can be much faster than volume sets.

  A. True

  B. False

  Answer: A

10. RAID level 0 increases the fault tolerance of your server.

  A. True

  B. False

  Answer: B

11. The system and boot partitions cannot be a part of a stripe set.

  A. True

  B. False

  Answer: A

12. You must use third-party tape backup software if you want to schedule unattended backups under Windows NT.

  A. True

  B. False

  Answer: B

13. Formatting a volume will destroy any data stored on that volume.

  A. True

  B. False

  Answer: A

14. Under NTFS, files created or copied into a directory retain their original permissions and attributes. Files moved into a directory inherit the security permissions of the directory.

  A. True

  B. False

  Answer: B

15. The memory in your computer is _____, which means that it goes away when the power is turned off.

  Answer: volatile

16. Hard disks and floppy disks (and to an increasing extent, CD-ROMs) are the most popular form of nonvolatile or _____ storage in personal computers.

  Answer: persistent

17. The two file systems for hard disks that Windows NT supports are _____ and _____.

  Answer: FAT, NTFS

18. Hard disks are subdivided into _____.

  Answer: partitions

19. The _____ _____ _____ is the first portion of data on a hard disk and is reserved for the BIOS bootstrap routine.

  Answer: master boot record

20. Windows NT supports converting _____ to NTFS for the purpose of easing the migration of a computer from OS/2 to Windows NT.

  Answer: HPFS

21. File names under NTFS are limited to _____ characters.

  Answer: 255

22. _____ is the preferred file system for use with Windows NT Server.

  Answer: NTFS

23. The maximum number of primary partitions on a hard disk is _____.

  Answer: four

24. The partition that your computer boots when it is turned on is the
_____ partition.

Answer: active

25. To recover a mirror set, you must _____ the existing mirror set to
remove the failed drive.

Answer: break

26. A _____ is one or more partitions treated as a single unit and given a
single drive letter.

Answer: volume

27. In a stripe set, the data is stored evenly across all of the disks, one row at
a time in _____ K blocks.

Answer: 64

28. Once you have created a partition, whether it be a single partition,
volume set, or stripe set, you must _____ the partition to make it usable
by Windows NT.

Answer: format

29. The recommended minimum partition size for NTFS is _____ MB.

Answer: 50

30. File _____ removes redundancy from files, thereby decreasing their
physical size.

Answer: compression

31. RAID level _____ describes mirroring.

A. 0

B. 1

C. 2

D. 3

E. 4

F. 5

Answer: B

32. Disk _____ creates fault tolerance by keeping an exact copy of the same volumes on two disks controlled by separate controllers.

A. duplexing

B. mirroring

C. striping

D. RAID

Answer: A

Chapter 6 Answers

1. Windows NT Server was designed to be the heart of your network.

A. True

B. False

Answer: A

2. The OSI model defines 12 layers for network communication.

A. True

B. False

Answer: B

3. The physical layer is simply responsible for sending bits from one computer to another.

A. True

B. False

Answer: A

4. The IEEE enhancements to the OSI model further subdivide the data link layer into the logical link control sublayer and the media access control sublayer.

A. True

B. False

Answer: A

5. The network layer and the transport layer are the layers at which Windows NT transport protocols such as TCP/IP and NWLink operate.

A. True

B. False

Answer: A

6. Boundary layers in the Windows NT network architecture isolate components to keep them from communicating with each other.

A. True

B. False

Answer: B

7. Boundary layers are the same thing as interfaces.

A. True

B. False

Answer: A

8. TCP/IP is the simplest transport protocol you can install.

A. True

B. False

Answer: B

9. NWLink supports accessing NetWare file servers.

A. True

B. False

Answer: A

10. NetBEUI is routable.

A. True

B. False

Answer: B

11. AppleTalk allows you to connect Macintosh computers to your Windows NT Server.

   A. True

   B. False

   Answer: A

12. When you install NWLink, any frame type or network number will do.

   A. True

   B. False

   Answer: B

13. AppleTalk is installed from the Protocol tab of the Network control panel just like TCP/IP, NWLink, or NetBEUI.

   A. True

   B. False

   Answer: B

14. A _____ _____ _____ links personal computers together.

   Answer: local area network

15. A _____ _____ _____ connects the computer to the cable and translates the data from the computer into a form that can be transmitted over the cable medium.

   Answer: network interface adapter

16. _____ define the meanings assigned to signals, which data is sent and in what order, and how the computers negotiate the sending and the receiving of data.

   Answer: Protocols

18. A _____ is a computer that not only executes programs for the user and interacts directly with the user (like a client) but also can share its hard disk space with other computers on the network (like a server).

Answer: peer

Chapter 7 Answers

1. All hardware devices require a driver in Windows NT.

   A. True

   B. False

   Answer: A

2. SCSI controllers are configured with the SCSI Adapters control panel.

   A. True

   B. False

   Answer: B

3. All control panels are vital to the functionality of a dedicated Windows NT Server.

   A. True

   B. False

   Answer: B

4. Windows NT prevents applications from directly accessing hardware devices.

   A. True

   B. False

   Answer: A

5. All the device drivers necessary for any Windows NT Server installation are included on the Windows NT Server CD-ROM.

A. True

B. False

Answer: B

6. File servers should always have a sound card so the system administrator can receive audible alerts.

A. True

B. False

Answer: B

7. The Add/Remove Programs control panel can be used to install any type of device driver.

A. True

B. False

Answer: B

8. The _____ control panel is used to stop and start device drivers.

Answer: Devices

9. Virtual memory settings are changed through the _____ control panel.

Answer: System

10. If your modem appears in the Modems control panel program and is set to the correct COM port but does not respond to the system, you should check settings in the _____ control panel.

A. Modems

B. Devices

C. Ports

D. Services

E. Internet

Answer: C

11. The Accessibility Options control panel controls:

   A. User input and output device alternatives

   B. Access to secure areas of the operating system.

   C. Security configuration

   D. Microsoft Access database connectivity

   Answer: A

12. User Profiles are managed in which control panel?

   A. Server

   B. System

   C. Licensing

   D. Services

   Answer: B

Chapter 8 Answers

1. Network browsers increase the amount of traffic on the network by storing a list of network resources centrally.

   A. True

   B. False

   Answer: B

2. Only Windows NT computers can perform the role of browser in a domain.

   A. True

   B. False

   Answer: B

3. A preferred master browser will win an election over a primary domain controller.

   A. True

   B. False

     Answer: B

4. A Windows 95 computer will be elected master browser over a Windows NT workstation.

   A. True

   B. False

     Answer: B

5. Because of the delay between the time when a computer goes down and the computer entry is removed from the browse list, up to 36 minutes can elapse before the master browser's list reflects computer's condition.

   A. True

   B. False

     Answer: A

6. The backup browser delay in combination with the delay for the computer to announce itself to the master browser could result in a resource not being available for as long as 99 minutes while a backup browser list maintains the resource in its browse list.

   A. True

   B. False

     Answer: B

7. The maximum number of backup browser in a domain is three, regardless of the size of the domain.

   A. True

   B. False

     Answer: A

8. NetBIOS is not an essential part of Windows NT Server networking services.

A. True

B. False

Answer: B

9. The logon process uses the RPC service.

A. True

B. False

Answer: A

10. Using the Workstation service means you are participating in a workgroup, and using the Server service means you are participating in a domain.

A. True

B. False

Answer: B

11. A workgroup is a good choice for your networking model if you have a large number of users and you need to centralize user account management and network security.

A. True

B. False

Answer: B

12. One and only one server in the domain must be the primary domain controller for the domain.

A. True

B. False

Answer: A

13. A network_____ maintains a list of currently available network resources for the domain.

> **Answer:** browser

14. The _____ browser is the computer that maintains the master list of resources available on the network.

> **Answer:** master

15. A _____ browser receives a copy of the browse list from the master browser and supplies the browse list to computers requesting the list.

> **Answer:** backup

16. A _____ browser can become a backup browser or a master browser.

> **Answer:** potential

17. A _____ will not be promoted to backup browser status nor will it assume master browser status in the absence of a master browser on the network.

> **Answer:** non-browser

18. Microsoft networks hold _____ to determine which computer will be the master browser.

> **Answer:** elections

19. When you connect to a network share, you are using the _____ service.

> **Answer:** Workstation

20. When you make a network share on your machine available to other computers, you are using the _____ service.

> **Answer:** Server

21. A Windows NT Server in a workgroup is called a _____ _____ _____ .

> **Answer:** stand-alone server

22. The _____ _____ _____ maintains a database that contains the user and group account information and the account and security policies.

> **Answer:** primary domain controller

23. The _____ _____ _____ maintain a copy of the primary domain controller's database.

Answer: backup domain controllers

24. A _____ _____ in a domain does not maintain the security database nor does it keep a copy of the security database.

Answer: member server

25. _____ _____ extend the utility of the single username and password logon to networks composed of multiple domains.

Answer: Trust relationships

26. Most of the resources provided by Windows NT are composed of _____.

Answer: objects

27. An object's _____ are the data contained in the object.

Answer: attributes

28. The actions that an object performs are called _____.

Answer: services

29. _____ are granted according to object and service.

Answer: Permissions

30. All objects have _____ _____ _____, or ACLs, so you can set access permissions for any NT resource based on a user's account or group membership.

Answer: access control lists

31. An _____ _____ is simply a representation of the user's account that Windows NT compares to entries in an object's access control list to determine if the user is permitted to perform the requested service.

Answer: access token

Chapter 9 Answers

1. Share permissions work on a computer even if it's not networked.

   A. True

   B. False

   Answer: B

2. Windows NT always favors file permissions over share permissions.

   A. True

   B. False

   Answer: B

3. A specific No Access denial always overrides specific access to a resource.

   A. True

   B. False

   Answer: A

4. When a user is a member of multiple groups, the user always has the combined permissions of all group memberships.

   A. True

   B. False

   Answer: A

5. Share permissions and file system permissions are the same thing.

   A. True

   B. False

   Answer: B

6. File system permissions increase control over security beyond that provided by share permissions.

    A. True

    B. False

      Answer: A

7. Windows NT makes file system permissions available to all supported file systems.

    A. True

    B. False

      Answer: B

8. Windows NT makes share permissions available to all supported file systems.

    A. True

    B. False

      Answer: A

9. File system permissions work on a computer even if it's not networked.

    A. True

    B. False

      Answer: A

10. Generally, you should create the fewest number of shares possible in your networking environment.

    A. True

    B. False

      Answer: A

11. Policy is set on a per group or per user basis.

    A. True

    B. False

      Answer: B

12. Shares allowing access to the Everyone group are available to members of trusted domains.

    A. True

    B. False

      Answer: A

13. Guests are members of the Everyone group, so they have permission to access any resource that allows Everyone access.

    A. True

    B. False

      Answer: A

14. Users who are members of a group have all the permissions assigned to that group.

    A. True

    B. False

      Answer: A

15. The Guest account does not save user preferences or configuration changes.

    A. True

    B. False

      Answer: A

16. Global groups are stored locally on each machine.

    A. True

    B. False

      Answer: B

17. You should always implement pessimistic security policies because you never know what might happen.

A. True

B. False

Answer: B

18. Account names must be _____.

Answer: unique

19. Permissions control access to _____ based on user account.

Answer: resources (or objects)

20. In a domain, user accounts are kept on the _____ and replicated to _____.

Answer: primary domain controller; backup domain controller

21. A good naming convention should be _____.

Answer: obvious

22. Security planning involves securing resources from _____.

Answer: unauthorized access

23. A logon script is usually implemented as a DOS _____ file.

Answer: batch

24. Your access token is created when you _____.

A. log on

B. launch an application

C. access a resource

D. share a resource

Answer: A

Chapter 10 Answers

1. File service is the primary function of most network servers.

A. True

B. False

Answer: A

2. When moving a file within a volume, Windows NT simply copies the file to a new location and deletes the original.

A. True

B. False

Answer: B

3. When you copy a file within the same volume, file permissions for the new file are inherited from the destination directory.

A. True

B. False

Answer: A

4. When you move a file within the same volume, the new file inherits file permissions from the destination directory.

A. True

B. False

Answer: B

5. When you copy a file between different volumes, the new file inherits file permissions from the destination directory.

A. True

B. False

Answer: A

6. When you move a file between different volumes, the new file inherits file permissions from the destination directory.

A. True

B. False

Answer: A

7. Files in copy and move operations always inherit directory permissions except when moving a file within the same volume.

A. True

B. False

Answer: A

8. The Server tools for Windows NT Workstation are the same tools provided with Windows NT Server.

A. True

B. False

Answer: A

9. Windows NT comes with a comprehensive suite of SNMP management tools.

A. True

B. False

Answer: B

10. Share permissions work no matter what the shared file system is.

A. True

B. False

Answer: A

11. The replication service cannot copy open files.

A. True

B. False

Answer: A

12. When you have both share and file permissions on a directory, Windows NT uses only the file permissions, because they are more restrictive.

  A. True

  B. False

  Answer: B

13. Users logged on locally are not limited by share-level security.

  A. True

  B. False

  Answer: A

14. For security reasons, you should enable file auditing on all files at all times.

  A. True

  B. False

  Answer: B

15. The distributed file system allows you to create a single unified hierarchy that actually consists of shares on many different machines.

  A. True

  B. False

  Answer: A

16. You can install Server tools on _____ and _____ client computers.

  Answer: Windows NT Workstation, Windows 95

17. The _____ server logs on to the _____ server to copy files in the Directory Replication Service.

  Answer: import, export

18. The status _____ means that although the Directory Replication Service has received updates in the past and can connect to the export server, it is not receiving them at the moment.

  Answer: No Sync

19. You can use the _____ to manage NTFS security after you've installed Server tools for Windows 95.

   A. Server Manager

   B. Policy Editor

   C. User Manager for Domains

   D. Windows 95 Explorer

   E. Event Viewer

   Answer: D

20. Enabling Audit policy is performed through the:

   A. Server Manager

   B. Security Manager

   C. User Manager for Domains

   D. File Manager

   E. Explorer

   Answer: C

Chapter 11 Answers

1. The purpose of RAS is to provide permanent network links over telephone lines leased from the phone company.

   A. True

   B. False

   Answer: B

2. You do not need a network interface adapter to use RAS.

   A. True

   B. False

   Answer: A

3. You do not need a transport protocol to use RAS.

   A. True

   B. False

     Answer: B

4. With RAS you can use a transport protocol that is not installed as one of the networking protocols in the Protocols portion of the Network control panel.

   A. True

   B. False

     Answer: B

5. Regular modems are much slower than regular Ethernet.

   A. True

   B. False

     Answer: A

6. RAS supports AppleTalk.

   A. True

   B. False

     Answer: B

7. RAS looks like a network interface adapter to Windows NT networking components.

   A. True

   B. False

     Answer: A

8. ISDN is more efficient than regular PSTN modems.

   A. True

   B. False

     Answer: A

9. RAS provides dial-in capability only. You must use the Dial Up Networking (DUN) service to dial out to a RAS server.

A. True

B. False

Answer: B

10. RAS supports SLIP for remote client dial-in.

A. True

B. False

Answer: B

11. RAS supports X.25 for wide area networking.

A. True

B. False

Answer: A

12. ISDN adapters can be installed only from the Modems control panel.

A. True

B. False

Answer: B

13. SLIP is a recent improvement on the PPP protocol.

A. True

B. False

Answer: B

14. RAS permissions are set per user rather than per RAS device.

A. True

B. False

Answer: A

15. You can use PPTP to allow remote clients to make secure connections to your RAS server using the Internet.

  A. True

  B. False

  Answer: A

16. RAS stands for _____ _____ _____.

  Answer: Remote Access Service

17. In practice, Ethernet is about _____ times faster than the fastest analog modems.

  Answer: 100

18. PSTN stands for _____ _____ _____ _____.

  Answer: Public Switched Telephone Network

19. ISDN stands for _____ _____ _____ _____.

  Answer: Integrated Services Digital Network

20. If you will connect to the Internet via RAS, you must use the _____ protocol.

  Answer: TCP/IP

21. SLIP stands for _____ _____ _____ _____.

  Answer: Serial Line Internet Protocol

22. PPP stands for _____ _____ _____.

  Answer: Point-to-Point Protocol

23. _____ is the simplest network transport protocol.

  Answer: NetBEUI

24. You modify RAS permissions in the _____ _____ _____ program.

  Answer: Remote Access Admin or User Manager for Domains

25. _____ functions by calling back the client computer after the client computer calls the RAS server and requests a network connection.

    Answer: Callback

26. The Require Microsoft encrypted authentication option uses the _____ authentication protocol.

    Answer: MS-CHAP

27. The Require encrypted authentication option uses the _____ authentication protocol.

    Answer: CHAP

28. The Allow any authentication including clear text option uses the _____ authentication protocol.

    Answer: PAP

29. _____ allows the combination of multiple serial data streams into one aggregate bundle.

    Answer: Multilink

30. PPTP stands for _____ _____ _____ _____.

    Answer: Point-to-Point Tunneling Protocol

Chapter 12 Answers

1. The Internet and the Web are two names for the same thing.

    A. True

    B. False

    Answer: B

2. The Internet is the largest network in the world

    A. True

    B. False

    Answer: A

3. The Internet is run by the U.S. government.

A. True

B. False

Answer: B

4. The only difference between an Internet server and an intranet server is where and how they are used.

A. True

B. False

Answer: A

5. An intranet is a private network running Internet protocols.

A. True

B. False

Answer: A

6. _____ _____ _____ are standards describing the Internet protocols.

Answer: Requests for Comment

7. Internet Information Server is administered using the _____ _____ _____ tool.

Answer: Internet Service Manager

8. The World Wide Web is based on which protocol:

A. HTTP

B. HTML

C. FTP

D. SMTP

E. PPP

Answer: A

9. You can use the _____ tool to create Web pages for the Internet

   A. Internet Explorer

   B. Internet Information Server

   C. Domain Name Server

   D. FrontPage

   Answer: D

10. The term *host* refers to

    A. A RAS server that hosts dial-up clients

    B. A terminal server that hosts dial-up clients

    C. A file that resolves domain names

    D. An Internet server

    E. A domain name server

    Answer: D

11. The traditional operating system of the Internet is

    A. Windows NT Server

    B. UNIX

    C. MacOS running Apple Internet Server

    D. OS/2 Warp Server

    E. NetWare for TCP/IP

    Answer: B

12. HTTP stands for

    A. High Speed Text Transfer Protocol

    B. Hierarchical Text Transfer Protocol

    C. Hypertext Transfer Protocol

D. Host-to-Terminal Text Protocol

E. None of the above.

Answer: C

13. Internet Information Server serves the following Internet protocols (choose all that are correct):

A. HTTP

B. SMTP

C. FTP

D. Gopher

E. NNTP

F. POP

Answer: A, C, D

Chapter 13 Answers

1. Microsoft Windows NT Server has the largest installed base of servers of any network operating system software.

A. True

B. False

Answer: B

2. Windows NT is more expensive than NetWare.

A. True

B. False

Answer: B

3. Microsoft Windows NT comes with software to make it look like a Net-Ware server.

  A. True

  B. False

  Answer: B

4. If you use a Windows NT server running GSNW to provide access to NetWare resources to Microsoft network clients, you must have as many client access licenses for Windows NT Server as you have Microsoft clients simultaneously accessing the NetWare resources.

  A. True

  B. False

  Answer: A

5. NetWare 4.1 provides a higher level of crash protection than Windows NT.

  A. True

  B. False

  Answer: B

6. If you use a Windows NT server running GSNW to provide access to NetWare resources for Microsoft network clients, you must have as many client access licenses for NetWare as you have Microsoft clients simultaneously accessing the NetWare resources.

  A. True

  B. False

  Answer: B

7. The Client for Microsoft Networks is built into all versions of Windows since 3.11 for Workgroups.

  A. True

  B. False

  Answer: A

8. Without GSNW or Services for NetWare, Windows NT servers would be useless in a NetWare network.

A. True

B. False

Answer: B

9. GSNW must be enabled before you can share NetWare print queues.

A. True

B. False

Answer: A

10. You can't use the same share name to refer to a Windows NT server share that used to be a gateway share because the security identifiers (SID) for the share name won't match.

A. True

B. False

Answer: B

11. GSNW provides all the functions of the CSNW included in Windows NT Workstation.

A. True

B. False

Answer: A

12. Although Windows NT can attach to NetWare 4.1 servers, it cannot browse the NDS tree structure.

A. True

B. False

Answer: B

13. The _____ _____ _____ service can make Windows NT computers act just like NetWare file servers.

> **Answer:** Services for NetWare

14. The NetWare _____ performs the same function as the Client for Microsoft Networks.

> **Answer:** requester

15. Services for NetWare includes which of these formerly separate products (choose two):

A. File and Print services for NetWare (FPNW)

B. Directory Services Manager for NetWare (DSMN)

C. Gateway Service for NetWare (GSNW)

D. NetWare Directory Services (NDS)

E. Distributed File System (DFS)

> **Answer:** A and B.

16. GSNW provides which of the following functions (choose two):

A. Makes Windows NT look like a NetWare server to clients running the NetWare Requester

B. Allows Windows NT server to attach as a client to NetWare servers

C. Allows Windows NT servers to trade user account information with NetWare servers

D. Allows Windows NT servers to request NetWare files and serve them to clients for Microsoft networks

> **Answer:** B and D

17. Services for NetWare provides which of the following functions (choose two):

A. Makes Windows NT look like a NetWare server to clients running the NetWare requester

B. Allows Windows NT server to attach as a client to NetWare servers

C. Allows Windows NT servers to trade user account information with NetWare servers

D. Allows Windows NT servers to request NetWare files and serve them to clients for Microsoft networks

Answer: A and C

Chapter 14 Answers

1. In Windows terminology a printer is not a physical device that produces printed pages.

A. True

B. False

Answer: A

2. A fax modem can be a print device.

A. True

B. False

Answer: A

3. You can have more print devices than you have printers.

A. True

B. False

Answer: A

4. You can have fewer print devices than you have printers.

A. True

B. False

Answer: A

5. Windows NT Server can provide printing services for Windows, UNIX, Apple Macintosh, and MS-DOS computers.

A. True

B. False

Answer: A

6. The GDI translates application print requests into DDI calls to the printer driver.

A. True

B. False

Answer: A

7. DDI calls are specific to the drawing characteristics of a printer.

A. True

B. False

Answer: A

8. A journal file print job contains DDI calls that must be made to the device driver to produce a raw print job.

A. True

B. False

Answer: A

9. The GDI will produce a journal file for a print job destined for a remote printer.

A. True

B. False

Answer: B

10. You may not have to have a print driver installed in your computer if you are connecting to a remote printer to print.

A. True

B. False

Answer: A

11. Windows NT can send print jobs to HP network printers and to UNIX printers.

A. True

B. False

Answer: A

12. The print provider is also known as the spooler.

A. True

B. False

Answer: A

13. Windows NT supports printing to Macintosh PostScript printers on an AppleTalk network.

A. True

B. False

Answer: A

14. You can schedule several times during the day when a printer is available and is not available from within the Printer Properties window.

A. True

B. False

Answer: B

15. You must install Gateway Services for NetWare in your Windows NT Server in order to connect to NetWare print queues from your Windows NT Server.

    A. True

    B. False

      Answer: A

16. You must use the Remote Printer Management tool to manage remote printers.

    A. True

    B. False

      Answer: B

17. The _____, in Windows terminology, is a software construct that will translate print requests from applications and forward the resulting print job to the appropriate printing device.

      Answer: printer

18. A _____ _____ consists of several printing devices fed by one printer.

      Answer: printer pool

19. GDI stands for _____ _____ _____.

      Answer: Graphics Device Interface

20. DDI stands for _____ _____ _____.

      Answer: Device Driver Interface

21. A _____ print job contains the sequence of instructions for the printer that will produce the printed document.

      Answer: raw

22. The _____ _____ is the software component that translates the printer-generic DDI calls generated by the GDI system into the printer-specific commands that are passed on to the actual printer

    Answer: print driver

23. The _____ _____ modifies the print job before it passes the print job to the print monitor.

    Answer: print processor

24. The _____ _____ is the software component that transmits the print job (by now transformed into the language of the printer) to the printing device.

    Answer: Print Monitor

Chapter 15 Answers

1. Storing client applications on the server has no drawbacks.

    A. True

    B. False

    Answer: B

2. TCP/IP is the easiest protocol to use.

    A. True

    B. False

    Answer: B

3. TCP/IP is more difficult to configure than any other protocol included with Windows NT Server.

    A. True

    B. False

    Answer: A

4. The Microsoft Mail Postoffice must reside on a domain controller.

    A. True.

    B. False.

      Answer: B

5. You must use the License Manager to maintain compliance with software copyright laws.

    A. True.

    B. False.

      Answer: B

6. The License Manager will keep you from exceeding the legal licensed limit for some software you have installed.

    A. True.

    B. False.

      Answer: B

7. AppleTalk is a TDI compliant network transport.

    A. True.

    B. False.

      Answer: B

8. Services for Macintosh will allow PCs to print to AppleShare PostScript printers.

    A. True.

    B. False.

      Answer: A

9. Because desktop explorer does not support Services for Macintosh, you must use _____ _____ or _____ to manage Macintosh accessible volumes.

      Answer: Server Manager or WinFile

10. The most effective way to reduce your client support burden is to

  A. Use the License Manager

  B. Standardize client hardware

  C. Standardize client software

  D. Use DCHP to automatically assign IP addresses.

  Answer: B

11. DHCP stands for

  A. Domain Host Configuration Protocol

  B. Domain Host Connection Protocol

  C. Dynamic Host Configuration Protocol

  D. Dynamic Host Connection Protocol

  Answer: C

12. The DNS service:

  A. Translates Microsoft network names into IP addresses

  B. Translates fully qualified Internet names into IP addresses

  C. Translates Domain security ID numbers into IP addresses

  D. Serves Web pages on the Internet

  Answer: B

13. The WINS service:

  A. Translates Microsoft network names into IP addresses

  B. Translates fully qualified Internet names into IP addresses

  C. Translates Domain security ID numbers into IP addresses

  D. Serves Web pages on the Internet

  Answer: A

Chapter 16 Answers

1. Running the performance monitor does not affect the performance of the computer.

   A. True

   B. False

   Answer: B

2. The performance monitor measures system performance.

   A. True

   B. False

   Answer: B

3. Upgrading your hardware is one way to eliminate bottlenecks.

   A. True

   B. False

   Answer: A

4. Bottlenecks are components that are not operating at peak performance.

   A. True

   B. False

   Answer: B.

5. Even the fastest computers have bottlenecks.

   A. True

   B. False

   Answer: A

6. Windows NT can vary priority levels up to _____ priorities higher or lower automatically.

> **Answer:** two

7. _____ performance counters are disabled by default to increase overall operating speed.

> **Answer:** Disk

8. _____ are the measures taken to reduce the impact of a bottleneck on performance.

> **Answer:** Optimizations

9. _____ are the basic units of division among processors in a multiprocessing environments.

> **Answer:** Threads

10. Windows NT supports which type of multiprocessing?

> **A.** Symmetrical
>
> **B.** Asymmetrical
>
> **C.** Both symmetrical and asymmetrical
>
> **D.** Windows NT supports Multitasking instead.

> **Answer:** A

11. Windows NT provides which tool for optimizing Windows NT performance?

> **A.** Microsoft Diagnostic tool (WinMSD)
>
> **B.** The performance tuner
>
> **C.** Windows NT Diagnostics (NTD)
>
> **D.** The performance monitor
>
> **E.** The task manager

> **Answer:** D

12. Which performance optimization is not implemented in the Windows NT operating system?

    A. Symmetric multiprocessing

    B. Swapping across multiple disks to increase performance

    C. Prioritizing threads and processes

    D. Caching RAM in the external processor cache

    E. Caching disk requests

    Answer: D

13. In Windows NT, memory is divided into pages of what size?

    A. 4KB

    B. 16KB

    C. 64KB

    D. 256KB

    Answer: A

14. NTFS uses which type of caching to improve performance?

    A. Write through

    B. Write back

    C. Write now

    D. Write optimization

    E. Buffered

    Answer: B

15. The biggest single bottleneck in most computers is _____ .

    A. the processor

    B. memory

    C. disks

    D. networks

    Answer: C

16. The best way to eliminate disks as bottlenecks is to _____ .

    A. create a stripe set

    B. use them as little as possible

    C. install a RAID controller

    D. use Ultra SCSI drives and controllers

    Answer: B

17. Which of the following can the network monitor in NT Server track? (choose all that apply)

    A. Any packet sent over the local network

    B. Any packet sent over the network, even packets across a router

    C. Packets sent to or from the server

    D. Broadcast packets

    Answer: C and D

18. If you want to use a fully functional network monitor, which additional package should you purchase?

    A. SQL

    B. SMS

    C. Network Monitor v2.0

    D. Network Monitor v3.0

    Answer: B

19. Assuming that NT Server has been installed to drive C in the WINNT directory, which directory does the network monitor use (by default) to save captured data?

    A. `C:\WINNT\SYSTEM32\NETMON\CAPTURES`

    B. `C:\WINNT\NETMON\CAPTURES`

    C. `C:\WINNT\SYSTEM32\REPL\NETMON\CAPTURES`

    D. `C:\NETMON\CAPTURES`

    Answer: A

20. Which properties can be filtered through the network monitor filter process? (Choose all that apply.)

A. Hex strings

B. Protocols

C. Computer address

D. Protocol properties

Answer: B, C, and D

Chapter 17 Answers

1. Release versions of Windows NT are bug free.

A. True

B. False

Answer: B

2. Windows NT runs on all computers capable of running Windows 95.

A. True

B. False

Answer: B

3. All Internet troubleshooting resources for Windows NT are maintained in the Windows NT knowledge base at the Microsoft Web site.

A. True

B. False

Answer: B

4. Microsoft does not certify hardware components as compatible with NT.

A. True

B. False

Answer: A

5. Recent changes are likely to be the cause of new malfunctions.

  A. True

  B. False

  Answer: A

6. If you use Windows NT, you no longer have any reason to use MS-DOS.

  A. True

  B. False

  Answer: B

7. The Microsoft Knowledge Base is the official repository for support information about all Microsoft products including Windows NT.

  A. True

  B. False

  Answer: A

8. With MS-DOS, you cannot access _____ volumes.

  Answer: NTFS

9. To create an emergency repair disk, use the _____ utility.

  Answer: rdisk

10. The _____ section of the Windows NT diagnostic tool is the most useful for troubleshooting.

  Answer: Resources

11. The _____ is by far the best troubleshooting resource for any computer problem.

  Answer: Internet

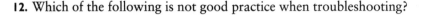

12. Which of the following is not good practice when troubleshooting?

    A. Be patient.

    B. Perform easy tests first.

    C. Change only one setting at a time.

    D. Make as many changes as possible.

    Answer: D

13. The most common hardware problem in PCs is

    A. Bad memory

    B. Hardware conflicts

    C. Loose cables

    D. Power supply failure

    Answer: B

14. Which of these failures is the most damaging of all computer component failures?

    A. Processor

    B. Memory

    C. Motherboard

    D. Hard disk

    Answer: D

15. An emergency repair disk can restore

    A. Missing System files

    B. Damaged user files

    C. Backup tapes

    D. Registry information

    Answer: A

16. To view the Event log, use the:

A. Event Monitor

B. User Manager

C. Notepad

D. Event Viewer

Answer: D

17. If none of your clients can reach the file server, but you can share files through Windows 95 peer networking, the most likely problem is the:

A. Client configurations

B. Data link devices

C. Cable plant

D. Server

Answer: D

18. If none of your clients can reach the file server, and you cannot share files through Windows 95 peer networking, the most likely problem is the:

A. Client configurations

B. Data link devices

C. Cable plant

D. server

Answer: B

19. If one of your clients cannot reach the file server, and you cannot share files through Windows 95 peer networking with that client, the most likely problem is the:

A. Client configurations

B. Data link devices

C. Cable plant

D. server

Answer: A

20. If none of the clients in the building next door can reach the server in the main building right after a contractor dug a trench in the road between the two buildings, the most likely problem is the:

A. Client configurations

B. Data link devices

C. Cable plant

D. Server

Answer: C

Glossary

A

Access Control Entries (ACE) Each ACL contains ACEs that are the permissions that have been granted or denied to the users and groups listed in the ACL. See also *Access Control List*.

Access Control List (ACL) A list of security identifiers contained by objects. Only processes identified in the list as having the appropriate permission can activate the services of that object. See also *Object, Security Identifier, Permissions*.

Access Tokens Objects containing the security identifier of a running process. A process started by another process inherits the starting process's access token. The access token is checked against each object's ACL to determine whether or not appropriate permissions are granted to perform any requested service. See also *Access Control List, Access Control Entries, Permissions, Object, Security Identifier, Process*.

Account Lockout Used to specify how many invalid logon attempts should be tolerated before a user account is locked out. Account lockout is set through User Manager for Domains. See also *Security, User Manager for Domains*.

Account Policies Account policies are used to determine password and logon requirements. Account policies are set through User Manager for Domains. See also *User Manager for Domains*.

Accounts Containers for security identifiers, passwords, permissions, group associations, and preferences for each user of a system. The User Manager for Domains utility is used to administer accounts. See also *Security Identifier, Preferences, Permissions, Passwords, Groups*.

ACE See *Access Control Entries*.

ACL See *Access Control List*.

Adapter Any hardware device that allows communications to occur through physically dissimilar systems. This term usually refers to peripheral cards permanently mounted inside computers that provide an interface from the computer's bus to another media such as a hard disk or a network. See also *Network Interface Card, SCSI*.

Address Resolution Protocol (ARP) An Internet protocol for resolving an IP address into a physical layer address (such as an Ethernet media access control address). See also *Physical Layer, Internet Protocol*.

Administrative Tools Program group on Windows NT servers that contain utilities such as User Manager for Domains, Server Manager, Disk Administrator, Performance Monitor, and Network Monitor. See also *User Manager for Domains, Server Manager, Disk Administrator, Performance Monitor, Network Monitor*.

Administrator Account A special account in Windows NT that has the ultimate set of security permissions and can assign any permission to any user or group. The Administrator account corrects security problems. See also *Permissions*.

Administrators Users who are part of the Administrators group. This group has the ultimate set of security permissions. See also *Administrator Account, Permissions, Groups*.

Advanced Research Projects Agency Network (ARPANET) Predecessor to the Internet that was developed by the Department of Defense in the late 1960s.

AppleTalk The built-in (to firmware) suite of network protocols that Macintosh computers use. Windows NT Server uses AppleTalk to service Macintosh clients by simulating an Apple server. See also *Macintosh, Network Protocol.*

Application Layer The layer of the OSI model that interfaces with User mode programs called applications by providing high-level network services based upon lower-level network layers. Network file systems like Named Pipes are an example of application layer software. See also *Named Pipes, OSI Model, Application.*

Applications Large software packages that perform a specific function, such as word processing, Web browsing, or database management. Applications typically consist of more than one program. See also *Programs.*

ARPANET See *Advanced Research Projects Agency Network.*

Asymmetrical Multiprocessing A multiple-processor architecture in which certain processors are designated to run certain threads or in which scheduling is not done on a fair-share basis. Asymmetrical multiprocessing is easier to implement than symmetrical multiprocessing, but does not scale well as processors are added. See also *Microprocessor, Symmetrical Multiprocessing.*

Asynchronous Transfer Mode (ATM) A wide-area transport protocol that runs at many different speeds and supports real-time, guaranteed packet delivery in hardware, as well as lower-quality levels of service on a bandwidth-available basis. ATM will eventually replace all other wide-area protocols, as most worldwide PTSN providers have declared their support for the international standard. See also *Public Switched Telephone Network, Wide Area Network.*

ATM See *Asynchronous Transfer Mode.*

Audit Policy Audit policy determines which user events you wish to track for security reasons. Audit policy can track the success or failure of specified security events; it is set in the User Manager for Domains. See also *Security, User Manager for Domains.*

B

Back Up The process of writing all the data contained in online mass storage devices to offline mass storage devices for the purpose of safekeeping. Backups are usually performed from hard disk drives to tape drives. Also referred to as archiving. See also *Hard Disk Drive.*

Backup Browser A computer on a Microsoft network that maintains a list of computers and services available on the network. The master browser supplies this list. The backup browser distributes the Browsing service load to a workgroup or domain. See also *Master Browser.*

Backup Domain Controllers Servers that contain accurate replications of the security and user databases; servers can authenticate workstations if the primary domain controller does not respond. See also *Primary Domain Controller.*

Baseline A snapshot of your computer's current performance statistics that can be used for analysis and planning purposes.

Basic Input/Output System (BIOS) A set of routines in firmware that provides the most basic software interface drivers for hardware attached to the computer. The BIOS contains the bootstrap routine. See also *Boot, Driver, Firmware.*

Bindery A NetWare structure that contains user accounts and permissions. It is similar to the Security Accounts Manager in Windows NT. See also *Security Accounts Manager.*

Binding The process of linking network services to network service providers. The binding facility allows users to define exactly how network services operate in order to optimize the performance of the system. By default, Windows enables all possible bindings. You can use the Network control panel to change bindings. See also *Network Layer, Data Link Layer.*

BIOS See *Basic Input/Output System.*

Bit A binary digit. A numeral having only two possible values, 0 or 1. Computers represent these two values as high (voltage present) or low (no voltage present) state on a control line. Bits are accumulated in sets of certain sizes to represent higher values. See also *Byte.*

Boot The process of loading a computer's operating system. Booting usually occurs in multiple phases, each successively more complex until the entire operating system and all its services are running. Also called bootstrap. The computer's BIOS must contain the first level of booting. See *Basic Input/Output System.*

Boot Partition The boot partition is the partition that contains the system files. The system files are located in C:\WINNT by default. See also *Partition, System Partition.*

BOOTP See *Bootstrap Protocol.*

Bootstrap Protocol (BOOTP) Predecessor to the DHCP protocol. BOOTP was used to assign IP addresses to disk-less workstations. See also *Dynamic Host Configuration Protocol.*

Bottlenecks Components operating at their peak capacity that restrict the flow of information through a system. Used singularly, the term indicates the single most restrictive component in a system.

Bridge A device that connects two networks of the same data link protocol by forwarding those packets destined for computers on the other side of the bridge. See also *Router, Data Link Layer.*

Browser A computer on a Microsoft network that maintains a list of computers and services available on the network.

Browsing The process of requesting the list of computers and services on a network from a browser.

C

Caching A speed optimization technique that keeps a copy of the most recently used data in a fast, high-cost, low-capacity storage device rather than in the device upon which the actual data resides. Caching assumes that recently used data is likely to be used again. Fetching data from the cache is faster than fetching data from the slower, larger storage device. Most caching algorithms also copy next-most-likely-to-be-used data and perform write caching to further increase speed gains. See also *Write-Back Caching, Write-through Caching.*

CD-ROM See *Compact Disk-Read-Only Memory*.

Central Processing Unit (CPU) The central processing unit of a computer. In microcomputers such as IBM PC-compatible machines, the CPU is the microprocessor. See also *Microprocessor*.

Client A computer on a network that subscribes to the services provided by a server. See also *Server*.

Client Services for NetWare (CSNW) A service provided with Windows NT that connects an NT client to NetWare file servers. See also *NetWare, Client Services for NetWare*.

Client/Server A network architecture that dedicates certain computers called servers to act as service providers to computers called clients, which users operate to perform work. Servers can be dedicated to providing one or more network services such as file storage, shared printing, communications, e-mail service, and Web response. See also *Share, Peer*.

Client/Server Applications Applications that split large applications into two components: computer-intensive processes that run on application servers and user interfaces that run on clients. Client/server applications communicate over the network through interprocess communication mechanisms. See also *Client, Server, Interprocess Communications*.

Code Synonymous with software but used when the software, rather than the utility it provides, is the object of discussion. See also *Software*.

COM Port Communications port. A serial hardware interface conforming to the RS-232 standard for low-speed serial communications. See also *Modem, Serial*.

Compact Disk-Read-Only Memory (CD-ROM) A media for storing extremely large software packages on optical read-only discs. CD-ROM is an adaptation of the CD medium used for distributing digitized music. CD-ROM discs can hold up to 650MB of information and cost very little to produce in mass quantity. See also *Hard Disk Drive*.

Components Interchangeable elements of a complex software or hardware system. See also *Module*.

Compression A space-optimization scheme that reduces the size (length) of a data set by exploiting the fact that most useful data contains a great deal of redundancy. Compression reduces redundancy by creating symbols smaller than the data they represent and an index that defines the value of the symbols for each compressed set of data.

Computer A device capable of performing automatic calculations based upon lists of instructions called programs. The computer feeds the results of these calculations (output) to peripheral devices that can represent them in useful ways, such as graphics on a screen or ink on paper. See also *Microprocessor*.

Computer Name A 1- to 15-character NetBIOS name used to uniquely identify a computer on the network. See also *Network Basic Input/Output System*.

Control Panel A software utility that controls the function of specific operating system services by allowing users to change default settings for the service to match their preferences. The Registry contains the Control Panel settings on a system and/or per user basis. See also *Registry, Account*.

Cooperative Multitasking A multitasking scheme in which each process must voluntarily return time to a central scheduling route. If any single process fails to return to the central scheduler, the computer will lock up. Both Windows and the Macintosh operating systems use this scheme. See also *Preemptive Multitasking, Windows for Workgroups 3.11*.

CPU See *Microprocessor*.

CSNW See *Client Services for NetWare*.

D

Data Link Control (DLC) An obsolete network transport protocol that allows PCs to connects to older IBM mainframes and HP printers. See also *TCP/IP*.

Data Link Layer In the OSI model, the layer that provides the digital interconnection of network devices and the software that directly operates these devices, such as network interface adapters. See also *Physical Layer, Network Layer, OSI Model*.

Database A related set of data organized by type and purpose. The term also can include the application software that manipulates the data. The Windows NT Registry (a database itself) contains a number of utility databases such as user account and security information. See also *Registry*.

Default Shares Resources shared by default when Windows NT is installed. See also *Share, Resource*.

Desktop A directory that the background of the Windows Explorer shell represents. By default, the desktop contains objects that contain the local storage devices and available network shares. Also a key operating part of the Windows GUI. See also *Explorer, Shell*.

DHCP See *Dynamic Host Configuration Protocol*.

Dial-Up Connections Data link layer digital connections made via modems over regular telephone lines. The term *dial-up* refers to temporary digital connections, as opposed to leased telephone lines, which provide permanent connections. See also *Data Link Layer, Public Switched Telephone Network, Modem*.

Directories In a file system directories are containers that store files or other directories. Mass storage devices have a root directory that contains all other directories, thus creating a hierarchy of directories sometimes referred to as a *directory tree*. See also *File, File System*.

Directory Replication The process of copying a directory structure from an export computer to an import computer(s). Anytime changes are made to the export computer, the import computer(s) is automatically updated with the changes.

Disk Administrator Graphical utility used to manage disks.

Disk Duplexing Disk mirroring with two separate controllers for better performance and reliability. See also *Disk Mirroring*.

Disk Mirroring The process of keeping an exact duplicate of data on two different partitions located on different physical drives. Used for fault tolerance. See also *Disk Duplexing*.

Disk Striping Data that is stored across partitions of identical size on different drives. Also referred to as RAID 0. See also *Redundant Array of Inexpensive Disks*.

Disk Striping with Parity Disk striping with parity distributed across the stripe set for fault toler-ance features. Also referred to as RAID 5. See also *Stripe Set, Redundant Array of Inexpensive Disks*.

DLC See *Data Link Control*.

DNS See *Domain Name Service*.

Domain In Microsoft networks a domain is an arrangement of client and server computers referenced by a specific name that share a single security permissions database. On the Internet a domain is a named collection of hosts and sub-domains, registered with a unique name by the InterNIC. See also *Work-group, InterNIC*.

Domain Controllers Servers that authenticate workstation network logon requests by comparing a username and password against account information stored in the user accounts database. A user cannot access a domain without authentication from a domain controller. See also *Primary Domain Controller, Backup Domain Controller, Domain*.

Domain Name The textual identifier of a specific Internet host. Domain names are in the form server.organization.type (www.microsoft.com) and are resolved to Internet addresses by domain name servers. See also *Domain Name Server*.

Domain Name Server An Internet host dedicated to the function of translating fully qualified domain names into IP addresses. See also *Domain Name*.

Domain Name Service (DNS) The TCP/IP network service that translates textual Internet net-work addresses into numerical Internet network addresses. See also *TCP/IP, Internet*.

Drive See *Hard Disk Drive*.

Drive Letters Single letters assigned as abbreviations to the mass storage volumes available to a computer. See also *Volumes*.

Driver A program that provides a software interface to a hardware device. Drivers are written for the specific device they control, but they present a common software interface to the computer's operating system, allowing all devices (of a similar type) to be controlled as if they were the same. See also *Data Link Layer, Operating System*.

Dynamic Data Exchange (DDE) A method of interprocess communication within the Microsoft Windows operating systems.

Dynamic Host Configuration Protocol (DHCP) A method of automatically assigning IP addresses to client computers on a network.

E

Electronic Mail (e-Mail) A type of client/server application that provides a routed, stored-message service between any two user e-mail accounts. E-mail accounts are not the same as user accounts, but a one-to-one relationship usually exists between them. Because all modern computers can attach to the Internet, users can send e-mail over the Internet to any location that has telephone or wireless digital ser-vice. See also *Internet*.

Emergency Repair Disk A floppy diskette created by the RDISK.EXE program that contains critical Registry information about a Windows NT installation. With an emergency repair disk, a Windows NT installation can be salvaged using the restore option when re-installing from CD-ROM. See also *Registry*.

Encryption The process of obscuring information by modifying it according to a mathematical function known only to the intended recipient. Encryption secures information being transmitted over non-secure or untrusted media. See also *Security*.

Enterprise Network A complex network consisting of multiple servers and multiple domains over a large geographic area.

Environment Variables Variables, such as the search path, that contain information available to programs and batch files about the current operating system environment.

Ethernet The most popular data link layer standard for local area networking. Ethernet implements the carrier sense multiple access with collision detection (CSMA/CD) method of arbitrating multiple computer access to the same network. This standard supports the use of Ethernet over any type of media including wireless broadcast. Standard Ethernet operates as 10 megabits per second. Fast Ethernet operates at 100 megabits per second. See also *Data Link Layer*.

Exchange Microsoft's messaging application. Exchange implements Microsoft's mail application programming interface (MAPI) as well as other messaging protocols such as POP, SNMP, and faxing to provide a flexible message composition and reception service. See also *Electronic Mail, Fax Modem*.

Explorer The default shell for Windows 95 and Windows NT 4.0. Explorer implements the more flexible desktop object paradigm rather than the Program Manager paradigm used in earlier versions of Windows. See also *Desktop*.

F

FAT See *File Allocation Table*.

Fault Tolerance Any method that prevents system failure by tolerating single faults, usually through hardware redundancy.

Fax Modems Special modems that include hardware to allow the transmission and reception of facsimiles. See also *Modem, Exchange*.

FDDI See *Fiber Distributed Data Interface*.

Fiber Distributed Data Interface (FDDI) A data link layer that implements two counter-rotating token rings at 100 megabits per second. FDDI has been a popular standard for interconnecting campus and metropolitan area networks because it allows distant digital connections at high speed, but ATM is replacing FDDI in many sites. See also *Asynchronous Transfer Mode, Data Link Layer*.

File Allocation Table (FAT) The file system used by MS-DOS and available to other operating systems such as Windows (all variations), OS/2, and the Macintosh. FAT has become something of a mass storage compatibility standard because of its simplicity and wide availability. FAT has few fault tolerance features and can become corrupted through normal use over time. See also *File System*.

File Attributes Bits that show the status of a file (e.g., archived, hidden, read-only) are stored along with the name and location of a file in a directory entry. Different operating systems use different file attributes to implement such services as sharing, compression, and security.

File System A software component that manages the storage of files on a mass storage device by providing services that can create, read, write, and delete files. File systems impose an ordered database of files, called volumes, on the mass storage device. Volumes use hierarchies of directories to organize files. See also *Mass Storage Device, Files, Database, Volumes, Directories.*

File Transfer Protocol (FTP) A simple Internet protocol that transfers complete files from an FTP server to a client running the FTP client. FTP provides a simple method of transferring files between computers, but cannot perform browsing functions. You must know the URL of the FTP server to which you wish to attach. See also *Internet, Uniform Resource Locator.*

Files A set of data stored on a mass storage device identified by a directory entry containing a name, file attributes, and the physical location of the file in the volume. See also *Volume, Mass Storage Device, Directory, File Attributes.*

Firmware Software stored permanently in nonvolatile memory and built into a computer to provide its BIOS and a bootstrap routine. Simple computers may have their entire operating system built into firmware. See also *BIOS, Boot, Software.*

Format The process of preparing a mass storage device for use with a file system. Low-level formatting writes a structure of sectors and tracks to the disk with bits used by the mass storage controller hardware. The controller hardware requires this format, and it is independent of the file system. High-level formatting creates file system structures such as an allocation table and a root directory in a partition, thus creating a volume. See also *Mass Storage Device, Volume.*

Frame A data structure that network hardware devices use to transmit data between computers. Frames consist of the addresses of the sending and receiving computers, size information, and a checksum. Frames are envelopes around packets of data that allow them to be addressed to specific computers on a shared media network. See also *Ethernet, FDDI, Token Ring.*

FTP See *File Transfer Protocol.*

G

Gateway A computer that serves as a router, a format translator, or a security filter for an entire network.

Gateway Services for NetWare (GSNW) An NT Server service that connects NT Servers and NT clients to NetWare resources via the gateway software. See also *Gateway, NetWare, Client Services for NetWare.*

GDI See *Graphical Device Interface.*

Global Group Group accounts maintained by the primary domain controller and visible to all computers in the domain. A global group can contain only members from within its domain. See also *Local Group, group indentifier*.

Gopher Serves text and links to other Gopher sites. Gopher predates HTTP by about a year, but has been made obsolete by the richer HTTP format. See also *Hypertext Transfer Protocol*.

Graphical Device Interface (GDI) The programming interface and graphical services provided to Win32 for programs to interact with graphical devices such as the screen and printer. See also *Programming Interface, Win32*.

Graphical User Interface (GUI) A computer shell program that represents mass storage devices, directories, and files as graphical objects on a screen. A cursor driven by a pointing device such as a mouse manipulates the objects. Typically, icons that can be opened into windows that show the data contained by the object represent the objects. See also *Shell, Explorer*.

Group Identifiers Security identifiers that contain the set of permissions allowed to a group. When a user account is part of a group, the group identifier is appended to that user's security identifier, thus granting the individual user all the permissions assigned to that group. See also *Security Identifier, Accounts, Permissions*.

Groups Security entities to which users can be assigned membership for the purpose of applying the broad set of group permissions to the user. By managing permissions for groups and assigning users to groups, rather than assigning permissions to users, security administrators can keep coherent control of very large security environments. See also *Permissions, Accounts, Security Local Group, Global Group*.

GSNW See *Gateway Services for NetWare*.

GUI See *Graphical User Interface*.

H

HAL See *Hardware Abstraction Layer*.

Hard Disk Drives Mass storage devices that read and write digital information magnetically on disks that spin under moving heads. Hard disk drives are precisely aligned and cannot normally be removed. Hard disk drives are an inexpensive way to store gigabytes of computer data permanently. Hard disk drives also store the installed software of a computer. See also *Mass Storage Device*.

Hardware Abstraction Layer (HAL) A Windows NT service that provides basic input/output services such as timers, interrupts, and multiprocessor management for computer hardware. The HAL is a device driver for the motherboard circuitry that allows the Windows NT operating system to treat different families of computers the same way. See also *Driver, Service, Interrupt Request*.

Hardware Compatibility List (HCL) The listing of all hardware devices supported by Windows NT. Hardware on the HCL has been tested and verified as being compatible with NT. You can view the current HCL at `http://microsoft.com/ntserver/hcl`.

Hardware Profiles Used to manage portable computers that have different configurations based on their location.

HCL See *Hardware Compatibility List.*

High Performance File System (HPFS) The file system native to OS/2 that performs many of the same functions of NTFS when run under OS/2. See also *File System, New Technology File System.*

Home Directory A directory that stores a user's personal files.

Home Page The default page returned by an HTTP server when a URL containing no specific document is requested. See also *Hypertext Transfer Protocol, Uniform Resource Locator.*

Host An Internet Server. Hosts are constantly connected to the Internet. See also *Internet.*

HPFS See *High Performance File System.*

HTML See *Hypertext Markup Language.*

HTTP See *Hypertext Transfer Protocol.*

Hyperlink A link in text or graphics files that have a Web address embedded within them. By clicking on the link, you jump to another Web address. You can identify a hyperlink because it is a different color than the rest of the Web page. See also *World Wide Web.*

Hypertext Markup Language (HTML) A textual data format that identifies sections of a document as headers, lists, hypertext links, etc. HTML is the data format used on the World Wide Web for the publication of Web pages. See also *Hypertext Transfer Protocol, World Wide Web.*

Hypertext Transfer Protocol (HTTP) Hypertext transfer protocol is an Internet protocol that transfers HTML documents over the Internet and responds to context changes that happen when a user clicks on a hypertext link. See also *Hypertext Markup Language, World Wide Web.*

I

Icon A graphical representation of a resource in a graphical user interface that usually takes the form of a small (32 x 32) bitmap. See also *Graphical User Interface.*

IDE A simple mass storage device interconnection bus that operates at 5Mbps and can handle no more than two attached devices. IDE devices are similar to but less expensive than SCSI devices. See also *Small Computer Systems Interface, Mass Storage Device.*

IIS See *Internet Information Server.*

Industry Standard Architecture (ISA) The design standard for 16-bit Intel compatible motherboards and peripheral buses. The 32/64-bit PCI bus standard is replacing the ISA standard. Adapters and interface cards must conform to the bus standard(s) used by the motherboard in order to be used with a computer.

Integrated Services Digital Network (ISDN) A direct, digital dial-up PSTN data link layer connection that operates at 64KB per channel over regular twisted-pair cable between a subscriber site and a PSTN central office. ISDN provides twice the data rate of the fastest modems per channel. Up to 24 channels can be multiplexed over two twisted pairs. See also *Public Switched Telephone Network, Data Link Layer, Modem.*

Intel Architecture A family of microprocessors descended directly from the Intel 8086, itself descended from the first microprocessor, the Intel 4004. The Intel architecture is the dominant microprocessor family. It was used in the original IBM PC microcomputer adopted by the business market and later adapted for home use.

Interactive User The user who physically logs on to a computer is considered interactive, as opposed to a user who logs on over the network. See also *Network User.*

Internet A voluntarily interconnected global network of computers based upon the TCP/IP protocol suite. TCP/IP was originally developed by the U.S. Department of Defense's Advanced Research Projects Agency to facilitate the interconnection of military networks and was provided free to universities. The obvious utility of worldwide digital network connectivity and the availability of free complex networking software developed at universities doing military research attracted other universities, research institutions, private organizations, businesses, and finally the individual home user. The Internet is now available to all current commercial computing platforms. See also *FTP, Telnet, World Wide Web, TCP/IP.*

Internet Explorer A World Wide Web browser produced by Microsoft and included free with Windows 95 and Windows NT 4.0. See also *World Wide Web, Internet.*

Internet Information Server (IIS) Serves Internet higher-level protocols like HTTP and FTP to clients using Web browsers. See also *Hypertext Transfer Protocol, File Transfer Protocol, World Wide Web.*

Internet Protocol (IP) The network layer protocol upon which the Internet is based. IP provides a simple connectionless packet exchange. Other protocols such as UDP or TCP use IP to perform their connection-oriented or guaranteed delivery services. See also *TCP/IP, Internet.*

Internet Service Provider (ISP) A company that provides dial-up connections to the Internet. See also *Internet.*

Internetwork Packet eXchange (IPX) The network protocol developed by Novell for its NetWare product. IPX is a routable, connection-oriented protocol similar to IP but much easier to manage and with lower communication overhead. The term IPX can also refer to the family of protocols that includes the Synchronous Packet eXchange (SPX) transport layer protocol, a connection-oriented protocol that guarantees delivery in order, similar to the service provided by TCP. See also *IP, NetWare, NWLink.*

InterNIC The agency that is responsible for assigning IP addresses. See also *Internet Protocol, IP Address.*

Interprocess Communications (IPC) A generic term describing any manner of client/server communication protocol, specifically those operating in the session, presentation, and application layers. Interprocess communications mechanisms provide a method for the client and server to trade information. See also *Named Pipes, Remote Procedure Call, NetBIOS, Mailslots, NetDDE, Local Procedure Call.*

Interrupt Request (IRQ) A hardware signal from a peripheral device to the microcomputer indicating that it has I/O traffic to send. If the microprocessor is not running a more important service, it will interrupt its current activity and handle the interrupt request. IBM PC's have 16 levels of interrupt request lines. Under Windows NT each device must have a unique interrupt request line. See also *Microprocessor, Driver, Peripheral.*

Intranet A privately owned network based on the TCP/IP protocol suite. See also *Transmission Control Protocol/Internet Protocol.*

IP See *Internet Protocol.*

IP Address A four-byte number that uniquely identifies a computer on an IP internetwork. InterNIC assigns the first bytes of Internet IP addresses and administers them in hierarchies. Huge organizations like the government or top-level ISPs have class A addresses, large organizations and most ISPs have class B addresses, and small companies have class C addresses. In a class A address, InterNIC assigns the first byte, and the owning organization assigns the remaining three bytes. In a class B address, InterNIC or the higher-level ISP assigns the first two bytes, and the organization assigns the remaining two bytes. In a class C address, InterNIC or the higher-level ISP assigns the first three bytes, and the organization assigns the remaining byte. Organizations not attached to the Internet are free to assign IP addresses as they please. See also *IP, Internet, InterNIC.*

IPC See *Interprocess Communications.*

IPX See *Internetwork Packet eXchange.*

IRQ See *Interrupt Request.*

ISA See *Industry Standard Architecture.*

ISDN See *Integrated Services Digital Network.*

ISP See *Internet Service Provider.*

K

Kernel The core process of a preemptive operating system, consisting of a multitasking scheduler and the basic services that provide security. Depending on the operating system, other services such as virtual memory drivers may be built into the kernel. The kernel is responsible for managing the scheduling of threads and processes. See also *Operating System, Drivers.*

L

LAN See *Local Area Network.*

LAN Manager The Microsoft brand of a network product jointly developed by IBM and Microsoft that provided an early client/server environment. LAN Manager/Server was eclipsed by NetWare, but was the genesis of many important protocols and IPC mechanisms used today, such as NetBIOS, Named Pipes, and NetBEUI. Portions of this product exist today in OS/2 Warp Server. See also *OS/2, Interprocess Communications.*

LAN Server The IBM brand of a network product jointly developed by IBM and Microsoft. See also *LAN Manager*.

Local Area Network (LAN) A network of computers operating on the same high-speed, shared media network data link layer. The size of a local area network is defined by the limitations of high-speed shared media networks to generally less than 1 kilometer in overall span. Some LAN backbone data link protocols such as FDDI can create larger LANs called metropolitan or medium area networks (MANs). See also *Wide Area Network, Data Link Layer*.

Local Group A group that exists in an NT computer's local accounts database. Local groups can reside on NT Workstations or NT Servers and can contain users or global groups. See also *Global Group*.

Local Printer A local printer is a printer that uses a physical port and that has not been shared. If a printer is defined as local, the only users who can use the printer are the local users of the computer that the printer is attached to. See also *Printer, Printing Device, Network Printer*.

Local Procedure Call (LPC) A mechanism that loops remote procedure calls without the presence of a network so that the client and server portion of an application can reside on the same machine. Local procedure calls look like remote procedure calls (RPCs) to the client and server sides of a distributed application. See also *Remote Procedure Call*.

Local Security Security that governs a local or interactive user. Local security can be set through NTFS partitions. See also *Security, Interactive User, New Technology File System, Network Security*.

LocalTalk A data link layer standard for local area networking used by Macintosh computers. Local-Talk is available on all Macintosh computers. The drawback of LocalTalk is that is transmits at only 230.4 kilobits per second (as opposed to Ethernet, which can transmit at 10 megabits per second). See also *Data Link Layer, Macintosh*.

Logging The process of recording information about activities and errors in the operating system.

Logoff The process of closing an open session with a server. See also *Logon*.

Logon The process of opening a network session by providing a valid authentication consisting of a user account name and a password to a domain controller. After logon, network resources are available to the user according to the user's assigned permissions. See also *Domain Controller, Logoff*.

Logon Script Command files that automate the logon process by performing utility functions such as attaching to additional server resources or automatically running different programs based upon the user account that established the logon. See also *Logon*.

Long Filename (LFN) A filename longer than the eight characters plus three-character extension allowed by MS-DOS. In Windows NT and Windows 95, filenames can contain up to 255 characters.

LPC See *Local Procedure Call*.

M

Macintosh A brand of computer manufactured by Apple. Macintosh is the only successful line of computers neither based upon the original IBM PC nor running the UNIX operating system. Windows NT Server supports Apple computers despite their use of proprietary network protocols.

MacOS The operating system that runs on an Apple Macintosh computer. See also *Macintosh*.

Mailslots A connectionless messaging IPC mechanism that Windows NT uses for browse request and logon authentication. See also *Interprocess Communications*.

Mandatory User Profile A profile that is created by an administrator and saved with a special extension (.man) so that the user cannot modify the profile in any way. Mandatory user profiles can be assigned to a single user or a group of users. See also *User Profile*.

Mass Storage Device Any device capable of storing many megabytes of information permanently, but especially those capable of random access to any portion of the information, such as hard disk drives and CD-ROM drives. See also *SCSI, IDE, Hard Disk Drive, CD-ROM Drive*.

Master Browser The computer on a network that maintains a list of computers and services available on the network and distributes the list to other browsers. The master browser may also promote potential browsers to be browsers. See also *Browser, Browsing, Potential Browser, Backup Browser*.

Member Server A NT server that has been installed as a non-domain controller. This allows the server to operate as a file, print and application server without the overhead of accounts administration.

Memory Any device capable of storing information. This term is usually used to indicate volatile random access semiconductor memory (RAM) capable of high-speed access to any portion of the memory space, but incapable of storing information without power. See also *Random Access Memory, Mass Storage Device*.

Microprocessor An integrated semiconductor circuit designed to automatically perform lists of logical and arithmetic operations. Modern microprocessors independently manage memory pools and support multiple instruction lists called threads. Microprocessors are also capable of responding to interrupt requests from peripherals and include onboard support for complex floating-point arithmetic. Microprocessors must have instructions when they are first powered on. These instructions are contained in nonvolatile firmware called a BIOS. See also *BIOS, Operating System*.

Microsoft Disk Operating System (MS-DOS) A 16-bit operating system designed for the 8086 chip that was used in the original IBM PC. MS-DOS is a simple program loader and file system that turns over complete control of the computer to the running program and provides very little service beyond file system support and that provided by the BIOS.

Migration Tool for NetWare A utility used to migrate NetWare users, groups, file structures, and security to a NT domain. See also *NetWare*.

Modem Modulator/demodulator. A data link layer device that can create an analog signal suitable for transmission over telephone lines from a digital data stream. Modern modems also include a command set for negotiating connections and data rates with remote modems and for setting their default behavior. The fastest modems run at about 33Kbps. See also *Data Link Layer*.

Module A software component of a modular operating system that provides a certain defined service. Modules can be installed or removed depending upon the service requirements of the software running on the computer. Modules allow operating systems and applications to be customized to fit the needs of the user.

MPR See *MultiProtocol Router*.

MS-DOS See *Microsoft Disk Operating System*.

Multilink A capability of RAS to combine multiple data streams into one network connection for the purpose of using more than one modem or ISDN channel in a single connection. This feature is new to Windows NT 4.0. See also *Remote Access Service*.

Multiprocessing Using two or more processors simultaneously to perform a computing task. Depending on the operating system, processing may be done asymmetrically, wherein certain processors are assigned certain threads independent of the load they create, or symmetrically, wherein threads are dynamically assigned to processors according to an equitable scheduling scheme. The term usually describes a multiprocessing capacity built into the computer at a hardware level in that the computer itself supports more than one processor. However, *multiprocessing* can also be applied to network computing applications achieved through interprocess communication mechanisms. Client/server applications are, in fact, examples of multiprocessing. See also *Asymmetrical Multiprocessing, Symmetrical Multiprocessing, Interprocess Communications*.

MultiProtocol Router (MPR) Services included with NT Server that allow you to route traffic between IPX and TCP/IP subnets. MPR also allows you to facilitate DHCP requests and forward BOOTP relay agents. See also *Internetwork Packet Exchange, Transmission Control Protocol/Internet Protocol, Dynamic Host Configuration Protocol, Bootstrap Protocol*.

Multitasking The capacity of an operating system to rapidly switch among threads of execution. Multitasking allows processor time to be divided among threads as if each thread ran on its own slower processor. Multitasking operating systems allow two or more applications to run at the same time and can provide a greater degree of service to applications than single-tasking operating systems like MS-DOS. See also *Multiprocessing, Multithreading*.

Multithreaded Multithreaded refers to programs that have more than one chain of execution, thus relying on the services of a multitasking or multiprocessing operating system to operate. Multiple chains of execution allow programs to simultaneously perform more than one task. In multitasking computers, multithreading is merely a convenience used to make programs run smoother and free the program from the burden of switching between tasks itself. On multiprocessing computers, multithreading allows the compute burden of the program to be spread across many processors. Programs that are not multithreaded cannot take advantage of multiple processors in a computer. See also *Multitasking, Multiprocessing*.

N

Named Pipes An interprocess communication mechanism that is implemented as a file system service, allowing programs to be modified to run on it without using a proprietary application programming interface. Named Pipes were developed to support more robust client/ server communications than those allowed by the simpler NetBIOS. See also *OS/2, File Systems, Interprocess Communications.*

NDIS See *Network Driver Interface Specification.*

NDS See *NetWare Directory Services.*

NetBEUI See *NetBIOS Extended User Interface.*

NetBIOS See *Network Basic Input/Output System.*

NetBIOS Extended User Interface (NetBEUI) A simple network layer transport developed to support NetBIOS installations. NetBEUI is not routable, and so it is not appropriate for larger networks. NetBEUI is the fastest transport protocol available for Windows NT.

NetBIOS Gateway A service provided by RAS that allows NetBIOS requests to be forwarded independent of transport protocol. For example, NetBIOS requests from a remote computer connected via NetBEUI can be sent over the network via NWLink. See also *Network Basic Input/Output System, NWLink, NetBIOS over TCP/IP, NetBEUI.*

NetBIOS over TCP/IP (NetBT) A network service that implements the NetBIOS IPC over the TCP/IP protocol stack. See also *NetBIOS, Interprocess Communications, TCP/IP.*

NetBT See *NetBIOS over TCP/IP.*

NetDDE See *Network Dynamic Data Exchange.*

NetWare A popular network operating system developed by Novell in the early 1980s. NetWare is a cooperative, multitasking, highly optimized, dedicated-server network operating system that has client support for most major operating systems. Recent versions of NetWare include graphical client tools for management from client stations. At one time, NetWare accounted for more than 70 percent of the network operating system market. See also *Windows NT, Client Services for NetWare, Gateway Services for NetWare, NWLink.*

NetWare Directory Services (NDS) In NetWare a distributed hierarchy of network services such as servers, shared volumes, and printers. NetWare implements NDS as a directory structure having elaborate security and administration mechanisms. The CSNW provided in Windows NT 4.0 supports the NDS tree. See also *NetWare, Client Services for NetWare, Gateway Services for NetWare.*

NetWare Link (NWLink) A Windows NT transport protocol that implements Novell's IPX/SPX protocol suite. NWLink is useful as a general purpose transport for Windows NT and for connecting to NetWare file servers through CSNW. See also *Internetwork Packet eXchange, Client Services for NetWare, Gateway Services for NetWare.*

NetWare NetBIOS Link (NWNBLink) NetBIOS implemented over NWLink. See also *NetBIOS, NWLink, NetBT.*

Network A group of computers connected via some digital medium for the purpose of exchanging information. Networks can be based upon many types of media, such as twisted pair, telephone-style cable, optical fiber, coaxial cable, radio, or infrared light. Certain computers are usually configured as service providers called *servers*. Computers that perform user tasks directly and that utilize the services of servers are called *clients*. See also *Client/Server, Server, Network Operating System.*

Network Basic Input/Output System (NetBIOS) A client/server interprocess communication service developed by IBM in the early 1980s. NetBIOS presents a relatively primitive mechanism for communication in client/server applications, but its widespread acceptance and availability across most operating systems makes it a logical choice for simple network applications. Many of the network IPC mechanisms in Windows NT are implemented over NetBIOS. See also *Interprocess Communication, Client/Server.*

Network Client Administrator A utility within the Administrative Tools group that can be used to make installation startup disks, make installation disk sets, copy client-based administration tools, and view remoteboot information.

Network Driver Interface Specification (NDIS) A Microsoft specification to which network adapter drivers must conform in order to work with Microsoft network operating systems. NDIS provides a many-to-many binding between network adapter drivers and transport protocols. See also *Transport Protocol.*

Network Dynamic Data Exchange (NetDDE) An interprocess communication mechanism developed by Microsoft to support the distribution of DDE applications over a network. See also *Interprocess Communication, DDE.*

Network Interface Card (NIC) A physical layer adapter device that allows a computer to connect to and communicate over a local area network. See also *Ethernet, Token Ring*, Adapter.

Network Layer The layer of the OSI model that creates a communication path between two computers via routed packets. Transport protocols implement both the network layer and the transport layer of the OSI stack. IP is a network layer service. See also *Internet Protocol, Transport Protocol, Open Systems Interconnect Model.*

Network Monitor A utility that captures and displays network traffic.

Network Operating System A computer operating system specifically designed to optimize a computer's ability to respond to service requests. Servers run network operating systems. Windows NT Server and NetWare are both network operating systems. See also *Windows NT, Server, NetWare.*

New Technology File System (NTFS) A secure, transaction-oriented file system developed for Windows NT that incorporates the Windows NT security model for assigning permissions and shares. NTFS is optimized for hard drives larger than 500MB and requires too much overhead to be used on hard disk drives smaller than 50MB.

Non-browser A computer on a network that will not maintain a list of other computers and services on the network. See also *Browser, Browsing.*

NT Directory Services The synchronized SAM database that exists between the PDC and the BDCs within a domain. Directory Services also controls the trust relationships that exist between domains. See also *Security Accounts Manager, Primary Domain Controller, Backup Domain Controller, Trust Relationship.*

NTFS See *New Technology File System.*

NWLink See *NetWare Link, Internetwork Packet eXchange.*

NWNBLink See *NetWare NetBIOS Link.*

O

Object A software service provider that encapsulates both the algorithm and the data structures necessary to provide a service. Usually, objects can inherit data and functionality from their parent objects, thus allowing complex services to be constructed from simpler objects. The term *object oriented* implies a tight relationship between algorithms and data structures. See also *Module.*

Object Counters Containers built into each service object in Windows NT that store a count of the number of times an object performs its service or to what degree. You can use performance monitors to access object counters and measure how the different objects in Windows NT are operating. See also *Object.*

Open Graphics Language (OpenGL) A standard interface for the presentation of two- and three-dimensional visual data.

Open Systems Interconnect Model (OSI Model) A model for network component interoperability developed by the International Standards Organization to promote cross-vendor compatibility of hardware and software network systems. The OSI model splits the process of networking into seven distinct services. Each layer uses the services of the layer below to provide its service to the layer above. See also *Physical Layer, Data Link Layer, Network Layer, Transport Layer, Session Layer, Presentation Layer, Application Layer.*

OpenGL See also *Open Graphics Language.*

Operating System A collection of services that form a foundation upon which applications run. Operating systems may be simple I/O service providers with a command shell, such as MS-DOS, or they may be sophisticated, preemptive, multitasking, multiprocessing applications platforms like Windows NT. See also *Network Operating System, Preemptive Multitasking, Kernel.*

Operating System 2 (OS/2) A 16-bit (and later, 32-bit) operating system developed jointly by Microsoft and IBM as a successor to MS-DOS. Microsoft bowed out of the 32-bit development effort and produced its own product, Windows NT, as a competitor to OS/2. OS/2 is now a preemptive, multitasking 32-bit operating system with strong support for networking and the ability to run MS-DOS and Win16 applications, but IBM has been unable to entice a large number of developers to produce software that runs native under OS/2. See also *Operating System, Preemptive Multitasking.*

Optimization Any effort to reduce the workload on a hardware component by eliminating, obviating, or reducing the amount of work required of the hardware component through any means. For instance, file caching is an optimization that reduces the workload of a hard disk drive.

OS/2 See *Operating System 2.*

OSI Model See *Open Systems Interconnect Model.*

Owner Used in conjunction with NTFS volumes. All NTFS files and directories have an associated owner who is able to control access and grant permissions to other users. See also *New Technology File System.*

P

Page File See *Swap File.*

Partition A section of a hard disk that can contain an independent file system volume. Partitions can be used to keep multiple operating systems and file systems on the same hard disk. See also *Volume, Hard Disk Drive.*

Password A secret code that validates the identity of a user of a secure system. Passwords are used with account names to log on to most computer systems.

PC See *Personal Computer.*

PCI See *Peripheral Connection Interface.*

PDC See *Primary Domain Controller.*

Peer A networked computer that both shares resources with other computers and accesses the shared resources of other computers. A nondedicated server. See also *Server, Client.*

Performance Monitor Utility provided with NT that provides graphical statistics that can be used to measure performance on your computer.

Peripheral An input/output device attached to a computer. Peripherals can be printers, hard disk drives, monitors, and so on.

Peripheral Connection Interface (PCI) A high-speed 32/64-bit bus interface developed by Intel and widely accepted as the successor to the 16-bit ISA interface. PCI devices support I/O throughput about 40 times faster than the ISA bus.

Permissions Assignments of levels of access to a resource made to groups or users. Security constructs that regulate access to resources by user name or group affiliation. Administrators can assign permissions to allow any level of access, such as read only, read/write, delete, by controlling the ability of users to initiate object services. Security is implemented by checking the user's security identifier against each object's access control list. See also *Security Identifier, Access Control List.*

Personal Computer (PC) A microcomputer used by one person at a time (i.e., not a multiuser computer). PCs are generally clients or peers in an networked environment. High-speed PCs are called *workstations.* Networks of PCs are called *LANs.* The term PC is often used to refer to computers compatible with the IBM PC.

Physical Layer The cables, connectors, and connection ports of a network. The passive physical components required to create a network. See also *OSI Model.*

Point-to-Point Protocol (PPP) A data link layer transport that performs over point-to-point network connections such as serial or modem lines. PPP can negotiate any transport protocol used by both systems involved in the link and can automatically assign IP, DNS, and gateway addresses when used with TCP/IP. See also *Internet Protocol, Domain Name Service, Gateway.*

Point-to-Point Tunneling Protocol (PPTP) Protocol used to create secure connections between private networks through the public Internet or an ISP. See also *Internet, Internet Service Provider.*

Policies General controls that enhance the security of an operating environment. In Windows NT, policies affect restrictions on password use and rights assignment and determine which events will be recorded in the Security log.

Potential Browser A computer on a network that may maintain a list of other computers and services on the network if requested to do so by a master browser. See also *Browser, Master Browser.*

PowerPC A microprocessor family developed by IBM to compete with the Intel family of microprocessors. The PowerPC is a RISC-architecture microprocessor with many advanced features that emulate other microprocessors. PowerPCs are currently used in a line of IBM computers and in the Apple Power Macintosh. Windows NT is available for the PowerPC.

PPP See *Point-to-Point Protocol.*

PPTP See *Point-to-Point Tunneling Protocol.*

Preemptive Multitasking A multitasking implementation in which an interrupt routine in the kernel manages the scheduling of processor time among running threads. The threads themselves do not need to support multitasking in any way because the microprocessor will preempt the thread with an interrupt, save its state, update all thread priorities according to its scheduling algorithm, and pass control to the highest priority thread awaiting execution. Because of the preemptive nature, a thread that crashes will not affect the operation of other executing threads. See also *Kernel, Thread, Operating System, Process.*

Preferences Characteristics of user accounts, such as password, profile location, home directory, and logon script.

Presentation Layer That layer of the OSI model that converts and translates (if necessary) information between the session and application layers. See also *OSI Model.*

Primary Domain Controller (PDC) The domain server that contains the master copy of the security, computer, and user accounts databases and that can authenticate workstations. The PDC can replicate its databases to one or more backup domain controllers. The PDC is usually also the master browser for the domain. See also *Backup Domain Controller, Domain, Master Browser.*

Print Device A physical device that produces printed output. See also *Printer.*

Print Driver The software component that interfaces the print device to the operating system. See also *Print Device.*

Print Server A computer to which printers are attached and connected via the network. See also *Printer, Print Device.*

Printer In NT terminology, a printer is the software interface between the physical printer (or print device) and the operating system. You can create printers through the Printers folder. See also *Print Device.*

Printing Pool A number of print devices controlled by the same printer. The printer directs the print job to an available print device in the pool. See also *Printer, Print Device.*

Priority A level of execution importance assigned to a thread. In combination with other factors, the priority level determines how often that thread will get computer time according to a scheduling algorithm. See also *Preemptive Multitasking.*

Process A running program containing one or more threads. A process encapsulates the protected memory and environment for its threads.

Processor A circuit designed to automatically perform lists of logical and arithmetic operations. Unlike microprocessors, processors may be designed from discrete components rather than be a monolithic integrated circuit. See also *Microprocessor.*

Program A list of processor instructions designed to perform a certain function. A running program is called a process. A package of one or more programs and attendant data designed to meet a certain application is called software. See also *Software, Application, Process, Microprocessor.*

Programming Interfaces Interprocess communications mechanisms that provide certain high-level services to running processes. Programming interfaces may provide network communication, graphical presentation, or any other type of software service. See also *Interprocess Communication.*

Protocol An established communication method that the parties involved understand. Protocols provide a context in which to interpret communicated information. Computer protocols are rules used by communicating devices and software services to format data in a way that all participants understand. See also *Transport Protocol.*

PSTN See *Public Switched Telephone Network.*

Public Switched Telephone Network (PSTN) A global network of interconnected digital and analog communication links originally designed to support voice communication between any two points in the world, but quickly adapted to handle digital data traffic when the computer revolution occurred. In addition to its traditional voice support role, the PSTN now functions as the physical layer of the Internet by providing dial-up and leased lines for the interconnections. See also *Internet, Modem, Physical Layer.*

R

RAID See *Redundant Array of Inexpensive Disks.*

RAID Controllers Hard disk drive controllers that implement RAID in hardware. See also *Redundant Array of Inexpensive Disks.*

RAM See *Random Access Memory*.

Random Access Memory (RAM) Integrated circuits that store digital bits in massive arrays of logical gates or capacitors. RAM is the primary memory store for modern computers, storing all running software processes and contextual data. See also *Microprocessor*.

RARP See *Reverse Address Resolution Protocol*.

RAS See *Remote Access Service*.

Real-Time Application A process that must respond to external events at least as fast as those events can occur. Real-time threads must run at very high priorities to ensure their ability to respond in real time. See also *Process*.

Redirector A software service that redirects user file I/O requests over the network. Novell implements the Workstation service and Client services for NetWare as redirectors. Redirectors allow servers to be used as mass storage devices that appear local to the user. See also *Client Services for NetWare, File System*.

Reduced Instruction Set Computer (RISC) A microprocessor technology that implements fewer and more primitive instructions than typical microprocessors and can therefore be implemented quickly with the most modern semiconductor technology and speeds. Programs written for RISC microprocessors require more instructions (longer programs) to perform the same task as a normal microprocessor but are capable of a greater degree of optimization and therefore usually run faster. See also *Microprocessor*.

Redundant Array of Inexpensive Disks (RAID) A collection of hard disk drives, coordinated by a special controller, that appears as one physical disk to a computer but stores its data across all the disks to take advantage of the speed and/or fault tolerance afforded by using more than one disk. RAID disk storage has several levels, including 0 (striping), 1 (mirroring), and 5 (striping with parity). RAID systems are typically used for very large storage volumes or to provide fault-tolerance features such as hot swapping of failed disks or automatically backing up data onto replacement disks.

Registry A database of settings required and maintained by Windows NT and its components. The Registry contains all the configuration information used by the computer. It is stored as a hierarchical structure and is made up of keys, hives, and value entries. You can use the Registry Editor (REGEDT32 command) to change these settings.

Remote Access Service (RAS) A service that allows network connections to be established over telephone lines with modems or digital adapters. The computer initiating the connection is called the RAS client; the answering computer is called the RAS host. See also *Modem, Public Switched Telephone Network*.

Remote Procedure Calls (RPC) A network interprocess communication mechanism that allows an application to be distributed among many computers on the same network. See also *Local Procedure Call, Interprocess Communications*.

Remoteboot The remoteboot service starts disk-less workstations over the network.

Requests for Comments (RFCs) The set of standards defining the Internet protocols as determined by the Internet Engineering Task Force and available in the public domain on the Internet. RFCs define the functions and services provided by each of the many Internet protocols. Compliance with the RFCs guarantees cross-vendor compatibility. See also *Internet*.

Resource Any useful service, such as a shared network directory or a printer. See also *Share*.

Reverse Address Resolution Protocol (RARP) The TCP/IP protocol that allows a computer that has a physical layer address (such as an Ethernet address) but does not have an IP address to request a numeric IP address from another computer on the network. See also *TCP/IP*.

RFC See *Request For Comments*.

RIP See *Routing Information Protocol*.

RISC See *Reduced Instruction Set Computer*.

Roaming User Profile A user profile that is stored and configured to be downloaded from a server. Roaming user profiles maintain a consistent environment for the user among computers on the network. See also *User Profile*.

Router A network layer device that moves packets between networks. Routers provide internetwork connectivity. See also *Network Layer*.

Routing Information Protocol (RIP) A protocol within the TCP/IP protocol suite that allows routers to exchange routing information with other routers. A variant of the RIP protocol also exists for the IPX/SPX protocol suite. See also *Transmission Control Protocol/Internet Protocol*.

RPC See *Remote Procedure Calls*.

S

SAM See *Security Accounts Manager*.

Scheduling The process of determining which threads should be executed according to their priority and other factors. See also *Preemptive Multitasking*.

SCSI See *Small Computer Systems Interface*.

Search Engine Web sites dedicated to responding to requests for specific information, searching massive locally stored databases of Web pages, and responding with the URLs of pages that fit the search phrase. See also *World Wide Web, Universal Resource Locator*.

Security Measures taken to secure a system against accidental or intentional loss, usually in the form of accountability procedures and use restriction. See also *Security Identifiers, Security Accounts Manager*.

Security Accounts Manager (SAM) The module of the Windows NT executive that authenticates a username and password against a database of accounts, generating an access token that includes the user's permissions. See also *Security, Security Identifier, Access Token*.

Security Identifiers (SID)   Unique codes that identify a specific user or group to the Windows NT security system. Security identifiers contain a complete set of permissions for that user or group.

Serial   A method of communication that transfers data across a medium one bit at a time, usually adding stop, start, and check bits to ensure quality transfer. See also *COM Port, Modem*.

Serial Line Internet Protocol (SLIP)   An implementation of the IP protocol over serial lines. SLIP has been obviated by PPP. See also *Point-to-Point Protocol, Internet Protocol*.

Server   A computer dedicated to servicing requests for resources from other computers on a network. Servers typically run network operating systems such as Windows NT Server or NetWare. See also *Windows NT, NetWare, Client/Server*.

Server Manager   Utility in the Administrative Tools group used to manage domains and computers.

Service   A process dedicated to implementing a specific function for other process. Most Windows NT components are services used by user-level applications.

Services for Macintosh   Service available through NT Server that allows Macintosh users to take advantage of NT file and print services. See also *Macintosh*.

Session layer   The layer of the OSI model dedicated to maintaining a bi-directional communication connection between two computers. The session layer uses the services of the transport layer to provide this service. See also *OSI Model, Transport Layer*.

Share   A resource (e.g., directory, printer) shared by a server or a peer on a network. See also *Resource, Server, Peer*.

Shell   The user interface of an operating system; the shell launches applications and manages file systems.

SID   See *Security Identifier*.

Simple Mail Transfer Protocol (SMTP)   An Internet protocol for transferring mail between Internet hosts. SMTP is often used to upload mail directly from the client to an Intermediate host, but can only be used to receive mail by computers constantly connected to the Internet. See also *Internet*.

Simple Network Management Protocol (SNMP)   An Internet protocol that manages network hardware such as routers, switches, servers, and clients from a single client on the network. See also *Internet Protocol*.

Site   A related collection of HTML documents at the same Internet address, usually oriented toward some specific information or purpose. See also *Hypertext Markup Language, Internet*.

SLIP   See *Serial Line Internet Protocol*.

Small Computer Systems Interface (SCSI)   A high-speed, parallel-bus interface that connects hard disk drives, CD-ROM drives, tape drives, and many other peripherals to a computer. SCSI is the mass storage connection standard among all computers except IBM compatibles, which use SCSI or IDE.

SMTP   See *Simple Mail Transfer Protocol*.

SNMP   See *Simple Network Management Protocol*.

Software A suite of programs sold as a unit and dedicated to a specific application. See also *Program, Application, Process.*

Spooler A service that buffers output to a low-speed device such as a printer so the software outputting to the device is not tied up waiting for it.

Stripe Set A single volume created across multiple hard disk drives and accessed in parallel for the purpose of optimizing disk access time. NTFS can create stripe sets. See also *NTFS, Volume, File System.*

Subdirectory A directory contained in another directory. See also *Directory.*

Subnet Mask A number mathematically applied to Internet protocol addresses to determine which IP addresses are a part of the same subnetwork as the computer applying the subnet mask.

Surf To browse the Web randomly looking for interesting information. See also *World Wide Web.*

Swap File The virtual memory file on a hard disk containing the memory pages that have been moved out to disk to increase available RAM. See also *Virtual Memory.*

Symmetrical Multiprocessing A multiprocessing methodology wherein processes are assigned to processors on a fair-share basis. This approach balances the processing load among processors and ensures that no processor will become a bottleneck. Implementing symmetrical multiprocessing is more difficult than implementing asymmetrical multiprocessing because certain hardware functions such as interrupt handling must be shared between processors. See also *Asymmetrical Multiprocessing, Multiprocessing.*

System Partition The system partition is the active partition on an Intel-based computer that contains the hardware-specific files used to load the NT operating system. See also *Partition, Boot Partition.*

T

TCP See *Transmission Control Protocol.*

TCP/IP See *Transmission Control Protocol/Internet Protocol.*

TDI See *Transport Driver Interface.*

Telnet A terminal application that allows a user to log on to a multiuser UNIX computer from any computer connected to the Internet. See also *Internet.*

Thread A list of instructions running in a computer to perform a certain task. Each thread runs in the context of a process, which embodies the protected memory space and the environment of the threads. Multithreaded processes can perform more than one task at the same time. See also *Process, Preemptive Multitasking, Program.*

Throughput The measure of information flow through a system in a specific time frame, usually one second. For instance, 28.8Kbps is the throughput of a modem: 28.8 kilobits per second can be transmitted.

Token Ring The second most popular data link layer standard for local area networking. Token Ring implements the token-passing method of arbitrating multiple-computer access to the same network. Token ring operates at either 4 or 16Mbps. FDDI is similar to Token Ring and operates at 100Mbps. See also *Data Link Layer*.

Transmission Control Protocol (TCP) A transport layer protocol that implements guaranteed packet delivery using the Internet Protocol (IP). See also *TCP/IP, Internet Protocol*.

Transmission Control Protocol/Internet Protocol (TCP/IP) A suite of network protocols upon which the global Internet is based. TCP/IP is a general term that can refer either to the TCP and IP protocols used together or to the complete set of Internet protocols. TCP/IP is the default protocol for Windows NT. See also *TCP, IP, SNMP, RIP, UDP, and all other acronyms ending in -P*.

Transport Driver Interface (TDI) A specification to which all Window NT transport protocols must be written in order to be used by higher-level services such as programming interfaces, file systems, and interprocess communications mechanisms. See also *Transport Protocol*.

Transport Layer The OSI model layer responsible for the guaranteed serial delivery of packets between two computers over an internetwork. TCP is the Transport layer protocol for the TCP/IP transport protocol.

Transport Protocol A service that delivers discreet packets of information between any two computers in a network. Transport protocols may operate at the Data-Link, Network, Transport, or Session layers of the OSI stack. Higher-level, connection-oriented services are built upon transport protocols. See also *TCP/IP, NWLink, NetBEUI, Transport Layer, IP, TCP, Internet*.

Trust Relationship Administrative link that joins two or more domains. With a trust relationship users can access resources in another domain if they have rights, even if they do not have a user account in the resource domain.

U

UDP See *User Datagram Protocol*.

UNC See *Universal Naming Convention*.

Uniform Resource Locator (URL) An Internet standard naming convention for identifying resources available via various TCP/IP application protocols. For example, `http://www.microsoft.com` is the URL for Microsoft's World Wide Web server site, while `ftp://gateway.dec.com` is a popular FTP site. A URL allows easy hypertext references to a particular resource from within a document or mail message. See also *HTTP, World Wide Web*.

Universal Naming Convention (UNC) A multivendor, multiplatform convention for identifying shared resources on a network. See also *MUP*.

UNIX A multitasking, kernel-based operating system developed at AT&T in the early 1970s and provided (originally) free to universities as a research operating system. Because of its availability and ability to scale down to microprocessor-based computers, UNIX became the standard operating system of the Internet and its attendant network protocols and is the closest approximation to a universal operating system that exists. Most computers can run some variant of the UNIX operating system. See also *Multitasking, Internet*.

User Datagram Protocol (UDP) A non-guaranteed network packet protocol implemented on IP that is far faster than TCP because it lacks flow-control overhead. UDP can be implemented reliably when some higher-level protocol (such as NetBIOS) exists to make sure that required data will eventually be retransmitted in local area environments. At the transport layer of the OSI model, UDP is connectionless service and TCP is connection-oriented service. See also *Transmission Control Protocol*.

User Manager for Domains A Windows NT application that administers user accounts, groups, and security policies at the domain level.

User Profile A directory that stores user environment information such as desktop and Start menu settings. See also *Roaming Profile, Mandatory Profile*.

Username A user's account name in a logon-authenticated system. See also *Security*.

V

VDM See *Virtual DOS Machine*.

Virtual DOS Machine (VDM) The DOS environment created by Windows NT for the execution of DOS and Win16 applications. See also *MS-DOS, Win16*.

Virtual Memory A kernel service that stores memory pages not currently in use on a mass storage device to free up the memory occupied for other uses. Virtual memory hides the memory swapping process from applications and higher-level services. See also *Swap File, Kernel*.

Volume A collection of data indexed by directories containing files and referred to by a drive letter. Volumes are normally contained in a single partition, but volume sets and stripe sets extend a single volume across multiple partitions.

W

WAN See *Wide Area Network*.

Web Browser An application that makes HTTP requests and formats the resultant HTML documents for the users. The preeminent Internet client, most Web browsers understand all standard Internet protocols. See also *Hypertext Transfer Protocol, Hypertext Markup Language, Internet*.

Web Page Any HTML document on an HTTP server. See also *Hypertext Transfer Protocol, Hypertext Markup Language, Internet*

Wide Area Network (WAN) A geographically dispersed network of networks, connected by routers and communication links. The Internet is the largest WAN. See also *Internet, Local Area Network*.

Win16 The set of application services provided by the 16-bit versions of Microsoft Windows: Windows 3.1 and Windows for Workgroups 3.11.

Win32 The set of application services provided by the 32-bit versions of Microsoft Windows: Windows 95 and Windows NT.

Windows 3.11 for Workgroups The current 16-bit version of Windows for less-powerful, Intel-based personal computers; this system includes peer-networking services.

Windows 95 The current 32-bit version of Microsoft Windows for medium-range, Intel-based personal computers; this system includes peer-networking services, Internet support, and strong support for older DOS applications and peripherals.

Windows Internet Name Service (WINS) A network service for Microsoft networks that provides Windows computers with Internet numbers for specified NetBIOS names, facilitating browsing and intercommunication over TCP/IP networks.

Windows NT The current 32-bit version of Microsoft Windows for powerful Intel, Alpha, PowerPC, or MIPS-based computers; the system includes peer-networking services, server-networking services, Internet client and server services, and a broad range of utilities.

Windows Sockets An interprocess communications protocol that delivers connection-oriented data streams used by Internet software and software ported from UNIX environments. See also *Interprocess Communications*.

WINS See *Windows Internet Name Service*.

Workgroup In Microsoft networks, a collection of related computers, such as a department, that don't require the uniform security and coordination of a domain. Workgroups are characterized by decentralized management as opposed to the centralized management that domains use. See also *Domain*.

Workstation A powerful personal computer, usually running a preemptive, multitasking operating system like UNIX or Windows NT.

World Wide Web (WWW) A collection of Internet servers providing hypertext formatted documents for Internet clients running Web browsers. The World Wide Web provided the first easy-to-use graphical interface for the Internet and is largely responsible for the Internet's explosive growth.

Write-Back Caching A caching optimization wherein data written to the slow store is cached until the cache is full or until a subsequent write operation overwrites the cached data. Write-back caching can significantly reduce the write operations to a slow store because many write operations are subsequently obviated by new information. Data in the write-back cache is also available for subsequent reads. If something happens to prevent the cache from writing data to the slow store, the cache data will be lost. See also *Caching, Write-through Caching*.

Write-through Caching A caching optimization wherein data written to a slow store is kept in a cache for subsequent rereading. Unlike write-back caching, write-through caching immediately writes the data to the slow store and is therefore less optimal but more secure.

WWW See *World Wide Web*.

X

X.25 Standard that defines packet-switching networks.

Index